Strategic
Human Resource
Management

Visit the *Strategic Human Resource Management* Companion Website at
www.pearsoned.co.uk/millmore to find valuable **student** learning material
including:

- Answers to self-check and reflect questions

Mike Millmore, Philip Lewis,
Mark Saunders, Adrian Thornhill
and Trevor Morrow

Strategic
Human Resource
Management

Contemporary Issues

FT Prentice Hall
FINANCIAL TIMES

An imprint of **Pearson Education**

Harlow, England • London • New York • Boston • San Francisco • Toronto • Sydney • Singapore • Hong Kong
Tokyo • Seoul • Taipei • New Delhi • Cape Town • Madrid • Mexico City • Amsterdam • Munich • Paris • Milan

Pearson Education Limited

Edinburgh Gate
Harlow
Essex CM20 2JE
England

and Associated Companies around the world

Visit us on the World Wide Web at:
www.pearsoned.co.uk

_____

First published 2007

ISBN: 978-0-273-68163-2

British Library Cataloguing-in-Publication Data
A catalogue record for this book can be obtained from the British Library.

10 9 8 7 6 5 4 3 2 1
12 11 10 09 08 07

Typeset in 10/12pt Minion by 30
Printed and bound by Ashford Colour Press Ltd., Gosport

The publisher's policy is to use paper manufactured from sustainable forests.

Contents

Part 1 Overview   1

Part 2 Strategic Interventions   157

Supporting resources
Visit **www.pearsoned.co.uk/millmore** to find valuable online resources

Companion Website for students
- Answers to self-check and reflect questions

For instructors
- Instructor's Manual containing:
  - learning outcomes and summaries
  - teaching and learning suggestions including comment, student preparation, in the classroom and follow-up work
  - answer to self-check and reflect questions
  - answer to case study questions
  - references
- PowerPoint slides

Also: The Companion Website provides the following features:
- Search tool to help locate specific items of content
- E-mail results and profile tools to send results of quizzes to instructors
- Online help and support to assist with website usage and troubleshooting

For more information please contact your local Pearson Education sales representative or visit **www.pearsoned.co.uk/millmore**

List of figures

List of tables

Preface

In teaching strategic approaches to the management of human resources (strategic human resource management – SHRM) to undergraduate and postgraduate students undertaking general business and management or more specialist human resource management (HRM) courses, as well as those studying towards membership of the Chartered Institute of Personnel and Development, we found it impossible to find a single text to adopt as a reader in support of their studies. Our dilemma was that available texts explicitly positioned to address the strategic development of HRM practice were either too inaccessible or insufficiently rigorous in their treatment of strategic integration. We therefore set about writing a book to bridge this 'divide'.

This book was conceived to bridge this perceived gap by providing comprehensive exploration of strategically directed management of human resources in a format that was easily accessible to students. We believe we have succeeded by ensuring that the subject domain is treated in an academically rigorous way but that, through the use of many illustrative devices, an undergraduate audience will be able to engage in its content. Early feedback on chapter drafts from our own undergraduate and postgraduate students provides evidence that we are well on the road to realising our aim.

The origins of SHRM lie in the burgeoning interest in strategic management evident from the late twentieth century onwards. Strategic management arguably became the dominant theme in management literature from 1980 onwards. Given the emphasis placed by strategic management on the strategic utilisation of an organisation's resource capability in the pursuit of organisational goals, it was hardly surprising that, within the personnel/human resources (HR) domain, attention turned to how human resources could be managed more strategically. This gave rise to the parallel development of HRM theory and practice. Advocates of HRM saw it as a natural development of more traditional approaches to personnel management that chimed with the strategic imperatives facing organisations in the late twentieth and early twenty-first century.

A number of distinguishing features were identified to differentiate HRM from its personnel management antecedents. These included: devolvement of HR activities to line managers so that they became more accountable for the performance of those that they managed; the adoption by HR specialists of a business partner role aimed at achieving greater congruence with business needs; and a movement in employee relations away from a collective focus (involving trade unions) towards the establishment of individual relationships with employees as a route to securing greater organisational commitment within a unitary perspective. However, underpinning the growing interest in HRM was the realisation that employees potentially represented an important, if not the most important, asset an organisation had at its disposal in its pursuit of strategic advantage. The feature that epitomises this ideology and underscores all interpretations of HRM is that of strategic integration where HR activities (or levers) are aligned vertically, with an organisation's mission and/or strategic objectives, and horizontally with each other to provide mutually supporting 'bundles'. In short, the one thing that commentators agree on is that what differentiates HRM from personnel management is its strategic focus and concern for strategic integration.

Given the overwhelming consensus that HRM is nothing if not strategic, deciding on the title for this book (*Strategic Human Resource Management*) provided us with something of a conundrum. If the essence of HRM, and its key feature for distinguishing it from personnel management, is its focus on strategic integration then the 'S' of 'SHRM' is tautological in that it simply adds the strategic element that is already accepted as a given in HRM! It was therefore with some misgiving that we opted for the SHRM title because of the possible confusion this may cause among our readership. However, we justify our decision on two grounds.

First, in our view the term HRM has come to be inappropriately used, such that it has been increasingly adopted in place of personnel management without due regard for its differentiating characteristics. In this sense, the term HRM is frequently used in the literature, too loosely, as a simile for personnel management. This has also been reflected in practice where organisations have relabelled their personnel function. It is not unusual to find that Personnel Departments have become HRM Departments, Personnel Managers HR Managers and Personnel Officers HR Officers with no commensurate change in their underpinning ideology or in the way functional roles are executed. This is akin to the proverbial case of 'old wine in new bottles'!

Second, this loose use of the term creates the possibility that some texts masquerade as HRM when they essentially cover the same ground found in earlier personnel management texts. An analysis of titles lining the bookshelves in one of our studies illustrates this point very well. This revealed that of those texts published in the last ten years (1996–2006): 58 per cent referred to HRM; 18 per cent to SHRM; 8 per cent to HR Strategies; 5 per cent to Management of Human Resources; 5 per cent to People Resourcing; and 5 per cent to Personnel Management. In summary, therefore, over 75 per cent used HRM in the title and only 5 per cent Personnel Management. An analysis of the content of these texts builds on the old wine in new bottles analogy. Many of these HRM texts and some of the SHRM texts allude to strategic integration but arguably after a nod in that direction proceed to present the material in a relatively standard way without maintaining an explicit strategic focus throughout.

We hope that when reading our text you will agree that the strategic component of HRM underpins the content throughout. We have attempted to build on the personnel foundations of HR theory and practice by exploring in detail what is meant by strategic integration, both generally and with specific reference to a selection of HR levers and issues around its development and delivery in practice. In order to stress this strategic focus and differentiate our work from those loosely titled HRM texts, we have adopted, with reservation, the title *Strategic Human Resource Management*. However, this leads to a second conundrum.

Throughout the period of the book's conception we found it difficult to reconcile two conflicting interests. First, we wanted to address our criticism of other HRM texts and discuss in detail how the various components of HR (or HR levers) such as recruitment and selection, reward management, employee relations and downsizing, etc., could be aligned to organisational strategy both conceptually and in practice. Second, it was recognised that to treat each area of HR in isolation of the other HR levers in this way would be inconsistent with the horizontal integration dimension of HRM identified above which anticipates their development as a bundle of practices. In the final analysis we could not find a way of doing this to our satisfaction and instead adopted a compromise position.

The book is divided into two parts. Part 1, through four chapters (Chapter 1, 'Strategy and human resource management'; Chapter 2, 'Strategic human resource management: a vital piece in the jigsaw of organisational success?'; Chapter 3, SHRM in a changing and shrinking world: internationalisation of business and the role of SHRM'; and Chapter 4, 'Evaluating SHRM: why bother and does it really happen in practice?'), provides an overview of the SHRM territory. In addressing the substance of their respective chapter titles, we have endeavoured in this part to present a holistic view of SHRM. A particular concern has been to surface the complexity lying behind the notion of strategic integration and to explore how this complexity impacts on the conceptual development and practical application of SHRM. In support of our attempts in Part 1 to present a holistic approach to the subject domain, we have used one integrated case study to cover all four chapters rather than the chapter case studies that are a feature of Part 2. This comprehensive, integrated case – Strategic human resource management at Halcrow Group Limited – appears at the end of Part 1 and hopefully sets the scene for the exploration of specific HR levers that follows.

The second part looks in detail at ten selected HRM levers and critically examines how they too can be conceived strategically and operationalised through organisation practice. The ten areas selected for Part 2 inevitably reflect our personal views. They are included because we feel that they all represent critical components of SHRM practice. Many of these selected levers (strategic human resource planning, strategic recruitment and selection, performance management, strategic human resource development, strategic reward management and strategic employee relations) will be found in the majority of HRM texts while others (organisation structures, culture, diversity and downsizing) are less frequently covered. This is not to say that our selection will find favour with everybody and we are already considering the possibility of including chapters on change management, competences and flexibility in any future edition. Hopefully, feedback on this first edition will throw up other possibilities for us to consider. However, in all cases our treatment of the ten selected topics concentrates on their strategic construction and organisational manifestation and consistently adopts a critical perspective that surfaces the difficulties of putting the rhetoric of SHRM into practice. However, in disaggregating this HRM 'bundle' to examine its constituent parts we have not abandoned the central HRM tenet of horizontal integration. Throughout the chapters making up Part 2, we provide cross-references to other HR levers to emphasise their interconnectedness and use other devices, selectively, to reinforce the essence of horizontal integration. For example, in Chapter 8 ('Strategic recruitment and selection') we provide a specific example to demonstrate how recruitment and selection can help facilitate the horizontal integration of the various HR levers, and in Chapter 7 ('Strategic human resource planning, the weakest link?') frequently use the theme of mergers and acquisitions to illustrate the need for 'joined-up' HRM thinking. Also, although each chapter concludes with its own topic-specific case study, it is possible to use the integrated Halcrow case to explore further the strategic connections of the various HR levers presented. Nevertheless we accept that our approach remains something of a compromise and runs the risk of falling between two stools. We accept that our position could alternatively be viewed positively as a pragmatic solution to our dilemma or negatively simply as a cop out.

We now leave it to you, our readers, to judge whether or not we have met our aims, which can be summarised as: to write a SHRM book that

- maintains a rigorous and critical focus on the 'S' of 'SHRM' throughout rather than resorting to a more traditional, personnel management, treatment of the subject domain;
- through its written style and supporting pedagogic features can be readily understood by its potential readership;
- conveys the central importance of vertical and horizontal strategic alignment in a way that enables the reader to appreciate the holistic nature of the concept and how it can be applied in practice to recognised specific areas of HR activity; and
- grounds the reader in the practicalities of organisational life in a way that enables them to distinguish between SHRM rhetoric and reality.

Although it could be said that 'we would say that any way', we would argue that there are early signs that we are well on the road to achieving our aims. During the course of writing this book we have 'test marketed' much of its content. Selected chapter drafts have been used as basic readings to support the teaching of SHRM to level three undergraduates and master's stage postgraduates. The majority of feedback has been that our work does treat the 'S' of 'SHRM' with more integrity than the majority of texts, through its rigorous exploration of the strategic alignment of HRM theory and practice, and does so in a way that can be understood. We are not quite sure how we should have reacted to the student who said that the readings were 'exhaustive if not exhausting' but are grateful to those students who have confessed that the readings were the inspiration behind their choice of dissertation or workplace management report topics. It is encouraging to know that we have budding researchers, currently out in the field, investigating the extent to which case organisations are practising respectively strategic recruitment and selection, and strategic human resource development. Indeed, one of these students has adapted their project to form the basis of the strategic recruitment and selection case study appearing at the end of Chapter 8! For those seeking ideas to kick-start their own research projects, each chapter concludes with 'Follow-up study suggestions' and 'Suggestions for research projects'. Hopefully these will not only serve as a vehicle for reinforcing the book's content but, for some, also help to maintain a growing interest in SHRM.

Acknowledgements

We would like to thank all those who helped to make the production of this book possible:

- those who granted us organisational access and support to produce a range of case studies that are a strong feature of this book;
- staff at Pearson Education who have helped steer us through the whole process, from the original book proposal right through to its publication; and
- friends, colleagues and, particularly, family who have had to put up with us while we endeavoured to bring the project to fruition.

Case studies are a commonly used vehicle for integrating theory and practice and help the reader actively engage in the subject material. We are, therefore, particularly grateful to those who granted access and provided cooperation and help to allow us to generate the case studies featured in this book.

The case studies in this book are all based on real organisations and examine their HR practice to explore its strategic credentials. Some of the cases, featuring named organisations, are based on published or publicly available information. However, the majority are based on data sourced directly from the organisations concerned and provided or written up by their staff. We would therefore like to thank the following people and their organisations who provided access to and supplied the data to generate these case studies and gave permission to use them.

Part 1 case study

Strategic human resource management at Halcrow Group Limited – an integrated case relating to the major themes developed in the first four chapters of this book which, taken together, provide an overview of the strategic human resource territory: Mandy Clarke, Director of Human Resources of Halcrow Group Limited, for permission to use the case study and for her considerable assistance and support in its preparation.

Part 2 case studies

- **Case 5 – DaimlerChrysler AG:** Professor Peter Weis, Dean, University of Applied Science, Kempten, Germany, for support and permission to develop and use this case.

- **Case 6 – Corporate culture and Group values at Dicom Group plc:** Kevin Davies, Managing Director of DICOM Technologies Ltd, for permission to use the case study, and the considerable assistance of Steve Barker, Operations Manager Dicom Technologies Ltd, in its preparation.

- **Case 8 – Recruitment and selection at Southco Europe Ltd:** Scott Duncan and Russ Pender, the outgoing and incoming Managing Directors of Southco Europe Ltd, for their support and permission to use this case, and Inge Studnik who was, at the time, Executive Assistant of Southco Europe Ltd, for taking the lead role in its preparation.

- **In Practice 8.3 – Recruitment and selection at the Dionysos:** Ahmet Senol, Managing Director of the Dionysos Hotel, for permission to use this case and for his considerable assistance and support in its preparation.

- **Case 9 – Performance management at Tyco:** Thanks are due to Tyco Ltd. for permission to use this case, and to Joanna Binstead for her support.

- **Case 12 – Strategic approaches to the employment relationship social partnership: the example of the Republic of Ireland:** Dr Terry Cradden, former Head of School, University of Ulster, for his support and guidance in developing this case.

- **Case 13 – Making diversity an issue in leafy Elgarshire:** Roger Britton, Development and Training Manager (Human Resources) of Worcestershire County Council, for permission to use the case study and for his considerable assistance and support in its development.

We would also like to thank all of the staff at Pearson Education (both past and present) who have supported us through all the stages of writing this book, from its inception to final production and appearance on the bookshelves, and Professor Denise Skinner of Coventry Business School, Coventry University, and Dr Savita Kumra of Oxford Brookes University Business School, for co-authoring Chapters 4 and 13 respectively.

Finally, our thanks go to Alice, Jenny, Jane, Jan, Roisin, Stephen, Jennifer, Jemma, Ben, Andrew and Katie for being so understanding and tolerant of our lengthy absences thinking about and writing our contributions to this book, and the pressures we have inevitably imposed on family life as a consequence.

Publisher's acknowledgements

We are grateful to the Financial Times Limited for permission to reprint the following material:

Chapter 1 'Strategic "Microsoft concern ad 'technology lag'", © *Financial Times*, 10 November 2005; Chapter 3 'The WTO smoothes the path to trade between US and China', © *Financial Times*, 22 April 2004; Chapter 14 'MG Rover staff benefit from speedy payout', © *Financial Times*, 3 May 2005; Chapter 14 'New employment found by 1,250 ex-Rover workers', © *Financial Times*, 22 June 2005; Chapter 14 'Waiting game ended in tears as SAIC deal for Rover failed to materialize', © *Financial Times*, 17 October 2005;

We are grateful to the following for permission to use copyright material:

'Shortage of people to run hot technologies' from *The Financial Times Limited*, 9 November 2005, © Ian Limbach; Extract from 'Capability procedures for teachers' is reproduced from Croner's The Teacher's Legal Guide and with kind permission of

Wolters Kluwer (UK) Limited (c) 2007. All rights reserved. No part of this documentation may be reproduced, stored in a retrieval system or transmitted in any form or by any means without the prior written permission of Wolters Kluwer (UK) Limited. Croner is a Trading Division of Wolters Kluwer (UK) Limited (www.croner.co.uk); Extract from 'Broadbanded pay: on the right track at EWS', from IRS Employment Review 796, 2004, reprinted by kind permission of Reed Business Information; Extract from 'Family breakdown: developing an explanatory theory of reward system change', from IRS Employment Review 796, 2004, by Lewis, P., Thornhill, A. and Saunders, M., from Personnel Review 33.2, 2004, reprinted by kind permission of Emerald Group Publishing Limited; Table 3.1 from *World Investment Report*, UNCTAD (Anon., 2003): the United Nations is the author of the original material; Table 3.4 from *Globalizing Human Resource Management*, Routledge (Sparrow, P., Brewster, C. and Harris, H., 2004); Figure 4.4 from *Research Methods for Business Students, 4th Edition*, FT Prentice Hall (Saunders, M., Lewis, P. Millmore, M. and Thornhill, A., 2006); Figure 6.4, Table 6.5 and Figure 6.7 from *Managing Change: A Human Resource Strategy Approach*, FT Prentice Hall (Thornhill, A., Lewis, P. Millmore, M. and Saunders, M.N.K., 2000); Figure 6.6 from *Exploring Corporate Strategy, Text and Cases, 6th Edition* (Johnson, G. and Scholes, K., 2003); Table 7.1 – this material is taken from *HR Forecasting and Planning*, by Turner, P. (2002), with the permission of the publisher, the Chartered Institute of Personnel and Development, London; Figure 8.3 from Just how extensive is the practice of strategic management and selection? in *The Irish Journal of Management*, Vol. 24, No. 1, Irish Academy of Management (Millmore, M., 2003).

In some instances we have been unable to trace the owners of copyright material, and we would appreciate any information that would enable us to do so.

Guided Tour of the Book

← Full page **chapter openers** list the **learning outcomes** that enable you to see what you should achieve from the chapter.

All chapters contain **summary maps** to help you grasp the overall picture. →

In practice boxes give you an idea of how the theory is applied in real-world situations. →

← **Key concepts** throughout the text highlight major or established theoretical ideas.

Figures in every chapter present information in diagrammatic form to aid your understanding.

Self-check and reflect questions are positioned at strategic points throughout the text to confirm your grasp of the learning points and understand both the theory and practice that has gone before.

End-of-chapter **summaries** provide an overview of what each chapter has covered and are a useful check and revision of the chapter content.

Follow-up study questions and **suggestions for research topics** will reinforce the book's content and help kick-start students' research projects.

Part 1 ends with a major **case study** that brings together all the ideas and issues discussed in chapters 1 to 4, and ends with **case study questions** that challenge your understanding.

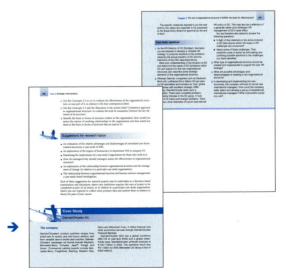

Each chapter in Part 2 ends with an end-of-chapter **case study** again with pertinent case study questions.

About the authors

Mike Millmore, BA, MSc, MA, PGCE, FCIPD, is a Visiting Fellow in Human Resource Management (HRM) at Gloucestershire Business School, University of Gloucestershire. As an HR generalist, he has taught a range of HRM subjects to postgraduate, undergraduate and professional students as well as supervising master's dissertations. Mike's main areas of interest and research are strategic human resource management, human resource development, human resource planning and, particularly, recruitment and selection, on which he has published several articles. He led the University's MA Management of Human Resources course for a number of years and has undertaken consultancy in both public and private sectors. He is co-author with Philip, Mark and Adrian of *Managing Change: A human resource strategy approach*, published by Financial Times Prentice Hall. Prior to his career in higher education, Mike worked for Hoover Ltd in both personnel and training roles. For roughly one-third of his career, Mike has worked in a variety of management roles including as a Training Manager and as a senior general manger within education. As Head of Department of Management and Business Studies and Dean of the University's Business School, Mike oversaw the development and implementation of three phases of faculty strategy designed to accommodate intra- and inter-organisational mergers. During this period the key focus was on integrating prior knowledge and experience of management and HR theory and practice to develop strategic HR responses to the changing strategic mosaic.

Philip Lewis, BA, PhD, MSc, MCIPD, PGDipM, Cert Ed, is a freelance lecturer and author of Human Resource Management. He teaches HRM and research methods to postgraduate, undergraduate and professional students, and is involved in research degree supervision. Philip's research interests are reward management and performance management, on which he has published several articles. He is co-author with Mark and Adrian of *Research Methods for Business Students* and *Employee Relations: Understanding the employment relationship* and with Adrian, Mike and Mark of *Managing Change: A human resource strategy approach*, all published by Financial Times Prentice Hall. He has undertaken consultancy in both public and private sectors. Prior to his career in higher education, Philip was a training advisor with the Distributive Industry Training Board.

Mark N.K. Saunders, BA, MSc, PGCE, PhD, MCIPD, is Assistant Dean: Director of Research and Doctoral Programmes at Oxford Brookes University Business School. He is also visiting professor at Newcastle Business School, University of Northumbria. Prior to this he was Head of the Human Resource Management Research Centre at Gloucestershire Business School. He currently teaches research methods to master's and doctoral students as well as supervising master's dissertations and research degrees in the area of human resource management. Mark has published a number of articles on trust and organisational justice perspectives on the management of change, research methods and service quality. He is co-author with Philip and Adrian of *Research Methods for Business Students* and *Employee Relations: Understanding the employment relationship*, and with Adrian, Philip and Mike of *Managing Change: A human resource strategy approach*, all published by Financial Times Prentice Hall, and has also co-authored a book on business statistics. He has undertaken consultancy in public, private and not-for-profit sectors, prior to which he had a variety of research jobs in local government.

Adrian Thornhill, BA, PhD, PGCE, FCIPD, is Head of the Department of Human Resource Management at Gloucestershire Business School, University of Gloucestershire. He teaches HRM and research methods to postgraduate, undergraduate and professional students, and is involved in research degree supervision. Adrian has published a number of articles principally associated with employee and justice perspectives related to managing change and the management of organisational downsizing and redundancy. He is co-author with Mark and Philip of *Research Methods for Business Students* and *Employee Relations: Understanding the employment relationship* and with Philip, Mike and Mark of *Managing Change: A human resource strategy approach*, all published by Financial Times Prentice Hall and has also co-authored a book on downsizing and redundancy. He has undertaken consultancy in both public and private sectors.

Trevor Morrow, BA, PGDIP, PGCUT, PhD, MCIPD, is a lecturer in Business Studies at the University of Ulster's School of International Business. He currently teaches human resource management and employee relations to undergraduate and master's students as well as supervising master's dissertations and research degrees in the area of human resource management. Trevor's primary research focus is within the field of international strategic human resource management. Trevor is the joint editor of the *Irish Journal of Management* and is the lead editor of *International Business in an Enlarging Europe* (Palgrave Macmillan, 2005). He has chaired three major international conferences and is course director of the University of Ulster's MSc in International Business. Trevor has published several articles within the area of SHRM. Trevor spent three years as a visiting lecturer, teaching on the International Executive MBA at the Michael Smurfit Graduate School of Business, University College Dublin. He has undertaken consultancy in both public and private sectors.

Professor Denise Skinner is Professor of Human Resource Management at Coventry Business School Coventry University.

Dr. Savita Kumra is Senior Lecturer in International Human Resource Management at Oxford Brookes University Business School.

Part 1

Overview

1 Strategy and human resource management

Learning Outcomes

By the end of this chapter you should be able to:

- Define the term strategy.
- Describe and evaluate a range of approaches to strategy making.
- Analyse links between different approaches to strategy and human resource management (HRM).
- Understand the significance of strategic integration to explore links between strategy and HRM and its multi-dimensional nature.
- Analyse the resource-based view of the organisation and describe key concepts related to this approach.
- Describe and evaluate links between resource-based theory and HRM.

Introduction

Strategic human resource management (SHRM) is concerned with the relationship between an organisation's strategic management and the management of its human resources (Boxall, 1996). *Strategic management* focuses on the scope and direction of an organisation, and often involves dealing with uncertainty and complexity. Johnson and Scholes (2002) define strategic management in terms of the following three main elements.

1. 'Understanding the strategic position of an organisation' (Johnson and Scholes, 2002: 16), which relates to management's understanding about:
   - the impact of the external environment on organisational strategy;
   - the organisation's strategic capability; and
   - the influence and expectations of its key stakeholders.

2. Management exercising 'strategic choice' about possible future strategies, to seek competitive advantage (or organisational effectiveness in the case of public sector or voluntary organisations).

3. 'Translating strategy into action', through the development of appropriate structures, processes and resources within the organisation and managing change (Johnson and Scholes, 2002: 21).

In Practice 1.1 is an illustration of a strategic response by one major multi-national: Sony Corporation.

In Practice   1.1

Restructuring Sony

In autumn 2005 Sony Corp.'s new management team looked set to announce another round of job cuts and new investment in fast-growing digital electronics as part of its strategy to turn the company around. The world's second-largest consumer electronics maker was aiming to strike a delicate balance between painful restructuring and forward-looking investments to drive growth and win back consumers and investors.

Sony was likely to accelerate the shift of resources to more promising digital ones, such as next-generation DVD recorders, high-definition camcorders and flat panel TVs, from analog products.

According to Reuters, analysts said that sizeable job cuts were likely as Sony downsized its cathode ray tube (CRT) TV operations, narrowed its research and development focus, and looked to eliminate head office staff. Sony had already slashed about 20,000 jobs under its current three-year restructuring plan that ran through to March 2006, but to no visible effect. Revenues had been shrinking and in 2005 Sony was flirting with an operating loss.

The company had been closing production lines for CRT sets over the past few years, but was still far behind rivals Matsushita Electric Industrial and Sharp Corp. in making the switch to flat panel TVs.

Some commentators were looking for wide-ranging restructuring across the electronics operations including its components business, its PC unit and its CD/MD Walkman operations, amid a rapid switch in the industry to digital music players. The inventor of the Walkman pioneered the portable music market a quarter-century ago, but has since been outfoxed in the digital era by Apple Computer Inc. and its popular iPod player and iTunes online music store.

Source: Reuters (2005).

People are a key resource, critically influencing each of these elements of strategic management. People form a significant component of an organisation's strategic capability and the ability to understand the organisation's strategic position will largely be a function of the capabilities of the organisation's people. People's capabilities also affect the exercise of strategic choice and the effectiveness of the way in which strategy is translated into action, as is considered in more depth later in this chapter. People's capabilities in an organisation result from the employment and management of its human resources. The relationship between an organisation's human resource strategy (in brief, how it selects, uses, develops, rewards and treats its employees) and its strategic management is therefore of great importance.

The exact nature of this relationship in practice, however, is likely to be difficult to analyse and evaluate, not least because strategic management is a far from simple matter. Strategy and strategy making, as the basis of strategic management, are problematic and contested areas. As Whittington (2001: 2) notes, 'there is not much agreement about strategy'. To develop an understanding of SHRM it is necessary to explore the relationship between strategic management and HRM. To do this Boxall (1996) maintains that two difficult questions have to be addressed:

1. what is strategy? (content); and

2. how is strategy formed? (process).

Building from these two questions, the chapter begins with a focus on strategy and, particularly, strategy making in order to provide a foundation for subsequent chapter sections that concentrate on developing their links to SHRM. When referring to the links between strategy and human resource management the term strategic integration is used and the second part of this chapter is designed to explore what is meant by this concept. This is initially done by examining how HRM can be linked to the different approaches to strategy making outlined in the opening section. Different perspectives on the nature of strategic integration that enable it to be constructed as a multi-dimensional concept are then considered.

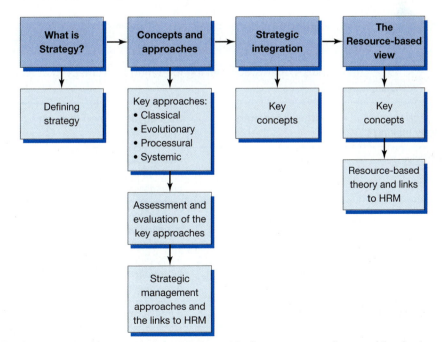

Figure 1.1 Mapping the strategy and human resource management territory: a summary diagram of the chapter content

The concluding section of the chapter explores the more recent recognition of a different approach to making strategy that places an organisation's human resource capabilities at the centre of this process. This is the resource-based view of the firm or resource-based theory. Traditional views of strategy see it as a process of analysing the external environment of an organisation in order to devise a strategic direction that matches the opportunities that this offers to ensure future success. The resource-based view shifts this view so that strategy making focuses on the internal capabilities of an organisation including its people, particularly those that give it some unique or valuable position, so that these can be used as the basis of its strategic direction to ensure future success.

Strategy and strategy making

Understanding strategy and strategy making is problematic. This leads to a lack of agreed definitions and explanations about the processes involved. A number of different approaches to strategy and strategy making are described and discussed in the literature (e.g. Mintzberg *et al.*, 1998; Whittington, 2001). In this section Whittington's (2001) framework will be followed, which outlines the four approaches to strategy and strategy making:

1. classical;
2. evolutionary;
3. processual; and
4. systemic.

These four approaches are supplemented by the more finely graded analysis of Mintzberg *et al.* (1998), who outline ten schools of strategy-making theory and practice (see Key Concepts 1.1). Each of these approaches will be described and discussed, and their respective links to human resource management will be explored below.

Key Concepts		**1.1**

Ten schools of strategy making identified by Mintzberg *et al.* (1998)

Approach to strategy making	School of strategy	Strategy is formed through
Prescriptive	Design	a *conceptual* process
	Planning	a *formal* process
	Positioning	an *analytical* process
Processual	Entrepreneurial	a *visionary* process
	Cognitive	a *mental* process
	Learning	an *emergent* process
	Power	a *negotiated* process
	Cultural	a *collective* process
	Environmental	a *reactive* process
Transformational	Configuration	a *transformational* process

Source: adapted from Mintzberg *et al.* (1998); Purcell (2001).

Classical approach

The *classical approach* was developed as a theoretical discipline in the 1960s (Chandler, 1962; Sloan, 1963; Ansoff, 1965) and emphasises strategy as being a rational, deliberate, linear and top-down process, where conception is separated from implementation through the creation of strategic plans that are passed down to others to implement. This process involves a number of strategic planning steps including:

- analysing an organisation's environment and its internal resources;
- identifying and evaluating strategic options;
- implementing the strategy chosen.

Integral to this approach to strategic management are a range of techniques and tools, ranging from a SWOT (strengths, weaknesses, opportunities and threats) analysis to a variety of diagrammatic and quantitative methods. SWOT analysis has been used widely to appraise the strengths and weaknesses of the organisation and the opportunities and threats evident in its external environment. The use of this and other analytical techniques theoretically leads senior managers to identify a range of strategic options from which the future strategy of the organisation will be chosen. This strategy will be intended to produce a match, or fit, between the organisation's internal resources and the opportunities available in its external environment. The goal is to achieve competitive advantage over its competitors or to produce a state of organisational effectiveness.

Mintzberg *et al.* (1998) essentially see this approach to strategy as a process of conception. Within the classical approach, they differentiate between what they term the design school, as outlined above, the planning school and the positioning school. Respectively, these schools of thought were developed in the 1960s, 1970s and 1980s. The *planning school* was different from the *design school* because it elaborated on and formalised strategic planning and stressed the importance of strategic planners to inform and advise an organisation's chief executive, who, instead of formulating strategy according to the design school, became responsible for choosing it. The *positioning school*, in contrast to the two previous schools of thought, advocated that, instead of an open choice of strategy, organisations should adopt one of a restricted choice of strategic positions to achieve competitive advantage. Porter's work (1980, 1985) is identified as the major focal point and driving force in the development of this school of thought. Porter (1985) identified three generic strategies: cost leadership, differentiation and focus (see Key Concepts 1.2). He believed that it would be necessary for a firm to choose one of these positions to gain competitive advantage.

Key Concepts 1.2

Porter's three generic strategies for competitive advantage

Cost leadership

This strategy is designed to achieve competitive advantage through operating as a low-cost producer. This can be achieved through large-scale production methods that incorporate economies of scale, controlling operating costs tightly and being very efficient.

Differentiation

This strategy is based on developing product differentiation, engendering brand recognition and customer loyalty. This can be achieved by developing high-quality products and/or superior performance, together with perceptions about quality and superiority, which can be reflected in the pricing position used.

Key concepts continued

Focus

This strategy is designed to achieve penetration into a particular market niche, where this is achieved in association with cost leadership or differentiation (see In Practice 1.2).

A key element in the classical approach is the process of identifying and choosing strategy, whether from an unrestricted or from a constrained choice. According to this approach, strategic choice will be determined by the logic of the analysis related to the appraisals that are undertaken of the organisation itself and the external environment within which it operates. The classical approach, as indicated above, is rooted in a rational and objective paradigm. However, the contested nature of these assumptions about the classical approach suggests that strategic choice will be much more problematic in practice. The theory of 'strategy choice' developed by Child (1972, 1997) will now be explored, followed by an examination of more general criticisms of the classical approach.

In Practice   1.2

Milking the market: rational analysis of the market for soft cheese

At the first of a series of Milk Development Council meetings covering on-farm processing, farmers were told that soft cheese, in particular, was a 'growth market'. Developing new farmhouse cheeses with a strong local identity is one of the best opportunities for dairy farmers considering on-farm processing. With UK cheese consumption now running at about 10 kg a head per year – compared with 18.5 kg in the rest of the EU – the regional cheese market is ripe for expansion.

Farmers were also told that UK consumption of imported soft cheeses is increasing, so there's a good opportunity for UK dairy farmers to develop the home-produced market. But, although there's potential, farmers must devise a strong concept for any new product launch. They were advised that as well as actually producing a high-quality food, farmers must ensure that they create the correct identity and marketing strategy.

Source: Farmers' Weekly Interactive (2006).

Evaluating the classical approach: strategic choice in practice

The classical approach implies that the strategy of an organisation should be determined by its organisational and environmental contingencies. Child published his 1972 paper on the nature of strategic choice as a 'corrective' to this deterministic view (1997: 43), which he believed to be inadequate because it fails 'to give due attention to the agency of choice by whoever have the power to direct the organisation' (1972: 2). This view recognises the existence of a political perspective in strategy making. The political perspective suggests that the preferences of key people in an organisation, its dominant coalition, to be reflected in the decisions taken. Child (1997: 45) therefore defines *strategic choice* as 'the process whereby power-holders within organisations decide upon courses of strategic action'. This recognises that managers in organisations will exercise some level of personal choice and behave proactively, rather than simply being directed by the constraints implied by environmental and organisational analyses and behaving reactively as a result (Child, 1972). However, Child (1997: 46) did not seek to substitute this view about agency of choice for determinism completely; rather he advocated a potential synthesis between the political process and functionalist perspectives because the power available to decision-makers was seen to be accountable in terms of the consequences for organisational performance that was the result of its exercise.

In reality, strategic choice will therefore be informed by political considerations that reflect the interests and values of the dominant coalition in an organisation. These considerations will affect decisions taken about strategy, as well as other aspects of organisational design. This will at least be the case when organisational performance is perceived as successful by key stakeholders such as shareholders. It highlights a subjective perspective to this process in practice, contrary to the presupposed position of the classical approach as entirely rational and objective. In this way, the exercise of political preference may be seen as a constraint on the nature of 'rational' strategy making. However, as Child indicates above, this view should not be used to assume that those in power will be able to exercise choice about strategy in a way that is entirely self-interested.

Child's 1997 paper recognises that there will be a wider range of constraints placed on the way in which decision makers exercise strategic choice in practice. In addition to the exercise of political considerations, strategic choice will also be likely to be constrained by cultural, psychological and logistical issues (see In Practice 1.3). Strategic decisions taken by multinational organisations, for example, will be taken with a number of considerations in mind, not the least of which is the attitude of the host country's government toward its operations. The development of theory related to national and organisational cultures (e.g. Hofstede, 1980) demonstrates how cultural values and institutionalised norms are likely to be internalised with the result that these constrain choice through the ways in which individuals perceive and interpret events and take action. This perspective will be returned to below when the systemic approach to strategy is considered, and also more fully in Chapter 6.

Points of view or norms about strategic action that are prevalent in an industry or organisation may also restrict a decision-maker's choice of strategy. Other psychological and logistical factors that may limit consideration about choice of strategy include time pressure and information load and the way in which individuals cope with these (Dutton, 1993; Child, 1997). Child also refers to imperfect information as a further factor that will constrain the choice of decision-makers in organisations. Information that is available may be limited in relation to its completeness and/or its ability to inform the decision-making process, especially where this is characterised by uncertainty.

In Practice 1.3

The impact of environmental concern on motor vehicle manufacturers

Throughout the world, the use of motor vehicles is growing. The environmental cost of this is well known. Throughout their life cycle, vehicles impact the environment in several ways: energy and resource consumption, waste generation during manufacturing and use, and disposal at the end of their useful lives. About 75 per cent of end-of-life vehicles, mainly metals, are recyclable in the European Union (Kanari et al., 2003). The remaining 25 per cent of the vehicle is considered waste and generally goes to landfills. Environmental legislation of the European Union (EU) requires the reduction of this waste to a maximum of 5 per cent by 2015.

On the face of it, this is a constraint upon the activity of motor vehicle manufacturers which forms part of the raft of considerations that need to be taken into account in the strategy-making process. But it is important that motor vehicle manufacturers keep track of the wider cultural nuances in society that move governments to take such legislative action.

Child (1997) concludes that these contributions have developed the scope of the original (1972) theory of strategic choice. The theory of strategic choice therefore encompasses a range of factors that place limitations on the presupposed rational and objective linkages implicit in the classical approach to determine strategy.

Evaluating the classical approach: intentions, outcomes and learning

The theory of strategic choice highlights limitations to human cognition. Simon (e.g. 1976) introduced the concept of *bounded rationality* to refer to the cognitive and behavioural limitations involved in collecting and processing information to make decisions. Perfectly rational behaviour would mean collecting all relevant information, considering this fully and evaluating it objectively to choose the best possible strategy (Simon, 1976). As has been seen above, this is unlikely to occur. Instead, what Simon calls bounds on human rationality result from the limitations involved in collecting and processing information. These bounds are linked to the existence of cultural filters and imperfect information, particularly in situations marked by complexity. If the classical approach sees strategy as being both rational and deliberate, then questions raised about the bounded rationality of decision-making will also reflect on the deliberate decisions that are taken. Decision-making processes that are not strictly rational will be likely to affect the nature of the outcomes that result, since all factors affecting the decision will not have been considered (e.g. Cyert and March, 1963; Simon, 1976).

In this context, Mintzberg *et al.* (1998) differentiate between realised and unrealised strategies. A *deliberate strategy* is one where strategic planning leads to a set of intended outcomes that are fully realised. However, in many cases, planned outcomes will not be realised in practice. These are intended strategies that are unrealised. Mintzberg *et al.* (1998) offer a number of reasons to explain why these become unrealised. These include the problem of coping with uncertainty, a factor which faces most organisations. This will make it difficult to anticipate future conditions and design an effective strategy. It may also lead to the development of an increasingly inappropriate strategy where changing conditions indicate the need for a different direction.

Evolutionary perspectives

Whereas the classical approach emphasises the role of planning, with senior managers responsible for ensuring that strategy achieves an effective fit or match between the organisation's resource capabilities and the external environment to be able to exploit evident opportunities, *evolutionary perspectives* on strategy place much greater emphasis on the role of environmental forces. Mintzberg *et al.* (1998) label this approach the *environmental school.* They say that those who advocate this view see an organisation and its managers as being subordinate to the external environment, with management's role as one of reacting to environmental forces. The role of management is to match strategy to these external forces. Contingency theory or the contingency approach, described in Chapter 5, identifies a number of broad dimensions including stability, complexity, diversity and hostility to which managers need to react. For example, environmental complexity would require the introduction of decentralised decision to facilitate organisational effectiveness. (Chapter 3 details the way in which this may be the response of some multi-national corporations.) In this way, organisations undergo adaptation to their environment.

However, for some who subscribe to an evolutionary approach, such as population ecologists (Hannan and Freeman, 1988), such interventions will only have limited effects. Organisational characteristics, which according to *population ecologists* are difficult to change, will determine whether an organisation survives in its environment or not in the fullness of time: as population increases and hence intensifies competition for resources, some organisations with particular characteristics will be selected out, while others remain. This approach introduces notions of natural selection and sees market competition as the determination of success or failure: that is, survival. The key emphasis in this construction is environmental fit or specialisation, rather than any strategic intervention by managers. This suggests that an environment will determine the criteria of fit and, therefore, which organisations survive over the longer term. Survival in this context will be demonstrated by superior performance and the achievement of profit maximisation (Mintzberg *et al.*, 1998; Whittington, 2001).

Evaluating evolutionary perspectives

This view has been contested on a number of grounds. For example, environmental systems may be more open than is being suggested and are therefore receptive to greater variation than is implied by the ecology approach. More fundamentally, the assumption that organisations are only acted upon, or selected, by their environment, rather than enacting with it, has been strongly contested (e.g. Mintzberg *et al.*, 1998). Whittington (2001) refers to the work of Penrose (1952), who points out that many large firms effectively select and dominate particular markets, rather than the market undertaking the selection. Organisations may also cooperate with each other through a number of formal and informal means to ensure their survival. These criticisms have lead to some reframing of this evolutionary perspective on strategy, although it appears to continue to find advocates, either explicitly or implicitly. Whittington (2001: 19) discusses the implications of this perspective for strategy; in competitive circumstances it is likely to lead to 'strategic conservatism', where organisational efforts are focused on the basics of production, costs are minimised and operating efficiencies sought. Apart from those who enjoy considerable market power, most firms according to this view should be attempting to operate as efficiently as possible.

Processual approach

The processual approach to strategy making commences from radically different assumptions from those of the classical approach. The classical approach conceives of strategy making as a rational, deliberate and linear process, resulting in the formulation of strategic plans that are handed down for implementation. But the *processual approach* identifies strategy as an adaptive and emergent process, driven by learning in an organisation. In this way, the formulation and implementation of strategy become, in practice, a more integrated or fluid process. Consequently, strategies are seen to form through action. Mintzberg (1987) refers to the approach of 'crafting strategy'. He sees the development of strategy as analogous to the approach of skilled experts, whose knowledge and skills mean that they conceive of (formulate) as well as execute (implement) their work in an integral manner. If you ask most skilled workers to distinguish between the formulation and implementation their work, they may find this difficult. In reality, the two are integrated. This provides a powerful contrast to the classical approach. Organisational strategies may emerge through opportunities that become apparent from the work of people employed at different levels in an organisation rather than just being deliberately planned from the top. Small, incremental steps, related to, say, product development or service delivery, lead to success and the emergence of a pattern of action. This then becomes recognised and established in an organisation. Moreover, recognition leads to this pattern of action becoming an organisational strategy in the formal sense (Quinn, 1980; Mintzberg, 1987, Mintzberg *et al.*, 1998).

Mintzberg and colleagues have termed this approach to strategy making, the *learning school*. Strategy is seen to emerge through a process of collective learning in an organisation (or outside the organisation, see In Practice 1.4). This is believed to be particularly important in the context of unstable environments, characterised by uncertainty. In such a context, advocates of this school believe that learning through time provides an effective means to develop strategy in circumstances that otherwise make it difficult to first develop a formal strategic plan prior to implementation.

In Practice   1.4

Product development at Microsoft

Napoleon is reported to have said, 'No battle plan survives contact with the enemy.' Similarly, no software product, no matter how well designed and conceived, survives first customer contact without requiring changes. As a result, at some point during the development process, product teams decide their product is far enough along to begin getting external feedback to help validate the features and architecture. To help get that feedback while there is still enough time to act, most product groups release alpha versions of their products.

Sometimes these alpha (or preview) releases are given to only select customers who have demonstrated a willingness to examine pre-release products and are known to give quality feedback. At other times (as with Microsoft Visual Studio and Windows 'Longhorn'), they are made available for download. Customers who are participating in a formal alpha program typically have dedicated Microsoft support resources available to them. Those in the download program have only public newsgroups to assist them.

In addition to providing Microsoft with feedback, alpha releases give customers an early look at the architecture of a product and help them make decisions on how and when to use the product. Customers using alpha releases in this fashion, however, must accept that the final product will differ, sometimes significantly, from the alpha, and any plans will need to be re-evaluated as the product nears completion.

Finally, an alpha release can serve a marketing purpose for Microsoft, particularly for products that require significant third-party developer support or which have long lead times for adoption. Publicising the availability of alpha builds helps Microsoft competitively by slowing the adoption of competing products and can draw developers and IT managers' attention towards its own offerings, even if they are not yet commercially available. Using pre-release builds to draw attention in this manner is by no means unique to Microsoft.

Source: DeMichillie (2004).

Evaluating the processual approach

Mintzberg *et al.* (1998) point out that while emergent strategy making emphasises learning, deliberate strategy emphasises control. In this way, the classical approach seeks to emphasise management control over strategy. They state that, 'all real strategic behaviour has to combine deliberate control with emergent learning' (1998: 195). The role of organisational leaders should be to develop an approach to strategic management that subtly exercises control while facilitating learning, so that strategies can emerge. Mintzberg (1987) had recognised earlier that in reality a purely deliberate or purely emergent strategy did not exist. Mintzberg and Waters (1985) developed a continuum along which real strategies could be identified, ranging from mainly deliberate to mainly emergent. These include strategies that are partly deliberate and partly emergent, which we now consider. Figure 1.2 shows a representation of this continuum.

Quinn (1980) introduced the concept of *logical incrementalism* to describe an approach to strategy making that commences with a conscious or evolving strategic vision, which is then realised or developed logically through a range of incrementally developed processes. These processes include the development of commitment towards, and consensus around, the strategic vision to help realise it. This approach indicates at least a degree of deliberate strategy making in a process that also relies on emergent or incrementally developed behaviours for success.

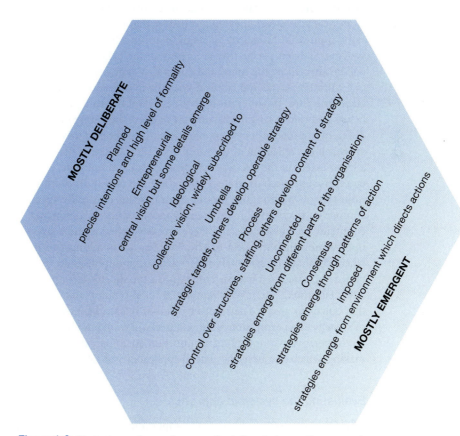

Figure 1.2 Strategic continuum from mostly deliberate to mostly emergent

Mintzberg and Waters (1985) describe what they term an *umbrella strategy*, which involves senior management defining strategic targets that others in the organisation use to develop the details of an operable strategy. The first part of this approach to strategy development is deliberately set out, while the second part is allowed to emerge. They also describe a *process strategy*, which involves senior management controlling processes such as organisational structures and staffing but allowing those within these structures to determine the content of strategy (i.e. which products or services to produce and how to provide them). This approach to strategy formation is again partly deliberate and partly emergent. Mintzberg (1987) recognises that these approaches to strategy are important in organisations where expertise and creativity are required, since it will be those deep down in an organisation's structure who will have such expertise and who will understand what is required to achieve strategic success in their market niche or area of service delivery. An organisation such as Microsoft (see In Practice 1.4) is a good example of this. Such organisations are likely to be structurally complex, most likely being structured as multi-divisional structures (see Chapter 5) where the corporate centre will be likely to develop umbrella and/or process strategies, allowing the operating divisions to form operable strategies more locally.

Systemic perspectives

Whittington (2001) states that systemic theorists also believe that organisations can plan strategically; however, they do not believe that the classical approach provides a universally applicable model of strategic planning because of variations between social systems. *Systemic perspectives* are based on the belief that strategy and strategy making will be affected by the social and cultural system within which this occurs. In this way, one country's social and cultural system will differ from another's due to variations in class structure, the operation of the market, the role of the state and underpinning beliefs and values, which will combine to affect the nature of strategy making, producing different approaches between countries. According to this interpretation, the classical approach is a reflection of the social and cultural system that prevails in the USA and to a lesser extent in the UK, where individualism and non-interventionism produce a free-enterprise approach to strategy and where the pursuit of profit is seen to be of primary importance. Whittington (2001) contrasts this culturally specific approach to other approaches that prevail in different types of society. In continental Europe, for example, countries such as France and Germany developed a much stronger tradition of state intervention than the USA or UK. This has led to a longer-term approach to strategy, where emphasis on national interest and social responsibility are also seen to be important, as opposed to a narrow emphasis on the shorter-term pursuit of profit (e.g. Price, 2001; Fulbrook, 2002). Whittington (2001) also points to cultures where people believe that outcomes are predetermined by God or by fate. In such cultures, the western notion of strategy as an expression of human free-will would not be accepted so easily. These different perspectives indicate an important sociological aspect to strategy and strategy making, which questions the general applicability of the classical approach in particular.

Evaluating the systemic approach

While this approach emphasises the importance of social and cultural differences and the ways these may impact on strategy and strategy making, there is also a need to beware of broad generalisations. Whittington (2001: 36) recognises that, 'Not all firms within a particular social system need be the same ... Societies are too complex and people too individualistic to expect bland uniformity.' Most societies encompass a wide range of acceptable beliefs and behaviours, making these pluralistic, within which different approaches to strategy and strategy making will prevail. Various types of organisational strategy may therefore be promoted and justified by reference to different beliefs and norms that are accepted within a society. However, just as it is important to recognise that there will be variations to strategy formation within a particular country, the systemic approach recognises that there will be differences related to cultural grounds between societies, thereby invalidating the idea of any universalistic model of strategy formulation.

Self-Check and Reflect Questions   1.1

Is it possible to reconcile any of these four approaches to strategy making in practice and if so how might this occur?

Strategic management and its links to HRM

The above review shows that there are a range of ways in which strategy may be formed. Like other human systems, practice is likely to vary on a case-by-case basis, informed in each situation by a particular combination of factors. These different approaches to strategic management have corresponding implications for the formation of human resource strategy. Ways in which the SHRM literature attempts to link strategic management and HRM will now be discussed.

To be strategic, HRM needs to demonstrate a two-way link to strategy. In this way, HRM will be informed by organisational strategy as well as helping to shape the nature of that strategy (Purcell, 2001). This idea of strategic integration is a key concept in definitions of SHRM (e.g. Guest, 1987; Storey, 1992; Wright and McMahan, 1992). Redman and Wilkinson (2001) refer to integration as a necessary condition for HRM to be considered strategic, although they recognise that it is not sufficient to consider it as the only condition. Other conditions for HRM to be considered strategic are discussed in Chapter 2. At this stage in the nature of the linkages between organisational strategy and HRM in relation to the different approaches outlined above to strategic management are specifically discussed.

Classical approach to strategy making and HRM

The behavioural perspective (Wright and McMahan, 1992) has been used to attempt to explain the link between the classical approach to strategy and HRM. This *behavioural perspective* is associated with the work of Schuler and Jackson (1987) and focuses on the types of employee behaviours required to realise organisational strategy. This theory assumes that employees possess the appropriate skills, knowledge and abilities for effectiveness and focuses, instead, on using these capabilities through the identification of 'required role behaviours' to achieve organisational strategy. Schuler and Jackson identify 12 types of role behaviour, each of which forms a continuum. For example, one type of behaviour varies between the requirement for predictability on the one hand and the need for innovation on the other. Another type varies between the requirement not to take risks and the need to take risks. A third one varies according to the need to engage in change. These types of employee role behaviour were used by Schuler and Jackson (1987) to predict the combinations of employee behaviours required to realise each of Porter's (1985) three generic strategies: cost leadership, differentiation and focus, which we discussed earlier. According to Schuler and Jackson, the identification of a set of required role behaviours to achieve one of these generic business strategies leads to the development of a particular human resource strategy to obtain and strengthen these behaviours. Table 2.3 provides a fuller representation of these theoretical links between each of Porter's three generic strategies, the employee role behaviours that are believed to be required for each and the appropriate HR practices that would make up a human resource strategy to realise each set of behaviours.

Adopting the behavioural perspective to find a link between organisational strategy and HRM, developed out of the tradition of contingency theory (Wright and McMahan, 1992). *Contingency theory*, in this context, is concerned with *matching* or *fitting* an organisation's HRM to its organisational strategy. A number of other matching models have been proposed in the literature. Fombrun *et al.* (1984) attempted to match or fit HR strategies not only to the nature of organisational strategy but also to the type of organisational structure associated with a particular type of strategy. Kochan and Barocci (1985) suggested that HR strategy should be linked to the *life cycle stage* of an organisation, related respectively to its start-up, growth, maturity and finally its decline. Each of these types of theoretical linkage between organisational strategy and HR strategy is discussed further in Chapter 2.

Returning more specifically to the behavioural perspective as a way of linking the classical approach to HRM, more recent work by Schuler *et al.* (2001) develops this linkage further by producing a model that looks at the role of HRM in the strategic management process. This model follows the assumptions of the classical approach in separating strategy formulation from its implementation in what appears as a rational, deliberate, linear and top-down process. Schuler *et al.* (2001) identify strategy formulation as being composed of three linear elements:

1. Establishing an organisation's vision, mission, values and general strategy, and then identifying the human resource management implications that arise from these activities.

2. Identifying a range of strategic business issues and establishing strategic business objectives, which also then lead to the identification of human resource implications that arise from these particular activities.

3. 'Crafting' specific plans to achieve the vision, mission, values and objectives, etc., which also lead to identifying the human resource implications of such business strategies.

Strategy implementation in their model includes developing and implementing HR plans that are based around what they call 'the four-task model of HRM' (Schuler *et al.*, 2001: 121). These four tasks require an organisation to:

1. engage in human resource planning;

2. develop required employee competences;

3. ensure required role behaviours; and

4. promote employee motivation.

This four-task model may be seen as an extension of the earlier 'role behaviours model' of Schuler and Jackson (1987), outlined above. HRM, in this four-task model, may also be seen as fulfilling the first, necessary condition to be strategic: the model recognises not only that HRM will be informed by organisational strategy but also that HR strategy will affect business strategy to some extent (Schuler *et al.*, 2001).

This type of model may be seen as epitomising the link between the classical approach to making strategy and HRM. However, the reality of such hypothesised links between corporate strategies, structures or life cycles, on the one hand, and HR strategies, on the other, is likely to be much more problematic than these reported formulations suggest. For example, it is important to recognise that strategy will change during an organisation's life cycle and that human resource strategy will be affected by this as well as by the nature of the organisation's strategy more generally. Similarly, the industrial sector within which the organisation operates and the nature of the occupational groups involved may have a significant effect (e.g. Purcell, 2001). However, such theorised linkages are based more on deduction than on empirical data (e.g. Hendry and Pettigrew, 1990), leading to an oversimplification of the processes involved in practice. It was seen earlier that the process of strategy development is affected by political, cultural and capability factors. It was also recognised above that when considering other approaches to strategy making it is unlikely to be an entirely top-down, rational and deliberate process, with business strategies emerging in parts of an organisation. Such factors suggest that a much more complex model of the relationship between strategy making and HRM is required to represent such linkages in reality.

Storey and Sisson (1993) point out that for a linkage even to be considered, a business strategy will need to be clearly apparent to the managers of an organisation. They suggest that 'where such strategies are available they are often extremely vague' (Storey and Sisson, 1993: 69). Mabey and Salaman (1995: 40) say straight out that 'experience suggests that strategic decision-making, either corporate or HR, is incremental, piecemeal, ad hoc, incomplete, and negotiated and only partly rational'. The complexity implied by these aspects needs to be considered alongside other factors that also question a straightforward linkage between business and HR strategies.

This conclusion does not discount the potential impact that particular strategies and structures may have on the use of HR strategy; rather, it discounts any straightforward and uniform linkage. Brews and Hunt (1999) recognised that organisations can derive a great deal of value from engaging in the type of strategic planning that incorporates flexibility, incrementalism and the involvement of line managers and others. Their remedy for bad planning is not to abandon it but to develop good planning that incorporates the attributes mentioned.

Evolutionary perspectives to strategy and HRM

This approach to strategy making stresses situational or environmental determinism to a much greater degree than does the classical approach (Poole, 1990). It follows that the matching model should be seen as even more appropriate for organisations that subscribe to this approach. Managers' strategic choice would be minimised in circumstances where environmental factors controlled the fate of an organisation and human resource strategy would need to be closely matched to the organisational strategy determined by these factors in order to achieve success.

Of course, this type of analysis may begin to appear theoretical in an unworldly way. In theory, success would depend on the capability of managers to identify and interpret key environmental variables, so that organisational and human resource strategies are as well adapted to environmental circumstances as possible. In practice, of course, the same criticisms made about strategy making in the classical approach can be applied to use of an environmental perspective. The same political, cultural and capability constraints will affect managements' ability to understand and interpret environmental factors appropriately, although the imperative to take action will be present. As a result, the approach developed to human resource strategy and to employee relations in such organisations is likely to be one that is dominated by the views of senior management. Opposition from other employee groups would be seen as dysfunctional, producing a senior managerial conviction for a strongly unitarist position.

The extent to which an organisation is adapted to its environment will affect its actions. A well-adapted organisation will be able to benefit from its environment, particularly if it faces limited competition. However, the implications for less well-adapted organisations, particularly in competitive situations, suggest more negative consequences. It was recognised earlier that this situation is likely to lead to strategic conservatism, where organisational efforts are focused on the basics of production. In this way, costs will be minimised, operating efficiencies sought, tight controls imposed with relatively short-term payback targets and performance monitoring (e.g. Goold and Campbell, 1987; Schuler and Jackson 1989; Whittington, 2001). This cost-efficiency strategy (Schuler and Jackson, 1989) or financial economies approach (Purcell, 1995) will have a number of implications for human resource strategy. These include restraints on pay budgets, employee discretion and staffing levels, and the use of performance controls, restructuring and downsizing (e.g. Purcell, 1989b; Schuler and Jackson, 1989). Such an approach may actually prove to be ineffective if it damages employee relations and leads to disaffection and higher levels of labour wastage (see In Practice 1.5).

In Practice   1.5

Pay problems at HSBC

The first strike at a UK high street bank in eight years was due to occur in 2006 after talks between trade union Amicus and HSBC broke down. Amicus said that the one-day action was in protest at a pay deal which, it alleged, would lead to a wage cut for thousands of workers. Amicus expected 9,500 workers to take action, on the same day as the bank's annual meeting. The bank said that it expected cash machines, telephone and online banking and major branches to be unaffected.

The dispute was over what the union said were inadequate pay arrangements at the bank. According to Amicus, 55 per cent of British HSBC workers covered by its pay negotiations got no salary rise or an increase below inflation in 2006. Tensions at HSBC have been on the rise during a wave of austerity, which has cost 3,500 jobs since the beginning of 2005. Lloyds TSB, a high street rival to HSBC, is also in the firing line for industrial action: workers there were also due to vote on a strike in the middle of 2006.

Source: BBC News Online (2006).

Redman and Wilkinson (2001) comment that such an approach can be seen as strategically integrated only in relation to the strategic imperative to control costs. For them, as for others, strategic human resource management requires a wider remit (see Chapter 2), where emphasis is also placed on developing and integrating the 'human' side as opposed to focusing simply on the 'resource utilisation' aspect of HRM (e.g. Guest, 1987; Storey, 1989, 1992). Inefficiencies that result from this broad focus may lead some organisations to incorporate human resource strategies aimed at developing and involving their employees rather than seeing them simply as a cost, although the use of these strategies will still be focused on maximising the interests of the organisation and achieving its goals.

Processual approach to strategy making and HRM

As noted above, the processual approach emphasises strategy making as an adaptive and emergent process, driven by learning in an organisation, with clear implications for the role of human resource strategy. The existence of an emergent strategy will need to be recognised (Mintzberg, 1987) and appropriate HR strategies introduced to encourage the behaviours required to promote and support this approach. These strategies may be divided into two categories. First, human resource, cultural and structural strategies can be used to help to foster the development of emergent strategies. Second, specific strategies also need to be designed to respond to the development of emergent strategies, in order to support them. As an example of the first category, Quinn's (1993) discussion about promoting an incremental approach to develop organisational strategy emphasises, in particular, the use of employee involvement as a key human resource strategy in this process (see Chapter 12). Related to both categories, Mintzberg (1987) believes that the development of emergent strategies in organisations is based on learning. This needs to be recognised and supported through human resource strategies related to, in particular, recruitment and selection, training and development, and reward, as well as through strategies related to organisational development and structure.

Organisational strategies which are emergent are likely to be understood by those who work in an organisation where they have been involved in the development of these strategies in some way. This contrasts with a situation where a strategic plan results in a low level of 'ownership' or even a lack of knowledge about it (Johnson and Scholes, 2002). This greater level of understanding and involvement may also, perhaps, be associated with the generation of increased levels of commitment to the goals of the organisation. Indeed, Quinn (1993) argues that one of the reasons for developing organisational strategy in an incremental manner is to generate employee effort and commitment in relation to an emerging strategy.

The earlier evaluation of the processual approach to strategy making discussed a number of strategies that are partly deliberate and partly emergent. It recognised that such a mixed approach is much more likely in reality than one which is completely deliberate or emergent. These approaches lend support to the idea of human resource strategy fulfilling multiple roles. These roles include responding to deliberate aspects of organisational strategy, fostering the capabilities and behaviours required to promote emergent aspects of the strategy and then supporting its development. They indicate a strategic approach to HRM, where human resource strategy is both informed by organisational strategy and helping to develop and realise it in practice.

Systemic perspectives to strategy and HRM

This approach recognises that strategy and strategy making will be affected by the social and cultural system within which this occurs. Institutional differences between countries will affect strategic choice about organisational and human resource strategies. The role of the state has been different in France and Germany, for example, when compared to the USA and the UK. These national institutional differences are related to underpinning cultural beliefs and values. Cultural differences may manifest themselves more generally. For example, the high prevalence of downsizing in some western-style societies has not been used in some Asian countries, where a stronger sense of collective values has led instead to the greater use of work-sharing strategies. However, even in China this is changing (Knight and Yueh, 2004). This suggests that the way in which human resource strategy is integrated into organisational strategy will vary, underpinned by societal values that may place, for example, much less emphasis on short-term, profit maximisation. Prevailing forms of ownership and size of organisation will also be likely to affect the nature of strategy. Whittington (2001) tells us, for example, that while a series of huge conglomerates developed in South Korea, nearby Taiwan's economy has been characterised by small and medium-sized family owned businesses. These factors suggest that the ways in which human resource strategy is conceived and integrated into organisational strategy will not only vary but that in many situations, in many different types of society, HRM will not be conceptualised in any intentional way as being strategic. The discussion of these aspects will principally be developed in two chapters: Chapter 3, which explores the international context of business and the role of SHRM, and Chapter 6, which looks at the role of culture in SHRM.

Self-Check and Reflect Questions	1.2

What is the scope for the strategic integration of HRM in relation to each of the four approaches to strategy making discussed in this section?

The multi-dimensional nature of strategic integration

Before discussing the resource-based view of the organisation in the next section, the nature of strategic integration wil be considered in more depth. Integration has been used through the previous part of this chapter as a means to explore possible links between different approaches to strategy and HRM. For this purpose integration was used because it is recognised as a necessary condition for HRM to be considered strategic (Redman and Wilkinson, 2001). So far, it has been recognised that integration may be a two-way process, where HRM informs the nature of organisational strategy as well as being informed by it. Alternatively, it may be a one-way process where organisational strategy informs HRM without being informed by it in any intended or planned way. The first of these situations implies full integration and the second partial integration. The discussion of these and other variants of strategic integration are now developed.

One may initially seek to achieve this by developing the use of the term organisational strategy, which so far as been used as a general expression to refer to any process of strategy making at the level of the organisation. In reality, strategy may be made at a number of levels in an organisation. The nature of an organisation's structure, discussed in Chapter 5, will thus be an important determinant of strategy making in practice. Strategy made at one level of an organisation will affect decision-making at other levels, with decisions taken at a higher level being most likely to affect those taken at a lower level. In general terms, three levels or 'orders' of strategy have been recognised (e.g. Purcell, 1989b).

The highest level is concerned with the overall or corporate strategy of an organisation. This relates to the way in which strategy was defined and used earlier in this chapter. Purcell (1989b: 70) refers to the nature of these strategies as '"upstream", first-order decisions' to indicate their status in relation to lower-order ones and the likely way in which other levels of strategy will flow from these higher-order strategies. These are concerned with the long-term direction and scope of the organisation. A further distinction may be made at this level between corporate and business strategies, related to the nature of multi-product and multi-divisional organisations. Purcell (1995: 66) succinctly summarises this distinction as follows:

> Multi-product and multi-divisional firms have to make a distinction between corporate and business strategies; between those taken at the centre covering the whole enterprise, and those taken lower down at division or business-unit level and related to the products made and the markets served.

Various strategic management writers identify a range of corporate strategies which may be grouped within a number of broad categories (e.g. Johnson and Scholes, 2002). Four such categories are shown in Key Concepts 1.3.

These corporate strategies will have implications for the nature of second- and third-level strategies including human resource strategy, as referred to earlier and will also be discussed further in Chapter 2.

The second and third levels of strategy are seen by Purcell (1989b) as being 'downstream' of corporate strategy. The *second* level of strategy concerns the organisational structures and operating procedures that are put into place to support first-order

Key Concepts 1.3

Four categories of corporate strategy

Stability	E.g. continuing with an existing strategy, consolidation
Growth	E.g. product development, market penetration, market development, or diversification involving internal investments, joint ventures, acquisition or merger
Retrenchment/ withdrawal	E.g. harvesting a business by using its existing competences and resources but reducing costs, investments and running it down; closing down some existing locations; relocation to reduce costs; divesting existing businesses
Combination	Using a particular mixture of the strategies referred to above

decisions. The *third level* concerns functional strategies, including those related to HRM, which are developed in the context of the first two levels. All three levels have strategic significance since they each affect the long-term direction of an organisation and the attainment of its goals, whether this is recognised and intended or not.

In relation to the second level of strategy, for example, a 'first-order' decision to merge with or take over another organisation would be likely to be followed by a set of decisions governing the structures and relationships of the 'new' organisation. These decisions might include delayering, increasing accountability to business units and decentralisation of business decision-making. Changes at this second level would, in turn, impact on human resource areas such as the roles performed by employees, their reporting relationships, and management style. The third level of strategy is therefore where functional areas define their strategies in accordance with first- and second-order decisions and the external environmental factors operating on the organisation (Purcell, 1989b). This direct strategic linkage of third-order, functional strategies with higher-order ones has also been referred to as *external integration* (e.g. Mabey and Iles, 1993: 16).

A limitation of these three types of strategic linkage is that they describe one-way, or 'downstream', relationships and as such do not meet the fuller definition of strategic integration, which incorporates a two-way relationship (i.e. moving 'upstream' as well as 'downstream'). From this perspective, external integration may only be achieved fully when human resource issues not only serve first- and second-order strategies in a downstream relationship but also operate upwards to influence strategic decision-making (e.g. Liff, 2000, Greer, 2001; Turner, 2002). At one level this upstream relationship could result in corporate strategy being informed by changes in the labour market and at another being formulated around the people and skills the organisation has at its disposal (Liff, 2000; Turner, 2002). Mabey and Iles (1993: 16) argue that this two-way relationship requires what they term 'institutional integration'. This is where the human resource function is strategically integrated into the organisation and is more likely to occur where the head of function is a board-level appointment. This ensures that a meaningful dialogue about the relationship between people and strategy will take place (Liff, 2000; Turner, 2002). This dialogue may surface a different perspective on opportunities and threats that might otherwise be overlooked and may also introduce a different set of values, for example in relation to diversity, that could influence strategy.

This two-way interpretation of strategic integration moves away from treating human resources as a 'dependent variable', where HRM simply reacts to predetermined organisational strategies (Liff, 2000), and is consistent with a number of themes explored in this book. It also reflects the resource-based view of the firm where strategy formation develops from the distinctive qualities inherent in the internal resources of the organisation that we consider in the next section. This two-way (upstream and downstream) relationship is central to our interpretation of SHRM and represents the fourth strand of the multi-dimensional nature of strategic integration. It supports the contention of Lengnick-Hall and Lengnick-Hall (1988) that organisations that engage in a process of strategy making that considers the interrelationships between competitive strategy and human resources will be more likely to improve their performance than those who simply use human resources to implement strategy. Of course the difficulties surrounding HRM in practice may reduce such views to no more than empty rhetoric. It assumes that human resources may operate as an element of first-order strategy formation whereas the evidence points to it being relegated to third-order status, consistent with the dominant view of HR as a dependent variable (e.g. Liff, 2000).

These first four strands of strategic integration all relate to external, or *vertical*, integration between the levels in the strategic hierarchy and HRM. The fifth strand relates to the *horizontal integration* of all the elements of HRM so that they fit together into a coherent whole. In this way, human resource activities need to be *internally integrated* in order to achieve full strategic integration (Mabey and Iles, 1993: 16–17). This would mean, for example, that within an organisation competing on the basis of quality, all the HR levers should be mutually supporting the acquisition, development and retention of a workforce that can deliver this type of competitive strategy. This means recruiting quality staff, investing significantly in the development of the organisation's skills base, defining and rewarding quality performance, involving employees in continuous improvement, etc.

Guest's (1987) interpretation of horizontal integration recognises that human resource activities not only need to be internally consistent but that they also need to cohere with other functional areas such as marketing, service provision or production, etc. Guest also identifies two further aspects of integration. The first of these relates to the attitudes and behaviours of line managers and the need for them to internalise and practise HR policies. The second relates to the full integration of employees into the business, leading to their identification with and commitment to the organisation. These additional aspects to achieve full integration are discussed further in Chapter 2 and the issue of employee involvement and commitment is evaluated in Chapter 12.

Taken together, this all begins to lead to a richer understanding of the nature of strategic integration but is still in itself insufficient. So far, what can only be seen as a static view of strategy has been presented which does not explicitly take account of uncertainty and the impact of unexpected change. Gratton (1999: 170) argues that a key challenge for organisations today 'is to continue to deliver sustained competitive advantage in the short-term whilst at the same time preparing for longer-term success'. This recognises that, as the future unfolds, changes to the business-operating environment will necessitate strategic shifts, sometimes of a transformational nature. This gives rise to the need for organisations to develop a pool of human capital that can not only achieve short-term business goals, derived from current organisational strategies, but also contribute to organisational transformation, through initiating, implementing and achieving change, including changes to business strategies (Gratton *et al.*, 1999). This presents an important temporal dimension to strategic integration that is sensitive to an uncertain future, where what lies over the horizon is hidden from view. It is this temporal dimension that represents the sixth and last strand. It also indicates another link to the resource-based view of the organisation, which is considered next.

For the various strands of integration for HRM to be considered strategic, SHRM needs to incorporate two-way vertical integration, horizontal integration within its own policy areas and with other functional areas, institutional integration, line management integration, the integration of employees with the goals of the organisation and its capacity to respond to change as the future unfolds. In practice, this may be asking a great deal for an organisation's approach to HRM to be classified as fully strategic. It does, however, provide an analytical framework against which organisational practice may be evaluated. A particular organisation's approach to HRM may thus be judged against these components for SHRM, in terms of whether each is present and also in terms of effectiveness, where simple presence does not imply this. Key Concepts 1.4 lists the six strands of strategic integration discussed above and Figure 1.3 represents these in diagrammatic form.

Key Concepts   1.4

Six strands of strategic integration

Responses to first-order strategic decisions
   Downstream, external or vertical integration

Responses to second-order strategic decisions
   Downstream, external or vertical integration

Responses to third-order strategic decisions
   Downstream, external or vertical integration

Interactions with strategy and as a potential driver of future strategic direction
   Upstream, external or vertical integration

Alignment of HR policies with themselves and with other functions; of line managers' practices with HR policies; and of employees with the organisation's strategic objectives
   Internal or horizontal integration

Responsiveness to future uncertainties and need for change.

Figure 1.4 develops this representation of strategic integration by showing its three levels or orders vertically. In relation to the third order, this figure shows horizontal integration between and within functional areas, focusing on HRM. Strategic integration within HRM is expanded to show links to the areas dealt with in subsequent chapters of

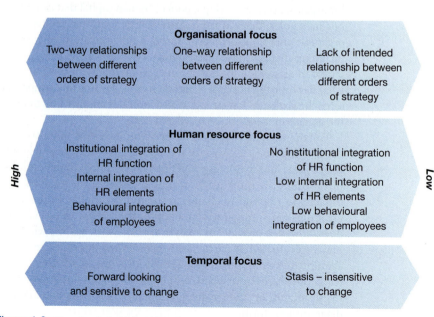

Figure 1.3 Strands of strategic integration

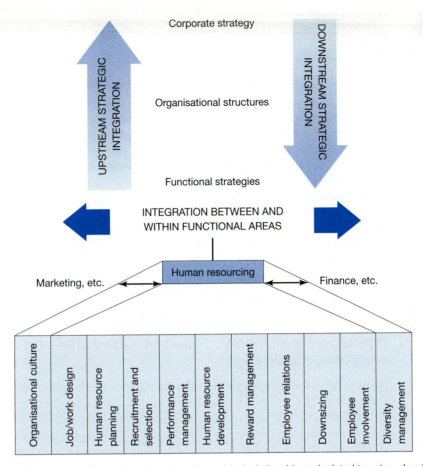

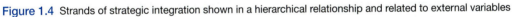

Figure 1.4 Strands of strategic integration shown in a hierarchical relationship and related to external variables

this book. This diagram also attempts to show environmental and temporal dimensions. Surrounding the figure are references to the external environment and change. Using traditional SWOT analysis, the environment can be seen as providing opportunities for an organisation as well as threats to it, while change shown on the right of the figure indicates the need to be capable of responding effectively to these variables.

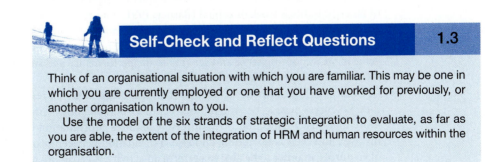

Self-Check and Reflect Questions   1.3

Think of an organisational situation with which you are familiar. This may be one in which you are currently employed or one that you have worked for previously, or another organisation known to you.

Use the model of the six strands of strategic integration to evaluate, as far as you are able, the extent of the integration of HRM and human resources within the organisation.

The resource-based view of the organisation and its links to HRM

Strategic management theorists traditionally focused their analysis on the product market or industry within which an organisation operated. Wernerfelt's (1984) analysis focused instead on the internal resources of organisations, to explore the implications of these for competitive advantage. This approach has led to the development of a major strand of strategic management literature, known as the resource-based view (RBV) or resource-based theory (RBT) of the firm (e.g. Dierickx and Cool, 1989; Wernerfelt, 1989, 1995; Prahalad and Hamel, 1990; Barney, 1991; Connor, 1991; Grant, 1991; Amit and Schoemaker, 1993; Peteraf, 1993; Connor and Prahalad, 1996). Wernerfelt based his idea of looking at organisations as sets of resources on the work of Penrose (1959). Penrose saw firms as being heterogeneous, in that their resources, both physical and human, varied and remained different over the course of time related to their differing qualities, including those of management and other employees. It follows from this analysis that competitive advantage and therefore superior firm performance might flow from the possession and development of better-quality resources.

Resource-based theory: resources, capabilities and competitive advantage

Resource-based theory conceives of organisational resources as unique bundles that have the power to give an organisation a competitive advantage over others in the same industry or sphere of operation (e.g. Boxall, 1996). Uniqueness or heterogeneity is stressed over sameness or homogeneity. Barney's (1991) conception of the *resources* of an organisation is widely drawn to include all of its strategic assets. These include its organisational attributes, capabilities and knowledge, and the processes (e.g. management decision-making) that it uses to make and implement strategy. More specifically, Barney identifies three categories of resources: physical, human and organisational. Of these, human resources are conceived in terms of the experience, knowledge and understanding that managers and workers bring to the context of the organisation. The third category of organisational resources is also important to the subject of this book. It includes formal organisational resources such as its structure and its systems for planning, coordinating and controlling as well as informal aspects such as the nature of internal and external relationships. These resource categories are each seen as being part of an organisation's stock of capital (Barney, 1991). Grant (1991) alternatively identifies six categories of resources: financial, physical, human, technological, reputation and organisational. He recognises that a number of these resources are intangible: difficult to value in an accounting sense and yet vital to the performance and success of the organisation which has assembled and developed them.

Grant (1991) also discusses the important distinction between resources and capabilities. Resources need to be brought together to form *capabilities*. However, a capability is more than just a collection of resources: it requires coordination between the people involved and their cooperation, and also coordination between people and other types of resources, in order to be able to perform an activity. A capability may also be seen as a collection of organisational routines, where those involved know and understand these routines and so are able to respond to a situation in a familiar, competent and productive manner. The establishment of organisational routines, and therefore capability, helps to demonstrate the link to *competitive advantage*. An organisation will develop a competitive advantage if it establishes routines or capabilities that others have yet to understand or perfect (Barney, 1991; Grant, 1991). Sustaining a competitive advantage involves an organisation maintaining this lead over others despite their best efforts to catch up (Barney, 1991).

Expressed more dynamically, an organisation may stay ahead of others and enjoy a *sustained competitive advantage* by proving to be more effective in adapting its routines and capabilities or learning and developing new ones (Grant, 1991) (see In Practice 1.6).

In Practice   1.6

Capabilities in action at Pret a Manger

Pret a Manger made its name as an environmentally friendly trader, banning genetically modified foods and sourcing chickens from humane cages in Seville (*The Guardian*, 2001). It also spelled the end of the brilliantly constructed illusion through which Pret seemed to offer a taste of sophistication for little more than the cost of an ordinary sandwich. In its early days, the chain's brushed steel stools, magenta labels and immaculate chrome bars seemed the ultimate in industrial chic. Its French name and comparatively adventurous menu all helped create an aura of exclusivity – instead of ham and tomato sandwiches, Pret offered Brie, tomato and basil baguettes.

The origins of Pret's classy £3 lunches lie in the mid-1980s, when its two creators met at the University of Westminster, where they were studying property law. According to one industry expert, Pret was in the right place, at the right time. There was a revolution going on in sandwiches – packaged sandwiches were finally taking off in a big way, mostly thanks to Marks & Spencer.

Pret has always been clear about who its customers are. Charging £1.20 for a tiny bottle of orange juice means it is targeting urban professionals with little time on their hands. In 2001 the chain had just over 100 shops in Britain, and one in New York. In 2000 it sold 25 million sandwiches, baguettes and wraps and just over 14 million cups of coffee. Pret sandwiches are still made on the premises, at every store. Shops receive fresh deliveries in the evenings, which are refrigerated every night until cooks arrive at 6.30am to prepare the day's sandwiches.

One of the partners holds the purse-strings. The other partner looks after the food, spending Thursday afternoons with a recipe committee, sampling different ideas. He goes for exotic mixtures, once remarking: 'The English respond to strong tastes – look at curry.' Recent additions include Scotch beef with crispy onions, 'more than mozzarella' sandwiches and Peking duck wraps.

In addition to the distinctive product offering, the company reduced labour turnover to 65 per cent in the first part of 2005, a difficult task in a sector where turnover normally runs at 100 per cent (*People Management*, 2005b). In 2002, Pret's turnover ran at 95 per cent. The following year it dropped to 86 per cent, then to 82 per cent in 2004, and then to 65 per cent in 2005. It seems that about 70 per cent of the turnover is due to staff taking time off to travel or return to their home country. Many of the frontline employees at Pret are non-UK nationals. The HR manager believes that some of the company's employees stay because Pret works hard to continually show its appreciation of its people. Perks include weekly drinks and an internal magazine that's allowed to appear uncensored by managers. In the HR manager's view, working at Pret is as much about social activities as business matters.

Barney (1991, 1995) identifies the attributes that an organisation's resources and capabilities must demonstrate in order to achieve sustained competitive advantage. These are shown in Key Concepts 1.5.

Key Concepts	**1.5**

Attributes of resources and capabilities that lead to competitive advantage

- Valuable

  Resources and capabilities that allow an organisation to develop strategies to exploit available opportunities and neutralise evident threats will be valuable. Valuable resources and capabilities provide the basis for competitive advantage.

- Rare

  Resources and capabilities also need to be rare, or unique to a particular organisation, in order to create a situation of competitive advantage. Commonly available (i.e. non-rare) resources and capabilities that are valuable may help an organisation survive but will not ensure competitive advantage.

- Inimitable

  Resources and capabilities that are valuable and rare are likely to lead to competitive advantage. Such an advantage will be eroded where others imitate or copy these resources and capabilities. For this advantage to be sustained these resources and capabilities will therefore need to be inimitable – that is, they cannot be imitated or copied. Such resources and capabilities are then labelled *imperfectly imitable* – they cannot be copied successfully.

- Non-substitutable

  An alternative means to challenge an organisation's competitive advantage, where its resources and capabilities remain inimitable, would be to use an alternative approach to implement the same strategy, where this is possible. Where inimitable resources and capabilities can be substituted this will allow a competitor to challenge an organisation's competitive advantage, either completely or partially depending on the nature of the substitutability of this alternative approach.

- Effectively organised

  In addition to possessing valuable, rare, inimitable and non-substitutable resources and capabilities, an organisation will need to be effectively organised to realise its potential competitive advantage and sustain this.

Source: Developed from Barney (1991, 1995).

The attributes described in Key Concepts 1.5 provide a useful conceptualisation to show, first, how competitive advantage may be gained through an organisation's resources and capabilities and, second, how this may be sustained in some cases or challenged and eroded in others. Resources and capabilities need to be both valuable and rare, as well as effectively organised, to create a situation of competitive advantage. For this to be sustained, resources and capabilities need to be both imperfectly imitable and non-substitutable. The literature identifies three possible reasons for resource inimitability.

1. *The history and timing of the organisation.* Firms may enjoy the effects of what Wernerfelt (1984) describes as a 'resource position barrier': they benefit from being a 'first mover' in developing an effective resource base which allows them to produce superior returns over other firms so long as they maintain this resource advantage. An example of this may be the UK vacuum cleaner manufacturer Dyson, which produced the first bagless vacuum cleaner. Valuable and rare resources by definition will be limited and the argument is made that organisations which set up at the time and place when these are developed should continue to benefit from the advantages that accrue, where other potential competitors have to contend with barriers to entry and resource position barriers (Wernerfelt, 1984; Barney, 1991).

2. *Causal ambiguity.* Basically, this is where the reasons for an organisation's competitive advantage are not understood clearly by it or by its competitors. In such circumstances, it will be difficult to know which resources and capabilities should be imitated to achieve similar success. If an organisation enjoying competitive advantage were able to analyse precisely why it enjoyed this success, competitors would be able to entice away its best managers to share their knowledge, just as top football teams persuade successful managers from smaller clubs to join them. Situations of complexity may actually make it difficult for organisations to analyse the reasons for their competitive advantage. In addition, much knowledge in an organisation is likely to remain tacitly in the heads of many different employees spread throughout the organisation.

3. *Social complexity.* The resources, capabilities and relationships in an organisation are very likely to be complex. While according to this reason it is possible to identify how success is achieved, for example because of good intra-organisational and/or supplier–customer relationships, the sheer complexity of these and other relevant factors would make it difficult to replicate them elsewhere. For example, understanding and manipulating a competitor's organisational culture to replicate that of the organisation enjoying competitive advantage would be most unlikely in practice. As Barney (1986) recognised, organisational culture may be a source of competitive advantage for this reason (see Chapter 6).

The attributes in Key Concepts 1.5 may also be seen as relating to a particular point in time. Other, exogenous variables, such as a major shift in technology, could shake up the status quo and lead to a reshaping of what constitutes valuable, rare, inimitable and non-substitutable resources and capabilities in such altered circumstances. Increasing use of computer applications and the rise of digitally based technologies provide current examples of how industrial boundaries and therefore previously enjoyed competitive advantages are being altered in the early twenty-first century. The major changes occurring at present in the retail industry as a result of the development of online shopping is just such a case. In Practice 1.7 illustrates the need for companies in the computer applications industry to revisit their capabilities to ensure future competitive advantage.

In summary, resources and capabilities that demonstrate the attributes shown in Key Concepts 1.5 are seen by resource-based theorists as the principal source of an organisation's competitive advantage. Figure 1.5 shows a simply portrayed causal link between these elements in the resource-based theory of the organisation.

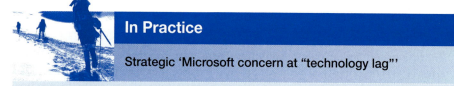

In Practice

1.7

Strategic 'Microsoft concern at "technology lag"'

Leaked internal memos from Microsoft have warned that its business would be under threat if it failed to respond quickly and decisively to key technologies in which it lagged competitors.

Ray Ozzie, chief technical officer and a newcomer to Microsoft, said in a memo to senior staff that the company had failed to achieve leadership in key areas of internet technology.

His memo suggested a shift in the technical leadership of the company, with Bill Gates, chairman and chief software architect, passing on authority for its most significant strategic change in five years to Mr Ozzie.

In an introduction to Mr Ozzie's memo, Mr Gates said the 'next sea change' was upon the company. He predicted the Ozzie memo would be as critical as 'the internet tidal wave' one he himself wrote 10 years ago when he issued a rallying cry to the company to embrace the internet.

The memo outlines a similar challenge whereby the growth of broadband, wireless networking and a new business model around advertising-supported web services and software 'has the potential to fundamentally impact how we build, deliver and monetise innovations'.

Mr Ozzie said Microsoft must respond quickly and decisively. 'It's clear that if we fail to do so, our business as we know it is at risk,' he said. He joined Microsoft in April and is regarded as an industry visionary.

'We knew search would be important but through Google's focus they've gained a tremendously strong position,' the memo said. And 'it was Skype, not us, who made VoIP [voice over internet protocol] broadly popular."

Source: *Financial Times* (2005b).

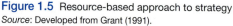

Figure 1.5 Resource-based approach to strategy
Source: Developed from Grant (1991).

However, not all organisational resources and capabilities will exhibit such attributes, even within an organisation that enjoys a competitive advantage, and we now consider in more depth the nature of the capabilities which do and differentiate them from those that do not.

Resource-based theory: core capabilities and competitive advantage

Capabilities which give an organisation a strategic advantage over its competitors have been called *core capabilities* (e.g. Leonard-Barton, 1992), although a number of alternative terms have been used to refer to the same concept, as Key Concepts 1.6 illustrates.

An important article by Prahalad and Hamel (1990), that helped to disseminate the resource-based view, refers to developing core competence in an organisation. *Core competence* develops from collective learning in an organisation, especially from being able to coordinate diverse sets of skills and integrate different technologies. Rather than

Key Concepts 1.6

Alternative terms for the concept of core capability

Leonard-Barton (1992, 1998) lists the various alternative terms used to refer to the concept of core capability:

Term	Source
Distinctive competences	Snow and Hrebiniak, 1980
Core competence	Prahalad and Hamel, 1990
Firm-specific competence	Pavitt, 1991
Resource deployments	Hofer and Schendel, 1978
Invisible assets	Itami, 1987

seeing a corporation as a set of diversified strategic business units, each producing a series of independently conceived end products, this perspective sees it as being composed of a small number of core competences, which are then used to derive a set of core products from which flow the range of end products. As examples, Prahalad and Hamel refer to companies such as Honda, Canon and Philips. Honda developed core competence in the production of engines and power trains. This was then used to produce a diverse range of end products including cars, motorcycles and generators. Canon developed core competences in imaging, optics and microprocessors, leading to the production of several end products including cameras, copiers and scanners. Philips developed core competence in optical media, leading to a wide range of laser disc-related end products. Rather than focusing on particular markets and the products that are sold within these to drive development, this perspective focuses instead on an organisation using its strategic intent to identify and build a small number of core competences and then using these as sources of competitive advantage through a range of commercial applications (Prahalad and Hamel, 1990; Hamel and Prahalad, 1994). Boxall and Purcell (2003: 79) refer to this perspective as being 'knowledge-based rather than ... product based ... [to understand]... strategic opportunities'.

Leonard-Barton (1992, 1998) also developed analysis of the operation of capabilities through her work on core capabilities and core rigidities. Each of these concepts will be examined in turn. For Leonard-Barton, capabilities can be considered as core if they are strategically important, leading to competitive advantage. She adopts what is termed a 'knowledge-based view' and defines core capability as a knowledge set, which is composed of four dimensions. These four dimensions are outlined in Key Concepts 1.7.

While core capability draws on accumulated knowledge sets within an organisation to achieve competitive advantage, Leonard-Barton (1992, 1998) identifies 'core rigidities' which lead to the loss of such advantage. *Core rigidities* are defined as knowledge sets that, while once appropriate for organisational success, have become inappropriate to achieve future advantage. They are the flip side of core capabilities. Because they have become part of the culture of an organisation they are difficult to change and therefore capable of damaging its future prospects, indicating the need to develop a new knowledge base. Leonard-Barton (1992) refers to the work of Itami (1987), who suggests that the time to develop new core capability is while the existing one is still effective. This

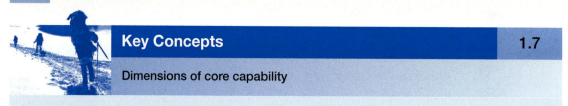

Key Concepts   1.7

Dimensions of core capability

Leonard-Barton (1992, 1998) develops four dimensions for the concept of core capability:

Employee knowledge and skill

This dimension is embodied in the organisation's employees and is composed of their general and organisationally specific technical knowledge and skills. Leonard-Barton comments that this dimension is particularly important during the development of new products.

Physical technical systems

This dimension recognises that employees' knowledge and skills will not only reside in people's heads but also lead to the development of organisational information systems over the course of time. These accumulated and formalised technical systems provide both a source of organisationally specific information and a set of procedural rules to shape and direct action.

Managerial systems

This dimension describes the sources that promote, guide and limit knowledge creation in an organisation, and which operate through both formal and informal channels. Knowledge creation related to desired core capability may be promoted and guided through types of development opportunities, organisational structures that facilitate this, appropriate rewards systems and internal and external networking, and so forth. Similarly, these systems can be used to inhibit types of knowledge creation that are not desired in relation to the strategic intent of the organisation.

Values and norms

This dimension is linked to the culture of an organisation and permeates the other three dimensions of core capability. Values and norms determine the types of knowledge created, and the means to generate and control it. Knowledge creation will emphasise areas of strategic importance in an organisation, e.g. development, design, information systems, production, service delivery and/or marketing. The means to generate knowledge will demonstrate which types of employees are important as well as their characteristics related to level and type of education or experience. The third element relates to the locus of control over knowledge. While the achievement of competitive advantage implies that knowledge creation will be available to the organisation and that management will exercise *de facto* control, this knowledge or resource-based view also implies that employee influence will be vital in order for this advantage to be realised.

Source: Developed from Leonard-Barton (1992, 1998).

implies proactivity related to foresighted strategic intent and indicates the need to avoid damaging periods of transition or even crisis.

Leonard-Barton (1998) recognises that not all resources within an organisation can be defined as core capability (i.e. leading to competitive advantage). She identifies two further categories for these other types of organisational capability, labelled supplemental capabilities and enabling capabilities. *Supplemental capabilities* add value to the activities of an organisation but are not necessary and can be imitated or copied by others. For example, an organisation's core capability may be in internet retailing but it may also have a strong distribution network; this supplements its core capability but is neither required nor unique when compared to other organisations (see In Practice 1.8).

In Practice   1.8

Amazon.co.uk develops distribution network

Amazon.co.uk's decision to open a second UK distribution centre was first announced in May 2004 and came following strong international sales growth. A total of 300 employees is expected to be employed at the centre in 2005 with further temporary staff being recruited to help with the busy Christmas months. The facility is operating in conjunction with Amazon.co.uk's existing UK distribution centre at Marston Gate, near Milton Keynes.

The Gourock distribution centre covers 300,000 sq ft – the size of five football pitches (this compares to Amazon.co.uk's existing distribution centre at Marston Gate which is 540,000 sq ft) with almost 3.5 miles of shelving and pallet racks. It handles customer orders from across Amazon.co.uk's product range in categories such as Books, Music, DVD, Video, Software, PC & Video Games, Electronics & Photo, DIY & Tools, Garden & Outdoors, Kitchen & Home, Personal Care and Toys. In addition to handling UK orders, the facility is dispatching orders to customers across the world.

Source: Scottish Enterprise (2004).

Enabling capabilities will be necessary but not by themselves sufficient to create a situation of competitive advantage. Leonard-Barton (1998) gives an example of manufacturing firms that need to establish very high levels of quality in order to compete but this attribute by itself is not sufficient to create competitive advantage since many such organisations need this just to stay in the industry (i.e. high quality is valuable but not rare). In this way, high-quality resources will serve an enabling role but other resource attributes will need to be developed to make these core capabilities.

A core capability distinguishes itself by its uniqueness, so that it is not easily copied, or imitated, in other organisations. It offers strategic superiority, leading to sustained competitive advantage. Core capability within an organisation will become institutionalised in its ways of operating, linked to the dimensions identified in Key Concepts 1.5. These dimensions will also contribute to the development and renewal of core capability if any competitive advantage is to be sustained (Leonard-Barton, 1992, 1998). Leonard-Barton's development of the concept of core capability is based, as noted above, on a 'knowledge-based view' of the organisation. The management of knowledge, particularly organisation-specific knowledge, is critical in this construction to achieve competitive advantage. However, as Boxall and Purcell (2003: 83) note: 'There is really no point in making a distinction between the resource-based view and the knowledge-based view of the firm. Whichever of these labels we apply, we end up with the same argument – that it is a firm's ability to learn faster than its rivals … that gives it competitive advantage.' Both the knowledge-based view and the resource-based view focus on the internal resources of an organisation and in particular the development of core competence or capability as the principal means to generate the scope for competitive advantage. The key attribute of these views, as far as this book is concerned, is that they place organisational resources and, in particular, human resources at the centre of strategy making and it is to the implications for SHRM that we now turn.

Resource-based theory: links to HRM

Different types of link between resource-based theory and HRM can be identified. Since resource-based theory sees resources and capabilities as the principal source of competitive advantage, it may be seen as placing human resources in a central position to realise this. For example, Barney (1991) includes 'human capital resources' as one of his three resource categories and Grant (1991) 'human resources' as one of his six. For Grant, intangible resources, including employee-based skills, are probably an organisation's most important strategic asset. Leonard-Barton (1992, 1998) also includes employee skills and knowledge as one of her four dimensions of core capability. Mueller (1996) takes an integrated view, seeing human resources combined with other key strategic assets, such as product reputation, as the source of competitive advantage. In either of these approaches, human resources in an organisation can be seen as a pool or stock of human capital, some of which may be linked directly to a situation of competitive advantage (Wright *et al.*, 1994).

However, no matter how strong the attributes and abilities in a human capital pool are, it is unlikely that these will be harnessed without a range of coordinating interventions. Wright *et al.* (1994) differentiate between the potential of human capital and its realisation through appropriate employee behaviours. The achievement of valuable outcomes in the case of human resources who offer supplemental or enabling capabilities, or competitive advantage in the case of human resources who are part of an organisation's core capability (Leonard-Barton, 1998), stems from the ways in which these resources are coordinated, developed and treated (cooperation was recognised earlier as being necessary) as well as integrated with other organisational resources (e.g. Grant, 1991). This indicates that the management of human resources in general terms is vital and provides a key link to resource-based theory.

Wright *et al.* (1994) consider the role of management in developing an organisation's capabilities. According to resource-based theory, capabilities need to be built or developed rather than being bought (e.g. Teece *et al.*, 1997). It is therefore management's role to build, recognise, develop and use an organisation's capability, including any core capability, to realise a situation of strategic or competitive advantage (Wright *et al.*, 1994). Management's role in achieving this aim is potentially multi-faceted. Management can identify the need to develop a core competence or capability through the statement of an organisation's strategic intent and then act on this (e.g. Prahalad and Hamel, 1990). Management may also identify the existence of a latent pool of human capital in an organisation, which has the potential to be developed into a capability for strategic or competitive advantage (Wright *et al.*, 1994). Management may also seek to improve the utilisation of an existing capability, particularly in a situation of rapid change. These possibilities demonstrate that level of managerial capability itself will be important in an organisation, in order for it to be able to recognise, develop and optimise resource-based opportunities.

Unlike other factors of production, people cannot be owned by the organisations that hire them. The effectiveness of a capability in which people play a part will be affected by the nature of relationships between them, their levels of cooperation and by their organisational treatment (Boxall, 1996; Grant, 1991). In the discussion earlier about whether an organisation's resources may be imitated by others, it was also recognised that the scope for this is likely to be adversely affected by causal ambiguity and social complexity (e.g. Dierickx and Cool, 1989). Given that causal linkages are generally more complex than imaged and difficult to understand, management will need to focus attention on developing organisational structures, organising work, fostering cooperative relation-ships and ensuring consistency of fair treatment to facilitate the development of an organisation's capability, rather than simply trying to exert overt forms of control.

This points to a further link between resource-based theory and HRM, related to the potential contribution of human resource policies or strategies. We may ask, 'What is the role of human resource strategies in helping to develop an organisation's capabilities and, in particular, how can these be used to promote the development of core compe-tence or capability?' At a fairly superficial level, it seems obvious that human resource strategies should be important in developing an organisation's capabilities. Human resource practices related to recruitment and selection, managing performance, training and development, and reward can be designed to attract, develop and retain high-quality employees (see Chapters 8, 9, 10 and 11 respectively for detailed coverage of these areas). Given that resource-based theory stresses the need to develop, rather than simply purchase, capabilities related to their organisation-specific nature, training and development appear to become particularly important. This is illustrated in 'In Practice' 1.9 where the need for companies to train very large numbers of skilled information technology (IT) workers to ensure future capabilities is demonstrated. The above discus-sion about developing capabilities, stressed that learning and knowledge application are key processes to achieve strategic and competitive advantage. This is a dimension of strategic human resource development (HRD) developed and explored in Chapter 10.

However, there are two problems in assuming that in practice there is a straightfor-ward, causal relationship between HRM and the generation of organisational capability in which a range of human resource strategies can be simply introduced to facilitate

In Practice   1.9

Shortage of people to run hot technologies

If IP [internet protocol] and wireless networks are such hot technologies at the moment, where are the people who can run them? Europe is facing a damaging shortage of skilled IT workers that could limit economic growth and international competitiveness in the region.

Three years from now, Europe will need nearly 500,000 more skilled resources than are available on the job market ... Eastern European nations face the widest skills gaps both today and in coming years, although Hungary and the Czech Republic fare notably better. Russia is expected to have a shortfall of 60,000 skilled technicians in 2008 ... But even in Europe's leading economies, demand will significantly outstrip supply. Although their gaps may be lower in percentage terms, the absolute number of resources needed will be significant. Germany could lack 88,000 technicians in 2008, while the UK and France could each face a gap of 40,000 people.

'There is a perception that ICT [training] is no big deal. But in 2005, no country is really well positioned. This is a wake up call for all of us,' warns Yvon Le Roux, a vice president at Cisco. And there are signs that Europe is already feeling the crunch. Half the organisations that had hired IT staff in the last 12 months reported difficulty in finding candidates with the right skills. 'When companies start stealing employees from each other, there's a gap,' says IDC analyst Marianne Kolding ...

The gap is being driven both by the success of new technologies and a failure of training pro-grammes to keep pace with adoption.

Source: Ian Limbach, Financial Times (2005a).

resource-based competitive advantage. The first of these concerns the scope for human resource strategies to become a source of competitive advantage, and is related to the assumptions of resource-based theory (Wright *et al.*, 1994). The second explores the evolutionary nature of developing resources and capabilities in practice and the implications of this for the role of human resource strategies (Mueller, 1996). Each of these is discussed in turn.

The first problem is related to the definition of capability as a source of competitive advantage that we discussed earlier. Barney (1991) defined resources and capabilities that lead to sustained competitive advantage as ones that are not only valuable to an organisation but also rare, inimitable and non-substitutable. Wright *et al.* (1994) argue that it would be very difficult for human resource strategies to be rare, inimitable and non-substitutable, since by their generic nature they can be developed in many different organisations. There is, for example, no shortage of books and articles about HRM, professing good practice and discussing links to strategy; for this reason, HRM can hardly be thought of as a mysterious set of practices, known only to those who enjoy competitive advantage in a particular industry or sphere of operation! However, Wright *et al.* (1994) argue that, while human resource practices cannot be a source of competitive advantage in themselves, they can nevertheless be linked to the development of core capability and competitive advantage through their role in developing the human capital pool within an organisation, and in particular by shaping employee behaviours that lead to effectiveness. In this way, they argue that human resource practices moderate the relationship between an organisation's pool of human capital and its competitive performance. The existence of a pool of human capital without appropriate human resource strategies, including practices related to selection, training, involvement, etc. as well as facilitative organisational structures and culture, may result in reduced organisational performance. Conversely, it is argued, appropriate human resource strategies will enhance organisational capabilities and performance, and could lead to competitive advantage where a capability is not only valuable but also rare, inimitable and non-substitutable.

Significantly, this position recognises an organisation's human resources as the source of competitive advantage, not the human resource strategies that are used to build them. It makes an important distinction between 'human resources as a pool of human capital and human resource practices' (Wright *et al.*, 1994: 317). Mueller (1996) follows this distinction by exploring the evolutionary nature of the ways in which resources are developed and the implications of this for the role of human resource strategies. He recognises that strategy and its relationship to human resource management have often been portrayed in an overly rationalistic way. Instead Mueller (1996: 757) 'proposes an evolutionary approach to strategic human resources … [where] … truly valuable strategic assets are unlikely to result directly from senior management policies'. This effectively returns us to the discussion earlier in this chapter about strategy as an emergent process, where this is formed from a pattern of activities over time. We recognised earlier that top-down planning approaches often make very simplified assumptions, do not recognise factors such as social complexity or bounded rationality, and are unlikely to be realised as intended.

Mueller proposes that strategic human resources are more likely to develop through a process of evolution rather than as the result of short-term managerial interventions. Mueller suggests that this can be facilitated by a number of factors. Management can pursue a state of persistent strategic intent, perhaps underpinned by a unifying theme such as the pursuit of continuous improvement. This will be important in terms of providing a focus around which strategy can develop over the longer term. Strategic human resources can also be promoted by focusing on skills development related to the organisational routines that underpin organisational capabilities rather than more superficial training and development programmes. They may also be promoted where there is organisational recognition of and support for the various forms of spontaneous cooperation and related employee behaviours that develop around organisational routines, linked to desired capabilities. The role for human resource strategies therefore becomes one of supporting these spontaneous forms of cooperation and behaviours to embed them into organisational processes linked to organisational routines and desired capabilities. Mueller also believes that human resources will be effective if they are integrated with other strategies or policies aimed at promoting and developing organisational capabilities. He sees this approach as a long-term one and refers to the development of 'social architecture' in an organisation, which 'results from ongoing skill formation activities, incidental or informal learning, forms of spontaneous cooperation, the tacit knowledge that accumulates as the – often unplanned – side-effect of intentional corporate behaviour'. Mueller's view, then, is that human resources may provide a source of competitive advantage but that the role and contribution of human resource strategies is likely to be a secondary and supporting one in terms of developing strategic human resources. HRM may be used to start a process of creating strategic human resources and also to help to develop them but is not sufficient in terms of their realisation.

Self-Check and Reflect Questions   1.4

How would you relate the resource-based view to the dichotomy between the planning school and the learning school that we discussed earlier?

Summary

- Strategic management focuses on the scope and direction of an organisation, and often involves dealing with uncertainty and complexity.

- Strategic human resource management is concerned with the relationship between an organisation's strategic management and the management of its human resources. The exact nature of this relationship in practice, however, is likely to be difficult to analyse and evaluate, not least because strategic management is a problematic area.

- Four approaches to strategy making were described and evaluated: the classical approach, evolutionary perspectives, processual approach and systemic perspectives. The implications of each of these approaches for human resource management were subsequently analysed.

- Strategic integration was used to explore possible links between approaches to strategy and human resource management. Integration has been recognised as a necessary condition for HRM to be considered strategic although it is not sufficient to treat it as the only link to define a strategic approach to HRM. Six possible strands of strategic integration were identified.

● Resource-based theory was analysed because of its recognition of an organisation's internal resources as a potential source of competitive advantage. Forms of organisational capability were analysed and their relationship to human resource management were evaluated.

Follow-up study suggestions

● Undertake a search of practitioner publications (related to HR and management), identify a number of short articles about case study organisations that often feature in these and select, say, two or three of them to identify references to or evidence of any of the strategic management themes discussed in this chapter and their relationships to the management of human resources.

● Seek out the possibility of talking to a senior manager in an organisation to discuss the organisation's approach to strategy making and the relationship between strategy and HRM.

● Seek to identify the strategy-making processes used in this organisation and the key influences that impact on and help to form the approach used.

Suggestions for research topics

● What are the key strategy-making processes used in organisation XYZ and what role does the HR function play in the conduct of these processes?

● How does overall organisational strategy influence HR strategy? A survey of private sector practice.

● To what degree are the organisation's human resources consciously used to develop strategically important capabilities in the organisation?

2 Strategic human resource management: a vital piece in the jigsaw of organisational success?

Learning Outcomes

By the end of this chapter you should be able to:

● identify the major principles which underpin the concept of strategic human resource management (SHRM);

● analyse the main theoretical approaches to SHRM;

● explain the history and origins of SHRM;

● evaluate the studies which aim to establish the link between SHRM and organisational performance.

Introduction

It is now to rather quaint and old-fashioned to hear the work undertaken by HR practitioners or HR departments referred to as 'personnel'. The change which has seen 'personnel'
re-titled as 'HR' has come about in the last few years. It is equally commonplace to hear
HR practitioners talk about the role they play in assisting the direction of the 'business' for
which they work (even HR practitioners in the public sector often refer to their organisations
as 'businesses'). There is obviously an element of fashion in all this. It is clearly leaping
much too far ahead to think that just because a personnel department calls itself 'HR'
and that it claims to play an important part in contributing to the organisation's strategic
direction that it is engaging in SHRM. The reality is much more complicated than that.

This chapter takes the two topics of defining SHRM and examining the degree to
which SHRM may be said to be contributing to organisational performance as twin
themes. It is a far from straightforward journey since the process of defining SHRM is
complex and the plotting of a straight path between the conduct of HR practices and
organisational performance is fraught with ambiguities.

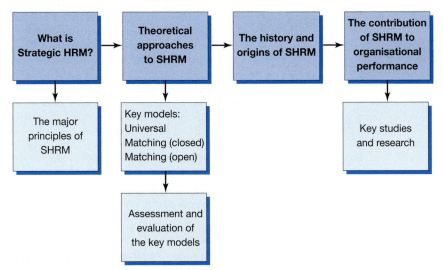

Figure 2.1 Mapping the strategic human resource management territory: a summary diagram of the chapter content

What is strategic human resource management? Major principles underpinning the concept

SHRM is such a complex, multi-faceted phenomenon that is not easy, nor is it particularly helpful, to arrive at a neat all-encompassing definition. Indeed, were one to do so it
would be at best simplistic and at worst misleading. This and the following section of
this chapter clarify some of the major principles fundamental to SHRM and then
explain some of the differing perspectives on SHRM. The intention is not to paint a
black and white portrait of SHRM but to give an overview of the main strands of SHRM
thinking, which set the scene for the remaining chapters in this book.

Sisson (1990: 5) comes as close as any writer in his assessment of the four main principles of SHRM, which are:

1. A stress on the integration of personnel policies to form a coherent package, and with business planning more generally.

2. The locus of responsibility for personnel management no longer resides with specialist managers but is now assumed by senior line management.

3. The focus shifts from management–trade union relations to management–employee relations, from collectivism to individualism.

4. There is stress on commitment and the exercise of initiative, with managers now assuming the role of 'enabler', 'empowerer' and 'facilitator'.

The first of Sisson's principles is perhaps the most fundamental. Indeed, Sisson (1990: 5) says that 'the management of people becomes a critical element – some would say *the* critical element – in the strategic management of the business'. SHRM derives its 'strategic' facet from the link to wider business strategy and integration between the various HR policies, procedures and practices: the first termed *vertical integration* and the second *horizontal integration* (Mabey *et al.*, 1998). The second component goes some way to explaining why so many HR practitioners in the larger organisations are now called 'HR consultants'. Their role is to support line managers with advice on the HR aspects of their roles, such as the disciplining of staff in a way which is consistent with the organisation's discipline policy and procedure. The third component of Sisson's assessment of the main principles of SHRM relates to a change in the focus of the employment relationship. This has changed from a concentration upon the relationship between management and trade unions to that between management and individual employees. This sounds self-evident in the second half of the first decade of the twenty-first century. The decline of trade union power and influence is well documented (see Lewis *et al.*, 2003c). Some of this decline may be attributed to the way in which managers have sought to get 'closer' to their employees through such initiatives as team briefing and other employee involvement techniques (for evidence of the growth employee involvement in the 1990s see Cully *et al.*, 1999). Another of these employee involvement initiatives is the setting up of problem-solving groups which are designed to achieve the commitment-seeking and empowering aims of management noted in the fourth element of Sisson's assessment.

Similarly Guest (1987) argues that there are four main principles of SHRM:

1. Integration of: relevant employment activities into general organisational strategies and policies; between HR practices themselves; of line managers in the process of people management; of all employees into the business.

2. High employee commitment to the goals and practices of the organisation.

3. High-quality staff and internal practices to achieve high-quality products.

4. Flexibility in terms of organisational structure, employee functions and job content to enable the organisation to respond quickly to change.

There appears to be two similarities with Sisson's four principles. They agree about the integration of relevant employment activities into general organisational strategies and policies and the existence of employee commitment to organisational goals.

It is difficult to argue with Guest's third principle of high-quality staff and internal practices producing high-quality products originating from general organisational strategies and policies which reflect the necessity for such staff and practices. An example of a company, the well-known DIY chain B&Q, using the internal HR practice of giving employees recognition in order to generate commitment and, therefore, quality customer service, is shown in 'In Practice' 2.1.

However, Guest's fourth element of SHRM – a fluid and adaptive organisational structure in which flexible employees perform flexible jobs – is less straightforward. On the face

In Practice   2.1

Recognising employee performance at B&Q

B&Q engaged consultants to measure employee engagement across its 327 stores, reflecting the company's strong belief that higher employee commitment and satisfaction translates to better customer service, which in turn drives higher profits.

A specific area that was targeted for company-wide improvement was that of 'recognition'. A question in the employee survey asked, 'In the last seven days, have you received recognition or praise for doing good work?' B&Q's HR director noted that the response to this question was satisfactory but that it was an easy one to improve. So in 2002 he introduced what he calls 'the best recognition schemes in retail'. These are:

- The big B&Q thank you – a monthly award of £50 in Kingfisher Group vouchers for each store and head office department for an employee with outstanding performance.

- The best of the best – an annual award for the highest-performing store staff adviser in each of six job types, such as cashiers, customer advisers and goods-in staff. Each store nominates its best performers in each category and they receive a small award, such as a bottle of champagne. The names go forward to the regional office, which then picks the best out of the region's stores and makes more awards. Finally, the six best across all stores each receive a £10,000 home makeover.

- B&Q heroes – staff are invited to submit details of a dream they would like to fulfil and the most imaginative each year receives a year's paid sabbatical plus £10,000 to try to pursue their ambition.

The three schemes cost around £500,000 a year and have brought a considerable rise in the recognition score in the employee survey. The results are part of the store managers' bonus scheme which covers managers, deputy managers, assistant managers and team leaders. It is based on store sales, as well as employee survey scores and customer service scores from 3,000 quarterly customer interviews conducted by Gallup.

Source: adapted from IRS Employment Review (2003b).

of it, it is plausible to recognise that an organisational structure that is responsive to change (e.g. enabling a project team comprising staff from different branches in different regions to open a new retail store) will lead to greater organisational effectiveness than an unresponsive, rigid structure. However, it is misleading to assume that all organisations are characterised by change. Some are relatively stable and unchanging. The primary school, for example, may have a stable staff, constant pupil numbers, and an unchanging organisational mission (notwithstanding curriculum change). Contrast this with Boots, the giant UK chemist chain, which has undergone a major restructuring programme in order to improve profitability (BBC News Online, 2004b). Structural change will clearly be necessary at Boots as it responds to a changing retail environment, whereas such a change may be quite unnecessary at the primary school. To deduce that SHRM is possible at Boots but not at the primary school seems too simple. Boots has obviously developed a business strategy embodying major change, part of which involves the trimming of staff costs, and to develop an HR strategy consistent with this is not only plausible but desirable. However, the primary school may also be in a position to pursue SHRM. If the school is deemed successful it may want to pursue a strategy of 'steady as we go' and develop an HR strategy to reflect this desire for stability. It seems that to have a flexible organisation is probably better than having an inflexible one, but that is not the same as saying that for HRM to be strategic it must be characterised by a flexible organisation structure.

Hendry and Pettigrew (1990: 21) also define SHRM in terms of four principles:

1. the use of planning;

2. a coherent approach to the design and management of personnel systems based on an employment policy and manpower strategy, and often underpinned by a 'philosophy';

3. matching HRM activities and policies to some explicit strategy;

4. seeing the people of the organisation as a 'strategic resource' for achieving competitive advantage.

The first of Hendry and Pettigrew's principles is implied in the emphasis upon strategy. They argue that HR planning is an important part of meeting business needs. This is particularly so if it is based on competence development and career planning rather than simply 'headcount'. The second and third are consistent with the principle of vertical integration included in the lists of Sisson and Guest, albeit that they include the notion of personnel systems being based on a 'philosophy'. Hendry and Pettigrew argue that having an HRM philosophy is a way of ensuring that HR practices are governed not just by 'technological, social and economic circumstances but by a degree of idealism as well' (Hendry and Pettigrew, 1990: 21). The notion of an HR philosophy has become increasingly important to many organisations in recent years and is often based on the well-known mission statement.

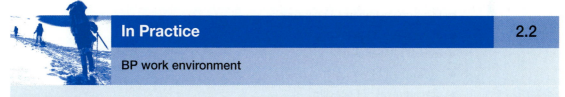

In Practice   2.2

BP work environment

We believe in creating a work environment of mutual trust, respect, inclusion and diversity. Everyone who works for BP should know what's expected of them in their jobs and have open and constructive conversations about their performance.

What to expect

We believe in creating an environment where you can improve your mind, learn more, gain professional qualifications within your discipline, improve your résumé, and work with and be inspired by like-minded individuals.

What do we expect?

We expect that you'll give it your all; that you'll share our vision for social responsibility and company, team and individual growth; and that you'll strive to make a difference every day. One thing is certain. When you join BP, we want you to be the best you can be. And be yourself.

Open communications

We aim for a radical openness – transparent, questioning, restless and inclusive. A new approach from a new company. We will be the magnet for people who want to change the world with new ideas, delivering a performance standard that challenges the world's best companies. Does that sound like you?

Benefits

Our benefits vary a great deal from country to country, largely because regions vary so much.

Stock options

BP offers most of its employees an opportunity to acquire shares in the company, through savings-related and matching arrangements. We also use a long-term performance plan and grant share options as a part of employee remuneration. The exact offerings vary, depending on the country.

Source: BP (2004).

It is easy to dismiss such statements as being little more than a series of meaningless clichés of the 'people are our most important asset' type. But such a statement of people management philosophy seems to us to be important in a large multi-national corporation such as BP. In Practice 2.2 portrays to prospective BP employees something of the nature of employment at BP which should apply to whichever part of the world that person is employed in.

Self-Check and Reflect Questions   2.1

What value would you place in a philosophy statement similar to the BP example above if you were searching for employment?

In a survey of 34 organisations (IRS, 2000) which have statements of employment philsophies, the most prevalent values expressed were:

- honesty and integrity (featured in 44 per cent of statements);
- valuing others and equality (41 per cent);
- focus on customers (35 per cent);
- innovation (32 per cent)
- respect (29 per cent)
- teamwork (24 per cent)
- development (24 per cent)
- partnership (15 per cent)
- responsiveness (15 per cent).

The fourth principle of Hendry and Pettigrew, seeing the people of the organisation as a 'strategic resource' for achieving competitive advantage, implies two important values. The first is contained in the B&Q policy statement on employee recognition (see In Practice 2.1) and in the list of values found to be prevalent among the organisations which responded to the IRS (2000) survey. It is the focus on customers in order to gain competitive advantage. Such focus has not restricted itself to the private sector, where one would expect to find the enterprise culture at its liveliest. As du Gay and Salaman (1998: 59) note:

There can hardly be a school, hospital, social services department, university or college in the UK that has not in some way been permeated by the language of enterprise. Enterprise has remorselessly reconceptualised and remodelled almost everything in its path.

Du Gay and Salaman go on to argue that the reconceptualisation of employment, for many, has found expression in the encouragement of competitiveness through small-group working and promoting individual accountability and responsibility through performance management schemes. Moreover, they argue, customer-focus philosophy has generated the values of: enhanced productivity, quality assurance, the fostering of innovation, and flexibility.

Those of us who are old enough to remember the pre-enterprise culture days are familiar with the interests of the producer dominating those of the consumer. Just such a tension can now be seen in China and parts of eastern Europe, where former Communist economies are grappling with the change to market economies with the result that employees in many organisations are having for the first time to ask themselves 'What is best for the customer?' not 'What is best for us?' It may be true that information technology has revolutionised customer service but so has the revolution in organisational attitudes. Computers have facilitated 24-hour banking but it needs management responsiveness to customer needs to have telephone lines staffed for 24 hours.

The second value enshrined in the fourth principle of Hendry and Pettigrew's is that of seeing the people of the organisation as a 'strategic resource'. This strikes at the heart of some of the earliest writing on HRM. It prompts the question of whether employees are to be seen as human resources or resourceful humans (Morris, 1974). The former term recalls Storey's (1992) oft-quoted phrase that employees, when seen as human resources, are seen as a 'headcount resource' and treated in as rational a way as 'any other factor of production' (Storey, 1992: 29). On the other hand, when employees are treated as 'resourceful humans', the emphasis is upon training and development, employee involvement and all the other HR practices which are designed to optimise the potential of employees. In reality, of course, it is rarely an either/or situation as both views can co-exist in any organisation at the same time. A major restructuring programme can, at the same time, involve major redundancies and initiatives to invest in those employees who are seen as key to the success of the restructuring programme. Whichever view is adopted, and whether the emphasis is upon cost reduction or investment in human capital, the human resource is, as Hendry and Pettigrew note, an important part of the organisation's strategy

So far all that has been done is discuss a list of major principles underpinning the concept of SHRM. They do not constitute a theory. It is important to articulate that theory clearly now. This is that if SHRM is introduced then certain benefits, such as the acquisition of a customer focused organisational culture, will be the consequence. Such theories are discussed in the next section.

Main theoretical approaches to SHRM

So far, all that has been done is to outline some of the principles that underpin SHRM. So, if one wanted to assess the extent to which the organisation's HRM activities were 'strategic', the best we could do would be to march along with these checklists and tick off those which we felt were present. This sounds straightforward but unfortunately organisational life is not as simple as that. The emphasis on integration, in the lists presented above, suggests that some indication of how the various components of SHRM fit together and interact may be more helpful. This introduces the idea of SHRM models which dominated the literature in the early writing on the topic. These models are helpful because they highlight different ways of thinking about SHRM, but, more importantly, they reinforce, and elaborate, that most significant of SHRM principles – the link between organisational strategy and HR strategy.

It is not possible to cover all the various SHRM models in this chapter, so some of the more influential ones in relation to the way in which they portray the link between organisational strategy and HR strategy are categorised. There are three categories, labelled: universal models; matching models (closed); and matching models (open) (see Figure 2.2). The universal approach assumes that there are 'best HR practices' which promise success irrespective of organisational circumstances. The matching models (closed) approach specifies HR policies and practices which are relevant to specific organisational situations, whereas the matching models (open) approach defines the employee behaviours necessitated by the organisation's overall strategy. These behaviours are to be delivered through the HR strategy. We now go into more detail on each of these.

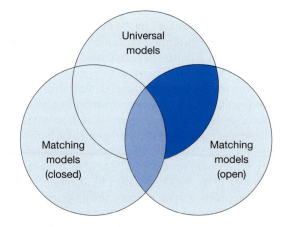

Figure 2.2 Three theoretical approaches to strategic HRM.

Universal models

The approach here is, on the face of it, very straightforward. It suggests that there is 'one best way' of achieving HR effectiveness. The link between organisational strategy and HR strategy is still emphasised but advocates of the universalistic school argue that this involves top management giving 'HR practices the profile they deserve in the senior management process' (Boxall and Purcell, 2003: 61). Boxall and Purcell go on to say that the universalists stress the importance of:

- top management commitment to key HR practices;
- researching the leading edge of best practice;
- publicising commitment to specific best practices;
- measuring progress towards the best practices;
- rewarding line managers for the consistent implementation of the best practices.

Everybody is familiar with the universalist approach. It can be seen in most prescriptive texts, particularly in the many 'how to be a successful manager' type of books which have appeared in recent years. Perhaps the most influential of these is *In search of Excellence* (Peters and Waterman, 1982). One of the eight key attributes that formed the basis of Peters and Waterman's prescription for organisational success was 'productivity through people' – where 'employees are seen as the key resources of the organisation and this is emphasised in involvement programmes and through activities designed to reinforce in employees the importance of their contribution to the success of the organisation and therefore to their own rewards' (Guest, 1992: 6).

The appeal of these books is their simplicity, but this is also their shortcoming. If the process of managing is as simple as following a magic number of golden rules then, presumably, the only unsuccessful managers would be those that never read the books! There is something a little demeaning in this. There are no books which promise to turn people into successful doctors, or lawyers or teachers in ten easy steps. Managing is a complex process underpinned by a wealth of social science theory. If it could be learned by following a few easy steps then presumably many readers of this book would not be spending valuable time and money studying the subject.

Before the idea of universalism is dismissed, some of the prescriptions must be examined. In doing so it must be admitted that there is some sense in the best-practice approach. Few would deny, for example, that it is better to select employees on the basis of the demands of the job rather than some vague notion of who may be the 'best' person. Similarly, to analyse training needs and set clear training objectives is preferable to adopting a haphazard approach to training. But we have already demonstrated that an important aspect of SHRM is that of integration. So immediately there appears to be a problem with universalism in that often the 'golden rules' are discrete; there is no clear sense of the way in which they interact with one another to produce an effective package.

But before critiquing the universalist approach, an examination of two of the HR-specific 'best practice' prescriptions is conducted. The first, that of Walton (1985), was extremely influential in early SHRM thinking, and, for that matter, still is. One then goes on to consider the more recent, and equally well-known, work of Pfeffer (1998).

Walton's (1985) argument was so influential because he did much to popularise the idea that certain HR practices implemented in specific ways gave rise to employee commitment; a theme that has subsequently been taken up with great enthusiasm by academics and managers alike. For Walton this was important because he felt that American managers (UK managers were little different) had failed to motivate their employees and realise their latent abilities. Moreover, there had been failure to engage employees in any sort of partnership, which Walton felt was necessary to serve the interests of the organisation's stakeholders. Walton made his theory quite clear. It sounds as persuasive today as it did 20 years ago.

> The strategy of eliciting employee commitment requires that management overhaul a large number of human resource policy areas. The common theme in the revision of these policies is the increased mutuality between workers and managers and between employees and employers. Thus, the new management strategy involves policies that promote mutuality in order to elicit employee commitment, which in turn can generate increased economic effectiveness and human development.
>
> *(Walton, 1985: 36)*

Walton contrasted his commitment model with the traditional model of employee control which owed much to the scientific management thinking of F.W. Taylor. The scientific management quest was to establish order and control to achieve efficiency. By contrast, the commitment model is designed to generate high levels of mutual trust without which 'management is forced to reinstitute controls to ensure acceptable performance' (Walton, 1985: 50).

The HR policy areas which Walton highlighted are shown in Table 2.1.

Pfeffer's (1998) seven practices of successful organisations are shown in Figure 2.3 and have some similarities with Walton's model, particularly in the policy areas of teams, reward, employment assurance and employee voice.

The seven practices are:

1. The provision of employment security.

2. Systematic recruitment and selection.

3. Self-managed teams and the decentralisation of decision making as the basic principles of organisational design.

4. Comparatively high levels of reward based on organisational performance.

5. High investment in staff training.

6. Reduced status differences.

7. Sharing financial and performance information with all the organisation's employees.

Table 2.1 HR policy areas and the main characteristics with which they are associated

HR policy area	Main characteristics
Job design	Jobs to be broader and combine planning and implementation; teams to be emphasised as units of accountability
Performance expectation	Emphasis on 'stretch objectives'; dynamic and based on continuous improvement
Management organisation	Flat; emphasises shared goals; based on expertise not position; status differences minimised
Reward	Emphasis upon reinforcing group achievement; emphasis upon contribution not job evaluation
Employment assurance	Great care to be taken to avoid redundancies
Employee voice	Mechanisms to be developed for employee involvement; importance placed on communication of information to employees
Employment relations	Less adversarial; develop scope for joint problem solving
Management philosophy	Inspiring; legitimate claims of all stakeholders acknowledged; employee needs as goal not means to end

Source: developed from Walton (1985).

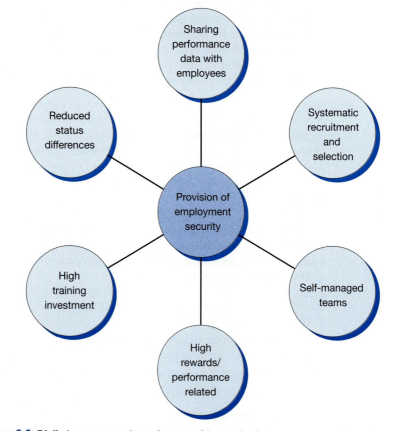

Figure 2.3 Pfeffer's seven practices of successful organisations

This chapter will not go into the detail of each of Pfeffer's seven practices, any more than it has done with Walton's, since only these approaches to SHRM are used as examples of best practice rather than definitive models. More detail on such issues as recruitment and selection, reward and training are found in later chapters of this book. However, it is appropriate to give some idea of the main thrust of Pfeffer's thinking.

Pfeffer argues that employment security is fundamental to the operation of his seven practices because organisations are unlikely to invest resources in the careful screening and training of new people if those people are not expected to be with the organisation long enough for it to recover these investments. He also argues that delegation of operating authority and the sharing of sensitive performance and strategic information require trust, which is much more likely to emerge in a system of mutual, long-term commitments.

Central to Pfeffer's list are the three practices which form the kernel of most HR systems: recruitment and selection; training; and reward. It is no surprise that Pfeffer emphasises the importance of systematic recruitment and selection of new employees with particular attention being paid to a fit between the critical skills, behaviours and attitudes necessary for successful job performance. Neither is it a surprise that high investment in staff training is advocated. But Pfeffer bemoans the fact that in the USA (and, all too often, in the UK) an irrational cycle occurs where training budgets are cut in times when organisations are not prospering and employees have more time to undertake training. The same budgets are plentiful in profitable times when employees have less time to pursue training. The linkage of reward to organisational performance is central to many high-performance work systems, as explained later in this chapter. It is also a fundamental component of strategic reward systems, as Chapter 12 illustrates.

There is a logical thread that runs through the remaining three of Pfeffer's seven practices of successful organisations: organisational design based on self-managed teams and the decentralisation of decision making; reduced status differences; and sharing financial and performance information with all the organisation's employees. Pfeffer claims a number of benefits for these practices, all of which have a plausible ring to them. The general thrust of his argument for all three is that better-quality decisions will result if those who have to implement the decisions are involved in their making and possess the necessary information to make those decisions. Moreover, the process of employee involvement, and the erosion of status differentials (particularly between white and blue collar employees) will send a symbolic message to employees that they are trusted and valued with the result that levels of motivation and job satisfaction will increase.

This chapter may be accused here of suggesting that both Walton and Pfeffer are oversimplifying their approaches. In fairness, both warn against assuming that implementing the policies they advocate is unproblematic. In addition, Pfeffer points out that implementing his seven practices piecemeal may be counter-productive. An example of this may be where organisations are unlikely to derive benefit from their commitment to training unless changes in work organisation permit these more skilled people to actually implement their knowledge.

Pfeffer acknowledges the point that the individual practices must be aligned with one another and be consistent with the overall direction of the organisation if they are to have a beneficial effect upon organisational performance.

Problems with the universalist models

The problem of list composition

The first problem for universalists is agreeing on which HR practices are essential for the delivery of enhanced organisational performance. The similarity between some of the practices in the lists of Walton and Pfeffer implies that agreement over some of the basics, such as effective selection and training activity, may be straightforward but there are areas, such as collective employee representation either through trade unions or internal employee committees, which may be much less so. Our immediate reaction to the question as to whether collective employee representation is likely to be associated with effective HR and organisational performance is that it depends on the context in which the organisation operates. It may be appropriate in a giant national employer in Sweden where there is a high level of trade union organisation, but less so in a small software design company in the USA.

The problem of context

The clearest difficulty with universalist models of SHRM is that they ignore the context in which SHRM operates. It seems an immediately plausible argument that a universalist recipe applied in one organisation may not yield the same results in another organisation. There may be a host of reasons for this which Boxall and Purcell (2003) classify as originating from differences in national, sectoral and organisation contexts.

There is a growing amount of international HRM literature which warns against the assumption that simply transplanting management practices from one country to another may result in widely differing consequences (see Key Concepts 2.1). The more those countries differ in relation to such factors as culture, work organisation, economic and political systems and what Gamble (2003) calls 'national business systems' (embeddedness in national institutional structures) the more care needs to be exercised.

Sectoral differences within countries may pose as many problems for universal advocacy of HR practices as transnational differences. Sectors of employment may, of course, be differentiated by the market for products or services in which they operate, organisational size or ownership. An obvious difference suggests itself between the large organisations operating in product markets characterised by the need for high added-value (e.g. telecommunications, computing) where sophisticated technology is used by professional and technical workers and small organisations using limited skills in low value-added operations (e.g. garment manufacturing, catering). The 1998 Workplace Employee Relations Survey (Cully *et al.*, 1999) notes, for example, that key HR practices, such as performance appraisal, were not operated by two-thirds of small workplaces (less than 100 employees). A major factor in the consideration of the difference between the likely consequences of implementing the same HR practices in large and small organisations is the level of sophistication in the management of employees. The following quote from Dundon *et al.*'s (1999) case study of a small commercial truck dealer illustrates this point. Here, managers outside the family circle tended to be time-served ex-mechanics or sales reps. Dundon *et al.* report one manager as recalling:

> The problem with motor trade managers is that they've had very little training – particularly in people and communication skills – they've got very rough and ready management skills.
>
> *(Dundon* et al.*, 1999: 255)*

The enormous amount of attention paid to organisational culture in recent years raises the obvious point that what is done in one organisation, even if all other variables

Key Concepts   2.1

Performance management in China

The development of performance management in Chinese organisations poses problems of cultural adaptation. This is particularly so in organisations owned by the state. These organisations have a greater legacy of management ineffectiveness to overcome than foreign – investing – companies. However, it is a potential difficulty for all organisations which employ Chinese nationals. Some of these problems are fundamental to performance management, including: the processes of assigning objectives; setting performance measures; giving performance feedback to employees; and tying pay to individual performance.

The major cultural barrier is the relative reluctance of Chinese society to embrace the concept of individualism – the very essence of performance management. Child (1994: 181) talks of 'the identification of merit by reference to objective performance criteria and the encouragement of personal ambition ... [as] ... the side of personnel management furthest removed from the collective norms of Chinese tradition and socialist ideology'. One consequence of this is that the notion of individual responsibility for the acceptance of personal job performance objectives is alien to traditional Chinese custom. The same applies to a spirit of openness in giving employees feedback (criticism or praise) on their job performance. This reluctance to engage in both objective setting and feedback giving, stems from several sources. Among the most telling of these is the complex sociological phenomenon of 'face' which imposes upon Chinese the need to maintain harmony in social settings. In addition, the legacy of the 'iron rice bowl' system of lifetime employment created an employment culture where high individual employee performance was of scant importance. There is also the traditional Chinese concern with bureaucracy, which may be used as a shield behind which those who do not wish to accept personal responsibility may hide. Bureaucracy also leads to the development of 'meaningless' performance objectives, which do little to improve individual job performance.

The traditional Chinese attitude to reward is also inconsistent with the concept of individual performance management. This has reflected the Communist concern with equality. Consequently, pay differences among those in different professions and at different levels of responsibility have been much lower than in Europe and North America. In China, rather than individual performance driving compensation levels, it has been seniority, political orientation and nepotism (Ding *et al.*, 1997).

Source: Lewis (2003a).

such as country, size and product market, are held constant may 'work' differently in another. This is why multi-national corporations, such as McDonald's, work so hard at attempting to inculcate a standard culture across countries. More is said about this in Chapter 3.

The problem of the absence of employee voice

The point is made below (in more detail) that one of the major problems with the universalist and matching (closed) models of SHRM is that they are essentially unitarist in that they assume a managerial view of the world without taking into account the employee perspective. The universalist position, as represented here by Walton and Pfeffer, is one that assumes unity of employee and employer interest and that if problems arise with the consequence that the desired results do not flow from the recommended HR practices then these are the result of faulty implementation rather than the substance of the practices themselves (Marchington and Grugulis, 2000).

Matching models (closed)

This school of SHRM thinking has argued that there is a clear and mutually supportive relationship between organisational strategy and HR strategy and goes on to say that this relationship gives rise to the implementation of *specific* HR initiatives. That is to say the match between the organisational strategy and HR strategy is closed and prescribed in the sense that a particular type of organisational strategy suggests the need for a specific HR strategy and set of practices.

The first of these comes from one of the earliest and most influential sources – Fombrun *et al.* (1984). They relate HRM activities to organisational strategy and structure (see Table 2.2). In this model it is simple to 'read off' what an organisation should do in terms of the various HR activities when it is at a particular stage of development.

Fombrun *et al.* (1984) describe their model as an attempt to fit their four generic HR systems (selection, appraisal, reward and development) to the different stages of growth that organisations go through from start-up to maturity. As such they were adapting the work of Galbraith and Nathanson (1978).

Fombrun *et al.* (1984) nail their colours firmly to the mast in their attempt to elevate their model to the status of a predictive theory. Their argument is that just as organisations will encouter inefficiencies when they try to implement new strategies with outmoded structures they will also face problems of implementation when they attempt to implement new strategies with inappropriate human resource systems. For Fombrun *et al.* the critical managerial task is to align the formal structure of the human resource systems so that they drive the strategic objectives of the organisation.

Baird and Meshoulam (1988) and Kochan and Barocci (1985) also link HR activities to stages in the organisation's development. Baird and Meshoulam's model moves from the first stage of initiation (the start-up stage) to the final stage of strategic integration (the management focus is upon flexibility, adaptability and integration across all business functions). As organisations move through the stages, the various HR components (e.g. management of the HR function, role of line managers and HR skills) become increasingly sophisticated. So management of the HR function moves from being absent or informal in the initiation stage to integrated with the strategic direction of the business in the strategic integration stage. Kochan and Barocci advocate three stages – growth, maturity and decline – and prescribe different HR activities under the headings of recruitment and staffing, compensation and benefits, training and development, and employee relations.

Schuler and Jackson's (1987) approach is a little different. They draw upon the well-known work of Porter (1985) and, in particular, his three main types of organisational strategies: innovation, quality enhancement and cost reduction (see Key Concepts 2.2). Schuler and Jackson's argument is that differing organisational strategies require from employees different behaviours which may be fostered through the practice of different HR techniques.

Table 2.2 HRM links to strategy and structure

Strategy	Structure	Selection	Appraisal	Reward	Development
Single product	Functional	Functionally oriented: subjective criteria used	Subjective: assessment through personal discussions	Unsystematic, determined in a paternalistic manner	Unsystematic, based on experience in the single function focus
Single product (vertically integrated)	Functional	Functionally oriented: standardised criteria used	Impersonal assessment based on cost and productivity data	Performance-related based on productivity data	Functional specialists with some generalists: largely job rotation.
Growth by acquisition (holding company) of an unrelated business	Separate self-contained businesses	Functionally oriented, but businesses may vary in extent of systematic approach	Impersonal: based on return on investment and profitability	Formula-based including return on investment and profitability	Cross-functional but not cross-business
Related diversification of product lines through internal growth and acquisition	Multi-divisional	Functionally and generalist oriented: systematic criteria used	Impersonal: based on return on investment, productivity and subjective assessment of contribution to the business	Large bonuses based on profitability and subjective assessment of contribution to the company	Cross-functional, cross-divisional and cross-corporate/divisional: formal
Multiple products in multiple countries	Global organisation (geographic centre and worldwide)	Functionally and generalist oriented: systematic criteria used	Impersonal: based on multiple goals such as return on investment, profit tailored to product and country	Bonuses: based on multiple planned goals with some top management discretion	Cross-divisional and cross-subsidiary to corporate: formal and systematic

Source: adapted from Fombrun *et al*. (1984).

Key Concepts   2.2

Porter's three main types of organisational strategies

Innovation

Developing products or services different from those offered by competitors – the primary focus on offering something new and different.

Enhancing product and/or service quality

Being right the first time every time – continual improvement.

Cost reduction

Gaining competitive advantage through being the lowest-cost producer by the use of tight controls, minimising overheads and pursuit of economies of scale.

Source: developed from Schuler and Jackson (1987).

Schuler and Jackson (1987: 208) define employee behaviours in terms of 'what is needed from an employee who works with other employees in a social environment ... rather than thinking about task-specific skills, knowledge and abilities to perform a specific task'. There are 12 such behaviours which may be assessed by the degree to which the role demands:

1. creativity;
2. a long/short time focus;
3. independence;
4. concern for quality;
5. concern for quantity;
6. risk taking;
7. concern for process;
8. the assumption of responsibility;
9. flexibility;
10. tolerance of unpredictability;
11. skill application;
12. job (or organisational) involvement.

Table 2.3 shows the required employee behaviours for each of Porter's three main types of organisational strategies and the HR techniques that are likely to foster these different behaviours from employees.

Such matching models are deceptively simple and contain a certain appeal. It must be of some comfort to the HR director to decide which of the strategies his or her organisation is pursuing and devise an HR strategy accordingly. But, as ever, life is not as simple as that. The matching models (closed) are not without their problems.

Table 2.3 Required employee behaviours for each of Porter's three main types of organisational strategy and the HR techniques needed to foster these behaviours

Type of strategy	Required employee behaviours	Accompanying HR techniques
Innovation	• High degree of creativity • Longer-term focus • High degree of cooperation and interdependence • Equal attention to process and results • High degree of risk-taking • High tolerance of ambiguity	• Select high-skill employees • Allow employees to develop skills which may be used in other organisational positions • Performance appraisal which assesses individual and group performance • Rewards which are lower in base pay but reflect organisational performance and internal equity • Broad career paths • Give employees discretion • High investment in human resources • Tolerance of occasional failure • Longer-term focus for performance management
Quality enhancement	• Repetitive and predictable behaviours • Long to intermediate-term focus • Modest degree of cooperation and interdependence • High concern for quality • Modest concern for quantity • High concern for process • Low risk-taking • High commitment to organisational goals	• Fixed and explicit job descriptions • Employee participation in job-level decisions • High emphasis upon empowerment • High emphasis upon teamwork • Concern for giving employees feedback • Some emphasis upon job security • High attention to training and development
Cost reduction	• Repetitive and predictable behaviours • Short–term focus • Primarily autonomous, individual activity • Modest concern for quality • High concern for quantity • High concern for results • Low risk-taking • Comfortable with stability	• Tightly defined jobs • Emphasis upon organisational 'rightsizing' • Monitoring of market rates to ensure no upward pay drift • High concern for results in performance management • Increased use of part-time employees and subcontactors • Work simplification • Temporal (i.e. flexible hours/shifts/days) flexibility • Little attention to training and development

Source: developed from Schuler and Jackson (1987).

Problems with the matching models (closed)

The problem of strategy ambiguity

Perhaps the most apparent difficulty with the idea of a neat matching of organisation strategy and HR strategy is that of assuming that both are defined clearly within the organisation. Moreover, that both are capable of clear definition. In Chapter 1 it is asserted that the formation of strategy is not as simple as managers sitting down and deciding which strategy to pursue. It may be as deliberate as this or may emerge as a process of trial and error (Mintzberg and Waters, 1989). So if the idea of strategy is accepted (both organisation strategy and HR strategy), emerging over time, then, the idea of HR strategy following organisation strategy becomes a somewhat messier and longer drawn-out process.

There has also been criticism (e.g. Boxall, 1992) of the extent to which it is possible to generalise about organisational strategies in the way in which they are portrayed in the models above. If Porter's three generic strategies are taken as an example, it appears that Schuler and Jackson are treating them as independent of one another, whereas the reality for many organisations is that they are pursued in tandem, as the example of Tesco (see In Practice 2.3) amply illustrates. Indeed, suggesting that these generic strategies are independent of one another seems illogical. While it may be that many organisations admit to not being particularly innovative, perhaps with good reason, there can be few who do not pursue the twin goals of quality enhancement and cost reduction. Both these goals point the way to competitive advantage. Neither is it only in the private sector that these twin goals are relevant. The explicit message of the 'best value' initiative in UK local government is to provide better-quality service from a reduced cost base.

> Best Value Performance Indicators exist because of the duty of best value, which requires local authorities (and other best value authorities) to seek to achieve continuous improvement by having regard to the efficiency, effectiveness and economy of their service delivery. To see if local authorities are achieving best value central government departments set measures of performance against key service delivery areas.
>
> *(Office of the Deputy Prime Minister, 2004)*

In Practice   2.3

Pursuing strategies of innovation and quality enhancement at Tesco

Tesco, the UK's biggest supermarket chain, is well known for its aggressive pricing policy. This was the way in which the company built its business from modest beginnings. Yet the company has grown to its present size pursuing simultaneously strategies of growth through quality, price and innovation.

Tesco operates more than 2,300 stores in 13 countries, including Japan, Poland, Turkey, Hungary, and a joint venture in China. Tesco said sales at its international operations in Asia and central and eastern Europe were up 13.1 per cent in 2004. It added that it intended to create 25,000 jobs worldwide in 2005, including about 11,000 in the UK (BBC News Online, 2005b).

Tesco's commitment to quality customer service is reflected in its HR policies. The company was one of the first to sign a partnership deal with its trade union, USDAW. The company reasoned that delivering the required level of customer service depended on enthusiastic staff who feel they are valued. The partnership deal allows for communication and consultation at all levels of the organisation (Thornhill *et al.*, 2000).

Another way in which the notion of organisational strategy is oversimplified concerns the tendency to assume that one organisation equates to one strategy. This ignores the multi-national, multi-divisional and multi-product companies where operational managers have limited knowledge of what is going on in other parts of the organisation (Purcell, 1999). This makes HR strategy forming even more confusing and complex. Purcell makes another point about the oversimplification of the closed matching models. He argues that they only look at business strategies and (with the obvious exception of HR) ignore those operational strategies that are needed to put the business strategies into effect. Such operational strategies may spell the need for different HR strategies from those suggested by the main business strategy. This highlights the problem of the difficulty of assuming that specific types of organisational strategy give rise to specific types of HR strategy. Purcell cites the example of the company (Pirelli Cables) which pursued cost minimisation through heavy investment in high-technology production systems. Schuler and Jackson's (1987) model prescribes little attention to training and development. Yet, in Purcell's example, the importance of maximising the potential of the new technology was such that learning new skills and knowledge became an important HR goal.

Another problem of strategic ambiguity is that the matching models (closed) make the assumption that the same HR techniques may be applied to all employees in the organisation pursuing the particular strategy. Intuitively this seems suspect. Schuler and Jackson's innovation strategy, for example, talks of low base pay in favour of rewards that link to organisational performance. However, the reality is that different employees prefer different reward packages due to differing personal circumstances. This is, of course, the theory behind flexible reward packages that enable employees to choose which package suits their needs.

The final ambiguity with this approach to SHRM theorising concerns the assumption that it is inevitable that HR strategy follows organisational strategy. It is by no means automatic that this may be so. The logical flow may be the other way around; that is that organisational strategy is determined largely by HR strategy. This is the so-called resource-based view of strategy which was covered Chapter 1. It may be that, particularly for small organisations in specialist product markets, the organisation's competitive advantage is built around the unique competences of key employees making HR-led organisational strategy formulation a real possibility. What this does point to is, perhaps, the key problem with the assumption that HR strategy neatly follows organisational strategy: that of the impossibility of defining and modelling all the contingent variables and their interconnection and of predicting the effect that changing one variable will have on others (Purcell, 1999).

The problem of managerialism

A rather basic weakness of the matching models (closed) is the way in which this approach assumes that managers will conceive and implement strategies without considering the perspective of employees. Given that HR strategies directly affect the working lives, and livelihoods, of employees this is a very considerable weakness. It betrays a unitarist perspective on the employment relationship (see Key Concepts 2.3) which is managerialist and pays no regard to the fact that employees may oppose the wishes of management. This may take several forms; for example, individual complaints, banding together with other employees to seek the help of a trade union, resignation or, at best, sullenly complying with management wishes.

The unitarist view of the employment relationship

- The employees of the organisation are seen as a team, unified by a common purpose with all employees pursuing the same goal.
- There is a single source of authority – that source being management.
- Since all employees are pursuing the same goal, conflict is irrational; it must be the result of poor communication or 'troublemakers' at work who do not share the common purpose.
- The presence of third parties to the employment relationship is intrusive, therefore there is no place for trade unions.

Source: developed from Fox (1966).

Such opposition is, of course, of vital importance to management implementing SHRM since all organisational strategies require at least the cooperation, if not the wholehearted commitment, of employees. Boxall and Purcell (2003) make the valid point that being mindful of employee interests is vital for organisations in highly competitive product and labour markets, where attracting and retaining key staff may pose real problems. Cooperation and commitment certainly cannot be taken for granted, yet the coverage of SHRM so far in this chapter has strangely little to say about the topic of employee motivation. This is curious as it is accepted that this is one of the central tenets of the management of people. As Boxall (1992: 68) says when he sums up the managerialist stance neatly: 'HRM appears as something that is "done to" passive human resources rather than something that is "done with" active human beings'. Similarly, Hendry and Pettigrew (1990: 23) reason that such an approach means that employees are 'excised from the equation'.

The problem of implementation

Boxall (1992) and Boxall and Purcell (2003) make the point that the SHRM matching models (closed) are rather 'static' in that they pay little attention to the fact that organisations' operating environments are constantly changing. On the one hand, 'fit' points to a certain unchanging rigidity, whereas 'flexibility' suggests dynamism and the ability to cope with ever-changing environments. Indeed, Wright and Snell (1998) note that the strategic fit and organisational flexibility are, on the face of it, in conflict. Clearly there are implications here for the management of HR which relate to the point made above about the assumption of a model of SHRM appearing as something that is 'done to' passive human resources. Dynamism implies the need for employees who can cope with change and an HR quest to attract, develop and retain key employees who can anticipate or, indeed, promote change as well as cope with the change when it occurs. The SHRM model in this case does not simply flow from organisational strategy to HR strategy but is constantly flowing between the two as change demands different responses from both.

A final point to be made here about problems of implementing the SHRM matching models (closed) is the unproblematic view that they take of organisational life. To think that simply designing the HR strategy in accordance with the prescription will yield 'success', ignores the host of variables that may conspire to render such an outcome unlikely. In short, the deterministic perspective is based on assumptions of rationality and unitarism which disregard the political realities of organisational life (Keenoy, 1990) not the least of which involve resistance to any threat to existing power bases (see In Practice 2.4).

In Practice   2.4

Lloyds TSB workers threaten to strike in protest over strategic plans to move call centre jobs to India

Members of finance union Unifi at Lloyds TSB are being balloted over the next few weeks after the move, which would lead to the loss of 1,000 jobs in Newcastle. The union national officer of Unifi, said: 'Staff at the call centre feel completely let down that the bank is putting profits before people. They want the opportunity to voice their disgust at the way they are being treated.'

A spokeswoman for Lloyds TSB has said the decision to close had been a difficult one and any staff reductions would hopefully be made through staff turnover and redeployment.

Source: BBC News Online (2003).

Matching models (open)

The open approach to SHRM also argues the existence of a clear and mutually support-ive relationship between organisational strategy and HR strategy. However, it differs from the closed approach in that the HR strategy initiatives should not be prescribed, following from the organisational strategy, but should be left open. In other words, the test of the degree to which the HR strategy is truly 'strategic' is a test of its *appropriate-ness* (Mabey *et al.*, 1998) to the organisational strategy.

In the authors' view the model that best summarises this approach is that of Mabey *et al.* (1998). These authors argue that the closed and open approaches to SHRM have much in common, not least that there should be a close and mutually supportive relationship between organisational strategy and HR strategy.

To summarise the Mabey *et al.* model, the operating environment (both external and internal) in which the organisation finds itself gives rise to the development of an organ-isational strategy that requires specific desired employee behaviours to be adopted if it is to be achieved. These desired behaviours are pursued through the HR strategy. This con-sists of three 'key levers' (structural, cultural and personnel strategies), which are intended to subsume all aspects of organisation that impact upon employees' behaviour. In the same way as there is to be a close and mutually supportive relationship between organisational strategy and HR strategy, so the same degree of mutual support is expected between the three components of the HR strategy.

This organisational strategy is called corporate strategy in the model (see Figure 2.4). Mabey and Salaman (1995) use the terms 'corporate strategy' and 'business strategy' interchangeably. This ignores Purcell's (1995) clear distinction between the two, which has the former as 'those taken at the centre covering the whole enterprise' (Purcell, 1995: 66) in multi-product and multi-divisional firms. Business strategies are 'lower down at the division or business unit level and related to the products made or the market served' (Purcell, 1995: 66). The absence of clear definition of this term means its use in

ENVIRONMENT

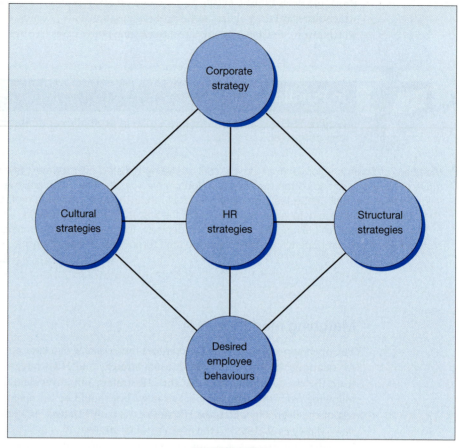

ENVIRONMENT

Figure 2.4 The 'open' SHRM model
Source: developed from Mabey *et al.* (1998).

Mabey *et al.*'s model is ambiguous. It could be used in either sense. But what is clear is the intention of the authors is to convey an impression of strategy driven by wider organisational purpose which has clear strategy, policy and practice implications for HRM (see Key Concepts 2.4).

Like all the models explained in this part of the chapter, Mabey *et al.*'s has a strong prescriptive ring to it. The authors argue that:

> ... competitive advantage will accrue to those organisations best able to exploit environ-
> mental opportunities and avoid or survive threats; and that the strategic management of
> human resources will assist organisations in this by encouraging and generating the
> appropriate sets of behaviours, attitudes and competences from employees.
>
> *(Mabey* et al.*, 1998: 71)*

However, the appeal of the Mabey *et al.* model is that the nature of the organisational strategy is not prescribed, neither is the content of the cultural, HR operational and structural strategies, or, indeed, the desired employee behaviours. It all depends upon

Key Concepts   2.4

Using the open SHRM model to change employee behaviours in a high street book multiple retailer

Bookworm was facing competition from a range of alternative suppliers of retail books, principally the specialist and generalist online suppliers. This meant that the company had to change dramatically from the way in which it had operated traditionally, which could be characterised as rather staid, formal, conservative and responding to the demands of the customer. The new retail book environment needed to be sharper and more entrepreneurial, always thinking up new ideas to anticipate and meet customer needs.

This meant that Bookworm needed to change the behaviours of its employees, with the emphasis being upon 'business-getting' salespeople rather than 'librarians'. The newly appointed HR director went about planning an HR strategy to deliver this change. This involved designing HR activities to complement the three 'key levers' (structural, cultural and personnel strategies) which would have an impact on employees' behaviour.

She started by defining the desired employee behaviours. One of these was that she particularly wanted employees to take responsibility, to think for themselves and not refer every minor decision (for example, on what specialist books to stock) to central managers. This involved changing the structure of the organisation with fewer managers and therefore shorter reporting lines.

In terms of personnel strategies, the HR director changed the template of required skills used for selection, training and appraisal purposes, and devised a new individual performance-related pay scheme to reflect the importance of employees demonstrating more responsibility in anticipating and meeting customer needs. She resisted the temptation to implement a major training programme under the banner of 'major cultural change', reasoning that making these changes to structure and personnel strategies would, by themselves, change the Bookworm culture over time.

the unique organisational context. That said, the Mabey *et al.* model should be treated with similar caution to the other models reviewed here. The authors themselves acknowledge that the model represents a:

> … fantastically idealised picture: in reality achieving it is extremely rare, and the risk in these rarefied discussions of abstract principles of HRS is that people begin to believe that the world is really like this. It is not.
>
> *(Mabey* et al.*, 1998: 70)*

Like all the SHRM models in this chapter, the Mabey *et al.* model is conceptually simple and, therefore, appealing. However, these authors agree with Mabey *et al.*, that the operationalisation of the model in order to achieve the desired results is extremely difficult. Each stage of the process provides its problems, not the least being that, as the authors themselves admit, the model tends to underestimate the dynamic nature of the context in which real-life organisations operate. This makes environmental analysis potentially unreliable for two principal reasons. First, in fast-moving sectors such as those employing high-technology applications, it is obviously problematic to keep track of what key actors, such as competitors, are doing in the external environment. Second, it also ignores the fact that organisational change initiatives, by definition, produce changing internal (and possibly external) environments.

Such processes as environmental analysis suggest that the Mabey *et al.* model adopts a highly rational approach with each step being taken in a cool, detached, systematic manner. As suggested earlier, this ignores the political dimension of organisational life and also assumes that employees' attitudes and behaviours can be changed in a simple cause–effect manner.

So far it has been shown that SHRM has a distinct identity, which marks it out as different from what has been known as personnel management. It is also more precise than HRM since it concentrates upon the strategic link between organisational strategy and HR strategy. Indeed, HRM, certainly in its 'soft' orientation, has been associated with a 'nurturing' approach to employees; the de-emphasising of conflict; increased communication; teamwork (Storey, 1992) as well as enhanced employee involvement; investment in training and development and employment security (Claydon, 2002). Claydon makes the point that this version of HRM has been portrayed as a 'win–win' situation in which the employer wins the benefit of higher labour productivity with resulting improvements to market share and profitability, and the employee gains a more interesting, better paid, more secure job with enhanced training and promotion opportunities.

Yet one of the notable aspects of the open approach is that it caters for all types of strategy, including a combination of the three Porter generic strategies which Schuler and Jackson used to drive their SHRM model, as analysed earlier. It is perfectly possible that an organisation (such as Tesco – see In Practice 2.3) may pursue strategies simultaneously giving rise to hybrid employee behaviours. For example, a high-tech computer games design house, which aims to be first in the market with high-quality games at a competitive price, will need designers who are flexible enough to learn new skills quickly as a result of a high degree of self-development, work across different projects and produce high-quality 'right first time' results.

What has not been shown is that SHRM, in any of the three orientations we have explained here, is any more effective in practical terms than any other approach to the management of employees. There has been increasing interest in providing such evidence in recent years and it is a summary of this which forms the last part of this chapter. But before we turn to this we describe the history and origins of SHRM.

The history and origins of SHRM

This chapter has explained that SHRM derives from the 1980s in North America and was adopted with enthusiasm in the UK in the latter part of the 1980s and 1990s. Therefore, the temptation is to look at that part of American business history to find the triggers which prompted such an interest in SHRM. Mabey *et al.* (1998) argue that this may be misleading, since SHRM is not that new; it was re-packaged in such a way that it resonated with other changes which happened in the external environment in that period. What was new, Mabey *et al.* (1999: 36) argue, was the 'combination of old elements in a new package'. Indeed, as Hendry and Pettigrew (1990) note, one of the doyens of management writing, Peter Drucker (1954), emphasised the importance of employees as a key organisational asset over 50 years ago.

Although there is some validity in the argument that SHRM did not arrive unannounced, there is no doubt that many of the changes that occurred in the external environment in which organisations operate had a profound influence upon the way in which managers viewed the importance of, and managed, their employees. That which is the most frequently quoted is the perceived crisis in American business performance which occurred in the early 1980s. This was due to the fact that American industry, particularly motor car production, was being outperformed significantly by Japanese companies. This produced the incentive to 're-invent' American organisations to restore their competitiveness; a re-invention in which the management of employees was to play an important part. This suggests that in North America, and later in the UK, the origins of SHRM were management driven, in response to a crisis of confidence. This is not so. SHRM also owes its momentum to other social, technological and labour market changes which occurred in the 1980s and 1990s. It is important to see these changes as interconnected in that one change stimulated another; for example, the drive to achieve competitiveness created the need for better use of human resources to achieve improved labour productivity, which spawned the practice of flexible work initiatives. So some changes were first-order changes which generated second-order changes in a constantly evolving dynamic cause–effect cycle of change from which it is often very difficult to say (if, indeed, it is useful to do so) which change came first. This section charts some of the most important of these changes which seem to us to be closely associated with the rise of interest in SHRM. These are summarised in Figure 2.5.

Crisis of under-performance in American industry

For many writers (e.g. Hendry and Pettigrew (1990) and Mabey *et al.* (1998)) one of the most significant triggers for the SHRM movement of the 1980s in the USA was the crisis

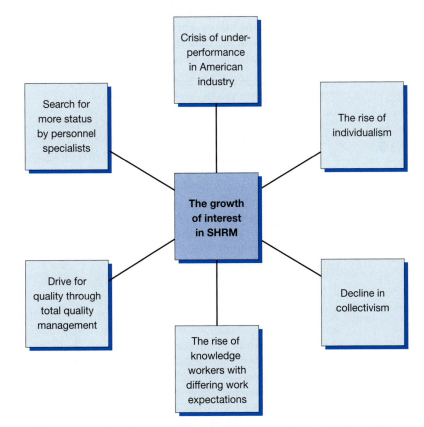

Figure 2.5 Changes in the HRM operating environment of the 1980s and 1990s which are associated with the growth of interest in SHRM

of under-performance in American industry. This was highlighted in an influential *Harvard Business Review* account by Abernathy *et al.* (1981). In this, Abernathy *et al.* charted the woes of US manufacturers of products such as cars, TVs, machine tools and computers. The problem arose because of the superior quality and cheaper cost of products from European and, particularly, Japanese manufacturers. Abernathy *et al.* attributed the success of these rival manufacturers to superiority in their manufacturing plants, especially in their production processes and workforce management. Abernathy *et al.* argued that the remedy was not to make incremental changes but to implement radical change, not least in the area of workforce management.

This bemoaning of the state of US industry and the call for radical changes in employee management, stimulated the growth of interest in SHRM in America. American scholars, notably Beer *et al.* and Fombrun *et al.*, occupied an almost evangelistic role in popularising SHRM through both their writing and their teaching. The latter activity attracted a notable following from the MBA student community for the first time. The American message was soon replicated by UK commentators, such as Storey (1989, 1992), and a decade of enhanced interest in employee management ensued.

The rise of the individualism

There has been a general change in western society in the past 20 years which has seen the growth of individualism and an accompanying decline in traditional family and community-based values. There may be a host of reasons for this upon which it is beyond the scope of this chapter to speculate. For example, in the UK, the Thatcher philosophy encapsulated in the former Prime Minister's famous comment:

> There is no such thing as Society. There are individual men and women and there are families, (cited in Kessler and Purcell, 1995)

set the tone for changes, replicated throughout Europe, which saw people encouraged to buy their publicly owned houses and buy shares in newly privatised public utilities such as gas, telecommunications and rail. Indeed, it may be argued that the decline in investment in public services for many years was an invitation for individuals to be more reliant on their own privately financed means and less on services to be provided for the community at large. The composition of the workforce and the jobs that workers do have also contributed to the rise in individualism. Jobs in the old 'smokestack' industries often bred a sense of community which grew from many workers doing the same jobs and often sharing in the hardships imposed by the difficult and physically demanding nature of these jobs.

The societal shift towards individualism in recent years has been mirrored in HR initiatives. SHRM has a distinctly individualist ring to it, as Sisson's (1990) list of SHRM principles demonstrates: 'the focus shifts from management – trade union relations to management – employee relations, from collectivism to individualism'. The clearest evidence of this is the growth of performance management (Bach, 2000) in which the individual employee is set targets and held accountable for their achievement. This approach forces the employee into a one-to-one relationship with that employee's manager. Therefore, the treatment that the employee receives from the manager is individualised according to the extent to which success has been achieved in pursuit of the targets.

Nothing illustrates the notion of individualism at work better than the idea of 'employability' where:

… the onus is placed on the individual to ensure accumulation of training and experience in order to remain attractive in the labour market, whether internal or external. The employer may provide opportunities for human capital development but it is up to the individual to take advantage of them. (Boxall and Purcell, 2003: 117–118)

Decline in collectivism

As Sisson's (1990) quote above notes, the workplace focus has shifted from management–trade union relations towards management–employee relations. It would be misleading to suggest that this has been caused by the rise of individualism. There are many other contributory factors of which changes in employment structure, particularly the decline of manufacturing industry, is an important one. However, the growing trend for employees to advance their own cause has been helped by the increasing amount of employment protection legislation in Europe aimed at the individual, much of it inspired by the EU. This has led to the membership of trade unions in the UK declining from approximately 13 million in 1980 to 7.8 million in 2000. At the same time, the proportion of workplaces without trade union recognition agreements has increased from approximately one-third to one-half. This decline in the influence of trade union organisation at the workplace has created a climate where managers can introduce policies of change, including SHRM initiatives based upon notions of individualism, such as performance management, without the need for extensive and time-consuming consultation and negotiation with trade unions. The desire of the UK Fire Service to introduce more flexible work practices and the resistance to this which led to a major strike after protracted negotiations, is a case in point. That is not to say that employers wedded to SHRM principles ride roughshod over employees by introducing change without consultation. Communication with employees by management has grown in importance as trade union influence has declined. The 1998 Workplace Employee Relations Survey (WERS) notes the prevalence of such communication methods as team briefings, the 'cascading' of information via the management chain, regular newsletters distributed to all employees and regular meetings with the workforce. All of these bypass the traditional method of communicating with employees in collectively organised workplaces. This is through the union representatives who sit on various committees and are charged with twin responsibilities. First, to represent their members' views at committees and, second, to disseminate the results of the committee meetings.

The rise of knowledge workers with differing work expectations

The decline in influence of trade unions is partly a consequence of the shift in western economies from the old 'smokestack' industries of, for example, coal, steel and shipbuilding to service and high-technology industries. It was in the smokestack industries that manual labour proliferated. The customary reliance on collective solutions to employee problems is not one that characterises employment in the newer industries. This is partly because trade unions have traditionally found it more difficult to recruit members in such industries as retail and catering because employers and workplaces tend to be small and geographically disparate. Consequently, there is less of a tradition of trade union organisation in these industries. But it is also in part due to the differing expectations of the increasing number of 'knowledge' workers who have the confidence, information and, often, labour market power gained through a shortage of key workers, necessary to pursue their interests.

The role which the proliferation of computer technology has played in increasing the amount of knowledge workers cannot be underestimated. This has changed the nature of many jobs and facilitated the emphasis of the workforces of the developed countries from the production of goods to the processing of information. In the twenty-year period to 2000 the proportion of manufacturing jobs in the UK declined by one-half whereas the proportion of financial services jobs doubled (Department for Education and Employment, 2000). Even many manufacturing jobs have changed in that they involve workers directing robotised machines by computer.

In general, it is often more of a challenge to employers to attract and retain key managerial, professional and technical workers than workers whose skills are more easily replaced. The ways in which this challenge is met are more likely to be individualistic, e.g. individualised reward packages rather than collective. The repertoire of HR initiatives designed to motivate the individual professional and thereby attract and retain that professional is different from the collective initiatives needed to render compliant the manual workforce.

Drive for quality

As noted above, Abernathy *et al.* (1981) commented upon the poor quality of many US manufactured products relative to those of Japanese manufacture. This stimulated the drive to produce higher-quality goods through processes which were subject to what became known as total quality management (TQM). The guru of this essentially Japanese movement was, ironically, the American W. Edwards Deming. Japanese industry had used TQM to regenerate its industries after the ravages of the Second World War. TQM differed from the traditional quality *inspection* approach through its emphasis upon quality problem prevention which emphasised employee involvement in all quality processes. Quality inspection had become associated with the management control approach, criticised by Walton (1985) as noted earlier. Involving employees in quality processes signalled the need for a radically different approach to employee management along the lines of the SHRM principles explained above, something which Deming advocated. Foremost among the principles of TQM is the notion of employee empowerment, which is necessary, for example, for employee participation in quality-problem-solving groups and suggestions for continuous improvement.

Search for more status by personnel specialists

In her reflections on the growth of HRM, Legge (1995) argued that there were certain stakeholders who had a vested interest in promoting HRM as a strategic function of considerable organisational importance, thus promoting it from the often mundane operational role it had traditionally occupied. These stakeholders were academics, line managers and personnel managers. The latter group has always suffered from low status relative to, for example, accountants and marketers. Torrington *et al.* (2002) categorise the personnel manager's role as historically being concerned principally with welfare, bureaucracy, industrial relations and manpower analysis. The accession of HRM to a place of strategic significance within the organisation presented the 1980s personnel manager with an opportunity to raise his or her status through developing HR strategies in line with organisational strategies. Some evidence that the personnel specialist has succeeded in this quest to move away from its low-status operational image may be seen in the latest development of the personnel specialist as 'internal consultant'; a role in which, for example, he or she may review the way in which HR activities are carried out and suggest resolutions to problems (Kenton and Moody, 2004). In addition, the internal HR consultant often has a key role to play in designing HR initiatives to generate and complement organisation change programmes.

Self-Check and Reflect Questions 2.3

How influential would you say that the factors noted in Figure 2.4 were in creating the drive to introduce SHRM in major organisations?

The contribution of SHRM to organisational performance

The content of this section is based on the theory that the practice of SHRM will contribute to the overall effectiveness of the organisation. The attempt to demonstrate a link between personnel management practices and such 'hard' outcomes as profit or, even less remote outputs as employee satisfaction, has been the Holy Grail of people management specialists for many years. The complaint has always been that so many other factors can impinge upon the relationship between the particular practice and the desired outcome that measurement is at best problematic, at worst pointless. This may be one explanation for the notorious reluctance of HR specialists to evaluate the effectiveness of HR policies and practices. What a blessing it would be if HR managers could present chief executive officers (CEOs) and finance directors with irrefutable proof that, say, an individual performance-related pay scheme produced a 50 per cent increase in production. The reality, of course, is that many other factors, for example, the general feel-good atmosphere created by a large order which guarantees future employment, may account for a significant proportion of the increase.

It follows that the attempt to show that there is a cause–effect link between HR and organisational effectiveness has been a major concern of researchers in recent years. Some of the most influential studies in this section are reviewed. All the studies reviewed have focused on SHRM in the sense that they assume vertical integration, a close relationship between HR and business strategy rather than simply attempting to measure the effectiveness of individual HR practices. Some of the studies treat HR practices as groups or 'bundles' of activities, thus emphasising the importance of horizontal integration between practices.

It is possible to trace a line of development chronologically through the studies covered here. The earlier studies from the mid-1990s concentrate on statistical relationships between HR practices and organisational effectiveness, whereas the later studies, in particular that of Purcell *et al.* (2003), attempt to explain what it is that people management practitioners actually 'do' that leads to organisational success. Each of the studies has its strengths and weaknesses but one thread seems to run through most of them: they are very confident about the effect of HR practices on the 'bottom line'. This confidence is shared by the UK's Chartered Institute of Personnel and Development (2001: 4) which states:

> More than 30 studies carried out in the UK and the US since the early 1990s leave no room to doubt that there is a correlation between people management and business performance, that the relationship is positive, and that it is cumulative: the more and the more effective the practices, the better the result.

Lack of space here prevents this chapter from giving little more than a taste of the studies chosen. However, although some thoughts have been offered on the strengths and weaknesses of each study, it is the intention here to allow readers to judge how justified the researchers are in their confidence that there is a clear link between HR and business performance.

One of the early studies by MacDuffie (1995) (Key Concepts 2.5) made a significant contribution to the HR–organisational performance debate by conceptualising SHRM as the application of 'bundles' of policies and practices rather than treating them as separate entities.

Key Concepts   2.5

MacDuffie (1995)

Industry sector: Automobiles.
Location: USA
No. of companies in study: 70 automobile plants

Theoretical background: MacDuffie's starting position was in the Walton (1985) tradition. He argued that innovative HR practices are the way to secure employee commitment to the organisation and such commitment is essential if employees are to apply the amount of discretionary effort required for high performance. In addition, he was interested in establishing the extent to which a specified 'bundle' of HR practices would be more effective than such practices implemented individually.

Research strategy and method: MacDuffie studied flexible production systems in the auto industry. Flexible production systems are characterised by the reduction of stock inventories and the elimination of 'buffer' areas such as those concerned with product repair space which create 'slack' in the production process. MacDuffie reasoned that these characteristics would have three major consequences: (1) the increase of interdependencies within the production process; (2) the highlighting of production problems; and (3) searches for improvements to the production process to solve these problems. His hypothesis was that innovative HR practices have an important role to play in such flexible production systems. MacDuffie argued that workers in flexible production systems need a good grasp of the production process and analytical skills to diagnose problems.

The data were collected by questionnaires and interviews with plant managers. The study sought to assess the effect upon labour productivity and quality of three variables: (1) the use of 'buffers'; (2) work systems (e.g. the use of work teams and employee involvement groups); and (3) HR policies, relating to those involved in the production process, of selection, performance-related reward, status differences and training and development.

MacDuffie developed two specific hypotheses: (1) that innovative HR practices affect performance not individually but as interrelated elements in an internally consistent 'bundle' and (2) the HR 'bundle' is effective in contributing to manufacturing plant productivity and product quality when they are integrated with flexible production systems.

Results and conclusions: MacDuffie argues that the evidence from his study supported the hypothesis that assembly plants using flexible production systems which use HR 'bundles' that are integrated with the production strategy outperform plants using traditional mass production systems on both measures of productivity and quality.

Study strengths: (1) Treats HR practices as integrated 'bundles' rather than separate practices. (2) Uses contextually relevant measures of organisational performance. (3) Study rooted in specialist knowledge of manufacturing production process.

Study limitations: (1) Employee commitment and competence are theoretical principles which are important to the study but they are not measured. One would expect the HR 'bundle' to promote high levels of commitment and competence which in turn would yield high productivity and quality measures. (2) It is not clear how the components of the HR 'bundle' were chosen. It seems that important elements (e.g. job security) may have been omitted (Richardson and Thompson, 1999). (3) The study is industry specific and may not generalise to other employment contexts. (4) The data are gathered from plant managers so there is no input from employees or HR specialists.

The research by Huselid (1995) (Key Concepts 2.6) was equally important in that he emphasised the 'strategic fit' aspect of SHRM. Like MacDuffie, Huselid concentrated on quantitative analysis of large data sets in the attempt to give validity and reliability to his results.

| **Key Concepts** | **2.6** |

Huselid (1995)

Industry sector: All major industries
Location: USA
No. of companies in study: 3,452 companies with more than 100 employees

Theoretical background: Huselid's position was that HR practices can affect HR performance in terms of their levels of skill and motivation and through adjustments to organisational structures which allow better job performance. Increased levels of employee skill and motivation will lead to lower employee turnover and higher productivity. As long as the expenditure on the HR practices designed to yield lower employee turnover and higher productivity does not exceed their true costs then lower employee turnover and higher productivity should lead to enhanced corporate financial performance. Furthermore, Huselid argued that the concept of strategic fit was important. Enhanced organisational performance will follow if HR practices complement and support one another. Similarly, enhanced organisational performance will be the consequence if the system of HR practices is aligned with the organisation's competitive business strategy.

Research strategy and method: Huselid sought to test four specific hypotheses: (1) systems of high-performance work practices will reduce employee turnover and increase productivity and corporate financial performance; (2) employee turnover and productivity will be the link between systems of high-performance work practices and corporate financial performance; (3) complementarities or synergies between high-performance work practices will reduce employee turnover and increase productivity; (4) alignment of a firm's high-performance work practices with its competitive strategy will reduce employee turnover and increase productivity.

Questionnaires were sent to 12,000 US firms which yielded 3,452 replies, a 28 per cent response rate. The questionnaire was sent to the senior HR manager in each firm. The questionnaire asked about 13 high-performance work practices which Huselid grouped into two main categories, which he called 'employee skills and organisational structures' and 'employee motivation'. The former category included practices designed to enhance employees' knowledge and skills and thereafter a structure in which those knowledge and skills could be applied in job performance. These practices included: job design; sophisticated employee selection; training and development; employee participation programmes, including profit-share schemes. The category he called 'employee motivation' included practices to recognise and reinforce the desired employee behaviours developed by practices in the first category. These included: performance appraisal; individual performance-related pay; and merit-based promotion. In addition, respondent views were sought on the extent to which there was consistency between the HR practices and between the HR practices and the firm's competitive strategy.

Employee turnover equated to the firm's average annual turnover rate and productivity was measured as sales per employee. Corporate financial performance was assessed in two ways: gross rate of return on capital and the market value of the firm divided by the costs of its assets.

Results and conclusions: Huselid found broad support for the hypothesis that systems of high-performance work practices will reduce employee turnover and increase productivity and corporate financial performance. This applied across industries and firm size. Indeed, the strength of the association was substantial. However, he found only modest support for the third and fourth hypotheses: that higher levels of internal and external fit will lead to better firm performance.

Study strengths: (1) Huselid adopts an explicitly strategic perspective in that he seeks to measure the effect of both internal and external fit. (2) He attempts to overcome one of the main methodological problems with this type of research, the problem of reverse causality. This means that, in this study, it is a concern that the firms may introduce high-performance work practices *because* they are successful rather than such practices *causing* organisational success. Huselid does this by introducing the intermediate measure of employee turnover and higher productivity rather than measuring directly the effect on firm performance of high-performance work practices. (It is difficult to imagine firms introducing high-performance work practices because they have low employee turnover and high employee productivity.) (3) Large sample size and breadth of industrial coverage.

Study limitations: (1) The data are gathered from HR specialists with no input from employees. (2) Data are collected at company level which does not allow for differences in separate workplaces in multi-workplace organisations (Richardson and Thompson, 1999). (3) The fact that this is a 'snapshot' piece of research rather than longitudinal (over a period of time) weakens any claim that high-performance work practices *cause* enhanced organisational performance.

The work of both MacDuffie and Huselid was carried out in the USA whereas Patterson *et al.* (1997) (Key Concepts 2.7) were commissioned by the UK's Institute of Personnel and Development. Theirs was a longitudinal study, which allowed the researchers to measure the effect of the introduction of HR practices over time. In addition it concentrated on single site and single-product workplaces in order to make comparisons more valid.

Key Concepts 2.7

Patterson et al. (1997)

Industry sector: Manufacturing
Location: UK
No. of companies in study: 67

Theoretical background: Patterson et al.'s point of departure was similar to that of other similar studies. They assumed that: (1) employees are the organisation's valuable resource; and (2) that the management of employees makes a difference to company performance. More specifically, they devised four research questions: (1) Is there any relationship between employee attitudes (i.e. job satisfaction and employees' commitment to their organisations) and company performance? (2) Does organisational culture predict subsequent organisational performance? (3) Do human resource management practices make a difference to organisational performance and, if so, which of these practices are the most important? (4) How do other management practices (i.e. competitive strategies, quality emphasis, research and development investment, investment in technology) compare with human resource management practices in terms of their influence upon organisational performance?

Research strategy and method: This was part of a ten-year study which began in 1991 aimed at establishing the factors that affect organisational effectiveness. Organisations' economic performance data were collected annually from 1990. Senior managers in the companies were interviewed every two years from 1991 and 36 of the companies' employees participated in employee attitude and organisation culture surveys in the early stages of the research. The companies were predominantly single-site, single-product operations with less than 1,000 employees.

Interviews were carried out with four or five senior managers in each of the 67 organisations, organisational documentation was gathered and observational tours of production plants were undertaken. In 36 of the organisations, employee attitude and culture survey questionnaires were sent to employees.

Company performance was measured by productivity (sales per employee) and profitability (profit per employee). For each company, performance data for two time periods were collected: (1) the average of the company's performance for the three years prior to the measurement of HRM practices, culture and employee attitudes; and (2) the average of the company's performance for the year following the measurement of HRM practices, culture and employee attitudes.

Job satisfaction was measured by 15 items ranging from relations with fellow team members and managers; to job autonomy, variety and responsibility; physical work conditions; pay; hours; recognition; job security; attention paid to suggestions; opportunities to use abilities; and promotion opportunities. Organisational commitment was measured by three components: identification with, involvement in and loyalty towards the company.

The HR practices measured were grouped under two headings which reflect the interrelated nature of the practices which Patterson et al. wished to portray: 'acquisition and development of employee skills' (selection, induction, training and appraisal) and 'job design' (skill flexibility, job responsibility, job variety and use of formal teams).

Two data analysis strategies were employed: (1) the HR practices culture and employee attitude data were related to the average of the company's performance for the year following the measurement of HRM practices, culture and employee attitudes; and (2) the researchers investigated whether higher levels of HRM practices, culture and employee attitudes were positively related to an increase in organisational performance by controlling for prior performance when predicting subsequent performance.

▶

Results and conclusions: Patterson *et al.* showed that:

1. Job satisfaction and organisational commitment each explained 5 per cent of the variation between companies in change of profitability. For productivity, job satisfaction explained 17 per cent and organisational commitment 7 per cent of the change in performance.

2. Organisational cultural factors explained 10 per cent of the variation between companies in change of profitability. In relation to productivity, organisational cultural factors explained 29 per cent of the change in performance over three to four years. The most important aspect of the organisational cultural factors was employee welfare.

3. HRM practices explained 19 per cent of the variation between companies in change of profitability. For productivity, job satisfaction explained 17 per cent and organisational commitment 7 per cent of the change in performance. For productivity, HRM practices explained 18 per cent of the change in performance.

4. Management practices other than HR (i.e. competitive strategies, quality emphasis, research and development investment, investment in technology) accounted for a very small proportion of the variation between companies in terms of their profitability and productivity.

Study strengths: (1) This is a longitudinal study with a before–after measurement and therefore does allow attempts to measure the effect of the introduction of HR practices over time. (2) The study does include employee as well as managerial interview data. (3) Mixed data collection methods were used which added to the validity of the data. (4) The single-site and single-product nature of the sample makes comparison more valid.

Study limitations: (1) The study was restricted to manufacturing companies, raising the question of generalisability. (2) Although the study is confident in its assertion that a link exists between HR and company performance, it does not explain why this link exists, i.e. what it is about the HR practices which cause enhanced company performance.

Like MacDuffie and Patterson *et al.*, Youndt *et al.* (1996) concentrated on the manufacturing industry. Their study is useful in the light of this chapter because they were concerned with the difference between what we have called the universal and the contingency (matching) approaches to SHRM. This study is interesting because of the performance measures the researchers use. Youndt *et al.* spurned what some may argue is a rather indefinite relationship between HR and financial performance measures and used manufacturing outputs such as production lead time. Although this study (like the others) has its limitations, in the authors' view it makes a valuable contribution to the debate (Key Concepts 2.8).

The research by Guest *et al.* (2000) (Key Concepts 2.9) was also commissioned by the Chartered (as it had become by then) Institute of Personnel and Development. It is based on a very clearly articulated model of HR–organisational effectiveness linking and a large-scale data set.

Key Concepts 2.8

Youndt *et al.* (1996)

Industry sector: Manufacturing
Location: USA
No. of companies in study: 97

Theoretical background: Youndt *et al.*'s starting position was that the value of human capital is particularly important in manufacturing companies that have invested in advanced manufacturing technologies since these technologies rely heavily upon employee skills and commitment to achieve superior performance. They were also particularly interested in drawing a comparison between the universal HR approach and the contingency (matching) approach. They had three overall research objectives: (1) determine the extent to which HR systems enhance performance; (2) analyse the moderating effects of manufacturing strategy on the relationship between HR and operational performance; (3) assess the extent to which particular manufacturing strategies and HR systems are actually used in conjunction with one another.

Research strategy and method: Youndt *et al.* calculated operational performance using eight measures: product quality, employee morale, on-time delivery, inventory management, employee productivity, equipment utilisation, production lead time and scrap minimisation. HR practices were grouped into aggregate indexes. One they called administrative HR system (including selection for manual skills, procedural training, results-based performance appraisal, hourly pay) and, the other, human capital enhancing system (including selection for technical and problem-solving skills, comprehensive training, developmental performance appraisal, skill-based pay). Manufacturing strategy was grouped into three types: cost reduction, quality enhancement and flexibility.

The research hypotheses developed were: (1) A human-capital enhancing HR system will be positively associated with operational performance. (2) Manufacturing strategy moderates the relationship between HR systems and operational performance. (3) A cost manufacturing strategy will positively moderate the relationship between an administrative HR system and operational performance. (4) A quality manufacturing strategy will positively moderate the relationship between an administrative HR system and operational performance. (5) A flexible manufacturing strategy will positively moderate the relationship between a human-capital enhancing HR system and operational performance.

Questionnaires were sent to plant general managers to ask them about HR activities and plant performance. Questionnaires were also sent to functional managers (operations, quality, production and HR) in the same plants to ask them about HR practices used in the plants. Eighteen months later a similar questionnaire was sent to all the managers who responded to the initial survey.

Results and conclusions: The study found general support for the contingency (matching) strategy particularly as the human-capital enhancing HR system delivered operational performance enhancements when linked to the quality enhancement manufacturing strategy. However, the researchers point out that administrative HR systems are appropriate in certain strategic contexts. They found that administrative HR systems interact with the cost manufacturing strategy to enhance employee productivity and also work in conjunction with a flexible manufacturing strategy to improve customer satisfaction. Although Youndt *et al.* hypothesised that flexible manufacturing strategies require high-skill employees, they point out that it may be that flexible manufacturing strategies may be based on flexible machines rather than flexible jobs.

Study strengths: (1) Particularly useful for the light it throws upon the distinction between the universal HR approach and the contingency (matching) approach. (2) Some longitudinal element in data collection.

▶

Study limitations: (1) Based upon self-report questionnaires with no data collected from public sources (e.g. financial performance). (2) No data collected from employees. (3) The study was restricted to manufacturing companies. (3) Little insight into why link exists between HR practices and operational performance. (4) This study only looked at the moderating effects of manufacturing strategy on the HR practices–operational performance link. The researches point out that there could be other variables (e.g. organisational structure or technology) which could have affected the results.

Key Concepts   2.9

Guest *et al.* (2000)

Industry sector: Various
Location: UK
No. of companies in study: 237

Theoretical background: The study is based on a model developed by Guest (1997). In this model Guest argues that the financial performance of companies is influenced by four factors: business and HR strategies; effectiveness of HR departments and HR practices; HR outcomes; and productivity coupled with product and service quality. Put simply, the model contends that business and HR strategies will point to the appropriateness of certain HR practices. The extent to which the HR practices are conducted effectively together with the effectiveness of the HR department will influence the achievement of the HR outcomes which Guest specifies: employee competence, commitment and flexibility. These three HR outcomes will in turn affect productivity and product and service quality which will have a significant influence upon the company's financial performance.

Research strategy and method: The study concentrated upon the private sector, both manufacturing and service. The respondents were heads of HR and CEOs. The research report is based upon interviews with 835 companies and over 1,000 managers. In 237 companies there were matched responses from both the head of HR and the CEO.

Two separate questionnaires were sent: one to CEOs and the other to heads of HR. The head of HR questionnaire asked questions about: the workforce, HR strategy and practices, HR outcomes and performance outcomes. The CEO questionnaire covered: HR strategy, a limited amount of HR practices, HR outcomes and performance outcomes, and additional questions on the business strategy and the state of the market in which the company operated.

Results and conclusions: (1) The most important factor in the defining of business strategies was responsiveness to customers (74 per cent) and high service quality (59 per cent), whereas beating competitors on price was rated lowly (10 per cent). (2) Only 10 per cent of managers thought issues concerning people were more important than finance or marketing. (3) Only one-quarter of organisations had more than 50 per cent of a list of 18 typical HR practices in place. (4) The most highly rated areas of HR activity were internal labour market practices (promotion from within) and employment security. (5) Managers rated employee flexibility and performance outputs highly. (6) Approximately one-half of CEOs rated their company's productivity and financial performance as above average for their industry. (7) Overall responses led the researchers to conclude that there was link between HR practices and HR department effectiveness, employee attitudes and behaviour and corporate performance.

Study strengths: (1) The sample size was one of the biggest in all the studies linking HR with corporate performance. (2) There was an attempt to measure the effectiveness, rather than simply the presence, of HR practices. (3) The clarity with which the research is based upon the variables which link HR and organisational performance.

Study limitations: (1) Interviews were by telephone, which limited the degree of 'insight' which could be developed by researchers (particularly when contrasted with, for example, the observational tours of production plants undertaken by Patterson *et al.*). (2) The absence of employee data. (3) The self-report nature of the managerial responses which raises questions about respondent objectivity. This is particularly relevant where questions about such items as organisational performance in relation to competitors are concerned. (4) Although the study points to the relationship between certain key variables it is less helpful in explaining the reasons for certain associations between variables.

The work of Purcell *et al.* (2003) (Key Concepts 2.10), also sponsored by the Chartered Institute of Personnel and Development (CIPD), is different from its predecessors. It sets out to be different in that is attempts to establish not only the extent to which HR is associated with organisation performance but, more importantly, 'to unlock the "black box" to show the way in which HR practices – or what the CIPD terms 'people management', meaning all aspects of how people are managed – impact on performance' (Purcell *et al.*, 2003: ix). The UK study is also different in that it does not concentrate on manufacturing companies. Of the 12 case study organisations featured in the research, only Jaguar Cars may be said to be a traditional manufacturer. The remaining organisations are in high-technology production, retail, financial services, health care and management services.

Key Concepts	2.10

Purcell *et al.* (2003)

Industry sector: Various
Location: UK
No. of companies in study: 12

Theoretical background: The theoretical framework which is tested in the study holds that employee performance is a function of ability + motivation + opportunity. That is that people perform when they possess the knowledge and skills necessary for the job, are motivated to perform and, finally, are given sufficient opportunity to deploy the skills and contribute to workgroup and organisational success.
    More specifically the theoretical propositions were:

● Performance-related HR practices work only if they induce discretionary behaviour.
● Discretionary behaviour is more likely to occur if employees have commitment to their organisation and/or they feel motivated to act in such a way that they exhibit discretionary behaviour and/or they gain job satisfaction.
● Commitment, motivation and job satisfaction are greater when they experience policies implemented to create a more able workforce, including opportunities to participate.
● A positive employee experience is improved if the HR policies designed to create ability + motivation + opportunity are in place and are mutually reinforcing.

▶

- Front-line managers have a key role in shaping the employee attitudes necessary to deliver discretionary behaviour through their implementation of HR policies and enactment of organisational values and culture.
- Success in achieving performance outcomes helps to reinforce positive attitudes.

Research strategy and method: The research was carried out over a two-and-a-half year period from 1999. In each organisation, interviews were carried out with one unit of analysis (e.g. one department). The interviews were with senior decision-makers, first-line managers/team leaders and front-line employees. Interviews were repeated 12 months later to allow changes to be noted. Questionnaires were administered face-to-face; there was no self-completion.

The HR practices which the researchers measured were those designed to deliver ability + motivation + opportunity and interrelate one with another. The list comprised 11 practices not dissimilar from those listed in the 'universalist' lists earlier in this chapter with the notable addition of job challenge/autonomy and work–life balance. The researchers also sought to measure employee commitment, motivation and job satisfaction as well as employee views of the way in which front-line managers did their job. The performance measures used for each organisation were unique to that organisation – those that each organisation felt were most important.

Results and conclusions: One of Purcell *et al.*'s key findings was that the HR–performance link was associated with the existence of a 'big idea' (e.g. quality at Jaguar), underpinned by similar values and culture. Another important finding was the centrality of the role played in employee management by front-line managers. By communicating, problem solving, listening to employee suggestions, coaching and showing employees fairness and respect, front-line managers brought HR policies to life. Such employee treatment by front-line managers was found to bring discretionary effort from employees – the desire to go the 'extra mile'. The existence of certain HR policies and practices was found to be less important than the way in which they were implemented.

There were distinct patterns in the association between certain HR policies and practices and enhanced employee commitment, job satisfaction and motivation, albeit that there were clear differences between occupational groups. Career opportunities, job influence, job challenge, training, performance appraisal, team working, involvement in decision-making, and work–life balance were all associated with enhanced employee commitment, job satisfaction and motivation. On the other hand, lower employee commitment was associated with poor execution of existing policies rather than the absence of those policies.

Overall, Purcell *et al.* found that the highest performing organisations were those that could sustain their performance over time and linked people management policies and practices with that performance. This meant that HR policies and practices fitted with business strategy and were flexible enough to help adapt to new environmental conditions.

Study strengths: (1) The most significant strength of this study is the 'black box' dimension. It is the only study that attempts to go beyond statistical associations and understand 'what is going on' in the key HR processes which lead to organisational performance. (2) Some longitudinal element in data collection. (3) Different performance measures for each organisation, which are likely to lead to more meaningful performance data. (4) The varied nature of the markets in which the case study organisations operate. (5) Employee responses gathered.

Study limitations: (1) The longitudinal element of the study meant that, inevitably, some of the respondents had left their organisations by the time the second round of interviews took place. (2) Not using standardised measures to assess organisational performance meant potentially more relevant measures were applied. However, in some organisations there was difficulty in obtaining performance data. Overall, the team noted difficulty in separating the impact of HR policies and practices on organisational performance from the impact of variables such as market fluctuations and technological changes.

Self-Check and Reflect Questions   2.4

What practical contribution do you think the studies linking HR and organisational performance listed in this section have made to the practice of SHRM?

Summary

- The main principles of SHRM include:
  - a stress on the integration of personnel policies both one with another and with business planning more generally;
  - the locus of responsibility for personnel management no longer resides with specialist managers but is now assumed by senior line management;
  - the focus shifts from management–trade union relations to management–employee relations, from collectivism to individualism.
  - there is stress on commitment and the exercise of initiative, with managers now assuming the role of 'enabler', 'empowerer' and 'facilitator'.

- The principal theoretical approaches to SHRM are termed: universalist, matching models (closed) and matching models (open). The universalist approach assumes that there are 'best HR practices' that promise success irrespective of organisational circumstances. The matching models (closed) approach specifies HR policies and practices that are relevant to specific organisational situations, whereas the matching models (open) approach defines the employee behaviours necessitated by the organisation's overall strategy. These behaviours are to be delivered through the HR strategy.

- All of the theoretical approaches to SHRM have their problems. Those concerned with the universalist approach are: defining the 'best practices' to apply; the low regard for organisational context; and the absence of employee input assumed. The problems with the matching models (closed) approach are: the ambiguity that attends the defining of strategy; the essentially managerialist stance assumed; and problems concerned with implementation. Problems attending the matching models (open) are the models' rather idealised nature and, like the other models, their prescriptive tone.

- The growth of interest in SHRM was due to a number of factors including: the crisis of under-performance in American industry; the rise of individualism; a decline in collectivism; the rise of knowledge workers with differing work expectations; and a search for more status by personnel specialists.

- In an attempt to establish the link between SHRM and organisational performance there have been numerous studies conducted since the mid-1990s in the USA and UK. In general, these have been very positive about the relationship between SHRM and organisational performance, although most have not offered an explanation as to why certain HR practices may lead to enhanced organisational performance.

Follow-up study suggestions

- Search the specialist practitioner HR literature for case studies that illustrate the way in which clear and cogent organisational philosophies inform HR strategy.
- From Pfeffer's (1998) book, make notes on the rationale for his recommendation of seven practices of successful organisations and assess the extent to which you think this rationale is valid.
- Look up 'employee competences' in an internet search engine and, from help offered on the sites you find, compile a list of desired employee behaviours consistent with the need to develop employees equipped to deliver high-quality customer service.
- Compare the research studies by MacDuffie (1995) and Huselid (1995) and assess the strengths and weaknesses of both.
- Read the research report by Purcell *et al.* (2003) as an HR manager and make a list of the lessons that you think you could apply in your organisation or one with which you are familiar.

Suggestions for research topics

- To what extent may the HRM activity in ABC organisation be termed 'strategic HRM'?
- What have been the effects of the major change programme in ABC organisation on HR strategy, policies and practices?
- Test the appropriateness of Mabey *et al.*'s open SHRM model in ABC organisation.
- Compare the validity of Pfeffer's list of key HR practices in private sector manufacturing and financial services.
- Does Purcell *et al.*'s theory that employee performance is a function of ability + motivation + opportunity apply equally in the public and private sectors of employment?

3

SHRM in a changing and shrinking world: internationalisation of business and the role of SHRM

Learning Outcomes

By the end of this chapter you should be able to:

- identify some of the key background issues relevant to the internationalisation of business;

- analyse the significance in the growth of multi-national companies;

- define strategic international human resource management;

- identify the key components of strategic international human resource management;

- explain the significance of the capability perspective on strategic international human resource management;

- evaluate the importance of the cultural perspective on strategic international human resource management.

Introduction

In any book or article on changes in the business environment in recent years there will be emphasis upon the growth in international business. The important effect this has had upon the way organisations conduct their affairs touches upon all aspects of the organisational life: not the least of which is HRM. This chapter examines the concept of strategic international HRM (SIHRM). Not surprisingly, this examination tends to concentrate upon the role of multi-national corporations (MNCs) in the conduct of SHRM, since it is in these organisations that SIHRM is more developed and more visible.

The chapter starts with an analysis of the background to international business. This analysis concentrates upon why organisations want to conduct international business and some of the main methods by which they pursue their international goals. It is argued that the time spent on this is worthwhile, in order to gain a greater understanding of the context in which SIHRM takes place. An example of this is the statistics which show the enormity of the scale of international trade. The main body of the chapter is an en examination of the concept of SIHRM. This uses a well-known conceptual model to structure the examination and examples from across the world. The chapter ends with a study of SIHRM from two important perspectives: capability and culture. Capability refers to the ability of those people, including HR professionals, responsible for international business. It is an area that is receiving an increased amount of attention. The importance of national cultures is more well known and no coverage of SIHRM would be complete without consideration of this key issue.

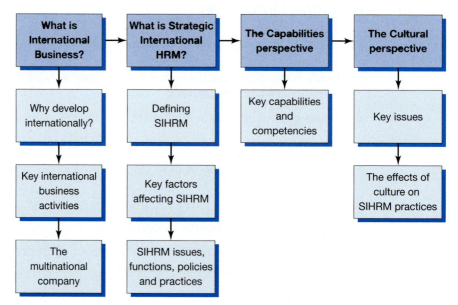

Figure 3.1 Mapping the international strategic human resource management territory: a summary diagram of the chapter content

Background to the internationalisation of business

Defining international business

Harrison *et al.* (2000) note that international business may be divided into two categories: international trade and international investment. International trade refers to the export and import of goods and services. However, the focus of this chapter is on international investment. International investment applies to the transfer by companies of resources in order that they may undertake business outside their country of origin. Such investment may take various forms, from the investment by multi-national companies (MNCs) in setting up wholly owned subsidiaries in foreign countries, to the licensing by MNCs of the right to use the licensers' intellectual property.

Why do companies wish to develop their international business?

As with all management decision-making, establishing the reasons why companies internationalise their business is not always as straightforward as might be imagined. Ghauri (2000), for example, talks of the 'bandwagon effect', where companies rush to emulate competitors by investing abroad for fear of losing competitive edge. However, there are solid reasons why companies will wish to invest abroad, as evidence from the past behaviour of companies shows. Some of these are listed below.

The desire to access international markets

An MNC will wish to expand its market by selling its products and services internationally because the domestic market is limited and the life cycle of the product is such that the commercial benefit to be gained from it means that the market has to be exploited while the product still has currency. A good example of this, as the illustration in In Practice 3.1 shows, is the market for Hollywood movies, in which the Walt Disney Corporation is a giant player.

In Practice	3.1

The clownfish nets shoals of bucks

Finding Nemo, the film about a clownfish's attempt to find his lost son, is the first animated movie to make more than $500 million in sales outside the USA. It has now made $504.2 million (£278.5million) outside the USA, including $93 million (£51.3 million) in Japan, reports UK industry newspaper *Screen International* (BBC News Online, 2004c). The film reached number one in the UK when it was released in October 2003. In France the film made $63 million (£34.8 million) and looks set to overtake the total made by the Disney-animated hit *The Lion King*. *Finding Nemo*'s records also included an opening weekend worth $310,000 (£171,000) in Turkey, a record for an animated film there. The film is produced by the animation studio Pixar, which has also made such hits as *Toy Story* and *Monsters, Inc.*

Subsequent DVD sales of the movie helped Pixar's net income in the first three months of 2005 to rise to $81.9 million (£43 million) compared with $26.7 million a year earlier. Sales rose to $161.2 million from $53.8 million a year ago (BBC News Online, 2005a).

The desire to access production advantages offered by other countries

One of the most familiar images of MNCs' operations is the ease with which they seem to move freely across the world seeking operational advantages that render the production of their products or services more cost effective. From the HR perspective the most significant advantage that MNCs seek is alternative sources of labour. This may be motivated simply by cost: workers in other countries may demand much less in wages than their counterparts in the MNC's country of origin. It may be that a greater pool of skilled labour is available in another country, thus enabling the MNC to overcome skilled labour shortages in the countries in which it normally operates. In the former case, the decision by many UK companies to set up call centres in Asia has attracted a lot of publicity. For example, in 2004, HSBC decided to cut 4,000 UK call centre jobs in order to set up a call centre in the Philippines, a country that has good-quality telecommunications and potential workers with good English-language skills. HSBC also has service centres in India, Malaysia and China (BBC News Online, 2004d). Similarly, the case of Dyson, the UK manufacturer of the 'bagless' vacuum cleaner, attracted a lot of publicity when it decided to move production to Malaysia, causing the loss of 800 jobs in Wiltshire. Dyson argued that the hourly wage of a Malaysian worker was one-third of a UK worker and office rental rates offered similar cost advantages. The company also cited the fact that its suppliers were increasingly based in the Far East and Far Eastern markets were also in its sights (BBC News Online, 2002).

Much publicity has been given to the availability of pools of highly qualified young IT workers in India. In 2004, IBM had a headcount in India of about 10,000 and is still expanding, while one of IBM's rivals, the US company Computer Sciences, aimed to more than triple its staff in India to 5,000 in about two years (ZDNetUK, 2004). Google planned to open a research centre in India's southern city of Bangalore, known as India's Silicon Valley. Microsoft, too, planned to expand its activities in India, increasing the number of engineers at its software development centre in Hyderabad from 150 to 500 in 2005. Around 20 per cent of the company's software engineers are of Indian extraction.

To grasp opportunities in developing markets

In May 2004, ten new countries gained admittance to the European Community. Of course, one of the principal reasons for their joining is that enormous trading opportunities are opened up not only to the companies in the joining countries but to those in the existing member states. Poland is a good example. It has a relatively under-developed economy but a population of 40 million, which presents excellent growth opportunities for European countries who have hitherto not sought to develop the Polish market.

However, the best example of the phenomenon of an emerging market ready to be cultivated is China. With an economy growing at approximately 10 per cent annually, and a growing prosperous middle class whose members are no longer content to use the bicycle as their main form of transport, the automobile market in China presents massive potential for western manufacturers such as Volkswagen (see In Practice 3.2).

To take advantage of financial inducements

Much of the inward investment by MNCs has been assisted by financial inducements offered by host countries. These may take the form of direct financial assistance; agreements to defray some of the initial operational costs, or favourable corporate tax rates (Harrison *et al.*, 2000). Car manufacturers in the UK, such as Nissan at Tyne and Wear and Toyota in Derby, have created factories and employment opportunities, with grants available in European development areas. South Korean giant Hyundai has picked Slovakia as the site for a new £466 million car plant. The factory, which will open in 2006, will produce

In Practice   3.2

China stands out in Volkswagen's global sales

German auto giant, Volkswagen AG, reported a sales growth of 32.9 per cent in the booming Chinese market for the first nine months of 2003, selling nearly half a million vehicles. The growing demand in the Chinese auto sector contributed to the group's 26.8 per cent sales growth in the Asia-Pacific region, which saw 570,000 vehicles sold from January to September, said a statement from Volkswagen Automobile (China) Investment Co., Ltd.

Meanwhile, car sales in the company's traditional European and North American markets shrank by 3.5 per cent and 6.3 per cent respectively compared with the same period in 2002. Sales in Canada dropped by 6.4 per cent and in Japan by 7.4 per cent, according to the Volkswagen's statement.

The company, affected by the slow recovery of the world economy, a strong euro, plus losses in its Brazilian market, saw a 1.2 per cent drop in global auto sales over last year to 3.71 million in the first nine months.

Volkswagen, the biggest automaker in China, is ambitious about expanding in the world's fastest growing economy. The company announced earlier this year that it planned to increase capacity to one million units by 2007 and that it would build two more factories by 2008.

Source: China Daily (2003).

up to 200,000 vehicles every year under Hyundai's Kia brand. Hyundai were thought to be influenced by Slovakia's low labour costs and financial incentives offered by the host country (BBC News Online, 2004g).

Following the example of competitors

Ghauri (2000) makes the point that a decision by a company to enter a new foreign market induces a chain reaction from leading firms in the same market as they do not wish to lose their competitive position. The rush of leading companies to the emerging markets of China and India is a case in point, as is their decision to source certain products from particular countries (e.g. consumer electronics in Taiwan, South Korea and Malaysia, and textiles in Pakistan, the Philippines and China).

To avoid host country protectionism

In order to protect their domestic markets, governments construct trade barriers that make efforts by foreign competitors' to enter those markets more difficult and costly. Such barriers may be tariffs and quotas or specific rules and regulations (Harrison *et al.*, 2000). Among the responses by companies to this, is to set up production facilities in the foreign country, as with the examples of Volkswagen in China and Toyota and Nissan in the UK, mentioned above. It is also an incentive for governments to join common trading arrangements such as the World Trade Organization (WTO) (see Key Concepts 3.1).

Principal international business activities

Import and export

Although it is not the most significant category of international business for the purposes of this chapter, import and export are vitally important to the operation of any country's economy and the prosperity of its companies. Exporting and importing may take two forms: direct and indirect. Direct exporting, on the one hand, takes the form of a company producing and selling goods to foreign customers. On the other hand, indirect exporting may be a domestic manufacturer importing goods from a foreign exporter and incorporating these goods as components in the manufacture of a product, which may in turn be exported. Some idea of the growth of importing and exporting can be seen from the fact that during the 30-year period from 1948, annual world exports grew by 6 per cent against a background of output growing by 3.8 per cent (Harrison *et al.*, 2000). In the UK alone, exports accounted for approximately £189,000 million and imports £250,000 million in 2002 (uktradeinfo, 2005).

Foreign direct investment

Foreign direct investment (FDI) involves a company gaining a controlling interest in a foreign company, usually through acquiring 30 per cent or more of the foreign company's equity. Where two or more companies share ownership of a FDI, the operation is termed a joint venture. According to Daniels *et al.* (2004), about 63,000 companies worldwide have FDIs that range across a variety of goods and services. Companies are likely to pursue FDI for the commercial reasons outlined above, but the enormous growth of FDI across the world has been eased by trade liberalisation policies practised by governments. A similar growth rate is evident in developing economies. The ten developing economies most active in terms of FDI increased investment from approximately US$60,000 million in 1997 to approximately US$161,000 in 2001 (UNCTAD, 2003). Harrison *et al.* (2000) make the point that it would be misleading to assume that most company FDI was a consequence of

Key Concepts   3.2

FDI outflows from US hit record $252 billion in 2004

Foreign direct investment (FDI) outflows from the USA reached $252 billion in 2004 – up from $141 billion in 2003 to hit an all-time record. While this to some extent was reflected in the weakness of the dollar, it also confirmed continuing strong interest among US companies in acquiring corporate assets abroad.

Of the largest 25 cross-border mergers and acquisitions (M&A) in 2004, five had a US-based company as the acquirer. A recovery of M&A activity in 2004, meanwhile, has carried on into 2005. On present trends, both inward and outward FDI in OECD (Organisations for Cooperation and Development) countries could increase by 10–15 per cent in 2005, OECD estimates suggest.

Inward FDI into Germany and France, the two largest economies of the European continent, fell sharply in 2004. In France, inward investment almost halved, falling from $43 billion to $24 billion. In the case of Germany, foreign investors actually withdrew about $39 billion from the country, reversing the inflow of $27 billion recorded in 2003. (Inward FDI figures include transactions, which can involve both inflows and withdrawals, between foreign-invested enterprises and their foreign mother companies. The downturn in 2004 largely reflected repayments to recipients outside Europe of inter-company loans and other transactions between related enterprises.)

For the OECD area as a whole, according to OECD figures, FDI inflows continued on a downward trend, falling to $407 billion in 2004 from $459 billion in 2003. Outflows, on the other hand, rose from $593 billion in 2003 to $668 billion in 2004. Against this background, net FDI outflows from OECD countries to the rest of the world reached record high levels in 2004: the OECD area was a net contributor of $261 billion worth of direct investment – most of which went to developing countries. In 2003, OECD countries invested a net $134 billion outside the OECD area.

China continued to receive a large share of the direct investment in developing countries, with inward FDI into mainland China rising to a record $55 billion in 2004 from $47 billion in 2003.

Source: Organisation for Economic Cooperation and Development (2005).

In Practice   3.3

Royal Bank of Scotland expands into the US market

The UK's Royal Bank of Scotland (RBS) is expanding its push into the USA by spending £5.8 billion on the US bank Charter One, based in Cleveland, Ohio. The purchase is to take place through Citizens Financial Group, RBS's main vehicle in the USA. The acquisition will give RBS access to six Midwestern states, including the cities of Chicago, Detroit and Cleveland. RBS has been an aggressive acquirer of US financial services companies, although Charter One is its biggest buy to date. RBS became the second largest in the UK when it bought NatWest in 2000.

RBS state that merging Charter One into Citizens will make the resulting bank one of the ten biggest in the USA, with assets of almost $130 billion and 24,000 employees. Charter One has 616 branches in the Northeast and Midwest.

RBS chief executive Fred Goodwin said 'this is a highly logical and natural acquisition for Citizens to make … it consolidates Citizens' position as one of the leading banks in the US'. RBS hopes to get one-quarter of its future profits from its US operations.

Source: adapted from BBC News Online (2004e).

companies establishing greenfield production sites in foreign countries. Much FDI activity involves mergers and acquisitions, such as has occurred in international car production, an example being the 36.8 per cent share in the Japanese manufacturer Nissan acquired by the French manufacturer Renault (Morrison, 2002). Morrison makes the point that cars are now truly international products in that the country in which they seemingly originate may be quite misleading since they may be assembled with products sourced from across the globe. In 2003, UK companies acquired 243 companies abroad at a total cost of over £21 billion whereas foreign companies investing in the UK acquired 129 companies at a total cost of £9.3 billion (Office for National Statistics (2004). Some idea of the scale of FDI growth may be seen from Key Concepts 3.2 and In Practice 3.3, which show how the top ten FDI host economies grew in trems of FDI activity in the period 1997–2001.

Licensing and franchises

Licensing involves the licenser allowing the licensee to use the licenser's intellectual property rights in return for a fee. These intellectual property rights may include technical expertise, patents, commercial knowledge and, most importantly, brand names. So, for example, a foreign company may be licensed to manufacture the brands of the licensing company or use the brand name of a company as an intrinsic part of a product being manufactured (e.g. the use of Nike or Adidas on sports shirts).

Franchising is a type of licensing agreement whereby the franchiser allows the franchisee to use the franchiser's intellectual property to undertake a specific business activity. This is seen by the franchising company as an effective way of spreading its brand name throughout the world without the risk and expense of setting up companies in foreign countries. Such arrangements are particularly popular in the retail and service industries. Fashion retailer Benetton, for example, sells 93 per cent of its products worldwide through franchises (*Business Week*, 2003). The US company Burger King has over 11,000 restaurants in over 50 other countries and franchises over 90 per cent of its restaurants.

The importance of the multi-national company

Much of the coverage of what follows in this chapter assumes that the most important aspect of the internationalisation of business is the predominance of the multi-national company. It is these companies that are significant in terms of SIHRM because it is they that develop strategies for the management of employees affected by the multi-national nature of their activities. This is the case whether those employees are international managers, for whom sophisticated international placement policies need to be developed, or production employees made redundant as a consequence of the MNC locating production in a lower-cost country.

Bennet (1999: 163) notes that defining the MNC is a confusing affair but argues that 'the essence of multinationality in a company's operations lies in the globalisation of its management systems, perspectives and approaches to strategic decisions. An MNC's profits are maximised across the world as a whole, regardless of the location of various activities, the whereabouts of head office or the nationality of its senior management. Resources are allocated to the areas that yield the highest return; there is no presumption that investments have to be restricted to certain countries.' The multi-national context in which the MNC functions is such that strategy plays an important role on the MNC's operations, hence the importance of strategic decisions in respect of employee management.

Such is the importance of MNCs that they now control one-third of the world's output and two-thirds of world trade (Morrison, 2002). Table 3.1 shows the world's top ten MNCs.

Table 3.1 The world's top ten non-financial MNCs, ranked by foreign assets (millions of US dollars and number of employees)

Rank	Company (home economy)	Foreign assets	Total assets	Number of foreign employees	Total employees
1.	Vodafone (UK)	187,792	207,458	56,430	67,178
2.	General Electric (USA)	180,031	495,210	152,000	310,000
3.	BP (UK)	111,207	141,158	90,500	110,150
4.	Vivendi Universal (France)	91,120	123,156	256,725	381,504
5.	Deutsche Telekom AG (Germany)	90,657	145,802	78,722	257,058
6.	Exxonmobil Corporation (USA)	89,426	143,174	61,148	97,900
7.	Ford Motor Company (USA)	81,169	276,543	189,919	354,431
8.	General Motors (USA)	75,379	323,969	148,000	365,000
9.	Royal Dutch Shell Group (UK/Netherlands)	73,492	111,543	52,109	89,939
10.	TotalFinaElf (France)	70,030	78,500	69,037	122,025

Source: UNCTAD (2003).

It is one of the curious contradictions of modern life that while, in general, the image of MNCs does not enjoy great public acclaim (see Key Concepts 3.3), we all use their goods and services every day of our lives with little thought of the consequences. The anti-globalisation movement has done much to promote opposition to the large MNCs. Most of the movement's supporters believe that globalisation leads to exploitation of the world's poor workers and the environment. The movement's key mode of protest is organising mass demonstrations. It first came to the attention of the international media in 1999 when 100,000 demonstrators marched on the opening ceremony of the WTO's third ministerial meeting in Seattle, Washington. Although the majority of protesters were peaceful, a minority caused major damage in the city. There were 500 arrests and damage to buildings and business losses was valued at £12.5 million.

Key Concepts   3.3

The case for and against MNCs

The case for:
   MNCs create economic advantages for society as a whole by:

- using the world's resources efficiently by concentrating economic activity in countries which possess specialist resources;
- creating employment opportunities in countries where these are needed;
- developing the knowledge and skills base of people throughout the world;

▶

- creating economies of scale, thereby bringing to consumers goods at prices they otherwise may not be able to afford;
- enabling technology transfer throughout the world;
- expanding host countries' economies by earning foreign finance, which can be used to fund economic development in the host country.

Global Envision takes the free market system as a starting point for reducing world poverty. Providing the poor with opportunities to improve their own lives is the catalyst for creating a more fair, hopeful and stable future. We support economic development and responsible free markets as the most reliable and sustainable strategies for global poverty alleviation. (Global Envision, 2004)

The case against:

- MNCs are owned and controlled by the world's largest and richest countries (see Table 3.1) which amounts to a form of 'economic imperialism' practised by the rich countries.
- MNCs seek to impose their cultural values upon, often, ancient cultures and traditions, thereby amounting to 'cultural imperialism'.
- MNCs operate in countries with weak employment and environmental legislation, thereby exploiting those countries and their people.
- MNCs too often pay little attention to environmental issues in the countries in which they operate.
- MNCs often concentrate low-skill operations in developing countries, preserving high-skill activities, such as research and development, for developed countries.
- MNCs are often accused of paying scant attention to employees' rights in such ways as: paying very low wages to and expecting long working hours from production employees; offering little health and safety protection; not granting collective bargaining opportunities and using expatriate managers rather than developing the management skills of local employees.

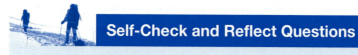

Self-Check and Reflect Questions   3.2

As a senior HR manager in a major MNC, what arguments would you anticipate using to defend your company against the anti-globalisation lobby's position that globalisation was disadvantageous to your company's employees?

SIHRM: definition and analytical framework

So far, this chapter has sketched in a little background in order to convey some of the growing importance of international business. In view of this it is not surprising that an increasing amount of attention in the management literature is paid to international human resource management. However, much of this literature has concerned the management of expatriate employees. The importance of this topic is undeniable. However, the scope of the remainder of this chapter is much broader. It is intended to examine a specifically strategic perspective on IHRM. This section starts by defining SIHRM and examining a conceptual framework which is useful for considering some of the main issues that attend SIHRM. Two perspectives on SIHRM are then considered: the organisational capability perspective and the cultural perspective.

Defining SIHRM

Harris *et al.* (2003: 135) take domestic SHRM as their starting point for defining SIHRM. In pointing out that strategic HRM is concerned with the linkage of HRM with the strategic management processes of the organisation and the integration between various HRM practices, they simply add that SIHRM 'is used explicitly to link international HRM with the strategy of the MNC'. While the essence of this definition cannot be denied, the richness of the additional issues with which SIHRM is concerned seems to us to be lost in this simple adaptation of the domestic definition. Schuler *et al.* (1993) note that the importance of SIHRM lies in the HRM policies and practices that result from the strategic activities of MNCs and the impact that SIHRM has on the international concerns and goals of those organisations.

Schuler *et al.* use the term multi-national *enterprises* as opposed to multi-national *companies* quite deliberately. Although the term is not generally used, it may be more appropriate to refer to multi-national *organisations*. This term would cover the huge not-for-profit organisations, such as the United Nations and the International Federation of the Red Cross, which employ large international workforces. However, Schuler *et al.*'s framework (see Figure 3.2) does imply that it is designed with companies in mind, and it is the term multi-national *companies* that is used in this chapter.

Close consideration of this definition raises immediate questions: what are the human resource management issues, functions, and policies and practices?; and what are the likely international concerns and goals of those enterprises? Schuler *et al.* provide the answers to these questions in the useful framework they develop with the intention of helping us to differentiate between domestic SHRM and SIHRM (see Figure 3.2). Each of the factors in Schuler *et al.*'s model are analysed below. In the model, classic MNC components and factors relevant to the MNC's external and internal operating environments influence the SIHRM issues, functions, and policies and practices which in turn affect the concerns and goals of the MNC.

Strategic MNC components

Schuler *et al.* (1993: 424) argue that there are two major strategic components of MNCs that give rise to and influence SIHRM: these are inter-unit linkages and internal operations.

Inter-unit linkages

MNCs that operate globally have key decisions to make about how best they structure their organisations in order that they may conduct business effectively. Schuler *et al.* argue that the key factor which determines success is the way in which the MNC differentiates its operating units throughout the world and, at the same time, integrates, controls and coordinates its activities. The key objective seems to be to balance the need

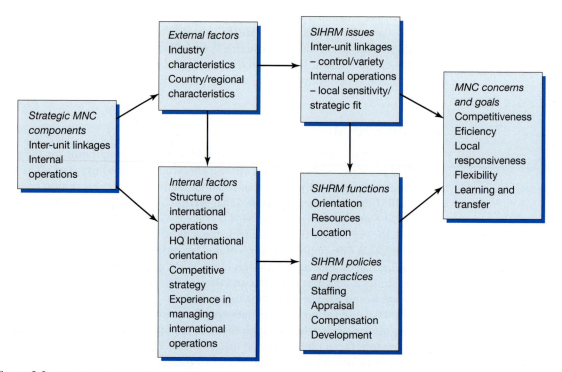

Figure 3.2 Integrative framework of SIHRM in MNCs.
Source: adapted from Schuler *et al*. (1993: 423).

for diversity with the needs of coordination and control to produce an organisation that is globally competitive, flexible and is capable of organisational learning. Diversity stems from the need to operate in a responsive way in the variety of environments experienced throughout the world. This chapter later goes into detail, for example, about different national cultures which demand operational diversity from MNCs. Coordination and control are classic organisation design factors which have long dominated the organisational literature.

Internal operations

There are two key imperatives for the MNC here. First, to fit activities with the local environment of the host country (see In Practice 3.4) and, second, to play a part in contributing to the competitive strategy of the MNC as a whole and the local unit itself. The local environment will dictate differential responses in terms of legal, political, cultural, economic and social issues which have the potential to threaten integration with overall MNC strategy, thus the need for coordination and control mentioned above.

In addition to the strategic MNC components, Schuler *et al*. note the importance of the external and internal factors which affect the SIHRM conditions, issues, functions, and policies and practices.

In Practice   3.4

Pfizer's community values

One of Pfizer's values is to play an active role in making the community in which the company operates a better place to live and work. Throughout the world, Pfizer strives to improve the local environment and help in worthwhile initiatives. An example of this is Pfizer's South African Diflucan™ Partnership Programme.

The programme was developed by Pfizer in cooperation with the United Nations and the World Health Organization (WHO). As of April 2004, 22 developing countries hit hardest by HIV/AIDS are now receiving Diflucan™ free of charge from Pfizer.

Through the Diflucan™ Partnership, the company is working closely with governments, non-governmental organisations, the UN and the WHO to ensure that Diflucan™ reaches all eligible patients who cannot afford treatment. The partnership offers medically responsible treatment programmes, which include the education of patients and health-care providers, appropriate dispensing of medications, ongoing monitoring and support from partner governments. The company's support has no time or money limits. The Diflucan™ Partnership has distributed over 4 million free doses of Pfizer's antibiotic and trained over 18,000 health-care professionals.

Source: Pfizer (2005)

External factors

The external factors affecting SIHRM may be grouped under seven main headings: industry type; competitor activity; extent of change facing the MNC; political; economic; legal; and socio-cultural.

The type of industry in which the MNC operates is important in determining SIHRM activity. Schuler *et al.* distinguish between global and multi-domestic industries. In the global industry, the MNC's competitive position in one country will be influenced by its competitive position in other countries. The major domestic electronic manufacturers, such as Sony and Samsung, are examples of MNCs that operate in a global industry. Such is the strength of their brands, fostered by global distribution and marketing, that they enjoy a competitive position across the world. In a multi-domestic industry, such as retailing, competition in one country is largely independent of competition in other countries. The traditionally highly successful UK retailer Marks and Spencer found, to its cost, that success in one country did not necessarily equal success overseas. At the beginning of 2001 the company took the decision to sell most of its stores abroad, including 18 stores in France and ten in Hong Kong, plus 220 Brooks Brothers sales outlets (men's apparel) in the USA and Asia and 25 Kings Super Market (food stores) based in New Jersey (USA). Conversely, the US fashion retailer Gap has forged a strong international competitive position with over 3,000 stores worldwide.

Schuler *et al.* propose that MNCs in global industries are likely to have an HR function which is more internationally oriented than multi-domestic industries. Coordination and control in global industries will have an international focus, whereas multi-domestic industries will have a more national orientation to these activities.

The main argument concerning competitor activity is that, unless careful attention is paid to this the strategy of the MNC may prove ineffective. This attention should be devoted to the geographical scale of the competitors' activities (e.g. whether they are global or multi-national players) and their overall business strategies, including the degree to which competitors may wish to be market leaders and their position with regards to merger and acquisitions. Schuler *et al.* argue that the more global and intense the activity of the main competition, the more significance is attached to SIHRM issues.

The extent and speed of change which the MNC faces will also affect SIHRM activity. Such changes may include product innovations, technological change, and entry and exit of major market competitors. Since this change occurs on a global scale, the more intense the scope and speed of change the greater necessity for coordination and cooperation (see Key Concepts 3.4). Consequently, the attention that needs to be paid to SIHRM increases in significance. This may lead to more importance being attached to such issues as management development, inter-unit communication mechanisms, such as video-conferencing, and job rotation among key personnel.

Key Concepts   3.4

The importance of intra-company communication

In a persuasive article, which stresses the importance of intra-company communication, Steinberg (1998) warns that corporate horror stories often are a result of management never getting its message about integrity and management control across to employees, or employees not bringing critical information to management, or both. He cites a Coopers & Lybrand USA survey of 100 CEOs, 100 chief financial officers, 100 middle managers and 200 non-management employees. The study found that 82 per cent of CEOs believe they lead by positive personal example but fewer than 40 per cent of non-management employees agreed.

Upwards communication from employees was equally ineffective. CEOs often are among the last to know of a potential crisis. The survey found that while 95 per cent of CEOs say they truly have an open-door policy and will reward those who communicate potentially bad news, half of all employees believe the bad news messenger runs a real risk. Indeed, Steinberg reports that in his role as a Coopers & Lybrand executive, he found that employees at hundreds of companies knew of very serious problems, while top management did not.

Steinberg argues that it might seem that some companies get into trouble because their chief executives turn a blind eye even when they sensed possible wrongdoing. Actually, top management is so often focused on new strategic initiatives, reorganisations, acquisitions or making the quarterly numbers, they sometimes do not mind day-to-day business closely enough.

Schuler *et al.* contend that MNCs can face political and economic risk in global operations. Political risk, for example, may involve a change in the degree of political stability in a particular country. A good example of the political risk that flows from global operations is the case of the US-based oil services MNC, Halliburton. This company was one of the first to win a contract for the post-Iraq war reconstruction following the 2003 war. At the time of writing (summer, 2004) the Iraqi environment is fraught with post-war difficulties so much so that dangerous conditions exist for parent-country national employees in Iraq, particularly those that come from western countries, such as the USA and UK, which were involved in the war. Added to those problems are the vulnerabilities involved where MNCs expose themselves to sensitive political situations played out on an international stage. Not the least allegation waged against Halliburton, for example, was one of favouritism, since the US government awarded the contract to Halliburton whose CEO from 1995 to 2000 was Dick Cheney, the US vice-president at the time the contract was awarded (*The Guardian*, 2004).

Schuler *et al.* maintain that the level of financial complexity involved in global operations generates a degree of economic risk that is much greater for the MNC than its domestic counterpart. Coupled with the heightened political risk attending global operations, this creates a source of uncertainty that the MNC will seek to control through monitoring the activities of its units. Part of this control will come from SIHRM policies and practices such as extra attention to welfare policies to deal with possibly vulnerable ex-patriate employees and flexible staffing to cope with changes in location consequent upon decisions to place operations in alternative locations.

Key Concepts   3.5

Workers' rights in India

The labour laws which apply in the manufacturing sector in India are as follows:

a. The right of association. India's Constitution gives workers the right of association. Workers may form and join trade unions of their choice. However, trade unions represent only approximately 2 per cent of the total workforce, and about 25 per cent of industrial and service workers in the sectors organised by unions.

b. The right to organise and bargain collectively. Indian law recognises the right of workers to organise and bargain collectively. Procedural mechanisms exist to adjudicate labour disputes that cannot be resolved through collective bargaining. However, state and local authorities occasionally use their power to declare strikes 'illegal' and force adjudication.

c. Prohibition of forced or compulsory labour. Forced labour is prohibited by the Constitution. A 1976 law specifically prohibits the formerly common practice of 'bonded labour'. However, the practice of bonded labour continues in many rural areas. Efforts to eradicate the practice are complicated by extreme poverty and jurisdictional disputes between the central and state governments; legislation is a central government function, while enforcement is the responsibility of the states.

d. Minimum age for employment of children. Poor social and economic conditions and lack of compulsory education make child labour a major problem in India. The government's 1991 census estimated that 11.3 million Indian children from ages 5 to 15 are working. Non-governmental organisations estimate that there may be more than 55 million child labourers. A 1986 law bans employment of children under the age of 14 in hazardous occupations and strictly regulates child employment in other fields. Nevertheless, hundreds of thousands of children are employed in the glass, pottery, carpet and fireworks industries, among others. Resource constraints and the sheer magnitude of the problem limit ability to enforce child-labour legislation.

e. Acceptable conditions of work. India has a maximum eight-hour workday and 48-hour work week. This maximum is generally observed by employers in the formal sector. Occupational safety and health measures vary widely from state to state and among industries, as does the minimum wage.

Source: adapted from US Department of State (2004).

Finally, there may be significant legal and socio-cultural differences between coun-tries in which the MNC operates. The early part of this century saw a notable trend by western MNCs to outsource much of their routinised work to developing countries such as India (People Management, 2004). In general, the labour laws in India are similar to those in the EU and do not pose great constraints upon MNCs planning to, say, set up a call centre. However, the manufacturing sector is somewhat different in that labour laws offer protection to, in particular, children who are exploited in a society which is charac-terised by extreme poverty.

Schuler *et al.* note that socio-cultural factors are important external factors affecting SIHRM. The next section of this chapter is devoted to the cultural perspective on SIHRM. The significance of these differences led UK outsourcing company Vertex to send workers from their call centre in India to undergo a week-long cultural awareness training programme in the UK, at which they watched UK TV and listened to soccer commentaries in an attempt to better understand UK culture (People Management, 2004a).

Internal factors

Schuler *et al.* list the internal factors affecting SIHRM as: the structure of the MNC's international operations; the orientation of the MNC to its international business; the MNC's competitive strategy; and the MNC's experience in dealing with international operations.

The structure of the MNC's international operations

There are five main options for the MNC in structuring its international operations: the international division structure; multi-national; global; international; and transnational. The characteristics of each of these are illustrated in Table 3.2.

| In Practice | 3.5 |

Virgin goes global

In 2005 Virgin started operation of its new USA low-cost airline (BBC News Online, 2004f). The airline created 600 jobs in the first five years in New York City, the location of the HQ. In addition, 1,800 workers were hired in two years in San Francisco, the location of the operations. Virgin is the first air-line to have operations based in California. It is US-owned and operated. Flight attendants, engineers and workers in related functions are hired in San Francisco.

Virgin USA said a minority stake in the new airline would be held by the Virgin Group, the conglom-erate that also operates carriers Virgin Atlantic and Virgin Express. The company said it plans to offer a customer-focused, low-cost airline providing more comfort and entertainment.

Under US law, foreign companies are only allowed to own 25 per cent of the voting rights in a US airline, and up to 49 per cent of the equity.

Table 3.2 Characteristics of principal organisational structures for international business

Focus	International division	Multi-national	Global	International	Transnational
Structural	MNC adds unit to domestic structure to deal with international business Key decisions still made at centre Knowledge developed at centre	Based on geographical divisions – very decentralised Responsive to local needs Loss of economies of scale	Operates on global scale to achieve economies of scale Spreads development costs over larger area Strategic decisions made at centre Local units implement major strategic decisions made at centre	Establishes discrete local units Strategic decisions made at centre Local units implement strategic decisions made at centre	Goals are seeking economies of scale; sensitivity to local needs; global competitiveness; flexibility and organisational learning The goals of the MNC are more important than the structure adopted which may be a hybrid of the others
SIHRM	Appointment of international management based at centre and expatriate staff	Developing HR practices to suit local environments and staffing local operations with local staff	Operating MNC as single global operation; deciding whether to appoint local managers or expatriates; ensuring sensitivity to local conditions (see In Practice 3.5)	Ensuring local units implement strategic decisions effectively (see In Practice 3.5)	Selection and development of managers who can balance effectively global and local perspectives

Source: adapted from Schuler *et al*. (1993).

The orientation of the MNC to its international business

The orientation of the MNC to its international business is an important, and well-documented factor, which influences the company's approach to SIHRM. The most well-known way of characterising the potential orientations is the work of Perlmutter (1969) and Heenan and Perlmutter (1979). They portrayed the characteristics as: ethnocentric; polycentric; and geocentric.

The ethnocentric orientation

The main orientation of the MNC here is to direct foreign operations from parent-country HQ. Key jobs at both HQ and local operations are held by parent-country nationals. Perlmutter (1969: 11) depicts the MNC's senior management attitude as 'Let us manufacture the simple products overseas. Those foreign nationals are not yet ready or reliable. We should manufacture the complex products in our country and keep the secrets among our trusted home country nationals.'

The polycentric orientation

Here the MNC treats each separate foreign operation as a distinct national entity with some decision-making autonomy. Foreign subsidiaries manage local operations albeit that they are seldom promoted to parent-country HQ. Perlmutter (1969) notes that senior executives work with the assumption that host country cultures are different and foreigners are difficult to understand. They tend to think that local people know what is best for them and the part of the organisation which is located in the host country should principally be as local in identity as possible. In this situation, Perlmutter views the organisation being held together by sound financial controls.

The geocentric orientation

The major concern of the MNC here is to employ the best people in key positions, irrespective of nationality. The ultimate goal is a worldwide approach to the organisation of the MNC. The focus is on corporate objectives as well as local objectives with each part making its unique contribution with its unique competence. Some of the organisational drivers and obstacles to geocentrism are illustrated in Table 3.3.

The MNC's competitive strategy

This factor is considered in detail in Chapter 2, in particular the work of Schuler and Jackson (1987) who use Porter's (1985) three main types of organisational strategies: innovation, quality enhancement and cost reduction (see Chapter 2 Key Concepts 2.2). Schuler and Jackson's argument is that differing organisational strategies require from employees different behaviours which may be fostered through the practice of different HR techniques.

Although conceived with domestic HRM in mind, Schuler and Jackson's thinking has relevance for SIHRM. Differing organisational strategies require different employee behaviours fostered through different HR techniques but these behaviours are unlikely to be affected by international location. In view of this it seems that the sharing of knowledge and expertise across the MNC's units is likely to be an effective strategy. Such a strategy may be assisted by the MNC's decision to devote some units to specialist activities and to develop mechanisms for sharing the resultant expertise across the organisation.

The MNC's experience in managing international operations

Finally, Schuler *et al.* (1993) suggest that MNCs with considerable international experience, such as Royal Dutch Shell and Ford, are more likely to have a diverse set of HR practices than those with limited international experience. Experience of dealing with complex international situations may have taught the MNC to be flexible by accommodating diverse local demands.

Table 3.3 Organisational drivers towards and obstacles to geocentrism

Environmental forces towards geocentrism	Intra-organisational forces towards geocentrism	Environmental obstacles to geocentrism	Intra-organisational obstacles to geocentrism
Increase in technical and managerial knowledge globally	Desire to use all resources (including human) optimally	Economic nationalism, in host and parent countries	Management inexperience in foreign operations
Local demand for product quality and competitive price	Evidence of increasing cost of polycentric approach	Political sensitivities involved in host-country operations	Mutual distrust between host-country and parent-country senior managers
Growth of world markets	Risk diversification through global production and distribution arrangements	Lack of international monetary system	Potential costs and risks
Global competition among MNCs for scarce resources (including human resources)	Necessity to secure services of best possible staff on a global basis	Growing differences between rich and poor countries	Nationalistic attitudes of staff
Advances in global transport and telecommunications systems	Need for development of global information system	Host country resentment of parent country tendency to get greater allocation of profits	Immobility of staff
Integration of global political and economic communities	Globalisation of products and services	Parent-country management desire to control MNC policy	Language and cultural barriers
	Senior management commitment to geocentrism		

Source: adapted from Perlmutter (1969).

SIHRM issues: functions, policies and practices

Earlier it was explained that Schuler *et al.* (1993) argue that there are two major strategic components of MNCs that give rise to and influence SIHRM: inter-unit linkages and internal operations. Here, we note some of the major ways in which they affect SIHRM issues; functions; policies and practices.

Inter-unit linkages

SIHRM policies and practices most associated with inter-unit linkages are: establishing a mix of employees in the local operation which is a mix of parent-country nationals (PCNs), host-country nationals (HCNs) and third-country nationals (TCNs); establishing HR policies and practices that link units but allow local adaptation; and using management development to ensure organisational coherence.

Establishing a mix of employees in the local operation which is a mix of PCNs, HCNs and TCNs

Traditionally, the objective of coordination and control has been achieved through means such as placing parent-country nationals as managers in the early stages of a foreign operation in the way that Japanese companies, for example the truck manufacturer Iveco locating in the West, did in the 1980s and 1990s. More recently, a leading UK DIY retailer opened stores in China with key positions occupied by UK senior managers (Gamble, 2003). Consequently, activities designed to prepare ex-patriates for overseas assignments (Dowling *et al.*, 1999) are likely to be important. However, as the case study of Halcrow at the end of Chapter 3, related to this chapter, shows, this can be a costly option. In the past, Halcrow's international staffing policy has been to send expatriates from the UK to work on overseas projects. This is now too expensive an option (IRS, 2002) as the relative cost of employing TCNs from countries such as China and Pakistan means that this is an increasingly attractive option for Halcrow. It is also an increasingly viable option as the amount of skilled potential staff in these countries is growing.

The move towards greater reliance on HCNs and TCNs does, of course, raise the problem of securing coordination and control. This may be accomplished through such measures as developing clear policies and procedures to which the foreign operation's managers are to adhere. Similarly, it may be done by tight financial control targets being imposed upon the operation. In addition, coordination and control may be achieved through what Gamble (2003) calls imparting 'explicit' and 'tacit knowledge'. In the case of the leading UK DIY retailer which has opened stores in China with key positions occupied by UK senior managers, explicit knowledge was conveyed to HCNs through such means as 'the introduction and dissemination of employee handbooks, training manuals and standard operating procedures' (Gamble, 2003: 374). Gamble notes that invariably the transmission of explicit and tacit knowledge overlap.

> Thus, at DecoStore, the expatriate managers not only introduced and activated training, selection and recruitment, and promotion procedures, they also participated in and oversaw their operation. In selection procedures, for instance, they introduced and established the recruitment criteria and actively selected recruits who possessed the 'motivational characteristics and skills appropriate to the imported form of organisational practice'. In addition, in their daily behaviour and example they indicated to local employees the kind of work style and approach that was 'sought, sanctioned and would be rewarded by the firm'.
>
> *(Gamble, 2003: 374)*

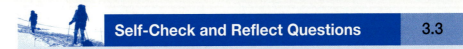

Self-Check and Reflect Questions 3.3

In what other ways may the expatriate managers at DecoStore have established tacit knowledge?

Establishing HR policies and practices that link units but allow local adaptation

It seems logical to assume that the demands of coordination and control should not be so overwhelming that HR policies and practices cannot be adapted to local conditions. This logical assumption was confirmed in an IRS Employment Review study (IRS, 1999) of senior HR managers across a range of transnational companies, see In Practice 3.6.

In Practice 3.6

HR policies and practices in MNCs: centralisation and local adaptation

IRS carried out case study work covering firms representing a variety of industrial sectors, countries of ownership and countries of operation. The focus was on the extent of internationalisation within five key areas of people management:

- employee relations and communications;
- remuneration and benefits;
- working time;
- selection and recruitment; and
- performance management and career development.

What was the overall finding of the research?

The IRS research revealed a mixed picture, characterised by important differences both between and within companies. The case studies showed a marked difference between those firms with a general policy of delegating decision-making to national subsidiaries and individual business units and those with a policy of internationalising aspects of human resource management.

Which areas of people management were decentralised?

The companies that give national subsidiaries considerable autonomy in, for example, selection and recruitment tended to have an international outlook when it comes to high-level succession planning and filling senior posts. In several cases, a key criterion for recruitment (and promotion) to top jobs was international mobility.

Not even the most centralising of the case-study firms favoured harmonising pay rates between countries where the relevant market rates are different. Basic pay levels provided one area where centralisation and decentralisation can appear paradoxically to amount to the same thing. The decentralised firms leave it to local managers to determine pay according to prevailing labour market conditions, while the centralised companies make it a matter of worldwide corporate strategy that

▶

people are rewarded in relation to the relevant market. In both cases the outcome is the same: base pay levels determined according to the market.

What was the main conclusion of the research?

The reason for the unevenness found in the international harmonisation of HRM policies and practices both between and within individual firms was that the scope for internationalisation is not the same for every aspect of the employment relationship. Some areas, such as performance management and staff development, readily lend themselves in some companies to a consistent cross-border approach. However, others, such as working time, are subject to a multitude of national regulations and local arrangements, which effectively rule out substantial harmonisation.

There was unanimity among the case study firms on the question of barriers to harmonisation of employee relations and communications strategies and policies. The most important obstacle cited was the existence of widely differing national frameworks of employment law and labour market regulation. In addition, the role of trade unions, works councils and collective bargaining in different countries was important. However, there was no agreement among the firms on the desirability of moving towards a cross-border approach to managing employee relations. One company illustrated this point. US-owned computer giant, IBM, while acknowledging that a country focus is to some extent inevitable because laws and institutions are different in each country, seeks as far as possible to apply a single employment philosophy in every location. A key part of its philosophy is that the firm should communicate directly with individual employees, rather than going through intermediaries such as trade unions. Although the situation on union recognition for collective bargaining varies from country to country, there are no cases where the union is the main channel of communication at IBM. IBM is actively seeking to break down the barriers to international management of employee relations and communications. The development of information and communication technologies is widely seen as one of the most important means to this end.

Source: adapted from IRS (1999)

Using management development to ensure organisational coherence

If MNCs are to use PCN managers located in foreign operations as a major part of the quest for inter-unit coordination and control, then it is apparent that the development of those managers is an important part of an MNC's HR strategy.

Briscoe and Schuler (2004) offer a series of 'tips' which American firms have adopted in order to develop the managerial competence of their international managers. These emphasise the importance of international mobility and experience for managers and the importance of integrating the managers who have received this international development into the mainstream of the organisation. Among the 'tips' are sending 'rising stars' on international assignments for two or three years, incorporating overseas placements into the main management development programme and considering moving certain foreign operations to other countries to facilitate greater global interaction. Above all, Briscoe and Schuler (2004) advocate the development of a 'global mind-set' among international managers. Among the attributes of managers with a global mind-set are the ability to: conduct business on a global as well as domestic scale; work and communicate with multiple cultures; manage the inevitable complexity that is involved in international business; manage cross-cultural teams and manage their own personal global learning. There is more on the competences of global managers in the next section of the chapter.

Internal operations

Schuler *et al.* (1993) note that the main objective of MNCs sums up the explanation of this important strategic component made earlier. This is being responsive to, and effective in, the local environment, yet being willing and ready to act in a coordinated fashion with the rest of the MNC units.

Schuler *et al.* note a number of ways in which this objective may be achieved. These are:

- matching and adapting HR practices with the competitive strategy of the unit and the local cultural and legislative system;
- creating a *modus operandi* whereby these HR policies can be modified to fit changing conditions;
- developing global HR policies flexible enough to be adapted for local HR practice.

Matching and adapting HR practices with the competitive strategy of the unit and the local cultural and legislative system

Schuler *et al.* (1993) argue that one of the most important ways of ensuring that the needs of the competitive strategy of the unit and the local cultural and legislative system are simultaneously met is to appoint an HCN as HR manager. This will ensure that knowledge of the local environment (e.g. legislation, acceptability of pay methods) is used as a positive aid in meeting business needs. Indeed, Schuler *et al.* contend that managing in a way that reflects local cultural needs is the key difference between domestic SHRM and SIHRM, given that both demand integration between business and HR strategy and between the components of HR strategy themselves.

Creating a modus operandi *whereby these HR policies can be modified to fit changing conditions*

As in other business contexts, it is important that sufficient flexibility exists in the local operation to be sensitive to changes in the operating environment and to adapt to these. To a large extent this hinges on the structure adopted for HR management in MNCs. In the giant French oil and chemicals MNC Elf Aquitaine, for example, there is a single, group HR and communications division which covers the whole of the HR area. Each of the three branches of the business has its own international HR division. The operating subsidiaries in each of the 62 individual countries in which the company operates each have an HR function, which reports to the head of the subsidiary; but there is also a 'dotted line' (two-way communication in relation to corporate HR policy and guidelines where they exist) to the heads of HR of the three branches (IRS, 1999). Such flexibility of structure gives companies like Elf Aquitaine sufficient capacity to respond quickly to operating environment changes at local level while ensuring consistency with MNC strategy.

Developing global HR policies flexible enough to be adapted for local HR practice

This imperative suggests the importance of the 'dotted line' in MNCs such as Elf Aquitaine above. Two-way communication in relation to corporate HR policies is important if the MNC's global HR policies are to be flexible enough to be adapted for local HR practice.

MNC concerns and goals

This is the last component of the Schuler *et al.* (1993) framework and represents the central issues on which the MNC's SIHRM function will be focused. The concerns and goals are:

1. global competitiveness;
2. efficiency;
3. local responsiveness;
4. flexibility;
5. learning and transfer of knowledge.

To a large extent these concerns and goals are integrated in many of the considerations that have been discussed earlier in this part of the chapter, in particular local responsiveness; flexibility; and learning and transfer of knowledge. Schuler *et al.* (1993) make the point that the degree of importance of each of these to the individual MNC will vary according to the circumstances of the organisation. But is it certain that global competitiveness and efficiency will apply to all MNCs. To assist in achievement of these two goals (and, for that matter, the remaining three goals), is the concern of those charged with the responsibility of devising and implementing SIHRM. The next part of this chapter deals in more detail with the capabilities required to fulfil this aim.

The capabilities needed to devise and implement SIHRM

It was noted above that management development is a major component of the drive to achieve inter-unit coordination and control. This section goes further than this and advocates that the development of key competences and capabilities is an important aspect of SIHRM. It can be seen as applying at three levels: organisation; line management; and HR professional. As can be seen in other chapters of this book, the development of competences and capabilities is an intrinsic part of domestic SHRM. This section deals particularly with those which relate to SIHRM.

Organisational capability

Interest in the concept of organisational capability has been evident for several years. It has its roots in the fields of management of change, organisational design and leadership (Sparrow *et al.*, 2004). Organisational capability focuses on the organisation's internal processes, systems and management practices to meet customer needs and directing the skills and efforts of the employees to achieving the goals of the organisation. A particularly important strand of organisational capability was explained in Chapter 1: the so-called 'resource-based view of the firm'. This emphasises the intangible nature of the so-called core competence that the organisation may possess. It is the sum of learning across individual skill sets and organisational units, which result in a bundle of skills and technologies that enable the organisation to provide particular benefits to customers (Hamel and Prahalad, 1994). Sparrow *et al.* (2004: 44) contend that building international organisational capability may mean creating many new competences, or applying existing competences to generate new strengths, for example by:

- exploiting core competence globally in a large number of countries and markets;
- identifying new resources found in untapped markets or countries and using them to strengthen an existing core competence; and
- reconfiguring value-adding activities across a wider geography and range of operations in order to enhance an existing competence.

All this sounds rather mysterious and begs the question: 'how will international HR managers recognise organisation core competence?' and 'when they have recognised the answer to this first question, how will they exploit, strengthen and enhance core competence?' A pointer to the answer to the first of these questions is provided by Ulrich (2000) who has listed the following as some of the indicators of organisational capability. These are the existence of:

- organisational structures which enable rapid decision-making by de-emphasising bureaucratic processes;
- strong organisational identity (or 'brand') against which employees can align their efforts;
- talented employees;
- a culture of innovation and learning;
- communication and information sharing across international boundaries;
- clear accountability for decision-making.

To a large extent the answer to the second question is to be found in the more concrete fields of management development and competence development of HR professionals. It is to these that the chapter now turns.

Line management competences

There are several studies which arrive at lists of management competences for the global manager (see Briscoe and Schuler, 2004). Typical among these is that of Dalton *et al.* (2002). These researchers argue that global managers need not only the core capabilities (managing action, people, information, coping with pressure and understanding how business works) but as global managers they need to see the world through the eyes of others. Consequently, Dalton *et al.* argue that they should develop four key global capabilities:

- international business knowledge;
- cultural adaptability;
- perspective taking (i.e. taking into account the views of others);
- ability to take the role of innovator by seeing old problems in new ways and trying new methods of solving them.

Much more is said about the need for cultural adaptability in the next section on the cultural perspective on SIHRM. Meanwhile, taking into account the views of others on the international stage is possessing what is similar to Schneider and Barsoux's (2003) 'global mindset'. This they define as a 'state of mind' achieved by managers who are able to work effectively across organisational, functional and cross-cultural boundaries. They argue that a global mind-set requires broad scanning, peripheral vision, and keeping in mind that multiple interpretations of a situation are needed. Moreover, they warn against the sort of 'our way is the only way and the best way' type of thinking to which adopting stereotyped views of 'foreign' operations can lead.

The competences of HR professionals

The aspect of the capability perspective on SIHRM which is most important to this book is that on the competences of international HR professionals. This is informed by work carried out by Sparrow *et al.* (2004) for the UK/Irish Chartered Institute of Personnel and Development. Part of the work involved a questionnaire with over 700 international HR professionals in UK organisations. It sought to find which HR activities were the most important in terms of the amount of people involved in them and the demands made upon their knowledge base.

The research revealed that international HR professionals pay more attention to communication processes, recruitment and selection, pay and benefits, training and management development, performance management, culture change and strategic planning, as well as, naturally enough, IHR administration. Sparrow *et al.* argue that it is predictable that these functions dominate given that they make a direct contribution to overall organisational effectiveness across the whole of their operations. On the other hand, Sparrow *et al.* contend that industrial relations, including employment law and equality and diversity issues, are often given a more domestic focus because they are related to legal and regulatory regimes that are more country specific. It is less clear why cost reduction and business process re-engineering issues do not feature more prominently. Sparrow *et al.* conjecture that it may have more to do with the concern of many international HR professionals with matters concerning international transferees than with the undoubted importance of these topics.

Self-Check and Reflect Questions	3.4

Which of the line manager competences do you think are particularly important for HR professionals?

The importance of communication

The research of Sparrow *et al.* (2004) concluded that that international HR professionals pay a good deal of attention to communication processes. Sparrow *et al.* see this as a consequence of the increased focus in global organisations on knowledge management. They argue that HR professionals have assumed the responsibility for the exploitation of knowledge that key employees carry with them, knowledge that is often the key to competitive advantage. The challenge for HR professionals is to develop mechanisms which can be used to share this knowledge throughout the organisation. Inevitably this means that the development of information technology solutions facilitates knowledge sharing through such means as company intranets. Many respondents in the research carried out by Sparrow *et al.* reported that they had started this process but that it was in its early stages at that time. Their general conclusion was that this would have an important effect upon the role of HR in global organisations.

In Practice   3.7

Fate of BAe merger hinges on exchange of knowledge

The success of the 1999 merger of British Aerospace and the defence arm of GEC Marconi to form BAE Systems depended on whether the two groups were willing to share corporate knowledge and best practice – in particular, the huge reserves of knowledge stored in BAe's then newly established virtual university. BAe management warned that the leverage of knowledge would be a more crucial factor in the merger than the integration of traditional business factors. Alan Millican, director of the virtual university, said, 'ideally, there will be an openness to look at what we can both bring to the table'. But he admitted that there were many barriers to information sharing. 'There is a massive problem in corporations that occurs when employees adopt an 'over my dead body' attitude to using other people's ideas and expertise. We're not very good at sharing best practice.'

The virtual university team were already aware of the legacy of BAe's own corporate past: the failure of its military and civilian divisions to exchange knowledge. 'People have been locked into individual areas and, when we merge with GEC, that will be even more evident,' Millican said. He admitted that GEC's 'entirely different' culture would present a challenge for management, but said the organisation was pinning its hopes on the more open, relationship-focused virtual workplace.

Millican argued that the intranet is a powerful tool to communicate the need to share. His view was that the new company could start to shape behaviour by disseminating values'. In the four years prior to the merger with GEC Marconi, BAe had been running a cultural change programme designed to face the challenge of global competition. The scheme spawned 'sharing events' such as a best-practice forum and employee-run master classes on best practice. The company had put all of this on its intranet which it was contemplating sharing with GEC. Millican added that 'mergers like this don't have a big success rate. We need to get staff excited about sharing their knowledge, and the virtual university is a good place to start.'

Source: *People Management* (1999).

Sparrow *et al.*'s (2004) study asked organisations questions about the key competences for global HR professionals. Table 3.4 notes the responses in terms of both those factors which the respondents thought the HR function needed to practise in order to be effective and the extent to which they felt that they were being practised.

In addition to the factors noted in Table 3.4, respondents were asked about the degree to which their organisations positioned the HR function as a strategic partner in global business, seen by Sparrow *et al.* as a crucial determinant of HR effectiveness in global organisations. This relates to most of the factors listed immediately prior to the chapter summary, in particular the ability to market HR globally as a source of strategic advantage,

Table 3.4 Factors HR function needs to practise in order to be effective and
the extent to which they are practised

Factor	Cited as important (%)	Reported as being practised (%)
Ensure flexibility in HR programmes and processes	51.6	37.5
Have ability to express the relative worth of HR programmes in terms of their bottom-line contribution to the organisation	37.5	35.9
Have ability to market HR globally as a source of strategic advantage	35.9	35.0
Develop global leadership through developmental cross-cultural assignments	29.7	29.7
Foster the global mind-set of all employees through training and development	29.7	29.7
Design and implement international HR information system	29.7	29.7
Develop relationships with international HR counterparts to encourage information exchange	23.4	23.4

Source: Sparrow *et al.* (2004).

to develop global leadership through developmental cross-cultural assignments and to foster the global mind-set of all employees through training and development. Not surprisingly, this produced a very positive response with nearly 70 per cent of organisations reporting that they felt this was practised in their organisations.

The cultural perspective on SIHRM

Briscoe and Schuler (2004) argue that the most important issue in the conduct of both international business and IHRM is culture. To anyone who has read about the cultural blunders made by MNCs in disregarding the cultural differences between countries this may seem self-evident. The same HR policies will not produce the same results in different cultural contexts. If this is accepted this as a valid statement in terms of domestic HRM how much more this is the case when the layer of complexity of different national cultures is added. An example of this occurred when a US company published a new diary for international distribution. The diary contained a note for Tuesday, April 30, followed by the detail: 'Queen's Birthday (Uruguay)'. In fact, Uruguay has no queen and no monarchy. The company's top customer in Uruguay personally called the publisher's general manager to ask just what it would take for the company to understand the basic culture of their market.

What is national culture?

Chapter 6 goes into much more detail on the issue of culture, in particular that which relates to the importance of culture at the organisational level. This section concentrates on the impact that national cultures have upon the efforts by global organisations to implement their HR strategies.

Chapter 6 also defines the concept of culture, at whatever level it applies. So this section does not want to complicate the issue by adding definitions which stress the national element of culture. However, it may be useful to introduce this section by noting what Briscoe and Schuler (2004) say about the impact that culture has upon the people who share a common culture which seems to us to be particularly appropriate to national culture. They contend that a people's culture:

- gives them a sense of who they are; a sense of belonging;
- equips them with the knowledge of how to behave in particular circumstances;
- enables them to pass the sense of who they are and the knowledge of how to behave in particular circumstances to succeeding generations;
- affects all aspects of how people think, solve problems and make decisions both within and outside their employing organisations.

This last reference to organisational life leads to a consideration of the relevance of national cultures for SIHRM. The last part of this section deals with the effects of national cultural differences on specific SIHRM practices. But different national cultural emphases have an impact upon the notion of strategy itself. By definition, strategy is concerned with longer-term organisation planning, a concept that sits uncomfortably with some national cultures. Briscoe and Schuler (2004) cite the work of Gesteland (1999) who categorised four key national cultural differences which helped him to better understand international marketing, negotiating and management behaviours. One of these four is attitudes to time. For some cultures time is vital, whereas others have a much more relaxed attitude to planning, scheduling and time. This difference may pose potential problems for MNCs in 'time conscious' cultures who expect the same attention to strategy and planning to be paid in 'time relaxed' cultures.

Before the chapter goes any further in this debate, a general warning is issued about generalising and stereotyping. It is obviously misleading to think of all members of an organisation as possessing similar characteristics. It is even more tempting to adopt the same approach with people from different national cultures. It is so easy to slip into the 'all Germans are formal and bureaucratic' while 'Americans communicate openly' mode of stereotyping, but this bears little relation to the complex reality of social life. In addition, this type of thinking assumes that national cultures are static. Yet everbody knows from the understanding of our own national culture that it is constantly evolving. Indeed, it would be surprising were this not the case, given the impact upon all our lives of rapidly developing international transport and electronic communication. Nonetheless, understanding that there may be differences in thinking about work issues which have their roots in traditional culture is clearly important to organisations which wish to implement effective international HR strategies.

How can differences in national cultures be measured?

Having advocated the importance of understanding national cultures it is of limited use if managers are aware of the existence of different cultures and their effects but cannot formalise this understanding through some attempt to render it tangible. This may be done through definition and, particularly importantly, an attempt to measure differences. This is why the work of academics such as Hofstede (1980, 1991, 2001) and Trompenaars (1993) and Trompenaars and Hampden-Turner (1997) has received so much attention. Their work is evaluated in detail in Chapter 6. But here their work is summarised to highlight the differences in national cultures.

Hofstede measured national cultural characteristics on five dimensions, the first four of which are:

1. Power distance (relates to the views societies have about the exercise of power in organisations).

2. Uncertainty avoidance (relates to actions members of societies take in respect of ambiguous and uncertain situations.)

3. Individualism–collectivism (relates to the views societies have about preferred ways of social organisation, as individual members or collective groups).

4. Masculinity–femininity (relates to the importance societies put upon the values of assertiveness or caring for others).

On the power distance dimension, Malaysia and the Philippines ranked as having high power distance, in that society members accepted the legitimacy of managers' power whereas the reverse was the case in the USA, UK, Ireland and Israel. For uncertainty avoidance, Greece and France were notable among societies with high uncertainty avoidance, thus pointing to the need for attention to bureaucracies and procedures, whereas Denmark and Sweden ranked low which signals the need for greater flexibility of approach in organisational processes. The USA emerged as a highly individualist society as opposed to Japan and Hong Kong, which rated as more collective. Japan was ranked the most masculine society, with Norway, Sweden, Denmark and the Netherlands the most feminine.

In addition, Hofstede refers to a long-term–short-term orientation. This relates to the views societies have about the importance of time horizons (see the reference to Gesteland (1999) in the previous section). Hofstede's original research did not include the long-term–short-term orientation dimension. This stemmed from the work of the Chinese Culture Connection (1987). This is a critical dimension given the importance of long-term decisions such as investment in training and development. Countries such as Japan tend to traditionally have a focus on the future as opposed to western countries which have a shorter-term view of, for example, company results.

Trompenaars identified seven distinct cultural factors by which countries in his study could be categorised. He contended that these seven value orientations greatly influence our ways of conducting business and managing. The relative position of people along these dimensions guides their belief and actions through life.

These were:

1. universal v. particular (emphasis on rules v. relationships);

2. collectivism v. individualism;

3. range of emotions expressed (neutral v. emotional);

4. specific v. diffuse relationships (e.g. in specific cultures people compartmentalise their lives into separate spheres (e.g. work and home) but in diffuse cultures there is less compartmentalisation so, for example, work relationships may be carried over into employees' private lives);

5. method of according status to other people (e.g. by performance or social status);

6. inner v. outer directedness (the degree to which individuals feel that they have control over their environment. Inner-directed individuals will, for example, have a much greater belief in planning than outer-directed individuals who will tend to believe that 'events' will dictate outcomes);

7. emphasis placed upon the past, present and future in orientation to action.

Trompenaars' conclusions were similar to those of Hofstede, albeit the different emphases in the dimensions used to measure culture. This research prompted Ronen and Shenkar (1985, 1988) to devise a general grouping of national cultures. These are:

- Anglo (Australia, Canada, Ireland, New Zealand, South Africa, the UK and USA);
- Arab (Abu-Dhabi, Bahrain, Kuwait, Oman, Saudi Arabia and UAE);
- Far Eastern (Hong Kong, China, Indonesia, Malaysia, Philippines, Singapore, Vietnam, Taiwan and Thailand);
- Germanic (Austria, Germany and Switzerland);
- Latin American (Argentina, Chile, Colombia, Mexico, Peru and Venezuela);
- Latin European (Belgium, France, Italy, Portugal and Spain);
- Near Eastern (Greece, Iran and Turkey);
- Nordic (Denmark, Finland, Norway and Sweden);
- Independent (Brazil, India, Israel, Japan and South Korea).

Self-Check and Reflect Questions	3.5

Of what value is this general grouping of national cultures to managers in their SIHRM activities?

How can differences between national cultures be managed?

Earlier in the chapter the three different orientations of MNCs to their international business were explained: ethnocentric, polycentric and geocentric (Perlmutter (1969) and Heenan and Perlmutter (1979)). Schneider and Barsoux (2003) present a similar categorisation of strategies that MNCs may employ in dealing with cultural differences. The three main categories noted are: ignoring the differences; minimising the differences; and utilising the differences.

Ignoring cultural differences

The thrust of this strategy is to see cultural differences as irrelevant, or at least to push them to one side in the pursuit of standardisation and efficiency. This may an important part of MNC overall business strategy since the strength of international brands, such as Wal-Mart and Starbucks, depends upon the customer receiving a similar experience in whichever part of the world the store is situated. So, in terms of marketing strategy at least, such MNCs are making a virtue of the 'one size fits all' approach.

But in relation to HR, ignoring cultural differences is similar to the ethnocentric (HQ knows best) orientation which is more complex to manage than presenting a uniform company face to the customer because it may fall foul of, for example, local legislation and trade union regulation. But to draw such a sharp distinction between marketing and HR strategy may be too tempting. Schneider and Barsoux (2003) note the case of Disney, which invests enormous resources in ensuring that the Disney visitor experience is exactly the same irrespective of location. This means that Disney employees must be trained to 'perform' in an identical fashion at all times in all places. Disney employees are an intrinsic part of the marketing strategy: a significant challenge for Disney training and HR specialists.

Perhaps the most revealing phrase in the Disney University example in 'In Practice' 3.8 is 'Nonconformists needn't apply.' Conformity is the byword for MNCs which pursue a 'one best way' approach to managing culture. But it is this desire for conformity which leads to difficulties in cultural adaptation of HR strategy and, ultimately, to charges of 'inhumanity' from those such as Ritzer (2002) who argue against the worst effects of globalisation.

Minimising cultural differences

This perspective sees cultural differences as a problem but does not ignore such differences. As with Perlmutter's (1969) polycentric orientation to international business, each foreign operating company is given some decision-making autonomy. To echo Perlmutter's view: local people know what is best for them and the part of the organisation that is located in the host country should be as local in identity as possible. This approach does not rule out the possibility of the MNC developing a strong corporate culture: but there is sufficient flexibility to adapt that culture to local conditions.

This is akin to the approach taken by many of the Japanese companies setting up in Europe in the past 20 years. One of the distinctive features of HR strategy the large Japanese corporations introduced is to work with a company union that represents workers but nonetheless is essentially part of the management structure of the company. The trade union structure in most European countries is quite different in that unions are independent of the organisations whose employees they represent. Japanese companies, such as Nissan (Wickens, 1987), adapted the company union idea in the UK by entering into agreements with British trade unions whereby a single union in partnership with the company represents the interests of its workers.

Utilising cultural differences

Here the MNC is concerned to use cultural differences as a learning opportunity and a source of competitive advantage. Rather as in the geocentric orientation, where the best people are placed in key positions, irrespective of nationality, MNCs that wish to utilise

In Practice   3.8

The role of the Disney University in presenting a uniform face to the visitor

The secret to Disney's success isn't magic; it's much easier to replicate. It's a well-trained, enthusiastic and motivated workforce: a secret that Walt Disney himself realised a long time ago. 'You can dream, create, design and build the most wonderful place in the world but it requires people to make the dream a reality,' he said.

All of Walt Disney World's 'cast members' begin their careers with Disney at the casting office. It's here that Disney 'auditions' prospective cast members. Disney's casting building was specifically designed to introduce prospective cast members to the idea that they are not simply doing a job but performing on stage. Cast members assigned to work in the casting office come from all different parts of the Disney organisation. They work on 12-month assignments. Disney believes it's important to have people who actually work in different parts of the company do the selection. An assignment to the casting office is a coveted job: one that most don't want to give up after their assignment ends.

While prospective cast members wait for their initial interviews, they watch a short video that describes the interview process and outlines Disney's expectations of its future cast members. Non-conformists needn't apply. Once hired, all new cast members go through the same one-and-one-half day training programme called 'Traditions'. It's here that they learn the basics of being good cast members, from Disney history to direction on how to meet and exceed guest expectations. It's also their first taste of something that is a large part of all cast members' careers: the Disney University.

Disney University

Walt Disney established the Disney University after opening Disneyland, when he realised the need for a structured learning environment to teach the unique skills that are required of Disney cast members. It was the first corporate university and remains one of the largest corporate training facilities in the world.

Disney University claims that it provides all cast members with world-class training in diverse skills ranging from computer applications to culinary arts. Cast members are also eligible to participate in the company's Educational Reimbursement Plan, which allows cast members to attend courses to pursue a college education at Disney's expense.

Disney University utilises a number of advanced training technologies that allow all cast members to receive training when it's convenient for them. Mobile Training Units allow cast members to receive computer training at their work site. In addition, training via satellite from some of America's top business schools is available to front-line supervisors and mid- to upper-level managers. The Disney University Learning Centre also provides cast members with dozens of self-paced courses in a variety of subjects that allow cast members to study whenever time allows.

A variety of visiting tutors is available for specialised training at various times.

Source: adapted from Patton (1997).

cultural differences are likely to spread their operations throughout the globe. This enables them to take advantage of different ideas and insights from wherever they may come. Earlier in the chapter there were examples of MNCs that had located some of their specialist functions in different parts of the world, largely for reasons for efficiency. But Schneider and Barsoux (2003) cite the case of pharmaceutical giant P & G which gave an element of product development responsibility to its Indian operation with the result that successful products for the Indian market were developed based on traditional herbal medicines.

The P & G example tempts Schneider and Barsoux (2003: 270) to suggest a new form of MNC where 'specialised units are co-ordinated into integrated networks'.

> Rather than be an assemblage of semi-independent units which contribute individually to HQ coffers, the MNC becomes a heterarchy with many centres playing a strategic role in formulating as well as implementing strategy. This fosters a broader range of strategic thinking, and encourages a global mentality among all employees. These approaches provide opportunities for organisational innovation and learning from any direction. They encourage reflecting on which local innovations may have applications in other national units or might even warrant global diffusion. They force companies to consider what is the opportunity or incentive for 'local for global' organisational learning, or transfer of 'best practice' from the subsidiaries to the headquarters.

What are the effects of national cultural differences on SIHRM practices?

The categorisation of strategies that MNCs may employ in dealing with cultural differences, explained above, only paints a rather general picture of what HR managers in MNCs may do to adapt to cultural differences. The reality of such differences is really felt at the level of HR practices. Being aware of a general strategy is one thing; knowing how to devise a pay system to promote a favourable reaction from Vietnamese workers is quite another. This final section examines briefly some of the issues that face MNC HR managers when making key decisions which have to take into account cultural differences. The decision areas we cover are: selection, training, performance management and pay.

Selection

Among the questions, which are interrelated, which need to be asked when selecting in unfamiliar cultures are:

- What emphasis needs to be put upon what people know as opposed to what they can do?
- How important is educational background?
- How important is social and family background?
- How important is it to be a generalist rather than a specialist?
- How important are issues of gender, disability, race, religion and age in selection?

Clearly the answers to these questions are important in informing selection decisions not only in ensuring that the most suitable person for the job is selected but that the successful candidate can become integrated into the organisation. It is always tempting to think that selection is a process of rational decision-making where the most competent person gets the job, irrespective of other considerations. However, we all know that this is not the case, despite the move to more apparent rationality in selection – decisions in the West through the development of such techniques as job specifications and competence frameworks.

Schneider and Barsoux (2003) report the tale from K-Mart, the USA retail giant, which bought the former state-owned *Maj* department store in Prague. Part of the selection criteria for the new company was that sales staff that would smile and greet customers in the way we have become used to in the West. However, this contradicted typical Czech behaviour which is characterised 'moodiness' and 'cynicism'. New appointees soon found that they could not adapt to the required behaviour and left.

Training

Many of the key issues for HR managers in MNCs in relation to training are similar to domestic concerns. However, there are two key issues which need to be considered: who does the training and to what extent do the content and method of the training provision (including the language used) need to be tailored to the country in which the training takes place.

There is considerable scope for ethnocentrism in the approach adopted. Of all the HR practices, training perhaps has the highest potential for delivering a 'MNC HQ knows best' message by adopting the content and method of the HQ country, delivered by training professionals from that country in (usually) English. Not only is there the spirit of ethnocentrism evident in the message sent here but the content of the training may be inappropriate for host-country needs. This strikes a familiar chord with the enduring claim that business and management education tends to be too American dominated.

The US publisher McGraw-Hill seems to be aware of the dangers of ethnocentrism in its training provision and is moving towards a more polycentric approach designed to minimise cultural differences (see In Practice 3.9).

In Practice   3.9

International training at McGraw-Hill

The vice-president at McGraw-Hill in charge of international training often delivers the training to the company's 17 locations, which are mainly in Europe and Asia. There are two McGraw-Hill divisions: USA and International, and training is seen as a way of developing a common corporate culture. Historically there was little training carried out in the International division.

The company is conscious of the need not to be too American in its training provision. Trainers network with other international trainers and host-country managers in order to tailor provision to host-country needs. In addition, trainers arrive at the location well before the training event in an attempt to familiarise themselves with the location's specific culture.

However, McGraw-Hill's goal is to develop instructors in each of the locations.

Source: adapted from Briscoe and Schuler (2004).

Performance management

Performance management is a particularly complex practice to transfer between cultures without philosophical and practical conflicts. The types of questions that may arise in considering the extent to which performance management may be transferred across cultures are: how prepared are individuals to accept individual responsibility as opposed to identifying their activities as part of a team effort?; how prepared are individuals to accept personal performance objectives?; how prepared are individuals to accept performance feedback?; and how equipped are managers to give feedback?

Schneider and Barsoux (2003) give two examples of the difficulties, one from Russia and the other from the USA. They note that Russian managers are often reluctant to set performance objectives for their employees because this is reminiscent of the regime of Lenin's Young Communist League in which individuals had to report on objectives achieved, such as the number of streets cleaned as part of community service expectations and the amount of papers by Lenin that had been mastered.

In the USA there is considerable sensitivity over what is being assessed: the individual or the individual's job performance. Such is the importance of the distinction that the US courts will uphold complaints from appraised individuals who can prove that their evaluation was based on their personal traits rather than their job performance, unless it can be demonstrated that there is a direct link between personality and performance.

Pay

Some of the issues that relate to performance management also concern pay; a classic example being the degree to which individual, team or organisational performance may be linked to pay. There are also cultural differences over the differentials that exist over the pay of employee groups, for example senior managers and production operatives. A large gap is expected and tolerated in the West, this will be less so in countries with a recent socialist history. For example the history of egalitarianism in China is clearly part of the 'old' values which are still influential in Chinese organisations. For example, so-called 'red-eye disease' (jealousy) is evident in many Chinese organisations where there is resentment over differing levels of pay.

In addition, the resistance to the principle of paying individuals differently according to their performance also highlights another difficulty in Chinese organisations, particularly those that are, or have until recently, been state owned. The absence of any real employee understanding of entrepreneurialism is a problem. Individual performance-related pay serves as an embodiment of the tension that exists in China between the 'old' values and the realisation that economic necessity dictates a set of 'new' values, a set in which old egalitarianism plays little part. Part of this set of 'new' values is using job effectiveness as a pay differentiator. This poses practical barriers for many Chinese organisations where there is no effective performance management system, in addition to the cultural barriers.

This section concludes wth a summary list of those HR activities that the authors consider cultural differences impact upon the most:

- strategic planning
- organisational structure in reaction to degree of formalisation and hierarchy
- management decision-making
- recruitment and selection
- the socialisation of employees into the organisation
- performance management
- content and structure of training
- career development
- employee involvement

- pay and benefits
- facility for gaining employee commitment to goals of organisation
- attitudes towards change management programmes
- attitudes of employers and employees towards collective employee representation.

There is little doubt that the future for many HR professionals will involve much more attention to international issues. As can be seen from this chapter, SIHRM is a wide-ranging and complex topic that merits careful attention. What will be interesting to note, as global business develops, is the attention that non-European and North American companies pay to HR issues as they spread their influence throughout the world. This chapter has taken a very western perspective on SIHRM. The future will undoubtedly be even more complex and varied.

Summary

- MNCs pursue international business for a variety of reasons in a variety of ways.
- The importance of MNCs is not new but their growth in recent years has been rapid and significant.
- SIHRM may be better understood by the examination of a model in which classic MNC components and factors relevant to the MNC's external and internal operating environments influence the SIHRM issues, functions, and policies and practices, which in turn affect the concerns and goals of the MNC.
- The development of key competences by MNCs is important at three levels: organisational, line management and HR professionals.
- National cultural differences are an important aspect of SIHRM and have been measured by a number of authors allowing these differences to be categorised.
- Strategies for managing cultural differences include: ignoring them, minimising them and utilising them.
- The effects of national cultural differences on HR practices can be quite profound with the consequence that the transferability of many of these practices is suspect.

Follow-up study suggestions

- Investigate official international business web sites (e.g. UNCTAD) to determine growth patterns in MNCs (i.e. country of origin, economic sector, size).
- Examine company reports of MNCs to identify the markets into which they are spreading and the discernible patterns among these developments.
- Interview key managers in an organisation known to you which has a substantial amount of international business in order to establish the key competences for managing international business.
- Search in key practitioner texts for examples of HR practices which have necessitated modification in the light of significant cultural differences.

Suggestions for research topics

In a particular organisation for which international HRM is important:

- Study the international HRM activities of the organisation and assess the degree to which they differ from the organisation's domestic HR activities.
- Evaluate the opportunities and threats posed to the effective operation of the organisation's HR activities by the international environment in which the organisation operates.
- What cultural challenges are posed by the different national cultures in which the organisation operates?
- What strategies are used by the organisation to manage cultural differences and to what degree do these seem to be successful?

4

Evaluating SHRM: why bother and does it really happen in practice?*
With Denise Skinner

Learning Outcomes

By the end of this chapter you should be able to:

- explain the importance and contribution of evaluation to strategic human resource management;

- identify the range of different purposes an evaluation can serve;

- assess the barriers to evaluation and their causes;

- identify the various stakeholders in any evaluation and their need both to contribute and to receive feedback;

- assess the choices to be made in respect of the evaluation process and make suitably informed decisions;

- outline a range of strategies and data collection techniques involving both primary and secondary data, which may be used to evaluate strategic human resource management;

- identify the complexity of issues associated with feeding back the findings of evaluations.

* This Chapter was co-authored with Denise Skinner

Introduction

Within all of our lives we are constantly evaluating as part of our normal daily activities. As this book was being researched the value or worth of many academics' work in the field of strategic human resource management (SHRM) was assessed. As this book is being read its contents will be evaluated, the style in which it is written, the design and pedagogic features and the ideas and issues that are raised. The relevance of the contents will probably be evaluated to the reader's context, her or his ability to understand the material and the suitability of the place and time in which it is being read. Such 'personal' or 'informal' evaluations of situations and experiences affect one's perception of the world and underpin the choices that are made.

Given that this process is so central to what people do, it is perhaps surprising that evaluation, as a planned and formal activity, appears to be so problematic in an organisational context. Effective evaluation and the promotion of HR strategies requires the systematic collection of data that are subsequently analysed, the findings being presented in a meaningful and useful form. These data may have been collected through monitoring what is happening within an organisation over time, perhaps as part of a balanced scorecard approach to performance management or an HR information system, or specifically to evaluate a particular strategic HR intervention. However, without the ensuing evaluation, the effectiveness of one or a series of strategic HR interventions may be unclear. The knowledge and understanding gained through this process of research, the authors would argue, enables organisations to have a clearer understanding of the impact of different strategies and, of equal importance, to adjust their HR interventions to help promote these strategies. Yet despite this, it is widely recognised that the implementation of HR strategies has rarely included a planned evaluation (Doyle *et al.*, 2000) and, on those occasions that they do, the findings are rarely utilised at all, let alone strategically.

Toracco (1997) argues that this lack of evaluation is due to difficulties associated with the long timeframes required for strategic change in organisations. In particular, it is often difficult to be certain of the precise impact of specific interventions. These observations are supported by others (for example Randell, 1994; Skinner, 2004) who emphasise the difficulty of designing evaluation studies and obtaining data of sufficient quality to disentangle the effect of a specific HR intervention from other stimuli. Even in the context of training and development, where there is a great deal of literature written about the need to evaluate and a widespread acceptance among practitioners of its importance, the reality is that evaluation rarely progresses beyond the end of course 'happy sheet', asking participants about the operational practicalities of the training experience. Despite such problems, the need for evaluation is emphasised by models of strategy formulation and development. These usually incorporate an information gathering and analysis stage, which emphasises the importance of knowing and understanding an organisation's current situation as part of developing strategy. For example, as was seen in Chapter 1, top-down development of strategy involves a number of steps, including analysing an organisation's environment and its internal resources, within which it is recognised that this information is likely to be incomplete and therefore imperfect. Similarly, the processual approach to strategy development involves reflection, evaluation and understanding.

Such research is likely to include data on the external environment as well as internal objectives, organisational (including HR) capabilities and the need to communicate within the organisation (Prahalad and Hamel, 1990).

Typical 'scientific' approaches to research often seek to minimise the amount of involvement between those collecting and analysing the data (the researchers) and those from whom data are collected on the grounds of maintaining objectivity (Robson, 2002). Within such a scientific evaluation, evaluators are seen as separate from, rather than working alongside, an organisation. Findings are disseminated only to the sponsor of the evaluation rather than all those affected. This conflicts with much that we discuss in this book in terms of the importance of an employee involvement to develop strategy ownership and understanding (Chapter 12). Such conflict is, perhaps, not too surprising if the purpose attributed to the evaluation is to understand and explain. We would argue that evaluation can also provide useful insights about HR issues associated with specific strategies. However, in evaluating and promoting HR strategies, we believe it is often necessary for the person undertaking the evaluation to be within or to become part of the organisation. Analysis of data collected should not take place in a vacuum and judgements need to be made within the context of the organisation.

In this chapter we therefore argue that the evaluation of HR strategies needs to involve those affected within the organisation as fully as possible. This is not to say that evaluation can only be undertaken by people within the organisation. Rather it implies that where people external to the organisation are used, their role should be to help those within to perceive, understand and act to improve the situation; an approach akin to Schein's (1999) 'process consultation'. As part of this it is recognised that, depending upon the purpose of the evaluation, one or a number of research strategies might be more appropriate. Evaluation may take place over a range of time horizons. These can range from one-off case studies, perhaps answering the question 'Where are we now?', through cross-sectional studies which benchmark HR practices, to longitudinal evaluations perhaps using a series of employee attitude surveys. Similarly, we recognise that to address particular strategic objectives some data collection techniques are likely to collect more appropriate data than others. For example, a questionnaire survey of employees is less likely to discover their in-depth feelings about a recent downsizing than face-to-face interviews in which an interviewer takes time to gain the employee's confidence.

Self-Check and Reflect Questions 4.1

Think about the last time you were asked to evaluate a course in which you were participating. A possible course could be a module on your current programme or a training course at your workplace.

a. What aspects of the course were you asked to comment about?

b. How do you think your evaluation and that of your fellow students was used subsequently?

This chapter begins by considering the nature of evaluation in terms of what it is, its benefits and why it may not be undertaken (Figure 4.1). The choices that have to be made about the process once a decision has been made to evaluate are then explored. Commencing with a discussion of purpose and context, typical and action research approaches are considered and different evaluation strategies and data gathering techniques outlined. The implications of different tools and techniques, and issues relating to the feeding back of findings, are then discussed. However, we would stress that while this chapter provides an overview of a range of evaluation strategies and techniques, there is still a need to read far more widely about these prior to undertaking an evaluation yourself. This is because the space available is insufficient to enable us to explain the strategies and techniques in sufficient detail.

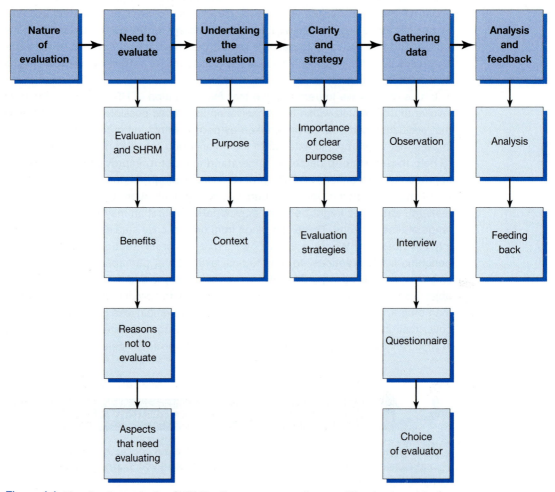

Figure 4.1 Mapping the evaluating SHRM territory: a summary diagram of the chapter content

The nature of evaluation

If one were to ask a group of people to define evaluation, it would probably be found that the term meant different things to individuals depending on their background and experience. As the thinking and practice relating to evaluation have evolved over the last 40 years, a variety of strategies and data collection techniques has developed and there has been a range of definitions to match. Patton (1997: 192), for example, identifies 57 types of evaluation as 'illustrative' of the many types available! Key issues in differentiating between evaluation types include:

- when they occur;
- their purpose;
- what is being evaluated;
- the evaluation strategy adopted;
- who undertakes the evaluation.

These issues have been used to differentiate between some examples of the evaluation types that Patton identifies in Table 4.1.

This process of planned or formal evaluation, as distinct from the personal, informal evaluation such as 'gut feeling', has variously been defined as: an activity for providing information for decision-making (Alkin, 1969), an activity focused on assessing the achievement of objectives (Eisner, 1979; Guba and Lincoln, 1981) or an activity focused on assessing actual effects and outcomes regardless of stated goals (Scriven, 1972).

Table 4.1 Illustrative examples of different types of evaluation

	Example of evaluation type or focus	Central question or defining approach
Purpose	Outcomes	To what extent have the desired outcomes been achieved and what has been the impact on those involved?
	Decisions	What information is needed to inform future decisions?
	Cost–benefit analysis	What is the relationship between the cost of the initiative/intervention and the outcomes in monetary terms?
	Efficiency	Could the same level of output be achieved with reduced input or could greater output be achieved with the same level of input?
When	Longtitudinal	What happens to the initiative/intervention and those involved/affected over time?
	Needs assessment	What do the client/participants/employees need and how might those needs be met?

Table 4.1 Continued

What is being evaluated	Effort	What are the inputs in terms of the level of activity and effort being put into the initiative or intervention, e.g. resources, ratios?
	Process	What are strengths of the day-to-day processes, how can these processes be improved?
	Quality	Are acceptable standards being consistently maintained?
Evaluation strategy	Monitoring	Data are routinely collected and analysed, often through a human resource information system, on an ongoing basis
	Developmental	The evaluator is part of the team working on the initiative's continued development long term
Who	Collaborative	The intended users work with the evaluators on the evaluation
	Connoisseurship	Experts apply their own criteria and judgement
	External	The evaluation is conducted by independent outsiders to increase credibility
	Internal	Those involved evaluate the initiative/ intervention

Source: adapted from Patton (1997).

Although different definitions take slightly different views, they all emphasise the need for evaluation to be conducted as a planned and purposeful activity rather than as an afterthought (In Practice 4.1). As such, evaluation is concerned with finding things out in a systematic way. The term 'systematic' emphasises that evaluation will be based on logical relationships and not just beliefs or hunches often associated with informal evaluations. The term 'finding out' highlights the importance of data as the basis upon which decisions are made as opposed to a reliance upon assumptions and guesswork. Patton (2002) highlights the contribution of evaluation to improvement, describing evaluation as any effort to increase human effectiveness through systematic data-based inquiry. Drawing these ideas together, Russ-Eft and Preskill (2001) argue that evaluation should be a systematic process for enhancing knowledge and decision-making which involves the collection of data.

In Practice   4.1

Planned evaluation of sustainability support for small businesses

Business Boffins Ltd provides mentoring and support to new and young businesses. Working with the South East England Development Agency and Oxford Brookes University, Business Boffins developed a business mentoring programme for small businesses. The programme was pilot tested with 147 small businesses in the south east of England. During this first year of operation, participants were asked to evaluate the programme three times using purpose-designed questionnaires. The data collected allowed the programme to be further tailored to the needs of the small businesses during the year. At the end of the first year, over 95 per cent of the small businesses agreed that the programme had been helpful. This contrasted with a recent Federation of Small Businesses' survey which indicated that, although 70 per cent of small businesses seek help and advice, only 10 per cent are satisfied with the help they receive (Business Boffins, 2005).

The need to evaluate

Evaluation and SHRM

Inevitably, given the turbulent business environment of the late twentieth and early twenty-first centuries, organisations have to contend with a world in which the only constant is change (Carnall, 1995). In this context, an important aspect of SHRM is to ensure that the organisation is able to respond in a timely and positive manner to its internal and external environments. As early as 1987, Guest identified a key role for HR managers within the global scenario of organisations faced with increasing external and internal pressures, when he asserted that the capacity to implement strategic plans was an important feature of successful SHRM. Since then, the literature has frequently argued for the strategic role of the HR function and authors such as Purcell (1999), Tyson (1999) and Ulrich (1998) have emphasised the need to manage human resources strategically in order that an organisation's capacity for change can be improved. Tyson (1999) maintains that HR managers are major players in the creation of organisational capability. He also suggests that evaluation is an area where the HR function can make a significant contribution to increase understanding of the appropriateness of interventions, in effect to learn from experience, and to change strategy as a consequence.

The benefits of evaluation

As discussed in Chapter 10, an integral part of effective learning is the reflection on experience – the evaluation of process and outcomes that enables informed progression to the next stage. Writing on organisational change, Doyle *et al.* (2000) ask the question, if this is not monitored how can the experience contribute to organisational learning? Pedler *et al.* (1991) include the conscious structuring of evaluation as a characteristic of learning organisations and the role of evaluation in successful change initiatives is widely acknowledged within the change management literature. Similarly, Patrickson *et al.* (1995: 6) argue that evaluation is a necessary precursor to more change 'in a cycle of continuous improvement', a pivotal point that provides an opportunity for analysis and reflection before making adjustments to the course of change. Nelson (2003) also asserts that the management of any change should incorporate the regular review of progress and that strategy should change in response to feedback.

Other authors specifically identify important contributions that the inclusion of a planned process of evaluation can make to successful SHRM. Love (1991), for example, outlines the role of effective evaluation in improving management decision-making through the provision of information and the development of shared understanding. Kirkpatrick (1985) argues the importance of feedback in gaining acceptance and commitment to organisational initiatives, while Carnall (1995) suggests that people need information to understand new systems and their place in them. Preskill and Torres (1999) argue that evaluative inquiry helps organisation members reduce uncertainty, clarify direction, build community, and ensure that learning is part of everyone's job. The sharing of information, they argue, is essential if new insights and mutual understanding are to be created.

Many of these benefits relate to the common themes of information gathering and developing shared understanding. At the start of this chapter, the reality that every individual evaluates on a personal basis and how the same is true in relation to our individual organisational experiences was highlighted. Reichers *et al.* (1997) argue that people need to understand not only the reasons for change but also its ongoing progress and its results. Individuals at all levels will make their own assessments, constructing their own 'reality' relating to the necessity for, and the effectiveness of, new initiatives and strategies, often even when these do not affect them directly. In some cases, these views are shared and tested with colleagues but, despite this, much may remain tacit rather than explicit. Yet individuals' future actions will almost certainly be influenced by these assessments, even when they are based solely on personal perceptions and the subjective evaluations that result from relatively narrow perspectives.

The extent of individual understanding is inevitably determined by the information that is available, whether through formal or informal channels. The conclusions that are reached will be affected by the quality of that information; in particular its relevance, accuracy, comprehensiveness and up-to-dateness (Calder, 1994). Patton (1997) maintains that an evaluation process is, in itself, a benefit, due to the learning that occurs among those involved in it. This, he argues, is because evaluation both depends on, and facilitates, clear communication. Every strategic HR intervention is unique and can only be understood from the experience of the participants but this needs to happen within a more general analytical framework. A planned process of evaluation can provide a mechanism for capturing the individual learning which has occurred and for the sharing of this learning across the organisation. This helps ensure that valuable knowledge will not be lost (Anderson and Boocock, 2002) and that there will be a sense of closure to the experiential learning cycle (Hendry, 1996). Without an evaluation process to capture and share the learning, the evidence is that valuable knowledge will escape, and it is highly likely that both individuals and organisations will repeat the, often unsuccessful, past (Garvin, 1993) increasing the likelihood of repeated mistakes (Gustafson *et al.*, 2003; Key Concepts 4.1).

Key Concepts   4.1

Thinking about whether to evaluate?

Chapter 9 considers the widely accepted management mantra that what gets measured, gets done. This highlights the importance of the link between performance and the evaluation or assessment of that performance. This and the issues discussed in the previous section can be summarised as four questions to consider in relation to whether SHRM should be evaluated:

1. If you don't measure outcomes and impact, how can you tell success from failure and explain it to others?
2. If success isn't visible, acknowledged and shared how can you reward it and build on it?
3. If you can't reward success, then how can you be sure that you are not rewarding failure?
4. If you can't recognise failure, how can you avoid its repetition and how can you improve?

Source: adapted from Patton (1997).

Self-Check and Reflect Questions   4.2

List the arguments you would use to justify the need for an organisation to justify evaluating SHRM interventions.

Reasons not to evaluate

Self-Check and Reflect Questions   4.3

Before you read on, based on your own experience make a list of reasons why you might be reluctant to undertake an evaluation of an HR process.

As you read this section compare the reasons you have listed with those we identify. To what extent are they the same or similar to those you have identified?

From reading and thinking about the arguments put forward in the previous subsection and answering Self-Check Question 4.2, you will have identified a range of reasons to justify the evaluation of SHRM. If asked, most mangers would probably come up with a similar list. Yet, despite the benefits that evaluation can provide, the reality for many organisations is that evaluation simply does not happen. Reasons given for this can be grouped into three overlapping categories:

- the difficulties of undertaking evaluation;
- the perceived lack of a need to evaluate;
- the difficulties associated with dealing with negative outcomes.

Difficulties of undertaking evaluation

Difficulties of undertaking evaluation in relation to HRM strategies have long been considered greater than for other business functions. Unlike the finance or production aspects of an organisation, the contribution of HR has been widely considered to be virtually unmeasurable because it deals with the 'soft', people side of the business. In the past it was not considered possible for HR to be fully accountable in the same terms as other functional areas, as its performance could not easily be measured or quantified in financial terms or business metrics (Key Concept 4.2). This belief has not served the cause of the HR function well, making it difficult for HR managers to demonstrate the value of the function's contribution to the business and to compete for resources. It is, however, a position that is changing, as there has been increasing recognition of the need to assess the contribution of strategies to manage human resources (often referred to as human capital management) to the bottom line. This highlights that, while there is no consensus on a set of universally relevant indicators, there is growing agreement that the performance of human resources is linked to practice in areas such as recruitment, training and development, remuneration and job design. These, it is argued, need to be measured and reported combining hard (quantifiable) data with narrative (Kingsmill, 2003). In the UK this has been reinforced by the move to introduce regulations requiring human capital management reporting to become a statutory requirement for listed companies as part of their operating financial review (Department for Trade and Industry, 2004; Key Concept 4.2).

Linked to the perception that some things are impossible to measure is the, often unfounded, assumption that an organisation's members do not possess the necessary skills to produce a credible or competent evaluation. This may lead to a belief that to acquire the necessary skills is likely to be both time consuming and costly or that an evaluation must involve the use of expensive external consultants.

The perceived lack of a need to evaluate

The perceived lack of a need to evaluate is often characterised by the phrase: 'we know the impact will be positive'. This is especially the case for interventions that are fashionable. Not surprisingly, writers such as Asch and Salaman (2002) caution that 'fashionable' ideas may not always be good. An intervention which fails to identify, or takes a simplistic view of, the origins and nature of HR difficulties, may simply replace one set of problems with another. Despite this there is often little or no evidence of a detailed or considered assessment of either the organisational need or the appropriateness of particular HR strategies before they are introduced. Given that the academic and practitioner literature promote the beneficial effects of HR initiatives and the positive experiences of others, it is not surprising that senior managers responsible for initiating the process often begin from the premise that there is an inherent value in the initiative in question (Brunnson and Olsen, 1998) and that benefits will therefore inevitably result from their implementation of a new or revised strategy.

In situations where managers are under increasing pressure, 'quick fixes' may be attractive (Swanson, 1997) and it may appear easier to imitate rather than innovate (Brunsson and Olsen, 1998). This unquestioned belief also serves to reduce the perceived need to evaluate formally as those responsible already 'know' the effect will be positive (Skinner, 2004). The power and impact of such assessments is recognised widely in the literature. Writing about the measurement of business excellence, Kanji (2002) observes

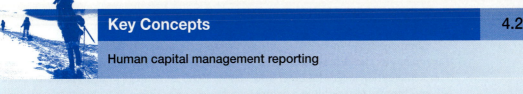

Key Concepts   4.2

Human capital management reporting

Human capital management reporting is based on the premise that, if an organisation's human capital drives its success, human capital should be reflected in the organisation's annual report. Within the UK, the government set up a task force 'Accounting for People' in January 2003 to:

- look at the performance measures used to assess investment in human capital;
- consider best practice in human capital reporting, and performance measures most helpful to stakeholders;
- establish and champion the business case for such reports.

The task force published its report in November 2003. In this they recommended that reports on human capital management should be balanced and objective, following a process which could be audited. In particular reports should:

- be strategic in focus;
- communicate the board's understanding of the links between human capital management policies and practices and its business strategy and performance;
- include information on:
  - workforce size and composition;
  - motivation and retention of employees;
  - competences, necessary skills and training;
  - remuneration;
  - fair employment practices;
  - leadership and succession planning;
- provide information that enables comparison over time using commonly accepted definitions where appropriate.

However, while the requirements published by the Financial Reporting Council state that the operating financial review should include information about employees, policies and the extent to which these have been successfully implemented; it does not define the precise content (Accounting Standards Board, 2005). These major references to employee reporting appear in a separate guide that is not part of the standard itself.

Sources: adapted from Kingsmill (2003); Scarborough (2003); *People Management* (2005a).

that 'gut feelings' rather than fact and measurement are the basis of too many management decisions. Such informal evaluations are made on the basis of unverified information, experience, instinct or the opinion of the most influential people rather than on information extracted correctly from reliable data (Conti, 1997). Easterby-Smith (1994) notes also a preference of managers, particularly at senior levels, for information received via their own informal information channels and observes that this information tends to be far more influential than that produced via more formal channels. Clark and Salaman's (1998) ideology of management reinforces the belief of managers in the value of their own judgements, making them unlikely to question their own interpretations or to acknowledge the limits of their own understanding. These factors serve not only to undermine a perceived need for a planned evaluation but may also mean that objectives and expected outcomes of SHRM initiatives are unclear and unarticulated.

Compounding this lack of a perceived need to evaluate formally among senior management is the focus of senior management on the initiation rather than implementation stages (Skinner and Mabey, 1997) of strategic human resource initiatives. This may also result in a failure to define success criteria or to assign responsibility for monitoring progress. Russ-Eft and Preskill (2001) note that, in their experience, the number one reason people give for not undertaking an evaluation is that no-one requires it. Managers at all levels of organisations struggle constantly with the pressure to succeed and the pressure of time (Swanson, 1997). Consequently, time for evaluation may appear an indulgence. Managers have limited resources available and, in the interests of their own security, satisfaction and longer-term goals are likely to use their resources in pursuit of outcomes and activities which they perceive to be valued by those in a position to reward success. They are therefore unlikely to undertake activities that they consider are not seen as priorities in the minds of their superiors and for which they have not been given specific responsibility or resources.

Allied to the discussion of the lack of a perceived need to evaluate is the implicit recognition that, for many, evaluation is an afterthought. You will probably have noticed that, in many of your HRM textbooks, discussion of evaluation occurs rarely and, if it does, tends to appear towards the end. The implication is that evaluation of HR strategies and associated interventions is something that is only thought about after the event has happened and is not central to the implementation process. However, the end of the

In Practice   4.2

Difficulties of measurement

During research relating to the evaluation of HR change initiatives, undertaken by Skinner (2004), managers in two organisations made the following comments with regard to problems associated with measurement:

A higher education institute

I don't think that managers are encouraged to think in evaluative terms and I think little of the literature suggests any kind of systematic approach. ... I mean, I've worked in a number of soft change areas and I think it's particularly hard to pin down evaluation techniques that are useful for those areas.

A government agency

... there are no established measuring devices for the less tangible criteria.

We don't tend to evaluate 'touchy-feely'.

There are some people that say it can't be measured because it's about people's views and feelings and that's not objective data ...

... we can't measure people's feelings and views.

implementation is the point at which those who have been involved are likely to be looking towards the next project and evaluation of what is perceived as a past event is not high on their personal agenda. In addition, if an evaluation process is not included in implementation plans from the beginning it is unlikely that thought will have been given to the systems, processes and resources that will be needed to collect information that will enable the evaluation to take place.

The difficulties associated with dealing with negative outcomes

The difficulties associated with dealing with negative outcomes provide the final category of reasons why evaluation of SHRM initiatives may not happen. For many HR managers, their previous experience of evaluation has been negative and divisive rather than as a positive process of improvement and shared learning. This is largely due to the blame culture which exists in a wide range of companies (In Practice 4.3). Bloomfield (2003) characterises such cultures as ones in which it is sensible to keep your head down, cover your back, do your best to hide mistakes, or, at the very least, ensure there is always someone else to share the blame. Not surprisingly, the expectation is that any planned, explicit evaluation will inevitably focus upon accountability and this will inexorably lead to criticism and the apportioning of responsibility for failure. As Tyson (1999) notes, managers are more than passive bystanders when it comes to the importa-

In Practice   4.3

Learning from accidents – the Ladbroke Grove train crash

On 5 October 1999 at Ladbroke Grove junction, about two miles west of Paddington Station, London, there was a head-on crash between two trains travelling at high speed. This crash caused the death of 31 people and injured over 400 others. The findings of the public inquiry into the Ladbroke Grove rail crash were reported in 2001. In its consideration of essential elements for the management of safety on Britain's railways, the report indicated that a high proportion of accidents, incidents and near misses followed unsafe actions resulting from underlying deficiencies in the management of safety. The evaluation report highlighted the existence of a blame culture within the rail industry in which there was a tendency to attribute blame rather than to seek to understand what had occurred and the reasons behind it. This, it was argued, inhibited proper investigation of rail accidents and incidents, and the open sharing of information. The blame culture was also said to deter staff from reporting non-serious accidents.

Lord Cullen, who chaired the inquiry, identified the need for the blame culture to be replaced by one of continuous learning in which the rail industry should study the lessons from previous accidents, near misses and other incidents in order to prevent them from recurring. In addition, the industry needed to establish clear and consistent processes to enable that to happen. The lessons that were learned from accidents, near misses and other incidents should be shared subsequently with all parts of the industry, and actions taken to prevent them being repeated. Regardless of whether they were major or minor incidents, the report said that accidents and other failures of procedures and systems provided an opportunity for a company or an industry to learn from its mistakes.

Source: adapted from Cullen (2001).

tion of new ideas, often selecting, reinterpreting and giving relative emphasis to ideas according to their own agendas. For these reasons, they become the obvious targets in a blame culture. Inevitably on this basis, defensive reasoning and routines at both an individual and an organisational level (Argyris, 1994) are unlikely to encourage the pursuit of planned, explicit, evaluation of strategic human resource management. HR managers are likely to be aware of the risks involved in terms both of personal criticism and of the activity being unpopular with peers and others who may also feel vulnerable.

Aspects of SHRM that need to be evaluated

The question that most probably arises at this stage is: 'Which aspects of SHRM should be evaluated?' It would, perhaps, appear unconvincing to answer 'all of them'. However, if an HR intervention is of strategic importance to an organisation, then the organisation needs to evaluate its impact. For some aspects of SHRM, such as recruitment and selection (Chapter 8) and human resource development (Chapter 10), data may already be collected and held on the organisation's human resource information system (In Practice 4.4). In such instances, the key issues will be ensuring that:

● the data held is both up to date and relevant;

● routine monitoring using these data are undertaken;

● the findings from the routine monitoring are acted upon.

For other aspects, such as the introduction of a new performance management system (Chapter 9) or the impact of an organisational downsizing on those who remain employed (Chapter 14), data are likely to need to be collected specifically to evaluate parts of that strategy. Similarly, for specific training interventions (Chapter 10), it is

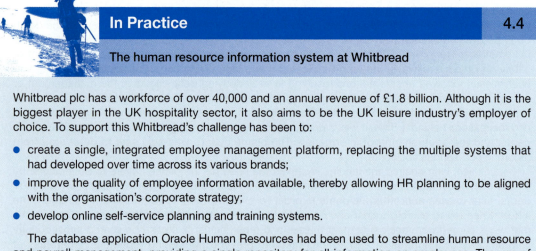

In Practice   4.4

The human resource information system at Whitbread

Whitbread plc has a workforce of over 40,000 and an annual revenue of £1.8 billion. Although it is the biggest player in the UK hospitality sector, it also aims to be the UK leisure industry's employer of choice. To support this Whitbread's challenge has been to:

● create a single, integrated employee management platform, replacing the multiple systems that had developed over time across its various brands;

● improve the quality of employee information available, thereby allowing HR planning to be aligned with the organisation's corporate strategy;

● develop online self-service planning and training systems.

The database application Oracle Human Resources had been used to streamline human resource and payroll management, providing a single repository for all information on employees. The use of Oracle's iLearning package allows staff to train at their own pace, while minimising disruption at work. Through these IT-based systems, Whitbread has been able to meet the challenges outlined above.

Source: developed from Allen (2005).

likely to be necessary to design evaluation strategies that measure the impact of the intervention on employees' performance, rather than whether or not the participants felt the trainer helped them to learn!

Undertaking the evaluation

The purpose of evaluation

Business research textbooks, for example Saunders *et al.* (2007), often place research projects on a continuum according to their purpose and context (Figure 4.2). At one end of this continuum are evaluations undertaken to advance knowledge and theoretical understanding of processes and outcomes including SHRM. This basic research is therefore of a fundamental rather than applied nature, the questions being set and solved by academics with very little, if any, focus on use of research findings by HR managers. At the other end are evaluations that are of direct and immediate relevance to organisations, address issues which they consider to be important and present findings in ways which can be understood easily and acted upon. This is usually termed applied research and is governed by the world of practice. The evaluation of SHRM is, not surprisingly, placed towards the applied end of this continuum. Such research is oriented clearly towards examining practical problems associated with strategic HR interventions or making strategic decisions about particular courses of action for managing human resources within organisations. It therefore includes monitoring of operational aspects of HRM such as absence (Chapter 9), turnover and recruitment (Chapter 8), thereby helping organisations to establish what is happening and assess effectiveness of particular HR interventions.

Evaluation should take place as an integrated part of the ongoing monitoring of existing HR policies or procedures as well as during the introduction and implementa-

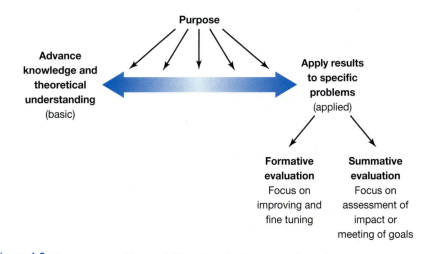

Figure 4.2 The purpose and focus of different evaluation approaches
Source: adapted from Thornhill *et al.* (2000).

tion of new HR policies or procedures. Evaluation where the focus is on improving and fine tuning is often referred to as formative evaluation (Table 4.1). In such cases data collection is often undertaken as part of regular ongoing measurement of an organisation's performance. For example, where a balanced scorecard approach (Kaplan and Norton, 1992; Huselid *et al.*, 2001) is adopted, data are collected on those measures that are considered to be most critical to that organisation's vision for success (Key Concepts 4.3). This is likely to include HR strategies such as learning and development and its ability to enhance the organisation's future leadership capabilities, or the extent to which the management of employee performance enables revenue growth. That which occurs towards the latter stages, perhaps to assess impact, determine the extent to which goals have been met or establish whether to continue with the intervention is termed summative evaluation. For such evaluations, data collection is likely to be less frequent or regular.

Key Concepts 4.3

The balanced scorecard

Balanced scorecards are an organisation-specific tool designed to monitor the impact of management's actions from four strategic perspectives (Ritter, 2003):

- financial – how do shareholders see the organisation?
- customer – how do customers see the organisation?
- internal processes – what must the organisation excel at?
- human resources, learning and innovation – can the organisation continue to improve and create value?

Devised in the early 1990s, the scorecard aims to provide an integrated view of an organisation's performance, including both financial and non-financial indicators, and from both internal and external perspectives (Kaplan and Norton, 1992).

Measures included in the scorecard are designed to focus employees and managers on the overall strategic vision of the organisation. Data overload is prevented by minimising the number of measures used but, at the same time, managers are forced to consider all the data together (Kaplan and Norton, 1992).

Within any evaluation, it is important to establish the purpose of both the evaluation and the strategic HR intervention or process that is being evaluated. Easterby-Smith (1994) defines four possible purposes of an evaluation but cautions that it is unrealistic to expect any evaluation to serve more than one. These are:

- *improving* where the need is to identify what should happen next;
- *controlling* is about monitoring for quality and efficiency;
- *proving* involves measuring and making judgements about worth and impact;
- *learning* in which the process of evaluation itself has a positive impact on the learning experience.

It would, however, be dangerous to assume that the identification of purpose will be straightforward. Many strategic HR initiatives lack either clear objectives or stated success criteria. This may make it difficult to identify what should be evaluated and how. Often evaluations need to include a variety of stakeholders, not all of whom may wish to pursue the same purpose. In addition, individuals and groups may not be able or willing to share their true intentions or expectations with each other or those who are undertaking the evaluation.

The context of evaluation

Not surprisingly, given the discussions in the previous paragraph, it is also important to identify who the stakeholders are in relation to the HR initiative being evaluated and the evaluation itself. Any changes resulting from the evaluation are likely to affect a range of individuals and groups who are likely to be both internal and external to the organisation. These stakeholders are likely to differ in the extent of their interest, their priorities and their level of influence for, as Easterby-Smith (1994) observes, any evaluation process is a complex one which cannot be divorced from issues of power, politics and value judgements. Organisational politics can affect any stage of an evaluation (Russ-Eft and Preskill, 2001) from influencing the decision to evaluate through to the way in which the findings are used. In any evaluation there is likely to be a commissioning or dominant stakeholder or stakeholder group (often referred to as principal client or sponsor) and in an organisational setting this is often a management group. However, the nature of HRM strategies and initiatives is such that in each case there will be others who have both a legitimate interest and a stake in the findings of any evaluation process. Not least, those managers and employees whose participation in the evaluation is necessary and who, through sharing their views and experience, might feel that they were owed access to the findings they had helped create as well as those who will use the evaluation findings.

Identifying the intended audience for the findings is important in terms of understanding expectation, defining purpose, involving those who need to participate and in providing feedback in an appropriate way. Although not a barrier to evaluation in itself the way in which the findings are used inevitably determines the effect, if any, that an evaluation has. Patton (1997) goes so far as to suggest that evaluations ought to be judged on their actual use, for as we will discuss in more detail in 'Analysing and feeding back, later in this chapter, non-utilisation of findings is a commonly identified and widely bemoaned problem. In this context, it is only realistic to recognise that it is the values of the commissioner and intended users, those who have the responsibility to apply evaluation findings and implement recommendations that need to frame the evaluation. This need not, however, preclude responding to the needs of other stakeholders. Evaluation can serve an important function in facilitating bottom-up feedback, ensuring that the experience of those on the receiving end of strategies is captured and shared outside their immediate peer group and used to refine the strategy.

Evaluation can take place at a number of different levels based upon its focus. Although the labels used differ, evaluation models in effect distinguish between levels that range from an operational level measuring reactions through to a more strategic focus on organisational performance. Developed in 1959 in relation to training evaluation, Kirkpatrick's model is still the most widely recognised (Phillips, 1991; Russ-Eft and Preskill, 2001). This highlights that evaluation can be undertaken to assess operational interventions (level 1 and occasionally 2), to support medium-term or tactical interventions (level 3 and occasionally level 2) or it can focus on more strategic interventions (level 4). As can be seen from Table 4.2, Kirkpatrick's first two levels focus on the effectiveness of the intervention as judged by the recipients. They relate primarily to the operational level and while they may affect the design of the HR intervention, such as a training event, evaluation at these two levels is unlikely to have any strategic impact. In contrast, evaluation at levels 3 and 4 have an increasingly strategic impact. These consider the effect of the process or policy being evaluated on the wider organisation, the achievement of its goals and ultimately the implications for organisational performance. Subsequent researchers, for example Hamblin (1974), have added a further strategic level of evaluation (5) which focuses on the wider contribution the organisation is now able to make. However, despite these observations, it is worth noting that Kirkpatrick did not describe his model originally as hierarchical or suggest that one level would impact upon the next.

Table 4.2 Levels of evaluation

Level	Measures	Comment	Impact
1	Reaction	Commonly measured soon after a training programme. Although this measurement is often referred to rather derisively as 'happy sheets', it provides an assessment of participants' reaction to the programme	Operational
2	Learning	Measures amount participants believe they have learned but does not measure whether the learning or the training has contributed to the organisation in any way	Operational to tactical
3	Behaviour	Measures behaviour change that has happened since the training: whether what has been learned transferred into the workplace	Tactical
4	Result	Assesses the impact of the training on the achievement of organisational goals	Strategic

Sources: adapted from Phillips (1991); Russ-Eft and Preskill (2001).

Clarity of purpose and evaluation strategies

In terms of approach, as with any evaluation, decisions have to be made regarding the techniques to be used to collect data. These should reflect the choices that have been made in relation to the topics covered in the preceding section. In terms of evaluation, the use of sound method and reliable data are critical (Stern, 2004). The decision about purpose will also determine whether the evaluation needs to be formative or summative in nature. A formative evaluation takes place during the implementation with the intention of feeding back into the process and improving both the process and the outcomes of the initiative where appropriate. A summative evaluation usually occurs at the end of the implementation and is about determining the worth or value of what has been done, whether success criteria were met, if the results justified the cost. It would therefore be possible to undertake both a formative and summative evaluation of the same initiative.

The importance of a clear purpose

Probably the most difficult aspect of any evaluation is coming to a clear understanding of what is being evaluated and why; in other words the precise purpose and objectives (Saunders *et al.*, 2007). However, this issue is often bypassed within the evaluation process. For example, typical corporate measures of the success of a redundancy programme are often related to profit, production levels, return on investment and perhaps customer satisfaction (Chapter 14). A numerical rise in such measures may be interpreted as the programme being successful and, perhaps, having a positive impact on employee commitment. However, these numbers do not actually measure employees' commitment to the organisation or any link between redundancies and commitment. Similarly, training courses are often evaluated in terms of the trainees' enjoyment and thoughts on the perceived usefulness of the intervention rather than the impact upon their observed behaviour in the work environment (Chapter 10). Simply enjoying a training intervention does not prove that it is effective, unless producing enjoyment is one of the aims (Rushmer, 1997).

One way of helping ensure clarity of purpose and objectives is to spend time establishing and agreeing these with the sponsor of the evaluation. This is unlikely to be as easy as it might seem and will be time consuming. As part of the process, it can be argued that it is essential to ensure that both the person undertaking the evaluation and the sponsor have the same understanding. Another, and equally important, aspect of ensuring clarity of purpose relates to the understanding and insight the person undertaking the evaluation brings. While her or his previous experience is likely to be important, this understanding is also likely to be drawn from reading about others' experiences in similar situations; a process more often referred to as reviewing the literature. Indeed, your reading of this book is based upon the assumption that you will be able to apply some of the theories, conceptual frameworks and ideas written about in this book to your strategic management of HR.

Evaluation strategies

Once a clear purpose for evaluation has been established, a variety of evaluation strategies may be adopted. Typically, evaluations are concerned with finding out the extent to which the objectives of any given action, activity or process, such as the introduction of a new training intervention, has been achieved. In other words, it is concerned with testing the value or impact of the action, activity or process, usually with the view to making some form of recommendation for change (Clarke, 1999). As part of the evaluation, it is necessary to gather data about what is happening or has happened and analyse them. This can be undertaken either as a snapshot or longitudinally using a variety of data collection techniques such as interrogating existing HR databases, interview, question-naire and observation. Findings based upon the analysis of these data are subsequently disseminated back to the sponsor whose responsibility it is to take action (In Practice 4.5). Consequently, there is no specific requirement upon those involved in the research to take action (Figure 4.3). This is in contrast to action research which will be discussed later.

In Practice 4.5

Evaluation at Barclays Edotech

Barclays Edotech is part of Barclays Technology Services, the division that is responsible for service delivery, production and marketing of information technology services principally to the Barclays Group. Each year, employees at the Computer Centre have taken part in the annual staff attitude survey for the division. The aims of this survey are outlined clearly in the letter that accompanies the questionnaire, with a strong focus upon identifying strengths and areas that require improvement. The content of the questionnaire remains substantially the same between years to enable comparisons. Approximately 80 questions are used to ascertain employees' views on areas of leadership, policy and strategy, people management, resources and processes, customer satisfaction, people satisfac-tion, the impact of the organisation upon society and business results.

In the late 1990s, consideration of the data from the annual staff attitude survey and an additional local staff survey indicated HR interventions required revision, in particular with regard to production staff salary grades, people management, leadership, and policy and strategy. Based upon this, actions were planned. These included:

- a review of salary grade bandings so that staff could be rewarded according to their skills and responsibilities;
- walkabouts by management team members;
- the introduction of regular question-and-answer sessions at which staff could raise local issues with a senior site manager.

These interventions were evaluated using a range of techniques including subsequent annual staff attitude surveys and the business excellence model self-assessment process. Findings indi-cated improvements of at least 25 per cent in the areas of people management, leadership and policy strategy and suggested that the interventions introduced were having a positive impact (Thornhill *et al.*, 2000).

Saunders *et al.* (2007) emphasise that, when making choices, what matters is not the label attached to a particular strategy, but whether the strategy is appropriate to the pur-pose and objectives. In particular, the use of a sound evaluation strategy and the collection of reliable data are critical (Stern, 2004). Four evaluation strategies tend to be used in the evaluation of SHRM:

- survey;
- case study;
- experiment;
- existing (secondary) data.

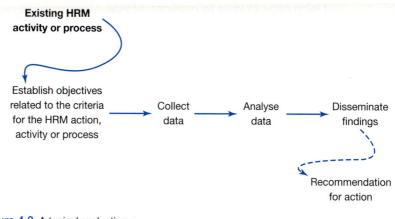

Figure 4.3 A typical evaluation
Source: adapted from Thornhill *et al.* (2000).

Each strategy should not be thought of as mutually exclusive, for example a case study in an organisation may well involve using a survey to collect data and combine these data with existing (secondary) data from the organisation's HR information system. Similarly, an experimental design, such as testing the relative impact of a number of different HR interventions, will often be undertaken using a number of different case studies. In addition, these strategies can be applied either longitudinally or cross-sectionally. The main strength of a longitudinal perspective is the ability it offers to evaluate the impact of SHRM interventions over time. By gathering data over time, some indication of the impact of interventions upon those variables that are likely to affect the change can be obtained (Adams and Schvaneveldt, 1991). In contrast a cross-sectional perspective seeks to describe the incidence of a particular phenomenon or particular phenomena, such as the information technology skills possessed by managers and their attitude to training, at one particular time.

Using surveys to evaluate SHRM

Surveys are perhaps the most popular strategy for obtaining data to evaluate SHRM interventions. Using this strategy, a large amount of data can be collected from a sizeable population in an economic way (Saunders *et al.*, 2007). This strategy is often based around a questionnaire. Questionnaires enable standardised data to be collected, thereby allowing easy comparison. They are also relatively easily understood and perceived as authoritative by most employees. However, the questionnaire is not the only data collection technique that can be used within a survey strategy. Structured observations, such as those frequently associated with organisation and methods (O&M) evaluations and structured interviews involving standardised questions can also be used.

Survey questions can be put to both individual employees and groups of employees. Where groups are interviewed, their selection will need to be thought about carefully. We would advocate taking a horizontal slice through the organisation to select each group. By doing this, each member of an interview group is likely to have similar status. In contrast, using a vertical slice would introduce perceptions about status differences within each group (Saunders *et al.*, 2007).

Using case studies to evaluate SHRM

Robson (2002: 178) defines case study as 'a strategy for doing research which involves an empirical investigation of a particular contemporary phenomenon within its real life context using multiple sources of evidence'. This strategy is widely used when researching the impact of HR interventions within an organisation or part of an organisation such as a division. The data collection techniques used can be various including interviews, observation, analysis of existing documents and, like the survey strategy, questionnaires. However, this is not to negate the importance of comparative work, benchmarking or setting a case study in a wider organisational, industrial or national context. This might be achieved by combining a case study strategy with the analysis of existing (secondary) data that have already been collected for some other purpose.

Using experiment to evaluate SHRM

An experimental strategy owes much to research in the natural sciences, although it also features strongly in the social sciences, in particular psychology (Saunders *et al.*, 2007). Typically, it will involve the introduction of a planned HR intervention, such as a new form of bonus, to one or more groups during which as many of the other factors likely to influence the groups are controlled. Comparison is then made between the groups and a control group where the HR intervention has not been introduced. However, although the origins of evaluation practice and theory lie in an experimental strategy, in many organisations, experiments such as that outlined may be impracticable.

Using existing (secondary) data to evaluate SHRM

The increasing use of existing data as a strategy to evaluate SHRM has been facilitated by the rapid growth in computerised personnel information systems over the past decade. These relational databases store HR data in a series of tables. Each table can be thought of as a drawer in a conventional filing cabinet containing the electronic equivalent of filing cards. For example, one table (drawer) may contain data about individual employees. Another table may contain data about jobs within the organisation, another about grades and associated salaries, while another may contain data on responses to recruitment advertisements. These tables are linked together electronically within the database by common pieces of data such as an employee's name or a job title.

Although these data have been collected for a specific purpose, they can also be used for other purposes. Data collected as part of performance and development appraisals might be combined with data on competences and recruitment and selection to support the development of a talent management strategy. As part of this, reports would be produced which match current employees' profiles with future requirements due to likely retirements within the organisation, thereby highlighting specific training needs.

External sources of secondary data tend to provide summaries rather than raw data. Sources include quality daily newspapers, government departments' surveys and published official statistics covering social, demographic and economic topics. Publications from research and trade organisations such as the Institute for Employment Studies at Sussex University and Income Data Services Ltd, cover a wide range of human resource topics, such as performance-related pay and relocation packages.

For certain SHRM evaluations, possible improvements will be sought by comparing data collected about particular HR processes in an organisation with data already collected from other organisations using one or more of numerous evaluation models available, such as the European Foundation for Quality Management's (EFQM) European Excellence Model (Chartered Management Institute, 2004; Key Concepts 4.4). Such process benchmarking is concerned not only with the measure of performance, but also with the exploration of why there are differences, how comparable the data are between different contexts and how potential improvements may be transferred (Bendell *et al.*, 1993). However, where limited appropriate secondary data are available within the organisation, primary data will also need to be collected specifically for the purpose (Key Concepts 4.3).

Key Concepts	4.4

The EFQM European Excellence Model

The EFQM European Excellence Model (known previously as the Business Excellence Model) argues that excellent business performance is dependent upon an organisation's impact on its customers, its people, and society at large. The model provides a framework for business improvement by identifying gaps and weaknesses that require addressing as well as strengths for consolidation and improvement and allows benchmarking against other organisations (Chartered Management Institute, 2004).

The model considers nine criteria:

- leadership and best practice in communication, empowerment and how change and improvement work in the organisation;
- policy, strategy and how organisational values, vision and goals are established;
- people management and how the organisation energises the full potential of its employees to improve their own skills and the business;
- partnership and resources and how they are managed effectively to contribute to business goals;
- processes to deliver products and services to customers;
- people's perceptions of the organisation and how their needs and expectations are met;
- customers' perceptions of the organisation and how their needs and expectations are met;
- society's view of the organisation and what is done to improve this;
- how the above feed into financial results and how targets are met and reviewed.

These are divided into 32 sub-criteria about each of which data are gathered through a variety of possible techniques.

Action research: an alternative to the typical evaluation

An alternative way to approach evaluation is that of action research, within which there is an inherent need for those involved to take some form of action. Action research makes use of the same set of data collection techniques as used for other evaluation approaches. Although it has been interpreted by management researchers in a variety of ways, there are four common themes within the literature. The first focuses upon and emphasises the purpose: research in action rather than research about action (Coghlan and Brannick, 2005) so that, for example, the evaluation is concerned with the resolution of organisational issues, such as downsizing, by working with those who experience the issues directly.

The second emphasises the iterative nature of the process of diagnosing, planning, taking action and evaluating (Figure 4.4). The action research spiral commences within a specific context and with a clear purpose. This is likely to be expressed as an objective (Robson, 2002). Diagnosis, sometimes referred to as fact finding and analysis, is undertaken to enable action planning and a decision about the actions to be taken. These are then taken and the actions evaluated (cycle 1). Subsequent cycles involve further diagnosis taking into account previous evaluations, planning further actions, taking these actions and evaluating.

The third theme relates to the involvement of practitioners in the evaluation and in particular a collaborative democratic partnership between practitioners and evaluators, be they academics, other practitioners or internal or external consultants. Eden and Huxham (1996: 75) argue that the findings of action research result from 'involvement with members of an organization over a matter which is of genuine concern to them'. Therefore, the evaluator is part of the organisation within which the evaluation and change process are taking place (Coghlan and Brannick, 2005) rather than more typical evaluation where, for example, survivors of downsizing are subjects or objects of study.

Finally, action research should have implications beyond the immediate project; in other words it must be clear that the results could inform other contexts. For academics

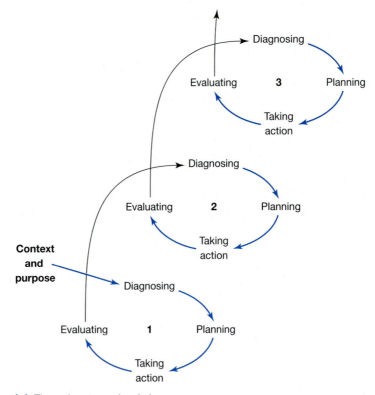

Figure 4.4 The action research spiral
Source: Saunders *et al.* (2007). Reproduced with permission.

undertaking action research the Eden and Huxham (1996) link this to an explicit concern for the development of theory. However, they emphasise that for both internal and external consultants this is more likely to focus upon the subsequent transfer of knowledge gained from one specific context to another. Such use of knowledge to inform other contexts, the authors believe, also applies to others, undertaking action research such as practitioners.

Thus action research differs from typical evaluation due to:

- a focus upon change;
- the recognition that it is an iterative process involving diagnosis, planning, action and evaluation;
- the involvement of employees (practitioners) throughout the process.

Schein (1999) emphasises the importance of employee involvement throughout evaluation processes, as employees are more likely to implement change they have helped to create. Once employees have identified a need for changes in HR polices and procedures and widely shared this need it becomes difficult to ignore and the pressure for change comes from within the organisation. Action research therefore combines both information gathering and facilitation of change. The diagnosis stage is often seen by employees as recognition of the need to do something (Cunningham, 1995). Planning encourages people to meet and discuss the most appropriate action steps and can help encourage group ownership by involving people. These plans are then implemented. Once monitoring and evaluation have taken place there is a responsibility to use the findings to revise the intervention as necessary.

Action research can have two distinct foci (Schein, 1999). The first of these, while involving those being evaluated in the process, aims to fulfil those undertaking the evaluation's agenda rather than that of the sponsor. This does not, however, preclude the sponsor from also benefiting from any changes brought about by the evaluation. The second starts with the needs of the sponsor and involves those undertaking the evaluation in the sponsor's issues, rather than the sponsor in their issues. Such consultant activities are termed 'process consultation' by Schein (1999). The consultant, he argues, assists the client to perceive, understand and act upon the process events that occur within their environment in order to improve the situation as the client sees it. Within this definition, the term 'client' refers to the persons or person, often senior managers, who sponsor the evaluation. Using Schein's analogy of a clinician and clinical enquiry, the consultant (evaluator) is involved by the sponsor in the diagnosis (action research) which is driven by the sponsor's needs. It therefore follows that subsequent interventions are jointly owned by the consultant and the sponsor, who is involved at all stages. The process consultant therefore helps the sponsor to gain the skills of diagnosis and fixing organisational problems so that he or she can continue to improve the organisation on his or her own.

Schein (1999) argues that the process consultation approach to action research is more appropriate because it better fits the realities of organisational life and is more likely to reveal important organisational dynamics. However, it is still dependent upon obtaining data which meet the purpose of the change evaluation and are of sufficient quality to allow causal conclusions to be drawn. Many authors (for example Randell, 1994), have emphasised the difficulties associated with obtaining such data. For example, the data collected may well be unreliable, such as where there are low response rates, or in the case of HR information systems, incomplete or out of date. We now turn to the need to identifying appropriate techniques for obtaining credible data whichever type pf evaluation is being undertaken.

Self-Check and Reflect Questions   4.4

Outline the relative advantages of action research and more typical approaches to evaluation from the perspective of the HR manager sponsoring an evaluation.

Gathering primary data for analysis

The data gathering techniques used need to be related closely to the purpose of the evaluation. For all change evaluations, it is important that data appear credible and actually represent the situation. This issue is summarised by Raimond (1993: 55) as the 'How do I know?' test and can be addressed by paying careful attention to data gathering techniques. This is especially important for longitudinal evaluation as techniques used and the questions asked at the start of a change process may be inappropriate if transformational change has occurred (Golembiewski *et al.*, 1976). For cross-sectional evaluations or evaluations over shorter time periods, the likelihood of techniques and questions no longer being appropriate is far lower. For example, the impact of a management development programme might be evaluated using data gathered by one or a number of different techniques dependent upon the focus of the analysis. These might be cross-sectional, such as in-course and post-course questionnaires and observations by trainers and others, and/or longitudinal attitude surveys and psychometric tests before and after the event. Secondary data regarding employee performance, already gathered by existing appraisal systems, might also be used.

However, before considering primary data gathering techniques, it is important to note that, in practice, evaluators' choices are likely to be influenced by pragmatic considerations. HR managers are often working within a very quantitatively oriented environment, where numbers convey accuracy and a sense of precision. In addition, they may have little experience or training in qualitative methods (Skinner *et al.*, 2000). Consequently, the use of qualitative data can be problematic as managers may not be comfortable with judgements based on such evidence.

Using observation

Where evaluation is concerned with what people do, such as how they respond after a particular training intervention, an obvious way to collect the data is to observe them. This is essentially what observation involves: the systematic observation, recording description, analysis and interpretation of people's behaviour (Saunders *et al.*, 2007). There are two main types of observation: participant and structured. Participant observation is qualitative and derives from the work of social anthropologists in the twentieth century. It has been used widely to study changing social phenomena. As part of this, the evaluator attempts to become fully involved in the lives and activities of those being evaluated and shares their experiences not only by observing but also by feeling those experiences (Gill and Johnson, 2002).

By contrast structured observation is quantitative and, as its name suggests, has a high level of predetermined structure. It is concerned with the frequency of actions, such as in time and motion studies, and tends to be concerned with fact finding. This may seem a long way from the discussion of evaluating SHRM with which this chapter began. However, re-examining the typical evaluation and action research processes (Figures 4.3 and 4.4) emphasises that this is not the case. Both these processes require facts (data to be collected or diagnosis to take place) before evaluation can occur and, in the case of action research, action taken.

We would discourage you from thinking of one observational technique, or indeed any single technique, as your sole method of collecting data to evaluate SHRM. In many instances, the decision to undertake formal evaluation is based, at least partially, on informal evaluation drawing upon observation in which the role of complete participant has been adopted.

However, on its own, participant observation is unlikely to provide insufficient evidence for an organisation's senior management team. Consequently, it is often necessary to supplement observation with other methods of data collection, such as interviews and questionnaires, to triangulate (check) the findings. If findings based on data from different sources all suggest the same conclusion, then you can be more certain that the data have captured the reality of the situation rather than your findings being spurious.

Using interviews

Interviews are often described as purposeful conversations, the purpose being to gather valid and reliable data. They may be unstructured and informal conversations or they may be highly structured using standard questions for each respondent. In between these extremes are intermediate positions, often referred to as semi-structured interviews. Unstructured and semi-structured interviews are non-standardised. Unstructured interviews are normally used for exploratory or in-depth evaluations and are, not surprisingly, also referred to as 'in-depth' interviews. There is no predetermined list of questions, although the person undertaking the interview needs to have a clear idea of those aspects of the change she or he wishes to explore. These are often noted down prior to the interview as a checklist. The interviewee is encouraged to talk freely about events, behaviours and beliefs in relation to the changes and it is their perceptions which guide the interview (Easterby-Smith *et al.*, 2002).

In semi-structured interviews, the interviewer will have a list of themes and questions to be covered. In these interviews, questions may vary from interview to interview to reflect those areas most appropriate to respondents' knowledge and understanding. This means that some questions may be inappropriate to particular interviewees. Additional questions may also be required in some semi-structured interviews to enable the objectives of the evaluation to be explored more fully. The nature of the questions and the ensuing discussion means that data from semi-structured interviews are usually recorded by note taking. However, as with in-depth interviews, audio recording may be used, provided this does not have a negative effect on interaction within the interview (Easterby-Smith *et al.*, 2002).

Using questionnaires

Saunders *et al.* (2007) argue that structured interviews are in reality a form of questionnaire. This is because, like other ways of administering questionnaires, the respondent is asked to respond to the same set of questions in a predetermined order (de Vaus, 2001). Because each respondent is asked to respond to the same set of questions, a questionnaire provides an efficient method of gathering data from a large sample prior to analysis.

Responses to questionnaires are easier to record as they are based on a predetermined and standardised set of questions. In structured interviews, there is face-to-face contact as the interviewer reads out each question from an interview schedule and records the response, usually on the same schedule. Answers are often pre-coded in the same way as those for questionnaires. There is limited social interaction between the interviewer and the respondent, such as when explanations are provided, and the questions need to be read out in the same tone of voice so as not to indicate any bias.

Questionnaire data may also be collected over the telephone, by post, by delivering and collecting the questionnaire personally or, as is increasingly the case in organisations' annual staff attitude surveys, by an online questionnaire. Some organisations use questionnaires developed by external organisations to evaluate SHRM interventions and benchmark themselves against other organisations, for example Cooper, *et al.*'s (1994) Occupational Stress Indicator. Others, either use consultants to develop a bespoke questionnaire, or develop their own in house. However, before deciding to use a questionnaire we would like to include a note of caution. Many authors (for example Oppenheim, 2000; Bell, 2005) argue that it is far harder to produce a questionnaire that collects the data you need than you might think. Each question will need to be clearly worded and, for closed questions (Key Concepts 4.5), possible responses identified. Like other data collection techniques, the questionnaire will need to be pilot tested and

Key Concepts	4.5

Open and closed questions

Open questions are used widely in in-depth and semi-structured interviews. In questionnaires they are useful if you are unsure of the response, or when you wish to find out what is uppermost in the respondent's mind. For example:

Please tell me what you like most about your current job?

In contrast, closed questions, sometimes known as forced-choice questions, provide a number of alternative answers from which the respondent chooses. These are normally quicker and easier to answer as they require minimal writing. Responses are also easier to compare as they have been predetermined:

For the following statement, please tick ✓ the box that matches your view most closely:

	agree	tend to agree	neither agree nor disagree	tend to disagree	disagree
I believe there are 'us and them' barriers to communication in the company now	☐5	☐4	☐3	☐2	☐1

amended as necessary. The piloting process is of paramount importance as there is unlikely to be a second chance to collect data. Even if finance for another questionnaire were available, people are unlikely to be willing to provide further responses.

Self-Check and Reflect Questions 4.5

Outline the advantages that are likely to accrue to an organisation using a range of techniques, rather than just one, to obtain data to evaluate SHRM.

The choice of evaluator

Another important aspect is identifying who should undertake the evaluation. A choice must be made between an evaluator who is an employee of the organisation or an external consultant and, within that, whether the individual needs to be experienced and/or trained as an evaluator, termed in Table 4.3 'professional'. Table 4.3 highlights some of the factors that may be associated with each choice.

Table 4.3 Choice of evaluator

	Internal evaluator: Advantages	Disadvantages	External evaluator: Advantages	Disadvantages
Amateur	☺ Knows organisation ☺ Understands internal processes ☺ Unlikely to be additional salary cost	☠ Vulnerability to dominant stakeholder ☠ Familiarity diminishes ability to question and challenge ☠ Conflict with other duties	☺ May find it easier to be objective ☺ Credibility as perceived as independent ☺ Not reliant on organisation for long-term career prospects	☠ Significant additional costs ☠ Limited understanding of organisation
Professional	☺ Knows organisation ☺ Understands internal processes ☺ Unlikely to be additional salary cost ☺ Well-developed evaluation skills ☺ Credibility within organisation as evaluator	☠ Vulnerability to dominant stakeholder ☠ Familiarity diminishes ability to question and challenge ☠ Conflict with other duties	☺ May find it easier to be objective ☺ Credibility as perceived as independent ☺ Not reliant on organisation for long-term career prospects ☺ Well-developed evaluation skills ☺ Experience of evaluation in other organisations	☠ Vulnerability to dominant stakeholder ☠ Familiarity diminishes ability to question and challenge

Sources: adapted from Nevo (1986); Torres *et al*. (1996).

Analysing and feeding back

Analysis and feedback are important in both typical evaluations and action research. Typical evaluation ends usually with the report and a presentation to the sponsor of findings from the analysis. In contrast, an evaluator involved in an action research project, perhaps as a process consultant, is likely to be involved also in developing actions and revising the intervention as necessary.

Analysis

Analysis of data is obviously a precursor to feedback. While a full discussion of the techniques available is outside the scope of this chapter, some key observations can be made. The most important of these is to ensure that the evaluation is undertaken against the agreed objectives (see 'Clarity of purpose and evaluation strategies' earlier in this chapter).

Analysis of large amounts of data, whether quantitative or qualitative, will inevitably involve the use of a personal computer. It almost goes without saying that those undertaking this analysis should be familiar with the analysis software for quantitative data (e.g. SPSS) or qualitative data (e.g. NVivo) used. However, we believe it is important that those who are going to analyse the data are also involved in the design stages of the evaluation. People who are inexperienced often believe it is a simple linear process in which they first collect the data and then a person familiar with the computer software shows them the analysis to carry out. This is not the case and it is extremely easy to end up with data that can only be analysed partially. If objectives, strategy, data collection techniques and analysis had been better integrated then data could analysed more easily. Another pitfall is that readily available software for data analysis means it is much easier to generate what Robson (2002: 393) describes concisely as 'elegantly presented rubbish'!

Feeding back

Findings based upon data analysis are fed back to the sponsor, usually in the form of a report and, perhaps, a presentation. Where the report contains findings that may be considered critical of the organisation in some way, this may create problems. However, we would argue that to maximise benefit it is important that these findings are fed back rather than being filtered so as not to offend. Typically, especially where large groups are involved, a summary of the feedback is cascaded from the top down the organisation. This may make use of existing communication structures such as newsletters, notice boards and team briefings. Alternatively, if rapid feedback is required then additional newsletters and team briefings might be used. The evaluation sponsor sees the full report of the findings first. Subsequently, a summary may be provided for circulation to all employees or posted on the organisation's intranet. As part of the team briefing process, each managerial level within the hierarchy is likely to see its own data and is obliged to feed the findings down to its own subordinates. Managers at each level are expected subsequently to report about what they are doing about any problems identified, in other words the actions they intend to take.

Schein (1999) argues that such a top-down approach may be problematic as it reinforces dependency on the organisation's hierarchy to address issues identified. If some issues raised by the evaluation are ignored, then employee morale may go down. It also places managers in a difficult position as they are in effect telling their subordinates about issues that the subordinates thought were important. Then they tell them what they (the managers) are going to do about it.

Instead, Schein advocates an alternative of bottom-up feedback that he argues also helps to promote change from within. In bottom-up feedback, data are shared initially with each workgroup that generated them. This process concentrates upon understanding the data and clarifying any concerns. Consequently the focus is on the evaluation rather than the whole organisation. Issues arising from the data are divided into those that can be dealt with by the group and those that need to be fed back to the organisation. The workgroup is therefore empowered by more senior managers to deal with problems, rather than being dependent upon the organisation's hierarchy. Feedback continues with each group in an 'upward cascading' process. Each organisational level therefore only receives data that pertain to their own and higher levels. Each level must think about issues and take responsibility for what they will work on and what they will feed back up the line. Schein (1999) argues that this helps build ownership, involvement and commitment, and signals management's wish to address the issues. In addition, it emphasises that higher levels of the organisation only need to know about those things that are uniquely theirs to deal with. While it may take longer to get data to the top level, Schein believes that this approach is quicker for implementing actions based upon the evaluation.

Thus, a top-down approach to disseminating evaluation findings can enable relatively rapid communication. It also allows management to maintain control of the process and decide the nature of the message, who receives it and any actions that will be taken. By contrast, a bottom-up approach involves employees thinking about issues, deciding and taking responsibility for the actions they will take, and selecting those issues they need to feed back to their line managers. The latter is inevitably more time consuming, but will only work where an organisation's culture allows employees to be empowered by managers to take ownership of the evaluation and any forthcoming actions. However, it would be wrong to think of these two approaches as mutually exclusive. Rather, the approach to feedback like the rest of the evaluation of SHRM needs to be tailored to the precise requirements of the organisation.

Summary

- Evaluation has the potential to make an important contribution in relation to the implementation of specific HR initiatives but also to wider SHRM.
- Evaluation takes place continuously on an informal and personal basis and will affect people's choices and behaviours at work.
- There are a number of valid reasons relating to organisational culture, unchallenged assumptions and previous experience that explain why planned formal evaluation of strategic HR has rarely taken place.

- A planned systematic process of evaluation should be included at the beginning of the implementation process for all HR interventions.

- Within evaluation of SHRM, a distinction can be made between typical evaluations and action research. While both use the same strategies and data collection techniques, action research has explicit foci on involvement of participants and subsequent action. Both can make use of both secondary and primary data.

- Prior to evaluating SHRM, it is important that a clear understanding of the precise purpose and objectives of the evaluation is reached. This needs to reflect the context and purpose of the evaluation and be agreed between those undertaking the evaluation and the sponsor.

- Evaluation of SHRM involves multiple stakeholders and cannot be divorced from issues of power, politics and value judgement.

- Feedback typically involves cascading a summary of findings from the top-down organisation. Alternatively, the findings can be shared first with those who generated the data. This can help promote ownership of subsequent actions. Issues that cannot be dealt with may be fed up from the bottom to high levels of the organisation.

Follow-up study suggestions

1. Choose a large UK quoted company (there are over 1,000, many of which are listed in the financial pages of quality daily newspapers) and visit that organisation's web site. Obtain a copy of that organisation's annual report. To what extent is the organisation's policy towards its employees reported? What quantitative measures are used for human resources?

2. Working with a colleague obtain copies of the evaluation questionnaires used to evaluate two different courses in which you have participated. Examples could be a module on your current programme of study or a one-day training course. Examine these questionnaires carefully and make an assessment regarding the levels of each evaluation. For evaluations that appear to be at the operational level, what would need to be done to address tactical or strategic issues?

3. Using the information in Key Concepts 4.4 as your starting point, consider how the criteria for the EFQM European Excellence Model support the evaluation of SHRM. (Hint: you may find it useful to visit the EFQM's web site http://www.efqm.org/)

4. Use an internet search engine, such as Google, to search for organisations that offer to undertake evaluations of human resource interventions. To what extent do you consider the evaluations they are offering to undertake to have a strategic, tactical or operational focus? Note down your reasons for this.

Suggestions for research topics

1. Despite the evidence, why do organisations fail to evaluate human resource interventions?

2. An exploration of the utility of training evaluations/exit interviews/equal opportunities monitoring in the public sector/not for profit/automotive sector...

3. To what extent does human capital management reporting support the strategic management of human resources: a comparison of companies WX and YZ.

4. A widely recognised problem relating to evaluation is that organisations fail to use the findings. Why might this be so and what can be done to increase the likelihood of findings being utilised?

5. Design an evaluation for an HR intervention in a case study organisation and justify the choices made.

Halcrow

Introduction to Halcrow

Halcrow Group Limited is a multidisciplinary consultancy group specialising in the provision of planning, design and management services for infrastructure development throughout the world. Within this, the Group's main interests are transportation, water, property and consulting. Although Halcrow has a background in civil engineering and associated specialisms, in recent years the group has extended its range of disciplines to cover architecture, project management, environmental science, transport planning and other non-engineering but related skills. Unlike many organisations, Halcrow does not have a mission statement, arguing that their 'purpose … to sustain and improve the quality of people's lives' describes their approach better (Halcrow, 2003). This purpose is underpinned by a series of values which outline those things that are important to the Group: 'Skills and innovation; Enjoying what we do; Delivering within time and budget', codes of business behaviour and business principles.

Halcrow's first projects outside the UK were undertaken in the 1890s, such work now accounting for nearly 40 per cent of an annual turnover in excess of £200 million with the Group currently undertaking projects in over 70 countries. Recent projects in which Halcrow have been involved include the Channel Tunnel Rail Link, road construction near the Stonehenge World Heritage Site, the International Congress Centre in Rome, Kuala Lumpur International Airport, new and refurbished stands for Chelsea Football Club, coordination of wetland conservation and river basin management for the Danube and its tributaries and managing pollution risk from the animal mass burial sites arising from the UK's 2001 foot and mouth disease outbreak.

Halcrow was founded in 1868 by Thomas Meik, the company becoming Sir William Halcrow & Partners in 1941. In 1985 a private limited company bearing the same name was formed, the most recent change being in 1998, when the various Halcrow businesses and departments became Halcrow Group Limited. The Halcrow Trust owns 90 per cent of Halcrow, with the remaining 10 per cent by its employees. Halcrow has grown extensively over the past decade and now operates through a network of 29 UK and 32 international offices. As part of this growth, the number of employees has increased from 1,700 to nearly 5,000 worldwide. Approximately 80 per cent of Halcrow's employees are classified by the Group as professional and technical (P&T) staff who have a minimum of an undergraduate degree in engineering or a related subject. The majority are engineers who are also members of a relevant professional institution or are undergoing training to gain membership. The remaining 20 per cent of employees, including those in human resources, are classified by Halcrow as non-P&T and provide corporate support services.

Halcrow Group's strategy

As a result of restructuring to meet the future needs of the business environment, Halcrow's operations were brought together in 2001 as four main business groups: Consulting, Property, Transport and Water. These operate as a matrix structure across the Group's eight geographical regions, this structure facilitating appropriate employees or teams to be brought together for specific projects throughout the world (Figure 1). Each of the four business groups is led by a management team comprising five people including a Group board director or managing director. Within each business group, P&T staff are assigned to technical skills groups the leader of whom is responsible for their training and career development. Employees are also assigned to an office in one of the regions. These vary in size from less than ten to more than 500 employees. The business groups and regional offices are supported by Corporate Support Services, comprising all the corporate and business support functions, including human resources, and located predominantly within

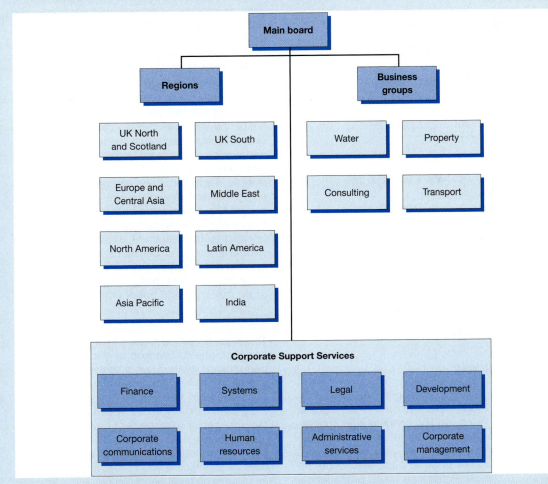

Figure 1 Halcrow Group Limited structure
Source: Halcrow (2004a).

the UK. At the time of writing, the human resource function had 31 employees divided between three teams: Personnel (22), Pensions (3) and Training (6) with a director at the executive level.

In 2004, Halcrow launched its change programme, 'Act now', which was designed to help the Group 'to continue to develop in a dynamic and sustainable way'. The focus of 'Act now' was to align employees' behaviours and approaches to Halcrow's purpose, values, codes of behaviour and business principles thereby improving individual, team and overall business performance. This was summarised in *Act Now: Your Pocket Guide to Halcrow's Change Programme* (Halcrow, 2004b: 8) as:

To take Halcrow's existing personality, strengthen all those things that are good about it, for example, our …
- technical competence
- dependability
- friendliness
- reputation for being a safe pair of hands
- commitment
- pride in one's profession

… and give it some added extras …
- passion
- dynamism
- fleetness of foot
- better listening skills
- excitement
- innovation
- confidence (with a clear sense of self)
- being more celebratory
- consistent delivery to expectation
- greater commercial edge
- being performance driven.

This change programme is intended to be continuous rather than having a specific end date. It emphasises the need for flexibility and the sharing of good practices and learning throughout the Group, the centrality of employees to achieving this, and the need to monitor and evaluate.

SHRM at Halcrow

The 'Act now' change programme is central to everything that Halcrow plans to do in relation to the HRM strategy. The overriding concern is to change the organisation's culture. It is often said that the Group is full of people who are professional engineers and who take pride in a job well done. In essence, technical excellence takes precedence

over commercial success. By the very nature of their training, Halcrow people tend to be concerned with 'detail' rather than seeing the bigger picture. This has served the Group well. But a recent client satisfaction survey commissioned by the Group did not show Halcrow in a uniformly glowing light. It reported that Halcrow emerged as technically excellent and a 'safe pair of hands' but that clients were looking for much more than technical competence and a track record. They wanted business partners whose behaviours were aligned to their own needs. In addition the Group was also seen as rather 'grey'. The challenge for Halcrow is to retain the reputation for technical excellence and reliability while becoming increasingly commercially aware, flexible and, above all, more responsive to customer needs.

Halcrow has designed several key HRM initiatives to support the change programme. These are:

- the development of core competences. This is seen as important because Halcrow employees have traditionally emphasised the importance of professional qualifications above all else. The development of a core competence programme is designed to move the emphasis from what people know to what they can do.

- The introduction of 360-degree appraisal. It is envisaged that this will make a significant contribution the 'Act now' culture change initiative. The Group's culture has always tended to reinforce the importance of hierarchy in that employees have been very conscious of their position in the organisation. In addition, there had been something of an 'ignore and deflect culture' in which people sought to evade responsibility for mistakes rather than being open enough to learn from them. By opening up the system of employee appraisal to people above and below the individual being appraised and by seeking the views of significant other stakeholders, particularly customers, Halcrow management believe that a far greater degree of openness will be developed.

- The instigation of a profit share bonus scheme. This is particularly designed to create in employees a greater awareness of the Group's profit performance. In the view of senior Halcrow management, this has the potential to make a major contribution to fostering in Halcrow employees more commercially aware values. In view of the fact that senior management have set clear targets for increases in Halcrow's profit performance, greater knowledge of the Group's profitability is seen as an effective way of focusing the minds of employees on profit performance.

- The development of 'ideas labs'. This is an important part of the Halcrow management of innovation programme which is designed to promote innovative thinking and enable commercially valuable ideas to be implemented. It is designed to:
  - add value to the business;
  - encourage cross-fertilisation between disciplines; and
  - give staff ownership of the ideas put forward.

Overall, the key change issue that is driving SHRM is the need for Halcrow to be more responsive in the light of a more competitive industry. Therefore, the principal aim of the new HR initiatives is to generate more competitive employee behaviours which, in turn, is envisaged will generate better all-round employee and business performance.

There are other critical issues facing HR at Halcrow. An important one of these is a consequence of customer feedback. Increasingly this shows that customers are taking technical excellence for granted when making decisions about which consultancy group to employ. In view of Halcrow's reputation for technical excellence among customers, this is bad news for the Group. As the HR director explained the world has moved on. Clients are now more demanding and want more all the time. Among the most demanding clients are the public sector. In the UK, Halcrow management feel that the UK government's Private Finance Initiative (PFI) has contributed to change in the industry. (The PFI is a mechanism developed by the government to raise money to pay for new buildings and services. Under PFI schemes a public authority buys the services of private-sector companies to design, build, finance and operate a public facility, such as a hospital. The private-sector companies borrow the money for the scheme and then the government pays an annual fee to the companies under a long-term operating contract for the services.)

Three examples of the more demanding nature of clients are evident, each of which demands an HR response. The first is clients asking for an assurance that the staff commencing work on a project will stay with the Group for the duration of the project. This is a key issue in an industry where the reputation of the consultancy is such that, in effect, the staff appointed to a project can be a more important factor in the client's decision to engage a particular consultancy than the consultancy group itself. The implications for HR are twofold. First, it must assure both external and internal clients that succession planning is in place. In the past this was not an HR strength at Halcrow or other similar consultancies, but is an issue that is now receiving more attention.

The second implication is the problem of retention. There is a shortage of high-quality consultants throughout the construction and engineering sectors and competition for consultants is high. Like the sector in general, staff turnover is high at Halcrow. This is an issue that senior management know must be addressed. The problem is exacerbated by the declining number of construction-related graduates in the UK, the number of students studying relevant courses in the UK dropping by 10 per cent in the late 1990s.

A second example of the more demanding nature of clients is the requirement that companies state their policy and practice on employee diversity and equal opportunities. Again this presents a problem for companies in this sector, like Halcrow, which has been traditionally male dominated and has, until recently, employed considerable numbers of expatriates in its overseas operations. In the UK construction industry as a whole, the proportion of women employed is less than 9 per cent (Egan, 1998).

The third example of client demands is the requirement that companies offer assurances over corporate governance. In the light of corporate scandals such as Enron and Parmalat, this is understandable. The HR response to this is to ensure that global training of key staff to ensure compliance with industry standards takes place. In addition, organisational structure issues, such as the revision of reporting relationships to ensure greater transparency, are receiving attention.

The level of staff turnover at Halcrow and decline in the number of graduates entering the construction-related industry has shaped another HR priority for the Group. This is to define more clearly a people statement that states more precisely what is meant by 'employer of choice'. In particular, Halcrow is concerned about losing high-quality graduates to the financial sector, both at the time of graduation and after they have worked with the Group for a short period. High-quality graduates can earn more money in financial services. In addition, younger graduates are more concerned with the work–life balance issues and their own staff development than were their predecessors. A measure of the siginificance of this issue to Halcrow is the large number of graduates employed each year, this being 133 in 2003. There is also worry over an ageing workforce in the construction industry in general.

It is felt by the HR director that employees and employee issues at Halcrow need to be higher on the list of Group priorities. Staff turnover is now a key performance indicator for the HR director. In her view 'it is no good imposing things upon people at Halcrow – the Group need to win hearts and minds'. This is typical of companies employing a high proportion of professional staff who tend to define, and act upon, their own standards of professional behaviour.

An HR strategy can be seen to be emerging at Halcrow, one that will demand vision and skill from the HR function. According to the HR director these are not qualities which the function has always displayed. She feels that HR has a major job to do because it has been perceived by Halcrow managers as ineffective in the past. Halcrow managers are critical and demanding and expect to receive effective assistance from the service functions. However, the importance accorded to technical excellence within Halcrow had created a culture where service functions, such as HR, were under-valued. Halcrow has traditionally called its staff 'professional and technical' and 'non-professional and technical' – the language reinforcing the message of P&T staff as fee-earners being the most important people in the Group. In addition, the HR function has been largely administrative rather than strategic, a situation that is now changing because of the HR challenges that Halcrow faces. The HR director is very conscious of developing professionalism in the HR team by developing team members' confidence and helping them acquire professional qualifications through the Chartered Institute of Personnel and Development (CIPD). The HR director argues that it is essential to develop a more customer-focused HR team. The lead provided by the HR director is important. Both she and the training manager have experience in leading change programmes in their previous companies. It is also a help that the HR director has a close link with the chief executive officer. This enables her to ask for the support necessary to drive through the HR initiatives. The HR director has also started giving increasing amounts of 'professional' work to her team members. An example of this was a case where redundancies flowed from business restructuring in one part of the Group. One member of the HR team handled all aspects of this. The HR director is also paying attention to mentoring and coaching her team.

International SHRM at Halcrow

Halcrow has a clear strategic aim in relation to its international business. It wishes to be a genuinely international business rather than a UK business with international operations. It is part of Halcrow's corporate business strategy that the Group wants to develop the scale of its international business. The plan is to pursue this growth through acquisitions in countries overseas. Business groups

(e.g. Water) have to prepare business plans which include plans for acquisitions. These plans are reviewed by senior management. Plans with regard to acquisitions have to be coherent with the overall business strategy, particularly in relation to the business sectors in which the companies to be acquired reside.

The scale of Halcrow's international business can be seen from the fact that approximately 40 per cent of the Group's workforce are engaged overseas. In the past, the Group's international staffing policy was to send expatriates from the UK to work on overseas projects. However, in recent years this has altered. The level of expertise of the available workforce in developing countries such as China and Pakistan, and the relative cost of labour in the developing countries compared with the UK, means that this option is now far less attractive. At the time of writing, only 3 per cent of the international Halcrow workforce was UK expatriates.

The Halcrow overseas offices operate as separate companies within the Group, albeit that the UK-based Corporate Support Services provide support to these offices. There has been no HR function in any of these offices until recently. The first overseas HR manager has been appointed in Dubai, UAE, where there are approximately 750 employees in the region. In addition to the small number of expatriate employees and the staff employed in the overseas companies there is a group of transnational employees who come form Halcrow's eastern European, Chinese and Asian operations. The Group has also established a computer-aided design bureau in Dubai.

The fact that there has been no HR function in any of the offices until recently suggests that HR has experienced a very low profile in Halcrow's international operations. In fact, the function in all but the most basic administrative sense has been non-existent. However, the HR director is keen for that to change and is pursuing a vigorous programme of visits to the regional offices within the Group to promote the advantages of HR. A catalyst for this drive is the Group's recently published codes of behaviour. These stress the need for honesty, transparency and integrity in all Halcrow's business operations and state that all employees will:

- Treat everyone with respect, trust and dignity
- Help each other – share experiences and lessons learned
- Be polite
- Never undermine anyone directly or indirectly
- Work together to resolve disagreements
- Be professional and ethical at all times

- Listen to others' points of view
- Be honest and open (Halcrow, 2003: 3).

Two aspects of the code of behaviours are important here: the need to help each other and learn from experiences and to be professional and ethical at all times. It is felt that HR has an important part to play in affecting the values of all employees. The HR director's predecessor did not see promoting the HR role in generating the appropriate code of behaviours as an important activity, but this is now being pursued through the writing of HR policies and disseminating them in the overseas operations. The HR director is also keen to act as a sounding board for international managers and is generally keen to promote the visibility of HR. Gradually, good relations are being built between HR and the international management teams to the extent that they now see the point of taking HR seriously. They can appreciate that having a local HR presence would provide them with useful support. Hitherto there have been no policies as there has been no HR presence. It is felt that it is important to support the regional offices in achieving the Group's strategy of making Halcrow a first choice employer for the best people and the place where its employees want to work.

Evaluation of SHRM at Halcrow

Although Halcrow has had a staff council for nearly 30 years, and through this has involved employees in the formulation of group policy and direction, there has until recently been only limited formal evaluation of HR initiatives including strategic HRM. Training courses were and continue to be evaluated by traditional end of course questionnaires but, prior to 2000, only limited attempts had been made to link evaluation of HR initiatives to the strategic direction of the Group.

In 2000, Halcrow introduced the Group-wide 'employee survey' to measure staff satisfaction, and provide information to help the organisation improve its leadership, management and skills base. This questionnaire is administered biennially to employees worldwide by an independent company, Kaisen Consulting Ltd, who undertake the data analysis, provide Halcrow with a report and, in conjunction with Halcrow, run follow-up workshops. The aims of the survey are outlined clearly in an accompanying letter with a clear focus upon identifying strengths as well as areas that require improvement.

The core content of the questionnaire has remained substantially the same between years to enable benchmark comparisons, although some new questions have been added. In 2004 approximately 30 questions were used to ascertain employees' views on ten key areas. These included the direction (of the Group), clarity about their job, client focus, their competence, resources to do their job, empowerment, involvement, cooperation from others, feedback to them and recognition. Supplementary questions to assess employee commitment were also included. Virtually all questions employ five-point Likert-type scales to record answers. In addition there are spaces for comments and a few open questions to provide further opportunity for respondents to highlight key issues. Locational information such as regional office, business group and skill group, is included to enable comparisons although, to preserve confidentiality, results for a sub-group are not provided if less than three people in that group completed the survey. Response rates for the survey are high, with over 67 per cent of employees worldwide returning their questionnaire in 2002 and 72 per cent in 2004.

Through the 2000 employee survey, Halcrow was able to identify those areas of strategic human resource management highlighted by employees as being most in need of attention. These were: feedback, recognition and involvement of employees. Benchmarking the surveys in 2002 and 2004 against the 2000 employee survey, has allowed Halcrow to establish the extent to which these issues are being addressed through HR initiatives. Results from the surveys suggest that there have been improvements in all three areas. However, data from the survey and other sources suggest that there is still more to be done to improve these and other aspects of human resource management such as employee engagement. Halcrow's senior managers are currently working with Kaisen Consulting Ltd to explore the precise meaning behind these results and develop clear action plans to improve the managerial environment. As part of this they are creating a process through which employees are involved in developing the actions.

Using data from Halcrow's employee survey the consulting company calculates an HR Enablement Index for the Group. This is an average score of responses to all the questions in each of the ten key areas. This index provides an overall indication of the extent to which employees are engaged with their work within the Group. Average scores for each of the ten key areas are then be used to highlight those aspects where satisfaction is relatively low and where action may need to be taken. Comparison of the 2004 HR Enablement Index score with that for 2002 revealed that there had been no significant change in employees' engagement. Retention rate data for the same period revealed that this was within a context of declining labour turnover and led the HR director to ask why engagement had only remained constant in a labour market characterised by a shortage of suitably qualified people? The answer to this question is currently being sought from a range of data including employee exit interviews, staff workshops around the world to discuss issues associated with employee engagement and further analysis of the employee survey data.

Data from other surveys are also used to evaluate SHRM within Halcrow. These include the use of the Business Excellence Model (BEM) self-assessment process (British Quality Foundation, 2001) to help illuminate issues raised in employee surveys, staff workshops focusing upon issues of particular importance, and internal customer satisfaction surveys. In addition they argue that an employee 'feel-good factor' is also important.

A range of secondary data provides further information from which to monitor, evaluate, learn and improve SHRM initiatives. For example, Non Compliance Reports from external auditing by the British Standards Institute (BSI) in relation to quality standards and by clients had highlighted a range of issues. These related to a number of employee inductions not having been undertaken properly and in some cases records of training being incomplete. These have now been addressed. Similarly, the new 360-degree feedback and client satisfaction surveys, such as those discussed earlier, have emphasised the importance of initiatives to ensure employees engage with the company and also understand and empathise with the client's needs.

Increasingly, Halcrow compares itself with other companies in the sector using a variety of approaches. In some instances this benchmarking is undertaken for prospective clients as part of the tendering for new contracts process. For example, the UK Highways Agency uses 'Capability Assessment Testing' to benchmark potential suppliers and assess their alignment to what they require. Informal benchmarking is conducted through contacts in joint-venture companies or other industry contacts to share best practice, discuss issues that are pertinent to the sector such as skills shortages and, through surveys, to establish benchmarking data relating to salaries, benefits and the like.

Halcrow sees monitoring and evaluation as essential to knowing whether or not SHRM initiatives within the 'Act now' programme are effective. Within these means of evaluation, the HR director recognises that the nature of the measures is still evolving and needs to be more closely aligned to the future direction of the Group and the centrality of the human resources to this.

Case study questions

1. Provide a brief overview of Halcrow Group's strategy.

2. Outline the linkages between Halcrow Group's strategy and its strategic human resource management.

3. What obstacles do you think that Halcrow management will face as it works to change the Group's culture from one dominated by technical excellence to one that also embraces commercial awareness?

4. What measures might Halcrow take to increase its retention of young professional graduates?

5. (a) What hurdles do you think that Halcrow will have to overcome in its attempt to ensure international employees adopt the Group's codes of behaviour?

   (b) Now visit the Halcrow Group web site (http:/www.halcrow.com) and read Halcrow's *Statement of Business Principles*, paying particular attention to the Code of Business Practice. Expand your answer in the light of what this tells you about the Group's views regarding business integrity, and what is expected of Halcrow staff.

6. To what extent do the data collected by the employee survey allow the HR director to evaluate the extent to which HR initiatives are supporting the Group's strategic direction?

7. (a) How does Halcrow currently make use of primary and secondary data to evaluate the extent to which initiatives to engage employees within the Group are working?

   (b) What other measures do you think they might adopt?

Acknowledgements

The considerable assistance and support of Mandy Clarke, Director of Human Resources at Halcrow Group Limited, in the preparation of this case is gratefully acknowledged.

Part 2

Strategic Interventions

5

The role of organisational structure in SHRM: the basis for effectiveness?

Learning Outcomes

By the end of this chapter you should be able to:

- define the term organisational structure and evaluate its links to strategy;

- describe and analyse conceptual approaches to the design of organisational structures and discuss their strategic implications;

- identify principal forms of organisational structure and explore their main effects on those who work within them at both a theoretical and practical level;

- analyse the relationship between organisational structure and SHRM.

Introduction

In general strategy terms, one of the most important resources an organisation has is its employees. Within the context of SHRM models and theories a central theme emerging is that people are the organisation's most important 'asset', so how they are organised is crucial to the effectiveness of a strategic approach to the management of human resources. Traditional views about controlling the organisation through structure can be traced back to the early twentieth-century management scientists, such as F.W. Taylor and Elton Mayo. These approaches can be directly linked to a view of strategy making that is essentially top-down. Strategy is developed at the top of the organisation and the rest of the organisation, including the HR function, is utilised as a supporting mechanism in the implementation of the strategy. In this approach to strategic management, the organisational structure becomes a method for achieving top-down control. Such a principle of control is known as *bureaucratic* or *mechanistic*. This chapter considers organisational structure in the context of SHRM. The fact that there is a need to regulate the implementation of an HR strategy is accepted but this needs to take of a wide variety of influences into account. For example the types and range of issues and problems the organisation faces in developing and implementing a strategic approach to the management of its human resources. Key issue to consider include:

- The operating environment of the organisation: it may operate in a highly complex or changing environment or in a relatively stable one.
- How diverse the organisation is, for example the needs of a multi-national company with a wide range of products and services and a globally dispersed customer base will be dramatically different from those of a small local firm.
- How accountable the senior executives of the organisation are to external influences, for example is the organisation a public body, perhaps reporting to a government minister or is it a publicly quoted company reporting to a board of directors and a variety of internal shareholders or is the business privately owned by a family or group of partners who may be owner managers and have complete control over the current and future direction of the business?

If the structure of the organisation is bureaucratic or mechanistic and focuses on the implementation of a top-down strategy, this can have a major impact. In the context of SHRM, a structure such as the one mentioned above may result in the HR function finding it difficult, if not impossible, to operate in a strategic manner: many of the goals will not be achievable, as the ability to influence and develop strategy will be firmly placed at the top of the organisation.

Defining organisational structure

Organisational structure is more than just a way of representing working relationships. Its importance is much more fundamental and strategic to organisations than simply producing organisational charts to show who reports to whom. Jackson and Carter

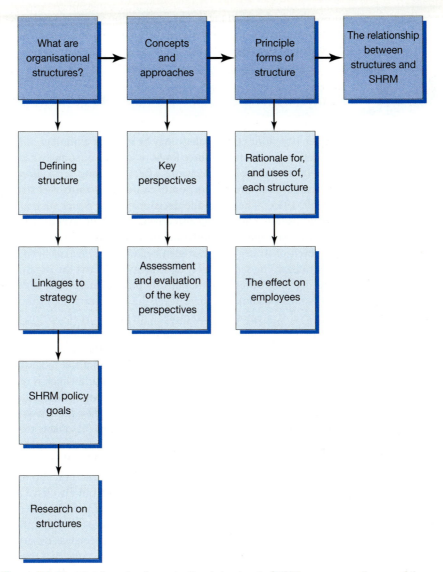

Figure 5.1 Mapping the role of organisational structure in SHRM: a summary diagram of the chapter content

(2000) recognise that, 'without structure there would be no organisation'. At a strategic level, the ways in which organisations are structured affect their scope to interact with their environment and fulfil their strategic purpose, their abilities to operationalise and the nature of working relationships and behaviours in them.

This chapter therefore sets out to discuss four relationships; the aim is to discuss these relationship at both a theoretical and a practical level. This section examines the relationship between organisational structure and human resource strategies, also recognising links to corporate strategy. The next section explores the relationships between approaches to the design of structure and implications for strategic effectiveness. The following section discusses the forms of organisational structure and their effects on those who work within them. The final section summarises the elements of the relationship between organisational structure and SHRM that have emerged through the discussion in the previous three sections.

Organisational structure: linkages to strategy and SHRM

Chapter 1 identifies that strategy may be made at a number of levels in an organisation and that, in general terms, three levels or 'orders' of strategy have been recognised (Purcell, 1989a). First-order decisions affect the long-term direction and scope of the organisation and involve corporate or business-unit-level strategic decision-making (Purcell, 1995). These include decisions about issues such as mergers, acquisitions, market position, cost cutting and downsizing. This level of strategic decision-making is generally taken ahead, or 'upstream', of other types of strategic decision. The second and third levels of strategy are thus seen by Purcell (1989a) as being 'downstream' of corporate strategy. The second level of strategy concerns the organisational structures and operating procedures that are put into place to support first-order decisions, with decisions taken at both of these levels having strategic implications for subsequent, third-level strategies. For example, a merger or cost-cutting strategy will impact on organisational structure and human resource strategies.

The nature of an organisation's structure is therefore an important part of strategy making in practice. Of course, this top-down method to strategy making reflects the classical approach that is discussed in Chapter 1 and which is recognised to be rationalistic and not so perfectly evident in practice. An evaluation of this approach to the formulation of organisational strategy will take place in various places in this chapter. At this point in the discussion, it nevertheless seems reasonable to recognise that organisational structure has strategic implications, whether an organisation seeks to adopt a top-down approach to strategy making or something that is messier in practice, involving recursive relationships between corporate, structural and functional strategies. The structures organisations choose to implement can also have a significant impact on SHRM. The development of key theories relating to SHRM focuses on the achievement of key policy goals or outcomes. Guest (1991) recognises that the four SHRM outcomes specified by Beer *et al.* (1984) (commitment, competence, congruence and cost effectiveness) constitute an 'implicit theory' and go on to construct their own theory of SHRM as a 'particular approach' to managing people. Guest (1991) identified the following as the four key outcomes of SHRM:

- strategic integration;
- high commitment;
- high quality;
- high flexibility.

It can argued that the strategic management of key elements of the HR function, such as recruitment and selection, pay and rewards, training and development, etc., will result in truly strategic HR policies and practices. This is undoubtedly true, but it may be difficult if not impossible to achieve this strategic approach without an organisational structure that supports current and future activities in these key HR areas.

If an organisation wishes to achieve the four key SHRM policy goals previously mentioned it must create, implement and, where necessary, develop and amend an appropriate organisation structure. Let us consider the role that structure may have to play in achieving its SHRM outcomes.

- *Strategic integration* refers to the integration of the corporate strategy and HR strategy. To fully achieve this integration, the most senior HR professional must hold a senior position within the organisational structure, ideally holding a seat on the board of directors or equivalent body and being able to play a full role in the development and implementation of corporate strategy. The corporate strategy should be driven by current and future HR capabilities within the organisation. The reverse of this can occur in many organisations, the most senior HR professional is seen by senior executives as having a solely operational role, does not contribute to corporate strategy development and is faced with a corporate strategy that does not take the organisation's HR capabilities into account. The HR decision, taken by the HR function in this example, can often be reactive and result in very low levels of strategic integration.

- *High commitment* relates to the relationship between employees and their employer, highly committed employees perform at high levels, are innovative and respond very well to changes in the internal and external operating environment. To achieve high levels of commitment, the employer must ensure that their employees remain motivated. A well-established way of doing this is to offer opportunities for career progression through promotions. The organisational structure chosen by an organisation should give high-performing employees an opportunity to gain promotions and establish a wide range of knowledge and skills. If the organisation structure is designed in such a way that it limits opportunities for progression, employee commitment may become low and employees may seek opportunities outside the organisation. This is a problem for the organisation as it may lose high-performing, talented members of staff. Chief executives and senior managers in organisations constantly highlight the fact that staff retention is a major issue in achieving an SHRM approach.

- *High flexibility* refers the range of skills and knowledge of an individual employee or group of employees. Flexibility relates to the context of their current job, their ability to do other jobs that currently exist in the organisation and, possibly more importantly, future tasks and jobs that may emerge in the organisation. In strategy terms, this concept has been covered in the flexible firm literature (see Atkinson, 1984; Thompson and McHugh, 2002). In SHRM, this flexible approach may create an organisational structure that focuses on core and periphery workers. The core reflects the need for the organisation to develop a permanent, highly skilled group of employees with internal career paths. In SHRM terms, 'core' employees experience a high degree of job security, with resource provided from training in company-specific skills not readily available in the external labour market. In contrast, peripheral workers have a low position within the organisational structure, perform jobs that are seen as having little or no strategic importance, are often on fixed-term contracts and appear to be easy to replace.

- *High quality* refers to the quality of goods or services the organisation creates and sells or offers to customers and clients. How high quality is defined will be unique to individual organisations. Quality levels are driven by the needs of the organisation's current and future customers, and the policies and procedures of its major competitors. SHRM can be viewed as being of vital importance to ensuring that the organisation recruits, develops and retains highly talented employees who are the key element in achieving high quality. Organisational structures can be considered as the building block required to facilitate integration at the job, team, departmental and organisational levels. The correct choice of structure can make high quality a true organisational reality; an inappropriate organisational structure can make it difficult, if not impossible, to achieve high quality.

There are potentially a number of different ways in which an organisation may be structured. A number of dimensions or components of organisational structure have been identified from previous research (e.g. Pugh *et al.*, 1968; Child, 1984, 2005). Key Concepts 5.1 briefly summarises some of these dimensions to illustrate the underlying components of organisational structure.

Key Concepts   5.1

The Aston Studies: research that identified the dimensions of organisational structure

Important research on the measurement of organisational structure was undertaken by a group of researchers in the 1960s who were based principally at the University of Aston. Outputs from this research became known as the Aston Studies and were continued by researchers who went on to work at a number of different universities. They developed a number of different ways to measure organisational structure and used these to survey organisations. A paper published by Pugh *et al.* in 1968 identified six primary dimensions of organisational structure based on a review of the literature on organisations. These primary dimensions are:

1. *Specialisation* – this is concerned with the extent to which activities in an organisation are divided into different and therefore specialised roles.

2. *Standardisation* – this is concerned with the extent to which work in organisations becomes subject to standard procedures and rules during its conduct.

3. *Formalisation* – this is concerned with the extent to which such procedures, rules and other instructions and policies about work are written down.

4. *Centralisation* – this is the extent to which decision-making authority is located at the top of the organisation's management hierarchy, known as the locus of authority.

5. *Configuration* – this is concerned with the 'shape' of the role structure in an organisation, in terms of the number of levels in an organisation's management hierarchy, the span of control at each level (i.e. the number of subordinates that report to a manager) as well as the nature of personnel in the organisation.

6. *Traditionalism* – this is concerned with the extent to which the nature of work in organisations is standardised around implicitly understood customs and practices – i.e. that people know what to do based on established traditions that do not need to be written down.

Pugh *et al.* (1968) constructed a series of scales to measure these dimensions in a range of organisations in different industries and services. Their subsequent analysis led to the identification of four basic or underlying dimensions of organisational structure:

1. The extent to which work is structured through the adoption of specialisation, standardisation and formalisation. The nature of work in organisations that scored highly

in relation to these would be highly structured and regulated, through the extensive use of specialised roles and high levels of standardisation and formalisation. An example of this type of structure could the National Health Service (NHS). In the context of the NHS, individual hospital trusts are expected to follow nationally agreed standards of practice and the structure of organisations is formalised to support the achievement of national standards. Within a hospital trust there is also the issue of specialisation: structures will reflect the fact that the organisations employ staff who have specialised knowledge and skills. Three broad specialist areas can be identified in hospitals:

- clerical and manual staff such as receptionists, cleaners and porters;
- professional and technical staff such as doctors and nurses;
- management specialists such as accountants, human resource managers, etc.

2. The extent to which authority is concentrated in an organisation. A structure may be associated with centralised decision-making and low levels of autonomy elsewhere in the organisation; conversely, this may vary along a continuum where organisational structures encourage decentralised decision-making and greater levels of autonomy. Public-sector bodies, such as the UK's civil service, can be considered to have highly centralised decision-making and low levels of autonomy. In the civil service and its various departments, decision-making is very centralised with the rationale being that all the organisation's customers and clients require consistency of approach. In this type of organisational structure, junior managers appear to have little autonomy. At the opposite end, many major retail organisations, such as Tesco, can be viewed as having high levels of decentralised decision-making; at a store level, managers have relatively high levels of autonomy and, although organisations such as Tesco develop an overall centralised corporate strategy there can be significant variations with regard to the implementation and development of the strategy at the store level; these variations may be evident in how employees in stores are managed.

3. The extent to which line management exercise control over work rather than this being exercised through impersonal forms of control, such as operating procedures. This dimension can be evident in organisations in which team working is highly important and the key products or services of the organisation are predominantly developed within the boundaries of this team or department. An example of this is the manufacturing organisation, such as Caterpillar or General Electric, that offers customers a wide range of products and services. Line mangers with responsibility for a team or department that is manufacturing a key product have high levels of control over the work of the team/departmental members. This line management control may also be focused at a geographical level, where line managers will exercise control over all the employees who are in their area or territory. In sales-driven environments, such as retailing, area managers can exercise high levels of control over work.

4. The relative size of the workforce in an organisation's structure engaged in support roles, as opposed to those that contribute directly to the goals of the organisation. This dimension is highly evident within the UK's various regional police forces; within most UK police forces there is now a high percentage of employees who are considered as providing essential support services for the police officers who are contributing directly to achievement of the goals of the organisation. The recruitment of employees who will work in support services for various police forces has in recent years required dramatic changes in the traditional organisational structure of virtually every police force in the UK.

As these underlying dimensions are mutually independent, they were seen as helpful to characterise the nature of organisational structure since each could be applied to understand the structure of a particular organisation.

Child's (1984) later summary of the dimensions of organisational structure reinforces and develops the conclusions from this earlier work. His list of major dimensions includes:

1. The way in which work is allocated to individuals in an organisation. This relates to specialisation, standardisation and formalisation.

2. The way in which reporting relationships are determined. This relates to configuration, including the number of levels in an organisational hierarchy and resulting spans of control.

3. The way in which work is grouped together into sections or departments, and then how these are grouped together into larger operating units and divisions, and finally how these are grouped in the organisation as a whole. This also relates to configuration.

4. The way in which organisational systems are incorporated to integrate effort, ensure effective communication and information sharing, and promote necessary participation.

5. The way in which organisational systems are designed to motivate employees, through appraising performance and structuring rewards, rather than alienating them.

More recent work by Child (2005) recognises that the original emphasis on these dimensions or components of organisational structure remains just as valid as when it was first subject to academic research, nearly 40 years before. The context has changed in varying ways over this period of time, so that the way these components are used in practice has been subject to some change. For example, some organisational forms now lay greater stress on reducing levels of management, through delayering the hierarchy and espousing greater discretion over the carrying out of tasks. They also emphasise leadership as a relationship-based process rather than the exercise of authority, with fewer, perhaps more wide-ranging and possibly unclear, management roles (Child, 2005). In general terms, though, the relevance of these dimensions or components of organisational structure remains unchallenged, which is not at all surprising given that they rest on the observation of organisational practices.

These dimensions indicate the complex range of factors to be understood by managers in deciding how they should structure an organisation's activities to meet its current and future strategic objectives. They also indicate that an organisation's structure will involve the exercise of choice, made by those managers able to influence and control such decisions. A particular structure will be judged as effective if it enables the objectives and goals of an organisation to be realised. However, even these seemingly logical points about organisational structure decision-making are unlikely to be as straightforward in practice. In Chapter 1, Child's theory of strategic choice was discussed (1972, 1997). It must be recognised that strategic choice, including decisions taken about organisational structures, will be constrained by a range of factors, a number of these factors are presented in Key Concepts 5.2.

Decisions taken about organisational structure will be affected by economic, personal and political considerations that reflect the interests and values of the dominant coalition in an organisation. Decisions may also be affected by cultural, psychological and logistical constraints. These may potentially constrain the way managers understand organisational and environmental contingencies and make decisions about organisational structures. These types of constraint are therefore likely to affect choice about

Key Concepts 5.2

Factors constraining strategic choice

- The culture of the business including the leadership style operated.
- The industries and markets the business operates in.
- The level of competition the business faces.
- The level at which the business operates, e.g. local, regional, national, international, etc.
- The size of the business in a number of areas, including the total number of employees, their market share for key products and services, the level of profits the business makes.
- The current and future needs of customers.
- The geographical location of the business.
- The skills and knowledge of the existing workforce.
- The ability to recruit and retain high-performing employees.
- The level of legal regulation at the industry and national levels.

organisational structure. Since organisational structure contributes towards organisational effectiveness and the performance of an organisation, an inappropriate choice will be less likely to enable the objectives and goals of an organisation to be realised. While organisational performance will be affected by factors other than structure, this will have at least some impact on an organisation's effectiveness.

Child (1984, 2005) recognises the adverse effects on an organisation's performance that arise from an inadequately designed organisational structure. He identifies a number of organisational consequences that may arise from structural deficiencies, including those summarised in Key Concepts 5.3.

Key Concepts 5.3

Organisational consequences from structural deficiencies

- *Reduced sense of morale and motivation*
  This may result because decisions about structure are poorly understood, or are seen to be poorly conceived, perhaps because they do not provide scope for employee development, growth, recognition and reward, or because structural decisions fail to lead to adequate job definitions, perhaps associated with role conflict and work overload, or because of some combination of such factors as well as others.

- *Poor quality and delayed decision-making*
  This may result from inadequate mechanisms for integration between different decision-makers in a structure and resulting poor coordination between them, or because of the inadequate transmission of information linked to structural weaknesses, or because decision-makers are overloaded, or because of some combination of such factors as well as others.

▶

- *Ineffective coordination between functions or groups, with the potential for conflict*
  This may result from inadequate mechanisms for integration between parts of an organisation's structure, or because of conflicting objectives between different functions or groups within it, especially where some functions or groups are highly dependent on others. An example may be a group of employees whose work is dependent on information provided by another department but who only receive inadequate information without being able to negotiate any improvement.

- *Lack of adaptability to changing circumstances*.
  This may result from lack of roles within a structure to identify the nature and implications of change, lack of systems and senior management support to recognise and respond to this, and failure to use adaptive structural mechanisms such as project teams composed of relevant experts or involvement approaches to help to develop and implement new strategies.

Sources: adapted and developed from Child (1984, 2005).

For Child (1984), structure needs to be designed to fulfil three requirements, as follows:

1. It should help the organisation to cope with its strategic direction and related objectives, and the environmental circumstances confronting it.

2. It needs to ensure consistency between its constituent parts – organisational structure involves differentiation to cope with uncertainty and different objectives but also the need for overall integration (see Key Concepts 5.4).

Key Concepts   5.4

Differentiation and integration

Lawrence and Lorsch (1967) developed the concepts of differentiation and integration, which help us to understand the functions of organisational design.

Differentiation is the process of subdividing the work of an organisation into different operating units, such as divisions, departments or business units. Each unit focuses on a particular organisational objective or area of activity.

Lawrence and Lorsch found that when environments became more uncertain, managers responded by increasing the degree of differentiation within the organisation to allow it to respond to each of its areas of activity more effectively. Differentiation is associated with the development of organisational subcultures and the design of unit-level operating procedures. Differentiated structures, particularly highly differentiated ones, may lead to conflict between operating units and require appropriate mechanisms to ensure effective coordination.

Integration is the process of coordinating the respective areas of work and operating units within an organisation. As the degree of organisational differentiation increases, so too does the need for greater integration. This may take a number of forms including introducing levels of management, cross-functional teams, working groups or committee structures, as well as corporate-driven procedures and guidelines and other interventions, such as standard human resource policies.

Consistency will be achieved where the level of differentiation is matched by an appropriate approach to integration. For example, a differentiated structure that did not include sufficient integrating mechanisms would be likely to be ineffective. The concept and importance of consistency in organisational design will be discussed further in the following section.

3. Finally, it needs to be adaptable to changing circumstances that affect the organisation. In relation to this final point, Fritz (1994) believes that structure is a key variable to be able to manage change.

These requirements illustrate the strategic nature of organisational structure, demonstrating that it implies more than simply a means to subdivide the work of an organisation and to coordinate the various tasks that result.

If the discussion in this section shows how structure is related to corporate- or business-level strategic decisions, it also begins to indicate how structure interacts with third-level or functional strategies, particularly human resource ones. The extent to which work is structured and authority is concentrated is likely to have a profound impact on those who work within an organisation in the following ways:

- the role of line managers and use of bureaucratic procedures;
- the ways in which work is grouped;
- the nature and use of systems to communicate with, involve, appraise the performance of, and reward participants.

This shows strategic linkages connecting strategy, organisational structure and human resource strategies. Child's reference, above, to consistency, illustrates the importance of this to help ensure effectiveness across these strategic levels. In Practice 5.1 provides an example where inconsistency between organisational structure, human resource strategies and corporate strategy did not occur, with implications for integration between these levels of strategy and organisational effectiveness.

In Practice   5.1

The impact of inconsistency between strategy and structure

A company in the financial services sector, which will be called Finco, invested considerable effort in developing its new organisational structure. This was underpinned by the development of a competences framework that provided the basis for job evaluation to position individuals within the new structure. The intention was to use this competences framework not only to determine employees' grades, and therefore reward, within the new structure but also to link this framework to a range of other human resource management strategies, including recruitment, training and development and career management, for example. The use of the competences framework suggested implications for the way in which work in the new organisational structure should be grouped and for the role of managers. This led to the belief that the new structure in Finco would be more transparent and effective than the one it replaced. These developments held out the promise of greater consistency between the components of its new structure, with positive implications for human resource as well as organisational effectiveness.

However, at the same time as Finco was developing this new organisational structure it was also facing an increasingly tough competitive situation. Finco decided its corporate strategy should be to maintain its market share in this tough climate by competing more on price while also reducing its cost base.

The impact of Finco's strategy now meant that greater emphasis was placed on holding down labour costs and there was also a sharpened emphasis on relating pay to performance. This had a negative impact on the use of the competences framework, which was widely seen by many of

▶

Finco's managers as only likely to produce potential benefits in the longer term, while Finco was placing its new emphasis on shoring up its market share in the short term, through price- and cost-based competition. As a result of this altered corporate strategy, the competences framework became a secondary consideration and the internal, third-level strategies, which had been envisaged to link to the new organisational structure, became less important in practice, crowded out by the need to engage in more aggressive price- and cost-based competitive strategies. The new organisational structure remained but it did not achieve the consistency with other levels of strategy that had originally been envisaged.

These relationships will be considered more fully below but at this point in the discussion linkages between organisational structure and human resource strategies, as well as corporate strategy, may be recognised. Organisational structure will affect a wide range of human resource strategies, such as human resource planning, recruitment and selection, training and development, performance management, reward, employee relations and employee involvement as well as others.

The relationship between organisational structure and human resource strategies may also be considered in relation to other practices that develop in an organisation. An organisation's structure is, of course, composed of people and arguably the managers in a structure have a strong influence on how it works in practice. In this way, the effectiveness of an organisational structure and its links to human resource strategy will be affected by the styles of management that prevail within the organisation. The effectiveness of organisational structure will similarly be affected by the nature of the culture and climate that exists within an organisation (see Chapters 13 and 6). The organisational practices that develop as a result of these influences may, for example, undermine or support a structure designed to encourage employee involvement in an organisation. Of course, organisational structure will help to influence the nature of managerial attitudes and styles and the culture and climate in an organisation. Organisational structure may thus significantly affect levels of employee morale and commitment, the nature of communication between those in the structure, the development of informal, as well as formal, relationships, conflict, and resulting motivation (Child, 1984; Francis, 1994; Fritz, 1994; Mintzberg, 1993).

Self-Check and Reflect Questions   5.1

Drawing on the dimensions of organisational structure outlined above, use the list of potential organisational consequences from structural deficiencies to evaluate the structure of an organisation known to you.

Conceptual approaches to the design of organisational structures for strategic effectiveness

In the section above, the dimensions of organisational structure were identified through previous research and observed organisational practice.

It is important to recognise that organisational structure has strategic and operational implications for organisational effectiveness and performance, indicating that its design is an important issue. This raises a key question about how a group of managers should design the structure of its organisation and what factors it should take into account if the organisation is well established and requires restructuring. The theory of strategic choice suggests that managers will exercise choice in determining structure (Child, 1972, 1997). This approach suggests that organisational structure will be a political process as key managers make a choice based on those factors that reflect their own interests and values where possible. However, such a suggestion is keenly contested by some theorists. In this way, other conceptual approaches have been advanced to explain how organisations should be structured, advocating at least a degree of prescription for the design of structure.

Three other perspectives or schools of thought that offer explanations about the relationship between the design of organisational structure and strategic effectiveness will now be discussed.

1. The first of these perspectives is clearly prescriptive since it claims that a universal set of principles should be used to design the structure of any organisation. This is the *classical universal approach* to organisational structure, which was promulgated in the first 60 to 70 years of the twentieth century (e.g. Child, 1984; Francis, 1994). However, the notion of a set of universal principles to structure organisations was also re-advanced in the 1980s through the publication of the 'excellence' literature (Peters and Waterman, 1982). Some formulations of universal principles suggest an ideal form of organisational structure which, if attained, would restrict, if not eliminate, the need to alter this in response to changing environmental circumstances.

2. The second perspective relates to contingency theory. This theory suggests that an effective organisational strategy and structure will be *contingent* on the circumstances confronting an organisation. Thus, as these circumstances change, there will be a need to alter both strategy and structure (e.g. Child, 1984; Mintzberg, 1993; Francis, 1994). Donaldson (1996) refers to this as *structural contingency theory*.

3. A third perspective relates to the need to achieve consistency between the various facets of organisational design within a particular organisation (e.g. Child, 1984; Mintzberg, 1991, 1993). This *internal consistency* approach places greater emphasis on the fit between the various elements of an organisation's structure in order to achieve strategic and operational effectiveness than its fit to the external environment.

Classical universal approach to organisational structure

The approach can be considered as a development of the so-called 'scientific management' approach in organisations in the early twentieth century which, along with technological changes, led to increasing standardisation of work and the notion that there was 'one best way' to organise it. This approach was designed to increase managerial control over organisational work. A similar idea, focusing on universally applicable principles, was applied to the design of organisational structure. A number of structural principles were advanced which were believed to be applicable in all organisations (see, for example, Francis, 1994).

This classical universal approach, at least as an idea, appears to have been popular for some time, until it was challenged by contingency theory. The work of early contingency theorists (Burns and Stalker, 1961; Woodward, 1965), as well as that of subsequent ones, demonstrated that the notion of universally applicable principles for the design of organisational structures was incorrect. The notion of 'one best way' was in effect substituted by a recognition that the design of an appropriate structure for an organisation will depend on a number of characteristics of that organisation and the environmental factors that confront it. In other words, an appropriate structure will be contingent on the nature of these characteristics and factors.

A body of literature and research, which is known as the 'excellence' literature, emerged in the 1980s and led to the advancement of yet more universal principles. These principles were based on a number of attributes of chosen organisations that had performed successfully, in terms of growth and financial returns, over a number of years. The belief was that if other organisations applied the principles derived from this excellence group, they would also benefit. While a number of the attributes derived by Peters and Waterman (1982) have structural, as well as cultural, characteristics, three of these attributes have particular relevance to structure as follows:

1. The belief that high-performing organisations were adopting 'leanness' in relation to the design of the organisation and its staffing. This concept of leanness has a major impact on how organisations develop a strategic approach to human resource management. It is often associated with a hard approach to SHRM and may require downsizing of the workforce and will require existing or future workforces to be multi-skilled and be fully committed to the current and future strategic direction of the business.

2. A model of accountability based on devolving responsibility through decentralisation while ensuring centralised control over core values and through financial targets.

3. A third advocates the creation of small, empowered teams on a flexible basis, whose sole task would be to find a relatively rapid solution to a significant business problem, rather than working through a bureaucratic or formal route to solve the issue.

Assessing the classical universal approach to organisational structure

The extent to which the publication of the 'excellence' literature and the dissemination of its ideas actually affected the thinking of those who were responsible for making decisions about corporate strategy and organisational structures may never be known. It is the case that strategies related to these principles have been particularly influential in organisations in many countries over the last 25 years. These strategies include structural changes related to leanness such as:

- delayering;
- downsizing;

- decentralisation;
- autonomy;
- team working; and
- flexibility.

The widespread practical adoption of these strategies may therefore be taken as evidence of a tendency towards the adoption and implementation of a universal approach to structuring organisations. However, the use of these strategies may also be explained by other causes. These include changes in organisations' operating environments, such as those related to globalisation, and the subsequent need to increase competitiveness. In addition, some of these structural strategies may be claimed to exhibit a much longer history than some current writing suggests, e.g. aspects of flexibility. Widespread adoption of these structural strategies may be explained by a 'universal' inclination to adopt cost reduction strategies, rather than dissemination of a management theory related to the advocacy of a generally applicable set of principles.

In any case, the universal applicability of these principles or attributes is questionable. Simple, lean structures may be applicable in some situations but not in others. The resulting use of delayering and downsizing (see Chapter 14), aimed at producing lean and efficient organisations which are responsive to their environment, may instead produce under-resourced ones that are associated with what employees view as being difficult environments rather than having the strategic underpinning and benefits associated with leanness (Kinnie *et al.*, 1998). Devolving responsibility through decentralisation may also be inappropriate in particular situations (Child, 1984). This issue will be discussed in more detail later in this subsection. In addition, the reliability of the universal principles or attributes has been questioned because of both the methodology used to derive them (e.g. Raimond, 1993) and the subsequent performance of the 'excellence' group of companies. The nature of these organisations' subsequent performance in changing environmental circumstances has raised questions about any approach to structure adopted by them that does not take into account key current and potential future factors evident in the internal and external operating environments. Organisations successful in one period cannot guarantee success in future periods – not without making changes that adapt them to new circumstances. A good example of this is presented in 'In Practice' 5.2.

In Practice 5.2

The decline of big blue's PC division

International Business Machines (IBM) is the world's top provider of computer products and services. It is ranked in the world's top ten companies by *Fortune* (the leading practitioner business journal); it ranks among the leaders in almost every market in which it competes. The company makes mainframes and servers, storage systems, and peripherals. Its service arm is the largest in the world, and IBM is also one of the largest providers of both software (ranking number 2, behind Microsoft) and semiconductors. The one sector in which IBM has struggled in recent years is its PC division. IBM was the market leader in the personal computer (PC) market during the 1970s and 1980s. The organisation was so successful, generating huge profits, and employing thousands of employees across the globe, that it became known by its senior managers and industry analysts as 'big blue'. The perception was that it had such a large market share that its future operating success would never be in question regardless of the emerging competition. This may have created a false sense of confidence in the IBM senior executives who were responsible for the PC division. This confidence appears to have resulted in complacency with regard to strategic decision-making and necessary changes to the corporate structure required to respond to the dramatic changes taking place in the global PC market. The essential design and implementation of new strategies and structures for a series of key management functions did not emerge. New competitors began to emerge, such as Compaq, Apple, Fujitsu, Siemens and Dell. Dell is now the world number 1 PC manufacturer. These organisations were offering customers more competitively priced products and were developing organisational structures that were much more responsive to the needs of both their customers and employees. The emergence of Microsoft and its new Windows operating system opened up the home PC market and created a dramatically larger global customer base. Bill Gates, founder and CEO of Microsoft, offered to sell his Windows operating system to IBM and he claims they refused point blank and were very dismissive of Microsoft which was at that time only a tiny company employing a very small number of people. Microsoft is now one of the world's most successful corporations and generates billions of dollars in sales every year.

Throughout the 1990s, IBM's share of the PC market decreased year upon year and many people reading this book may have heard of IBM but would not know that they made PCs. Students of business and management in the 1980s and early 1990s would have all been very familiar with the IBM Corporation and, in particular, its highly successful PC division. IBM completed the sale of its PC operations to the Chinese corporation Lenovo for approximately $1.75 billion in 2005. It is possible to conclude that this was an indication by senior executives that the PC division not longer fitted well with IBM's overall organisational structure.

| **Self-Check and Reflect Questions** | **5.2** |

What other criticisms do you think may be made against the classical universal approach to the design of organisational structure?

Contingency approach to organisational structure

A number of contingency factors have been recognised in the literature (e.g. Child, 1984; Mintzberg, 1993). These include the companies' growth rate, size, range of products and services and number of markets in which they operate, including how internationally diverse they are, the nature and impact of the environmental factors that have an effect upon them, and the level of difficulty of the technologies that they use. The subsequent discussion will focus on the organisational and environmental contingencies in order to explore and evaluate this approach to designing organisational structures. Writers on contingency theory believe that where an organisation's structure has not been designed to take account of the demands created by the current and future operating environment and the characteristics of the organisation this will have an negative effect on its effectiveness and performance. Where this approach is applied in practice, it may lead to a wide range of structural solutions. In reality, other factors are likely to make the use of this approach difficult or unachievable. These factors will be discussed later in this section.

A series of structural changes is likely to become necessary as organisations grow and employ greater numbers of staff. Small organisations are likely to be characterised by a simple structure within which there is departmental or role flexibility, and a high level of direction and control from the manager or chief executive, who may also be the owner of the business. For example, the owners of a small restaurant may run the kitchen, wait on tables as well as manage the finance of the business, recruit and train employees. This type of manager will expect a high level of flexibility from the few staff they employ. In contrast, large organisations have traditionally developed their structures to incorporate departmental and task specialisation, delegation of authority, and highly formalised standard policies and procedures. This approach can create a situation of greater internal complexity. This latter type of structure, associated with large organisations, is mechanistic and bureaucratic, as defined by the presence of specialised tasks and jobs, clearly identified procedures and responsibilities, and hierarchical structures. An example of this can be seen in 'In Practice' 5.3.

In Practice 5.3

The changing context of public sector organisations

Examples of this type of situation include organisations such as the civil service and central and local government. The public sector, in general, has been heavily criticised for being mechanistic and bureaucratic. Those individuals who are in senior positions within these organisations are aware that the structures can cause major problems for those who work in them and can make it very difficult to respond to the changing needs of their customers and clients. Historically, the desire of senior managers to make dramatic changes to these types of organisations may not be as great as it is in the private sector simply because of the nature of their operating environments. Traditionally, public-sector organisations have a constant customer or client base, low level of competition, are focused on regional or national markets and appear to have little difficulty in recruiting employees. But things are changing for the public sector, the current UK Labour government has set out clear policies for the restructuring of the public sector. The drive to modernise the UK civil service, and central and local government, has been part of the Labour Party's agenda since its election in 1997. At time of writing, the most recent initiatives are being led by the Chancellor of the Exchequer, Gordon Brown. Key elements already completed include the merger of Customs and Excise with the Inland Revenue and the next phase will see the downsizing and restructuring of various government departments. The central aim is to respond to the criticism of the electorate, groups representing the private sector and government ministers who are keen to see a dramatic reduction in the cost of managing the public sector. Some of the changes have been widespread and involved significant external consultant processes under the title Review of Public Administration. The outcome of this review includes the reduction of the number of councils in local government, reductions in the number of hospital trusts and health authorities, and the reduction in the number of political forces. The practical implication of these changes can be dramatic and will require the merger of current organisations to cover a greater geographical area and also provide a wider range of services. The public in these areas still require these services but the civil service of the future will undoubtedly have a smaller number of total employees as will local government. The mergers of hospital trusts and of police forces will create larger and more complex organisations. These changes to the public sector will require significant change to the existing organisational structures and the creation of new structures to support the creation and development of the new organisations.

In large organisations, coordination becomes a significant issue, as do the design of jobs, the motivation of those who work in such a system and the identification and management of effective performance. In Practice 5.4 considers the reverse of the example given previously of a small restaurant: the opposite of this type of organisational structure might exist in the restaurant of a large hotel.

In Practice   5.4

The structure of a large hotel

For the purpose of discussion, let us use a Hilton hotel as an example. The restaurant in a Hilton hotel is likely to be structured as a department of the business (in this context the business is the hotel rather than the overall Hilton Hotel corporation) with a range of specialist jobs and staff. There will be a restaurant manager who reports to the overall hotel manager. The restaurant manger will be responsible for managing the waitresses and waiters, bar staff, customer service, cleaning staff, etc. Within the context of the restaurant the kitchen is of vital importance; the head chef will have a high degree of control over what happens in relation to this area and the structure should reflect this. In the context of a prestige hotel such as a Hilton hotel, the chef running the kitchen will also have significant expertise and a high degree of autonomy over how he or she manages the staff in the kitchen. The staff in the kitchen are likely to report directly to the head chef rather than the restaurant manager. In this context, the organisation structure will need to reflect the fact that professional staff, such as a chef, are as important as a restaurant manager in achieving the strategic goals of the organisation. To support this type of structure the head chef and the restaurant manager will need to work in partnership.

In a less prestigious or smaller hotel chain, the skill and expertise required of the head chef will be lower and his or her role in the hierarchy may be reflected by the fact that the head chef will have to report to the restaurant manager.

Child (1984: 223) believes that organisational structure will be affected by 'multiple elements and factors, such as environment plus size'. Because of the resulting interaction between these factors and elements, size will not act as the sole determinant in choosing an appropriate structure, even though it is seen as a very significant factor according to contingency theory. At this point it is important to consider the impact of environmental factors on the design of organisational structure.

Mintzberg (1993) identifies four environmental dimensions. These relate to stability, complexity, diversity and hostility in the environment.

- Stability refers to the level of certainty or predictability that is evident, with a dynamic or variable environment being characterised by uncertainty or low predictability.

- Complexity concerns the number of environmental elements that confront an organisation, with a complex environment being characterised by the presence of numerous external factors.

- Diversity relates to the range of activities of an organisation, so that a business would be likely to face greater uncertainty where it had diversified into a number of different markets.

● Finally, hostility refers to the level of competition faced by an organisation, as well as the presence of other threats to its competitive position.

These environmental dimensions can interact with each other, affecting the type of organisational structure that will be appropriate in a particular combination of circumstances, according to contingency theory. Figure 5.2 shows the interaction between only two of these environmental dimensions, namely complexity and stability, and the structural implications of these interactions that are believed to result according to this contingency approach.

Figure 5.2 shows that it will not be appropriate for all large organisations to adopt a mechanistic and bureaucratic approach to the design of their organisational structure because of the interaction between these variables. Traditionally, this type of bureaucratic structure was likely to be more appropriate in large organisations, such as public-sector bodies, banks and utility companies, that operate in relatively stable and simple environments (e.g. Mintzberg, 1993), organisations in these sectors have experienced significant change in the last ten years. This type of company produces standard products and services, where its technology and market remain relatively stable. This type of structure will also be more appropriate for organisations that supply one market, especially where they enjoy a position of market leadership or domination. In each of these cases, the level of environmental uncertainty is (fairly) low.

However, in environments characterised by varying conditions, an alternative structural model will be more appropriate. Similarly, where an organisation faces environmental complexity, or where it has diversified into different markets and created a situation of complexity of its own making, an alternative set of structural arrangements will be necessary. Intense competition can also require a higher level of responsiveness than that offered by the adoption of a mechanistic and bureaucratic structure. The alternatives to such a mechanistic and bureaucratic structure are characterised by greater flexibility and differing levels of decentralisation or centralisation. Some of the examples discussed later in this chapter illustrate these more flexible forms of structure.

		Environmental complexity	
		Simple ←——————————→ Complex	
Environmental stability	Stable	The stable environment promotes a bureaucratically based structure and the limited environmental interaction encourages centralised decision-making	While the stable environment promotes a bureaucratically based structure, the environmental complexity requires decentralised decision-making linked to a divisional structure
	Variable	Environmental variability requires a structure that encourages flexibility, adaptability and responsiveness. Limited environmental interaction makes centralised decision-making possible, while the variable or dynamic nature of this environmental niche means that this is also desirable	Environmental variability requires a structure that encourages flexibility, adaptability and responsiveness. However, environmental complexity also requires decentralised decision-making. This will result in an organisational structue with a high level of internal complexity

Figure 5.2 Structural types related to the interaction between environmental complexity and stability

Evaluating the contingency approach to organisational structure

In reality, choice of organisational structure will be subject to aspects other than the elements suggested above, and these other aspects may prove to be more important in practice than such contingent variables. Child (1984) provides a very useful assessment of contingency theory when applied to organisational design. His assessment includes consideration of the following aspects related to organisational performance:

● environmental dependency;
● the impact of multiple contingencies;
● structural variations and choice (that may be based on non-technical factors) and an absence of rationalistic assumptions.

Some examples from the work of Child (1984) will illustrate the essence of these aspects. Structure is only one of several factors that will affect organisational performance. It is therefore possible for a relatively successful organisation to be operating with a structure that is apparently a poor fit in relation to its operating environment (and vice versa). Organisations in a position of market dominance may not recognise the consequences of poor operating choice. They will therefore be able to exercise greater freedom in relation to choice about organisational structures without having to suffer the consequences of resultant inefficiencies, at least in the short term.

Child's (1984) discussion on contingency theory may be seen to cope with this by pointing to the adoption of an internally differentiated structure, or structures, in an organisation, this reality also leads to structural variations and the exercise of choice. Such choice may be based on suboptimal or social considerations. It may also be based on lack of knowledge about structural alternatives, constrained by current ('fashionable') thinking and affected by previous organisational policy and practice. This is likely to lead to significant differences between apparently similar organisations operating in the same environment (Stacey, 1993). It is also the case that organisations will seek to affect their operating environments and markets in a way that is beneficial to their current and future financial interest. A large organisation may seek to do this by using its market position and through the use of marketing techniques. Such actions may encourage structural variations as organisations adopt different strategies to attempt to achieve this beneficial environmental planning and to achieve and maintain competitive advantage.

Consistency approach to organisational structure

In reality it is likely to be difficult to use such a rational approach as suggested by contingency theory to design an organisational structure. An alternative approach recognises that effectiveness may nevertheless be achieved where an organisation attains a high level of integration within its organisational structure and in relation to other key internal attributes, such as its culture (Chapter 6), leadership and internal operating systems, including the strategic approach taken by the human resource function. The essence of this approach is based on achieving a high level of internal consistency between the components of organisational structure, as outlined above, and the creation of clear and concise linkages with other organisational characteristics. Strategic effectiveness is derived in this way through the creation of internal consistencies and efficiencies rather than through fit with the factors operating in the organisation's external environment, although, of course, effectiveness may be achieved through some combination of fit with both internal and external factors. Similar organisations operating in the same environment but with different structures may thus each be effective where they achieve a high level of internal consistency (e.g. Child, 1984; Mintzberg, 1991).

This is demonstrated in relation to *centralised* and *decentralised* forms of organisational decision-making and related structures. Child (1984) provides examples of organisations in the same industry that adopted either a centralised form of decision-making and structure, or a decentralised form, but which were both effective because of the high levels of internal consistency within each approach in practice. He contrasts this with other organisations in the same industry that adopted decentralised structural forms but also maintained tight centralised controls over decision-making and supporting centralised structures, with the result that they were much less effective due to these structural inconsistencies. Such inconsistencies are likely to lead to conflict and to the frustration and demotivation of managers in operating divisions or business units who feel unable to manage in their areas of apparent responsibility without having to keep obtaining authority from higher levels of the organisation. In contrast a truly decentralised organisation will be likely to have delayered its structure, reducing centralised managerial overheads and support staff, and therefore reducing the overall size of its workforce. Structural consistency is therefore associated with improved organisational performance as well as effectiveness (Child, 1984). However, configuration and relative workforce size may not tell the whole story. Control may continue to be exercised through formalisation and bureaucracy even though centralised structures have been reduced, as In Practice 5.5 illustrates.

| In Practice | 5.5 |

Inconsistencies in Publicserviceorg

Publicserviceorg had made periodic changes to its organisational structure, related to attempts to resolve tensions between centralised and decentralised decision-making. It had a long history of centralised decision-making and control but the nature of its work meant that tensions existed between the centre of the organisation and its operating divisions, which were seen to impair its performance and effectiveness. Over a number of years, the central managerial overhead was reduced and attempts made to devolve greater responsibility to these operating divisions. However, the need for accountability of the public funds deployed in the organisation and measurement of its performance in relation to similar organisations, via controls exercised through central government reporting and accounting procedures, meant that the organisation remained highly formalised and subject to bureaucratic control. As a result, managers and staff in its operating divisions enjoyed little autonomy in practice, spending more of their time engaged on formal reporting procedures than interfacing with their client groups.

Evaluating the consistency approach to organisational structure

Recognition of the importance of internal consistency in organisational structure offers an alternative to the prescriptive approaches of both the classical universal and contingency approaches. The consistency approach recognises choice in determining a structure that can lead to strategic effectiveness linked to organisational performance. Seeking to match organisational structure to a complex and rapidly changing set of environmental factors may be difficult to achieve in practice and the consequences of trying to achieve this may not always produce the necessary outcomes. Equally, following a claimed set of best practices may or may not be appropriate. Even where either of these approaches might be followed, however, the importance of achieving internal structural consistency for strategic effectiveness will remain.

In Chapter 6 it is recognised that seeking to change culture is likely to be problematic; while possible to change perhaps, it is not a given entity that may be manipulated according to the predetermined design of a particular group of managers. Many so-called culture change programmes have failed because of this reason. In a similar way, organisational structure, which may appear to be more tangible than culture when represented as a formal chart or as an 'artefact' or 'visible symbol' of culture, also involves human perceptions, beliefs and behaviours. Relationships between individuals and groups in an organisation cannot easily be changed, so that restructuring that is aimed at changing an organisation's culture is likely to be problematic. The consistency approach may be seen as implying at least some sense of continuity because changes in the environment will not automatically lead to a change in organisational structure. It also implies relative simplicity because the key need is for the components of structure to fit together effectively. Child (1984) believes that company traditions and practices are likely to be important in developing consistency. This also has the benefit of allowing those who work in such a structure to develop long-lasting relationships, develop trust and potentially to identify with and be committed to the organisation, perhaps to a greater extent than they might to one that is subject to continuous restructuring. Of course, as Child recognises, change will be necessary over time but this will be observable as an occasional process rather than continuous one.

From an SHRM perspective, the conclusion to be drawn from this approach is that an organisational structure that is internally inconsistent is more likely to lead to negative human resource implications than one that is consistent. This theme will be returned to in the final section of this chapter.

Self-Check and Reflect Questions   5.3

How would you summarise the key differences between the classical universal, contingency and consistency approaches to the design of organisational structure?

Principal forms of organisational structure and the effect on employees

Organisational structures have changed in relation to the development of increasingly complex and variable or dynamic environments, including changes in the scope of organisations such as diversification or globalisation (e.g. Chandler, 1962; Miles and Snow, 1984b; Child, 2005). Chandler's (1962) work on the rise of industrial enterprise in the USA charted the development of organisational structures that were used to adapt to the changing nature and strategies of American capitalism. Miles and Snow (1984a, 1984b) summarised these developments and produced a typology of five organisational forms as follow:

- agency or simple;
- functional;
- divisional;
- matrix; and
- network structures.

Further work by Miles, Snow and other colleagues (Miles *et al.*, 1997) suggests the addition of what they call *cellular* structures. Some types of network and cellular structures are often referred to as virtual organisations. The development of new organisational forms has been characterised by Clegg and Hardy (1996) as a movement from bureaucracy towards much greater fluidity, associated with decentralisation, collaboration and alternatives to hierarchy. Each of these forms and their effects on those who work within them will now be reviewed.

Simple organisational structures

A simple organisational structure is often associated with small organisations. These organisations commonly employ less that 25 people, supplying a single product or service, or related products or services, within a defined market. An example may be a professional practice such as a small firm of financial advisers or a doctors' surgery serving a particular location (see In Practice 5.6). A *simple structure* is inherently centralised, with one person or perhaps a small number of people exercising control over the direction and operation of the organisation. The nature of both the managerial style adopted and the work undertaken will significantly affect the character of working relations in this type of structure. In this sense, its impact on those who work within it will depend also on these factors. Simple structures encourage flexibility and should be responsive to changes in its environment, although the degree of responsiveness will depend on the abilities and attributes of the person who exercises control over the organisation.

Functional and divisionalised forms of organistional structure

These are the most prevalent forms of organisational structure among large industrial companies commonly employing over 250 people (Mayer and Whittington, 2004). Introducing a *functional structure* is designed to overcome the inability of a simple structure to respond to an organisation's increasing internal complexity arising from its growth. The

Most organisations employ no more than a 'handful' of people.

There is a tendency to think of large organisations when studying subjects such as SHRM but when there is a need to call a plumber or an electrician, take a car to the garage, visit a doctor, call in to the local takeaway, or take a pet to the vet, there is probably interaction with a small business, run by one person or no more than a few and which employs only a small number of people at most.

You might care to think about the small businesses whose services you use, how these are structured and what it would be like to work for them.

adoption of a functional structure therefore leads to the creation of a number of specialised managerial roles and departments that typically include areas such as production or service provision, product development, sales and marketing, finance and human resources (Figure 5.3). Although this type of structure involves some delegation of authority (vertical decentralisation), power and control continue to be vested in line managers and focused on those in the most senior positions (Mintzberg, 1993). This type of structure is associated with the bureaucratic model that was briefly outlined earlier. Mintzberg (1979, 1993) called the developed form of this type of structure the 'machine bureaucracy' because of its mechanistic and standardised approach to organising work. Many types of organisation have traditionally been organised in this way.

However, functionally arranged organisations, characterised by bureaucratic principles of standardisation and formalisation, have been criticised for not being sufficiently responsive to complex environmental circumstances (e.g. Chandler, 1962; Miles and Snow, 1984b). Organisations require a different form of structure to be able to respond to a complex or diverse operating environment. For these organisations, the third type of structure in Miles and Snow's (1984a) typology is more appropriate. This is the divisionalised form of organisational structure. In a *divisionalised structure*, different products, or groups of products, or service areas are organised into separate operating divisions (Figure 5.4). Different regions supplied by an organisation may also be organised into corresponding operating divisions (e.g. Child, 1984). Many well-known organisations, such as Marks and Spencer, General Electric, Vodafone and Virgin, structure themselves using one or more of these divisional forms. The managers of a semi-autonomous division will thus be able to focus on the particular issues faced by their operating unit and take more rapid action. This type of structure is often referred to as the multi-divisional or M-form of structure (e.g. Purcell, 1995). Mayer and Whittington (2004) report that, despite national differences about choice of structural forms,

Figure 5.3 Representation of a functional structure

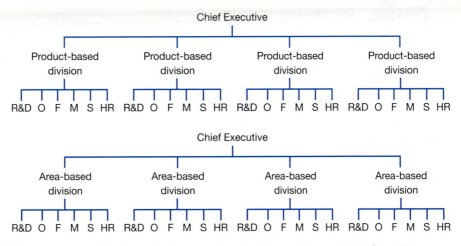

R&D = research and development; O = operations; F = finance; M = marketing; S = sales;
HR = human resources.

Figure 5.4 Representations of a divisionalised structure

the multi-divisional form is the dominant type in western European countries, as well as in other developed countries, such as the USA and Japan.

While Mintzberg (1993) recognises that the use of a divisionalised structure will involve some decentralisation of decision-making, he points out that this will be restricted. This will only occur vertically down to the senior managers of each division, so that these middle-ranking managers in the organisation are permitted to exercise power along with its corporate managers. From a human resource perspective, this may help to motivate these divisional managers, providing them with developmental experience and a clear route for career progression and promotion (Child, 1984). However, there may be little effective difference for others who work in each product division, other than the fact that a centralised bureaucratic structure has been replaced by a similar functional structure for that particular division. In other words, a divisionalised structure may continue to be characterised by a mechanistic and bureaucratic design affecting most of the people who work within it, although this does not have to be the case (Mintzberg, 1993). See In Practice 5.7 for an example of this structure type.

The human costs of working in such mechanistic and bureaucratic structures under Tayloristic principles of managing people have been recognised for a long time (see, for example, Mintzberg, 1993; Francis, 1994). Structures that emphasise managerial control over work are likely to be met by forms of employee resistance and attempts at counter-control. Employees may develop forms of job control that restrict their work effort and output. Indeed, Crozier (1964) found that the employees he studied used the bureaucratic procedures imposed by their organisations to their own ends in order to prevent their managers from treating them in an arbitrary way. These types of structure are therefore associated with a range of potential outcomes that may impact adversely on human resource strategies aimed at engendering employee involvement and performance as well as broader strategies related to innovation and change.

As recognised earlier, a bureaucratic structure may also prove to be inappropriate when an organisation is confronted by variable/dynamic or hostile environmental conditions. Such an organisation would operate according to established rules which

In Practice   5.7

Trad Manufacturing Co.: assessing the nature of its structural components

Trad Manufacturing Co. (TMC) has an organisational structure that reflects a highly functional and mechanistic form. Analysis of its structure using the components reported earlier shows how this works in practice.

Specialisation	Specialised job roles are prevalent among both TMC operatives and office staff
Standardisation	There is a high level of standardisation arising from the use of internal operating procedures and quality management systems in TMC
Formalisation	Operations in TMC are highly formalised. This is partly because its parent company maintains control through issuing formal policy guidelines to direct its operations. TMC has also adopted various quality management systems to meet the quality standards required by the organisations to whom it supplies its products
Centralisation	Vertical hierarchy is important in TMC, with authority centralised in its senior management team and ultimately in its parent company, of which it forms one operating division
Configuration	In spite of a long period of downsizing and some delayering, TMC remains hierarchical, with five levels of authority and fairly narrow spans of control, although it has used ad hoc project teams on particular occasions to capitalise on the expertise embedded in different parts of the company
Traditionalism	In spite of significant change and the introduction of forms of flexibility in TMC, embedded custom and practice still informs the conduct of work in certain areas of its operations

wouldn't necessarily be suitable to cope with their changing environment. Contingency theory suggests that in these situations the appropriate form of organisational structure is likely to be a centralised one that permits an 'entrepreneurial' approach rather than one characterised by pre-established bureaucratic routines and behaviour. For example, Child (1984: 223) found that 'high performing companies in a changing environment tended to be particularly free of a bureaucratic style of structure: they were highly centralised and without much formalisation'. Mintzberg (1993) suggests that a centralised organisational structure will need to be introduced, at least on a temporary basis, where an organisation is confronted by a situation of particular difficulty from its environment (see also Morgan, 1989). Where an organisation has already been adversely affected by such environmental conditions and needs where possible to make improvements, these improvements usually occur under a new management regime: an entrepreneurial and centralised organisational structure will also be appropriate (e.g. Mintzberg, 1991).

The discussion in this section so far has highlighted some of the tensions around the dimensions of organisational structure. These include:

- determining the appropriate level of behavioural or procedural standardisation;
- the extent to which decision-making should be centralised or decentralised;
- the extent of specialisation that is appropriate (e.g. Pugh et al., 1968).

A problematic relationship is particularly evident between the respective desires for managerial control, organisational efficiency and responsiveness to external conditions and intended markets. The simple organisational structure allows for the achievement of these three goals in variable or dynamic environmental conditions, where the leading manager(s) adopts an appropriate approach – perhaps encapsulated by the term 'entrepreneurial'. Because of the lack of standardisation and formalisation, this type of organisation remains organic and adaptable.

As previously discussed, standardisation and specialisation are likely to develop in an organisation that develops a functional structure where it operates in a fairly stable and simple environment. This may help to preserve managerial control and organisational efficiency but may also impair the organisation's ability to be responsive where the operating environment becomes more changeable or dynamic, or where the organisation itself changes and encounters a more complex operating environment. Responsiveness may be regained in the event of diversification by introducing some vertical decentralisation through a divisionalised structure, while seeking to maintain managerial control and efficiency by retaining other elements of a bureaucratic structure. However, a more difficult situation will confront an organisation that faces both a more complex and variable or dynamic environment. The desire to achieve managerial control, organisational efficiency and responsiveness in this situation is likely to lead to a more complicated organisational structure. Such a structure will be designed to promote managerial control and optimise efficiency while allowing a greater measure of decentralisation and more flexiblity, in order to be responsive to the uncertain conditions confronting the organisation. One manifestation of this type of organisation is the matrix form of organisational structure, the fourth type in Miles and Snow's (1984a) typology. This type will now be discussed before discussing other possible forms.

Matrix forms of organisational structure

A *matrix* structure combines a functional, hierarchical form with a lateral, project-based approach. As an illustrative example of this type of organisational design, Figure 5.5 shows the functional structure on the vertical axis and the project-based approach linked to a particular product or market location on the horizontal axis of this structure. In other words, one of these approaches to managing is overlaid on the other, to create an integrated or multi-dimensional structure (Child, 1984). This type of structure is designed to combine the efficiency suggested by a functional approach to organisational design with the responsiveness implied by a product- or market-centred approach (e.g. Miles and Snow, 1984b). In this way, a matrix form is seen to be more likely to be suited to an operating environment characterised by both variability and complexity (Mintzberg, 1993). However, because it operates on the basis of a shared, dual approach to decision-making and control it may well be problematic to operate in practice because of differences between the people who exercise, and share, authority within this type of structure. Some of these human resource focused issues of this type of organisational structure will be considered in the discussion that follows in this subsection.

As may be expected, in practice this organisational structure has a number of variations. It may be introduced on a temporary or permanent basis, and as a structure for the whole or a part, or parts, of an organisation. The 'temporary' use of this type of structure is likely to be characterised by the use of project- and team-based teams. The level of uncertainty confronting an organisation may lead it to establish special project

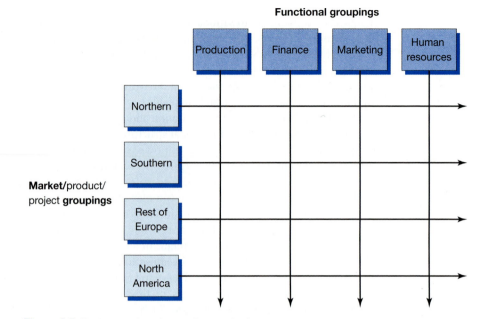

Figure 5.5 Representation of a matrix organisation

teams to deal with the problems that face it and in order to utilise effectively the specialised, and perhaps limited range of, skills that it possesses. Such project teams may be formed or re-formed according to the needs of the organisation and the environmental or market problems confronting it. A recent example of this was the use of cross-functional teams by many organisations to ensure Year 2000 compliance in relation to the operation of their computing systems.

The use of this project-based approach suggests a number of potential advantages, related to the organisation and its employees. For the organisation, it suggests responsiveness to circumstances, the attainment of employee flexibility, as well as, perhaps, effective employee performance arising from a stream of interesting and challenging work, concomitant development and a greater acceptance of change. For affected employees, it suggests scope for development, motivation, involvement and satisfaction. However, it also suggests scope for role and interpersonal conflict, resulting in stress, that may have the opposite effect in relation to these work dimensions (e.g. Child, 1984).

A matrix structure will involve the establishment of both project and functional managers, which will affect the way in which these personnel, as well as others involved, need to work together. In a negative scenario, there is scope for confusion and interpersonal conflict between these different types of manager and for the creation of stress, with implications for effectiveness and performance. Even in a more positive scenario, there are implications about the level of communication and nature of decision-making processes required to realise the potential benefits of this type of organisational structure in practice. A matrix structure will require intensive communication and the use of joint decision-making processes. Adopting a permanent form of matrix structure is likely to have significant repercussions within an organisation. It may well signify a culture change, or at least the final stage of one, for the organisation (Bartol and Martin, 1994). It will also require great care in relation to the selection and training, as well as defining the roles, of those who are placed into the management and other key jobs in this type of structure. The significance of the need to define these roles and to select and train for them carefully is illustrated by the potential for shifts in power and struggles for control where this is not considered or achieved effectively.

There are three forms of control in a matrix structure (Knight, 1977). In an 'absolute' or 'pure' matrix structure, which Knight called the 'overlay form', functional managers and project or product managers jointly share power and exercise authority. These managers still commence their roles within this structure from different perspectives: in other words, from their functional or project/product perspective; but will need to work closely together to achieve an outcome. Francis (1994: 68–69) summarised this position of interdependency:

> Every individual in the organisation is responsible to a functional manager for the technical aspects of the work and to a product or project manager for the way in which the task in hand is co-ordinated with other tasks relating to the same product or project.

The requirements of matrix structures indicate the potential for conflict to occur and to become standard practice. Other employees may be affected adversely where they are exposed to conflict in situations where they undertake different roles and answer to various managers, resulting in stress.

An alternative to the pure or absolute form of matrix structure is for either the functional manager or the project/product manager to hold overall authority. The first scenario has been called the 'coordination' matrix and the second situation the 'secondment' matrix (Knight, 1977). The authors' experience suggests a further variation, whereby overall authority switches between the functional manager and project/product manager, depending on the particular context or project. This is referred to as the 'variable control' matrix (Figure 5.6). Each of these variations suggests that there is still scope for conflict, even where overall, formal power and control has been established. This potential for conflict has led Mintzberg (1993) to suggest that this type of structure is

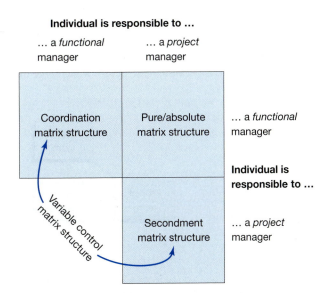

Figure 5.6 Individual responsibility under different types of matrix structure

only really suitable for organisations that have achieved operational and interpersonal 'maturity'. This may be characterised by an organisational culture that emphasises openness, cooperation and learning (see Chapters 6 and 11 in particular). This will be in addition to other requirements before this type of structure is adopted (e.g. Davis and Lawrence, 1977; Child, 1984).

Project-based organisational structures

Another variation of this type of organisational design is a *project-based structure*. In this type of structure, project-based teams are responsible for undertaking the core activities of the organisation (Figure 5.7). This organisational design may also continue to have a functional structure, although this will play a secondary role in the business of the organisation and the relationship between the project-based and functional structures will be different from that in a matrix structure. An organisation's capacity to respond to its environment and to innovate in this design is therefore generated by the use of project teams rather than through its functional arrangements (Morgan, 1989). In this way the project-based organisation will be more fluid than bureaucratic (Clegg and Hardy, 1996).

This is similar to the 'task alignment' approach advocated by Beer *et al.* (1990) (see Chapter 6 for a fuller discussion of this approach). They advocate the introduction of ad hoc organisational structures, centring on various types of project teams, to help bring about more permanent organisational change. This approach is intended to engage employees in the generation of solutions to the problems faced by an organisation – to some extent, as a 'bottom-up' approach to strategy formation and implementation. Beer *et al.* (1990) believe that the use of project teams in this type of situation will lead to a number of specific benefits, culminating in the generation of more effective change in comparison with a top-down, 'programmatic' approach. These benefits include: the opportunity for participants to develop an understanding of the problems facing that part of the organisation for which they work and to devise solutions that are 'owned' jointly; as a result, the development of commitment to this work and those engaged on it; and the development of competences to be able to contribute. Whether such an approach generates, or is more likely to generate, these benefits must be open to examination in the context of particular change situations. In relation to organisational structure, Beer *et al.* (1990) believe that a more effective structure should emerge from a 'task alignment' approach. This is because the structure will emerge through the experiences of the project

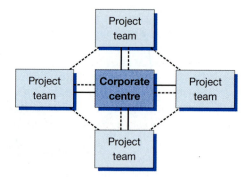

Figure 5.7 Representation of a project-based structure

teams. It will be reflective of those areas of interdependency that become evident, which require coordination. When such a structure has emerged fully, it can be formalised in the organisation. This, they contend, will be a more effective way in which to generate an efficient structure for the future, than imposing one from above at the outset of a purely 'top-down' change programme. A project-based organisation may therefore be used as a means to move from one formal structure to another, and thus it may be seen as a transitional structural state and a facilitator of other types of change.

Project-based structures, according to these two formulations, may be either permanent or transitional structural arrangements. In either case, some of the concerns expressed above about the involvement of organisational participants in either approach are relevant here. Such arrangements will need to be based on effective working relationships and genuine forms of employee involvement and participation. There are undoubtedly risks to using this type of structure as well as potential benefits. This project-based approach to organisational design should benefit from the use of a range of human resource strategies that are designed to foster and support it. These include the introduction of appropriate recruitment and selection, training and development, performance management and employee involvement strategies and practices. Project-based structures require the expertise of those who are involved in them and their commitment to develop solutions and a new direction in order to achieve success. This will involve human resource strategies including employee involvement and communication that need to be developed in an 'integrated' manner rather than imposed from the top down. Beer *et al.* (1990) distinguish between approaches to human resource strategy by seeing top-down, imposed approaches as aimed at changing attitudes and more grounded, emergent and context-specific approaches as being aimed at altering behaviours. The behavioural approach is seen as being much more effective; the attitudinal one being likely to become 'overtaken' by other organisational events (e.g. Guest *et al.*, 1993).

Network forms of organisation

Matrix and project-based structures are more suited to environmental conditions characterised by both complex and variable or dynamic conditions. Another form of organisation suited to this type of environment is the so-called *network organisation*. Such organisations are seen as being flexible and responsive to market changes and segments, again stressing fluidity rather than bureaucracy in their operations. There are different categories or types of network structure. These have been termed internal networks, vertical or stable networks and dynamic or loosely coupled networks (e.g. Miles and Snow, 1984a; Morgan, 1989; Snow *et al.*, 1992; Senior, 2002; see Figure 5.8 below).

Internal networks are essentially strategic business units or profit centres that use market pricing as the basis for supplying components or services from one part of an organisation to another. This arrangement is used to promote organisational efficiency and innovation. Many large organisations have moved to establish this type of internal structural arrangement.

Vertical or *stable networks* involve different organisations, centred on a core organisation, working together to produce and supply a good or service. The example often cited is that of the motor industry. Vertical integration is limited in this industry, so that at least some of the parts of the car that you drive may have been made by a range of firms that supply the company whose name your car displays. The distribution network for a particular make of car will also be owned by a range of other organisations, approved by and contracted to the particular manufacturer. These types of network generally remain stable over long periods. For the core organisation in such a network, this has the benefit of spreading the costs of investment, their exposure to risk and controlling their supply costs. For the organisations that supply parts or distribute the final product, this should generally ensure a steady flow of work and income. For the core organisation, this type of organisational arrangement is also known as outsourcing. Other examples of vertical networks may be found in a range of other industries such as manufacturing, clothing and retail (e.g. Benetton, Next and Debenhams).

Dynamic or *loosely coupled networks* differ from the previous form in that they are less likely to be dependent on a particular organisation and, by definition, are also likely to be less stable. This type of arrangement is essentially a cooperative one between a number of organisations to develop and exploit a perceived commercial opportunity, perhaps where none is large enough or resource capable to achieve this in isolation. Examples may be found in construction, in order to undertake large projects that bring together a range of capabilities. Such a network arrangement therefore has the benefit of allowing a number of specialised organisations to pool their resources to mutual advantage. Larger organisations that cooperate to pool their resources in some way, in relation to a particular opportunity, may prefer to develop a more permanent organisational arrangement. This has occurred in manufacturing, where companies have shared the large investment costs necessary. This may lead to the creation of a strategic alliance or joint venture. These arrangements indicate the increased importance of interorganisational relationships and resulting structures.

In general terms, there appears to be a number of human resource implications arising from these types of network arrangements and structural relationships. These include issues related to coordination, cooperation, communication, product quality, training and development, performance management, involvement and commitment. The use of an internal network will affect the nature of coordination and communication within the organisation, suggesting the need for the development of cooperative relations based on internal customer relationships. In turn, this is likely to have implica-

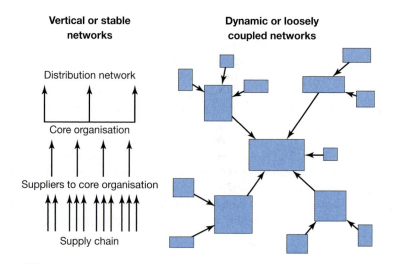

Figure 5.8 Representations of network forms

tions for the nature of human resource strategies relating to, among others, recruitment and selection, training and development, and the design and management of appropriate performance standards.

A vertical network adds a further layer of complexity to the effective management of people engaged in this type of arrangement. Coordination, cooperation and communication will not only need to be achieved within each constituent organisation in this type of network but also between them. The core organisation may seek to ensure the adoption of particular standards in supplying organisations within the network by requiring them to adopt an approved and verifiable system of quality management. This in turn will raise human resource implications related to, most obviously, employee training and selection. The core organisation may also use its supplier network, or part of it, to hold down costs in this area, with particular implications for the nature of the treatment of those who work in one of these supplier organisations. When a core organisation decides to develop its strategy of outsourcing, this may lead it to restructure and reduce its workforce as it downsizes. In effect, this vertical network strategy may allow the core organisation to become smaller with an altered internal organisational structure. This outcome may therefore lead to a lower level of internal complexity, but a need to engage 'key' personnel to coordinate effectively its vital external relationships.

The issue of external complexity and coordination is most evident in relation to the use of a loosely coupled network. This type of network arrangement suggests the need to generate a high level of shared understanding, communication, trust and cooperation. It seems likely that each core employee of an organisation in such a network will need to become a 'key' member in ensuring the success of this type of arrangement. This has clear implications for the selection of employees and the management of performance, as well as the commitment characteristics, of people who work in organisations that adopt the network approach.

Cellular forms of organisation

Another variation of a flexible, adaptive and responsive form of organisational structure is described by Miles *et al.* (1997). The *cellular form* of organisational design is based on principles of self-organisation and entrepreneurship. It has been used by a, as yet, small number of companies according to the literature to re-create themselves into a number of individual but linked organisations, each of which operates independently of the others but which also act interdependently when circumstances warrant this. Each cell or company will be capable of maintaining an independent existence through working in network relationships with other, external organisations, for its own customers. It will also work with other cells or companies in its parent organisation, where there is scope to combine their respective competence and knowledge base to exploit a particular market opportunity. Figure 5.9 provides an example of this type of organisation.

This organisational design emphasises the importance of entrepreneurial behaviours, adaptability, creativity, participation and innovation. It appears suited to knowledge-based companies and Miles *et al.* (see In Practice 5.8) describe its use in two companies in the computing industry as well as its partial use in other types of company.

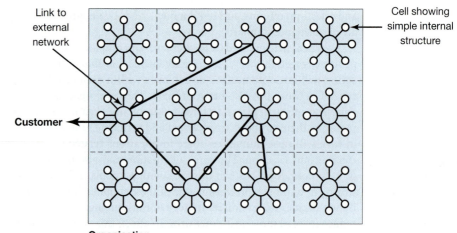

Figure 5.9 Representation of a cellular form

In Practice   5.8

Building a cellular structure

Miles *et al.* (1997) describe an Australian-based computer graphics company which exemplifies cellular organisation. This organisation developed a number of information technology capabilities leading to a range of products and services. The company organised itself into 13 small firms, each acting as an independent cell with its own purpose and ability to develop and conduct business, specialising in different aspects or products of the overall organisation. Business is developed through partnerships that involve one or more cells of the organisation working with an external firm in a joint-venture relationship and with an important customer, which provide equity capital and an advanced order respectively. Each cell typically operates with up to 20 professionals.

Virtual organisations

The idea that organisational structures can demonstrate fluidity reaches its height, perhaps, in relation to descriptions of virtual organisations. The *virtual organisation* is seen as a developed form of the network organisation (Child, 2005): a flexible and transient structure specifically assembled from cells or companies to respond to a particular opportunity, which will either cease once this goal has been fulfilled or reform in an appropriate way to pursue another. It lacks its own physical assets and structures, relying instead on those of its constituents and on the use of electronic communications technology. In this sense, the organisation may be thought of as virtual because of its reliance on the internet and the mobility of working that this permits. Its presence as an organisation may be more evident through the internet than based on the existence of a particular physical location. It may be truly international, with work being sourced from anywhere in the world where there is an appropriate capability and access to the internet. Work will be fragmented into tasks, carried out by constituent individuals, cells or companies and then integrated into a whole elsewhere in this virtual organisation (e.g. Davidow and Malone, 1992; Warner and Witzel, 2003).

The concept of the virtual organisation appears suited to knowledge-based work that utilises technologies such as the internet. It epitomises the human resource implications described above for network and cellular organisations. In particular it may be seen as epitomising the alternative to hierarchy that was referred to in the introduction to this section, or at least demonstrating a new approach to hierarchy, where this may shift according to the particular task or project being undertaken within the virtual organisation. The relationships implied by this approach suggest the need for high levels of cooperation and commitment. However, this is not to say that control is absent within such a virtual organisation, since the scope to change the supply of a particular service or product exists by using alternative suppliers on a global basis, suggesting that poor performance would not need to be tolerated by other contributors to the virtual organisation. A summary of structural types is produced in Key Concepts 5.5.

Self-Check and Reflect Questions 5.4

Using the ideas discussed above, how would you summarise 'organisational fluidity'?

Key Concepts 5.5

Summarising structural types

Simple

A centralised structure, where one person or a few people exercise control over the direction and operation of the organisation.

Functional and divisionalised

A functional structure is associated with a number of specialised managerial roles and operating departments. In a divisionalised structure, different products or services are organised into separate operating divisions.

Matrix

A matrix structure combines a functional hierarchical structure with a lateral, project-based approach.

Project based

In this structure, project-based teams are responsible for undertaking the activities of the organisation.

Network

An organisational form designed to be flexible and responsive to change. There are different types of network organisation: internal; vertical; and dynamic.

▶

Cellular

Another form of organisation designed to be flexible, based on principles of self-organisation and entrepreneurship.

Virtual

A highly flexible and transient form, which exists for a given period and purpose.

Summarising the relationship between organisational structure and SHRM

The relationship between organisational structure and SHRM has emerged through three strands of our discussion. Firstly, it has emerged in relation to the discussion about the links between corporate strategy, organisational structure and human resource management strategies.

- The first substantive section of this chapter recognises that there will be links between strategy and structure as well as between structure and human resource strategies. This is not an attempt to advocate a rationalist, planned approach by this recognition or to be prescriptive about the nature of these links. Whether strategy is attempted in a planned way or achieved through an emergent approach, these linkages will exist. In this way all aspects of organisation – strategy, structure and human resource strategies in our context – need to be considered in relation to one another. Without this, incongruence or inconsistency may result in practice. Components of structure need to be consistent with strategy and between themselves, while these same dimensions of structure will impact on the nature of work and of working relationships (Key Concepts 5.2 and 5.3 help to illustrate some of these relationships, as does the discussion in the section within which these are located).

- Second, the relationship between organisational structure and SHRM has emerged in relation to the discussion about conceptual approaches to understand the design of organisational structures. While these approaches are conceptual and, in practice, structure may emerge in many organisations through a more pragmatic and intuitive process of decision-making, each of these approaches nevertheless suggests implications about the relationship between organisational structure and the management of human resources. Adopting universal principles appears to suggest a lack of focus on the outward context of the organisation. Adopting leanness or decentralisation, for example, because of adherence to some universal set of principles will have particular consequences for the management of human resources, whether or not this is the most appropriate course to take. Attempting to achieve a contingency approach demonstrates an explicit attempt to match strategy to contextual circumstances, with implications for the nature of both structure and human resource strategies. Of course an organisation's ability to comprehend and match all of its contextual circumstances may be limited for a number of reasons, as was recognised above and in Chapter 1. Strategic choice and the influence of organisational politics and power recognise instead the role of individual agency and gain, with consequential implications for the management of human resources.

● Third, the relationship between organisational structure and SHRM also emerges in the discussion about structural forms. Each form of organisational structure will have different effects on those who work within it, as well as particular implications about the nature of the capabilities and attributes of the people required to make it effective in practice. This may be most evident in relation to the more decentralised forms of structure discussed in the above section. In these decentralised forms, high levels of competence, communication and cooperation are often required, particularly among core employees or workers. This has clear implications for the nature of human resource strategies, both to facilitate these types of structure and working relationships, and to support their maintenance and development. The scope of human resource strategies in such decentralised organisations may, however, be limited to particular divisions, constituent companies or cells within a larger organisation, with implications for consistency and integration across the organisation as a whole.

The consistency approach to structural design recognises that effectiveness will be linked to congruence between the elements of structure within each organisation, with clear implications for consistency with SHRM as well.

Some discussion about the scope of human resource strategies in decentralised structures will be developed below, after seeking to summarise the human resource implications arising from organisational structures in general terms. As can be seen in the following list, organisational structure can be seen to influence:

● the nature and fulfilment of organisational strategy;
● organisational responsiveness to external change and competitiveness;
● scope for innovation;
● organisational capability to cope with uncertainty;
● organisational performance and effectiveness;
● product and service quality;
● the nature and effectiveness of coordination;
● the organisation of work and job design;
● the nature of decision-making (accountability and responsibility);
● the location and exercise of power and control;
● the generation and level of organisational conflict (and cooperation);
● organisational culture;
● motivation and commitment/alienation;
● the scope for and nature of employee involvement and performance;
● the nature of and channels for communication;
● formal and informal relationships;
● group processes, team working and network relationships;
● career paths and scope for development;
● the nature of employees' psychological contracts (discussed in Chapter 8);
● work-related stress.

What items can you add to this general list of implications?

The focus now turns towards the way in which decentralised structures may affect the scope for and nature of human resource strategies in organisations. In the section above, discussions on divisional structures and their implications for those who work within them took place. The use of complex and vertically decentralised organisational structures, characterised by a multi-divisional structure, can lead to a reduction in the scope for human resource strategies to develop or embed themselves across an organisation. Business unit managers in such a structure may become more concerned to meet the financial targets established for them than to focus on corporate human resource issues and approaches, even where these have been identified and developed (Purcell, 1989b). This decentralised focus is also likely to depend on the strategic focus of particular organisations. Some divisionalised organisations may promote a short-term focus on financial control and returns that reduces their scope to develop organisation-wide human resource strategies. Conversely, other divisionalised organisations may adopt a longer-term strategic focus that encourages the development and use of integrative human resource strategies across the organisation (Goold and Campbell, 1987). The nature of human resource strategies may also be affected by a combination of a divisionalised organisational structure and the particular strategic focus of the organisation.

In a similar way, other decentralised forms of organisational structure, such as network or cellular structures, may affect the scope for organisation-wide human resource strategies. Again, this effect is likely to be in combination with the strategic focus of an organisation. The use of these structures may thus lead some organisations to recognise the importance of the contribution of their core groups of staff, in particular, and to adopt a developmental and strategic approach to the management of these people. Conversely, other organisations may adopt a more short-term focus based on financial controls and returns. These organisations may believe that they can 'poach' key members of staff from an external pool of labour, by rewarding them well. This second approach is based on pragmatism and opportunism and would not encourage the development of a range of integrated and longer-term human resource strategies.

Self-Check and Reflect Questions   5.5

The discussion in this section has considered the impact of decentralised organisational structures on the development of human resource strategies. How do you think a more centralised and bureaucratic form of organisational structure will affect the development of human resource strategies?

Summary

- Strategic linkages exist between corporate strategy, organisational structure and human resource strategies, demonstrating the strategic nature of structure.
- Dimensions of organisational structure have been identified that can be used to analyse the nature and evaluate the effectiveness of an organisation's structure.

- These dimensions indicate the complex range of variables to be understood by managers in deciding how they should structure an organisation's activities to meet its strategic objectives. They also indicate that the design of organisational structure involves managerial or strategic choice.

- Three perspectives were considered that offer explanations about the relationship between the design of organisational structure and strategic effectiveness. These relate to the classical universal, contingency and consistency approaches to the design of organisational structure. A fourth perspective relates to the role of organisational politics and the exercise of power that has already been considered and discussed in depth in Chapter 1.

- Principal forms of organisational structure were reviewed and their effects on those who work within them analysed and evaluated. These forms include: simple; functional; divisionalised; matrix; project-based; network, cellular and virtual structures. Theoretical linkages between these organisational forms and contingency variables have been recognised. The development of these forms indicates some degree of movement from centralised and bureaucratic structures to decentralised and more fluid ones.

- Organisations need to promote human resource strategies that are congruent with the nature of the organisational structure that they chose (or recognise the impact of their structure on their espoused human resource policies and the practice and outcomes of the human resource strategies that they promote).

- Choice of organisational structure has been recognised as leading to a problematic relationship between the respective desires for managerial control, organisational efficiency and responsiveness to external conditions and intended markets. Attempts to maximise centralised managerial control in situations requiring greater organisational responsiveness are likely to affect the pursuit of effectiveness and working relationships adversely.

- Decentralised forms of organisational structure may adversely affect the scope for and nature of organisation-wide human resource strategies. In practice, this is likely to be a function of both the nature of the structural form that is chosen and the strategy of the organisation.

Follow-up study suggestions

Either:

Undertake a search of practitioner publications (related to human resource and management) and identify a number of short articles about case study organisations that often feature in these and select, say, two or three of them that discuss structural change, perhaps due to downsizing or a restructuring, and use one or more theories discussed above to try to evaluate what these organisations did and its likely effectiveness.

Or:

Using an organisation with which you are familiar, which may be one in which you are currently employed or have worked for, or one known to you:

1. Use the list of dimensions of organisational structure in Key Concepts 5.1 to analyse the nature of this organisation's structure.

2. Use Key Concepts 5.2 to try to evaluate the effectiveness of the organisation's structure, or one part of it, in relation to the four consequences listed.

3. Use Key Concepts 5.3 and the discussion in the section titled 'Consistency approach to organisational structure' to evaluate the level of consistency between the key elements of its structure.

4. Identify the form or forms of structure evident in this organisation. How would you assess the nature of working relationships in the organisation and how suited are these to the form or forms of structure that are used in it?

Suggestions for research topics

- An evaluation of the relative advantages and disadvantages of centralised and decentralised structures: a case study of ABC.
- An exploration of the impact of bureaucracy in department WX in company YZ.
- Examining the implications of a case study's organisation for those who work in it.
- How do managers/why should managers assess the effectiveness of organisational structure?
- An exploration of the relationship between organisational structure and the management of change (in relation to a particular case study organisation).
- The relationship between organisational structure and human resource management: a case study-based investigation.

Each of these suggestions for research projects may be undertaken as a literature-based examination and discussion, where your institution requires this type of project to be completed as part of an award, or in relation to a particular case study organisation, where you are required to collect some primary data and analyse these in relation to theory for part of your course.

Case Study

DaimlerChrysler AG

The company

DaimlerChryslers' product portfolio ranges from small cars to sports cars and luxury sedans; and from versatile vans to trucks and coaches. Daimler-Chryslers' passenger car brands include Maybach, Mercedes-Benz, Chrysler, Jeep®, Dodge and Smart. Commercial vehicle brands include Mercedes-Benz, Freightliner, Sterling, Western Star,

Setra and Mitsubishi Fuso. It offers financial and other automotive services through DaimlerChrysler Financial Services.

DaimlerChrysler (DC) has a global workforce (382,723 at year-end 2005) and a global shareholder base. DaimlerChrysler achieved revenues of €149.7 billion in 2005. The operative result was €5.1 billion for 2005 (Mercedes Car Group a loss of €505 million!).

DC has been described as a very traditional German company. For a long time its culture has been described as technology- and quality-focused: brilliant engineers and craftsmen were producing well-designed, reliable, high-quality cars. Under the shining Mercedes star, managers could afford to buy companies all over the world as the coffer was full. Unfortunately, too often they paid too much for companies which did not fit in their organisational structure.

Meanwhile, the reputation of the Mercedes star has dimmed and Mercedes has slid dramatically in consumer rankings and loyalty. DC appears to have quality problems, manufacturing efficiency has declined (while costs are relatively high) and there has been excess production capacity for years. Also, its technological prowess is more and more disputed.

The giant head office (HO) in Stuttgart-Möhringen monitors hundreds of national and international companies in different industries. There are manufacturing facilities in 17 countries. Most Group companies are in fact (economically) more or less independent as it is very difficult to stir these companies 'virtually' from the HO.

Dieter Zetsche became group chief executive at the start of the year 2006 succeeding Jürgen Schrempp.

In September 2005 Zetsche warned: 'We should not let ourselves become overconfident. There is still a long and difficult road ahead of us before we can become truly competitive again.' The company continues to drag around excess production capacity, he wrote, and its costs remain 'significantly higher than those of the best competitors'. To redress the situation, he announced, DaimlerChrysler's board was cutting 8,500 Mercedes jobs in Germany, or about 9 per cent of the total.

New 'leadership model'

On 24 January 2006 the board published a new 'leadership model', which was focused on making specific changes to the existing organisational structure. Within minutes the share prise rose by about 5 per cent to €45. This model was widely reported in the print media:

Integration leads to organization that is faster, more flexible, leaner and more efficient

Together with other ongoing efficiency programmes, G&A [general and administrative] costs are expected to be reduced by EUR 1.5 billion per year, G&A staff reduced by up to 20 per cent over three years

Supervisory Board agrees to realignment of functions within the Board of Management

Shortly after the board's announcement the following text was published on DC's web site (http:www.daimlerchrysler.com):

DaimlerChrysler today introduced a new management structure designed to enhance competitiveness and promote further profitable growth. The new structure will further integrate the company's functions, focus the operations within DaimlerChrysler on core processes, and encourage internal collaboration. Moreover, it will reduce redundancies and remove management layers.

'Our objective in taking these actions is to create a lean, agile structure, with streamlined and stable processes that will unleash DaimlerChrysler's full potential,' said Dieter Zetsche, Chairman of the Board of Management (BoM) of DaimlerChrysler AG. 'We're going to build on a strong product portfolio.' In 2005 alone, DaimlerChrysler launched 17 new products, giving it one of the youngest product lines in the automotive industry. The company plans to continue its aggressive level of investment.

'Over the last several years, we focused on our automotive business and started to streamline the core processes in our divisions,' said Zetsche. 'But to safeguard our future in this competitive global industry, we need to apply that same equation across all general and administrative (G&A) functions with the added dimension of adapting to the needs of our business.'

The preliminary work for this new structure began in mid-2005 with a high-level internal team.

The program focuses on the company organization and the processes that are used throughout the DaimlerChrysler enterprise.

Among structural changes is a consolidation and integration of G&A functions, such as Finance and Controlling, Human Resources and Strategy. These areas will be centralized to report to the respective head of that function throughout the entire company. Redundancies between staff functions at the corporate and operating levels will be eliminated, thereby reducing the complexity of the organization. A more integrated G&A organization will result in more consistent processes, and reporting and decision-making will become shorter, faster and more efficient.

'We want our divisions to concentrate on the automotive core processes – development, production and sales,' added Zetsche.

The consolidation of corporate functions will occur throughout the company. The earlier decision for Dieter Zetsche to serve a dual role as Chairman of the Board of Management and concurrently as Head of the Mercedes Car Group, will now be reflected in the organizational structure as well. BoM members Bodo Uebber and Ruediger Grube will also continue to have dual roles: Uebber for Finance and Controlling, as well as DaimlerChrysler Financial Services; Grube for Corporate Development (including Information Technology) and DaimlerChrysler's participation in EADS (European Aeronautic Defense and Space company). That will effectively reduce the number of BoM members to nine (from 12 about one year ago).

The German BoM members currently based in Stuttgart-Moehringen will relocate in May 2006, along with their staff, to Stuttgart-Untertuerkheim, and therefore closer to production. This means the DaimlerChrysler headquarters function will be located in Stuttgart-Untertuerkheim and Auburn Hills, Michigan. Several support functions and non-G&A functions will stay in Stuttgart-Moehringen.

On the basis of the new structure, the company will standardize the most important processes within and across divisions, according to best-practice criteria.

Cooperation between the Mercedes Car Group and the Chrysler Group will become markedly closer, according to Zetsche, but 'a clear priority within this effort will continue to further strengthen brand identity. You can expect to see more examples of collaboration especially when we can transfer knowledge between the groups, much as Chrysler Group tapped the rear-wheel-drive expertise of Mercedes-Benz in the development of the Chrysler 300C.

'Beyond that,' added Zetsche, 'you will also see more examples of clearly defined "*project houses*" where engineers from different divisions work together for the benefit of the whole company.' A current example is the joint project to develop hybrids, where Mercedes-Benz and Chrysler engineers are working side-by-side (with General Motors and BMW specialists). This joint team is creating a new two-mode hybrid system that will power future vehicles from the brands of both divisions ...

Several other organizational changes will also be made. Corporate-wide Research and Technology will be merged with product development of Mercedes Car Group under BoM member Thomas Weber. The new organization – Group Research & MCG Development – will continue as the research center of competence for the entire company. Within this realignment, the new function will take on more responsibility for advanced engineering activities of all automotive divisions.

This action is expected to reduce the time-to-market of future technologies, keep research focused on customer-relevant innovations, and eliminate redundancies.

The Commercial Vehicles Division, headed by BoM member Andreas Renschler, will also undergo changes. It will focus on commercial trucks as its core business and operate under the name Truck Group, while the Bus and Van business will be reported elsewhere. The following operations will continue in Truck Group: Trucks Europe/Latin America (Mercedes-Benz), Trucks NAFTA (Freightliner, Sterling, Thomas Built Buses), Mitsubishi Fuso Bus and Truck Corporation, and Truck Product Creation. The new structure will create further synergies between the regional truck units and brands, and allow the Truck Group to accelerate its profit potential initiative called Global Excellence ...

In total, the new management model will reduce the cost of administrative functions at DaimlerChrysler, in an effort to reach benchmark levels. Together with other ongoing efficiency programs, G&A costs are expected to be reduced by EUR 1.5 billion per year. The net effect of today's announcement will be EUR 1 billion per year.

Preparation to implement this comprehensive program will start immediately, and take three years to fully implement. It is expected to require an overall expenditure of about EUR 2 billion from 2006 to the end of 2008. Due to the elimination of redundancies, consolidation of staffs and optimization of processes, headcount will be reduced by about 6,000 employees over the three-year span. This represents roughly 20 percent of general and administrative staff (30 percent at management levels). These reductions will take place in G&A functions around the world. At a meeting today, the DaimlerChrysler Supervisory Board agreed to the realignment of functions in the Board of Management, which will be implemented by March 1st, 2006.

The specific measures required to put the new actions into place are expected to be presented to the Supervisory Board for approval by the end of April.

Case study questions

1. As the HR-Director of DC (Stuttgart, Germany) you are required to develop a 'suitable HR strategy' to propose solutions to the problems raised by the actual situation of DC and the intentions of the CEO described above.

   State your understanding of the situation at DC and determine the needs of DC (problems within DC and reasons for the new organisational structure); also describe some strategic elements of the organisational structure.

2. Whereas German companies such as Deutsche Bank AG, Lufthansa AG or Allianz AG are seen by HR specialists and scholars as 'truly' global companies with excellent strategic HRM policies, DaimlerChrysler lacks such a reputation. There were incredible problems integrating Chrysler in the DC group. It took years to fix many post-merger problems. There are many other examples of a poor international HR policy of DC. This may also be a reflection of a generally rather poor (strategic) HR management of DC's head office.

   You are therefore also asked to answer the following questions:

   - In light of the intentions in the announcement of DC (text above) which HR areas or HR challenges are concerned?

   - Name some of these challenges. Then establish a plan of action by formulating and justifying possible solutions to the challenges you have identified.

3. What type of organisational structure should be created and implemented to support the new HR strategy?

4. What are possible advantages (and disadvantages) of creating a new organisational structure?

5. In developing and implementing the new structures, the company will have to recruit new international managers. How could the company really select and develop a group of experienced international managers? What instruments would you use?

6

Relationships between culture and SHRM: do values have consequences?

Learning Outcomes

By the end of this chapter you should be able to:

- explain the meanings of national and organisational cultures and the debates relating to their existence;

- discuss the importance of organisational and national cultures in managing SHRM interventions;

- explore the three main perspectives through which culture has been explored within organisations: integration, differentiation and fragmentation;

- assess the complexity of issues associated with aligning culture to an organisation's strategic direction;

- analyse the linkages between organisational and other cultural spheres and SHRM interventions.

Introduction

Over the past 50 years, culture has become one of the most widely written about concepts in management literature in both the populist and academic press (Cooper *et al.*, 2001). At the national level, writers such as Hofstede (2001) and Tayeb (1996) have highlighted the implications for both multi-national organisations and uni-national organisations employing a multi-cultural workforce, while at the organisational level, writers such as Handy (1993) and Peters and Waterman (1995) have highlighted the importance of an effective culture to organisational success. Messages relating to organisations from a vast range of culture studies have been summarised by Hendry (1995) as twofold. First, culture matters and, more importantly, the right organisational culture can lead to improved organisational performance. Linked to this there is a second implicit message: an organisation's culture is a tangible phenomenon, which can be manipulated and altered. The importance of organisational culture might therefore be considered a result of the search by organisations for competitive advantage linked to 'buzz phrases' of the 1980s, such as 'competitive advantage' and 'models of excellence' (Legge, 1994: 397). The implication of this is that, through a strong culture, an organisation can deliver sustained superior performance gaining competitive advantage and corporate success (Barney, 1986).

An organisation does not, however, exist within a cultural vacuum. Rather, its operations are affected by what Schneider and Barsoux (2003: 51) term 'interacting spheres of culture'. In addition to the organisation's culture, these spheres include national and regional cultures, industry cultures, functional or professional cultures. All of these impact upon each other and the culture of the organisation and, as a consequence, the management of human resources within the organisation. The implication is that an understanding of these spheres of culture and their interactions is central to the success of business activities, such as mergers and acquisitions, joint ventures and the like.

Despite this, research evidence (reviewed by Hendry, 1995) suggests that the link between an organisation's culture and its performance is weak. He argues that an organisation's culture is unlikely to accentuate positive attributes already possessed such as competitive advantage, overall performance or success. Rather the way in which an organisation's employees behave, and the assumptions upon which they base their behaviours, are likely to reduce the impact of negative attributes such as resistance to necessary change. With regard to this, Whipp *et al.*'s (1989) contention is that culture is one factor influencing an organisation's competitiveness over time. This implies that an understanding of an organisation's culture, and the other spheres of culture that influence it, can assist in the selection and application of more effective SHRM interventions relating to recruitment and selection, performance management, training and development programmes. At the same time, SHRM interventions can influence the culture of the organisation.

This chapter starts by considering the different meanings of culture and exploring different typologies of national cultures (Figure 6.1). Building upon this, frameworks for understanding organisational cultures and typologies of organisational cultures are examined. Within this the implications of different cultures for different SHRM interventions are considered. In this consideration the standpoint is adopted that an organisation's culture is an objective entity and, in particular, that it is 'something an organisation has' (Legge, 1994: 405). This implies that an organisation's culture, as well as impacting upon HR policies and practices, is something that can, at least theoretically, be manipulated and managed to achieve alignment with an organisation's strategic direction. To this end we offer an analysis of a variety of ways in which this might be achieved and the contribution SHRM might make. Within this analysis it is recognised that, while a large number of views and prescriptions for realigning or changing an organisation's culture abound, in reality the process is long term and complex needing careful study prior to attempting any strategy of change (Thompson, 1992; Bate, 1995).

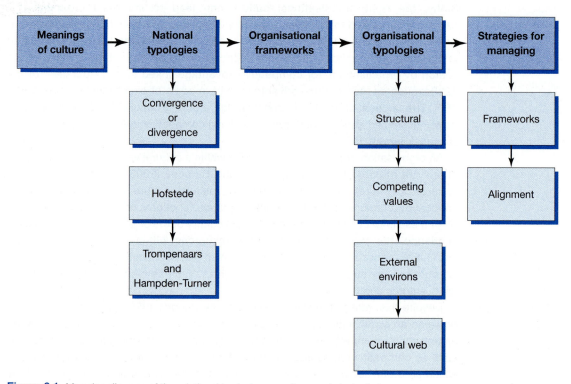

Figure 6.1 Mapping diagram of the relationships between culture and strategic human resource management: a summary diagram of the chapter content

Meanings of culture

Within the literature there are numerous definitions of culture. Schneider and Barsoux (2003) note that anthropologists alone have proposed over 164 different definitions and, in their discussion, argue that culture is both shared patterns of behaviours and the meanings that are attributed to these behaviours. They stress that the interrelationship between meanings and behaviours is crucial to understanding cultures, emphasising not only that the same shared behaviour can have different meanings but also that different shared behaviours can have the same meaning. This is illustrated in 'In Practice' 6.1. They also highlight that these meanings may not be readily apparent, suggesting that, although culture can be observed, like a code it still needs to be deciphered.

In Practice 6.1

The world's local bank

A recent television advertisement campaign by the international banking corporation HSBC highlighted differences in national cultures and their importance to understanding the bank's customers. In the advertisement, the meanings attributed to different gestures and gifts were contrasted between countries in a humorous manner. For example, while the giving of chrysanthemums is welcomed in the UK, the same flowers are associated with funerals and death in France. However, the underlying message put over by the advertisement was serious. Although HSBC is a global company it understands the importance and takes account of local cultural differences in its operations. This was emphasised by the advertisement's final comment 'HSBC The World's local bank'.

Schein (1997: 12) captures these ideas of shared behaviours and meanings in his definition of culture. In this he states that culture is:

> A pattern of shared basic assumptions that the group learned as it solved its problems of external adaptation and internal integration, that has worked well enough to be considered valid and, therefore, to be taught to new members as the correct way to perceive, think and feel in relation to those problems.

This definition emphasises that culture consists of shared assumptions that not only belong to a group but, because they have worked, have been internalised and are taken for granted. Within this a group could be, for example, a nation, region, industry, profession, organisation or function within an organisation. Consequently, it can be argued that these assumptions represent why people within a group behave the way they do and why they hold the values and beliefs they espouse. This definition has additional appeal as it emphasises key issues faced by SHRM: finding solutions to problems of adaptation to the external environment and determining practices that will promote internal integration.

When considering organisational culture specifically, most writers adopt one of two approaches. Either they view culture as one of a series of metaphors, such as the organisation as a machine, used to help understand the complexity of organisations (for example Morgan, 1997); or (the majority) see it as an objective entity. Those writers who view culture as an objective entity use two distinct approaches. The first of these considers culture in a similar way to anthropologists; that is as something an organisation *is* rather than a variable that can be manipulated by managers. The *is* approach argues that all of an organisation's features and behaviours, including its systems, procedures, policies and processes, are part of its culture. As a consequence, the culture cannot be manipulated as a whole, or turned on or off; although it may be intentionally influenced (Pacanowsky and O'Donnell-Trujillo, 1982; Meek, 1992). Legge (1994) argues that this approach is self-defeating. By defining culture as an organisation's features and behaviours, its management becomes equivalent to managing behaviour in organisations, including SHRM. The alternative approach is to think of culture as a variable that an organisation has, such as the set psychological predispositions that members of an organisation possess which lead them to respond in certain ways (Schein, 1997). This implies that it is possible for an organisation to manage at least some aspects of its own culture.

Drawing upon these arguments, the relationship between organisational culture and SHRM is examined from the viewpoint of culture being something an organisation *has*. Despite this, it is recognised that some implications for SHRM associated with the *is* approach are still likely to be of relevance, in particular the complexity and time-consuming nature of the change process. As the basis for this examination, Brown's (1998: 9) definition is used:

> Organisational culture refers to the pattern of beliefs, values and learned ways of coping with experience that have developed during the course of an organisation's history, and which tend to be manifested in its material arrangements and in the behaviours of its members.

This definition is similar to Schein's wider definition of culture. The term 'culture' is used collectively to refer to more than a single set of attitudes or beliefs within any one organisation. A particular pattern of beliefs, values and behaviours will have proven valid and useful for the organisational group(s) that use this, and will therefore have been shared with new group members (Schein, 1992a). It therefore follows that a culture will need to change when the beliefs, values and learned ways no longer work or when the external environment necessitates different responses. Brown's (1998) definition also acknowledges the possibility of a multi-national organisation having different cultures in different countries owing, at least in part, to the influence of national or regional cultures as well as political, economic, technical and social factors. In addition, it allows for the possibility of more than one culture co-existing within an organisation, such as different cultures for different professional groups.

Typologies of national cultures and their implications for managing human resources strategically

All HR interventions are influenced, at least to some extent, by the cultures within which they are enacted. In particular, the efficacy of differing HR interventions depends upon the national culture and context within which an organisation operates. Over the last 30 years, large numbers of typologies of culture, particularly within the national and organisational spheres, have been developed. These provide differing overviews of the variations that exist between cultures and some indication of the associated dimensions. Although these typologies are not applicable to all nations or organisations, they can be used as a series of idealised types through which to begin to understand aspects of cultures and subcultures and explore the implications of these for SHRM. To this end the section starts by considering national cultures.

The influence of national cultures – converging or diverging?

As suggested earlier in relation to Schneider and Barsoux's (2003) cultural spheres of influence, one of the influences upon an organisation's culture is the national culture or cultures within which it is located. Within the literature, there is a long-standing discussion as to whether national cultural differences and their impact are declining or increasing. This is known as the convergence–divergence debate. Those favouring the convergence view highlight that, due to advances in telecommunications, the world is becoming smaller and that we are increasingly buying global brands, such as Levi jeans and Nike trainers, and eating global food, such as McDonald's. They argue that the rapidly increasing use of technology and the growing numbers of multi-national organisations will result in a convergence of organisational configurations in terms of strategy, structure and management practice (Ritzer, 1998; Senior, 2002). In 2002 the United Nations estimated that there were more than 65,000 multi-national companies in the world and that the total sales of these companies accounted for more than one-tenth of the world's gross domestic product (GDP) and one-third of the world's exports (International Labour Office, 2003). Consequently, it is argued that the impact of national cultures on organisational cultures appears likely to continue to decline where such organisations have no national allegiance, only an international common purpose (Ohmae, 1994).

Management education has also been argued to encourage convergence (Schneider and Barsoux, 2003). For example, training provided in western business schools provides students with an understanding of basic business disciplines including finance, marketing, operations and human resource management. This is often underpinned by a particular ideology based upon the need for businesses to make money and the importance of shareholders' rights underpinned by the fundamental of free enterprise. Despite this, the business norms associated with these ideologies suggest a common culture management which, it is argued, may not be relevant or useful for some contexts (Schneider and Barsoux, 2003). Consequently an implicit promotion of convergence through education may be counter-productive.

Writers like Hofstede (2001) and Tayeb (1996) support the opposing 'divergence' view. They argue that, despite the growth in multi-national organisations and the technical and economic forces for convergence, between-country differences, such as language, religious beliefs, laws, political systems and education, mean that their cultures will diverge. Organisations therefore increasingly need to be aware of differences in national cultures, the influence of these differences upon the organisation's culture or subcultures and the implications for the organisation's policies and procedures and differing management practices. While advances in telecommunications technology are increasingly enabling organisations to locate work (for example call centres) anywhere, thereby taking advantage of economic differences between countries, the management of the people employed still needs to take account of cultural differences between countries. These will influence both the culture of organisations operating within these countries and the human resource interventions utilised within these organisations. In addition, an increasingly culturally diverse workforce within countries, such as the UK, further emphasises the need to understand the implications of national cultures within organisational HR practices, such as training and development (In Practice 6.2).

Self-Check and Reflect Questions 6.1

Produce a table summarising the arguments for convergence and for divergence of national cultures using the following structure:

Arguments for convergence	Arguments for divergence

In Practice   6.2

Ethnic minority police are more likely to quit

According to UK government targets, the proportion of recruits to London's Metropolitan Police from ethnic minorities needs to reach 25.9 per cent by 2009. Speaking to the BBC (British Broadcasting Corporation) in April 2004, the Metropolitan Police Force's head of human resources said the current rate of progress meant the force did not 'stand a prospect of getting anywhere near that target'. In 2002–2003 some 9.8 per cent of recruits to London's Metropolitan Police were from ethnic minorities.

Despite the need to meet such targets, the 2004 Skills Foresight report for the police sector in England, Wales and Northern Ireland reveals that nearly a quarter of police recruits from ethnic minority backgrounds quit before they finish their training programme. Recruits from ethnic minority backgrounds are twice as likely to drop out of training within the first six months as those from white backgrounds.

Research conducted by the Commission for Racial Equality (2004: 27) reports that for one group of police probationers undergoing initial training there was a 'dominant "bar culture" which reinforced macho and anti-diversity attitudes and excluded participants from minority groups who abjured alcohol or heavy drinking'. Based upon this and other evidence, the report highlighted that ethnic minority probationers often felt culturally isolated and vulnerable. The report recommended the establishment of effective pastoral care and a safe complaints process for trainees.

Hofstede's dimensions

The best-known work on national cultures has been undertaken by the Dutch academic Geert Hofstede, the most recent version being published in 2001. As outlined briefly in Chapter 3, this focuses on the differences and similarities between national cultures across, initially, four dimensions using survey data drawn from a pre-existing bank of employee attitude surveys undertaken in the 1960s and 1970s within IBM subsidiaries in 66 countries. Based upon analysis of these and some additional data, Hofstede was able to define four bi-polar dimensions of national culture, giving a comparative score to 40 out of the 66 countries in which the IBM subsidiaries were located for each. These dimensions were:

- power distance;
- individualism/collectivism;
- masculinity/femininity;
- uncertainty avoidance.

Subsequent research in the 1980s (Bond, 1988) resulted in a fifth dimension:

- Confucian dynamism.

Power distance relates to the extent to which less powerful employees accept that power is distributed unequally. Thus, within low power distance countries, such as the UK, Sweden and Denmark, inequalities between people are more likely to be minimised and consultative decision-making is more likely to be used. In contrast, in high power distance countries such as Malaysia and the Philippines, inequalities are considered desirable and there are greater differentials between employers and senior managers in terms of pay and privileges.

Individualism/collectivism refers to the extent to which individuals are oriented to themselves and their immediate family, rather than wider strong cohesive in-groups that offer protection in exchange for unquestioning loyalty. This is likely to have implications for the psychological contract. In high individualist countries, such as the USA and the UK, contracts of employment are based on mutual advantage in which the employer provides training and good physical conditions are taken for granted and are relatively unimportant. For low individualist countries, such as Pakistan and Indonesia, contracts with employers tend to be viewed in moral terms, like a family relationship. Consequently, hiring and promotion decisions are more likely to take into account the employee's in-group. Employer-provided training, and the like, is less likely to occur, and where it does, it is unlikely to be taken for granted.

The masculinity/femininity dimension refers to the extent to which assertiveness and decisiveness are prioritised over more caring values, such as nurturing and concern for quality of life, Hofstede's label attributing these to specific genders. Although you may find the use of such gendered labels annoying, it is worth putting aside your feelings and exploring briefly the meanings Hofstede attributes to these words. In 'masculine' countries, such as the UK and Italy, organisations place greater emphasis on competition and high performance. Employment disputes tend to be resolved by conflict and there is often a stronger ethos of living to work. In more 'feminine' countries, such as Sweden and the Netherlands, conflicts tend to be resolved by compromise and negotiation, and there is often an ethos of working to live.

Uncertainty avoidance relates to the extent to which people feel threatened by ambiguous or unknown situations. In low uncertainty avoidance countries, such as the UK and Hong Kong, there is greater tolerance of risk and ambiguous situations, and people are likely to be motivated by achievement and esteem. For high-uncertainty avoidance countries, such as Portugal and France, there is a fear of ambiguous situations and people are more likely to be motivated by security.

The final dimension, Confucian dynamism, captures the long- or short-term orientation of cultures. Countries with a high long-term orientation, such as China and Japan, emphasise the adaptation of traditions to a modern context, are sparing with resources and stress perseverance. In contrast, countries with a low long-term orientation, such as the USA and the UK, tend to have less respect for traditions, place lower emphasis on the importance of social and status obligations, approve conspicuous consumption and demand quick results.

Table 6.1 notes the relative scores on Hofstede's dimensions of national culture for selected countries. These can be thought of as stereotypes based on the mean score of the respondents from each country and so represent an average around which scores for individual members of that country will be dispersed. Consequently, when cultural dimensions are compared among members of a country, there is likely to be less variation than when they are compared between countries. This can be represented diagrammatically, such as when comparing the cultures of the UK and Japan in relation to their long-term orientation (Figure 6.2). Although it may be possible to find some Japanese who have less of a long-term orientation than some people from the UK (represented by the shaded area), overall we can expect people from the UK to have a relatively short-term orientation and those from Japan a relatively long-term orientation.

Hofstede has emphasised that, while his work and that of others such as Laurent (1983) on upper and middle managers has focused on the nature of national cultures, these nations are largely a creation of the twentieth century. For example, within the past two decades, both the Soviet Union and Yugoslavia have split into constituent countries

Table 6.1 Relative scores on Hofstede's dimensions of national culture for selected countries

Country	Power distance (high = greater differentials)	Individualism/ collectivism (high = individualism)	Masculinity/ femininity (high = masculinity)	Uncertainty avoidance (high = fear of ambiguity)	Confucian dynamism (high = long-term orientation)
Germany (West)	Low	High	High	Moderate	Moderate
Hong Kong	High	Low	Moderate	Low	High
Japan	Moderate	Moderate	High	High	High
Netherlands	Low	High	Low	Moderate	Moderate
Pakistan	Moderate	Low	Moderate	Moderate	Low
Sweden	Low	High	Low	Low	Moderate
Switzerland	Low	High	High	Moderate	Moderate
Taiwan	Moderate	Low	Moderate	Moderate	High
UK	Low	High	High	Low	Low
USA	Low	High	High	Low	Low

Source: adapted from Hofstede (2001).

and Germany has been re-unified. Despite this, Hofstede argues that differences between countries in language, education and laws mean that national cultures are still powerful forces in shaping the patterns of beliefs, values and learned ways of coping with experiences for employees within organisations.

Although Hofstede's work has been adopted widely, it has also been subject to criticism, a recent example being that by McSweeney (2002a). As part of this he criticises the assumptions implicit within Hofstede's method, namely that:

● an individual's organisational, occupational and national cultural spheres are discrete;

● national cultures can actually be identified at the micro or local level;

● national cultural differences can be shown by differences in questionnaire responses;

● national cultures can be identified by analysing such responses;

● national cultures are situationally (in this instance, organisationally) non-specific.

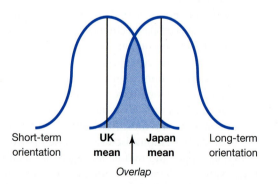

Figure 6.2 Schematic distribution of the Confucian dynamism dimension for the UK and Japan

McSweeney (2002a) also argues that Hofstede's research fails to show a causal link between the dimensions of a particular national culture and specific actions. He states that, while Hofstede acknowledges the existence of other levels and types of culture, he appears to suggest that they have little influence. McSweeney argues that other levels and types of culture and non-cultural influences are likely to also be important. For example, in one country uncertainty avoidance may be the cause of low labour turnover, while in another it may be due to high unemployment (Tayeb, 2000). This might be equated, at least in part, to the importance given by Schneider and Barsoux (2003) to the interaction between their different spheres of cultural influence and other factors. Hofstede (2002) responded to McSweeney's criticisms, arguing that many had been addressed elsewhere (for example, Hofstede, 1980, 2001). In his response Hofstede emphasised that while organisational practices could be modified, national cultural values, as measured in his research, were hardly changeable. It should be noted that in a rejoinder, McSweeney (2002b) argued that Hofstede had failed to rebut his initial criticisms. However, whether you agree or disagree with McSweeney's (2002a) criticisms, they:

- provide insights into the methodological assumptions behind Hofstede's work;
- raise awareness of possible interactions between different spheres of culture;
- question the extent to which national cultures have preferred management styles;
- question the extent to which national cultures have discrete influences on specific actions such as SHRM interventions.

Your own view on such issues will inevitably influence the way in which you consider the implications of national cultures for SHRM, an issue which you can explore further through Self-Check and Reflect Question 6.2.

Trompenaars and Hampden-Turner's dimensions

In contrast Trompenaars and Hampden-Turner (1997) identify seven dimensions of culture. Although these are different, they appear conceptually related to Hofstede's dimensions (Tayeb, 2000). Trompenaars and Hampden-Turner sampled over 30,000 employees from 30 companies, with departments in 50 countries worldwide, a minimum of 100 people with similar backgrounds and occupations being included from each of these countries. Approximately 75 per cent of their sample were managers, the remaining 25 per cent being general administrative staff. Based on these data, Trompenaars and Hampden-Turner proposed a series of seven dimensions which, they argue, are the basis of cultural differences. These dimensions are grouped into three distinct areas that are summarised in Figure 6.3 and listed below:

- relationships with people;
- attitudes to time;
- attitudes to the environment.

As can be seen from Figure 6.3, Trompenaars and Hampden-Turner (1997) group five dimensions within the area 'relationships with people'. The first of these is universalism versus particularism. Societies, which are universalist, have a relative rigidity in which contractual agreements and rules are important in defining individuals' conduct within the workplace as well as in the relationships between organisations. Personal relationships are not anticipated to impact upon business decisions. These are expected to

Figure 6.3 Trompenaars' and Hampden-Turner's dimensions of cultural differences

be made logically, impartially and professionally. In contrast, in societies which are more particularist, obligations to both friends and family are considered to be important and morally right. Consequently, specific situations, such as whom to recruit or promote, are likely to be considered more flexibly.

The individualism versus communitarianism dimension emphasises that societies can be individualistic or collectivist. It can therefore be considered to be almost identical to Hofstede's individualist/collectivist dimension (Tayeb, 2000). Within societies, communitarianism (collectivism) can take many forms such as the importance of the organisation in Japan, or the family in Italy. However, the relevance of this to managing human resources strategically relates to the extent to which employees regard themselves as individuals or as part of a group and has associated implications for policies and practices, such as performance-related pay and team working (Trompenaars and Hampden-Turner, 2004).

The extent to which it is acceptable to express emotions publicly, such as within interpersonal communications, is highlighted by the neutral versus emotional dimension. This can be considered as the extent to which individuals should communicate the full extent of their personal feelings. Within North America and, to a lesser extent, north west Europe, Trompenaars and Hampden-Turner (1997) argue that business relationships are typically instrumental and focused upon achieving objectives; personal feelings being subdued as they only confuse issues. In contrast, they argue that in cultures that are more open about their emotions (affective), such as Russia and Egypt, more overt displays such as laughter and anger are typically considered part of business (Table 6.2). Trompenaars and Hampden-Turner (2004) consider that this dimension is particularly important when managing employees and, in particular, enabling employees to learn through honest evaluations of their work performance. They argue that, by establishing rapport between individuals in a supportive environment, it is possible to 'make tough reports and still be credible' (2004: 120), while if there is no rapport such reports may be ignored or seen as personal attacks.

The specific versus diffuse dimension highlights the relative importance ascribed by different cultures to focusing on the specific, for example analysing issues by reducing them to specific facts, tasks, numbers or bullet points. This is contrasted with a focus upon analysing issues by integrating and configuring them into relationships, understandings and contexts. Trompenaars and Hampden-Turner (2004) illustrate this by contrasting specific and diffuse approaches to ascribing blame in a workplace where a trainee has made a serious and costly error. In a more specific culture, such as Australia or Russia, blame would be more likely to be placed on the individual who made the mis-

Table 6.2 Relative positions on Trompenaars' and Hampden-Turner's dimensions for selected countries

Country	Relationships with people					Attitudes to time	Attitudes to the environment
	Universalism v. particularism	Individualism v. communitarianism	Neutral v. emotional	Specific v. diffuse	Achievement v. ascription		
China	Particular	Communitarian	Middling	Diffuse	Ascription	Sequential	External
Egypt	Middling	Communitarian	Emotional	Middling	Ascription	Middling	External
Finland	Universal	Middling	Middling	Specific	Middling	Middling	Middling
Germany	Universal	Middling	Middling	Specific	Middling	Middling	Middling
India	Middling	Communitarian	Middling	Diffuse	Ascription	Sequential	Middling
Japan	Middling	Communitarian	Neutral	Middling	Ascription	Synchronic	Middling
Netherlands	Universal	Middling	Middling	Specific	Middling	Middling	Internal
Russia	Universal	Middling	Emotional	Specific	Middling	Sequential	External
Switzerland	Universal	Middling	Middling	Specific	Middling	Middling	Internal
UK	Universal	Middling	Middling	Specific	Achievement	Middling	Internal
USA	Universal	Individual	Middling	Specific	Achievement	Middling	Internal

Source: adapted from Trompenaars and Hampden-Turner (1997, 2004).

take. In contrast, within a more diffuse culture such a mistake is more likely to be considered as due to a failure in a wider system, such as the procedures for training, supervising and developing new employees.

The fifth dimension, concerned with relationships with people, achievement versus ascription, focuses upon the way in which status is accorded. Cultures that place relatively high values on achievement are more likely to focus on what has been accomplished with, for example, selection, promotion and reward decisions being more likely to be based upon this. In contrast, cultures that place a higher value on status than what has been accomplished are more likely to focus upon kinship, gender, age, connections and past record, such as the university attended. In ascription cultures, seniority and promotion are more likely to be linked, for example, to age or time served in the organisation. Comparing Tables 6.1 and 6.2, it can be seen that this dimension has some similarities with Hofstede's power distance. For example, countries that have relatively low power distance scores, such as the UK and the USA, tend to accord status through achievement. In contrast, countries that ascribe status, such as Japan, tend to have at least a moderate power distance score.

The dimension 'attitudes to time' (Figure 6.3) focuses particularly on whether time is viewed as linear and sequential (past, present and future), or circular and synchronic (seasons and rhythms). These differences are likely to impact on how planning and organising takes place and can be differentiated by contrasting a focus on the concept of doing things in sequence as quickly as possible (sequential), often attributed to North America, with the concept of coordinating processes so that things are done just in time (synchronic), often attributed to Japan. This is illustrated in 'In Practice' 6.3.

In Practice   6.3

Just in time *and* time and motion

In their book *Managing People Across Cultures*, Trompenaars and Hampden-Turner (2004) recount how Taichi Ohno, the person who first set up the Toyota motor company's assembly operation in the 1950s, used to kick any pile of inventory he saw on the assembly plant floor. Such piles of 'work in progress inventory' highlighted where there was poor synchronisation between different parts of the assembly operation and so emphasised where improvements were needed to shorten the process. Reflecting on Toyota's current vehicle assembly operations, Trompenaars and Hampden-Turner argue that the combination of this just-in-time philosophy of good synchronisation with rapid sequencing based upon time and motion studies has enabled Toyota to maintain its lead in automobile manufacturing.

The final dimension, attitudes to the environment, focuses on the relationship between individuals and the environment (Figure 6.3). Some cultures, for example the UK, see the major focus affecting individuals' lives and the origins of the way that people act as residing within the individual or internally. Other cultures, for example China, are more likely to consider an individual as a product of their environment and so influenced externally. This interrelationship with the surrounding environment is illustrated by the reasons some people in large conurbations wear face masks over their mouth and nose. In Tokyo, people tend to wear such masks when they have a cold or virus in order not to infect other people by breathing on them. This can be considered as seeing themselves as part of the environment and not wishing to impose upon it. In London, face masks tend to be worn by people such as cyclists who do not want to breathe environmental pollution, in other words to be imposed upon by the environment (Trompenaars and Hampden-Turner, 1997).

Self-Check and Reflect Questions   6.2

Examine Tables 6.1 and 6.2 and select two countries with contrasting profiles. Use Hofstede's dimensions to suggest how SHRM interventions to motivate employees and appraise employees might differ between these countries. Now repeat this process using Trompenaars and Hampden-Turner's dimensions. To what extent do your suggestions differ?

The discussion of Hofstede's work on national cultures emphasised the importance of power and the way it is exercised for the strategic management of human resources. However, it has also highlighted the importance of other factors, such as the tolerance by employees of uncertainty and whether the time orientation is over the shorter or longer term. Alongside Trompenaars and Hampden-Turner's research, it has also been emphasised that the relative focus on the individual and differences in the way in which conflicts are resolved are also likely to influence an organisation's culture and subcultures and, consequently, the way in which human resources are managed. Following a discussion of frameworks for understanding organisational cultures the discussion turns to the implications of cultures and their management for SHRM.

Frameworks for understanding organisational cultures

Among the best-known representations of culture are Hofstede's (2001: 11) 'onion diagram' subtitled 'manifestations of culture at different levels of depth' and Schein's (1997) 'levels' of culture. Each emphasises that cultures manifest themselves in many ways. Some of these are visible and therefore relatively easy to discern, such as when studying an organisation. However, because of their shallow or superficial nature, the true meaning is difficult to decipher. These manifestations are Hofstede's 'symbols', 'heroes' and 'rituals' and Schein's 'artefacts' (Figure 6.4). Managers often think that just through changing these visible practices or artefacts they are able to effect a culture change. Unfortunately, for real change the process also needs to occur far more deeply, in the less visible levels.

The deepest levels of culture (Hofstede's 'values' and Schein's 'basic underlying assumptions') are invisible and, as a consequence, extremely difficult to discover (Figure 6.4). They provide what Argyris (1995: 21) terms the 'theories in use' upon which the more visible 'practices' or 'artefacts' of organisational culture are built. Hofstede (2001: 10) refers to these 'values' as a 'core element of culture'. Such values are likely to have become so taken for granted that there will be little variation in them within a culture or subculture (Schein, 1997). They will be communicated to new employees, thereby transferring the culture. If these basic underlying assumptions are held strongly, then group members will find behaviour on any other premise inconceivable. For this reason, changing these is likely to result in a true culture change, which will also be reflected in 'practices' and 'artefacts'. However, because they are deeply and strongly held in individuals' subconscious, they are extremely difficult to change.

Between the deepest and shallowest levels, Schein (1997) introduces 'espoused values'. These are values connected with moral and ethical codes and determine what people think

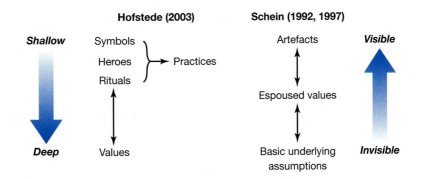

Figure 6.4 A comparison of Hofstede's and Schein's representations of organisational cultures
Source: Thornhill *et al.* (2000). Reproduced with permission.

ought to be done, rather than what they necessarily will do. Often, organisations present a particular view of their culture through formal documents, such as annual reports, mission statements and speeches by senior managers (In Practice 6.4). While these predict much of the behaviour that is observed at the 'practice' or 'artefact' level, especially with regard to what people say, they may conflict with what people do (Schein, 1997).

In Practice 6.4

Smile while you work

Employees at the Disneyland theme parks and, in particular, the practices they adopt while working, have a major impact on the guests' (customers') experiences. While the symbolic resources within the parks are an important part of the experience, it is the workforce's eagerness or otherwise in greeting guests, helping them into rides, delivering food in restaurants, keeping the streets clean and undertaking many other jobs, that will decide whether or not customer expectations are met.

Disney employees are expected to adopt a prescribed demeanour. This is governed by three rules:

- a friendly smile;
- using only friendly and courteous phrases; and
- not being stuffy.

Language is also important with, for example, customers being referred to as 'guests', and rides as 'attractions'. Employees are expected to be happy and helpful at all times. They are also expected to conform to park procedures and policies set down in codebooks with which they must be familiar. Supervisors keep close watch on what is going on and employees know they can lose their jobs by not conforming to expectations and breaking these rules.

Despite this, it has been suggested that at times during the working day some employees adopt an emotional numbness during which, although they appear as if they are fully engaged in their work, they are not. This has been argued to be a passive resistance to the prescribed culture.

Source: Van Maanen (1991).

So there is a problem. The outward manifestations of culture are clearly visible and relatively easy to discern. Unfortunately, if only these are considered, we cannot be certain that they are congruent with the less visible underlying values or basic assumptions of the culture. Yet, in order for SHRM interventions to be aligned with an organisation's culture, it is necessary to ensure that not only are the practices or artefacts, such as messages provided through training sessions, appropriate but that they are also internalised as values or basic underlying assumptions by individual employees (Mabey and Mallory, 1994/5). Conversely, where SHRM interventions are used to change an organisation's culture, it is necessary to ensure that not only can new values be observed through artefacts, such as answering the telephone within four rings, but that these new values are espoused by employees and the relationship between these and the desired culture has been internalised as part of the employees' underlying beliefs.

Martin (1992) identified three perspectives for looking at organisations' cultures.

These she termed:

- integration;
- differentiation;
- fragmentation.

The integration perspective implies that all members of an organisation share a common culture and there is consensus regarding the beliefs held and the behaviours expected. While this idea of one culture is easy to comprehend, Schneider and Barsoux's (2003) concept of interacting spheres of culture emphasise that this is unlikely to exist in its purest form. Although there may be some aspects of the way in which people in organisations behave and beliefs that are accepted by everyone, it is unlikely that all the beliefs and behaviours of organisational members in, for example, different professional groups will be universally accepted. Rather, different employee groups and their representatives are likely to have different beliefs about some aspects of the organisation. Martin terms this perspective 'cultural differentiation', arguing that, for this, manifestations of culture within the organisation will at times be inconsistent. Subcultures, perhaps formed around different work groups, such as shop-floor workers, professions or management, will exist, consensus regarding some aspects being found only within, as opposed to between, these groups. Martin's fragmentation perspective offers a further, if somewhat extreme, alternative to the other two. Within this, researchers argue that they can detect very little cultural consensus in what they are studying other than around time-specific sensitive issues, such as an imminent downsizing. Inevitably, these issues will change over time and, as a consequence, cultures are ambiguous and uncertain.

In reality, therefore, the idea of an integrated whole organisational culture, in which all members hold precisely the same beliefs, is unlikely to occur. Rather, organisations will exhibit only some organisational-wide cultural consensus and consistency. In addition, there will be differentiation between groups of employees. Research at the global nylon manufacturer DuPont's Gloucester site (Thornhill et al., 2000) emphasises this, highlighting how some employees had embraced the new culture introduced by management as part of a change process. Although these employees were now taking responsibility for their own actions, others, in particular production workers, still believed that this was not part of their job. This example also emphasises that culture is not a static entity, rather an organic process that is created, sustained and changed by people (Bate, 1995).

Self-Check and Reflect Questions   6.3

Why do you think it is difficult for managers to describe their organisation's culture in detail?

Typologies of organisational cultures and their implications for managing human resources strategically

Structural views

Structural views of organisational culture inevitably use structural artefacts or symbols as outward expressions of an organisation's culture. Of these, the most widely known and influential is probably Handy's (1993) typology. This was developed in the 1970s from work by Harrison (1972) and is concerned with how authority is exercised within an organisation and is the basis for power. These artefacts through which power is expressed can be used to help explore the likely cultural implications for managing the employment relationship. Handy proposes four main types of organisational culture:

- power;
- role;
- task;
- person.

He argues that, although these types do not have a high level of rigour, the differing power structures they encapsulate impact upon the way the organisation does things; in other words, the organisation's ways of coping with experiences that have developed during the course of its history.

In a power culture, Handy argues that there is a single source of power from which rays of influence spread out. He likens this to the power radiated by the god Zeus in Greek mythology, who was believed to be the supreme god, and protector and ruler of all humankind. The internal organisation of power is highly dependent upon trust, empathy and personal communication for its effectiveness. Authority comes from the resources controlled and the leader's charisma. This means that the strength of the culture comes from the willingness of employees to defer to the leader and, presumably, accept his or her power. Within such a culture, Handy argues that employees are unlikely to be concerned about taking risks or issues of job security. In contrast, within a role culture, power comes from the bureaucracy (rules and procedures) and the logic and rationality of the way functions/specialisms are structured (Chapter 5). Position power and, to a lesser extent, expert power are therefore the main bases for authority and it seems likely that the organisation's values will reflect ideals of security and predictability. Handy likens the role culture to a Greek temple, suggesting that any individual's power is determined by the rules and structures of the organisation rather than its leader.

Within a task culture, power is based upon employees' expertise rather than charisma. This is likely to necessitate a different approach to managing human resources, as flexibility and adaptability are valued and authority is based upon the employee's ability rather than position or seniority until a crisis occurs. When this happens, such cultures can, Handy argues, quickly change into a power or role culture with rules or procedures or internal political influences becoming the dominant way of managing employees. Handy continues with his Greek analogy, suggesting that the goddess Athene's emphasis was on task and getting the job done. Like Senior (2002), the authors find this analogy for a task culture somewhat curious, as Athene was typically allegorised into a personification of wisdom. Within Handy's fourth type, the person culture, power and authority lie within each of the individual members, rules and procedures being of minimal importance. The person culture is represented by Dionysos who, as the Greek god of wine and altered states, was considered the god of the self-oriented individual. This, Handy argues, occurs in very few organisations and represents a group of people who decide that it is in their own interests to come together as a cluster of individuals, for example in a doctors' or solicitors' practice. Later work by Pheysey (1993) has linked task and person cultures, in particular, with processes of support and achievement used within organisations, thereby emphasising the importance of culture in motivating and controlling employees.

Competing values

Work by Quinn and McGrath (1985) uses the nature of information exchange within organisations to distinguish between different organisational cultures. Within their typology, the focus is on the values that determine how things are done rather than the status that these processes give to both individuals and groups within the organisation. As part of their work, they argue that the manner in which these transactions are conducted (the artefact) is governed by a set of values or norms, which reflect the basic underlying assumptions within the organisation. From this they identified four generic cultures determined by the dominant values:

- rational or 'market' culture;
- ideological culture or 'adhocracy';
- consensual or 'clan' culture;
- the hierarchical culture – 'hierarchy'.

Although there is a concern about the nature and use of power within these, they also appear to have some parallel to Hofstede's individualism/collectivism and masculinity/femininity dimensions.

A market culture is directive and goal oriented, with individuals being judged according to their output and achievement. These values are likely to be reflected in artefacts such as pay and reward systems (Chapter 9). The 'boss' is firmly in charge of the organisation and their competence is the basis of authority. Decisions are made decisively and intuitively, compliance being guaranteed by employees' contracts. In contrast, within an adhocracy, individuals are judged according to their intensity of effort, rather than achievement. Authority in an adhocracy is maintained by charisma, while power comes from reference to the espoused organisational values.

Within a clan culture, authority is based upon the informal status of organisation members. Consultation and participation are valued, employees complying with decisions because they have shared in the process by which these were reached. Individuals are evaluated in terms of the quality of relationships they enjoy with others and are expected to show loyalty to the organisation. In a hierarchy culture, authority is vested in the rules, and those with technical knowledge exercise power. Decisions are made on the basis of factual analysis and leaders are conservative. Compliance of employees is maintained by surveillance and control, and they are evaluated against formally agreed criteria. They are expected to value security. Thus, the artefact of the nature of transactions within an organisation provides a means of helping distinguish the underlying values of the culture.

The external environment

Deal and Kennedy's (1982) typology of organisational culture is explained through artefacts related to the importance of the external environment (market place). They identify four generic cultures (Figure 6.5) based upon the interaction of two market-place factors:

- degree of risk associated with organisation's activities;
- speed at which the organisation and employees receive feedback on their decisions and strategies.

The latter of these, speed of feedback, can be argued to incorporate aspects of the short- or long-term orientation of the culture; Hofstede's Confucian dynamism dimension and Trompenaars and Hampden-Turner's sequential versus synchronic attitudes to time. While Deal and Kennedy recognise that organisations will not fit into any one of their four cultures perfectly, they argue that this framework is useful in helping managers identify their own organisation's culture(s).

Within tough guy/macho cultures the focus is on speed and the short-term, which places enormous pressures on employees to take risks and get results quickly. As a result, internal competition, tension and conflict are common suggesting both masculine and individualist dimensions in which employees are unlikely to make a long-term commitment to the organisation. Work hard/play hard cultures also focus on short-term feedback for performance but at the same time each individual action is unlikely to have high risks for the organisation as a whole.

Bet-your-company cultures are associated with risk but feedback takes a long time. As a consequence, decision-making tends to be top-down and there is a strong respect for authority, technical competence and cooperative working, linking to power distance and uncertainty avoidance dimensions. The process culture is a low risk and slow feedback culture, which operates well in a known predictable environment, with employees receiving relatively little feedback on their work and memos and reports seemingly disappearing into a void. Those employees who remain in such organisations tend to be orderly, punctual and attentive to detail.

Figure 6.5 Deal and Kennedy's typology of organisational culture
Source: adapted from Deal and Kennedy (1982).

Johnson and Scholes' cultural web

An organisation's culture is therefore likely to influence, and be reflected in, the way that an organisation manages its human resources. This in turn will have been influenced by internal factors, including the organisation's subcultures and external factors, such as the national cultures within which the organisation is operating. Earlier in this chapter, an organisation's culture was defined in terms of artefacts, espoused values and basic underlying assumptions. Artefacts, as the most visible of these, often have symbolic value for employees over and above their normal associations. Johnson and Scholes (2003) refer to the:

● stories;

● symbols;

● power structures;

● organisational structures;

● control systems;

● rituals and routines

and their interrelationships as the cultural web which define the core values and beliefs of the organisation. These elements combine together in different ways to determine and reinforce the paradigm that makes up the organisation's culture and the way in which it is acted out through day-to-day actions (Figure 6.6).

Within an organisation, aspects of the way in which human resources are managed are likely to have strong symbolic associations for employees and provide clues to the organisation's culture. Organisational rituals and routines, such as training programmes, recruitment and promotion, provide clues as to what the organisation values and considers important. Similarly, the manner in which employees usually behave towards each other can be seen to represent the accepted way of doing things. Such

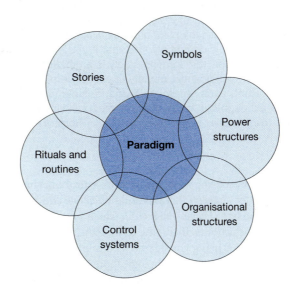

Figure 6.6 Johnson and Scholes' cultural web
*Source:*Johnson and Scholes (2003: 230).

rituals and routines will manifest themselves in particular control systems, as set out through procedures or policies, such as individual or team-based performance-related pay (Chapter 9) or an avoidance of redundancy procedure (Chapter 14), but are likely to be based upon the underlying basic assumptions of that organisation. Organisational structures will also provide clues as to the real value placed upon SHRM, for example whether the HR director has a board-level appointment. Similar clues are provided by informal power structures, such as relationships between senior human resources' personnel and other managerial groupings within the organisation. Symbols, such as logos, offices and reserved car parking spaces, are also likely to reflect the organisation's culture while stories and myths are used to reinforce key aspects of the culture (In Practice 6.5). From these elements, individuals are likely to obtain the information they need to understand how the organisation operates, and the forms of behaviour that are acceptable and unacceptable.

In Practice   6.5

DuPont's safety culture

Safety has always been, and continues to be, of paramount importance to the global corporation DuPont. The corporation's web site states that 'since its founding, DuPont has held fast to core values of safety, health, ethics, fair and respectful treatment of people and environmental stewardship' (DuPont, 2004). Although, today, DuPont provides science-based solutions in areas such as food and nutrition, health care, apparel, safety and security, construction, electronics and transportation, it was originally an explosives manufacturing company (DuPont, 2004).

A corporation story tells of an accidental explosion in 1818 at the gun-powder plant on the Brandywine River in Delaware, Massachusetts. Subsequent to this, the du Pont family rebuilt the plant, including its own house within the plant grounds. E.I. du Pont justified this, arguing that if the factory was safe for his employees it would be safe for him and his family. The du Pont family also agreed that one partner should always remain in the yards and that lower-level managers should reside, as the family did, within the plant grounds (DuPont, 2004).

Today, within DuPont, it is commonly said that if you make an error regarding safety it is 'a good career opportunity', in other words acting safely is a condition of continued employment. The focus upon safety has wider significance, namely that every employee is responsible for his or her own actions. Within DuPont, each employee is responsible for creating a safe environment. DuPont emphasises that, although it is the managers' responsibility to create a safe environment, it is also each individual's responsibility to act safely within it (Thornhill *et al.*, 2000).

Considering an organisation's culture in the way that has so far been made in this chapter, suggests that it is as an objective entity and, in particular, 'something an organisation has' (Legge, 1994: 405), which manifests itself visibly in the organisation's features and behaviours, including its systems, procedures, policies and processes. In doing this, culture is being considered as one of a number of variables that an organisation has, such as the set of psychological predispositions that employees possess which lead them to act in certain ways (Schein, 1997). This implies that culture is a distinct influencing variable that needs to be understood in managing human resources but also that it can be managed by organisations through SHRM interventions.

Human resource strategies for managing organisational cultures

As outlined earlier ('Meanings of culture') there has been considerable debate as to whether culture can be managed, much of it focusing on whether or not it can be modified. Given that it can be altered, it therefore follows it can be managed and, where necessary, realigned to the strategic direction an organisation wishes to take. Bate (1995) argues that, within organisations, culture is a dynamic continuously developing phenomenon. It therefore follows that, if managers can manage organisations' cultures, they can not only realign culture but also prevent its realignment as well as abandon or destroy it (Ogbonna, 1993). In this section possible frameworks for realigning an organisation's culture through both gradual or incremental changes as well as more radical or transformational changes to a new culture are explored. In particular, the use of top-down and bottom-up approaches and the role of SHRM interventions within these are looked at.

Frameworks for cultural alignment

Lewis (1996) reviews a range of frameworks for cultural change. These, he argues, consist 'overwhelmingly of a number of steps' or questions (Lewis, 1996: 9) which outline an overall process and emphasise the importance of knowing and understanding the current culture and strategic direction of the organisation prior to commencing realignment. In essence, the process consists of:

1. working out the desired culture;
2. ensuring that the HR strategy and desired culture match;
3. identifying gaps between actual and desired culture;
4. taking steps to move the actual culture to the desired culture.

One of the most widely quoted of these is Lewin's (1952) three steps of unfreezing, moving and refreezing. Lewin's framework emphasises that before an organisation's culture can be transformed, the existing embedded culture must be unfrozen and made more susceptible to being altered. Subsequent to the transformation, his framework highlights the importance of stabilising and institutionalising the new culture, in Lewin's words refreezing.

However, the reality of achieving this is more complex. Organisations are dynamic phenomena and even those within similar backgrounds in similar environments are likely to develop different cultures (Hassard and Sharifi, 1989). As highlighted particularly by Handy's (1993) typology of organisational cultures and Johnson and Scholes' (2003) cultural web, power relationships within the organisation and the transformation process will need to be managed (In Practice 6.6). Similarly, the resources available will need to be sufficient to ensure that any cultural realignment is permanent (Beckhard, 1992). These, and other principles, have been illustrated by numerous case studies which 'purport to demonstrate successful cultural change' (Lewis, 1996: 10) and are summarised in the following list:

- Accepted and appropriate patterns of behaviours within organisations are defined by values and basic underlying assumptions.
- Successful organisations tend to be those where the values and basic underlying assumptions encourage practices and behaviours, which match the organisations' strategies.

- Where values and basic underlying assumptions are incompatible with an organisation's strategy, successful cultural change may be difficult to achieve.
- If an organisation is contemplating change, it first needs to establish whether or not the strategy necessitates a shift in values and basic underlying assumptions or if change can be achieved in another way.
- Prior to any culture change, senior management must understand the implications of the new culture for their own practices, artefacts and espoused values, and be involved in all the main change phases.
- Adequate resources need to be allocated to support culture change and maintain it once it has been achieved.
- Culture change programmes must pay careful attention to the organisations' power bases and opinion leaders, such as trade unions and employees' associations.
- Culture change programmes must take into account an organisation's existing practices or artefacts such as approaches to recruitment, selection and retention, training, performance management and employee relations.
- In order to create a change in culture, organisations need to decide how practices or artefacts will be amended to support the new espoused values and contradictory practices removed.
- Every opportunity should be taken to reinforce the practices or artefacts and restate the espoused values of the new culture's values and basic underlying assumptions.

Source: adapted from Hassard and Sharifi (1989); Beckhard (1992).

In Practice   6.6

HP merges with Compaq

In 2002 Hewlett-Packard (HP) merged with Compaq to create the world's largest consumer IT company, the world's largest small and medium-sized business IT company and a leading enterprise IT company. The merger involved 145,000 employees in 170 countries (Hewlett-Packard, 2004) and, according to press reports at the time, resulted in a culture clash between the two firms. Two years on from the merger, Hugo Bagué, vice president HR, stresses that HP is now one company (Edwards, 2004). He states that the attitudes of the company's employees are aligned to the future of HP, citing evidence from the employee attitude survey. Much of this success is attributed to HP's global HR team. They developed a three-part people strategy (Edwards, 2004):

1. Ensuring a solid foundation in which all employees had access to the latest information on HP's strategies and objectives through a company-wide information portal. The portal streamlined processes into one company-wide approach, while still taking account of cultural and linguistic differences as well as legislative differences between countries.

2. Creating a high-performance workplace by linking together performance systems, salary planning, the performance review process and reward and payroll. This enables employees to see how their performance impacts upon the rest of the business.

3. Energising people to feel HP is the best place to work by addressing a range of HR issues, such as diversity and talent management.

Self-Check and Reflect Questions   6.4

Visit HP's corporate web site at http://www.hp.com. Use the menus to go to the pages headed 'Company information: About us – History and Facts'.

What clues do these give you about the culture of HP?

Which culture do you consider was dominant in the merger between HP and Compaq?

From earlier discussion it is clear that, prior to utilising SHRM interventions to align an organisation's culture, a variety of elements need to be taken into account. Bate (1995) groups these into five foci. The first is a need to have a clear appreciation of the existing culture. To enhance appreciation, the current culture needs to be placed within an historical context so that the ways in which it has developed are clearly understood. This second focus allows learning from past experience as well as avoiding 'corporate amnesia … and the associated problems of repeating the same mistakes or endlessly re-inventing the wheel' (Bate, 1995: 141). Understanding of the current organisational culture needs to be integrated with the nature of the required change. In particular, whether the existing culture can be further developed or a transformational change to a new culture is necessary. Bate (1995) refers to this third focus as the life-cycle stage of the culture in the organisation. Through doing this, the most appropriate SHRM interventions can start to be identified as well as potential problems.

Typologies of organisational culture reviewed earlier in this chapter (for example, Deal and Kennedy, 1982) suggest the external environment will also impact upon individuals' behaviours and an organisation's culture. This environmental context provides Bate's fourth focus and, taking a broad interpretation, could be considered to emphasise that other cultural spheres are also influential. Bate's last focus returns to the organisation and contrasts what people in an organisation want with that organisation's needs. This emphasises the importance of understanding organisational politics, power bases and opinion leaders (highlighted by the cultural web – Figure 6.6) prior to attempting to alter culture (Harrison, 1972; Handy, 1978). Changes required for cultural realignment will therefore occur from and within an existing organisational culture and be influenced by other cultural spheres, such as the professional and national.

Strategies for cultural alignment: top-down or bottom-up?

Strategies for cultural alignment are characterised as two alternative approaches: top-down and bottom-up. Those in the former category, often termed 'programmatic change', are typically initiated and led from the top (Beer *et al.*, 1990) and have often been inspired by writers on corporate excellence (Hendry, 1995). Those in the latter focus on incremental approaches, in which alignment is developed from the bottom up, tied to an organisation's 'critical path' (Beer *et al.*, 1990) and spread through that organisation. For either approach to succeed, it is crucial that employees have the capabilities to deliver the behaviours necessary to realise cultural alignment (Mabey and Mallory, 1994/5). It therefore follows that an organisation can make a number of HR responses to support either approach, ranging from strategic to tactical, coherent to piecemeal or, maybe just after thought!

Top-down approaches

Cultural alignment initiated by senior managers typically looks towards organisation-wide consensus, focusing on the artefacts of culture (including employees' overt behaviour) and to a lesser extent their espoused values (Legge, 1994). As a consequence, senior managers often rely on the HR function to manage the associated cultural symbols, such as the organisational structure, the management of office space, and car parking allocations, as well as provide educational and training interventions to change them directly. SHRM initiatives, such as organisation-wide human resource development programmes (Chapter 10) to enhance quality, excellence or empowerment, might be introduced as part of top-down approaches, although the outcome is likely to be representational learning (i.e. in the way participants talk) rather than behavioural learning (the way they do things).

Often managers will try a succession of HR interventions using only anecdotal evidence to evaluate the impact each is having rather than having a clear strategic focus. For example, the introduction of performance-related pay (Chapter 9) might force managers to differentiate between better and poorer performers. However, on its own it will not help them to internalise the cultural context of the new standards by which performance is to be judged, or the way in which poor performers will be dealt with. Ultimately it may therefore fail to create the desired realignment of culture resulting in, perhaps, another HR intervention, such as training to manage poor performance. Consequently, the focus is on the process rather than understanding the organisation's problems and the consequent need for strategic integration. In addition the succession of interventions tends to promote cynicism and scepticism thereby inhibiting real change. Hendry (1995: 135) summarises these arguments:

> Programmatic change does not work because it typically fails to tackle three interrelated structural-cum-attitudinal factors – the requirement for co-ordination through teamwork, the need for commitment, and the need to develop new competencies. Company-wide change programmes address one only or, at best, two of these. Culture change programmes in particular dwell on the creation of commitment, but only at a very superficial level.

Programmes involving top-down culture change also suffer from three interrelated paradoxes (Legge, 1994). First, messages of initiative, autonomy and innovation are usually conveyed through highly bureaucratic methods, such as team briefings or company-wide training initiatives. This can be problematic when, as in the case of the NHS, such public promises have in some instances only been delivered in part (In Practice 6.7). Second, transformation to the new culture is often seen as the task of a new leader. This can create problems if employees believe the new culture conflicts with their existing occupational culture. Finally, and building upon Legge's second point, if the values espoused by senior management are discordant with employees' sense of reality the new culture may be acted out cynically and without being internalised into employees' basic underlying assumptions.

This is not to say that HR interventions, such as those we have mentioned, are inappropriate to managing cultural realignment. They can play a valuable role when used strategically in an integrative manner, ensuring that the implicit and explicit message provide 'consistent cues' to the desired culture (Brown, 1998: 166). Indeed research into significant factors behind successful interventions at organisations, such as BT (British Telecom), Royal Dutch Shell, BA (British Airways) and Manchester Airport, emphasise the importance of deliberately modifying organisation-wide HR practices such as reward systems (Chapter 11) to reinforce desired cultural changes (Mabey and Mallory, 1994/5).

In Practice 6.7

Improving working lives?

Recent research argues that organisations' HR policies can be seen as a visible manifestation of management promises. Skinner *et al.* (2004) considered the Improving Working Lives (IWL) policy within the UK National Health Service (NHS) as an example of one such 'promise' that has been made to staff. Improving Working Lives publicly acknowledged the centrality of staff in attaining the achievements and changes required and the reciprocal need for the NHS to invest in its human resources. Using an anonymous questionnaire, data were collected from employees in five primary care trusts in relation to their experiences and awareness of what was being done to address working-life issues as part of a wider culture alignment. Their research found that although the IWL standard makes very public promises about work–life balance, harassment, equality and the valuing of staff, employees in these five primary care trusts perceived these promises had been met only in part.

Bottom-up approaches

In contrast to a programmatic or top-down approach, Beer *et al.* (1990) found that successful change usually started in one part of an organisation away from corporate headquarters. As you would expect, change in these organisations was led by general rather than senior managers. Rather than creating formal structures and systems, these managers focused upon solving concrete business problems; a process Beer *et al.* (1990) termed 'task alignment'. The role of senior management in change, such as cultural realignment, was to specify the general direction and provide a climate for change as well as to spread lessons from both successes and failures. Task alignment, Beer *et al.* argued, could be achieved through a series of overlapping steps (their critical path) taken at the business unit or site level (Figure 6.7).

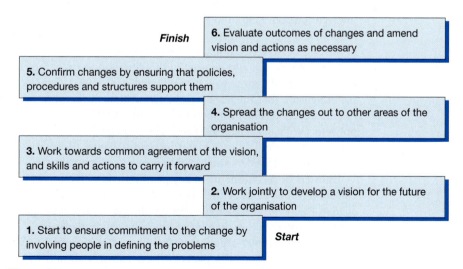

Figure 6.7 Beer *et al.*'s 'bottom-up' approach to task alignment
Source: Thornhill *et al.* (2000). Reproduced with permission.

As can be seen, there are some similarities between the bottom-up approach and the general framework for culture re-alignment outlined earlier. Despite these, it can be argued that bottom-up task alignment offers a different approach for managing culture re-alignment within organisations. In particular it focuses on the part of the organisation away from corporate headquarters, emphasising individuals' shared commitment and vision as a prerequisite. As in other frameworks, re-alignment is enabled by HR interventions, such as developing people's abilities, although now the desire to learn is enhanced by improved coordination and the need to work differently to solve concrete problems. Subsequent results generate stronger commitment to change, resulting in a mutually reinforcing cycle of increasing commitment, coordination and abilities. This provides a role model for other parts of the organisation. Organisation-wide SHR policies, procedures and structures provide a framework within which this is allowed to take place, with strategies, such as those relating to recruitment and selection, or roles and responsibilities within the hierarchies, only being revised subsequently to reinforce and support the re-alignment.

Consequently, within a bottom-up approach, HR-related strategies can be used to support such a process of culture re-alignment. In the early stages of Beer *et al.*'s (1990) bottom-up task alignment, this is likely to involve managing or enabling employees from different levels and functions within that part of the organisation to meet, mobilise commitment and develop their shared vision. Once the vision has been defined, employees will need to develop the skills required by the new culture. As part of this stage (three), HR initiatives, such as training and management development programmes might be used (Chapter 10). Such programmes can play a very important role in indoctrinating the desired culture as illustrated by use of employee training at Disneyland (Van Maanan, 1991; In Practice 6.4). However, unlike the Disneyland experience, training within a bottom-up approach will usually aim to address needs directly identified by employees. As a consequence, it is more likely to influence their basic underlying assumptions.

By stage three in the re-alignment process, employees who have not accepted the new culture are likely to be highly visible. It will be apparent if the total number of employees is too large or too small for the new vision of the organisation. For both scenarios, HR interventions can help to foster consensus of the new vision and generate the cohesion to move it along. Redundancy or early retirement programmes (Chapter 14) perhaps, as in the case of Abbey National in the mid-1980s, accompanied by the offer of generous severance terms, can also be used in this situation to encourage those people who hold onto the original culture to leave (Williams *et al.*, 1993). Considerable care will need to paid to ensure that the negative impact of these programmes on those who remain is minimised. Alongside this, recruitment and selection of new staff involving realistic job previews (Williams *et al.*, 1993) and selection exercises to discover whether interviewees support the desired culture might be used (Chapter 8). Internal and external promotions, as well as transfers and secondments, can support this.

Transfers or secondments of key people are also likely to be used to spread the new culture to other parts of the organisation (Figure 6.7, stage four). As with the initial change, Beer *et al.* (1990) argue that the change in these other parts must again be managed from within rather than being forced by senior managers.

Beer *et al.* (1990) argue that strategic alterations to policies, procedures and structures to support the process (new culture) should only be made once it is entrenched within part of the organisation, the right people are in place and it is working (Figure 6.7, stage five). Through working together, employees have already learned what interdependencies are necessary and so the organisational structures to support this can be developed. As discussed later, performance appraisal systems (Chapter 9) need to be tailored to emphasise the basic underlying assumptions of the new culture. Answers to questions such as: 'are past achievements or future potential more important?', 'should objective or subjective techniques be used?' and 'who undertakes the appraisal?' need to be aligned to the culture. Reward systems (Chapter 11) need to reflect the espoused values of the culture through what is rewarded, the relative importance of individuals or teams and the way bonuses are given. Similarly, defining job roles, writing new policies and applying human resource development systems (Chapter 10) will, whether intended or not, send out messages to employees about accepted and desirable behaviour and the new culture. Many of the problems with implementing strategies to re-align culture occur because such systems are either projecting inappropriate values or because they are giving out mixed messages (Hendry, 1995). The HR function can help coordinate, providing direction and control to overcome this.

The final stage in the process of bottom-up task alignment relates to evaluating and adjusting strategies in response to problems. This emphasises the evolving nature of culture as it interacts with both the internal and external environments. However, as in earlier stages, it also emphasises the importance of evaluating interventions and sharing the outcomes of evaluations undertaken as part of the process (Chapter 4).

Having just read the arguments above, one might gain the impression that a bottom-up approach is always the best way to manage culture re-alignment. However, this is not always the case. While Beer *et al.*'s (1990) research has shown that a bottom-up approach is more likely to achieve effective re-alignment, this does not mean that top-down approaches will not work. Every organisation's culture is unique and, as discussed, a product of that organisation's past as well as the wider environment within which it exists. The appropriateness of the chosen strategy will consequently depend upon what an organisation wishes to achieve through culture re-alignment (In Practice 6.8).

In Practice　　　　　　　　　　　　　6.8

Establishing a culture of trust at Richer Sounds

The UK's hi-fi retailer Richer Sounds has, for a number of years, been using a variety of HR interventions to enhance the working environment and create a culture of trust. Employees are offered a range of benefits on top of their basic pay package, including a subsidised health-care plan, a hardship fund and performance-related bonuses. Staff who have been employed by Richer Sounds for over a year receive short paid holidays in holiday homes owned by the company on top of the normal leave entitlement. They are encouraged to invite both family and friends to join them on these holidays. While some may argue that this is a risky thing to do, as the majority of employees are male and under 35, it is argued that this helps reinforce a culture of trust. For the same reason, employees who win performance-related bonuses are allowed to take the cash directly out of the till. The company's scheme for employee feedback channels complaints via a named representative. This means that no individual is held back by fear of repercussions. In addition, the company has formal procedures to ensure that employees do not work beyond their allocated hours. Consequently, it is as strict about employees staying late as it is about their arriving at work on time.

Source: Allen (2004).

Bate (1995) identifies a series of parameters through which an organisation can explore what it wishes to achieve through cultural re-alignment and the appropriateness of different cultural change strategies and associated SHRM interventions. Bate (1995: 203) argues that the relative importance, weight and value of these 'design parameters for cultural change' will differ both between organisations and over time within an organisation. These are outlined in Table 6.3.

Table 6.3 Design parameters for cultural change

Parameter	Aspect of the organisation	Description
Expressiveness	Affective component (feelings)	The ability of the approach adopted and associated SHRM interventions to express a new symbol, which captures employees' attention, and excites or converts them
Commonality	Social component (relationships)	The ability of the approach adopted and associated SHRM interventions to create a shared common understanding and sense of common purpose among a group of employees or the whole organisation
Penetration	Demographic component (number/depth)	The ability of the approach adopted and associated SHRM interventions to spread throughout all levels of an organisation and to affect employees' basic underlying assumptions
Adaptability	Development component (process)	The ability of the approach adopted and associated SHRM interventions to adjust to changing organisational and wider environmental circumstances
Durability	Institutional component (structure)	The ability of the approach adopted and associated SHRM interventions to create a lasting culture

Source: adapted from Bate (1995).

Thus, what might be effective or appropriate in one situation may not be in another. For example, 'expressiveness' is unlikely to be important where culture re-alignment is concerned with further developing an existing culture, in effect more of the same. Conversely, where transformational re-alignment is desired, expressiveness is an essential component. Requirements of an organisation are also likely to change over time. At the start of a culture re-alignment process, expressiveness may be considered more important, while commonality and penetration are considered less important. However, as the process continues and the new culture is spread throughout all levels of the organisation, commonality and penetration may become more important.

Relationships between these parameters and the top-down and bottom-up approaches are summarised in Table 6.4. As can be seen, the two approaches' effectiveness differs across the parameters. This emphasises that it is not just a case of choosing which approach will fit best with an organisation, as no one approach will provide everything required. Rather, the HR strategy for culture re-alignment needs to be tailored to the organisation's precise requirements at that particular time, taking into account the wider cultural spheres within which it is operating. A top-down approach can enable relatively rapid change in an organisation's practices. SHRM interventions, such as organisation-wide training and communication, can be used to help inspire employees to adopt the new culture at the practice or artefact level, offering the impression of culture re-alignment. However, if the culture re-alignment is also required to be durable, it will need to be combined with a bottom-up approach over a longer time period. This can help ensure the new culture becomes part of the employees' basic underlying assumptions.

Managing an organisation's cultural re-alignment change is therefore extremely complex. It needs to take account of the existing culture, whether developmental or transformational re-alignment is required, as well as a range of internal and external

Table 6.4 Relative effectiveness of top-down and bottom-up approaches to cultural re-alignment across different parameters

Parameter	Level of effectiveness of: top-down approaches	bottom-up approaches
Expressiveness	**High** – deal in simple messages and specialise in communicating these effectively and reasonably quickly at the practice/artefact level	**Low** in short term – focus on concrete problem generates lots of detail rather than a new symbol
Commonality	**Low** – promoted unifying feeling often ceases after formal programme ends. Methods often lead to resistance and lack of common ownership	**High** – operate through shared understanding and create a culture of trust and understanding
Penetration	**Variable** – depends on ability of interventions to affect more than just practices or artefacts; – highly structured programmes likely to reach all employees	**Low** in short-term – involve only part of the organisation **High** in long term – involve discussing proposals and implications with employees
Adaptability	**Low** – tend to be inflexible and imply instant fix; programmed nature implies conformity and devalues deviance	**High** – concrete-problem-led, willing to accommodate new views and find best fit with organisational requirements
Durability	**Low** – based on senior management's desires; – lack of ownership by employees likely to be highest with transformational re-alignment.	**High** – employees are keen to preserve what they have created; – especially high when a development of existing practices which employees own rather than transformational re-alignment

Source: Thornhill *et al.* (2000). Reproduced with permission.

factors. As part of this process, employees need to be managed. The reality of this challenge is clearly summarised by Whipp *et al.* (1989: 583) who state: 'culture is a Pandora's box: both academics and practitioners should not make any easy assumptions about their control of the contents'.

Self-Check and Reflect Questions　　　6.5

How might an organisation use SHRM interventions to support a culture re-alignment process?

Self-Check and Reflect Questions　　　6.6

Why might organisations choose a top-down approach to cultural re-alignment?

Summary

- An understanding of culture, and the interactions between different spheres of culture, such as national and organisational, can assist in the selection and application of effective HRM interventions and the hierarchies in which they are placed. At the same time, SHRM interventions can influence the culture within an organisation.

- Culture consists of shared attitudes, beliefs, values and behaviours that belong to and have been learned by a group and, because they are considered to be valid, have been internalised and are taken for granted. These are taught to new members of the group as the correct way to perceive, think and feel.

- Culture is one of a range of factors that can influence an organisation's competitiveness.

- There is long-standing debate as to whether the impact of national cultural differences is declining or increasing. This is known as the convergence/divergence debate.

- Researchers have developed dimensions upon which national cultures can be placed. These emphasise the importance of power and the way it is exercised, alongside other factors, such as tolerance of uncertainty, orientation to time, the relative focus on individuals and the way in which conflicts are resolved.

- Nations' scores against dimensions of national cultures can be thought of as stereotypes representing the mean around which scores for individual members of that country are dispersed. There is likely to be less variation within countries than between countries.

- Within organisations culture is most visible in practices or artefacts and, to a lesser extent, espoused values. SHRM interventions are largely concerned with structural means of influencing and supporting these visible manifestations.

- To re-align an organisation's culture, the basic underlying assumptions upon which these practices or artefacts are based need to be changed. As these are deeply and strongly held within each employee's subconscious they are difficult to change, especially over the short term.
- Realigning an organisation's culture is a complex process utilising a range of strategies. These are often divided into top-down (programmatic) and bottom-up (critical path) approaches.

Follow-up study suggestions

1. Working with a colleague from another culture, first describe your national culture as you see it. Now describe your colleague's culture. Compare your view with that of your colleague for the two cultures. What does this suggest to you about stereotypes of national cultures?

2. Use your understanding of culture to create a cultural web for an organisation or a department within an organisation that you know well.

3. Re-examine the cultural web you drew in answer to suggestion 2. If you wished to re-align the organisation's culture, how would you use HR interventions to support changes to the rituals, routines, stories and symbols?

4. Choose a large multi-national organisation and visit that organisation's web site. Based upon the web site, what do you think are the main features of that organisation's corporate culture?

Suggestions for research topics

1. Can typologies of organisational and national cultures help organisations manage their human resources more effectively?

2. To what extent are the human resource practices in XYZ aligned to that organisation's culture?

3. To what extent does an organisation's culture act as a barrier to change? A case study of company XYZ.

4. What are the implications of a lack of congruence between an organisation's espoused values and its actual HRM practices?

5. How do national cultures impact upon HRM practices in different countries?

Dicom Group plc is the global market leader in the information capture market, providing document imaging scanning hardware and software, and associated support services. Operating through two distinct divisions, the information capture and the Samsung General Agency Division, the Group has wholly owned subsidiaries in Europe and Asia and over 10,000 customers in more than 60 countries (Dicom, 2004). In the financial year ending 30 June 2004, the Group achieved a turnover of £156.2 million, the information capture division accounting for 77 per cent of this and 92 per cent of the Group's profits (Dicom, 2004).

Founded in Switzerland in 1991 by Otto Schmid, Dicom Group grew rapidly during the 1990s via a combination of acquisitions and organic growth and now employs over 840 people across the subsidiary companies. Although the Group headquarters are in Basingstoke, UK, the senior management team operate from an international base, due to the Group's broad global coverage (Dicom, 2004). A visit to the Group's web site reveals both the vision:

> The Dicom team will be the world leader in enabling organisations to automate their business transactions by accelerating the collection, transformation and delivery of mission critical documents

and the mission:

- We care for our customers better than anyone else in our industry.
- We are a premier business partner of the world's leading system integrators, software developers, IT resellers and OEMs [original equipment manufacturers].
- We only compete with superior products and services in fast-growing information technology sectors in which we can achieve and maintain a dominant market share.
- We hire the highest calibre employees available and continually invest in their development.
- We constantly aim to achieve attractive returns for our shareholders.

- To us respect, integrity and loyalty constitute very important values, reflected in a co-operative relationship with the society and the environment in which we operate.

The Group promotes itself to employees in the subsidiary companies as the 'Dicom Family'. The unofficial (although heavily endorsed by senior management) aim of the Group is 'to make money and have fun doing it'. Announcements regarding Group performance and other news are communicated regularly to all employees via email from the Chief Executive Officer. These emails always begin 'Dear Friends,' and finish by thanking everyone for their hard work and commitment. Within emails, subsidiaries' newsletters and face-to-face communications, a Group language has evolved in which some everyday words and phrases have particular organisational meanings. For example, employees throughout Dicom are likely to say 'Standards!' when a colleague or the organisation has done well, thereby offering congratulations for the setting of a standard which competitors will find difficult to achieve. Group members argue that the use of such language reinforces the feeling of camaraderie, and their membership of an exclusive club.

Stories are used to illustrate the Group's values to visitors, prospective and new employees. One story concerns the Group's tenth anniversary celebrations. All 800 employees from around the world and their partners were invited to Switzerland for an all expenses paid weekend of celebrations at the Lucerne Opera House. This was hired exclusively by the Group for the whole weekend and, according to Dicom legend, was partly funded by the Chairman out of his own pocket. This and other stories are used to illustrate the humanity and caring nature of the Board of Directors and how this permeates the entire Group.

Virtually all Dicom's employees work in open-plan offices, symbols and displays of rank or seniority being discouraged. Employees are introduced as 'colleagues' to visitors by their managers, the phrases 'these people work for me' and 'these are my staff' being considered unacceptable. All employees are given freedom to undertake their jobs in their own way, albeit within the confines of company procedures and policies. One UK manager described this approach as 'We like to steer with very long reins'. Wherever possible, employees are quickly given as much responsibility as they can handle in both their working lives and their own personal development. Dicom Group aims to 'bring people on', and takes responsibility for the personal development of its employees. Wherever possible, employees are promoted internally into managerial positions as they arise. Where this is not possible, employees are involved in the writing of the job specification and the subsequent recruitment process, including interviews and selection.

Employee training and development is considered essential by Dicom. All employees, whatever their level, are encouraged to take advantage of both in-group and external training programmes. If there is a business advantage to be gained from the training, then the Group will both provide the finance and allow individuals time to complete it. At the time of writing, employees based at the UK subsidiary, Dicom Technologies Ltd, were attending courses including a Certificate in Management Studies, a Diploma in Personnel Management, Chartered Institute of Management Accountants Certification and Microsoft Certification training. Alongside external courses, Dicom has recently launched 'The Dicom Academy'. This offers all Dicom Group managers and those identified as future managers the opportunity to attend a series of one-week courses on areas such as marketing and leadership at various venues around the world. These are tutored by Harvard Business School professors alongside Dicom Group board members.

Performance appraisal is carried out at least annually for all employees, with employees in some subsidiaries receiving three-monthly reviews. Each appraisal focuses upon a joint review of an individual's own performance using an appraisal schedule. This asks a series of questions, for example 'How do you rate your punctuality on a scale of one to ten?' If an employee has a different rating from his or her manager, then a discussion is held and a compromise reached. Where an individual employee's performance is exceptional, the manager has discretion to reward him or her in the way that is likely to be of most value. This might be the granting of extra holiday, a meal for them and their partner, or a public display of gratitude at an award ceremony. Every year, at the Group's Christmas celebration, awards and prizes are given out to individuals and to work groups that have been voted as exceptional by colleagues. Each subsidiary company has a display cabinet where these shields, trophies and award certificates are displayed for all to see.

Alongside performance review, performance measurement is a continual process. Within each subsidiary, work groups normally meet on a monthly basis to discuss problems and progress. All work-group members are encouraged to make suggestions to improve performance against measurable criteria. All subsidiary companies report annually on promotions, hires of people who are disabled, and donations to charity. This is done with the aim of promoting ethical awareness among Dicom Group's management.

Case study questions

1. Drawing on the information given in this case, construct a cultural web for Dicom Group.

2. Assess the extent to which Dicom Group's culture is aligned to its vision and mission.

3. To what extent do you consider that Dicom Group's culture exhibits characteristics identified by Hofstede (Table 6.1) and by Trompenaars and Hampden-Turner (Table 6.2) for Switzerland? Give reasons for your answer.

Acknowledgements

The support of Kevin Davies, Managing Director of DICOM Technologies Ltd., in granting permission to use this case, and the assistance of Stephen Barker, Operations Manager of DICOM Technologies Ltd., in the preparation of this case are both acknowledged gratefully.

7 Strategic human resource planning:
the weakest link?

Learning Outcomes

By the end of this chapter you should be able to:

● identify and discuss the core principles that underpin the concept of strategic human resource planning;

● critically evaluate the extent to which strategic human resource planning represents the vital connecting link between organisational strategy and SHRM practice;

● analyse the conceptual and operational difficulties surrounding the practice of strategic human resource planning;

● assess the relevance of strategic human resource planning to organisations facing an increasingly changing business environment;

● review potential avenues for addressing the difficulties associated with human resource planning in order to enhance its operational viability.

Introduction

> Human resource planning is about ensuring that the correct number and mix of
> employees is available at the right place at the right time. The success of HRP is
> paramount to the survival of the organisation and the complexities associated with
> the planning process are enormous.
>
> *(Parker and Caine, 1996: 30)*

This opening definition captures three important themes that have been used to
help structure the chapter. First, it starts with a beguilingly simple definition of
human resource planning (HRP) that is frequently echoed elsewhere in the literature.
Although this definition can be criticised as being too simplistic, it provides a useful
starting point for getting to grips with the question, 'What is strategic human resource
planning?'

Second, the claim that HRP is 'paramount to the survival of the organisation'
reflects its potential strategic significance and critical position within SHRM. Recognising that similar claims might be made for other dimensions of SHRM explored in
this book, it is necessary to subject Parker and Caine's statement to closer scrutiny.
To do this a case for representing strategic human resource planning (SHRP) as the
vital connecting link between organisational strategies and SHRM practices is developed. However, it is accepted that viewing SHRP in this way provides no guarantee
that it will be either practised or practised effectively.

The third theme relates to the complexities underpinning the theory and practice of
SHRP referred to in Parker and Caine's definition. The nature of these complexities is
deconstructed in order to better understand the difficulties that might confront organisations wishing to practise SHRP. This leads to the conclusion that conceptual and
operational complexities associated with SHRP contribute to its limited take-up by organisations. This presents something of an organisational conundrum, whereby, despite its
potential as a vital connecting link between organisational strategies and SHRM practices, the difficulties associated with SHRP may preclude its practice by organisations.

This potential dilemma is particularly pronounced when the case for SHRP is set
against the challenges presented by an uncertain future. The paradox that arises here
is captured well by Turner (2002: 19) who argues, 'There are those who say it is useless trying to plan when no one can predict what is going to happen … and there are
those who would claim that it is now more than ever necessary to plan.' However,
where such dilemmas militate against its practice, SHRP can be viewed as the missing link between organisational strategies and SHRM practices, or, to borrow the
vernacular of a popular game show, 'the weakest link' of SHRM. These apparent
paradoxes are more fully explored as a further chapter theme and can be para-
phrased in the question 'To plan or not to plan?'

As a final chapter theme, how SHRP practices and processes might be shaped in
order to enable it to fulfil its potential role as a crucial link between organisation strategy and SHRM practice is discussed.

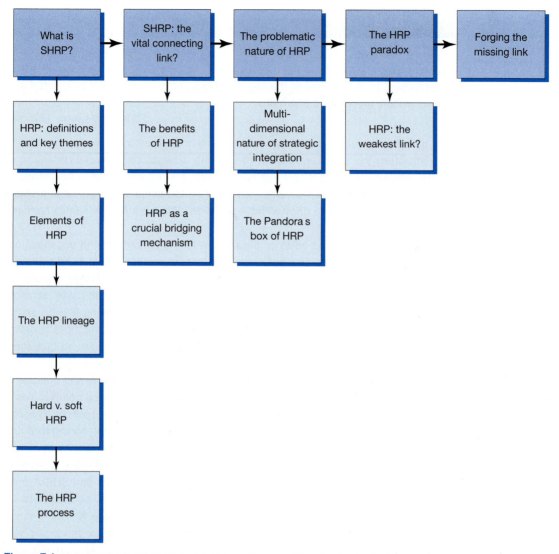

Figure 7.1 Mapping the SHRP territory: a summary diagram of the chapter content

This chapter introduction concludes with an illustrative example of SHRP in practice (In Practice 7.1). The focus here is on evidence of failures in mergers and acquisitions that particularly illustrates the problems that can arise when SHRP is a missing element in important corporate-level decision-making. It is in stark contrast to the concluding chapter case, where SHRP is identified as a critical factor in successful merger cases.

In Practice | 7.1

The role of HRP in mergers and acquisitions

From 1980 onwards, the number of mergers and acquisitions increased, largely as a result of the strategic possibilities they offered (Appelbaum and Gandell, 2003; Schraeder and Self, 2003). For the organisations involved, they constitute major change at the first-order level of corporate strategy decisions (Purcell, 1991) and are designed to achieve, through strategic integration, objectives such as diversification and economies of scale, as well as opportunities for obtaining a speedy global presence (Schraeder and Self, 2003). In contrast to the relatively slow speed of internal development, mergers/acquisitions offer unique potential for accelerated organisational transformation and renewal and have the capacity to contribute to rapid market repositioning (Salama *et al.*, 2003). However, their track record of success is very poor. Based on research evidence in the USA, the failure rate of mergers/acquisitions to meet their financial and strategic objectives has been variously assessed at 55–70 per cent (Schraeder and Self, 2003) or 60–80 per cent (Appelbaum and Gandell, 2003).

Increasingly it is held that such failures are due to poor HRP throughout the merger/acquisition process (Greer, 2001; Appelbaum and Gandell, 2003). The argument runs that while financial, legal and operational aspects, together with strategic synergy, are well planned, HR areas, such as culture, communication, management style and leadership of change, are neglected. It has been argued that the success of mergers/acquisitions depends on the extent to which the human resources of the combining organisations are integrated. The repeated failure to consider these issues demonstrates that HRP is not integral to the process of strategic planning (Greer, 2001). Somewhat ironically, evidence also exists of cases where planning still fails to sufficiently account for HR issues even where the prime motivation behind the merger was to acquire another organisation's human resources (Greer, 2001). Cultural issues are particularly identified as a cause of merger failures and can be the factor that makes or breaks the merger success (Salama *et al.*, 2003; Schraeder and Self, 2003).

Importantly, the extent to which HR issues are neglected throughout the planning stages of mergers/acquisitions impacts on employees as well as the success of the venture itself. Buono and Bowditch (1989) discuss two contrasting strategies for integrating human resources. A 'love and marriage' strategy strives for high levels of HR collaboration between the organisations involved in attempts to secure employee commitment, despite the hard realities that may accompany the merger (e.g. downsizing). In contrast, an 'abuse and plunder' strategy is seen as synonymous with asset stripping. They conclude that evidence points to the latter being much more common than the former (Buono and Bowditch, 1989).

What is strategic human resource planning?

Definitions of SHRP

Returning to Parker and Caine's (1996: 30) definition that 'Human resource planning is about ensuring that the correct number and mix of employees is available at the right place at the right time', it can be argued that reducing SHRP to one all-encompassing definition is too simplistic and not particularly helpful. However, by considering a range of definitions it is possible to surface a number of important features that, as with SHRM (Chapter 2), reveal SHRP to be a complex and multi-faceted phenomenon.

'Manpower planning may be defined as a strategy for the organisation, utilisation, improvement and preservation of an enterprise's human resources' (Department of Employment and Productivity, 1968: 2).

'HRP consists of a range of tasks designed to ensure that the appropriate number of the right people are in the right place at the right time' (Zeffane and Mayo, 1994: 36).

'A management process designed to translate strategic objectives into targeted quantitative and qualitative skill requirements, to identify the human resource strategies and objectives necessary to fulfil those requirements over both the shorter and longer terms, and to provide necessary feedback mechanisms to assess progress. Overall the purpose of the planning is to invoke an institutional learning process and to generate information which can be utilised to support management decision making in all staffing areas' (bin Idris and Eldridge, 1998: 346).

'Human resource planning is the process of systematically forecasting the future demand and supply for employees and the deployment of their skills within the strategic objectives of the organization' (Bratton and Gold, 2003: 191).

'HRP is the process for identifying an organisation's current and future human resource requirements, developing and implementing plans to meet these requirements and monitoring their overall effectiveness' (Beardwell, 2004: 159).

Key features of SHRP

From the above definitions it is possible to surface a number of important features that have been used to inform the exploration of SHRP.

- HRP is viewed as a process (Parker and Caine, 1996; bin Idris and Eldridge, 1998; Bratton and Gold, 2003; Beardwell, 2004).
- There is a temporal perspective such that HRP is directed at meeting both current and future needs (Zeffane and Mayo, 1994; Parker and Caine, 1996; bin Idris and Eldridge, 1998; Beardwell, 2004).
- HRP is seen to progress through distinct phases primarily involving forecasting the demand for and supply of human resources and then developing plans to address any mismatches arising (bin Idris and Eldridge, 1998; Bratton and Gold, 2003; Beardwell, 2004).
- Monitoring and evaluating outcomes and feeding back results are viewed as integral parts of the process (bin Idris and Eldridge, 1998; Beardwell, 2004).
- The process should be driven by the strategic objectives of the organisation and its purpose is to help achieve their fulfilment (Parker and Caine, 1996; bin Idris and Eldridge, 1998; Bratton and Gold, 2003).

Conceptual limitations of SHRP definitions

While the above definitions and key features provide a useful starting point, they carry with them a number of limitations:

- First, the notion that HRP is about ensuring that 'the right people are in the right place at the right time' is somewhat simplistic. Although it trips readily off the tongue and finds popular expression, it provides no insight as to what might be construed as 'right'.

- Second, there is little or no explanation as to what is meant by the term 'process'. Although the importance of viewing HRP as a continuous process is discussed later in the chapter, this facet does not emerge from the above definitions, with the possible exception of that provided by bin Idris and Eldridge (1998). At best, HRP as a continual process is only implicit in the definitions cited.

- Third, the strategic linkage consistently appears to be portrayed as one-way with HRP being clearly positioned downstream of corporate decision-making. This reflects a narrow interpretation of vertical strategic integration falling short of the two-way strategic linkage advocated in Chapter 1.

- Fourth, references to the planning stage reflect a compartmentalised mentality where HR plans developed to address mismatches between the demand and supply of labour could be conceived as stand-alone activities with little thought to their horizontal integration.

- Last, the very use of the word 'planning' in HRP could be viewed as something of a misnomer when applied to the forecasting stage. Arguably, planning responds to the outcomes of the forecasting process and is about developing solutions to perceived HR problems.

This last point is crystallised by Turner (2002) who separates the two concepts of forecasting and planning. He reserves the term HRP for what others regard as the latter (planning) stage of the process. He interprets HRP as an output arising from strategy formulation concerned with managing the organisation's human resources. In contrast strategic human resource forecasting is interpreted as an input to strategy formulation, rather than a dimension of planning. These relationships are captured diagrammatically in Figure 7.2 .

However, strategic human resource forecasting can also lie downstream as an output of strategy formulation. It is argued here that it also represents an input into HRP. This reflects the more conventional view that forecasts of labour demand and supply are made against corporate strategies with any resultant mismatches between them being the concern of HRP. Figure 7.3 illustrates how the input–output relationships described by Turner can be reconstructed to reflect all these possible relationships.

Figure 7.2 Input and output relationships between strategic human resource forecasting, strategy formulation and HRP

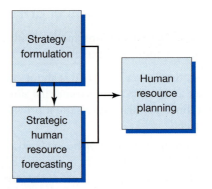

Figure 7.3 Input–output relationships between strategic human resource forecasting, strategy formulation and HRP – a revised model

To better understand the distinctions drawn by Turner between strategic human resource forecasting and HRP his definitions of these two elements are reproduced in Table 7.1.

Table 7.1 Strategic human resource forecasting versus human resource planning

Strategic human resource forecasting (SHRF) is defined as:	Human resource planning is defined as:
A process by which an organisation looks ahead at the people implications of business and organisational strategy, and facilitates a dialogue within the organisation about these implications. Its objective is to give direction to the people decisions to be made at strategic level that will enable the organisation to achieve sustained success ... The SHRF deals with the quantification of the people implications of business or organisational strategy and the likely qualitative inputs or outputs of the strategy. The SHRF comprises a process intended to form an intervention into the strategic planning process or the strategy-setting process of the organisation. It consists of groups of strategic HR activities: • dialogue with strategy-makers • scenario planning aligned to the business or organisational strategy • demand-and-supply forecasts for the people aspects of strategy • gap analysis • input to the HR plan	The output that arises from the process of business or organisational strategy setting as it affects the people in an organisation. It contains quantitative analyses of HR data ranging from headcount and costs to qualitative analyses about culture, learning and knowledge management. The HRP is a dynamic entity that can be changed if turbulence or unpredicted extraneous factors affect the business strategy. It consists of a range of plans within the key HR activities. These can be grouped as follows: • resourcing through specific organisational design, quantified HR plans and resource allocation • employee commitment and relations • learning, training and development • reward and recognition

Source: This material is taken from *HR Forecasting and Planning*, by Turner, P. (2002), with the permission of the publisher, the Chartered Institute of Personnel and Development, London

Taken together, the two elements of Turner's (2002) model go some way to addressing the earlier critique of HRP definitions. He is more explicit about the nature of process features and his use of the word 'dialogue' suggests a continuous process that incorporates two-way strategic fit. However, the lack of focus on horizontal integration is again evident.

Elements of HRP

From Turner's (2002) definitions of SHRF and planning, it is possible to identify the key elements involved in the two processes. Table 7.2 summarises the key elements of HRP identified elsewhere in the literature, which can be compared with Turner's framework (Table 7.1).

Table 7.2 The elements of HRP

Key elements of HRP	Description
Strategic planning	Environmental scanning Identification of key business issues Strategy formulation
Demand forecasting	Determining HR implications of strategy Forecasting future HR requirements to meet business objectives
Auditing current HR capability	Analysing current labour resources Auditing internal labour supply Reviewing labour utilisation
Supply forecasting	Forecasting internal labour supply Forecasting external labour supply
Gap analysis	Comparing demand and supply forecasts Identifying gaps between needs (demand) and availability (supply)
Planning	Developing HR objectives and goals to address identified labour shortages and surpluses Designing HR strategies, policies, programmes and practices (action planning) to deliver objectives and goals
Implementation and evaluation	Implementing action plan Monitoring and evaluating outcomes Feedback results Revising and refocusing HR objectives and plans

Sources: Hercus (1992); Hendry (1995); Tansley (1999).

Although these elements of HRP are frequently brought together in explanatory models, it is very difficult to capture fully the complexities of the HRP process in this way. However, many examples exist within the HRP literature that you can refer to for a diagrammatic summary of the process (for example Galpin, 1999; Turner, 2002; Beardwell, 2004).

The HRP lineage: the historical development of HRP

Historically, two labels have commonly been applied to the formal process designed to plan future organisational HR requirements. The term 'manpower planning' was widely adopted up to the mid-1980s (as reflected in the Department of Employment and Productivity's (1968) definition appearing in Key Concepts 7.1), after which it became increasingly replaced by the term 'human resource planning' (or HRP). This change paralleled the shift in terminology from personnel management to HRM and prompted similar debates around whether it simply represented a cosmetic name change or something more fundamental. Most commentators, however, argue that HRP is conceptually different from manpower planning. The most commonly identified differences have been summarised in Table 7.3.

Table 7.3 Distinguishing features of manpower planning and human resource planning

Manpower planning	Human resource planning
• Human resources viewed as a factor of production to be deployed efficiently – employees seen as costs	• Human resources viewed as the organisational key to sustained competitive advantage – employees seen as assets
• Emphasis is on managing the headcount	• Emphasis is on human capability
• Concentration on generating and storing HR data	• Creative and integrated approach to knowledge management
• Represents a downstream, tactical response to strategy formulation	• Represents both an input into strategy formulation and an output to meet strategic objectives
• Adopts a quantitative 'hard' approach with a focus on forecasting and controlling labour to ensure its efficient utilisation	• Adopts a quantitative and qualitative approach by building on hard elements to incorporate 'soft' elements such as culture, management, and development and retention of talent
• Follows rational, prescriptive decision-making approach	• Adopts a processual approach
• Tactical	• Dynamic

Sources: Bramham (1997); Tansley (1999); Liff (2000); Beardwell (2004).

Ulrich (1987: 42) went further in differentiating three phases in the development of SHRP: 'regulation'; 'control'; and 'shape'. These phases in the transition to SHRP are described in Table 7.4.

Table 7.4 Transitions in SHRP: from policeman to business partner

Phase	Guiding principle	Objective of HRP	HRP metaphor	Responsibility for HRP
1	Regulation	Ensure compliance with internal, corporate and external, government regulations and policies	Policeman	HR specialists
2	Control	Modify HR practices to match corporate strategies and support their achievement	Professional	HR specialists and strategic planning staff
3	Shape	Create competitive advantage through development of core HR competences	Business partner	Line managers and HR specialists

Source: after Ulrich (1987: 42).

This three-phase interpretation of the development of SHRP introduces two important dimensions that will be explored in more detail later in the chapter. First, it is possible to distinguish a temporal dimension between short-term, operational and longer-term strategic HR requirements. Second, it is possible to discern two different types of strategic fit: one-way (traditional HRP and the control phase) and two-way (strategic HRP and the shape phase). This last point leads to potential confusion in terminology between HRP and SHRP. However, irrespective of whether it is translated as one-way or two-way, the essential characteristic of HRP definitions discussed earlier is that of strategic integration. For this reason, from this point onwards, the conventional acronym HRP has been adopted and its strategic prefix taken as a given. These different types of strategic integration are returned to later in the chapter with a reminder of and reference back to the multi-dimensional nature of strategic integration discussed in Chapter 1.

Hard versus soft HRP

Running alongside the manpower versus HRP debate is the frequently drawn distinction between hard quantitative and soft qualitative variants of HRP. Indeed some of the distinguishing features of the hard and soft variants reflect definitions of manpower planning and HRP respectively. The commonly identified characteristics of the hard and soft variants of HRP are summarised in Table 7.5.

Table 7.5 Distinguishing characteristics of hard and soft HRP

Hard HRP	Soft HRP
• Focuses on human resources	• Focuses on resourceful humans
• HR strategies directed at exploiting this resource to the benefit of the organisation	• HR strategies directed at developing employee capability to the mutual benefit of both employees and employers
• Management of human resources reflects a unitary perspective and operates through direct control via the exercise of managerial prerogative	• Management of human resources reflects a pluralist perspective and operates through indirect control enabled through employee involvement and measures aimed at gaining their commitment
• Synonymous with manpower planning and efficient utilisation of labour	• Synonymous with SHRM with an emphasis on integrating employee values, beliefs and behaviours with organisational goals through culture management
• Driven by HR specialists intent on demonstrating their strategic awareness and ability to contribute to the bottom-line	• Driven by a multi-stakeholder perspective with particular emphasis on the role of line managers in executing organisational strategies and contributing to their formulation
• Champions the cost-effective use of human resources as a major contributor to meeting organisation objectives	• Champions a resource-based view of the firm where employees represent assets that can produce sustainable competitive advantage

Sources: Mabey *et al.* (1998); Tansley (1999); Liff (2000); Bratton and Gold (2003); Beardwell (2004).

Self-Check and Reflect Questions   7.1

To what extent can the hard and soft variants of HRP be regarded as mutually exclusive?

Taken together with manpower planning, the hard variant can be criticised for reducing HRP to little more than a numbers game. Here HRP can be likened to a form of stock control with a concentration on headcount, staff inventories and the movement of staff within the organisation. This perspective has little regard for the qualitative skills possessed by staff, such as their knowledge, motivation and values, or their relevance to job performance (Hendry, 1995). Criticisms of the hard variant are brought together well by Liff (2000: 94) who reminds us of 'the need to remember the humanness of human resources'. However, these criticisms do not mean the hard variant cannot be strategic. It is highly relevant to organisational strategies directed at cost minimisation and as such is arguably more likely to be found in practice than soft HRP. Moreover, the harsh realities of business life may lead to organisations having to take hard HRP decisions irrespective of their business ethos. This is evidenced below in 'In Practice' 7.2 which reports on the case of the Co-operative Financial Services Group, recognised as one of Britain's leading proponents of ethical business behaviour, which in 2004 was undertaking large-scale job cuts in one of its business divisions.

In Practice   7.2

Co-operative Insurance to axe 2,500 jobs

In July 2004 the Co-operative Insurance Society (CIS), part of the Co-operative Financial Services Group, announced it was cutting its headcount from 9,000 to 6,500 over the next two years. In response to the increasingly competitive nature of the market, the move was designed to reduce costs and increase CIS's competitiveness in the financial services sector.

The job losses were to be part of a re-organisation programme and might involve compulsory redundancies. Union officials of Amicus said that while they recognise the need for change and modernisation, such a drastic reduction in headcount was to be regretted and that any compulsory redundancies would be vigorously opposed.

The chief executive of the Co-operative Financial Services Group maintained that the job losses would help to ensure the future viability of CIS so that it would be well placed to fulfil its mandate of meeting the needs of millions of ordinary households in the UK.

Source: Griffiths (2004).

To reinforce the strategic relevance of the hard variant you might like to return to Table 2.3 in Chapter 2 and reflect on the employee behaviours and HR techniques that Schuler and Jackson (1987) associate with a cost reduction strategy. Similarly you could usefully reflect on the appropriateness of hard HRP to Miles and Snow's (1984b) defender strategy. In contrast, the report on Pret a Manger summarised in 'In Practice' 7.3 reveals evidence of the softer side of HRP in operation. Its business revolves around the quality of its product and the passion and service quality displayed by its staff. Here HRP needs to translate this into HRM strategies and practices that will provide the necessary staffing base to deliver these prerequisites.

In Practice   7.3

What can be softer than passion?

Pret a Manger has established in the UK, and increasingly internationally, a niche business with a distinctive culture. Its success is based around the quality of its product – high-quality sandwiches – and the passion for the business demonstrated by the people who serve them.

According to the chief executive, Andrew Rolfe, passion for the product, the staff and the whole business is the driving force behind Pret. Part of the business philosophy is to obtain consistency of purpose throughout the business so that customers will recognise the Pret experience within minutes of walking into one of its shops. This is achieved through attention to customer and supplier relations and new product development. It requires clear specification of personal responsibilities and staffing the organisation with people with the talent to carry out those responsibilities.

Pret deploys an integrated set of HR practices to ensure that its shops are staffed with people who display the necessary passion, including:

1. Unorthodox selection procedures where candidates attend a general interview and are sent to their closest shop for a further interview with the general manager before working a paid day in the shop. The whole shop team then vote on which applicants to accept. Successful candidates receive ten days training in the shop and kitchen working side-by-side with a personal trainer who takes them through all aspects of the company. Recruits are formally appraised after working four weeks and successfully completing their training, with subsequent promotion into a team member after three months. Only 5 per cent of applicants are selected.

2. Use of extrinsic and intrinsic reward strategies including: visits by managers to pass on congratulations to team members specifically singled out by customers through their feedback; giving praise consistently for effective job performance; taking over a pub every Friday night and inviting all team members; a weekly bonus every time a shop hits its performance target; surprise rewards – in 2001 the company granted an across-the-board pay increase that had not previously been budgeted or planned for (after its introduction, sales and profits went up); and cash vouchers awarded to employers at various 'graduation' stages that can be distributed to colleagues who have been instrumental in their progress.

3. Keeping employees close to the business through ensuring that: every new employee, including senior managers, works for two weeks in one of the Pret shops without the team members knowing their position; all head-office staff are sent out five times a year to work in their adopted 'buddy' shop.

4. Open communication through 15-minute team briefings held every morning in every shop.

Source: *Human Resource Management International Digest* (2002).

In contrast to hard HRP, soft HRP has been criticised for being too broad and telling us little about how it might be applied in practice. It lacks the methodological precision associated with the hard variant and, if seen to embrace all dimensions of human resourcing, becomes difficult to differentiate from SHRM (Marchington and Wilkinson, 1996; Tansley, 1999). However, despite the difficulties associated with translating it into practice the soft variant of HRP may be critical to organisational success as exemplified in the cases cited in 'In Practice' 7.4.

In Practice 7.4

Soft HRP: applications and examples

Williams (2002) identifies that the failure of organisational mission statements to impact on employee behaviour and the implementation failures of business initiatives designed to provide competitive edge (e.g. business process re-engineering) can arise from a lack of commitment to long-term planning and core organisational values. She argues that an organisation's core values need to be articulated at all levels of the organisation and translated into strategic human resource plans and practice. She concludes that where shared values and their cultural context cannot be easily replicated they assume the status of an important source of sustained competitive advantage.

A study by Deutsche Bank (Steffens-Duch, 2001, cited in Turner, 2002: 58–59) concluded that employee commitment embedded in organisation culture was a significant differentiating factor between successful and less successful businesses operating in the service sector. Employee commitment was therefore held to be a pre-condition for business success.

The global telecommunications giant Ericsson established clear linkages between values, behaviour and culture. The values of professionalism, respect and perseverance were ultimately converted into the behaviours of passion to win, dedication to customer success, fast urgent creativity and value-adding teamwork. In recognition of the criticality of these 'soft' HR dimensions Ericsson appointed a senior vice-president to be responsible for people and culture (Reigo, 2001, cited in Turner, 2002: 59).

Self-Check and Reflect Questions 7.2

To what extent can the view that HRP is all about ensuring that the right person is in the right place at the right time be interpreted as a soft, as well as a hard, approach to HRP?

The HRP process

In concluding this section, the question 'What is SHRP?' is addressed by briefly reviewing one further area of debate within the HRP literature. This relates to the process of HRP itself where two different approaches – systems and processual – emerge from the different theoretical perspectives underpinning strategy formulation discussed in Chapter 1. Tansley (1999: 45) provides a helpful analysis of these relationships. She argues that the systems approach to HRP equates to rational planning models where management exercise decision-making prerogative 'through deliberate calculation and analysis'. This reflects the prescriptive classical approach to strategy and strategy making discussed in detail in Chapter 1. Here, in summary, the organisation is viewed as having a separate existence from the employees that make it up and is characterised by: a controlled interface with the external environment; detailed internal structures; clearly defined objectives; and a unitary ideology with its stress on shared goals and values. Relating these strategy formulation perspectives to HRP, Tansley (1999) argues that within a systems model, planning precedes action, as illustrated in Figure 7.4.

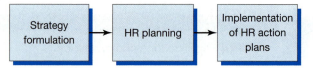

Figure 7.4 A systems perspective of the HRP process
Source: adapted from Tansley (1999: 51).

This systems perspective is synonymous with the hard, manpower planning dimensions of HRP illustrated respectively in Tables 7.5 and 7.3. Although criticised for its narrow, rationalist and prescriptive foundations (Mintzberg, 1994; Liff, 2000) this should not lead to its wholesale rejection particularly when viewed as an integral component of HRP practice. In Table 7.3 it was argued that HRP 'adopts a quantitative and qualitative approach by building on hard elements to incorporate soft elements such as culture, management and development, and retention of talent'. Therefore the inherent limitations of this perspective become particularly dangerous to organisations only when it is used in isolation.

In contrast, the processual approach to strategy and strategy making, again discussed in detail in Chapter 1, reverses the basic premise such that organisations are viewed as creations arising from the social interactions of their stakeholders. This chimes with the emergent view of strategy to create a dynamic where organisations and their patterns of beliefs and behaviours are forged over time as a result of a continuous process of social exchange and negotiation (Tansley, 1999). From this perspective, the HRP process can be viewed as being based on continual interactions between those responsible for HR strategy and those responsible for business strategy (Liff, 2000). Compared with a systems perspective, the processual perspective is arguably more able to accommodate unforeseen events arising from an uncertain future and the 'humanness' of people with their idiosyncrasies and is also better equipped to support the types of behaviours necessary to survive in an increasingly turbulent, global economy (Tansley, 1999). In HRP terms, adopting a processual perspective means that it becomes a continuous process where action can precede planning as well as planning precede action, as illustrated in Figure 7.5.

Of the definitions of HRP reviewed earlier, arguably that of bin Idris and Eldridge (1998) comes closest to reflecting this processual perspective. They view HRP as a continual learning process brought about through the interactions of stakeholders affected by the HRP process, with managers being particularly identified as crucial participants. Their construction of HRP also incorporates a systems approach to formalise the continuous process and thereby draws on the strengths of both the systems and processual perspectives. They maintain that:

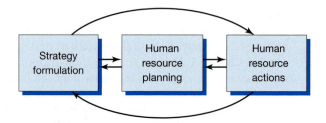

Figure 7.5 A processual perspective of the HRP process
Source: adapted from Tansley (1999: 52).

Fundamentally, through transformation an internal capability is developed to face the opportunities and threats posed by the external environment. Successive cycles of planning work build internal robustness in decision making by increasingly directing attention to areas of human resource weakness and opportunity. The ability to respond more effectively over time in this way represents a learning to learn capability jointly acquired by stakeholders which builds as cycles [of the process] are completed in successive rounds of planning activity.

(bin Idris and Eldridge, 1998: 355)

The operation of such a continuous process carries with it the possibility for HRP to provide the crucial link between corporate strategies (prescribed or emergent) and SHRM practices (short or long term).

Human resource planning: the vital connecting link?

Reflecting Parker and Caine's (1996: 30) view that 'The success of HRP is paramount to the survival of the organisation', Mills (1985) argues that HRP helps organisations to ascertain that strategic plans may be unrealisable because of HR factors before rather than after they have been implemented. However, he goes on to argue that, despite the compelling nature of this benefit, many organisations do not practise HRP, thereby running the risk of costly strategic implementation failures.

His argument provides a powerful rationale for HRP and illustrates the importance of the potential two-way (upstream and downstream) relationship that exists between organisational and HR strategies. It also throws up the possibility that the evident lack of formal HRP practice is inconsistent with its importance. This possibility is considered further in a later section examining the HRP paradox. Mills' analysis also accords with the introductory discussion on the role of HRP in mergers and acquisitions (see In Practice 7.1). Here it was revealed that a failure to plan for the HR dimension of mergers and acquisitions was a key reason for their subsequent failure. It might have been thought that those planning mergers would have had a vested interest in identifying and attending to the human factors that could threaten their success! Building on this initial position, the chapter now goes on to focus on the perceived benefits of HRP and how these can be used as a platform for constructing an argument in support of the role of HRP as the crucial link between organisational strategies and SHRM.

The benefits of HRP

Frequently identified benefits of HRP have been captured in Key Concepts 7.3 and these provide powerful arguments to justify its formal practice by organisations.

An analysis of the benefits claimed (Key Concepts 7.3) shows that the majority relate to the link between HRP and strategic planning. This is reflected at three levels:

- where HR plans are aligned with corporate strategies to further their accomplishment in a downstream relationship;
- where HRP can reveal HR issues that threaten the viability of corporate strategies and thereby lead to their reformulation; and

Key Concepts 7.3

Benefits of HRP

1. Ensures that the HR dimension receives due attention in the strategy-making process.
2. Enables HR strategies to be linked to and integrated with organisational strategies.
3. Surfaces and recognises the potentially unique contribution an organisation's human capital can make to long-term strategic direction.
4. Provides a formalised process that encourages organisations to take account of HR issues early on in strategy making thereby reducing the risk of implementation failures due to a lack of HR capability.
5. Provides a formalised process for generating plans to tackle the HR issues arising from strategic planning.
6. Generates a detailed audit of an organisation's human capital.
7. Enables the appropriateness of the organisation's current skills, knowledge and attitudes mix to be analysed.
8. Provides a mechanism for forecasting labour demand against internal and external supply in terms of numbers, knowledge, skills and attitudes.
9. Matches labour demand and supply and through gap analysis surfaces mismatches between the two that need to be addressed.
10. Generates a variety of HR solutions for tackling the complexity of problems arising from strategy making.
11. Enables HR strategies, policies, procedures and practice to be developed as a coherent bundle of activities.
12. Provides detailed information that enables tighter control over staffing numbers and costs.

Sources: Greer (2001); Marchington and Wilkinson (2002); Turner (2002).

● where a reciprocal relationship means that HR issues can represent an important input into the strategy formulation process from the outset in an upstream relationship.

The operation of these three levels of strategic linkage is consistent with those who advocate that two-way external or vertical integration is a core dimension of SHRM. Where HRP successfully contributes to these three types of linkage it is difficult to deny its utility as a linking mechanism between organisational strategy and HR strategies and practices.

In contrast, identified benefits provide little emphasis on the potential contribution HRP can make to integrating HR strategies horizontally despite the centrality of this dimension to the concept of SHRM. This is addressed to an extent by Marchington and Wilkinson (2002: 280) who argue that 'It enables employers to make more informed judgements about the skills and attitude mix in the organisation, and prepare integrated HR strategies.' Their view is reinforced by Beardwell (2004: 181) who argues that HRP can contribute to organisational performance through 'the integration of HR policies and practices with each other and with the business strategy, i.e. horizontal and vertical integration'.

The notion that the route to competitive advantage lies through an organisation's human resources and the way they are managed is an increasingly recurrent theme in the SHRM literature. HRP as a specific contributor to business performance is supported by Marchington and Wilkinson (2002: 280) who argue that irrespective of whether HRP is operating in a downstream or upstream relationship with corporate strategy it 'is perceived as a major facilitator of competitive advantage'. Using HRP as a vehicle for managing people as strategic assets can also facilitate the pursuit of the high-performance organisations commonly associated with SHRM by focusing on a high commitment, productivity and trust agenda (Godard and Delaney, 2000).

The claimed contribution of HRP to organisational performance may, however, be more difficult to establish in practice. In Chapter 2, following an examination and critique of a number of studies investigating the link between SHRM and organisational performance, it was concluded that the studies were generally positive about this relationship. However, as was pointed out, all of the studies reviewed focused on SHRM rather than the effectiveness of individual HR practices such as HRP. In comparison there has been little empirical research on the extent of HRP practice or its link to organisational performance. One notable exception is the work of Nkomo (1986, 1987) who found evidence two decades ago that the introduction of formalised, strategically linked HRP was frequently followed by improvements in organisational performance and that inferior organisational performance was linked to its absence. Her last point accords with earlier arguments that the failure of mergers and acquisitions frequently arise from deficiencies in formal HRP. More recently, evidence has established links between HRP and labour productivity (Kock and McGrath, 1996) and sustained organisational profitability (Caulkin, 2001). What limited evidence there is of the link between HRP and organisational performance seems, at least, to mirror that found for HRM more generally and lends weight to the argument that HRP can operate as the vital connecting link between organisational and HR strategies.

For Zeffane and Mayo (1994) the process of HRP contains within it an important boundary-spanning role that is crucial in helping organisations to adapt the workforce to meet changing demands arriving from a dynamic socio-economic climate. It can be argued that human resources are the key factor in managing change because they are far more adaptable than other sources of production, such as capital investment. As a consequence, HRP may help manage the unpredictability of business life by exercising a degree of control over medium-term and incremental change through exploiting the flexibility and adaptability of the workforce to meet new contingencies as they arise (Beardwell, 2004). However, this claim is open to question as it can be argued that a lack of flexibility and adaptability in the workforce can potentially frustrate using human resources in this way. Elsewhere in this book the difficulties of culture change and the political realities of organisational life that can, for a variety of reasons, fuel employee resistance and intransigence have been discussed. Also, the pace at which it is possible to adapt and shape the workforce is debatable. As Gratton (1999: 173) graphically points out:

- It takes ten to fifteen years to select and develop an international senior executive cadre.
- It takes a minimum of three years to pilot and implement a reward system refocused on supporting a new set of competences.
- It takes at least five years to reshape the technological skill base of employees.

These facets of an organisation's human resources remind us of Liff's (2000: 94) clarion call 'to remember the humanness of human resources' and it is surprising how little of the discussion in the literature on the benefits of HRP focuses on workforce considerations. However, at least Bratton and Gold (2003) go some way towards this by pointing out that HRP has an important role to play in reconciling the needs of individual employees and the needs of the organisation. This has echoes of the employee-centred HR practices associated with soft HRP.

Self-Check and Reflect Questions	7.3

How would you map out the benefits of HRP identified in the above analysis against the 'regulation', 'control' and 'shape' phases of Ulrich's (1987) model of transitions in SHRP (see Table 7.4)? You might find it helpful to structure your answer in tabular format. To get you started one example under each of the three phases identified by Ulrich has been provided below.

Phase I Regulation	Phase II Control	Phase III Shape
Provides detailed information that enables tighter control over staffing numbers and costs	Enables HR strategies to be linked to and integrated with organisational strategies	Surfaces and recognises the potentially unique contribution an organisation's human capital can make to long-term strategic direction

HRP as a crucial bridging mechanism

Given the benefits claimed for formal HRP it is easy to appreciate its potential value as an SHRM tool. However, to what extent does this justify a view that HRP can represent the crucial link that facilitates the two-way integration between organisational strategy and SHRM? As identified in the chapter introduction, HRP can arguably be considered from two perspectives. Conceptually, HRP can be viewed as a vital boundary-spanning function operating between organisational strategies and the human resources that determine their successful realisation (or otherwise) and as such could be construed as the focal point for human resource practice in the organisation (Zeffane and Mayo, 1994). However, its conceptual relevance does not mean that HRP will be formally practised in organisations or, if practised, make an effective contribution to organisational effectiveness. Therefore, a second perspective is that HRP is either a potential link that is in reality missing or is the weakest link of SHRM practice. Either of these perspectives may account for failures of organisations to realise their strategic objectives because of failures to plan the people dimension. This second perspective is discussed later in the chapter in a search for evidence of HRP practice. The perspective of HRP as the vital connecting link between organisational and HR strategies is now considered further.

In establishing a conceptual linkage, initial reference is made to the oft-cited frameworks of Miles and Snow (1984b) and Schuler and Jackson (1987) who provided early and powerful arguments for developing strategically integrated HR practices (Chapters 1 and 2). By way of a reminder, if you refer back to Table 2.3 it is possible to track the employee role behaviours and accompanying HR techniques that Schuler and Jackson identified against each of three competitive strategies: 'innovation'; 'quality enhancement'; and 'cost reduction'. However, valuable though they are, a number of reservations were raised about such frameworks in Chapter 2. For example, they are overly prescriptive and do not, therefore, cater sufficiently for the contingencies operating in specific organisational settings. They are also more appropriate to earlier definitions of manpower planning in that the nature of strategic integration is ostensibly one-way: top down. As such, it fails to address employee diversity (Chapter 13) and the political realities of organisation life.

More importantly, with respect to HRP, such frameworks do not detail the process used to forge the strategic linkages exemplified. For example, using Schuler and Jackson's framework, how would an organisation move from strategy to needed employee role behaviours to accompanying HR techniques? Unfortunately such frameworks are not created by magic nor do they drop out of the sky into the laps of waiting managers and HR specialists. It is here that the formal processes of HRP come into play forming a bridge between an organisation's strategies and staffing processes. Spanning the boundaries between these two organisational dimensions is the territory of HRP (Zeffane and Mayo, 1994; Rothwell, 1995). To put it another way, HRP represents the formal expression of that linking function. Viewed from this perspective, for example, HRP is this missing connecting link in the Miles and Snow (1984b) and Schuler and Jackson (1987) frameworks. Here, HRP is the process necessary to identify the needed behaviours of employees and integrate the HR practices necessary to obtain, develop and sustain these behaviours.

Although these models, as already discussed, are ostensibly one-way – top-down (closed matching models) – the same argument about the capacity of HRP to act as a linking mechanism with strategy can be applied to models that reflect more the resource-based view of strategy with their emphasis on two-way vertical integration (open matching models). For example, taking the open model approach to human resource strategies portrayed by Mabey *et al.* (1998) and discussed in Chapter 2 it will be seen that there is no reference to HRP. The SHRM components in this model are identified as culture, personnel and structure, and are integrated vertically with corporate strategy and horizontally with each other. What is missing is reference to the process necessary to establish this vertical integration and the horizontal integration between the SHRM components themselves. Here again it can be argued that HRP has the potential to fill this void and create the necessary strategic linkages.

Building on the above, it is possible to identify a number of organisational roles played by HRP. It starts from the basis that if resourceful humans are to realise their potential to source competitive advantage, HRP becomes central to strategy formulation and implementation. On the one hand it can help steer HR practice to become more compatible with organisational prerogatives and on the other help to identify, address and resolve fundamental strategic issues related to corporate and people management (Greer, 2001). On this basis it has been argued that HRP represents the core of SHRM and that improvements to its processes and systems are likely to benefit both the organisation and the HR function (Khoong, 1996). However, in many ways, explaining the conceptual nature and heritage of HRP as well as its potentially pivotal role in SHRM is the easy part. Turning the HRP rhetoric into reality is an altogether more difficult proposition. As explored in the next section, there are many difficulties confronting the effective practice of HRP. These may well be sufficient to put many organisations off from even entertaining the prospect of introducing HRP such that it is cast aside to a different destiny altogether as the missing or weakest link.

The problematic nature of human resource planning practice

While not disagreeing with Parker and Caine's (1996: 30) view that 'The complexities associated with the planning process are enormous', there is a need to get to grips with what this means in practice if effective HRP is to become a reality. This section begins by briefly revisiting the discussion on the multi-dimensional nature of strategic integration in Chapter 1 in order to explore the problematic nature of establishing strategic linkage between organisational goals and HR practices. It then goes on to range more widely over a number of potential pitfalls, posers and problems associated with HRP which have been characterised here as 'the Pandora's box of HRP'.

The multi-dimensional nature of strategic integration

At the heart of the complexity surrounding HRP is the very strategic integration that it is meant to forge between an organisation's management of its human resources and its strategic goals. Too often in the SHRM literature the nature of strategic integration and its implications for SHRM practice is either taken as a given or not developed beyond the notion of vertical and horizontal integration. However, as discussed in Chapter 1, this is too simplistic and represents only part of the story. It is therefore sobering to be brought down to earth by Purcell's (1995: 63) rueful observation:

> All definitions of human resource management agree on one point: that there must be a link between a firm's strategy and the deployment and utilization of the human resource. Quite what that link is, where it is realized and how it is developed, are separate matters.

In Chapter 1, at least six strands to strategic integration were delineated, each one of which could be said to carry with it potentially different implications for HR planners. Within the context of HRP, these six strands of strategic integration can be summarised as:

- HRP responses to first-order strategic decisions, i.e. those concerned with the long-term direction of the enterprise or the scope of its activities;
- HRP responses to second-order strategic decisions, i.e. organisation structures and operating procedures put into place to support first-order decisions;
- HRP responses to third-order strategic decisions, i.e. where functional areas define their strategies in accordance with the first- and second-order decisions;
- two-way strategic integration where HRP operates both upstream to help shape future strategic direction as well as downstream to support organisational goals in a reciprocal relationship;

● horizontal integration where HRP operates to facilitate other HR initiatives and develop coherence between them;

● HRP sensitivity and responses to planned change and unplanned change arising from future uncertainties.

Summarised in 'In Practice' 7.5 and 7.6 are two HRP cases that illustrate the different strategic connections that can be forged within the multi-dimensional model of strategic integration. As you read the two In Practice boxes, think through which of the six strands of strategic integration are evident in each case. This will form the basis of the self-check and reflect question that follows them.

In Practice   7.5

Strategic HRP in a Chilean university library

Strategic HRP was introduced by a Chilean information organisation in the library system of the Pontifical Catholic University of Chile (SIBUC) in order to achieve the organisation's strategic objectives. The HRP process adopted starts from the premise that the management of human resources needs to be coherent with the library system's strategic plan.

The starting point is SIBUC's mission 'to contribute to the attainment of academic excellence by the university community of the Pontifical Catholic University of Chile' (Franco and Diaz, 1995: 15). To achieve the mission, strategic objectives were developed for each of the organisation's nine key management areas: human resources; users; management; image; financial resources; information and bibliographic resources; technological support; physical resources; and suppliers. For example:

● *Human resources*. To have human resources with a service vocation, who are achievement oriented, innovative, competent, informed and satisfied with their work in professional and financial terms, interacting effectively in a disciplined working environment.

● *Management*. To attain an organization oriented to the user, which is innovative, rapid in response, efficient, integrated, co-ordinated and austere, tending to the autonomy of its members, using a participative management system with working groups and consultations.

● *Suppliers*. To have a close collaboration with suppliers, by means of a mutually beneficial commercial relationship that ensures the efficient and timely provision of our services at the lowest possible cost (Franco and Diaz, 1995: 19–20).

Using a SWOT analysis, current human resources were analysed in relation to the organisation's operating environment and its nine strategic objectives. The findings of the SWOT analysis were then used to develop a suite of (six) human resource objectives and strategies designed 'to improve on the weaknesses, to take advantage of the opportunities, to diminish the threats and to maintain the strengths' of current human resources (Franco and Diaz, 1995: 21). The six HR objectives were:

● To have supervisors who are leaders who will permit the efficient attainment of strategic objectives.

● Staff who interact assertively and effectively with the user community, anticipating information needs.

● To have a staff selection system that will permit the incorporation of achievement-oriented people with innovative capabilities.

▶

- Decrease rotation of librarians in the high rotation levels without deteriorating the relative positions of the jobs.
- Promote self-instruction for professional development.
- Knowledge of the contribution of the present performance evaluation system to staff productivity and job well-being' (Franco and Diaz, 1995: 21–22).

Against each HR objective the following were developed: a strategy; a plan to achieve that strategy; and a series of controls against which achievement of the strategy could be evaluated.

Source: Franco and Diaz (1995).

In Practice   7.6

The man who moved east to make rooms: a case of hard HRP?

When one of Silicon Glen's biggest electronics manufacturers decided in 2001 to shut up shop in Scotland and relocate to low-cost eastern Europe, it started another local company thinking. Michael Shand, managing director of R.B. Farquhar, an Aberdeenshire-based maker of portable cabins and prefabricated rooms for construction projects, did some swift sums. 'I went on the internet, found some figures for labour costs in the Czech Republic and calculated on the back of a fag packet whether we could also produce there more cheaply,' he says. 'It looked very encouraging.'

He concluded then that labour costs for the manufacture of prefabricated bathroom pods, of the type Farquhar supplies to hotel chains, would be about 75 per cent lower. In the event, the saving has proved to be closer to 80 per cent. Three years after Mr Shand reached for the cigarette packet, Farquhar is winning significant orders from a new £3 million plant in the Czech Republic. Since coming on stream last November, the plant has won orders worth about £12 million, including a £10 million order from Travelodge, the budget hotel chain, for 3,000 pods.

Farquhar's pods business, which is also served by a plant at Huntly in Aberdeenshire, is now growing at more than 25 per cent a year thanks to the new plant, which is already in profit – six months earlier than Mr Shand had estimated. 'It's way ahead of our expectations,' he says. 'We can compete now with any producer of prefabs anywhere in Europe.'

The board had considered acquiring a local company, entering a joint venture or building a greenfield plant, but after due analysis opted for the latter. A site for the plant was found in a region of relatively high unemployment close to the German border. Mr Shand then went to the local labour office and won support for a training scheme for 90 potential workers. Farquhar provided the materials for the training scheme and the local authority paid the workers while they were being trained. About half the trainees were taken on as the first batch of workers at the factory, which now employs 60 staff and is hiring five to ten new people each month. The company also benefits from the fact that the Czech authorities pay half the wages of anyone joining the company from the unemployment list for the first two years of their work.

But, rather than their cost, it is the quality of the Czech workforce that has most impressed Mr Shand since the plant was completed last August. 'We found the workers absolutely excellent. They're responsive, they have good skills, a good work ethic,' he says. 'We were very surprised and very pleased at what we found. With no disrespect to our staff at home, they're as good as anything in the UK.' He also points out that the Czech facility was never designed to replace Farquhar's UK plant. 'This was firmly not about relocation. This was about opportunity and being more profitable,' he says.

Nonetheless, he suggests that opening the Czech plant may have provided 'a little bit of a wake-up call' to staff in the UK. Indeed, one unexpected result of opening an overseas plant has been the effect on production at Huntly. In the UK plant, for instance, workers move around the steel-framed pods as they are manufactured. In Chomutov, where it was easier to experiment with production methods, the company tried putting the pods on wheels and moving them among teams of workers. This cut working time per unit in the Czech plant by a fifth, so the practice is now being adopted in the UK operation.

Source: Nicholson (2004: 11).

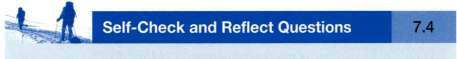

Self-Check and Reflect Questions   7.4

For each of the above In Practice Cases answer the following question and justify your answer with reference to case evidence:

● Which of the six strands of strategic integration are evident in the case company?

An example illustrating how the multi-dimensional framework of strategic integration can be applied to one SHRM lever, recruitment and selection, is provided in Chapter 8. This demonstrates how the multi-dimensional nature of strategic integration impacts on SHRM practice and will help you to apply the six strands of strategic integration to other SHRM levers covered in this book.

These different types of strategic integration can be applied to any HR activity to test its strategic credentials. Logic would seem to dictate that the more fully an HR practice reflects the different types of strategic integration over time the stronger its strategic credentials. However, the more strands of strategic integration that are woven into the HRP tapestry quite clearly the more complex it becomes. Unfortunately the multi-dimensional nature of strategic integration is not the only difficulty confronting practitioners of HRP. The chapter now goes on to surface other sets of difficulties that can arise from the process of strategy formulation itself as well as the context and realities of organisational life.

Potential pitfalls, posers and problems: the Pandora's box of HRP

Pandora's box has come to mean any source of great and unexpected troubles. In Greek mythology Pandora was given a box by Zeus but advised not to open it. She did, releasing its contents, which represented the ills of the world, except for hope which was left in the bottom of the box (Chambers, 1999). In previous chapters a number of problematical issues that are likely to be released upon those involved in practising HRP have surfaced. The intention here is not to go through them all again at length but to provide a brief bullet-point résumé of some of the main issues arising, leaving you to revisit earlier chapters for a fuller account if necessary.

Table 7.6 The Pandora's box of HRP: four different perspectives on the problems associated with HRP

The strategy jungle	Contextual contingencies	Cultural complexity	'Humanness' hiccups

• Questionable assumption that organisational strategy is:
  • defined clearly
  • communicated clearly
  • capable of clear definition
• Questionable assumption that one organisation equates to one strategy:
  • first-, second- and third-order strategies
  • corporate, business unit level strategies
• Conflicting strategies
• Limitations of rational planning model of strategy formulation when in reality it can be:
  • rational, deterministic
  • emergent
  • ad hoc
  • non-existent
	• International differences and the problems associated with transnational transportation of HR practices
	• Sectoral differences with different markets or products sometimes brought together in one holding company
	• Organisational differences including:
	  • size and technological sophistication
	  • operating environments
	  • managerial competence and sophistication
	  • multiple structures
	  • fluidity in structures
	• Organisational life cycles, e.g., start-up; growth; maturity and decline (Kochan and Barocci, 1985)
	• The temporal dimension and the challenge of change
		• The strategic choice of the dominant cultural viewpoint in multi-national organisations:
		  • polycentric
		  • ethnocentric
		  • geocentric
		  • regiocentric
		• Managing integrating spheres of cultures:
		  • national
		  • regional
		  • organisational
		  • functional
		  • professional
		  • conflicting
		• Organisational culture and change management:
		  • supportive or against?
		  • enabler or barrier?
		• Problems of changing the culture itself
		• Top-down versus bottom-up approaches to cultural alignment: which to choose?
		• Problems of definition and whether in reality, an organisation's culture can be managed.
			• Assumptions of rationality and unitarism adopt a managerialist view of the world and ignores or plays down employee perspectives
			• Employees, collectively or individually, may oppose managerialist prescriptions
			• One size fits all HR prescriptions ignore individual differences
			• Short-term focus militates against the long-term focus that underpins investment in human capital
			• Investment in employees is consistent with human resource issues being regarded as central to organisation strategy whereas this may not be the case in reality
			• Managers may give low priority to their HR role responsibilities and/or exclude the employee voice
			• The political nature of managerial decision-making rather than rational planning may more closely approximate organisational reality

Mills (1985) reports on the views of one business executive who argues that talk of HRP should be vetoed when failures to even adequately conduct business planning mean that effectively HRP is a non-starter	'International human resourcing is conducted within a multi-unit business organisation that operates in several countries, giving rise to conflicts and tensions associated with the inherently political relationship between managements of the parent company and its overseas subsidiaries' (Walsh, 1999: 124)	'The Prudential did not try to turn itself from Reliable Insurer to Online Bank – it gave birth to Egg: new people, new approach, new governance mechanics, and instant new culture (Turner, 2002: 66).	'For HR Planning to be strategic it needs to take place within an organization where human resource issues are seen as central to business strategy. However, this is not normally the case, certainly in the UK where financial considerations are invariably predominant (Liff, 2000: 108)

Despite the daunting range of complexities summarised in Table 7.6, the Pandora's box of HRP has not yet been emptied of all but hope as there are at least two further difficulties particularly relevant to HRP practitioners left in the box that need to be considered. First, there are limitations associated with techniques for forecasting labour supply and demand. This element of HRP has been previously identified as being essential to gap analysis and the subsequent development and implementation of HR plans to address mismatches between labour supply and demand. Despite the wide range of forecasting techniques available, they can often lack the precision necessary to be able to HR plan with certainty. Further, some of the statistical techniques employed are well beyond the capabilities and comprehension of many HR professionals.

Forecasting labour supply and demand has been identified as a central component of manpower planning. The difficulties associated with some forecasting methods and the questionable accuracy of the predictions generated contributed to the decline in interest in manpower planning before the advent of HRP. A particular difficulty is that HRP involves long-range planning, and reliability of forecasting generally diminishes as the time horizon increases, so, whereas projections several months ahead may be reasonably accurate, those over a three- to five-year timescale are likely to be less reliable (Mintzberg, 1994). Another difficulty with HRP, and a reason why it is sometimes shunned, is trying to forecast the future in an increasingly changing world. In Practice 7.7 provides a flavour of the forecasting headaches that can arise from the unplanned and unexpected, and illustrate well the difficulties that can confront HRP in a dynamic environment. All the examples are taken from events reported while writing this chapter.

In Practice 7.7

There may be trouble ahead!

In a deal between leadership of the Labour Party and trade unions, workplace rights will be extended for millions of workers. A European Union directive designed to provide agency and temporary workers with similar rights to those enjoyed by permanent employees had been opposed by the government. The government's decision to reverse its stance and withdraw its opposition will result in a guarantee of an extra eight days' holiday a year for millions of employees because under the directive employers will no longer be able to count Bank Holidays as part of the minimum entitlement to 20 days holiday per year (Grice and Clement, 2004).

Many companies are in danger of being 'burnt by soaring oil prices'. The managing director of a specialist glassmaker, where energy is the second highest cost after the wage bill, reported that the best quotes obtained for new contracts for electricity and gas were up 51 per cent and 34 per cent respectively. He said, 'This equates to a cost increase of £600,000, which is over half our annual profit prior to interest and tax.' According to the Energy Intensive Users' Group, manufacturers up and down the country are telling similar stories (Koenig and Kemeny, 2004: 7).

Spain's biggest bank, Santander Central Hispano, is set to announce a bid to take over Abbey National, Britain's sixth-largest bank, to create the world's eighth-largest bank (Cave, 2004a). The business analysts at Citigroup estimated that Santander would need to lay off 8,000 Abbey National employees to achieve its £300 million synergy targets. However, they predict that 6,000 jobs will actually be cut in measures to bring processing staff, as a percentage of the total workforce, in line with the ratio operating at Santander (Cave, 2004b).

There has also been a tendency to equate forecasting with the quantitative dimension of labour supply and demand to the neglect of the qualitative dimension. Forecasting the qualitative dimension of labour is arguably even more difficult than quantitative extrapolation. Consider for a moment the difficulties of pinning down the skills involved in performing a task. Employees may perform jobs in subtly different ways and, through exercising job control, may obscure relationships between skills and effective job performance. There may also be mismatches between an employee's actual skill base and their willingness to exercise their skills in practice. Further, if employees are involved in analysing the skills used in the performance of their job, they may conspire to exaggerate their prowess, particularly if the exercise is related to pay determination. This illustrates well the problematic and messy reality of organisational life as identified in Table 7.6 (Liff, 2000).

A second set of further difficulties emerge around the ability of HR specialists to perform as business partners (Lawler and Mohrman, 2003). Two important related points raised earlier are relevant here. An argument running throughout the chapter is that for HRP to become a reality the centrality of HR issues to organisational strategy needs to be recognised and acted on (Liff, 2000; Newell, 2002). However, as Liff (2000: 108) concludes, 'this is not normally the case'. The second point relates to the status and role of the HR function within organisations. In order for HR issues to take centre stage and be an integral component of organisational planning it has been argued that the head of the HR function must have equal status with other heads of function and sit at top table (Mabey and Iles, 1993; Greer, 2001; Turner, 2002). These two points are brought together eloquently by Liff (2000: 108) who posits that 'A factor which is arguably both a symptom and cause of the lack of importance given to human resource issues is the traditionally low status of HR specialists.' The development and successful implementation of HRP is highly unlikely in an organisational context where HR issues are not regarded as being of paramount importance.

This bleak scenario is consistent with the downstream HR role discussed earlier which anticipates that, once strategy has been formulated, HR activities will at best be directed to support its implementation. This creates a danger that HR practice will be piecemeal and lack horizontal integration and effectiveness (Galpin, 1999). Despite these dangers, recent research surveying how HR functionaries spend their time confirmed that their orientation and competence meant that traditional HR roles still predominate, with little evidence of the role of business partner emerging (Lawler and Mohrman, 2003). Of course, it may be the very competence of HR specialists and their lack of strategic acumen that militates against their achievement of business partner status (Greer, 2001; Beardwell, 2004). The devolvement of HR functions to line managers anticipated by SHRM may compensate in part for this deficiency but this presupposes the competence of those managers to perform strategically. The difficulty here is that managerial orientation tends to be towards more immediate concerns rather than longer-term planning, an orientation that may well be reinforced by reward management systems. The skill base of managers arguably reflects the needs of day-to-day problem solving rather than strategic planning and encourages a focus on operational issues (Greer, 2001). This leads to a somewhat circular argument where a strategically oriented, interventionary HR presence is necessary to support line managers in their planning roles but may well be absent, with the consequence that managers lack help in moving from their short-term orientation.

The above analysis presents a formidable set of barriers and difficulties confronting the effective practice of HRP and could well be sufficient to prevent HRP ever being entertained by organisations. This is a possibility that is considered next but not before a quick reminder that, according to Greek mythology, it should still be possible to find hope residing at the bottom of Pandora's box.

The HRP paradox: to plan or not to plan?

In one sense, a paradox arises from juxtaposing the benefits of HRP against the problematic nature of its practice. On the one hand, claims that 'the success of HRP is paramount to the survival of the organisation' (Parker and Caine, 1996: 30) have been examined. Here it could be argued that the numerous benefits associated with HRP and its potential role as the vital link between organisational strategy and HR strategy and practice support such claims. On the other hand, Parker and Caine's (1996: 30) contention that 'the complexities associated with the planning process are enormous' has also been considered. The problematic nature of strategic integration and the potential pitfalls, posers and problems associated with HRP certainly give credence to their viewpoint and may conspire to inhibit its practice. This leads us to a position where it is difficult to establish HRP as a vital connecting link because the strategic linkage is difficult to forge, i.e. the reasons that argue for its adoption conspire to thwart its effective execution.

A more commonly identified paradox, however, arises specifically from the relationship between HRP and the unpredictability of the future. This generates a dilemma that has been captured by a number of commentators in Key Concepts 7.4.

Key Concepts	7.4

The HRP paradox

'Is it realistic even to consider strategy, planning and forecasting in a dynamic and unpredictable world?' (Turner, 2002: 13).

'It is sometimes implied that planning is irrelevant or misguided in a turbulent and increasingly insecure environment' (Marchington and Wilkinson, 2002: 278).

'It is of course a paradox that as it becomes more difficult to predict and select, so it becomes more necessary to do so' (Bramham, 1988: 7).

Evidence of HRP: another rhetoric versus reality gap?

Earlier in the chapter it was pointed out that, relative to SHRM, little empirical research has been conducted to establish the extent and nature of HRP (Lam and Schaubroeck, 1998; Liff, 2000; Beardwell, 2004) making it difficult to establish the significance it plays in linking organisation and SHRM strategies and practice. However, analysing what evidence there is leads us to four general conclusions. First, there is an optimistic and pessimistic divide. Some research evidence can be found which indicates that the majority of organisations and HR/personnel managers are involved with HRP (Tyson and Doherty, 1999; Millward *et al.*, 2000), whereas other studies demonstrate little evidence of HRP being practised (Lam and Schaubroeck, 1998; Wagner *et al.*, 2000).

In Practice 7.8 provides a recent and costly example where operational inadequacies in HRP appear to be evident in one of the UK's most prominent businesses. The HRP difficulties faced by British Airways also demonstrate internal (or horizontal) integration in operation, albeit negatively, as issues around absenteeism, employee commitment, employee development, employee relations, labour retention and turnover, recruitment and selection, and reward management come together in a dangerous cocktail to thwart day-to-day operational management.

Second, the survey methodology frequently adopted may lead to an exaggeration of the incidence of HRP practice. Here, surveys sometimes reveal an organisational intent to conduct HRP that, when subjected to more detailed case analysis, is found not to be converted into practice (Liff, 2000; Beardwell, 2004). Third, building on this apparent mismatch between organisational rhetoric and reality, HRP practice uncovered by

In Practice 7.8

What price HRP failures?

On Tuesday, normally the quietest day of the week, and for the second day running, British Airways was forced to cancel more than 30 flights out of Heathrow airport. 'BA bosses were forced to deploy the lamest excuse in travel: staff shortage' (Calder, 2004: 1). According to Calder (2004: 1) 'the origin of the chaotic scenes at Heathrow yesterday lies in a combination of low staff morale, absenteeism and technical resources', all of which represent dimensions of HRP.

On the day in question, 11 per cent of staff rostered on the morning shift failed to turn up for work. This may have been partly the result of a deal to pay bonuses to baggage handlers, check-in and ground staff who take less than the average annual sickness absence of 17 days. The deal, due to take effect in October, was agreed the previous week to avert a threatened strike and, according to one source, staff were 'getting their retaliation in early, racking up the days off while they can' (Calder, 2004: 1). It was also held that low staff morale was contributing to staff turnover as well as high levels of absenteeism. According to Calder (2004: 1) efforts to tackle staff shortages will be too late, 'BA is recruiting and training replacement workers who start work next month after the summer peak, a piece of timing described by the talk-radio host Mike Dickin as "like training Father Christmases in January".' One stranded passenger commented: 'It's a world-renowned company. They should have the infrastructure in place to ensure they have adequate staff' (Demetriou, 2004: 4).

Rod Eddington, BA's chief executive, admitted 'that staffing levels were inadequate to cope with the number of travellers and that appropriate decisions were not taken at the right time' (Simpkins, 2004: 3). BA has cut its workforce by 13,000 to 52,000 as part of his 'Future Size and Shape' strategy, 'but the big fear is that BA has cut too much' and that its 'obsession with costs is starting to hit the quality of service' (Simpkins, 2004: 3).

BA is reportedly going 'to give 17,500 staff two free tickets each to compensate them for stress and inconvenience suffered during last week's cancellations debacle at Heathrow' at an estimated cost of £4 million (O'Connell, 2004: 1). The full extent of the cost to BA will, however, only become clearer when the impact of its troubles on future revenue can be gauged. 'As Ms Baaske stated: "The next time I will fly Lufthansa"' (Demetriou, 2004: 4).

Sources: Calder (2004: 1, 4); Demetriou (2004: 4); O'Connell (2004: 1); Simpkins (2004: 3).

research evidence tends to be more focused at the operational rather than the strategic level (Nkomo, 1988; Lam and Schaubroeck, 1998; Wagner *et al.*, 2000; Beardwell, 2004). Last, the research may be too constrained by rational prescriptions of HRP and in searching for this may overlook evidence of HRP emerging from ad hoc, incremental and more tentative efforts (Hendry, 1995; Beardwell, 2004) that are more associated with a processual viewpoint.

HRP: the weakest link?

On balance, therefore, it is difficult to make a convincing case that HRP is alive and well and the missing, or weakest, link perspective seems more than a distinct possibility. Unfortunately there is little research evidence of substance to explain why this might be the case, although the earlier review of the complexity of the process will no doubt suggest a number of possible candidates. However, part of the problem may well be that HRP is avoided because it cannot deliver certainty, whereas, as pointed out above, less exacting expectations might demonstrate its utility and make less than perfect outcomes acceptable. For example, Boxall and Purcell (2003: 232) argue that 'it is vital to accept that change is inevitable and that some preparation for the future is therefore crucial'. Armstrong (2003: 367) stresses that even broad statements of intent can be used to guide HR practice and are better than nothing at all. Returning to the paradox, it is therefore possible to build up a case that, just because an uncertain future and the dynamics of change make HRP both more complex and difficult, it does not render it meaningless, but arguably makes it more necessary than ever (Liff, 2000). This has echoes of the adage, to fail to plan is to plan to fail.

> In the light of these realities, it seems that, rather than being seen as an anachronism, human resource planning may now be more important than ever, and remaining constantly aware of employees' strengths and weaknesses and catering for them in planning future needs should, therefore, form a primary thrust of human resource management.
>
> *(Wagner* et al.*, 2000: 384)*

This perspective is also consistent with the earlier review of the work of Brews and Hunt (1999) in Chapter 1 with respect to the processual approach to strategy and strategy making. There it was argued that in a reversal of received wisdom they advocate that more strategic planning is required in unstable environments and possibly less in stable ones.

Forging the missing link

Can hope be found at the bottom of Pandora's box?

Space does not permit an in-depth discussion of how each of the difficulties associated with HRP, identified above, might be tackled in order to forge HRP as the vital connecting link between organisational strategies and HR strategies and activities. The focus here therefore concentrates on addressing four particular areas of difficulty that need to be confronted if any hope of establishing HRP as such a link is to be realised.

Four key difficulties impeding HRP practice

The four areas of difficulty identified below have all been explored in some detail earlier in the chapter and are therefore only summarised here. However, each area is sufficiently significant such that, taken singularly or in combination, they can operate to thwart the introduction of formalised HRP or threaten its effective practice. First, the rationalistic presumption of strategy formulation places HRP in a downstream relationship relegating the importance of HR to a level far removed from that envisaged by SHRM. Second, the lack of importance attached to HR and the low status frequently afforded to professional practitioners makes it difficult to challenge this presumption. Third are the complications arising from the need for HRP to address both short- to medium-term and long-term strategic concerns – the temporal perspective. These different time perspectives arguably demand different HRP approaches (Gratton, 1999). Fourth, longer-term perspectives are difficult to sustain in an increasingly dynamic environment where rapidly changing circumstances can frustrate and/or invalidate the best of planning intentions. Here it can be argued that change can make any static HR plans rapidly obsolete and that forecasting future HR requirements is futile when organisations cannot predict what lies over the horizon with any degree of certainty.

Potential routes towards effective HRP practice

In response, it is possible to identify at least four avenues that have the potential to address the 'key' difficulties identified.

Elevating the credibility of HR and its specialist practitioners

The first potential avenue revolves around the status of HR and its practitioners. In a hostile organisation environment the onus for improving the lot of HR will almost certainly fall on its specialist practitioners. A possible way forward is for any HR function to develop its own HR plan for increasing its competence, influence and strategic relevance, while at the same time developing the HR capabilities of line managers to contribute to HRP. This approach is referred to by Beardwell (2004: 178) as 'micro-planning'. This means that those responsible for HR must be proactive in getting their voice heard on matters of strategy, even if they are not represented at board level. Where there is no representation, Turner (2002) offers some practical guidelines to the HR function for getting the board to take account of the people dimension in their deliberations:

- Become fully acquainted with corporate objectives and how the organisation's board of directors operates in order to provide the information necessary to plan strategies for securing a higher profile for HR issues.
- Ask the board to sign off specific HR issues to raise their profile and secure greater organisational commitment.
- Endeavour to get regular presentations on HR included on the agenda of board meetings and include annual performance evaluations of the HR function.
- Lobby the chief executive to represent HR initiatives at board meetings.
- Lobby other board members to champion and/or support HR initiatives.
- Become technically proficient on complex and critical HR matters and seek acknowledgement of this expertise as a way of gaining credibility and extending the sphere of HR influence.

Such a proactive stance may not come naturally hence the need to HR plan the HR function to ensure that, longer term, it can achieve its own strategic objectives. Indeed, success for HRP at this micro, functional level might in itself go a long way to enhancing the credibility and elevating the status of HR in the organisation and the profile of HRP itself. It is also likely to help HR specialists hone their HRP skills, possibly to the subsequent wider benefit of the organisation. Without such a stance it is difficult to see how two-way strategic integration will be achieved, a situation that leaves organisations vulnerable to strategic and operational failure because of its lack of attention to the people dimension (Appelbaum and Gandell, 2003; Greer, 2001).

Flexible forecasting

The second potential avenue focuses on confronting the problematic nature of forecasting in an increasingly uncertain and unpredictable world through contingency and scenario planning. These approaches are 'predicated on the assumption that if you cannot predict the future, then by speculating on a variety of them, you might just hit upon the right one' (Mintzberg, 1994: 248). The two approaches are broadly similar, although it could be argued that scenario planning is about identifying a number of possible hypothetical positions and contingency planning is about producing HR plans to match the different scenarios identified and their possible outcomes (Turner, 2002; Beardwell, 2004). In Practice 7.9 provides some examples to illustrate these approaches.

In Practice 7.9

Examples of scenario and contingency planning

HRP might need to take account of uncertainties such as:

- extreme movements in the cost of commodities, energy and raw materials, e.g. oil, cement, etc., that drive up costs and product prices and lead to unanticipated adverse market conditions;
- political changes in government, economic direction and legislative priorities;
- enlargement of the European Community;
- major national disasters that have a global impact or adversely affect certain industries.

HRP might need to cater for different outcomes to a planned event, e.g. the establishment of an autonomous, new business venture:

- the business launch goes to plan, meeting market projections and planned performance indicators;
- the business launch far exceeds original market projection expectations with the consequence that product or service demand cannot be met within current human resource capability;
- the business launch flops and leads to a public relations disaster for the parent company and a position of chronic over-staffing;
- the planning permission necessary for a greenfield development to accommodate the new venture is not granted.

The importance of this type of contingent thinking is well illustrated by Manzini (1988), who argued that:

> Large sectors of our industry have plainly failed to anticipate possibly threatening future events, and the impact such events would have on the organization. In fact, many organizations even failed to plan appropriate action to address the 'worst case' scenario, other than reacting after the fact by directing large-scale layoffs and other 'economies' which should have been paid attention to in the first place.
>
> *(Manzini, 1988: 79)*

However, despite their potential, scenario and contingency planning are not without their problems. It is possible that, as the future unfolds, unplanned scenarios may still emerge and such approaches demand an HRP sophistication or resource base likely to be lacking in many organisations (Mintzberg, 1994). This places a stress on the need for HRP to be a continuous process so that deviations from forecasts and plans can be rapidly identified and tackled.

Human resource flexibility

The third potential avenue approaches the problem of uncertainty and unpredictability from a different direction in a way consistent with the resource-based view of the firm by creating an adaptable and flexible workforce. Whereas scenario and contingency planning attempt to anticipate threats and create a capacity to change HR plans even at short notice, this approach is intent on building into the workforce the capacity to cope with planned and unplanned change. It is unlikely that significant changes to HR plans arising from a dynamic, changing environment could be managed effectively without a flexible HR capacity. Under this approach a central strand of HRP becomes the creation of a flexible workforce that will enable adjustments to be made to the strategy–HR link to reflect changing circumstances that could vary from incremental to transformational change.

A number of possible routes for achieving this flexibility may come to mind. One approach, perhaps as part of the 'flexible firm' construct, is to build functional and numerical flexibility into the workforce. Another is to identify competences associated with managing change and to embed them in the organisation through HR practices, such as recruitment and selection (Chapter 8), performance management (Chapter 9), human resource development (Chapter 10) and reward management (Chapter 11). Indeed this might be developed to the point where the competences for change become the core competences of the organisation (Prahalad and Hamel, 1990). The notion of core competences was discussed in Chapter 1 as a facet of resource-based theory. Here, it is argued more generally that in order to develop HR capability as a source of competitive advantage management need to focus attention on developing organisational structures, organising work, fostering cooperative relationships and ensuring consistency of fair treatment to facilitate the development of this capability. HRP provides a vehicle for management to do this irrespective of the competences to be developed and supported. Yet another route to flexibility is through diversity management, as discussed in Chapter 13.

These various routes can be brought together through the planning process. For example Wright and Snell (1999) have developed a framework that sets out to reconcile the potentially competing demands of strategic fit and flexibility. They argue that planning is necessary to ensure that the necessary HR practices, employee skills and employee behaviours are in place to achieve both planned strategies and future flexibility in order to achieve effective organisation performance.

HRP as continuous process

The work of Wright and Snell (1999) shifts the focus to the HRP process itself. This is the fourth and probably most important avenue for confronting the myriad of difficulties associated with HRP. The argument here is that there is a need to develop HRP processes that are continuous, not static, so that they have the capacity to inform strategy formulation and provide an early warning system for when events begin to deviate from plans. This enables contingency plans to be brought into effect or, in their absence, adjustments made to HR plans to reflect the new reality. To achieve all of this it is likely that HRP processes must involve all relevant stakeholders so that emerging threats and opportunities are not overlooked. The stakeholders themselves need to be sufficiently competent to add meaningfully to the HRP process, and senior managers must be open to accepting inputs into the planning process and strategy formulation from all quarters. Planning to achieve this might in itself be an example of the micro-planning referred to earlier. It also necessitates a formalised and integrated feedback and evaluation mechanism in order to surface deviations from plan and elicit changes in direction that otherwise might be left to chance.

Wright and Snell's (1999) framework referred to above, taken together with process models produced by Ainsworth (1995), Gratton (1999) and Turner (2002), provides various possible ways forward. To illustrate this potential the work of Gratton (1999) and Ainsworth (1995) is summarised below.

Gratton (1999), using case study methodology, has mapped out relationships between organisational strategy and employee performance. The 'people process map' developed by Gratton *et al.* (1999) is based on three propositions:

> That the delivery of business strategy is most successful when linkage occurs on three dimensions; that at the core of the linkage are a set of key clusters of processes; and that the linkage between business strategy and these people processes can vary from weak to strong.
>
> *Gratton (1999: 172)*

The three dimensions of her strategic linkage are the, by now, familiar ones of vertical, horizontal and temporal linkage, with the latter ensuring that both short- and long-term strategic considerations receive due attention. Interestingly, she identifies different clusters of people processes as being relevant to the achievement of short- and long-term strategies. For short-term strategic linkage, objective setting, performance metrics, rewards and short-term training are identified as being particularly relevant, whereas for long-term linkage, leadership development, workforce development and organisational development are identified. The strength of the linkage between organisational strategies and people processes are assessed along a continuum. At one end, changes in people processes mirror changes to organisational strategies, while at the other end there is, at worst, no relationship between the two and, at best, ad hoc linkage. Through continual monitoring and feedback, gaps between strategies and HR capability can be identified and people strategies developed to redirect the people processes as necessary to address both short- and long-term requirements. Taken together these relationships are captured below in an adaptation of Gratton's (1999: 185) 'people process map', as depicted in Figure 7.6.

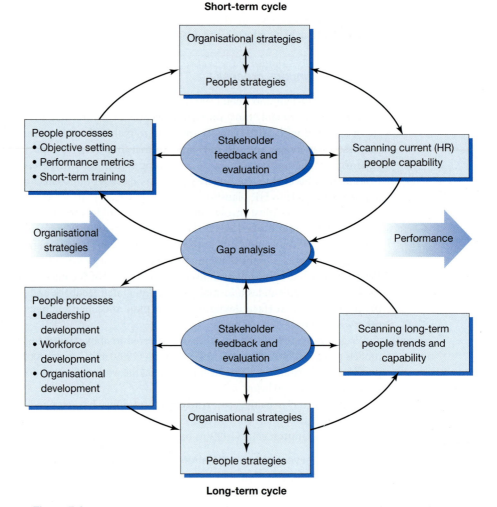

Figure 7.6 The 'people process map'
Source: after Gratton (1999).

Within the case companies studied, people process–strategy linkages were found to be stronger within the short-term cycle and significantly weaker within the long-term cycle. The main reasons put forward for this lack of long-term strategic linkage were 'the complexity of embedding these processes and the general short-term view of the companies' (Gratton, 1999: 195). Given the previous discussion this does not come as any surprise but once again reinforces the difficulties associated with HRP.

In Practice 7.10 summarises an alternative HRP process developed by Zeneca Pharmaceuticals. However, like Gratton's (1999) 'people process map', it places heavy emphasis on continual feedback and evaluation and also stresses the importance of multi-stakeholder participation in an open and collaborative process.

It is now left to you, the reader, to reach your own conclusion on the extent to which HRP can be viewed as either the vital link or the missing/weakest link between organisational strategies and SHRM.

In Practice 7.10

A window on HRP practice at Zeneca

The strategic HRP process developed at Zeneca Pharmaceuticals was in response to a need to move the business from a relatively stable and centralised operation to one that could address the realities of a rapidly changing business environment. Creative and innovative science, speed to market and effective marketing were identified as the organisation's critical success factors and it was accepted that all three were dependent on HR excellence. At this time, however, although accountability for HR had been increasingly devolved to line managers, the HR function had little previous strategic involvement. In response to these contextual factors a rolling six-stage framework for devising strategic HR plans with senior line management teams was developed and implemented.

Stage 1 – initial analysis by core team

For each particular line function, a core HR team analyses: the key HR implications arising from each of the line function's objectives; which HR activities or processes are vital to achieving those objectives; and the extent to which the function is currently deploying those HR activities and processes effectively.

Stage 2 – sharing the analysis with function head and agreeing key themes

The HR team present the function head with their analysis and its relationship to the business (not function) strategy with a view to producing an HR plan for the function. During this process the function head may rework the core team's analysis and conclusions.

Stage 3 – function head engages with (their) management team through existing business processes to confirm key themes

The outcome of stage 2 is shared with the functional management team through one of their normal business planning processes. Where possible, a current area of HR interest is used as a hook to facilitate line management involvement.

Stage 4 – work with management team to agree strategic plan

Key HR themes are worked up into a detailed HR plan for the future.

Stage 5 – implementation of plan

This is led by the line management with the support of the HR team.

Stage 6 – continual review of progress and currency of plan

Where possible the review is conducted through the same business planning process utilised at stage 3 and aims to integrate HRP and the HR function's objectives with organisational objectives as they change over time.

Source: Ainsworth (1995).

Summary

- HRP is the name given to formal processes designed to ensure that an organisation's human resource capability can support the achievement of its strategic objectives. It involves forecasting the future demand for and supply of labour and drawing up HR plans to reconcile mismatches between the two.

- When viewed as the vital link between organisation and HR strategies, HRP can be regarded as a bridging mechanism fulfilling three vital roles: aligning HR plans to organisational strategies to further their achievement; uncovering HR issues that can threaten the viability of organisational strategies and thereby lead to their reformulation; and acting in a reciprocal relationship with organisational strategies such that HR issues become a central input into the strategy formation process.

- Numerous difficulties surrounding the practice of HRP may thwart its potential to serve as the link between organisational strategy and SHRM practice. These difficulties may be sufficient to lead organisations to abandon any thoughts of practising HRP, may conspire to reduce the effectiveness of HRP practice, or may limit its application to short-term, operational matters.

- Patchy and limited data on HRP practice points to its low level of take-up by organisations leading to an alternative perspective of HRP as the missing or weakest link between organisational and HR strategies. This leads to a paradox where the more the complexities of organisational life warrant the establishment of HRP as the vital link the more these complexities are likely to cause HRP to be cast aside to become the missing/weakest link.

- Avenues for confronting operational difficulties and forging HRP as the pivotal bridging mechanism between organisational strategy and SHRM practice focused on: raising the profile of HR issues generally and the status and credibility of HR practitioners particularly; using contingency and scenario planning to introduce flexibility into the HRP process; building towards a flexible workforce that can manage the vagaries arising from unplanned developments and an uncertain future; and developing an HRP process centred on continual review, evaluation and adaptation and adopting a multi-stakeholder approach to make this a realistic possibility.

Follow-up study suggestions

- Access and read the cited articles of Miles and Snow (1984b) and Schuler and Jackson (1987). Analyse the extent to which you believe their approaches to human resourcing can be construed as HRP using the conceptual frameworks discussed in this chapter.

- Review Chapter 7 and determine what you believe are the key features of an effective HRP process. Then, access and read the frameworks, maps and models developed respectively by Ainsworth (1995), Gratton *et al.* (1999), Turner (2002) and Wright and Snell (1999) and analyse these against the evaluative framework you have just created.

- Drawing on research methods literature, design a research project to test the extent to which HRP is practised in UK organisations. Critique your research design to identify its strengths and weaknesses.

- Access the international SHRM literature and identify and explore the key HRP issues arising. Those wishing to conduct a deeper level of analysis can go on to complete this task against the different organisation forms adopted by businesses operating across national boundaries, i.e. multi-national; global; international; and trans-national companies.

- Use the internet to explore the HRP practices of different 'case' organisations and develop explanations that account for similarities and differences between their practices.

Suggestions for research topics

- How do the processes and practices of HRP vary between SMEs and large organisations?
- To what extent and how do organisations conduct longer-term HRP?
- How do HR professionals perceive their role in HRP? An exploration of the differences between their aspirations and perceptions of reality.
- How extensive is HRP in organisations? A survey of current HRP practice in the UK.
- *Vive la difference!* How do organisations based in different countries view the utility of HRP? A comparative study of European HR practice.

Case Study

Human resource planning in mergers and acquisitions

The three cases outlined briefly below are drawn from the work of Salama *et al.* (2003) who are investigating changes and opportunities presented by mergers and acquisitions (M&A) involving companies within related industries but which cross national boundaries. Such M&A frequently bring together people of diverse cultural backgrounds which create the potential either to enhance competitive advantage or to derail the M&A process and lead to its subsequent failure.

Their research provides an interesting counterpoint to the literature that emphasises how inappropriate integration strategies contribute to the high failure rate of M&A (see In Practice 7.1). In contrast, they report on three M&A success stories and have focused on researching the integration processes adopted to maximise potential synergies and minimise the potential negative effects of cultural differences between the organisations involved. Their central argument is that

value-added outcomes arising from M&A are only likely to be realised if people from both organisations, and particularly their managers, have both the will and the ability to work collaboratively. They argue that 'The key to integration is to obtain the participation of the people involved without compromising the strategic task' (Salama *et al.*, 2003: 313). This represents a critical agenda for HRP. One approach here would be to minimise the difficulties by establishing cultural compatibility as one important criterion for selecting possible M&A candidates. However, as exemplified in Chapter 6, a more realistic scenario is that cultural differences will exist and need to be managed. This scenario is a feature of all three cases and underpins their interest in integration strategies designed to encourage: tolerance of diversity; organisational learning; knowledge transfer; and acculturation (culture change resulting from the interaction of different organisational cultures).

Deutsche Bank and Bankers Trust

Deutsche Bank was in the process of strategic transformation from a German bank to a global organisation but lacked sufficient presence in the USA. It acquired Bankers Trust to address this and was particularly interested in the investment bank Alex Brown acquired by Bankers Trust two years earlier. The success of the acquisition has been largely attributed to the pre-integration period or 'courting phase' (Salama et al., 2003: 316). Here, during the due diligence period (the period of time between announcing and closing the M&A deal), an independent cultural assessment exercise was commissioned by Deutsche Bank senior management. The cross-organisational perceptions of employees revealed that:

● Deutsche Bank employees did not feel the acquisition of Bankers Trust would enhance their business;

● the integration of Alex Brown and Bankers Trust had not been managed effectively, causing internal conflict and a loss of identity among Alex Brown employees;

● Bankers Trust felt that Deutsche Bank typified the traits of bureaucracy, hierarchy and slow decision-making that they associated with German companies.

These findings led senior management to:

● enhance employee communication to close what was perceived to be a validity information gap by sharing the rationale behind the acquisition;

● name the merged company in the USA The Deutsche Bank-Alex Brown Investment Bank to reinforce the brand identity that was one of the prime moves behind the acquisition in the first place (this led to the perception among Alex Brown employees that they had been rescued from Bankers Trust by Deutsche Bank);

● start challenging the prevailing Deutsche Bank working values and embracing alternative ones.

During the 'integration phase: the "marriage"' (Salama et al., 2003: 316) a number of HR initiatives were introduced to facilitate organisational integration:

● the establishment of an integration team, comprising key executives, charged with making the tough integration decisions, one of which was the decision to 'strip out' those parts of Bankers Trust that could not be integrated into the new business;

● redundancy packages incorporating incentives for 'redundant' Bankers Trust employees to work through until the acquisition process was completed;

● incentive schemes to encourage 'key' Bankers Trust staff (only) to commit to the new organisation in order to avoid damaging employee turnover.

British Petroleum (BP) and Amoco

The merger between two large British and US petroleum companies has been hailed as a success by its managers because it was achieved faster and created greater synergy than forecast. As with Deutsche Bank, the management of the pre-merger phase was seen as crucial to this success. This involved the creation of an integration team who used the due-diligence period to assess the potential synergies that could be produced by combining head offices and merging operating divisions (e.g. finance, HR).

Managing the post-merger 'marriage phase' revolved around five areas:

1. Integrating areas of duplication where, continuing the marriage analogy, partners analysed and dealt with duplication of assets brought into the marriage and worked from current patterns of behaviour to develop and pursue desired behaviours.

2. Appointing into managerial roles in a way that creates opportunities for employees from both constituent companies. Here, for example, the top 500 appointments in the new company were sourced 60 per cent from BP and 40 per cent from Amoco, directly in line with their respective share of the business.

3. Integrating systems and processes on the basis of what was considered to be best practice across the constituent companies. Here integrating HR processes, such as job grading and remuneration management, were particularly problematic not because of any technical complexity but because of strong emotional attachments of employees to their HR heritage.

4. Building a new corporate culture where regular meetings of the top managers were used to explain the operating philosophy of BP and to encourage socialisation and the breakdown of barriers between BP and Amoco managers.

5. Regular monitoring of employee attitudes as the merger unfolded so that managerial action could be directed towards influencing their 'hearts and minds' and obtaining full commitment to the new company.

Volvo and Ford

This merger between a large Swedish organisation and huge Anglo-Saxon corporation had to confront many cultural differences between the two. Employees perceived Volvo as operating within a decentralised and participative management philosophy where teamwork and devolved decision-making were the accepted norm and where personal credibility was derived from expertise not position in the organisation hierarchy. These characteristics were reflected in the management of industrial relations where union representatives and management worked closely together to improve business performance. In contrast, Ford was perceived as highly structured and hierarchical, with status differentials between blue- and white-collar workers and with a more confrontational industrial relations climate. For Volvo employees, the transition was also more marked as they moved from a position where Volvo represented 51 per cent of the previous AB Volvo group to where it represented only 8 per cent of Ford's total business.

Structural re-organisation was a key outcome of the mergers. Two major divisions were created. The first brought the premium products under one roof (Jaguar, Land Rover, Aston Martin and Volvo) – the Premium Automotive Group. The second, Ford Cars, covers the more traditional, mass-market product offerings.

The due-diligence period focused on exploring the potential for financial synergies. Cultural issues were not explored at this time, but immediately after the merger was finalised an integration team comprising 18 matched pairs of Ford and Volvo executives was formed. They were tasked to work together on an equal basis to establish further synergies in specified areas such as marketing, purchasing and research. The integration team was seen as an important vehicle for overcoming cultural differences.

Source: Salama *et al*. (2003).

Case study questions

1. Compare and contrast the three outline cases from an HRP perspective. What are the main similarities and differences between them?

2. If you had been responsible for the HRP dimension of each of the three merger situations which do you think was handled most effectively and why?

3. If you had been responsible for the HRP dimension of each of the three merger situations what would you have done differently and why?

4. Critically evaluate the HRP process and practice evident in the three cases against the subject content of the chapter.

8 Strategic recruitment and selection:
Much ado about nothing?

Learning Outcomes

By the end of this chapter you should be able to:

- provide an underpinning rationale in support of the development and practice of strategically integrated recruitment and selection;

- identify and explain the major features of strategic recruitment and selection, and summarise these through an explanatory model;

- analyse how recruitment and selection can be developed to fit a variety of strategic scenarios using illustrative examples to support your analysis;

- explain how recruitment and selection practice can be shaped to accommodate the demands of strategic change and unplanned change arising from an uncertain future;

- evaluate evidence to determine the extent of strategic recruitment and selection practice;

- account for the apparent mismatch between the rationale for strategic recruitment and selection and the paucity of evidence of its practice.

Introduction

The focus of this chapter is on how recruitment and selection practice can be developed in support of SHRM to apply strategic leverage in organisations. The chapter begins by developing a rationale for the adoption of a strategic approach to recruitment and selection by organisations. However, irrespective of how persuasive this rationale might be, there is limited evidence of the adoption of strategic recruitment and selection by organisations. This lack of organisational take-up and the problematic nature of the concept and how it can be put into practice are important challenges confronting the development of strategic recruitment and selection.

Unfortunately, despite passing reference to strategic recruitment and selection in mainstream texts, there is little detailed development of the concept or reported evidence of its practice in academic journals, as illustrated in Key Concepts 8.1.

Key Concepts   8.1

Food for thought?

In the 1980s and 1990s the occasional chapter dedicated to strategic recruitment and selection could be found in mainstream HR texts (see, for example, Borucki and Lafley, 1984; Miller, 1984; Evenden, 1993; Lundy and Cowling, 1996; Williams and Dobson, 1997). Now, most chapters on recruitment and selection in mainline HR texts make some reference to strategic perspectives (see, for example, Iles, 2001; Bratton and Gold, 2003; Beardwell and Wright, 2004). However, such references tend to be cursory in nature and this, together with the lack of coverage of strategic recruitment and selection in academic journals, suggests that research into the subject is somewhat sparse. When strategic recruitment and selection does get a mention it tends to be buried in a wider management or HR investigation.

In April 2004 a search of the Emerald Fulltext database using strategic recruitment and selection as the search words was conducted. One thousand and forty-nine hits were scored but only one bull's-eye. Only one article title directly referred to the subject domain (Petrovic and Kakabadse, 2003). Further searches of four management and social sciences databases provided one further hit (Millmore, 2003) which is reported on in 'In Practice' 8.11, later in this chapter.

In order to address these issues, the chapter goes on to discuss the nature of strategic recruitment and selection and develops its principal characteristics into a conceptual framework and associated model. This is followed by a discussion on how the principles of strategic recruitment and selection might be applied to a multi-dimensional interpretation of strategic fit. This includes, as a further section, how strategic recruitment and selection can be applied to support strategic change specifically and to managing change more generally.

The final two sections review the extent of strategic recruitment and selection practice and analyse why evidence points to its low level of take-up by organisations.

The chapter themes identified above have been captured in a series of questions and correspondingly mapped in Figure 8.1:

1. What is the rationale for strategic recruitment and selection?

2. What is strategic recruitment and selection?

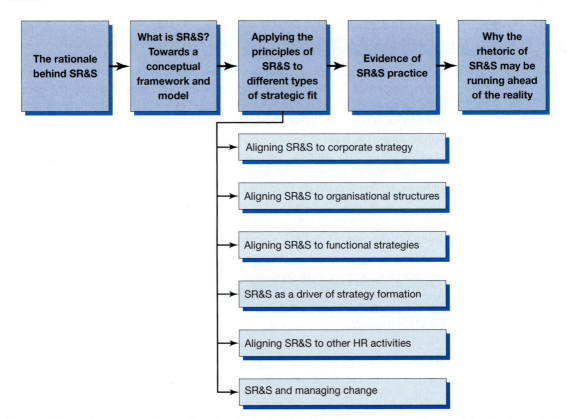

Figure 8.1 Mapping the strategic recruitment and selection (SR&S) territory: a summary diagram of the chapter content

3. How can strategic recruitment and selection be applied in practice?

4. How feasible is strategically aligned recruitment and selection in a changing world?

5. How extensive is strategic recruitment and selection practice?

6. What might account for the mismatch between the rhetoric and reality of strategic recruitment and selection?

What is the rationale for strategic recruitment and selection?

Self-Check and Reflect Questions   8.1

Imagine that you work as an HR officer for a company that is unhappy with the effectiveness of its current recruitment and selection practice. You have been asked to write a paper presenting a rationale for the development and subsequent implementation of strategic recruitment and selection.

Before you read on, take five minutes to think through the main arguments that you would use to structure such a paper. Write them down in note form. If you have already read Chapters 1, 2 and 7 you should find these helpful in developing your ideas.

Self-Check and Reflect Questions

Advance warning!
At the end of this section the following Self-Check and Reflect Question is posed:
   What potential features emerge from your reading of the section 'What is the rationale for strategic recruitment and selection?' that you would expect to be incorporated into the development of a conceptual framework of strategic recruitment and selection?
   You might therefore find it helpful to bear this question in mind as you read and try to identify emergent themes as you go along.

If the mantra of HRM is accepted then human resources represent an organisation's most valuable asset. From this perspective it can be argued that an organisation's human resource capability is a core competence and major source of competitive advantage. However, while this may be true for many organisations the discussion of the resource-based view of the firm in Chapter 1 pointed to how other resources, for example brands or capital stock, could also fulfil this role. Notwithstanding this rider to the HRM perspective, an organisation's human capital will still represent a critical resource because of its capacity to exploit these other resources for strategic advantage.

Against this backdrop it is easy to identify the importance recruitment and selection has in sourcing an organisation with employees capable of delivering sustainable competitive advantage. Although only one of a bundle of human resourcing practices, it has been argued that recruitment and selection lies at the very centre of human resourcing in organisations. The importance attached to recruitment and selection is evident in the assertion that appointment decisions are some of the most crucial ones ever taken by employers (IRS, 1991) and summarised neatly by Newell (2005: 141): 'if we get the wrong people in the organisation there will be problems'. However, this arguably shifts recruitment and selection practice from its traditional, narrow focus on identified job vacancies to a broader organisation concern to secure strategic leverage. The essence of the strategic variant is that recruitment and selection practice is driven by its alignment with organisational strategies rather than the immediate needs of specific job vacancies.

The strategic importance of recruitment and selection is given sharp focus by a number of writers. For example, Sparrow and Hiltrop (1994: 315) argue that recruitment, selection and assessment are central practices that 'provide the organization with a powerful basis for influencing and organizing human behaviour in line with the strategic direction of the organization'. Williams and Dobson (1997: 242) arguably go further in their hypothesis:

> that where SHRM strategies in general and selection specifically are coherent and aligned to current and future business strategy, personnel selection will make a significant contribution to organizational performance.

In making the shift in direction it begs the question as to whether traditional approaches to recruitment and selection can deliver the necessary strategic focus. Over many years, organisational recruitment and selection practice has evolved into a relatively standardised approach frequently labelled as 'traditional' (Newell and Shackleton,

2001: 24). This traditional approach has its roots in a psychometric model where organisational effort is directed at matching the different attributes of individuals to the different demands of specific jobs in order to establish a person–job fit (Newell, 2005). The psychometric tradition of recruitment and selection translates the process into a systematic sequence of activities as outlined in Key Concepts 8.2.

The limitations of this approach are that the stages of recruitment and selection and any subsequent evaluation of its effectiveness are prescribed by the demands of specific jobs rather than the strategic imperatives of the organisation. To shift recruitment and selection practice towards a strategic focus arguably requires the features of the psychometric tradition to be adapted to meet broader organisational concerns. How this might be achieved, both conceptually and in practice, are discussed in the next three sections.

The interrelated nature of the arguments presented immediately above has been illustrated in Figure 8.2.

Drawing on the above analysis it is possible to summarise the rationale for strategic recruitment and selection by reference to a series of propositions contained within the strategic management and human resource literature (Key Concepts 8.3).

Key Concepts 8.2

Essential features of the psychometric tradition of recruitment and selection

1. Jobs are analysed and defined in terms of their tasks and responsibilities (job description).
2. Human attributes associated with effective job performance are identified and assembled into a profile of the ideal candidate (person specification).
3. Jobs are marketed to attract applicants who fit the person specification (recruitment).
4. Applicants are assessed and profiled against the person specification using a variety of measures (selection).
5. Candidates are selected on the basis of the match between their personal profile and the person specification (offer/rejection decision).
6. Job performance of appointed candidates is measured to establish effectiveness of the recruitment and selection process (evaluation).

Source: adapted from Newell (2005: 142).

Key Concepts 8.3

The rationale for strategic recruitment and selection – summary propositions

- Organisation behaviour should be increasingly directed towards the strategic pursuit of competitive advantage (Porter, 1985).
- The strategic pursuit of competitive advantage involves matching resources to the long-term direction of the organisation (Johnson and Scholes, 2002).
- Human resource competence represents an important element of resource capability (Thornhill *et al.*, 2000) and is regarded by many as an organisation's most important asset (e.g. Bratton and Gold, 2003).

- Human resource management incorporates, as its principal feature, the alignment of HR practice with corporate strategy (e.g. Bratton and Gold, 2003).
- Recruitment and selection lies at the centre of human resourcing within organisations (Newell, 2005).
- Traditional approaches to recruitment and selection are ill-equipped to contribute to the strategic pursuit of competitive advantage (Thornhill *et al.*, 2000).
- Strategically directed recruitment and selection has the potential to make a significant contribution to organisational performance and the pursuit of competitive advantage (Williams and Dobson, 1997).

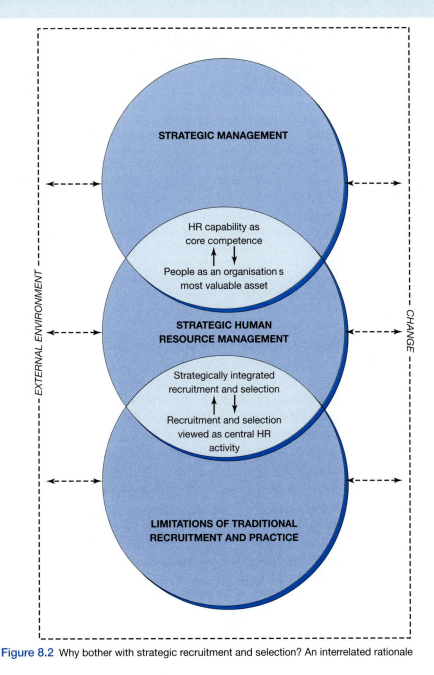

Figure 8.2 Why bother with strategic recruitment and selection? An interrelated rationale

Self-Check and Reflect Questions   8.2

What potential features emerge from your reading of the section 'What is the rationale for strategic recruitment and selection?' that you would expect to be incorporated into the development of a conceptual framework of strategic recruitment and selection?

What is strategic recruitment and selection? Towards a conceptual framework and model of strategic recruitment and selection

This section commences with a brief discussion of the seemingly straightforward relationship between strategy and recruitment and selection in order to generate an initial understanding of the concept of strategic recruitment and selection. The shortcomings of this opening position will then be exposed through reference back to Chapters 1 and 7 where a more detailed examination of the notion of strategic integration (or fit) revealed its true complexity. This will lead into a more in-depth exploration of how to develop strategic recruitment and selection practice from which a conceptual framework and model of the process is developed. What will become apparent is that the movement of recruitment and selection from its psychometric traditions to a strategic approach does not involve the proverbial 'throwing out the baby with the bath water'. It will be seen that while some fundamental differences exist, in other respects strategic recruitment and selection builds on many of the features of the psychometric approach.

Strategic recruitment and selection: an opening position

The central tenet of strategic recruitment and selection is its strategic thrust, where the suitability of potential recruits is defined by reference not only to specific job requirements but also to broader strategic concerns. Not surprisingly, this strategic thrust is captured in definitions of the concept. For example, Lundy and Cowling (1996: 240) argue that:

> If organisation selection is informed by the organisation's environment, linked to strategy, socially responsible, valid, periodically evaluated and maintained by knowledge of leading theory and practice, then selection is, indeed, strategic.

Their definition not only emphasises strategic integration but also points to other criteria that might need to be incorporated into a more demanding interpretation of the concept of strategic recruitment and selection. However, before examining such criteria in more depth the fact that this opening position throws little light on the nature of strategic integration, thereby masking its inherent complexity, is addressed. To do this, the multi-dimensional nature of strategic integration is reviewed briefly. This is necessary in order to understand the different types of strategic fit that need to be incorporated into strategically driven recruitment and selection.

The multi-dimensional nature of strategic integration

In Chapter 1 (and reinforced in Chapter 7) the notion of strategic integration and its multi-dimensional nature was explored. Without claiming to have covered all the angles it was demonstrated that strategic fit could relate to: different levels within a strategic hierarchy comprising first-, second- and third-order strategies; two-way, downstream and upstream relationships; internal, or horizontal, integration between HR activities; and strategic change and future uncertainties. These six strands of strategic integration were captured in Key Concepts 1.4 and Figure 1.3 and a quick look back at these will help to reinforce the multi-dimensional nature of strategic integration. These six strands of strategic fit have been related to recruitment and selection immediately below:

- Recruitment and selection responses to first-order strategic decisions (downstream, vertical or external integration).
- Recruitment and selection responses to second-order strategic decisions (downstream, vertical integration).
- Recruitment and selection responses to third-order strategic decisions (downstream, vertical integration).
- Recruitment and selection as an influencer of future strategic direction (upstream, vertical integration).
- Recruitment and selection responses to facilitate other HR initiatives (horizontal or internal integration).
- Recruitment and selection responses to planned change and future uncertainties.

In Figure 1.3 the complex strategic context of SHRM was captured with recruitment and selection clearly identified as one of a bundle of human resourcing activities. In terms of recruitment and selection, this begins to explain the nature of the strategic link identified by Purcell (1995: 63) but still falls short of explaining how that link will be *realised* and *developed* in practice in order to achieve the demands of strategic integration. The chapter now goes on to address these remaining matters and later sections takes each of the six strands of strategic integration and demonstrates how they can be supported by recruitment and selection practice.

How can strategic recruitment and selection practice be developed?

In Figure 8.3 the key features of strategic recruitment and selection are brought together in a model of the process.

The model captures the primary and secondary features underpinning strategic recruitment and selection. It also shows how HRP can be used as a linking mechanism between different orders (or levels) of organisational strategies and strategic recruitment and selection. The chapter now goes on to discuss the primary and secondary features depicted in the model.

Primary features of strategic recruitment and selection

Strategic recruitment and selection starts from the premise that an organisation's workforce makes a significant contribution to the achievement of both short-term and long-term strategic goals. The quality of an organisation's workforce is, in part, a func-

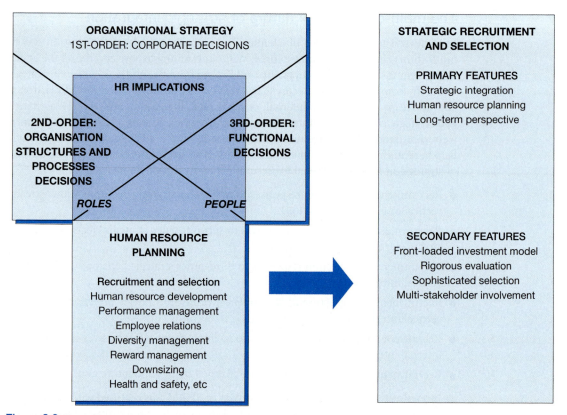

Figure 8.3 Strategic recruitment and selection: an explanatory model
Source: Millmore (2003: 92).

tion of the recruitment and selection process. The concern to meet current and future strategic requirements as well as facilitating organisational adaptation to cope with future uncertainties represents the starting point for a model of strategic recruitment and selection.

Millmore and Baker (1996) not only reinforce the links between recruitment and selection and corporate strategy but also begin to suggest how organisational strategies can be translated into recruitment and selection practice. For them strategic recruitment and selection occurs when practice is aligned with and integrated into the strategic planning process of organisations and involves the translation of mission statements and/or strategic plans into those employee attributes which are seen to be critical to their successful attainment. This provides a long-term focus where the intention is to develop recruitment and selection practice to source an organisation with those attributes deemed critical to its future success.

The emerging themes of strategic integration, identification of employee attributes necessary to service strategic goals and the adoption of a long-term focus are embedded in Miller's (1984) discussion of strategic staffing. He argues that it is essential to integrate recruitment and selection practice with business planning in order to staff the organisation with people who can best deliver its corporate strategy over the long run. This involves forecasting the human resource requirements necessary to ensure the successful implementation of an organisation's strategic plans and developing a range of staffing programmes and activities to find such people.

When compared to the 'traditional, systematic approach' (Wright and Storey, 1997: 211) the strategic variant has: a different starting point; is geared to longer-term considerations; and requires a bridging mechanism between strategy and recruitment and selection practice. Here, consistent with the concept of internal integration (Mabey and Iles, 1993), recruitment and selection is one of a number of integrated HR activities designed to deliver an organisation's strategic objectives rather than an isolated activity conducted in a vacuum (Millmore and Baker, 1996). For strategic recruitment and selection the starting point is not a job vacancy but the strategic objectives of the organisation which must be translated into the personal attributes required to achieve this strategy. This shifts the focus of recruitment and selection away from fitting the person to the job to fitting the person to the organisation or fitting the job to the person once recruited (see, for example, Bowen *et al.*, 1991; Beaumont and Hunter, 1992; Lawler, 1994). Here the HR requirements of an organisation are sometimes expressed as a common set of core values and/or competencies which are used to drive recruitment and selection and other related human resource practices (e.g. Cockerill, 1989; Sparrow, 1994). This is not dissimilar to the approach adopted by TGI Fridays as described in 'In Practice' 8.1.

In Practice   8.1

Strategic recruitment and selection at TGI Fridays

TGI Fridays is based on the American bar and diner concept, portrayed humorously in the US sitcom *Cheers*. It occupies a lead position in the themed dining market and actively pursues premium brand status. Within its niche market it aims for higher than average repeat business and customer spend. Central to this is the service performance of staff who are expected to achieve successful encounters with customers through offering a personal service within the context of a highly standardised business operation. This creates a tension between standardisation and customisation that has to be addressed through all business areas, including SHRM strategies.

Operating within tightly specified performance standards, employees are expected to take responsibility for customer satisfaction through:

- meeting unusual service requests;
- resolving customer complaints; and
- delighting customers.

This requires the interpersonal competence to adjust to varying clientele needs ranging from entertainment through showmanship to respecting customer space and managing conflict.

When researching employee empowerment at TGI Fridays, Lashley (2000) witnessed first-hand spontaneous examples of its service ethic performed by employees without management direction. On one occasion, during dinner, a succession of 'Dub-Dubs' (TGI Fridays speak for waiting staff) came and tied balloons to the chair of a highly amused young woman celebrating her birthday. On another, at a hen party, eight front of house and kitchen staff gathered around to sing 'I'm getting married in the morning'.

Recruiting and selecting against these role demands is arguably complicated in the UK by the lack of service ethic where, according to one TGI Fridays executive, too often service means servile. Not surprisingly, the organisation invests heavily in recruitment and selection procedures. These can include multiple interviews, psychometric testing and something tantamount to auditioning where candidates have to perform or act out role-play situations. The emphasis is primarily on recruiting staff with the right personality and is supported by front-loaded investment in training to develop operational skills.

Source: Lashley (2000).

To achieve the degree of integration between SHRM practice and strategy discussed above requires a bridging mechanism. As discussed in Chapter 7, the translation of corporate plans into human resource requirements and planned actions to deliver those requirements is the province of formalised human resource planning (HRP) (Rothwell, 1995; Iles, 2001). For Miller (1984) HRP is central to the HR function's development and implementation of recruitment and selection strategy.

It is not the intention to repeat the HRP content of Chapter 7 here but simply to remind you of its bridging potential. In a discussion that centred on HRP as the vital link between HR practice and organisational strategy, a two-way relationship was established. It was explained how HRP has both the potential to act as a downstream support mechanism geared to ensure that the necessary HR capabilities are in place to help realise organisational strategy and a shaping role where it operates as part of the strategy formulation process.

Based on the foregoing discussion of strategic recruitment and selection, it is possible to delineate three primary features of the concept:

- strategic integration;
- a long-term perspective; and
- the use of HRP as the bridging mechanism between organisation strategies and recruitment and selection practice.

Secondary features of strategic recruitment and selection

If the above primary features are developed to their logical conclusion, two consequential, interdependent outcomes arise. First, recruitment and selection acquires greater organisational importance and, second, it becomes more sophisticated and complex. When getting it right is evaluated against broader strategic concerns, the recruitment and selection process arguably becomes much more important than where it simply relates to satisfying more immediate job needs. However, the complex demands generated by such a strategic focus are likely to lead to more diverse and exacting personnel specifications. This in turn will require a greater array of recruitment and selection practices to be deployed in order to meet organisational staffing requirements. Under these circumstances the challenge for recruitment and selection is to develop and assess against composite personnel specifications, addressing the needs of specific job requirements, group and organisation fit for both now and in the future.

These consequential outcomes of strategically driven recruitment and selection have the potential to impact significantly on organisational practice in a number of particular ways. First, the perceived critical role of recruitment and selection and concern to get it right is likely to lead to a front-loaded investment model. Here the assumption is that up-front investment in recruitment and selection is made with the objective of recruiting the 'right' competences first time rather than investing later in rectifying 'poor' selection decisions and is exemplified by practice documented in inward investment companies such as Nissan and Toyota (Storey and Sisson, 1993) and a number of UK companies (Cockerill, 1989).

Second, the greater financial expenditure demanded by a front-loaded investment model will almost certainly lead to concerted calls for its effectiveness to be more rigorously evaluated. Full evaluation would include the assessment of the reliability and validity of the personnel specification, the selection methods utilised and the contribution recruitment and selection makes to the attainment of strategic objectives (Lawler, 1994). Third, heavy investment in the process, the consequential emphasis on getting 'it' right and the demands of a more complex and diverse person specification will necessitate the use of a greater array of selection methods to assess potential recruits (Evenden, 1993; Bratton and Gold, 2003) in order to deliver acceptable levels of reliability and validity. Fourth, the complex and critical nature of strategic recruitment and selection makes untenable the limited stakeholder involvement associated with the traditional variant and arguably demands a multi-stakeholder approach. Consistent with the social exchange view of recruitment and selection, the strategic model places much more emphasis on securing the active participation of relevant stakeholders within a more open decision-making framework. There is a concern throughout to provide a realistic preview of the job, role and organisation context to enable candidates to match their aptitudes and interests, etc. against any vacancy and thereby enable self-selection (Lawler, 1994). In addition the selection process itself will also be constructed with due regard to the impact it, and the decisions emanating from it, can have on the future lives of candidates and other organisation members. This leads naturally to the involvement of those who have a direct investment in any appointment, for example subordinates, peers and service providers as exemplified in 'In Practice' 8.2.

This analysis clearly positions these features as a natural corollary of strategically integrated recruitment and selection. As such they may be regarded as a set of secondary features that are needed to support the three primary features in order to achieve strategic recruitment and selection. However, it has to be accepted that they could just as easily be present as elements of good, professional practice within the psychometric tradition of recruitment and selection. Therefore on their own these features are not sufficient to evidence strategic recruitment and selection because they might be operating in a strategic vacuum. It is only when they are allied to the three, necessary, primary features that their strategic significance becomes apparent. Despite their centrality to strategic recruitment and selection, on their own the three primary features do not actually staff the organisation with effective recruits. To do this requires, in addition, the operation of the secondary features.

In Practice   8.2

Recruitment and selection at Pret a Manger

Pret a Manger is in the business of making and serving coffee and sandwiches through its shops, and involves hard, physical teamwork. Staff are recruited to shops against a set of core competences, such as enthusiasm, which are assessed via a two-stage selection process. First, there is a competence-based interview from which only a minority of candidates progress to the second stage: working one day in a shop where there is a vacancy. During the day candidates are exposed to as many different tasks and team members as possible, and are also interviewed by the shop manager. At the end of the day the candidate is assessed by team members against the core competences, who then vote on whether to appoint or not. The shop manger actively participates in the assessment discussion but cannot vote.

Source: Carrington (2002a).

It is now possible to assemble these primary and secondary features into a conceptual framework (Key Concepts 8.4) of strategic recruitment and selection. Taken together, the conceptual framework and model of strategic recruitment and selection depicted in Figure 8.3 provide a detailed specification against which the strategic pedigree of an organisation's recruitment and selection practice can be assessed.

Traditional recruitment and selection practice as a foundation for the strategic variant

It is important to stress that under the strategic variant developed above, the essential elements of the recruitment and selection process are broadly similar to those outlined earlier under the 'traditional' model. The key difference is that strategic concerns drive their operation. This will mean that job analysis moves away from a narrow concentra-

Key Concepts   8.4

Strategic recruitment and selection: a conceptual framework

Primary features

To be classified as strategic, recruitment and selection must exhibit three interdependent primary features: strategic integration; a long-term focus; and a mechanism for translating strategic demands into an appropriate recruitment and selection specification.

- *Strategic integration* occurs when recruitment and selection practice is aligned with an organisation's hierarchy of strategies and results in sourcing the organisation with employees who possess the necessary attributes to achieve those strategies.
- This represents a *long-term perspective* and anticipates recruitment and selection contributing to: the achievement of current strategies; planned changes in strategic direction; and emergent strategies and, in part, involves equipping organisations with a human resource capability that can cope successfully with future uncertainties.
- This requires a capacity to identify the HR attributes necessary to deliver the organisation's strategic plans over the long term and to develop staffing practices and activities to obtain such people. The translation of strategic plans into HR requirements and plans to deliver those requirements is the province of *formalised HRP*.

Secondary features

When recruitment and selection is strategically driven there are two consequential outcomes: it acquires greater organisational importance; and it becomes more sophisticated and complex. These outcomes lead to four interrelated secondary features that support the three, necessary, primary features:

- Substantial, *front-loaded investment* in the process.
- *Rigorous evaluation* of its effectiveness including its strategic contribution.
- The adoption of a greater array of more *sophisticated selection methods*.
- A *multi-stakeholder* approach.

Source: Millmore (2003).

tion on the current demands of specific tasks to a future-oriented process that also takes into account the wider demands of units or teams as well as the whole organisation itself (Bowen *et al.*, 1991). This changing requirement is encapsulated in the strategic job analysis technique developed by Schneider and Konz (1989). This sets out to specify the knowledge, skills and abilities that will be relevant to anticipated future job roles and tasks to ensure their effective performance as well as providing a procedure that can be applied to job roles and tasks that have not yet been anticipated. There is a similar change in emphasis in the generation of a personnel specification. The focus is no longer on identifying attributes associated with effective performance among current job incumbents but on those that are seen to be relevant to changing strategies and future uncertainties. The person specification could therefore reflect changing patterns of work, the consequences of organisational restructuring, different strategic priorities as well as be responsive to specific change programmes (e.g. culture change) and future uncertainties. It is critical that the specification provides sufficient detail for recruitment and selection processes to be targeted specifically at locating, attracting and assessing the desired attributes whatever they are.

The strategic variant does not therefore reject traditional recruitment and selection methods, but develops and deploys them in ways consistent with overriding strategic concerns. For recruitment more thought will be given to likely sources of potential recruits and how to reach them. For selection, the common reliance on shortlisting, interviews and references is likely to be put aside in favour of more reliable and valid selection methods. This may involve the use of purpose-built selection methods, such as work sampling exercises, as well as the use of a greater array of off-the-shelf assessment tools, such as psychometric tests. There will be concern to increase the reliability and validity of interviews and a more realistic appreciation of what they can and cannot measure as well as frequent adaptations to application forms and reference requests to reflect the explicit demands of different roles or jobs, for example based around core competences.

Overall there is an implicit assumption that it will be insufficient to simply update existing job descriptions, interpret the personnel specification narrowly in terms of immediate job requirements, use the same array of recruitment media, produce standardised application forms and select by interview in a relatively arbitrary and cavalier way. The focus switches from role to organisational requirements and in essence strategic recruitment and selection is interpreted as a tailor-made activity designed to relate specifically to many emerging demands. This construction makes redundant any pretence to a prescriptive model. Each recruitment and selection activity is therefore viewed through a contingency framework that recognises that it will need to be adapted to each changing scenario.

Based on the above discussion it is possible to distil a number of core practices that underpin the primary and secondary features of strategic recruitment and selection. These are captured in Figure 8.4.

These explanatory devices enable a more detailed exploration as to how the six types of strategic fit identified earlier might be realised through strategic recruitment and selection practice. However, before doing this a case example of recruitment and selection practice is presented in 'In Practice' 8.3 and you are invited to analyse this against the conceptual framework and model of strategic recruitment and selection outlined above.

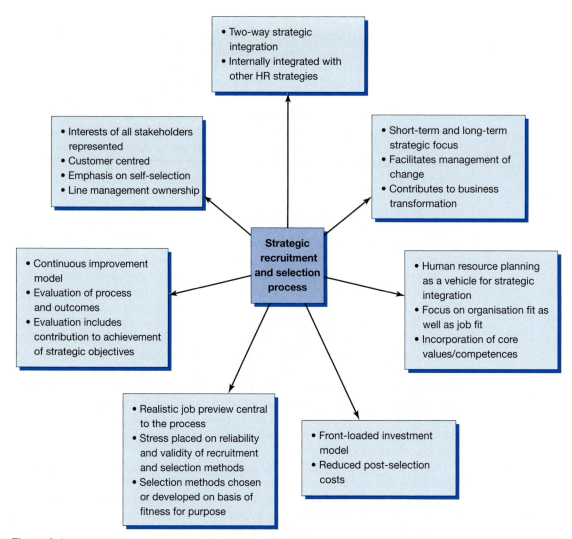

Figure 8.4 Core dimensions of strategic recruitment and selection

In Practice   8.3

Recruitment and selection at the Dionysos

The Dionysos is a luxury hotel located on the Turkish coast overlooking Kumlubuk on the Bozburun peninsular. It accommodates 85 guests and employs over 50 full-time equivalent staff. In Greek mythology Dionysos was the son of Zeus, and god of vegetation, fertility, wine and ecstasy.

The business goal of the owners, Rim and Ahmet Senol, is 'to create a special and unique environment, completely removed from the orthodox tourist experience – where service comes first and guests can relax in a truly stunning setting' (Exclusive Escapes, 2005: 55). The achievement of this business goal is based on two overriding principles. First, that the business represents a family where all staff and guests are members during their stay. Ahmet likens this to the traditional, matriarchal, Mediterranean, family business and this sets the pattern for how the hotel is managed. Second is a concern to deliver a quality of service that exceeds guests' expectations. Business performance is evaluated against three interrelated performance indicators: customer satisfaction; complaints; and repeat business. Another measure of success is where annual staff bonuses exceed their expectations.

Recruitment is largely through word of mouth and personal recommendation. Selection is based on two principal methods: a 'conversation'; and a probationary period. The 'conversation' has two main purposes. First, to assess candidates' ability to deliver the quality of service demanded as measured by the rather unconventional criterion of their ability to 'smile from the heart'. Second, is to establish what candidates are good at and what they want from their life. A major concern of Ahmet's is how working at the hotel can be used to support the aspirations of staff. The other key selection criterion is family fit, where staff exhibit the family values such as trust and mutual respect. Although assessed during the 'conversation', family fit is largely determined via the second selection method: the probation period.

Candidates progressing from the 'conversation' stage are provided with one month's paid employment. Candidates are allocated to job groups on the basis of their interests and assessment of their aptitudes. At month end, group members report on the suitability of candidates against the criteria of service performance and family fit. Successful candidates are offered employment and, once appointed, are encouraged to have further 'conversations' with Ahmet to track their interests and aspirations. Changes in role responsibilities and group membership are determined largely by these conversations.

Workgroups also play a key role in managing 'family relationships'. As well as providing inputs into the staff development process they are also largely responsible for dealing with performance problems, including discipline. Staff training and development is ongoing and based on issues arising out of day-to-day job performance. In addition financial support is provided to help staff realise their aspirations. This most frequently involves support for education to enhance the career opportunities of staff. Rim and Ahmet expect members of the Dionysos family to move on and believe that they should help provide additional life skills to enable this to happen. They also provide support to staff who encounter problems in their domestic lives.

Most recruitment takes place ahead of the new season so that there is time to weed out unsuccessful candidates. At the end of each season customer feedback is shared throughout the family and used to set group and corporate goals for the next season, in a kind of rolling performance-management cycle.

Based on participant observation over a two-week period, the level of customer satisfaction with service quality was exceptionally high. The only evident criticism was that because it was so good it might make guests reluctant to venture outside the hotel! The vast majority of guests vowed to return at the earliest opportunity with many making bookings for the following year while they were there.

Self-Check and Reflect Questions   8.3

To what extent do staffing processes at the Dionysos reflect the strategic approach to recruitment and selection encapsulated by the conceptual framework and model depicted in Key Concepts 8.4 and Figures 8.3 and 8.4?

How can strategic recruitment and selection be applied in practice?

This section discusses how recruitment and selection practice can be aligned to support different strategic scenarios. These strategic scenarios represent the six strands of strategic integration identified in Chapter 1 (as summarised in Key Concepts 1.4 and depicted in Figure 1.3) and developed through the discussion of the multi-dimensional nature of strategic integration. These six strands were further elaborated in Chapter 7 by applying them to HRP where, looking ahead, it was indicated that they would be used in the recruitment and selection chapter of this book as a vehicle for showing how SHRM practice could be related to these six different strategic scenarios.

How these six strands of strategic integration could be related to strategic recruitment and selection was identified earlier in this chapter. Converting these into questions, it is now possible to go on to explore in turn how recruitment and selection can support these different kinds of strategic relationships. In this section, the four different types of vertical (or external) integration identified are illustrated as well as exploring how recruitment and selection can be integrated horizontally (or internally) with other HR levers. In the following section the last strand of strategic fit is addressed through an examination of how recruitment and selection can contribute to strategic change and the vagaries of an uncertain future.

How can recruitment and selection contribute to first-order (downstream, vertical integration) strategic decisions?

In Chapter 1 it was identified that 'first-order decisions are concerned with the long-term direction of the enterprise' (Purcell, 1991: 70). These relate to what Purcell (1995: 63) calls 'the big decisions taken in the corporate office' and include: mergers or acquisitions; joint ventures; and divestment out of existing business (Purcell, 1995). Burnes (2004: 240–241) refers to 'six basic forms of strategy which organisations pursue at this level': stability; growth; portfolio extension; retrenchment; harvesting; and combination strategy. Elsewhere in the literature, first-order decisions are translated into different strategic choices for achieving competitive advantage, for example the defenders, prospectors and analysers developed by Miles and Snow (1984b) and the innovation, quality enhancement and cost reduction framework of Schuler and Jackson (1987). Irrespective of the strategic choice, the objective of strategic recruitment and selection under this scenario is to resource the organisation with employees whose role behaviours will enhance its capacity to deliver its chosen strategy. The key task is to identify these necessary role behaviours and to use them to drive recruitment and selection practice.

To illustrate this, reference is made to the work of Schuler and Jackson (1987), initially discussed in Chapter 2. They identified 12 behavioural continua that can be used to generate a personal profile of those enabling behaviours that would support the pursuit of three different competitive strategies: innovation; quality enhancement; and cost reduction. For example, reference to Table 2.3 reveals that the following employee behaviours would be particularly required to support an innovation strategy:

- high degree of creative behaviour;
- longer-term focus;
- high level of cooperative, interdependent behaviour;
- equal degree of concern for process and results;
- high degree of risk-taking activity;
- high tolerance of ambiguity and unpredictability.

When specific job-related requirements are added to this generic set of attributes this produces the more complex and diverse strategically driven person specification referred to in the development of the strategic recruitment and selection conceptual framework (Key Concepts 8.4) and its related core recruitment and selection dimensions (Figure 8.4). This person specification provides the framework against which recruitment and selection practice can then be developed and implemented. The role of recruitment will be to seek out and attract people with these necessary personal attributes. The role of selection will be to design a selection process that will deliver reliable and valid assessments of shortlisted candidates against these attributes. Here it is argued that the classic trio 'of application form, letter of reference and interview' (Cook, 2004: 3) are highly unlikely to suffice. What is more likely is that the use of a greater array of sophisticated selection methods will be needed to adequately assess candidates against these attributes.

Essentially this process represents how strategic recruitment and selection can be applied to all the types of strategic fit identified. It satisfies the three primary features where HRP is used as the vehicle to translate long-term strategic demands into human resource requirements. It also would necessitate front-loaded investment in the recruitment and selection process through, for example, the development of custom-made selection methods to address the demands of the complex person specification. The use of sophisticated methods of selection in itself is likely to be better served by multi-stakeholder involvement, particularly given the reference to cooperative, interdependent behaviour in the person specification. However, this would still need the subsequent rigorous evaluation of the process to realise the full set of secondary features.

In Practice   8.4

Strategic recruitment and selection at Signet

Like many high street retailers, Signet, owners of the H. Samuel and Ernest Jones chains of jewellers, is recruiting constantly. The organisation employs 6,000 staff but annually recruits 3,000 staff to cover labour turnover and 2,000 to provide Christmas cover.

Concerns about sales led to the development of a business goal to grow sales without increasing retail space. This placed a heavy emphasis on the recruitment of staff who would perform well in a sales environment. This led to proposals to overhaul Signet's whole HR strategy rather than to simply invest heavily in training. The rationale, successfully sold to the board, was that HR strategies were needed to avoid wasting resources on recruits who were likely to leave within a few months.

A business psychologist was employed to determine the key motivational factors associated with high-performing sales staff and all candidates for such roles now have to complete a motivational questionnaire prior to interview. Feedback from Signet's performance management system has already provided evidence that staff selected through this approach are delivering higher levels of performance.

Source: Carrington (2004).

Strategic recruitment and selection at the Pontifical Catholic University of Chile

In 'In Practice' 7.5 the work of Franco and Diaz (1995) was used to provide an example of the rational approach to HRP where the library system of the Pontifical Catholic University of Chile (SIBUC) set out to integrate its human resource objectives and strategies with corporate strategy. As part of the HRP process, six HR objectives were formulated to enable this strategic integration, one of which reflects downstream strategic recruitment and selection in action. This objective was to develop a staff selection system that would source the organisation with achievement-oriented people with innovative capabilities.

The 'strategy' for achieving this objective centred on employing a specialist consultant to work in partnership with SIBUC staff. The action plan formulated by this partnership to create the strategically integrated recruitment and selection system involved:

- identifying and formalising the core values and competences of the organisation emerging from its corporate strategy;
- determine job profiles based on these core values and competences;
- employ an expert psychologist in personnel selection to work with the partnership to evaluate the validity of the job profiles, and prepare a preliminary recruitment and selection policy to meet organisational requirements;
- communicate the policy to line managers and obtain their feedback;
- finalise the policy and develop related recruitment and selection procedures; and
- implement the action plan.

The effectiveness of the recruitment and selection process was to be monitored and controlled by three measures: specifying policies and procedures in a written document; the use of performance evaluation to assess the extent to which the policy was being achieved; and following up staff recruited through the new system to assess their degree of job satisfaction.

Source: developed from Franco and Diaz (1995).

Taken at face value it seems highly plausible that different employee role behaviours will underpin different competitive strategies. However, such frameworks may be overly prescriptive and should therefore be used cautiously. While such frameworks provide useful guidance, organisations will still need to identify and validate those role behaviours that support their own particular context in order to fully exploit the potential contribution that recruitment and selection can make to first-order strategic decisions.

The identification and validation of employee role behaviours is then a core dimension of strategic recruitment and selection. However, as discussed earlier, 'the big decisions taken in the corporate office' (Purcell, 1995: 63) extend beyond competitive strategies to include, for example, the demands of joint ventures, mergers, inward investment, and change to a service culture, etc. The same logic can be applied to shaping recruitment and selection to meet these first-order strategic demands. It is about identifying the key employee behaviours, values, etc. that are necessary to support these big decisions and then using recruitment and selection to actively acquire them whenever the opportunity presents itself.

How can recruitment and selection contribute to second-order (downstream, vertical integration) strategic decisions?

In Chapter 1 it was identified that 'second-order decisions' are concerned with the alignment of an organisation's internal structure and operating procedures and processes with its first-order strategic decisions (Purcell, 1991: 71). Similarly to first-order strategic decisions, there are likely to be contingent relationships between structures and processes on the one hand and staffing strategies and desired role behaviours on the other (Miller, 1984). For example, as you may have experienced, organisations regularly make major structural changes as they adapt to changing organisational circumstances. This has frequently involved the move away from bureaucratic, mechanistic structures towards more organic organisational forms and the imposition of delayering to reduce hierarchy and produce flatter organisational structures.

The impact that this shift from bureaucratic to organic structures has had on managerial roles has been researched by Cockerill (1989). In the relative stability of bureaucracies, planning, organising, monitoring and the use of rules, regulations and precedents to solve problems represent appropriate role behaviours that could be used to drive recruitment and selection. However, these role behaviours lose their value in organic organisations where the more turbulent nature of the business environment undermines their validity. Here management behaviours that include networking, team building, information retrieval and innovative problem solving and decision-making are likely to be more appropriate.

This focus on managerial roles, however, is only half the equation. To support changes to organisation structures more fully, similar thought also needs to be given to the necessary role behaviours for line staff. For example, in organic structures, or as a consequence of organisational delayering, employees are likely to be expected to:

- exercise higher degrees of discretion and autonomy in their work (empowerment);
- take more control of their personal development;
- be flexible and adaptable in their responses to changing patterns of work;
- work collaboratively within and across teams;
- multi-skilled in order to deliver the wider role responsibilities expected of them, both horizontally (job enlargement) and vertically (job enrichment).

This is likely to lead to greater emphasis being placed on the assessment of social skills, interaction ability and group fit and may lead to teams being given devolved responsibility for recruitment in a highly appropriate application of a multi-stakeholder approach.

How can recruitment and selection contribute to third-order (downstream, vertical integration) strategic decisions?

In Chapter 1 it was identified that 'downstream third-order decisions' (Purcell, 1991: 91) concern strategic choices made at the functional level that are necessary to support the achievement of corporate strategies. Here, by way of illustration, the focus is on the HR function and how recruitment and selection can be directed to support the move from traditional personnel management to SHRM. The presumption here is that the HR function is making this change to align itself with the prevailing corporate focus in its pursuit of competitive advantage.

As discussed in Chapter 2, SHRM has emerged as an approach to managing the human resources of an organisation partly in response to the increasing recognition given to employees as valuable assets but particularly because of its strategic alignment. To illustrate the impact recruitment and selection can have on the introduction of SHRM Guest's (1987) construction of HRM and its related series of theoretical propositions are utilised. His work is explained more fully in Chapter 2 but, by way of a reminder, it is built around four key human resource goals: integration; employee commitment; flexibility/adaptability; and quality.

Applying the strategic approach to recruitment and selection, developed above against first-order decisions, to Guest's (1987) analysis, the key issues will be to identify the attributes that are positively correlated with committed, flexible and high quality employees and to determine how to attract and select people who possess them.

Another key feature of SHRM is its emphasis on the devolvement of much of the work of HR specialists to line managers who are perceived as having a pivotal role in its successful introduction. This re-alignment is likely to impact significantly on their respective role responsibilities. For line managers, who are not generally noted for their interest or competence in handling HR issues, this redefinition of their role places particular demands on their selection and development. If the HR competence of line mangers cannot be assured, it is highly likely that any top-down intent to introduce SHRM will be frustrated by their skills gap and inappropriate attitudes. For HR specialists, SHRM may precipitate the development of an alternative model for delivering the department's work, create the need for the acquisition and development of a different skills base and possibly involve redundancy. For example, in one of many typologies of HR specialist roles, Storey (1992: 168–169) identifies four types of personnel management: 'handmaidens; advisers; regulators; and changemakers'. Of these it is the changemaker role that is closely identified with the SHRM approach. Any move towards the changemaker role from the other less interventionist and/or strategic types should have significant repercussions on the recruitment and selection of HR staff as the change in role orientation involves significantly different skills, behaviours, values and attitudes.

How can recruitment and selection contribute to strategy formulation (upstream, vertical integration)?

This section begins by illustrating the nature and potential organisational significance of upstream (or two-way, external integration) through reference to a real case (see In Practice 8.6), adapted to preserve anonymity.

This scenario illustrates the potential dangers of operating the external integration relationship between corporate strategy and human resourcing only through a one-way (downstream) interpretation. It may have also said something about the credibility and/or status of the personnel function in the case organisation (i.e. the 'institutional integration' of Mabey and Iles, 1993: 16). It also provides an example of how, through environmental scanning, human resource concerns can potentially influence higher levels of strategic planning and corporate level decision-making, as discussed in Chapter 7. Evenden (1993: 223) argues that this represents a 'business case' for upstream strategic integration. He contrasts this with a 'social responsibility' case for upstream integration where strategy formulation is influenced by human resource initiatives concerning moral and ethical issues (Evenden, 1993: 223). This could arise, for example, through proactive approaches to equal opportunities that target recruitment

In Practice   8.6

Rejection of HR's upstream strategic proposals contributes to business collapse

A large manufacturing company developed an aggressive growth strategy to defend its dominant market position. This involved both planned expansion of its product markets and increasing the company's share of those markets, thereby providing growth of sales on two counts. This required significant financial investment to fund increased production capacity through the installation of additional traditional production lines based on scientific management principles and to enhance the production support infrastructure. In order to service this strategy in a downstream relationship, the HR department was tasked to recruit employees to staff the new production lines and related growth in service departments in order to meet the increased production targets.

The HR department was aware that prevailing labour market conditions (virtually full employment leading to both general labour and specific skill shortages) precluded any large-scale recruitment. They argued that this would make the production and marketing plans untenable, thereby threatening the viability of the corporate strategy itself. As an alternative the HR department proposed a strategy based around the capital intensification of production work and associated business re-engineering as the mainstay of the organisation's growth and defender strategy. The rationale was that this would allow the increased sales and production demands to be met through greater utilisation of existing staff using extensive automation coupled with computerisation to generate the additional production capacity.

The department was basically instructed to stop messing up and get on with the recruitment campaign. Despite exhaustive recruitment efforts the increased demand for labour could not be met. This led in time to a staffing crisis where production lines could not be staffed. Consequently output fell well short of the increased demand generated by the successfully implemented marketing strategies and potential customers went elsewhere. The staffing crisis fuelled the collapse of the business strategy and, coupled with the inflow of cheaper foreign imports, contributed significantly to the eventual demise of the organisation.

strategies at the long-term unemployed, a group which is significantly over-represented by ethnic minorities.

Another example where upstream integration may be evident is the promotion by the HR function of a 'managing diversity' strategy (Chapter 13). 'Managing diversity' has been developed as a strategic response to the changing demographic complexion of the workforce and social values that emphasise the need for the full participation of all people in and at work. According to Kandola and Fullerton (1994a: 8):

> The basic concept of managing diversity accepts that the workforce consists of a diverse population of people. The diversity consists of visible and non-visible differences which include factors such as sex, age, background, race, disability, personality and workstyle. It is founded on the premiss that harnessing these differences will create a productive environment in which everybody feels valued, where their talents are being fully utilised and in which organisational goals are met.

As such, using Evenden's (1993: 223) analysis, the push for a diversity strategy could be construed as representing both a 'business' and 'social responsibility' case for upstream strategic integration. However, the likelihood is that its adoption is more likely to be driven by business arguments as the following examples of managing diversity summarised in 'In Practice' 8.7 illustrate.

In Practice   **8.7**

The search for diversity through the strategic integration of
recruitment and selection

A range of companies, for example Burger King and Sainsbury's, have developed recruitment and selection strategies to increase the number of employees from certain ethnic groups in order to exploit these groups' significant and growing importance as consumers (Evenden, 1993).

L'Oréal in France found that recruiting a diverse workforce enhanced the creative capacity of the workforce on which it depended (Sadler and Milmer, 1993).

Iles and Hayers (1997) point to how a number of organisations are selecting diverse, multi-national project teams to increase their flexibility and responsiveness in globally competitive markets.

Ford has targeted the distribution of more that 250,000 recruitment leaflets at London boroughs with large ethnic minority populations in an effort to attract more young Asian and black people to become apprentices. This appears to be part of a growing appreciation of the business case for diversity where large companies 'want to get the best talent from the widest possible pool, to understand fresh markets by having them represented in their workforce, and to drive innovation through diverse teams' (Maitland, 2004: 1).

The frequently cited positive policies on age diversity operated by B&Q are held to make good business sense. B&Q found 'that having older workers on its staff has enhanced sales and customer loyalty'. Similar arguments are held to apply to the financial services sector where increasing the average age of sales teams provides a better fit with the age profile of the customer base (Murray, 2004a: 6).

Barclays Bank found that many customers preferred to do business with older, more experienced staff, the very sort of employee who had been lost to the bank in successive rounds of redundancies in the 1990s. To address this and the future demographics of the labour pool they have been reviewing all policies and practices to ensure that they are as inclusive as possible. This has led to changes in advertising copy, recruitment media and the design of application forms (Murray, 2004b: 6).

It can also be argued that the recruitment of a diverse workforce adds generally to an organisation's ability to meet the challenges presented by an uncertain future through the creation of a more flexible and adaptable workforce (Sparrow, 1994). Recruitment and selection processes have a key role to play in securing a diverse workforce and may require innovative practices to identify and attract suitable candidates from target groups (Paddison, 1990). This use of recruitment and selection to help confront the challenge of change is explored in greater depth in the next section. This section concludes by examining recruitment and selection against the fifth strand of strategic fit: horizontal integration.

How can recruitment and selection facilitate other HR initiatives (horizontal integration)?

As discussed earlier, an important part of internal integration is the coherence between different elements of human resourcing (Guest, 1987; Mabey and Iles, 1993). Here, work restructuring is used to illustrate how recruitment and selection can support other human resource change initiatives. You might also like to work through how recruitment and selection can similarly be integrated with all the other HR areas covered by this book. For example, the next chapter deals with performance management and with respect to its internal integration with recruitment and selection the following questions could be legitimately asked:

1. Do different types of people respond better than others to a performance culture?
2. If so, how can what characterises such people be identified?
3. Where will such people be found?
4. How might the organisation attract their interest?
5. What selection methods would provide the most reliable and valid measures of these attributes among prospective candidates?

Earlier, when considering second-order strategies, it was observed that delayering might necessitate the redesign of jobs to achieve greater congruence with the demands placed on working arrangements and relationships by flatter structures (Lawler, 1994). A consistent feature emerging from the chapters on the role of organisation structure (Chapter 5) and downsizing (Chapter 14) is that jobs will require restructuring in order to cope with the consequences of delayering and the need 'to do more with less (staff)'.

A direct consequence of the introduction of delayering, and downsizing, has been a growing interest in autonomous workgroups (Flynn *et al.*, 1990), team working (Staniforth, 1996) and high-involvement organisations (Bowen *et al.*, 1991; Beaumont and Hunter, 1992). These approaches to job design are in many ways synonymous and involve the introduction of self-managed teams who are assigned delegated responsibility for task completion. Such teams exercise high degrees of autonomy over interrelated activities such as production control, quality control, work allocation and problem solving. This demands a high level of involvement from and interaction between team members. Evidence suggests, however, that, in practice work redesign along these lines has not always been successful because such changes have not been introduced within the context of a supportive human resourcing infrastructure (Staniforth, 1996). Staniforth (1996) argues that in order to ensure internal integration, team-working ability needs to be assessed during recruitment and selection, developed through training and reinforced through appraisal and reward systems. However, the composition of the team has been particularly identified as a critical success factor (McCombs *et al.*, 1994). This places considerable emphasis on the role of recruitment and selection in identifying, attracting and selecting those employees who are most likely to succeed under team-working conditions (Flynn *et al.*, 1990).

Two sets of employee characteristics have been identified as predictors of effective team performance. The first concerns individual characteristics, such as dependability, interpersonal skills, self-motivation and integrity. The second concerns group membership characteristics such as leadership potential, assertiveness, participation, tolerance of ambiguity and capacity to cope with stress (Flynn *et al.*, 1990). In reporting on case studies where autonomous workgroups (Flynn *et al.*, 1990) and high involvement work systems (Bowen *et al.*, 1991) have been successfully introduced, such characteristics have been assessed through the use of multiple selection devices. These included:

- application forms designed around the specified characteristics;
- surveying previous employers using structured questions to secure reference checks against dependability and integrity;
- work sampling;
- attendance at a pre-employment training programme;
- group interviews involving current team members;
- aptitude and personality testing; and
- a series of group exercises to assess decision-making skills, problem solving and values orientation.

There was also a heavy emphasis throughout on providing candidates with a realistic job preview, making selection genuinely a two-way process, and involving team members in the final selection decisions. Both the Bowen *et al.* (1991) and McCombs *et al.* (1994) studies also reported on methods used to evaluate the recruitment and selection process which were found to have promoted the formation of teams characterised by high productivity, high job satisfaction scores and low levels of absenteeism and labour turnover.

How feasible is strategic recruitment and selection in a changing world? Confronting the challenge of change

The demands of different time horizons and change on strategic recruitment and selection

From the preceding discussion it is argued that strategic recruitment and selection has three distinct temporal points of focus. First, they must be aligned with current strategic objectives in order to facilitate their achievement. Second, it must be aligned to future strategy in a way that will support the implementation and achievement of any new strategic direction. Third, it needs to facilitate continual, proactive change in order to help the organisation adapt successfully to future uncertainties. This might be broadly interpreted as focusing recruitment and selection activities on three different scenarios:

- maintaining the status quo;
- responding to planned, predictable change; or
- coping with an uncertain future characterised by unplanned, unpredictable change which might arise from either unintended consequences of planned change or new, emergent contingencies.

Through a contingency framework, it is possible to map out appropriate HRP approaches, strategic selection choices and selection criteria for each of these three scenarios (Snow and Snell, 1993; Sparrow, 1994; Williams and Dobson, 1997). Table 8.1 illustrates these contingent relationships and helps us to identify the recruitment and selection implications of the three different scenarios.

The primary concern in this section is to explore the relationship between recruitment and selection and two of these three scenarios: planned/predictable change; and unplanned/unpredictable change. This will enable us to explore the extent to which recruitment and selection can contribute to strategic change and staffing in readiness for future uncertainties.

However, the distinctions between planned/predictable change and unplanned/unpredictable change are arguably less clear-cut than Table 8.1 might suggest. For example, planned changes to strategy suggest a degree of rationality to change management that will not always accord with reality. Further, the distinction between selection choices relating to predictable and unpredictable change may be somewhat artificial. It could be argued that the human resource competences that Williams and Dobson (1997: 239) associate with 'transformational' selection criteria, such as envisioning, team building, conflict management and persuasiveness, are equally applicable as both attributes for securing some future planned strategy and enablers that facilitate adjustment to unpredictable change. In Practice 8.8 illustrates how recruitment and selection help planned change at Axa, the insurance conglomerate.

Table 8.1 Human resource planning choices

Scenario	HRP approaches	Strategic selection choices	Selection criteria
Status quo	Provision of human resources for existing jobs	Select for short-term proficiency and accept the possibility of high levels of turnover if employees cannot cope with change	Operational criteria: attributes required for successful current job performance, such as the abilities, knowledge, interpersonal skills and the beliefs and values required to meet current job demands
Planned/ predictable change	Provision of human resources for envisaged future jobs	Select for longer-term adaptability to change, but accept that there will be limited knowledge of future changes and therefore some difficulties in assessing adaptability	Visionary criteria: attributes that are hypothesised as necessary for successful future job performance
Future imperfect: unplanned/ unpredictable change	Provision of human resources for jobs that cannot be prescribed	Follow a path of continuous modifications as the future unfolds, with numerous changes to selection systems (where reliance is on the external labour market) or vocational training systems (where the reliance is on an internal labour market)	Transformational criteria: attributes that are required to enable change to happen: the competences for change rather than the changing competences

Sources: adapted from Snow and Snell (1993), Sparrow (1994: 15); Williams and Dobson (1997: 235).

In Practice   8.8

Changing core values at Axa

With increasing globalisation of its business and a desire to create a unifying employer brand, Axa found it necessary to undertake culture change. It sought to establish a new culture that could cross the diversity of culture, language and social barriers reflected in its international workforce. This led over time to the creation of a global set of five core values: innovation; integrity; pragmatism; professionalism; and team spirit.

To make these values accessible to HR practice they were deconstructed into the behavioural traits necessary to secure their delivery. These behaviours form the basis of recruitment and selection practice and are used to underpin induction, staff development and performance management systems. Over time, staff who could not operate within the changed value system have been replaced through recruitment and selection by staff who exhibit the necessary behavioural traits and share the organisation's core values.

Source: Higginbottom (2003).

The contribution of strategic recruitment and selection to unplanned and unpredictable change

A major difficulty is that it is not always possible to predict with any degree of certainty what lies ahead even within the adopted planning horizon, let alone what lies over the horizon. This is well illustrated by the events of 9/11 and its aftermath, which impacted differentially on the long- and short-haul airline industry. Within this context it is easy to see how the strategic relevance of human resource plans and contingent recruitment and selection strategies can quickly be overtaken by events in the wake of unfolding events. A change in business strategy and/or radical adjustments to future staffing requirements (downsizing) may turn previous human resource and recruitment and selection strategies on their head almost overnight. Such uncertainties place an onus on recruitment and selection to generate a workforce that will be able to cope with the unexpected as well as expected or planned change. Two possible strategies may be appropriate in such situations. First, to recruit people who can adapt readily to change and, second, recruit people who will become agents of change and/or shapers of the organisation's future destiny. This also gives rise to the prospect that recruitment and selection processes will be directed, in part, at jobs that do not yet exist! These approaches are congruent with the resource-based view of the firm where organisations seek to identify their core competences and exploit them to future strategic advantage. Even within circumstances of change this can provide a strategic direction to recruitment and selection and the building blocks for future job creation.

One approach, consistent with the recruitment of employees who can adapt to change, is managing diversity (Chapter 13). As identified earlier, this can build a rich mix of employees whose varied skills, experiences, values and culture increase the organisation's potential capacity to cope with change. Another approach is to recruit and select against the construct of the learning organisation, as discussed in Chapter 10. The implication for the staffing process is to incorporate characteristics appropriate to the learning organisation into the personnel specification – such as: 'experiments, admits mistakes, open, encourages ideas and makes joint decisions'; as opposed to 'cautious, rationalises mistakes, defensive, discourages ideas and dominates' (Evenden, 1993: 238–239) – and to develop recruitment and selection strategies to secure these attributes and evaluate their strategic significance.

Another approach is to consider the extent to which managers will hold the key to future organisational effectiveness in times of uncertainty. This has led to attempts to identify and select managers against appropriate change management competences. Cockerill (1989: 54–55) identified 11 competences that are associated with high-performance management in rapidly changing environments ('information search; concept formation; conceptual flexibility; interpersonal search; managing interaction; developmental orientation; impact; self-confidence; presentation; proactive orientation; and achievement orientation') and argued that they could be assessed reliably through direct observation and 'simulated assessment centre conditions'. Williams and Dobson (1997: 239) cited BP and NatWest as good examples of companies trying 'to ensure that they have the basic raw material in senior management to cope with a scenario where the only certain fact is that the future will be impregnated by change'. They see the use of what they termed 'transformational criteria' in recruitment and selection and training and development making a significant contribution to 'an organisation's renewal processes and the development of the learning organisation' (Williams and Dobson, 1997: 239).

The change agent role of managers is well documented. Beer *et al.* (1990) suggest that line managers might be expected to play a pivotal role in initiating and managing change, whereas Williams and Dobson (1997) point to the key role newly appointed chief executives might play in the process of strategic change. However, it is important to stress that change agents are not necessarily managers and may operate at various levels within the organisation. Therefore, it is arguably the characteristics of transformational leaders that are needed for organisations to manage change effectively. Bass (1990) stresses the increasing relevance of transformational leadership to future uncertainties in the business environment and suggests that research evidence identifies four key characteristics of such leaders:

- charisma – where the leader provides vision and is able to generate respect, trust and pride;
- inspiration – where high expectations are set and communicated;
- intellectual stimulation – where rational, intelligent approaches to problem solving are promoted; and
- individualised consideration – where the needs of individual employees are identified and supported through personalised approaches to their development needs.

Alternatively, Legge's (1978) 'deviant innovators' might be viewed as high-ranking HR change agents with the mission of challenging the criteria by which organisational success is evaluated and promoting change towards a different set of beliefs and values. This perhaps represents another perspective on diversity and will be particularly valuable as an antidote to organisations that, for whatever reason, find they have assembled a management team that is too homogeneous (Sparrow, 1994).

The potential for creating novel solutions to the problems that change can visit on organisations can also be enhanced by taking a team approach to recruitment and selection. Unfortunately the demanding lists of competences sought in change environments (see, for example, Cockerill, 1989) may only be found in individuals who can walk on water! It may, therefore be more appropriate to apply the competence template to teams so that members collectively have the capacity to initiate and manage change and cope with an uncertain future. This, however, implies that personnel specifications and appropriate recruitment and selection strategies need to be constantly recast as each team member is appointed in order to focus on the competence gaps that remain following each appointment. This would be important, for example, where new teams are being formed, perhaps along the lines of autonomous work groups described earlier. The identification of competences is not therefore a one-off exercise but a dynamic process in which refinement to and development of competency profiles is the order of the day. Each recruitment and selection activity is therefore viewed through a contingency framework that recognises that it will need to be adapted to each changing scenario.

How extensive is strategic recruitment and selection practice? A review of the evidence

Grounds for optimism

It was argued earlier that it is possible to construct a persuasive rationale in support of the adoption of strategically aligned recruitment and selection such that its practice might be expected to be widely and increasingly evident. However, it is legitimate to question the validity of this proposition particularly as it is frequently maintained that the rhetoric of SHRM runs well ahead of its practice (e.g. Legge, 2005). This section examines evidence of strategic recruitment and selection practice in order to address its opening question. It starts by considering the evidence of strategic recruitment and selection practice that emerges from four distinct fields of HR research investigating respectively: the use of HR systems to support the pursuit of different competitive strategies; general developments in HR practice; individual case companies (in search of SHRM); and specific developments in recruitment and selection practice. It then goes on to challenge the optimistic picture painted by this initial review using counter-evidence while at the same time developing a rationale to explain the apparent exaggeration of strategic recruitment and selection practice. Lastly it reports on recent survey evidence that provides a stark picture of the current state of play.

The use of HR systems to support the pursuit of different competitive strategies

On both sides of the Atlantic there has been a number of reported cases of strategic recruitment and selection in action. This evidence has sometimes been assembled against generic strategies of competitive advantage. This is well illustrated by the work of Schuler and Jackson (1987) referred to earlier. They were able to identify human resource practices, including recruitment and selection, that were congruent with the different competitive strategies of cost reduction, innovation and quality enhancement and found evidence of such practice in case companies.

General developments in HR practice

At other times, evidence of strategic recruitment and selection has emerged from studies investigating general developments in human resource practice. For example, from a case study investigation into how the management of human resources was developing in UK companies, Storey (1992) was able to identify 'selection' as one of 27 dimensions that could be used to differentiate SHRM from more traditional personnel management and industrial relations practice. Under SHRM, selection was identified as an 'integrated, key task' whereas under the personnel and industrial relations banner it was seen as a 'separate, marginal task' (Storey, 1992: 35). In his analysis of 15 major case companies Storey (1992: 83) found evidence of integrated selection in 80 per cent of them, suggesting a high incidence of strategic recruitment and selection.

Individual case companies (in search of SHRM)

Another strand in case study-based research has been to examine how human resourcing has supported particular corporate strategies and/or responded to environmental pressures to maintain leading edge competitive positions. Sparrow and Pettigrew (1988), through a study of companies operating in the UK computer industry, tracked how SHRM was responding to support radical strategic change flowing from a turbulent business environment. Strategic selection was identified as a critical lever for acquiring specialist skills necessary to support the delivery of high-quality service provision as companies moved progressively from concentration on selling hardware to providing total business solutions that incorporated non-hardware support services. In a review of their own case study research, Hendry *et al.* (1988) identified that strategic responses to changes in the business environment, such as restructuring, internationalisation and total quality management, were leading to demands for new employee skills to support such moves. Their delivery required a more strategic approach to recruitment and selection. Kydd and Oppenheim (1990) studied four successful industry leaders with excellent track records of SHRM practice and found that they were using recruitment and selection strategically to respond, albeit in different ways, to their particular labour market conditions to maintain their competitive position.

Specific developments in recruitment and selection practice

Elsewhere, case studies targeted specifically at recruitment and selection have also provided evidence that the strategic variant is being practised. In a study of Chase Manhattan Bank, Borucki and Lafley (1984) demonstrated how recruitment and selection practices were adapted over time to meet different strategic imperatives as they emerged. Research by Bowen *et al.* (1991) led them to develop an alternative model of recruitment and selection with a strategic thrust. Here their focus is on recruitment and selection directed against organisational and not specific job requirements. They illustrated how their model related to recruitment and selection practice in a manufacturing company adopting a high-performance and involvement strategy. In a detailed case study exploring the human resource practices of a paper production plant, Beaumont and Hunter (1992) uncovered strong evidence that recruitment and selection was being used strategically to bring about a more flexible workforce that was necessitated by the organisation's competitive strategy.

The emergence of a more pessimistic picture

These case study findings provide grounds for optimism about the extent of strategic recruitment and selection. However, an alternative perspective is supplied by Wright and Storey (1997). Although acknowledging evidence that some organisations were developing radically new approaches to support major corporate initiatives, such as business process re-engineering, they concluded that traditional approaches to recruitment and selection continue to dominate current practice. The true extent of strategic recruitment and selection practice may, therefore, be fairly limited and closer examination of the evidence supports this viewpoint on at least four counts.

Why the practice of strategic recruitment and selection may appear to be exaggerated

First, supporting Wright and Storey's (1997) more pessimistic analysis, it is possible that the simple reporting of evidence of strategic recruitment and selection practice can lead to an exaggerated impression of its incidence which does not accord with reality. Indeed, limited evidence of strategic recruitment and selection led Lundy and Cowling (1996: 212) to conclude that 'There is a paucity of cases which demonstrate strategic selection in action'. Scholarios and Lockyer (1996), following a review of British selection practice, point to a significant discrepancy between the rhetoric of many SHRM texts and the reality of organisational recruitment and selection practice. They found that there had been little movement towards 'better-integrated SHRM practices' and limited evidence of more sophisticated recruitment and selection practice (Scholarios and Lockyer, 1996:

189). They concluded that prevailing evidence supported Keep's (1992: 332) observation that, despite the importance attached to selection 'in many organisations, recruitment and selection are apparently conducted in a haphazard and informal fashion'. The survey results of recruitment and selection practice in the hotel industry summarised in 'In Practice' 8.9 appear to bear out these perspectives.

Second, it is possible that the validity of reported strategic recruitment and selection is in itself open to question. This suggestion can be explored by closer scrutiny of the evidence of strategic recruitment and selection practice. If, for example, Storey's (1992) case study analysis is reconsidered, it will be recalled that he identified recruitment and selection as an 'integrated key task' representing one of 27 dimensions used to construct his template of SHRM practice. This juxtaposition of 'integrated' recruitment and selection with SHRM might suggest that evidence of such practice in his case companies may be construed as strategic recruitment and selection. However, with respect to Storey's (1992) terminology, this may be an assumption too far and it is worth asking the question 'integrated to what?'

Storey's (1992) conclusions concerning integrated selection were based on evidence from the major case companies that they were responding to labour shortages by: attaching greater importance to recruitment and selection; developing innovative practices to appeal to a wider spectrum of potential applicants; using training and career development initiatives to aid retention; making greater use of testing and assessment centres to assess personal attributes; and attempting to improve the reliability and validity of interviewing practice through training line managers. Although these responses may be consistent with strategic recruitment and selection, and certainly seem to provide evidence of the secondary features of strategic recruitment and selection in action

In Practice   8.9

Does size matter? Research findings on recruitment and selection practice in the hotel industry

Hotels operate in the service sector where organisational success is largely determined by the quality of service provided by front-line (or customer facing) staff who engage with the clientele directly. However, within the industry there is little evidence of strategically focused recruitment and selection designed to identify the personal characteristics associated with quality service or of sophisticated selection practice to assess such qualities. The use of psychometric testing, structured interviews, biographical data, etc., is generally rare and where it is evident is limited to larger hotels and hotel chains. This suggests that the absence of a strategic connection in the recruitment and selection practices of small hotels is particularly marked.

This conclusion arises from a survey of recruitment and selection practice in Scottish hotels, using data from 81 questionnaire returns and nine interviews. Relative to larger hotels and hotel chains, it was found that recruitment and selection practice in smaller hotels:

- is less likely to be supported by professional personnel input;
- is more likely to be conducted by the manager/owner who is less likely to have received any training for the role;
- uses fewer and less valid methods of selection;
- relies more on informal methods bearing little relation to 'good practice' models.

Source: Lockyer and Scholarios (2004).

(see Figures 8.3 and 8.4), they do not necessarily provide evidence of vertical strategic integration. It could be argued, for example, that these responses were not strategically driven but represented no more than rational responses to changing labour-market conditions and as such are part of the normal diet of everyday recruitment and selection practice. As such they are clearly integrated to something but not necessarily to the organisation's corporate strategy.

Third, reported evidence of strategic recruitment and selection may be drawn from case companies which are not representative of organisations generally. For example, Kydd and Oppenheim (1990) based their work on what they termed excellent companies, Storey (1992) used 15 leading organisations while Sparrow and Pettigrew's (1988) work was positioned within the highly turbulent world of the computer supply industry. This potential lack of representativeness is highlighted by Scholarios and Lockyer (1996: 189) when they concluded that what limited evidence of more sophisticated recruitment and selection there was appeared 'to be restricted to relatively few companies, usually the largest'. To this list it is possible to add foreign owned, inward investment companies, as exemplified by Nissan (Garrahan and Stewart, 1992), those experiencing transformational change (van de Vliet, 1995) and those practising SHRM (Storey, 1992).

Fourth, evidence of strategic recruitment and selection has, arguably, been advanced on narrow foundations and against a concept that has not been fully explained. It is possible that all that is required for the existence of the strategic variant to be claimed is evidence that recruitment and selection policies and practice are clearly consistent with an organisation's corporate strategy. While this is clearly necessary it may not be sufficient and may mask the fact that any relationship between the two variables is more accidental than deliberate. This raises the not implausible suggestion that evidence of strategic recruitment and selection relates directly to how the concept is defined by the researcher.

In Practice   8.10

Recruitment and selection at Buckingham Palace

Breaking news, November 2003 – Ryan Parry, a *Daily Mirror* undercover reporter, worked undetected for two months as a trainee footman in Buckingham Palace. His role gave him unprecedented access to the Palace and compromised the Queen's personal security. His duties included attending at the Queen's breakfast table which he claimed gave him ample opportunity to poison her.

Ryan Parry had applied for the job under his real name but submitted a fake CV and one of his listed references was false. He attended a 30-minute interview and shortly afterwards was advised that he had been accepted for the job subject to security clearance. The personnel department handles the Palace's vetting procedure. One of the checks they made was a telephone reference request to a pub in North Wales where he had previously worked. The landlord had moved on but a barmaid taking the call shouted out Mr Parry's name to see if he was known by any of the regulars. A regular took the call, said he recognised the name and this was accepted by the caller.

Whitehall officials emphasised the need for careful selection of staff who would be working alongside members of the Royal Family, particularly as the country was on a heightened terrorist alert. The Palace accepted that its vetting procedures were insufficient. A simple internet search would have revealed Ryan Parry's true identity and highlighted that he had previously infiltrated security at the Wimbledon tennis tournament after posing as a security guard.

Sources: Pierce *et al.* (2003); Seamark (2003); Seamark and Greenhill (2003).

Self-Check and Reflect Questions   8.4

To what extent does the process used to recruit Ryan Parry reflect a strategic approach to recruitment and selection? It is recommended that you conduct your analysis against the conceptual framework and model of strategic recruitment and selection presented earlier in the chapter (Key Concepts 8.4 and Figures 8.3 and 8.4).

Evidence of strategic recruitment and selection practice

In Practice 8.11 concludes this section by reporting on evidence extracted from recent research that was clearly structured around a detailed exposition of strategic recruitment and selection that culminated in the conceptual framework and model presented earlier in the chapter (Key Concepts 8.4 and Figures 8.3 and 8.4). It was against these templates that evidence of strategic recruitment and selection was assessed.

In Practice   8.11

Is the strategic recruitment and selection glass half full or half empty? A summary of recent findings from survey data

Literature review:

- Research reported in the literature painted a contradictory picture. It was possible to construct both an optimistic view that strategic recruitment and selection was alive and well, and a pessimistic view that its practice was much exaggerated.

- A difficulty in resolving this contradictory position arose because the explicit criteria against which recruitment and selection practice was being evaluated to establish its strategic credentials were seldom made explicit.

- A conceptual framework of strategic recruitment and selection comprising three primary and four secondary features was developed as an evaluative tool (see Key Concepts 8.4).

The study:

- A longitudinal examination of recruitment and selection practice in organisations represented by management and HR students attending postgraduate programmes.

- Respondents (students) were asked to report on actual recruitment and selection exercises conducted in their organisations.

- Respondents were required to map out, through a flow chart, their perception of the entire recruitment and selection process that was used to fill an identified vacancy.

- Instructions for completing the flow chart emphasised the need to start from the very beginning of the recruitment and selection process and to work through to the very last element of the process.

- Prior to the production of flow charts, students had received inputs on strategic integration and HRP.

● 180 flow charts depicting recruitment and selection exercises conducted by 108 organisations over a four-year period were generated and analysed.

● Flow charts were analysed against the evaluative frameworks depicted in Key Concepts 8.4 and Figure 8.4 to establish evidence of strategic recruitment and selection practice.

Selected findings:

● Not one recruitment and selection exercise satisfied all the primary features.

● Only 2 per cent of exercises demonstrated any direct connection with strategy.

● If HRP was interpreted implicitly as fulfilling all three primary features, then evidence of strategically driven recruitment and selection rose to 8 per cent.

● In these 8 per cent of cases, evidence of secondary features was far more prevalent than in the remainder which reflected the traditional, systematic approach to recruitment and selection.

● There was no evidence of the strategic contribution of recruitment and selection practice being evaluated.

Conclusion:

● On the basis of this evidence the strategic recruitment and selection glass is virtually empty, albeit with a little froth in the bottom.

Source: Millmore (2003).

Self-Check and Reflect Questions   8.5

In Chapter 2 a number of studies exploring the contribution of SHRM to organisational performance were reported on. A critique of the research methodology used by each study was presented under the banner of 'Study limitations'. On a similar basis, what limitations can you identify in the study outlined in 'In Practice' 8.11 that might explain the low incidence of strategic recruitment and selection reported?

What might account for the mismatch between the rhetoric and the reality of strategic recruitment and selection?

The problematic nature of strategic fit

Many of the difficulties that may frustrate the development of strategic recruitment and selection coalesce around the nature of strategic fit itself. Much of the above analysis has within it a rational deliberative process of strategic formulation, which will not always be in evidence. As discussed in Chapter 1, legitimate challenges can be made against the rational, deterministic presumption. At one level, strategy may be seen to emerge over time (Mintzberg, 1987) on the 'I know it when I see it basis' or as a result of muddle and inertia. At another level, strategic change, like any change programme, may be more effectively driven by a bottom-up approach through task alignment (Beer *et al.*, 1990). However, irrespective of whether strategy is the outcome of a deliberate or an emergent process, there is still a requirement to translate it into 'people' terms, and, on this basis, where there is no evident strategy it can be held that one should be assumed, for only then is it possible to 'develop human resource policies and plans related to the organisation's future' (Evenden, 1993: 222).

There may also be insufficient integration between SHRM and strategic planning, a factor that has been identified as a common reason for SHRM policy implementation failures (Golden and Ramanujam, 1985). Another difficulty is that the central tenet of strategic fit is open to challenge. It may be simply that organisations fail to undertake strategic planning or that personnel managers cannot develop strategic approaches to human resourcing because they cannot gain access to the strategic plan even if it exists (Storey and Sisson, 1993). Alternatively, there may be more than one strategy operating at the same time. This is only to be expected in multi-divisional organisations, and when combined with decentralised decision-making it should be self-evident that the development of coherent, long-term, integrated human resource strategies will be problematic (Storey, 1992). Another difficulty is that strategic contradictions may be evident. For example, following Guest's (1987) construction of SHRM, an organisation may adopt core–periphery strategies to deliver 'flexibility/adaptability' but it is questionable whether 'quality' can be sustained solely on the backs of core employees and within a climate of cost-cutting and the casualisation of labour (Storey and Sisson, 1993).

The barriers of money and time

The strategic recruitment and selection model, with its emphasis on tailor-made procedures, is expensive in terms of both time and money. Because of this, the potential for front-loaded investment staffing processes may be restricted to large organisations and is, anyway, unlikely to be compatible with cost-reduction strategies. Strategies developed around cost competition may be the antithesis of strategic recruitment and selection, and are more likely to lead to an end-loaded rather than front-loaded investment model. Strategic recruitment and selection may also be perceived as demanding an unobtainable nirvana where selection is successfully made against a composite personnel specification embracing specific job requirements, group fit and organisation fit both now and in the future. Even if managers have time to work through all these scenarios, compromises between these different demands are likely and may necessitate suboptimal decisions that could then threaten the integrity of the whole process.

Short-termism

Another practical difficulty is the short-term perspective, rooted in accountancy traditions and traditional patterns of corporate ownership, said to characterise UK businesses. This outlook encourages managers to adopt quick-fix solutions (Storey and Sisson, 1993). A scenario, familiar to many managers, 'is that they may be under too much pressure to develop a strategic response of any kind – they may simply seek to muddle through' (Sisson, 1994a: 12). This is reminiscent of Legge's analysis (1978) of personnel managers who are caught in a vicious circle, where problem prevention is precluded by a focus on problem solving and fire fighting.

The evaluation of strategic contribution?

One last problem concerning strategic fit considered here is the difficulty of validating selection decisions within the strategic framework. Most attempts to validate recruitment and selection decisions use the predictive validity model where relationships between predictions from selection methods and subsequent measures of job perform-ance are correlated (Lundy and Cowling, 1996). However, the utility of this approach which is based essentially on current job performance, is questionable where selection is being directed towards organisation fit and the future capabilities of employees to manage change (Lawler, 1994). Organisations may therefore find it difficult to justify resource-intensive staffing processes without also investing in alternative concepts of validation (Lawler, 1994).

Issues of competence?

Another set of difficulties relate to the very competence of those responsible for recruit-ment and selection. Whatever strategic recruitment and selection is, it is not straightforward. HRP, strategic job analysis, sophisticated selection, evaluation, etc. are not exactly as easy to execute as falling off the proverbial log. They arguably demand a high degree of commitment and competence and these attributes may simply not be within the compass of those managers and HR specialists responsible for recruitment and selection. Here it can be questioned whether managers are psychologically fit to carry out their HR responsibilities effectively (Beer and Eisenstat, 1996). Consider, for example, the following questions:

- Have managers been selected with the necessary attributes and values to deliver their HR responsibilities successfully?
- Have managers been trained adequately to fulfil these responsibilities?
- Are overall managerial roles structured to provide sufficient prominence to and space for the effective delivery of their HR responsibilities?
- Do short-term performance demands preclude the longer-term perspective demanded by strategic recruitment and selection?
- Are managers assessed and rewarded for their ability to staff their section with either employees who can demonstrably contribute to the achievement of the longer-term strategic imperatives of the organisation or, who in terms of immediate job perform-ance, can hit the ground running?

Of course it is unfair to single out managers in this way as it is equally legitimate to question the capability of the HR specialists who support these managers in their recruitment and selection role responsibilities. This presents an interesting catch-22 where organisations may need to practise strategic recruitment and selection in order to staff their organisation with managers and HR specialists with the necessary compe-tences to develop strategic recruitment and selection practice!

Am I bothered?

These potential obstacles represent formidable barriers to the successful implementation of strategic recruitment and selection processes. However, as reported earlier, there are exam-ples of organisations that are moving in this direction, perhaps reflecting the adage 'to fail to plan is to plan to fail'. There are also, inherent within the strategic model, concepts whose careful application may serve to address and ameliorate these difficulties. Particular atten-tion is drawn to recruitment and selection geared around managing diversity, the learning organisation, competences associated with change management, managerial and key change agent appointments and using team selection as the basis for assembling the many disparate qualities likely to be demanded in the workforce of the future.

Summary

- The pursuit of competitive advantage, interest in SHRM and the role of recruitment and selection in securing one of an organisation's most valuable assets provide a powerful rationale for the development of strategic recruitment and selection.

- It is possible to construct a model of strategic recruitment and selection around three primary features: strategic integration; a long-term perspective; and the use of HRP as a bridging mechanism between strategy and HR practice. The strategic variant elevates the organisational importance of recruitment and selection, and leads to the generation of a more demanding person specification. These two outcomes generate four consequential interrelated, secondary features that are likely to shape strategic recruitment and selection practice: the adoption of a front-loaded investment model; rigorous evaluation of outcomes; the use of high validity, sophisticated selection methods; and multi-stakeholder involvement.

- Far from being a simple notion, strategic fit has been revealed as a multi-dimensional concept where it is possible to identify at least six different strands. This means that strategic recruitment and selection has potentially to be aligned with multiple interpretations of strategy if it is to satisfy its strategic credentials.

- Despite uncertainties surrounding strategy implementation and the business environment as it unfolds over time, recruitment and selection practice can be shaped to support long-term changes in strategic direction.

- On balance, and despite a powerful rationale to the contrary, organisational approaches to recruitment and selection practice appear to be dominated by traditional and not strategic approaches.

- The overall conclusion is that although the case for adopting strategic recruitment and selection may be seductively persuasive it is arguably another case in the HR arena where the rhetoric runs ahead of the reality.

Follow-up study suggestions

- Search the literature for material that explicitly addresses strategic recruitment and selection. From this, develop your own definition and conceptual framework of strategic recruitment and selection against which organisation practice could be tested to establish its strategic credentials.

- Compare and contrast your conceptual framework of strategic recruitment and selection with the constructions of strategic recruitment and selection presented in this chapter in Key Concepts 8.4 and Figures 8.3 and 8.4. Develop the arguments that you would present in defence of the similarities and differences identified.

- Drawing on research methods literature, design a research project to test the extent to which strategic recruitment and selection is practised in UK organisations. Critique your research design to identify its strengths and weaknesses.

- Access the international SHRM literature to establish whether discussion of strategic recruitment and selection theory and evidence of its practice is more or less prevalent in other countries.

- Use the internet and SHRM/recruitment and selection literature to determine those competences that you believe are positively associated with the effective management of change. Develop these into a person specification and think through how selection methods could be devised to provide valid assessments of candidates against these competences.

Suggestions for research topics

- How will we know it when we see it? The development of a conceptual and evaluative framework against which organisational recruitment and selection practice can be analysed to determine its strategic credentials.
- To what extent can recruitment and selection in XYZ organisation be termed 'strategic recruitment and selection'?
- How extensive is strategic recruitment and selection practice in UK organisations?
- Why is the apparent gap between the rhetoric and reality of strategic recruitment and selection so large?
- Does size matter? An examination of the feasibility of practising strategic recruitment and selection in SMEs.

Case Study

Recruitment and selection at Southco Europe Ltd

Southco is a medium-sized American-owned global manufacturer of access hardware solutions, such as latches and hinges, used for applications in the aircraft, railway, computer and automotive industry. Operating out of its headquarters in Philadelphia, by 2003 the company had manufacturing sites and sales offices in Connecticut and Florida and similar European operations with a head office in the UK. At this time, the company employed a global workforce of more than 1,479 employees referred to as 'associates'. This case is centred on the European head office of the business and details how recruitment and selection is being used to support the organisation's strategic goal of accelerated global expansion while serving local markets with local production.

The organisation's vision is to be the 'leading global source of engineered access control hardware, services and solutions' (Southco, 2004: 1). This is translated into the following mission statements, which are communicated throughout the organisation:

- to create continuous growth opportunities through strong customer connectivity and engineering excellence
- to seize these opportunities through seamless teamwork and by leveraging operational excellence and supply chain management
- to drive leadership, growth and extraordinary value for customers, associates and shareholders.

(Southco, 2004: 1)

The organisation's vision, mission statements and related annual key objectives are captured on a plastic card carried by every Southco associate:

- to drive profitable top line growth
- to drive and leverage process excellence
- to expand global reach and capabilities
- to strengthen and leverage financial position
- to strengthen people and performance management systems.

(Southco, 2004: 1)

Exposed to environmental factors, such as increasing political and economic insecurity and ever more aggressive competitors, Southco reflects a climate of constant change. An appreciation of cultural diversity is characteristic of the organisation as summarised by one of its cultural belief statements: 'Act Global/Think Local.' The company's continuing commitment to this objective has recently been demonstrated by its establishment of a direct sales presence in eastern Europe and a new Automotive Office in Germany to better serve local customers.

Case study question 1 – to be answered before reading on

1. Based on the information provided with respect to organisation context, strategy, vision, mission statements and annual key objectives, what core competences do you feel will underpin Southco's recruitment and selection processes?

Southco values its associates highly and its approach to human resource management could best be described as soft. This is reflected in its annual key objectives and evidenced by: generous health and benefits schemes; considerable investment in employee training and development; and initiatives that seek to improve employee relations such as interdepartmental or cultural training, where the associates are prepared for the challenges of a multi-cultural environment.

Despite being exposed to a rapidly and continuously changing business environment, the organisation regards itself as being extremely people-focused and is particularly committed to its internal labour market and proud of its many long-serving employees. When sourcing for the right pool of talent, Southco recruits from both the internal and external labour markets.

However, it will first strive to fill vacancies via the internal labour market rather than recruiting externally and it is company policy that every position is first advertised internally. The company regards people as its key success factor and places great emphasis on their development and training. The HR department seeks to continuously assess and develop the skills and talents of its associates in order to ensure that these match its strategic requirements.

With a strong focus on the rapid global expansion of the organisation, the pressure is on the HR function for timely and effective delivery. A critical success factor for achieving this is the coherent alignment of the HR function with corporate strategy and objectives. This is particularly evidenced through the corporate scorecard, where the HR function represents one of the key measurables relating to performance delivery against corporate goals, including internal and external customer satisfaction. Here, in short, Southco's HR function positions people processes as the link between corporate objectives and performance management. The strategic fit between Southco's corporate and HR strategies is also evidenced by the fact that the European Human Resource Development (HRD) Manager is regarded as an indispensable member of the senior management team.

Case study question 2 – to be answered before reading on

2. What do you think would be an appropriate recruitment and selection procedure for Southco to follow? Map out your answer providing as much detail as possible on the recruitment and selection methods you would use.

The organisation's recruitment policy could be summarised as 'right person, right job', a philosophy backed up by the argument that hiring the 'wrong' person will cause the company to incur substantial indirect (e.g. the impact on business efficiency of poor performers) and direct (e.g. training) costs. On the one hand, the match between the person and the skills and competence requirements of the job specification should be as accurate as possible. However, on the other hand, Southco also stresses the importance of the candidate's fit with organisational culture. Information material received by potential applicants clearly states the organisation's vision, mission statements and corporate goals, which are also included on Southco's web site. Therefore, prior to any application, interested parties are given the opportunity to assess for themselves whether they can identify with 'what

Southco is about', and decide whether or not to apply for a position. In addition, any candidate must also be able to adapt to the fast-paced business environment that characterises Southco.

In an organisation such as Southco, with a growing demand for globally mobile talent, and an ever increasing awareness of both internal and external customer service, the HR function views its core responsibility as 'identifying the right pool of talent for establishing the right candidate'. Applicants are shortlisted by the HR Advisor based on a competence-based approach. This means that there must be a very close match between the skills and competences detailed in the job and person specification and what is described in the written application. Therefore the match between the technical skills and work experience of the applicant and specific requirements of the job and person specification are important considerations. However, there is also a number of organisationally driven requirements that inform shortlisting decisions. These particularly focus on organisation fit, where an applicant should come across as a 'well-suited family member', but also correspond to the international nature of the business, assessed in terms of speaking at least another European language and/or demonstrating a 'global outlook', revealed ideally through work experience abroad or at least an expressed interest in travelling.

Not surprisingly, the selection processes are lengthy and complex. Dependent on the position, the selection procedure may last anywhere between 2 and 7 days. During the selection process candidates attend a series of interviews, skill and competence assessments, and are psychometrically tested to identify whether or not they would be suitable for the Southco environment. Consistent with the mission statement, particular emphasis is also placed on establishing whether a person interacts well within a team. The key recruitment and selection decision-makers include the HRD manager, the line manager and in some cases, for top management, the next-level manager.

On the first day, candidates are welcomed by the HRD manager and attend an informal introductory interview, followed by a two-hour psychometric testing procedure. On the second day, candidates attend a behaviourally based interview with the HRD manager, followed by an interview with the direct line manager which, taken together, are designed to establish both behavioural fit and technical competence. Following these standard arrangements, the procedure then varies according to the position. However, the focus remains on skill and competence testing supplemented by further introductions to the organisational context. An applicant for, say, a position in European Customer Services, will undergo various written and oral foreign language tests, and an applicant for a secretarial position will be tested on their IT skills. Having concluded the technical skills and competence testing procedures, all candidates meet with the person who currently holds the position of interest to them, in order to gain an insight into the daily working environment and to learn first-hand about the nature of the job. Candidates for managerial positions may be required to return to deliver presentations to their potential teams and, in some cases, particularly for senior managers, are sent to the corporate office in the US for further interviews and presentations.

Finally, the recruitment and selection team meet for discussion and ideally come to joint decisions on candidates based on their findings with respect to skill and competence and cultural fit assessments.

Case study questions 3 and 4

3. To what extent could Southco's approach to recruitment and selection be classified as strategic? Justify your answer with evidence drawn from case material.
4. What changes would you make to Southco's recruitment and selection processes in order to more fully meet the model, core dimensions and conceptual framework of strategic recruitment and selection captured respectively in Figures 8.3 and 8.4 and Key Concepts 8.4.

Acknowledgement

The support of Scott Duncan and Russ Pender, the outgoing and incoming Managing Director of Southco Europe Ltd., in granting permission to use this case and the lead role played by Inge Studnik, formerly Executive Assistant of Southco Europe Ltd., in its preparation are gratefully acknowledged.

9

Performance management: so much more than annual appraisal

Learning Outcomes

By the end of this chapter you should be able to:

- define performance management and explain its relationship to strategic human resource management;

- analyse the reasons for the growth in importance of performance management;

- explain the performance management systems model and the key processes embedded in the model;

- evaluate some of the major criticisms of performance management;

- suggest ways in which performance management may link more closely to strategic human resource management.

Introduction

What is performance management?

Rather like many other titles, the term 'performance management' originated in the USA. But in reality there is nothing new about performance management. It is an umbrella term to describe not a single activity but a range of activities that may be gathered together to enhance organisational performance. So, before defining what performance management is, it may be useful to clarify what it is not. First, it is not performance appraisal. It is easy to go through the annual ritual of performance appraisal, from which little action follows, and call this performance management. Performance appraisal is an important component of performance management, but the action that emanates from performance appraisal is crucial if organisational performance is to be enhanced. Second, performance management is not just defining performance indicators and setting these as targets to be achieved, either by individual employees, a department or organisation. This is much too narrow an approach, as is argued later in this part of the chapter. Third, performance management is not only performance-related pay. This may be an important consequence of the performance appraisal process, but it is only one consequence. Indeed, performance-related pay may be awarded to individuals without any formal attempt at appraising performance.

Given the wide-ranging nature of performance management, it is not surprising that defining the topic is not straightforward and many conventional HRM texts do not attempt a definition. However, Armstrong and Baron (1998: 7) address the issue of defining performance management by framing a short overall definition and then embellishing this with a further explanation of what performance management is about. This seems an effective way of capturing the complexity of a subject that is so all-embracing that a simple catch-all definition is unsatisfactory. Armstrong and Baron define performance management as:

> A strategic and integrated approach to delivering sustained success to organisations by improving the performance of people who work in them and by developing the capabilities of teams and individual contributors.

For the purposes of this book, the emphasis that Armstrong and Baron put upon the aspect of strategy and integration is highly appropriate. Performance management has the capacity to match the organisation's overall strategy, indeed these authors argue that performance management will not reach its full potential if that is not the case. In addition, Armstrong and Baron stress the aspect of integration. Ideally, performance management is integrated vertically with the strategic goals of the organisation and horizontally with the other aspects of HRM. Particular attention is paid to these two aspects of integration later in the chapter. The word 'ideally' is chosen deliberately to highlight the fact that performance management is often not strategic or integrated (IRS, 2003).

However, there are important additions to this definition that need to be made. In making these additions the scene is set for the content of this chapter. The terms 'development' and 'improvement' suggest a forward-looking element to performance management, which is captured in this chapter. Development in terms of both capability and longer-term career planning has long been an important element of effective performance appraisal systems – improvement less so. However, the role that performance management plays in seeking to improve the performance of under-performing employees is given due attention in this chapter. The aspect of team performance management is given much less attention, both in the literature and in practice. This is surprising given the current attention that is paid to teamwork in organisations. This is examined briefly in this chapter. All these aspects are important if a strategic and integrated approach to achieving success in organisations by improving the performance of people who work in them and by developing the capabilities of teams and individual contributors is to be realised.

As noted earlier, a major component of performance management in many organisations is that of individual performance-related pay. Although this topic is covered briefly in this chapter, it is dealt with in more detail in Chapter 11.

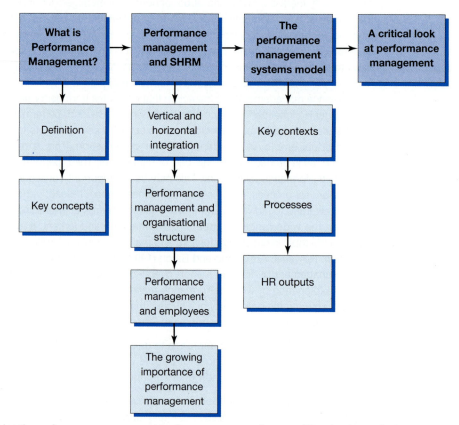

Figure 9.1 Mapping the performance management territory: a summary diagram of the chapter content

Performance measurement: only one element of performance management

The introduction makes clear that performance management is not simply the process of defining performance indicators and measuring achievement against those indicators. The difference between performance measurement and performance management is that performance measurement includes measures based on key success factors, which may include: measures of deviation from the 'norm'; measures to track past achievements; measures of output and input; whereas performance management involves such issues as training, teamwork, management style, attitudes, shared vision, employee involvement and rewards, etc. (Lebas, 1995).

Yet the performance measurement approach has proliferated in many organisations, following work such as that of Kaplan and Norton's (1992) 'balanced scorecard' approach (see Key Concepts 9.1) and the well-known European Foundation for Quality Management (EFQM) European Excellence Model. The EFQM model posits that business results are a function of leadership driving people management, resources, and policy and strategy, which in turn drive business processes. The outcome is people satisfaction, customer satisfaction and, through these, business results. (For more details on the European Excellence Model see Key Concepts 4.4).

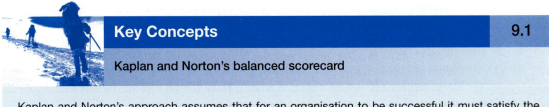

Key Concepts   9.1

Kaplan and Norton's balanced scorecard

Kaplan and Norton's approach assumes that for an organisation to be successful it must satisfy the demands of its key stakeholders: investors, customers and employees. Therefore, they suggest four key perspectives on business performance. These perspectives generate the following four questions:

1. Financial: 'to succeed financially how should we appear to our shareholders?';
2. Customer: 'to be successful how should we appear to our customers?';
3. Internal business processes: 'to meet the expectations of our shareholders and customers at what business processes should we excel?';
4. Learning and growth: 'to achieve our vision and strategy how will we sustain our ability to change and improve?'

Kaplan and Norton argue that the balanced scorecard strategy should have vision, not control, at the forefront. It establishes goals but assumes that people will adopt whatever behaviours and take whatever actions are necessary to arrive at those goals. The measures are designed to drive people towards the overall vision. Managers may know what the end result should be but they cannot tell employees exactly how to achieve that result, if only because the conditions in which employees operate are constantly changing.

Kaplan and Norton's view is that by combining the financial, customer, internal process and innovation, and organisational learning perspectives, the balanced scorecard helps managers to understand, at least implicitly, many interrelationships between different organisational functions. This understanding can help managers transcend traditional notions about functional barriers and ultimately lead to improved decision-making and problem solving. The balanced scorecard keeps organisations focused on the future not simply the past.

The issue of quantitative measures in HR, and the problems that flow from using this approach, are touched on in Chapters 2 and 4, where the subject of the contribution that HR makes to organisational performance is examined. Gratton (2004) echoes the authors' view that placing too much reliance in HR metrics is a dangerous path to tread. Yet it is tempting to pursue this approach to performance evaluation because it is the language that so many managers understand. For HR specialists to hide behind the sort of argument that runs – 'you can't measure soft HR process factors like the quality of interaction between colleagues' – is likely to be seen as, at best, an excuse and at worst an attempt to evade accountability. In either case it does little to enhance non-HR managers' view of the HR profession.

The main problem behind the performance indicators approach to performance management is that of validity. Put simply, can those who define the performance indicators be sure that the indicators are measuring what they want measured? Gratton (2004) gives the well-known metric of retention to illustrate the case. This is often used as a supposed indicator of such phenomena as employee commitment to the employing organisation. The theoretical assumption is that 'committed' employees will stay longer in the organisation than those who are not committed. Gratton draws on research which suggests that those employees who are highly mobile did form attachments and commitment during their relatively short stays in organisations and were just as committed as workers who stayed in a single company.

The other main problem with the concentration upon performance measurement is that it can see measurement as an end in itself whereas the performance management emphasis is upon following up the results and promoting action consequent upon those results. This is similar to the action research approach to evaluation outlined in Chapter 4.

The performance measurement approach has been particularly prevalent in the UK public sector, where it has been introduced as part of the drive to improve public services, through more effective use of resources, and to reinforce accountability so that organisations are accountable for resource usage and achievement of outcomes. The role that performance management plays in meeting these goals is explained in Key Concepts 9.2.

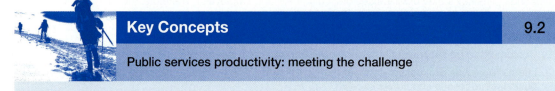

Key Concepts   9.2

Public services productivity: meeting the challenge

Effective performance management is essential for any organisation. Without the rigour that performance management provides, public services can (and do) lose sight of their objectives, accept mediocrity and fail to serve the customer.

The concept of performance management is well understood in the public sector and most organisations have some form of performance management system in place. But successful implementation of such systems is difficult and the quality is currently very mixed. We therefore regard performance management as very important and in October 1999 the Civil Service Management Board adopted the key elements of our framework as the new business planning structure for central government.

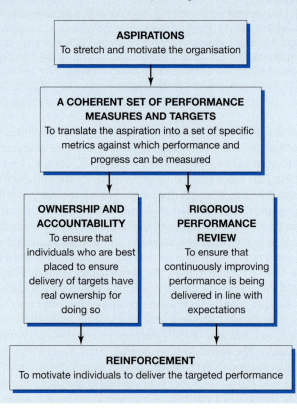

1. Bold aspirations to ensure that organisations have a clear and shared sense of direction that are derived from the needs and preferences of stakeholders, whether internal or external.
2. A coherent set of measures and targets that must be both demanding and manageable, with a mixture of targets that are cascaded throughout the organisation and are continually reviewed.
3. Ownership and accountability for targets, which may be at team or individual level, but specific responsibilities and accountabilities must be recognised.
4. Rigorous performance monitoring and review, when accountabilities have been defined.
5. Reinforcement so that success in delivering targeted performance should result in real consequences at an individual level, involving a mix of incentives such as financial rewards, career opportunities and non-pay incentives.

Source: Public Services Productivity Panel (2000).

The fear that performance measurement becomes an end in itself was borne out in case study research carried out by Radnor and McGuire (2004) in two UK public sector organisations: a health authority and a central government department. These researchers found four main weaknesses.

1. Performance was about measurement and evaluation, not about management. In both organisations too much time was spent 'form filling' and chasing information.
2. The systems in the two organisations were diagnostic not interactive or about allowing employee improvement.
3. The targets were not considered nor was there evaluation of the foundation upon which they were based.
4. There was a general lack of ownership of the targets, since those having to manage them were not responsible for the setting of the targets.

The last two weaknesses point to the observation that staff felt they had no direct influence over the targets and therefore quickly lost interest in them because they felt that they had little relevance to their daily work.

Self-Check and Reflect Questions 9.1

What factors do you think would explain the weaknesses Radnor and McGuire found in their research?

Performance management and SHRM

It was noted in Chapter 2 that SHRM derives its 'strategic' facet from the link to wider business strategy and integration between the various HR policies, procedures and practices: the first-termed vertical integration and the second 'horizontal integration' (Mabey *et al.*, 1998). In this section of the chapter the links that performance management has with both vertical and horizontal integration are analysed.

Performance management through vertical integration

There are two major ways in which senior management can enlist the services of performance management activities to underpin the strategic direction of the organisation: first, by reinforcing the organisation's mission and, second, through closely relating the organisation's business objectives to those of the individual.

Reinforcing the organisation's mission

It has become fashionable for organisations in all sectors of the economy to have clear statements of their mission. These tend to promote a good deal of scepticism, as often they are couched in rather bland language and express sentiments with which few would disagree. An extreme example is one of the world's leading computer companies which states:

> Our goal is simply stated. We want to be the best service organization in the world.

It goes without saying that employees are crucial to the pursuit of this mission and activities devoted to optimising employee performance are an intrinsic part of delivering the mission. However, this may not be as straightforward as it seems because it assumes that employees are able and willing to play their part in mission achievement.

Purcell *et al.* (2003), with their A+M+O model (see Chapter 2), assert that for people to perform effectively they must:

1. have the *ability* to do so by possessing the required skills and knowledge;

2. be *motivated* to do the work and do it well;

3. be given the *opportunity* to use their skills in playing their part in achieving team and organisational success.

Performance management has a direct role to play in the second and third of these factors. To return to the mission statement, as it does assume that employees will be motivated to play their part in its achievement, the challenge for managers is to get all employees to be committed to the mission.

The pursuit of employee commitment to the organisation's mission is something that has dominated people management thinking in recent years. As was noted in Chapter 2, Guest (1987) identified commitment as one of the four goals of HRM together with strategic integration, flexibility and quality.

Legge (1995b: 180) suggests that the orthodox interpretation of commitment 'is operationalised in terms of three factors: a strong desire to remain a member of the organisation; a strong belief in, and acceptance of, the values and goals of the organisation; and a readiness to exert considerable effort on behalf of the organisation'. Guest (1987) argues that the theoretical proposition that follows from this orthodox interpretation of commitment is that organisational commitment will result in high employee satisfaction, high performance, longer tenure and a willingness to accept change.

The research evidence on the effects of employee commitment is inconclusive, not the least reason being the difficulty of separating cause and effect in relation to HR processes and outcomes (Legge, 2001). For example, you may be asking: does the opportunity to negotiate individual performance objectives *cause* employee commitment or does a committed employee define the objective-setting process as negotiation where, in truth, it is little more than imposition with a cursory opportunity for the individual to disagree? What this suggests is that testing the theoretical proposition that employee commitment leads to specific outcomes is extremely difficult.

However, it is necessary to make two points here. The first is that managers have taken this theoretical proposition as an act of faith on the assumption that employees who 'sign on' to the organisation's goals are more likely to be effective performers than those who are, at best, apathetic or, at worst, alienated. Notwithstanding the complexity of the topic masked by its seeming simplicity, it is a compelling argument. The second is that without the communication of the organisation's mission, commitment to it is impossible. Performance management offers an excellent opportunity not only to introduce the mission but to reinforce it consistently through regular reviews of individual performance.

Relating the organisation's business objectives to those of the individual

Integrating human resource activities with the strategic objectives of the organisation may take the form of, for example, selecting the sort of people with the potential to deliver a contribution specifically to organisational objectives (the ability element of the Purcell *et al.* (2003) A+M+O model) and training them in such a way that such performance may be realised. But performance management offers the most obvious link. In Practice 9.1 is a good illustration of how organisational objectives, in this case based on Kaplan and Norton's (1992) balanced scorecard approach, inform the performance objectives throughout the organisation.

The design of a clear link between individual job and organisational objectives raises the question of the extent to which this link will be forged in practice. For reassurance, doubting managers may turn to goal-setting theory (Locke *et al.*, 1981). Goal-setting

In Practice   9.1

Performance management at Lever Fabergé

Lever Fabergé manufactures major international toiletry and home-care brands, such as Persil, Domestos, Dove, Sure and Sunsilk. It employs 2,700 people across four UK sites and introduced a new performance management system at its Leeds manufacturing plant.

The integrated approach to performance management is based on four related elements: objective setting; competence development; personal development planning; and reward and remuneration.

Objective setting is based on the balanced scorecard approach. There are six top-level objectives that are the foundations of the objectives that are then cascaded throughout the organisation. These are: safety; quality; service productivity; service delivery; cost; and morale. Annually, three work targets are agreed with relevant employees, which support key performance indicators (KPIs). The KPIs are based on the top-level objectives and represent work priorities or special tasks that need to be accomplished. The targets can apply to an individual, a team or a group of teams.

The top-level objectives also provide the basis for competence development. At the same time as targets are being set, employees agree their personal competence development targets. There is a list of core competences upon which the targets are based. These include such competences as influencing others; team working; self-development and creating a safe environment.

The work targets and competence targets form the basis of a personal development plan, which includes not only the targets but the way it is planned that they should be achieved. There are regular progress reviews and a final end of year evaluation to assess the extent of achievement.

The work targets and personal competence development targets drive individual performance-related pay. This takes two forms: a salary increment and a cash bonus.

Source: IDS (2003b).

theory has a long history that has been substantiated over 30 years of research. The components of the theory are that:

- clear and challenging goals lead to higher performance than easily attainable goals, goals at which you try your best, or no goals;
- goals affect performance by directing employees' attention and effort, increasing their determination to succeed and motivating them to develop strategies for achievement;
- goal-setting is most likely to improve employees' task performance when goals are clear and challenging; employees have sufficient ability to achieve them; supportive managers give regular feedback on the level of progress being made; tangible rewards, such as money, are given for goal achievement; and employees accept their goals.

Many performance management schemes involve setting employees challenging goals. Microsoft UK (IDS, 2003) calls them 'stretch goals'. An insurance company whose performance management scheme was studied (Lewis, 1998a) emphasised that rewards would only be given to those employees who demonstrated *improved* performance; performing at last year's level, however good, simply wasn't good enough. This reveals a particularly demanding aspect of performance management but what it does imply is the necessity for managers to ensure that the *opportunity* is available for individuals to demonstrate improved performance.

Locke *et al.*'s inclusion of the notion of employee acceptance by the individual of assigned goals suggests that mere imposition of goals by managers is unlikely to lead to goal acceptance and goal pursuit in line with strategic objectives. At Lever Fabergé (see In Practice 9.1) emphasis is placed upon the principle of joint ownership, with employees accepting their responsibility for performance development if they are to progress.

There may be two reasons why managers impose rather than negotiate objectives. The first relates to what Marsden and Richardson (1992) call 'information asymmetry'. This occurs when managers control all the information relevant to performance management. They set objectives, define performance measures, conduct appraisals and decide rewards. It is easy to see why some managers may prefer to do this: it enables them to retain the power that they derive from their managerial status and makes them less accountable for their actions.

The second reason why managers may impose rather than negotiate objectives is structural. In many large organisations, such as the building society in which the authors studied performance management, the objective-setting process is a mini-industry (Lewis, 1998a). Goals are 'handed down' to over 700 branch managers through their area managers. In reality there is little scope to amend the content of these goals which relate to the *outputs* (e.g. mortgage sales) the manager is expected to achieve. However, there is scope for area managers to negotiate *process* goals, on the way in which the branch manager performs his or her duties (e.g. leadership style of branch staff).

The provision of feedback to show progress in relation to the goal is a powerful indicator of performance management effectiveness. Some organisations have weekly, monthly or quarterly progress meetings and reviews. This is a very demanding and time-consuming process for managers. This element of the performance management cycle needs managers who are not only prepared to spend the time, but also committed to the style of management that is consistent with emphasis upon, giving feedback. This 'new style' managerialism is characterised by less concern for the technical side of individuals' jobs and more emphasis on talking to them about what they do to ensure that everything is right for them to do their jobs. The 'new style' manager is supportive, a team leader, a coach and facilitator. This is a style of management that is concerned with processes as well as outputs.

Self-Check and Reflect Questions	**9.2**

What obstacles do you think may stand in the way of an attempt by organisations to adopt a 'new style' of management in which the 'new style' manager is supportive, a team leader, a coach and facilitator?

Giving rewards, such as money, for goal attainment raises the contentious question of individual performance-related pay, which is covered in Chapter 11. Suffice it to say at this stage, that for some employees the achievement of goals is a reward in itself, without the existence of financial incentives.

Performance management through horizontal integration

It will become clear when performance management inputs, processes and outputs are considered later in this chapter, that the scope for performance management to link to other elements of HR is considerable. In this section, consideration is given to how this may be done by seeing performance management as: an important part of the so-called 'high performance (or 'high commitment') HR strategy; an approach which reinforces the organisation's structure; and a vital component of the drive to build employee skills, behaviours and attitudes consistent with the business strategy.

Performance management as an important part of the so-called 'high performance' HR strategy

Much attention has been paid to high performance (or, as they are sometimes called, high commitment) work systems in recent years. According to the Chartered Institute of Personnel and Development (CIPD, 2004b) these are characterised by the presence of:

- decentralised, devolved decision-making, with decisions made by those closest to the customer – so as constantly to renew and improve the offer to customers;
- development of people capacities through learning at all levels, with particular emphasis on self-management, team capabilities and project-based activities – to enable and support performance improvement and organisational potential;
- performance, operational and people management processes aligned to organisational objectives – to build trust, enthusiasm and commitment to the direction taken by the organisation;
- fair treatment for those who leave the organisation as it changes, and engagement with the needs of the community outside the organisation – this is an important component of trust- and commitment-based relationships, both within and outside the organisation.

The thinking behind such work systems is that they will create the conditions whereby employees will be more likely to be enthusiastic and involved with their work, thus demonstrating higher commitment to the organisation's goals. It is assumed that this will lead to enhannced employee and organisational performance. Much of the research that has been done on high performance work systems concentrates upon their ability to deliver improved organisational performance, a topic that was dealt with in some detail in Chapter 2. Boxall and Purcell (2003) point out that much works needs to be done to establish the conditions for and the components and consequences of high performance work systems.

The list of characteristics above puts performance management firmly at the centre of high performance activities. Cully *et al.* (1999), in the 1998 Workplace Employee Relations Survey, list performance tests and regular appraisals as part of the battery of high performance work practices, while Wood and de Menezes (1998) talk of 'new forms of assessment'. The contribution that performance management can make to high performance work systems is to act as part of a 'bundle' of HR activities, complementing and reinforcing them in order that the impact of the bundle may be increased.

To go into more detail on high performance work systems is not the concern of this chapter. Suffice to say that performance management has the facility to change the culture and therefore the working practices of organisations as part of a concerted effort to generate change.

Performance management and the reinforcement of the organisation's structure

The point was made in Chapter 2 that a key element of SHRM is a fluid and adaptive organisational structure in which flexible employees perform flexible jobs (Guest, 1987).

Performance management can play an important part in ensuring the effectiveness of an organisational structure. In order to understand this, it is necessary to return to basics: what is the purpose of any organisation's structure? This is concerned with:

- the allocation of resources in order that maximum efficiency may be gained;
- the organisation of work tasks;
- the distribution of responsibilities to organisational members;
- the monitoring of work patterns and standards to ensure efficient resource usage;
- establishing reporting patterns to clarify responsibilities;
- coordination of different parts of the organisation;
- ensuring a degree of flexibility in order that future changes may be accommodated.

As is explained later in this chapter, the essence of performance management is the series of communication processes between job holders and their managers. This communication is, for example, about: what tasks are to be performed; the standard to which the tasks are to be performed; and the identity of the person(s) responsible for monitoring the achievement of tasks and performance standards. Thus, effective communication between employees and their managers over these structural topics is an important part of ensuring that the purposes of an effective structure are achieved. Effective communication should lead to a better understanding of these structural topics.

This better understanding is achieved in two ways. First, it means that individuals and teams are likely to be much more responsible for their performance if they can see precisely the goals they are supposed to achieve, are given guidance on how the goals may be achieved and are provided with the resources to perform the tasks. This is particularly the case if they have been instrumental in setting the objectives. Second, performance management, through its close relationship between individual, unit goals and organisational goals, is potentially a powerful way of ensuring the optimum use of resources, as it should lead to a minimum of wasted resources through, for example, duplicated efforts or the pursuit of inappropriate tasks. The conduct of frequent, regular performance reviews ensures that tasks pursued by employees are as appropriate at the time of the review as they were when originally set.

Armstrong and Baron (1998) make the point that performance management is very much concerned with interrelationships, among the most important people – managers and individuals, managers and teams, and team members themselves. They note that contributors to their research often talked of the value of formal and semi-formal discussions that took place, which clarified many of the structural topics referred to earlier.

Key Concepts   9.3

Communication to foster effective interrelationships: a Chinese perspective

Some researchers (e.g. Child, 1991; Glover and Siu, 2000) have noted the absence of interpersonal communication in Chinese organisations. This is consistent with poor communication of information in organisations. In Child's (1994) view, this is because many Chinese employees see information as a personal rather than as a collective possession. As a consequence, there is often virtually no flow of information between departments. Child suggests that this is exacerbated by the absence of any notion of interdependence between departments and the inability of many Chinese employees to see how their efforts fit into the overall purpose of the organisation. In addition, it may be explained by the vertical authority chain in many Chinese organisations, where employees accept little responsibility because all decisions have to be referred to the senior executive at the top of the organisation. Glover and Siu (2000: 874) noted the 'low involvement, low initiative nature of employee attitudes to work', which accounted for production errors in the food processing plant they studied.

Questionable interpersonal communication skills may be attributed to the cultural value of the wish to preserve face. Feedback on job performance, if done with genuine intent, will inevitably involve some personal criticism. As one technician in an electronics plant studied by Lewis (2003a) explained:

> There is not a lot of talking between managers and staff in R and D at present, only about the everyday demands of the job. Individual review meetings would be welcomed if it could be assured that managers would listen to the views of their staff. They must give specific answers to problems. We seldom have discussions about personal development. Mr W... does not tell his staff they are promising but he sends the message in a subtle way by giving them responsible jobs.

Performance management as a vital component of the drive to build employee skills, behaviours and attitudes

Perhaps the most basic way of integrating the various HR practices is to use the skills, behaviours and attitudes (SBAs) necessary to deliver effective job performance as a way of assessing individual success. Skills, behaviours and attitudes (the term 'competences' has been deliberately avoided here to steer clear of a debate about the different definitions of the term) are what are needed for the employee to meet the performance targets (the 'how' to deliver the 'what'). Such skills, behaviours and attitudes may be used to define:

- the person specification at the time of recruitment. This specification can be the basis of the job advertisement;
- the job description;
- training and development objectives, which can inform both learning objectives and criteria for assessing training effectiveness;
- job performance targets;
- criteria for determining performance-related pay awards;
- promotion criteria;
- capability targets to be achieved by less-effective performers.

In Practice 9.2 contains a good illustration of how skills, behaviours and attitudes are used in the performance management system by a UK public service employer.

In Practice   9.2

The use of skills, behaviours and attitudes in performance management at the Scottish Prison Service

The Scottish Prison Service operates 15 prisons in Scotland with 4,500 staff and in 2000 embarked upon a new vision called 'correctional excellence', based on the principle of continuous improvement. An important part of the new vision was a revised performance management system which has three main components:

- a clear set of expected outputs against which employee performance is measured;
- desired skills, behaviours and attitudes that reflect how the outputs are to be attained;
- continuous improvement targets.

The desired SBAs' profile was a new initiative for the Scottish Prison Service. It used the skills framework that had already been drawn up for the purpose of drafting person specifications and job descriptions. Five core behaviours were defined.

- building and maintaining relationships (working with others, sharing ideas, experiences and effort to achieve common objectives);
- problem solving and decision-making;
- planning, implementation and control;
- adaptability;
- self-motivation.

In order to assist line managers in the measurement of the SBAs, illustrations of 'effective' and 'ineffective' behaviours were drafted for each of the five core behaviours. Examples for 'building and maintaining relationships' are: 'effective' – ensures people have the information they require; 'ineffective' – shows little consideration for the impact of decisions in other areas, gives misinformation.

Source: IDS (2003b).

The initiative by the Scottish Prison Service to measure SBAs is a bold one given the relative ease with which performance outputs, compared with SBAs, may be measured. Hard measures lend themselves to quantification, whereas soft measures, such as behaviours, do not. This also raises the question of the desirability of paying attention to soft measures. It is a plausible business argument that what counts is what is achieved, not the way it was achieved.

In addition, attention to SBAs' measurement may be challenged on basis of the underlying theory that prescribed SBAs lead to particular performance outcomes. To explain the authors' contention that this may not necessarily be the case, look at Figure 9.2. Scenarios A and B reflect the theoretical position on which the performance management system, which puts emphasis on the demonstration of SBAs, is based. There is a certain intuitive logic to this. It is similar to the 'high commitment work practices lead to enhanced organisational performance' theory. After all, it seems like common sense that the employee who can perform the sort of SBAs enshrined in the Scottish Prison Service's five core behaviours is more likely to meet his or her performance targets than the employee who cannot. Yet scenario C raises the possibility that the SBAs may be demonstrated, yet the performance outcomes may not be met. There may be a host of reasons for this. There may be inadequate resources provided by the organisation or external constraints, for example the economic context, may render target achievement very difficult. Scenario D is that situation to which many managers may be tempted to turn a blind eye: targets are achieved in spite of ineffective SBA demonstration. Such a situation may be common in sales situations where the salesperson may demonstrate poor customer relationship skills and behave in a manner that alienates his or her sales team colleagues yet still achieve high sales figures due to a buoyant product market or simple persistence (although this may, of course, be a relevant SBA). The manager may be swayed by the argument that long-term success in the job will only be sustained if there is demonstration of effective SBAs. This would lead to a poor performance rating for the salesperson. But it would be a brave sales manager who risked losing someone who produced high sales figures as a result of a poor SBA rating. That said, there are jobs where the link between SBAs and performance output achievement may be stronger. An example is a senior manager who is dependent upon others for the achievement of outputs.

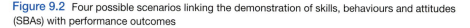

| | Outcomes | |
Effective ⟷		⟶ Ineffective
Scenario A Effective SBAs demonstrated, resulting in effective performance outcomes	**Scenario C** Effective SBAs demonstrated, albeit ineffective performance outcomes demonstrated
Scenario D Ineffective SBAs demonstrated, albeit effective performance outcomes demonstrated	**Scenario B** Ineffective SBAs demonstrated, resulting in ineffective performance outcomes

Figure 9.2 Four possible scenarios linking the demonstration of skills, behaviours and attitudes (SBAs) with performance outcomes

It is not the purpose of Figure 9.2. to undermine the promotion of SBAs in performance management. Far from it. Emphasis upon SBA achievement enhances the strategic thrust of performance management through the principle of generic SBAs, such as the five core behaviours evident in the Scottish Prison Service's system. The nature of these five SBAs is that they relate to the majority of jobs in the organisation. The fact that individual employees may reflect scenarios C and D does not threaten the principle that, in general, the inclusion of SBAs in performance management may enhance strategic significance, provided, of course, that the SBAs reflect the organisation's mission. The significance of Figure 9.2 is that scenario C points up that the context in which the job is performed needs to be conducive to effective performance, and scenario D may be seen as a 'test of resolve' for organisations and managers who espouse the value of attention to job processes as well as performance outcomes.

Reasons for growth in the importance of performance management

Any list of the reasons for the growth in importance of performance management in recent years in many respects mirrors the content of the list of reasons for the growth in importance of SHRM. This reinforces the claim for the centrality of performance management in SHRM.

An early survey of performance management by the (then) Institute of Personnel Management (1992) claims it offers several advantages to organisations. Among these are:

- more effective employees, able to meet increased product market competition;
- a greater opportunity for employees to share in the organisation's vision and the way to realise that vision;
- the pushing of key decisions down the organisational structure to line managers and supervisors;
- a greater acceptance of accountability by line managers of the necessity to make such decisions; and
- reward structures that forge a clear link between individual and/or group performance.

These claims seem as relevant now as they did in the early 1990s. Indeed, with the growth of global competition in many markets, the rationale that underpins performance management, which is reflected in the first factor in the list above, is more relevant now. Therefore, it is no surprise to note that in 2004 the most recent survey by the CIPD noted that 87 per cent of organisations surveyed had some form of performance management system (Baron and Armstrong, 2004).

But it is not just in the private sector that attention to cost, which leads to a quest for optimum contribution from all employees, has been apparent. Earlier, this chapter explained how performance measurement was a feature of performance management in the UK public sector. The best value initiative in UK local government is a good example of this drive for optimum employee contribution. Best value was introduced in 1998 with the aim of ensuring that management and business practices in local government deliver better and more responsive public services. Best value in local government is about local authorities:

- balancing quality service provision against costs;
- achieving sustainable development;
- being accountable and transparent, by engaging with the local community;
- ensuring equal opportunities;
- continuously improving the outcomes of the services they provide (Scottish Executive, 2004).

Similarly, performance management has been a key component in the campaign to introduce a performance culture in many organisations. Raising the status of individual employee performance assessment from an aspect of personnel bureaucracy (these forms have to be filled in once a year) to a managerial practice that has real meaning is an important symbol of the desire of the organisation to change. Chapter 6 explains how one view of culture has it that artefacts are an important visible manifestation of organisational culture (Schein, 1992a). Performance management is a powerful visible manifestation of the organisation's desire to change to a performance culture. This is particularly so when the outcomes lead to discernible management action, such as performance-related pay, promotion and development decisions or action to improve individual performance through the capability procedure.

The ability of performance management to differentiate between those employees whose performance is adequate, or less than adequate, and those who are high performers has acquired greater importance in these days of downsized, delayered and flexible organisations. It follows that if there are fewer people doing the same amount of work then a higher level of performance is required together with practices that generate higher levels of performance.

The final reason why performance management has grown in importance is the increasing dissatisfaction with traditional performance appraisal practices (Bach, 2000). Bach highlights the lack of objectivity of performance appraisal and the over-reliance on the annual appraisal interview as the most important reasons for general dissatisfaction with performance appraisal. This had led to a greater interest in so-called 360-degree appraisal in which performance assessments are secured from a wider range of sources: for example, the employee him- or herself and other stakeholders, such as customers and other line managers. This, in turn, generates performance information on a wider range of topics than if the assessment is done only by the employee's immediate line manager. Later in this chapter, 360-degree appraisal is discussed in more detail.

Consideration of the way in which performance management processes are changing leads us now to the major part of the chapter, which deals with the performance management system.

 Self-Check and Reflect Questions   **9.3**

To what extent do you think that the lack of objectivity in performance appraisal may be overcome in performance management?

The performance management systems model and the key processes embedded in it

It is normal for writers on performance management to represent the series of activities included in performance management as a cycle (e.g. Clark, 1998, Thornhill *et al.*, 2000). This is a valid approach, since there is a series of activities that start at a particular point in the organisation's calendar, are subject to regular review and end with discernible results. The cycle then starts again at the commencement of the following year. However, in this chapter, performance management is characterised as a systems model. The cyclical nature of performance management is included in the model, as are all the activities that form the cycle. We believe that by representing performance management in systems form we give greater emphasis to the inputs and outputs of the system as well as the processes. It is the processes that gain greater coverage in the literature. This is as it should be because the interaction between appraiser and appraisee is the very essence of performance management. However, the effectiveness of performance management is not only a consequence of how well the processes are enacted. It is also a function of, for example, the context in which the system operates.

In Figure 9.3, the inputs to the system (e.g. the existing SBAs of employees) are instrumental in creating the outputs through the application of a series of processes (e.g. performance appraisal). These outputs are both HR and the ultimate goals, enhanced employee and, eventually, organisational performance.

Stakeholders

The most important stakeholders in the performance management system are appraisers, appraisees, and those upon whom they have most immediate impact, for example recipients of the services provided by the appraisee.

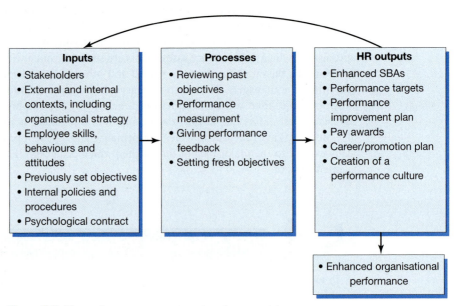

Figure 9.3 The performance management systems model

Traditionally the system has been driven by the individual employee's immediate manager who set objectives and assessed the extent that these were achieved. However, this is now changing, particularly with the growing popularity of 360-degree appraisal as is explained in the section on processes. This means that the population of significant stakeholders expands to include the appraisee's colleagues or subordinates, other managers and customers.

External and internal contexts including organisational strategy

It would be foolish to ignore the social, political, economic and technological contexts external to the organisation in which performance management operates. For example, the advent of a greater degree of democracy in performance appraisal process is a reflection of wider social change, and the very content of jobs and the SBAs they require for effective performance is affected by technological change. Similarly, as is evident in the thrust of this book, the organisation's overall strategy is a key input to the performance management system.

The aspect of the internal context that cannot be ignored is the organisation's culture (see Chapter 6). Perhaps the key determinant of the effectiveness of performance management is the degree to which the culture supports the aims of the system. If the overall emphasis is upon improving what managers perceive as sub-standard employee performance, then the culture will need to be different (results-driven) to one where the emphasis is upon self-development of individuals (nurturing).

Employee skills, behaviours and attitudes

SBAs are a central component of the performance management systems model. Existing levels of SBAs are brought to the system by employees as inputs. Often one of the intended outputs of performance management, as with the Scottish Prison Service (IDS, 2003) example above, is to improve the level of SBAs.

Previously set objectives

Part of the review process takes into account the extent to which the individual has achieved the objectives set at previous review(s).

Internal policies/procedures

The degree of comprehensiveness of internal policies and procedures may also play an important part in determining performance management system effectiveness. A good example of this is the way in which the discipline procedure caters for the improvement of employee capability, as shown in 'In Practice' 9.3.

In Practice 9.3

UK teachers' capability procedure

Informal stage

If a teacher is considered to be under-performing, the headteacher or line manager should investigate. Once the facts have been gathered, there are three options: (1) drop the matter because there is no case to answer; (2) arrange counselling in order to give support without using the formal procedures; (3) arrange a formal interview if the case is serious enough.

The counselling and informal coaching should aim to help and encourage the teacher. The teacher should be told what is required, how his or her performance will be reviewed and when. The teacher should also be told that the formal procedure will begin if there is no improvement. At the appointed time of the review, a clear decision should be taken either to drop the matter or arrange a formal interview.

Formal stage

The investigations into a teacher's capability and the various interviews, meetings and decision-making during the procedure can be carried out either by the head or by a senior colleague who has responsibility for the teacher's performance. Throughout the procedures, local education authority (LEA) advisers, or other advisers with educational and personnel experience, should advise the school and, if appropriate, assist with the process, including classroom observation and providing support to the teacher and to the investigators.

Formal interview

A formal interview will initiate the formal stage. At least five working days' (or if out of term time, seven consecutive days') notice of this initial formal interview must be given.

The teacher can be accompanied by a union official or a colleague.

At the end of the interview, there are two options available if new evidence has come to light or further investigation has shown that the matter is no longer as serious: either drop the matter or arrange counselling, unless this has already been done without improvement. Where there is continuing concern, there are two alternatives: oral or written warning, or a final written warning. The decision about which level of warning is appropriate will depend on the seriousness of the problem. Normally a written warning will be the next step. It is possible, however, in cases where the education of pupils is in jeopardy because of the lack of competence, that the head might move directly to a final written warning.

A written warning will trigger an assessment period of up to two terms. A final written warning will trigger an assessment period not exceeding four weeks. During the assessment period, those monitoring the performance should always offer periodic feedback and instruction to help the teacher to improve. Training courses should be arranged as soon as possible if these would be helpful, but they should not interrupt the timing of the procedure.

Appeal against a formal warning

An appeal could be heard by a senior manager, an LEA adviser or an individual governor. Meanwhile, the monitoring of the teacher's progress should continue.

First assessment stage

From week 1 to week 20, regular observation, monitoring and evaluation with guidance, training and support will be put in place. It would be possible to move to a final warning at any time during this stage if a more serious problem arose. At week 20 the process could stop if progress has been satisfactory but, if not, then a final written warning will be issued. The decision and main points must be recorded and communicated to the teacher in writing.

Second assessment stage

If a final written warning has been issued, regular monitoring will continue for a further four weeks. During week 24, the final evaluation meeting will take place. If performance is still unsatisfactory, the teacher should be told in writing that the matter will be referred to the governing body's Staff Dismissal Committee.

Source: Croners (2004).

Psychological contract

The final input to the performance management system considered here is the psychological contract. This is a term first used by Argyris (1960) to refer to the expectations of employer and employee which operate in addition to the formal contract of employment. It has been defined by Rousseau (1994 cited by Hiltrop, 1995: 287) as 'the understanding people have regarding the commitments made between themselves and their organisation'. As the central assertion is that the inputs to the performance management system are instrumental in creating the outputs through the application of a series of processes, it follows that performance management activities, which are consistent with the psychological contract, will assist the quest for performance management effectiveness. Conversely, if the psychological contract is breached, then the consequence may be that performance management will not achieve the aims planned by management.

Hiltrop's (1995) examination of the psychological contract, included contrasting characteristics of the 'old' and 'new' types of contract. It is clear from this that performance management has a central role to play in that it defines what is expected from the employee in terms of the parameters of performance criteria. He talks, for example, of a 'fair day's work for a fair day's pay' being replaced by 'high pay for high job performance'; 'making a difference to the organisation' replacing the 'old' contract expectation of 'good performance in the present job'; 'knowledge and skills' superseding 'time and effort' as a dominant aspect of the expectations of management; 'value added' being attributed more importance than loyalty.

Stiles *et al.* (1997) argue that performance management processes play a key role in creating a framework in which the psychological contract between employer and employee is determined. They specify three particular processes as being important: (1) setting objectives; (2) performance evaluation; and (3) the linkage between (1) and (2) to generate reward and development outputs in order to reward desired behaviour. They conducted research at three organisations which used performance management as an important part of their attempt to move from an 'old' type of psychological contract, emphasising job security and clear career paths, to one that supported the companies' aims of excellent customer service, commitment to teamwork, continuous improvement and professionalism. Stiles *et al.* concluded that the move towards redefining the psychological contract was hampered by ineffective implementation of performance management. In particular, they highlighted the presence of mixed messages from management and employees' doubts about the fairness and accuracy of ratings. The particular problems noted by the researchers were:

- short-term demands dictated that 'softer' targets were ignored;
- objectives were imposed by managers rather than negotiated;

- performance appraisal was perceived as bureaucratic and did not give rise to action; inconsistent appraisal ratings;
- performance pay in which the link between pay and performance was unclear and/or perceived as unfair;
- training outcomes that were based on the current job rather than the espoused aim of employability;
- insufficient opportunity to practise newly learned skills.

Self-Check and Reflect Questions	9.4

In what ways do you think the psychological contract is threatened by the short-comings in the implementation of performance management at Stiles *et al.*'s organisations?

Performance management processes

Reviewing past objectives

This is usually the first process in any performance appraisal interview. Too often it can be the first review of past objectives since they were originally set. This is the opposite approach to that which is trumpeted in the prescriptive texts: the need to have regular reviews to ensure that objectives are still relevant and to check progress against them. Clearly, modified past objectives may have an important influence upon the content of fresh objectives.

Performance measurement

The earlier section of this chapter, which dealt with performance measurement, is critical of too narrow a conception of performance measures – in particular that demonstrated by the 'performance indicators' approach adopted in some public-sector organisations. Recent research by the CIPD (2004a) confirms the impression that many organisations may not be broadening the criteria by which they assess employee performance. A survey of over 500 practitioners reported that 84 per cent of respondents thought that 'quantifiable measures of performance are essential to successful performance management'. In terms of the key factors used to determine the effectiveness of performance management, 'achievement of objectives' and 'achievement of financial targets' were rated as the most important by respondents.

Giving performance feedback

Performance appraisal was prevalent long before the term performance management achieved popular usage. Appraisal remains the cornerstone of performance management and the major vehicle for providing employees with feedback on their job performance. In the 1998 Workplace Employee Relations survey (Cully *et al.*, 1999)

80 per cent of UK workplaces conducted appraisals, albeit that they were more likely to be conducted among 'white collar' than manual employees. In an IRS (2003) survey of 49 UK organisations in both public and private sectors, 96 per cent used performance appraisal with 77 per cent of those organisations thinking that the technique had a 'lot' of effect upon employee performance.

All the organisations in the IDS (2003b) study conducted regular performance reviews with staff. The typical pattern was for there to be a minimum of two formal reviews: one in the middle of the review year and the other at the end of the year. Organisations such as Microsoft also encourage managers to meet regularly with their employees to give feedback, and employees are given a guarantee that they will be given time to talk to their managers about performance and development issues.

The model of the manager as the sole judge of employee progress, given in a top-down manner, is increasingly becoming outmoded in many organisations. So-called 360-degree appraisal is becoming more prevalent. In the IRS (2003) study of 49 organisations, one-half used 360-degree appraisal. This type of appraisal is so called simply because it does not rely on assessment from the line manager only but from a number of sources. These may include, in addition to the line manager: other managers such as those responsible for projects; peers (e.g. fellow team members); employees for whom the individual may be responsible; internal and external customers; and self-assessment. Since those sources, other than the immediate line manager, may not be familiar with the individual's performance objectives, skills and behaviours are usually the focus of the feedback. Therefore, the information gained from multiple sources is more likely to be used for developmental reasons than for the purpose of 'rating' the individual for the purposes of pay or promotion.

In Practice 9.4

Upward appraisal at Microsoft UK

At Microsoft UK, upward feedback is provided to line managers in advance of their own development discussions and formal performance reviews. Every member of the manager's team has the opportunity to give feedback to the managers through the online feedback tool, which is operational in April and December of each year. Employees are asked to rate certain areas of the manager's performance on a 5-point scale and also answer open-ended questions about the manager.

Although employees are given the opportunity to remain anonymous in giving their feedback, Microsoft believes that the feedback will be more useful if it comes from a known source.

Source: IDS (2003b).

There are potentially significant advantages to be gained from 360-degree appraisal not the least of which is the breadth of view that is lent to the feedback process. It may be argued that the subjectivity of performance appraisal by one manager is simply multiplied by the number of feedback givers in 360-degree appraisal. But if the feedback reveals significant trends that are reinforced by a number of sources, then the feedback may be more valid. Redman (2001) notes that senior managers may also find 360-degree appraisal a useful management development tool, since it is often this group that is ignored in traditional performance appraisal schemes. Redman also argues that 360-

degree appraisal has a strategic advantage in that feedback questionnaires may be designed to reflect the specific organisation's mission, culture, strategy, etc.

However, 360-degree appraisal is not without its potential problems. Perhaps the most important of these is the almost inevitable doubt about the validity of the data produced. Redman (2001) makes the point that information is only as good as the instrument that is used to collect it. He cites the example of the question posed to employees about their manager: 'does the manager deal with problems in a flexible manner?' The very ambiguity of such a question leads to doubt about the data it yields. This assumes that the employee is in position to answer the question. If he or she has not been in a position to witness the manager in situations where flexibility is required, then the doubts about the validity of the data multiply. It is not only wording of questions that may lead to different interpretations that attracts Redman's scepticism. He is similarly doubtful about the administration of standard evaluation instruments to a variety of raters that does not take into account the fact that the rater's contact with the person being evaluated may differ according to context. For example, the manager's secretary may have quite a different perspective on the manager's competence than a fellow manager or a colleague technical expert.

Setting fresh objectives

The principal questions to ask when considering performance objectives are: where do they come from?; who sets them?; how may they be characterised?; and for how long do they last?

The strategic thrust of this book and this chapter means that the answer to this first question is clear. Performance objectives flow from the organisation's business goals and values (as in the Lever Fabergé example in 'In Practice' 9.1). If this is not so, the risk is run that HR process and functions, such as the pursuit of performance objectives, operate in a vacuum (Hendry et al., 2000). All this assumes, of course, that there is clarity in the strategic objectives of the organisation and, as Chapter 1 points out, this may not always be the case.

It may be expected that if the individual's performance objectives are derived from the organisation's business goals and values, then their content is clear and the question of who sets the goals in unproblematic. However, this is not as straightforward as it appears. As was noted earlier in the research by Stiles et al. (1997), employees saw the imposition of objectives by managers as undesirable. It seems reasonable to assume that if employees are to pursue individual objectives with some enthusiasm then they should have some say in setting them. Increasingly this seems to be the trend. The IDS study (IDS, 2003b) notes how employees at AstraZeneca Global R&D group propose their own objectives to their line managers as the initial stage in a negotiation. At Microsoft UK, goal setting is seen as a three-way responsibility: with individual employees, line managers and HR playing a part. Here again, employees have overall ownership of the process but line managers, with guidance from HR, ensure that employee expectations are realistic and that there is sufficient 'stretch' in the objectives set.

Goal-setting theory (Locke et al., 1981) has long held that a relatively small amount of objectives with which employees can readily identify is better that a multiplicity of objectives. Having too many objectives makes focusing more difficult. In addition, the well-known SMART acronym suggests that objectives should be: specific (defined clearly); measurable (or, in the case of qualitative objectives, at least demonstrable);

agreed rather than imposed; realistic (to be perceived as fair by employees); and time-related (with clear target dates by which achievement may be evident). This last aspect heralds the final question about performance objectives that was heralds at the beginning of the section: for how long do they last? Clear target dates by which achievement may be evident suggest a rigidity that may be inconsistent with the organisation's desire to be flexible and responsive to external (and internal) pressures. There was a general pattern in the IDS study (IDS, 2003b) for organisations to have regular performance reviews during the annual cycle, at which the appropriateness of performance objectives were reviewed and changed as necessary to reflect changing circumstances.

HR outputs

Enhanced SBAs and performance targets

SBAs and performance targets have already been covered in some detail in this chapter and it is not our intention to re-visit these topics here. Suffice it to say that in the CIPD research noted above (CIPD, 2004a), 82 per cent of respondents thought that the focus of performance management should be developmental, suggesting that the employee SBAs, that serve as an input to the performance management systems model, should ideally emerge from the model in enhanced form. This is self-evidently the case where the intention is to remedy poor performance. But, with the possible exception of the organisation where the thrust of performance management is overt control (to ensure that employees are 'doing what they are paid to do), it seems that a golden opportunity to enhance employee SBAs is being missed if the system does not have a developmental focus. Performance appraisal has long been recognised as an important way of identifying training needs. However, the growth in popularity of defining SBAs has meant that, in many organisations, performance management is the precursor to specific activities, such as shadowing key employees or coaching by a recognised 'expert', designed to enhance the individual's SBA levels. This may be contrasted with the approach where appraisal is the annual ritual where managers assign employees to training courses which they think may be relevant. Often the appropriateness of the content of such courses is checked neither beforehand nor after attendance. Similarly, there is little effort to give the employee the opportunity to utilise the skills and knowledge gained on the course.

The model in Figure 9.2 includes performance targets set at the previous review as inputs, which are the focus of attention for the review, measurement and feedback processes. These processes lead to the setting of objectives for the coming review period, which are outputs in our model and feed back into the system as inputs for the next period.

Performance improvement plan

In recent years there has been much more attention paid to the question of employee capability. There are at least two reasons for this. First is the increasing importance of all employees performing to their maximum potential in the light of reduced headcount in organisations. The second is the development of management thinking, which accepts that sub-standard employee performance may be a result of insufficient preparation of the employee by his or her managers. This has led many organisations to develop a separate procedure for dealing with lack of capability – a procedure that is, in effect, part of the main disciplinary procedure.

As In Practice 9.5 points out, Acas guidance on the handling of capability issues (Acas, 2004) makes clear that performance management has a major role to play both in the prevention of capability problems and in the handling of them when they arise.

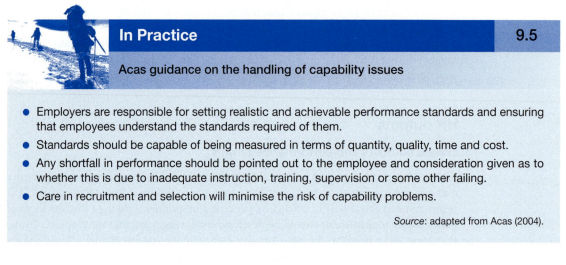

In Practice   **9.5**

Acas guidance on the handling of capability issues

- Employers are responsible for setting realistic and achievable performance standards and ensuring that employees understand the standards required of them.
- Standards should be capable of being measured in terms of quantity, quality, time and cost.
- Any shortfall in performance should be pointed out to the employee and consideration given as to whether this is due to inadequate instruction, training, supervision or some other failing.
- Care in recruitment and selection will minimise the risk of capability problems.

Source: adapted from Acas (2004).

Acas (2004) go on to recommend that in cases of unsatisfactory performance an employee should be given an 'improvement note', setting out:

- the performance problem;
- the improvement that is required;
- the timescale for achieving this improvement;
- a review date; and
- any support the employer will provide to assist the employee.

Acas advise that the employee should be informed that the note represents the first stage of a formal procedure and that failure to improve could lead to a final written warning and, ultimately, dismissal. A copy of the note should be kept and used as the basis for monitoring and reviewing performance over a specified period (e.g. six months).

However, if an employee's unsatisfactory performance – or continuance – is sufficiently serious, for example because it is having, or is likely to have, a serious harmful effect on the organisation, it may be justifiable to move directly to a final written warning. An example of this may be disregard of an important organisational rule, such as recording when a period of duty has finished.

The immediate problem in dealing with the poor performer is to establish whether the reason for poor performance is due to lack of capability or negligence. Poor performance may be evident when an employee does not have the ability to achieve the standards set by the manager, however hard that employee tries. Alternatively, the employee may possess the ability to meet the standards but, for whatever reason, is not prepared to make the effort to meet them. There is a clear need for the employer to distinguish between what the Employment Appeal Tribunal (EAT) termed 'sheer incapability due to an inherent incapacity to function or … one of failure to exercise to the full such talent as is possessed' (Croners, 1991: 1). This attempt to distinguish is made through the initial investigation which, for example, is detailed in the first principle of the procedure in 'In Practice' 9.3. The EAT went on to say that 'cases where a person has not come up to the required standard through his own carelessness, negligence or idleness are much more appropriately dealt with as cases of misconduct rather than incapability' (Croners, 1991: 1).

	Self-Check and Reflect Questions	**9.5**

What problems may be involved in distinguishing between lack of capability and negligence?

Pay awards

When the CIPD carried out research in 1992 and 1997 on performance management, one of the conclusions was that there was a dominance of individual performance-related pay (CIPD, 2004a). Indeed, for many respondents in the 1992 survey (Institute of Personnel Management, 1992) performance management was synonymous with performance-related pay. There is some evidence that the link with pay is not quite as direct as it was in the early 1990s. There is still a link between the achievement of individual performance targets and pay in many organisations but there are other drivers of individual pay. A typical example is the financial services organisation studied by the authors (Lewis *et al.*, 2004) which has introduced a new reward system. Here pay is determined by market rate, competence acquisition as well as achievement of individual performance targets. In the Lever Fabergé example cited earlier in this chapter (IDS, 2003b) similar arrangements exist although there are proposals to remove individual performance targets from pay considerations. At the Scottish Prison Service, employees move to the next pay point if they are rated as at least effective. However, at AstraZeneca performance reviews 'inform' rather than 'determine' employees' pay awards.

A trend that had developed is the payment of cash bonuses linked to the achievement of individual performance targets. These bonuses are not consolidated into basic pay. More consideration is given to variable pay in Chapter 11.

Career/promotion plan

For many employees, performance appraisal has been a traditional vehicle for recognising potential with a view to planning forthcoming activities so that the employee may move 'onwards and upwards' in the organisation. This may be, for example, in the form of training course attendance, expanding the current job to encompass new responsibilities, on the job coaching by an experienced employee, or temporary attachment to a project team. Here the emphasis has tended to be upon the individual's manager 'spotting' the potential of the employee and planning initiatives to develop that potential to the benefit of the organisation and the individual.

However, as noted earlier, there has been a move from the time-honoured top-down model of performance management to one where the emphasis has been on the individual to participate in his or her own objective setting and performance measurement. In the same vein, the flattening of organisational structures, with the consequent reduction in vertical promotion opportunities and the end for many employees of the 'job for life' psychological contract, has meant that the emphasis for career development has switched to the employee. Torrington *et al.* (2002) make the point that the career is the property of the individual and therefore the responsibility for planning the career rests with the individual, who should identify career goals and adopt strategies and plans to realise them. Clearly this may be within or outside the individual's current employing organisation.

It seems that the practice of defining employee SBAs in performance management is particularly helpful to employees in career planning. This approach clarifies the necessary ingredients for success in the current and future roles within the organisation. In addition, it enables the employee to assess his or her own competence in SBAs that may be considered generic for his or her chosen speciality which are likely to apply in other organisations. One aspiration of many organisations, such as that illustrated in 'In Practice' 9.6, is to create a so-called performance culture.

In Practice   9.6

Creating a performance culture in a UKAir

Many companies in the air industry suffered as a result of the very difficult product market following the events of 11 September 2001 and the consequent reluctance of travellers to use air transport. UKAir's profits declined by 60 per cent in the third quarter of 2003. However, despite the decline in profits, UKAir confirmed it achieved its sales target. As a result, it has overtaken its US rival for the first time in three decades of fierce competition. A company statement said: 'Our performance during the first nine months of 2003 is in line with our plans. We continue to reinforce our position in the industry's competitive environment and lay the foundation for future profitable growth through investments in new products.'

One of the consequences of this tighter financial climate has been the need to generate HR responses that match the strategic need to be more cost effective. As far as reward is concerned, the compensation and benefits specialist devised a new reward strategy. This was to replace the old one that was based on the principle of progress being made through annual increments up a steep hierarchical grading structure. The new strategy places much more emphasis upon individual job performance. The compensation and benefits specialist said we need to breed a performance culture here. It is not now enough for people to come and work, even for ten hours a day. They have to perform, make a difference. It's not how long you are here, or what qualifications you have: it's what you actually do that counts.'

Creation of a performance culture

As noted earlier in this chapter, the development of a performance culture is based on the principles of Schein (1992b, 1997) which were discussed in Chapter 6. Schein would argue that tying pay to the performance management system in the way UKAir has done (see In Practice 9.6) is a powerful visible manifestation of organisational culture which, if allowed to embed itself in organisation practices over a long period, may play a significant part in developing a performance culture in which the need to 'make a difference' is a taken for granted assumption within the organisation.

Performance management: built on shaky foundations?

So far, this chapter has struck a rather positive note in that it has sought to demonstrate that performance management has an important role to play in delivering significant HR outputs. However, not all commentators have been as encouraging in the performance management perspective they have adopted. In this final section a few issues are raised that summarise this less positive stance, with the intention of signalling the possible pitfalls that may lie in wait for the unwary designer of performance management schemes.

Performance management and the quest for management control

It is clear from this chapter that there is scope for managers to implement performance management in a variety of ways. At the 'soft' end of the continuum, the manager may adopt a highly democratic perspective in which employees play a major part in shaping the performance management processes outlined here, such as defining performance objectives and measures. At the 'hard' end, the emphasis may be upon imposition, with managers imposing a harsh regime of targets which if not met trigger the disciplinary procedure. The hard end appears to equate with what Friedman (1977) called direct control. Direct control involves close supervision of employees, a harsher regime of discipline characterised by threats of, say, pay reduction or dismissal. It also entails minimising the individual responsibility given to employees. As Morgan (1997) notes, direct control is part of the approach that sees the organisation, and its employees, as machine-like. It has somewhat militaristic overtones and, in industry, owes much to the work of F.W. Taylor, the father of scientific management (1911). The spirit of scientific management is reflected in Taylor's stress upon the manager's need to set goals and objectives and ensure that employees go for them; to organise rationally, efficiently and clearly and to specify every detail of the work in order that employees will be sure of the jobs that they have to perform. In short, Taylor's creed was to 'plan, organise and control'.

It seems that Taylorism is alive and well in the twenty-first century. Morgan (1997) cites the example of the fast-food chain that specifies the tasks that workers have to perform in careful detail. For example, when the food is ready at the counter to be handed to the customer, the observation checklist used to rate employee performance specifies that the bag in which the food is placed should be neatly double folded away from the customer with the company's logo facing the customer and the food should be placed on the tray neatly and evenly. The level of detail specified for effective employee performance in the Scottish Prison Service (see In Practice 9.2) may not be as great, but the principle is the same: management defining what has to be done and the way in which it should be done.

You may argue that this is perfectly legitimate. After all, many of us would rather be doing something else than selling our labour to our employer so it follows that if we would rather spend our time at work doing what *we* want to do, or at least doing what our employer wants us to do in the way we want to do it, then managers need to devise ways of making us do what *they* want us to do.

However, a regime of direct control is hardly an attractive proposition for many employees. Moreover, for the past 20 years it has also been somewhat unfashionable. Employers have realised that greater productivity it possible using a strategy of what

Friedman (1977) called responsible autonomy. This is very much the Theory Y approach of McGregor (1960), which assumes that human beings welcome the opportunity to take responsibility for their working lives: to be empowered. This school of thought is that of the human relations school. The assumptions on which its advocates' writing is based are summarised below:

- individuals have needs to satisfy in organisations; they do not exist in order to satisfy the purposes of the organisation;
- organisations and individuals both bring needs to the relationship; when they fit then both prosper;
- democratic leadership is the best way to ensure such a fit;
- openness and participation is the best way to demonstrate such leadership (Fineman and Mangham, 1987).

The views of Walton (1985) have also been influential for the past 20 years. He advocates that managerial policies of mutuality (where employers and employees share goals and agree on the means to achieve these goals) rather than direct control will elicit employee commitment, which in turn will generate both better economic performance and greater human development.

But it is misleading to think of 'hard' performance management as simply part of the apparatus of direct control. It may be that 'soft' performance management is equally controlling even if aligned to the principles of responsible autonomy. The performance management, which applies to UK schoolteachers, is a good example of a scheme which gives some autonomy to teachers in the controlling performance management processes; nonetheless it is an attempt by management to impose accountability for individual job performance upon employees who traditionally have not had to experience such measures.

What managers practising strategies of direct control and responsible autonomy have in common is that they both assume that their particular strategy will yield the best results in terms of organisational performance. When we think about management control we tend to think about direct control, but if the purpose of responsible autonomy is to elicit more effective employee performance, as Walton suggests, then it is equally controlling. It is just that it has a face, which is rather more acceptable in the twenty-first century.

Performance management and assumed employee compliance

The issue of management control is closely aligned with that of the assumption in much modern HR thinking, that when employees are given the 'right' treatment in terms of HR policies then positive outcomes will follow. The treatment of performance management in this chapter so far tends to follow this assumption. It gives little thought to the notion that employees simply will object to it in principle or (more likely) in practice. This objection may take the form of outright dissent, as with the National Union of Teachers' threat of strike action when the scheme was introduced (BBC Online, 1999). Alternatively, disgruntled employees (and their managers, for that matter) may simply 'go through the motions' with no meaningful results.

Much HRM thought and action is based on the principle of unitarism, which sees the employees of the organisation as a team, unified by a common purpose with all employees pursuing the same goal. It does not admit that there may be competing interests in the organisation, most relevantly between managers and employees. For many employees, the thought that they will readily commit to the goals of the organisation is simply fanciful. Their principal interest is their own personal concerns, such as family and career, and the role of their current employment is simply a means to an end.

The likelihood is that most employees are in favour of policies which recognise good and bad performance, and see these as intrinsically fair in principle. The problems arise when the implementation of such policies is perceived by employees as unfair. The principle of organisational justice (Greenberg, 1987) puts great emphasis upon procedures being perceived as fair and the way in which any benefits (e.g. pay and promotion) flow from management policies as being distributed fairly. Much of the hostility, or more likely apathy, towards performance management implementation stems from a lack of organisational justice.

Performance management and the danger of prescription

This chapter cannot be concluded without a reference to the dangers of prescribing particular performance management policies, procedures and processes: such prescription will be explicit in the solutions advanced by some management writers and consultants and even may be implicit in this chapter. An example of this is schemes that are centrally imposed by governments on employee groups such as teachers, university lecturers and doctors. This ignores the simple consideration that what may be appropriate for one school or university department or doctor's practice may be quite inappropriate for another. The concept of culture raises obvious points of difference, which those seeking to introducing performance management schemes would be foolish to ignore (Mabey *et al.*, 1998). Cultural differences may render performance management prescriptions questionable at national level (see Key Concepts 9.3), at the level of the organisation or department or occupation. The same may be said of structural differences. It has also become a discernible trend in HR prescriptive writing to assume an individualist perspective and ignore the possibility of trade union influence. There may be a case for this in many areas of the private sector where trade union recognition is increasingly limited but this is not so in the public sector. Trade union presence may, for example, constrain the ability of managers to introduce performance management, which includes individual performance-related pay, as this may be seen by trade union negotiators as undermining the principle of collective bargaining.

Ending the chapter by sounding these warnings makes the point that the introduction of performance management in itself will not guarantee that the part it is designed to play in delivering an effective HR strategy will be a success without careful consideration of the context in which it is managed and the way in which it is conducted. Indeed, this serves as reinforcement of the point made throughout this book: that effective SHRM depends upon the co-existence of various HR activities which are mutually reinforcing. There is little doubt in our minds that performance management plays a crucial role in this set of HR activities.

Self-Check and Reflect Questions 9.6

What other potential problems may be relevant to the introduction or implementation of performance management?

Summary

- Performance management is an umbrella term to describe not a single activity but a range of activities that may be gathered together to enhance organisational performance.

- Although the performance indicators approach to performance management has proliferated in many organisations, it offers a restricted perspective on performance management.

- Performance management may be linked to the organisation's strategy through horizontal and vertical integration.

- Performance management has the facility to change the culture and therefore the working practices of organisations as part of a concerted effort to generate change through its role as part of an organisation's 'high performance' HR strategy.

- An important way of integrating the HR practices is to use the skills, behaviours and attitudes necessary to deliver effective job performance as a way of assessing individual success.

- Among the reasons for the growth in importance of performance management, are the desire to achieve grater organisational effectiveness and the dissatisfaction with traditional performance appraisal.

- The performance management systems model includes inputs such as external and internal contexts and employee skills; processes including setting objectives and 360-degree appraisal; HR outputs such as performance plans and pay awards; and enhanced organisational performance.

- Included in the major conceptual flaws in performance management thinking are the potential preoccupation with management control, the assumed compliance of employees and the dangers of prescribing a particular model of performance management without paying due regard to the organisation's context.

Follow-up study suggestions

Using an organisation with which you are familiar, which may be one in which you are currently employed or have worked for, or one known to you:

- Identify the range of activities that may be deemed to be part of what is termed in the chapter 'performance management' and assess the extent to which those activities may be termed 'strategic'.

- Identify which are the most important skills, behaviours and attitudes to be developed by employees in the organisation and the degree to which performance management contributes towards this development.

- Using the performance management systems model in Figure 9.2, identify the key inputs, processes and HR outputs in the organisation's performance management system.

- Define what may be termed 'effective' performance management and evaluate the degree to which performance management in the organisation meets this definition.

Suggestions for research topics

Using an organisation with which you are familiar, which may be one in which you are currently employed or have worked for, or one known to you:

- How do managers manage employees' performance? An investigation of the formal activities embraced by performance management and the extent to which they play a secondary role to the informal day-to-day management of employee performance.
- What role does performance management play in the management of change?
- A study of the skills and behaviours required by managers to obtain the maximum benefit from 360-degree appraisal.

Case Study

Performance management at Tyco

Tyco employs 260,000 people in the USA and in more than 100 countries around the world. It is:

- a global leader in passive electronic components and major producer of active components;
- the number one worldwide company offering fire and security solutions;
- one of the largest medical device and disposables companies in the world;
- a leader in niche markets for plastics and adhesives products;
- the world's number one producer of sprinklers, valves and actuation.

The overall aim of Tyco's performance management system is to contribute to the company's goals of achieving operational excellence and becoming one unified company. The aim is to unite Tyco teams throughout the world into a single operating company with a healthy culture characterised by alignment and growth opportunities.

Performance management at Tyco has three particularly significant features. First, it is easy to understand; second, it empowers employees to take an active and influential part in the processes; and, third, it is designed to assess not only the results that employees achieve but the way in which these results are achieved.

Role and responsibilities of the participants in the performance management process

The handbook which outlines the details of the scheme makes it clear that employees, managers and the company have crucial responsibilities if the scheme is to operate effectively.

Employees must:

- work hard to achieve their goals;
- take responsibility for their own professional development;
- solicit, listen to and act upon feedback;
- assess their performance objectively.

Managers must:

- set and clarify employees' goals;
- support employee development and possible career progression;
- provide useful, frequent and candid feedback;
- assess performance fairly.

Tyco must:

- make performance management and employee development a business priority;

- ensure fairness, consistency and process integrity across all businesses;
- provide tools and processes to develop skills and behaviours that enhance performance.

Tyco's performance management system

Tyco's performance management system is a simple yet powerful three-step process. The three steps are:

1. setting goals;
2. providing feedback; and
3. conducting the assessment.

Setting goals

Performance goals should flow from the top of the organisation down through the various layers (e.g. departments) to be expressed in individual employee goals. Advice given to employees in the performance management handbook states: 'if you cannot state how your performance goals support the accomplishment of higher level goals, then your goals should be carefully re-examined'. The goal-setting sequence starts at the commencement of the fiscal year. At that point there is a meeting between the employee (or group of employees) and the manager at which departmental goals are discussed. The employee then uses these goals to write his or her individual goals. These are then submitted to the manager for approval. Employees and managers are reminded of the importance of reviewing goals throughout the year, as the goals may need to change to reflect changing business priorities. The goals are expected to be SMART (specific, measurable, agreed, realistic and time-related). Typically they may relate to factors such as: earnings before interest and taxes, revenue, operational excellence, cash, growth and safety. Each employee usually has between two and four performance goals.

In addition to performance goals, employees have development goals. These are individual to the employee and focus on the skills, knowledge and behavioural changes necessary to accomplish performance goals or prepare for future assignments. Typically, each employee has one or two development goals which may concentrate on developing strengths or improving development needs.

Providing feedback

Both managers and employees have responsibility for requesting and providing feedback. Employees are encouraged to request feedback at formal performance review meetings and as part of informal day-to-day conversations. Managers are reminded that providing feedback is a core responsibility of their job and that employees look to them for guidance, encouragement and advice. Managers are expected to encourage their employees to ask for feedback by letting them know that they as managers are open and keen to provide information on their employees' performance. At the same time, managers should ask for feedback from their employees on their performance as managers.

Conducting the assessment

This third part of the performance management process has three steps:

1. completing/updating the profile form;
2. writing the self-assessment;
3. a collaborative discussion between the individual employee and the manager.

Completing/updating the profile form
The profile form is an internal curriculum vitae (cv). It is annually updated by the employee and can be used in internal promotions and job transfers throughout the company. As with any cv, it contains details of Tyco and general work experience, qualifications and training undertaken, etc.

Writing the self-assessment
This step involves the completion of an assessment form which, like the profile form, should be no more than one side of paper. The employee is asked to summarise in bullet points his or her performance for the review year. Also, employees are asked to summarise their performance against Tyco's four key behaviours: integrity, excellence, teamwork and accountability. These values are supported by nine key behaviours:

1. champions integrity and trust;
2. managerial courage;
3. customer focus;
4. learning/change agility;
5. building effective teams;

6. managing vision and purpose;

7. managing diversity;

8. drive for results;

9. business acumen.

Employees are asked to note short examples of how they demonstrated (or failed to demonstrate) each behaviour. Examples are provided in the performance management handbook.

The self-assessment form also asks employees to include a brief description of their perceived strengths and development needs and one or two 'key questions'. These questions usually focus on contributions and flow from the perceived strengths and development needs (e.g. can I learn to provide candid, direct feedback?). Finally, there is a section for 'best next moves' which is the outcome of a discussion between the employee and the manager about the employee's potential for a lateral move, transfer or promotion within the next two years.

A collaborative discussion between the individual employee and the manager

The final stage in Tyco's performance management process is a two-way discussion between manager and employee, focusing on the profile and self-assessment forms. The performance management handbook suggests the following order for the discussion:

- performance summary;
- Tyco values/behaviours;
- strengths and development needs;
- key questions;

- best next moves;
- development plan;
- summary categories.

At the conclusion of the discussion, both manager and employee sign the assessment form which signifies that a discussion has taken place, although this does not necessarily mean that total agreement was reached.

Case study questions

1. What action is needed to ensure that Tyco managers play their full part in ensuring that the performance management system is effective?

2. What action is needed to ensure that Tyco employees are equipped to gain the maximum benefit from the performance management system?

3. What should be the priority concerns of Tyco HR specialists in their attempt to ensure that the performance management system is fully integrated with other HR activities?

4. What problems may be encountered in applying a standardised performance management system throughout the 100 countries in which Tyco operate?

Acknowledgement

Thanks are due to Tyco Ltd., for permission to use this case, and to Joanna Binstead for her support.

10 Strategic human resource development: pot of gold or chasing rainbows?

Learning Outcomes

By the end of this chapter you should be able to:

- develop and discuss a continuum of strategic maturity upon which different approaches to Human resource development (HRD) can be located;

- identify and explain the major features of Strategic human resource development (SHRD) and organise these into a conceptual framework;

- analyse how systematic approaches to HRD can be accommodated in conceptual frameworks of SHRD;

- analyse the significance of the learning organisation and knowledge management to SHRD;

- critically review the rhetoric and reality of the role of managers as key SHRD stakeholders.

Introduction

Similar to other HR activities explored in this book, SHRD is not portrayed as something completely new but as an approach to developing an organisation's human resource capability that builds on earlier traditions. The majority of readers will already be familiar with the term training and development, widely recognised as one of the fundamental components of HR practice. Training and development can broadly be represented as a planned process designed to improve the current and future capacity of an organisation's human resources to work effectively through modifying their skills, knowledge and attitudes. The process is frequently portrayed as a cycle of four systematic stages running through: identifying training needs, planning and designing training interventions, implementing training and evaluating its outcomes.

More recently, the term training and development has been replaced by human resource development (HRD). At one level this may simply reflect more general shifts in HR terminology that mirror more closely the language of HRM. At another level, HRD reflects a significant development from its training and development traditions. Whereas training and development is normally driven by top-down, planned interventions, HRD incorporates, in addition, a greater focus on individual and organisational learning that can give rise to accidental as well as planned changes to the skill, knowledge and attitude base of employees.

SHRD arguably represents the latest extension of the training and development lineage where training and learning are strategically integrated, vertically to an organisation's strategic goals and horizontally to other HR activities. This moves training and development from a process that is largely directed at solving specific gaps in HR competences as they are identified to a potentially proactive activity directed at improving corporate effectiveness.

Although many other terms covering the same or similar territory can be found within the literature, in this chapter, unless referring directly to the work of others, the terms HRD and SHRD have been adopted. SHRD is used to cover all those situations where the focus is clearly strategic, and HRD is used where the various interventions that make up its approach do not have an explicit strategic focus. However, it is worth pointing out that although the chapter concentrates on exploring the intricacies of SHRD, and its potential to contribute to organisational effectiveness, opposing viewpoints on the worth of even its more basic forerunner HRD exist. You may wish to reflect on the two viewpoints presented below.

Most investment in HRD is a waste of money!

Such a stark hypothesis may seem to be a strange way to introduce a chapter on SHRD. However, as a statement designed to provoke argument, it is worthy of further consideration. In Practice 10.1 provides examples of those circumstances that tend to support such a position.

In Practice   10.1

HRD as a waste of money?

- Investment in HRD is viewed as an organisational luxury. In reality it represents little more than an extension of the benefits package. This viewpoint is exemplified where HRD is drastically cut back at the outset of economic downturn.

- Investment in HRD is systematically wasted. This arises through failures to reinforce off-the-job learning and skills development in the workplace or to cascade HRD outputs throughout the organisation.

- Investment in HRD reflects an act of faith. There is little attempt to evaluate its organisational benefits and bottom-line contribution or even to establish the criteria against which its organisational payback could be evaluated.

- Investment in HRD is targeted primarily at remedying identified employee deficiencies with little or no connection to organisation strategy and goals, thereby contributing little to the pursuit of sustained competitive advantage.

The potential for this somewhat depressing portrayal of HRD to become an organisational reality is reflected by Helen Milner, Executive Director of Learndirect (Milner, 2004). She argues that training investment is wasted by:

- failures to take up places on courses already paid for because staff are too busy to be released;

- undertaking comprehensive training programmes when only a small part is relevant to the trainee's job; and

- failures to transfer and evaluate learning as a result of inadequate debriefing.

HRD as a source of competitive advantage

The pessimistic picture painted above is in sharp contrast to examples that demonstrate how investment in HRD has been used as an important, if not the key, vehicle for turning round organisational fortunes. This is well illustrated by the National Training Award winner Hindle Power, reported on in 'In Practice' 10.2 below, and the chapter case where, for INA, investment in HRD became an inextricable component of strategy making.

In this chapter the emphasis is on the second viewpoint. The focus is on the strategic potential of HRD, and its emphasis on the promotion of a learning culture, to contribute to achieving sustainable competitive advantage. The chapter begins with an exploration of the HRD/SHRD interface in order to delineate the defining characteristics of SHRD and different levels of HRD strategic maturity. This surfaces the role of a learning culture as a central characteristic of SHRD and the chapter goes on to explore two recent HRD approaches related to this facet: the learning organisation and knowledge management. However, the development of SHRD and/or a learning culture is to a large extent dependent on the HRD role responsibilities of managers and how effectively they are performed. The chapter is therefore concluded with an exploration of the pivotal position played by managers, as HRD stakeholders, in facilitating or impeding the development of SHRD.

In Practice   10.2

Bottom-line benefits of SHRD – a case of business turnaround at Hindle Power

Hindle Power faced the threat of losing its major contract, representing 75 per cent of its income, if it did not improve its customer service significantly. It responded by investing heavily in HRD in order to survive and built a platform for future growth.

- The pursuit of Investors in People (IiP) was used as a catalyst for business planning and improvement with an emphasis on improving communication between line managers and their staff.
- Career planning was aligned to a new system of performance appraisal and led to the internal promotion of over 25 per cent of staff.
- A training budget was established for the first time and was sufficient to support up to 26 days' training per annum for every employee.
- HRD interventions focused on business management and IT skills, induction, customer care and, in conjunction with suppliers, product awareness.
- Non-work-related HRD was also supported as an adjunct to career planning because it was recognised that the learning derived would result in unplanned organisational benefits.

Over a four-year period, a loss-making company with a turnover of £6 million was back in profit with a turnover of £15 million and a transformation in its organisational culture.

Source: Littlefield (2000).

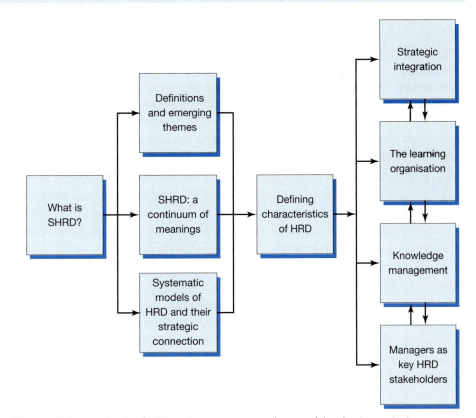

Figure 10.1 Mapping the SHRD territory: a summary diagram of the chapter content

Definitions and emerging themes

Definitions

The exploration of the HRD/SHRD territory begins, in Key Concepts 10.1, with a review of a number of definitions of the concepts. From these definitions a number of key themes that are used to inform later chapter sections are extracted.

Key Concepts	10.1

Definitions of the HRD/SHRD territory

'Human resource development encompasses activities and processes which are *intended* to have an impact on organisational and individual learning. The term assumes that organisations can be constructively conceived of as learning entities, and that the learning processes of both organisations and individuals are capable of influence and direction through deliberate and planned interventions. Thus, HRD is constituted by planned interventions in organisational and individual learning processes' (Stewart and McGoldrick, 1996: 1).

'A strategic approach to training and development can be depicted as one where all those involved are engaged in a connected, explicit and developmental purpose which helps to simultaneously fulfil an individual's learning goals and the organization's mission' (Mabey *et al.*, 1998: 158).

'SHRD could thus be defined as the creation of a learning culture, within which a range of training, development and learning strategies both respond to corporate strategy and also help to shape and influence it. It is about meeting the organisation's existing needs, but it is also about helping the organisation to change and develop, to thrive and grow. It is the reciprocal, mutually enhancing, nature of the relationship between HRD and corporate strategy which lies at the heart of SHRD and at the heart of the development of a learning culture' (McCracken and Wallace, 2000: 288).

'Strategic HRD may be considered as a range of culturally sensitive interventions linked vertically to business goals and strategy, and horizontally to other HR business activities, to actively encourage and support employee learning, commitment and involvement throughout the organisation' (Myers and Kirk, 2005: 359).

Key themes

From the above definitions, a number of key SHRD themes can be identified. Perhaps not surprisingly the most dominant theme arising is that of external or vertical strategic integration. However, this tends to be limited to a downstream, vertical strategic relationship where HRD interventions are designed to support the achievement of an organisation's mission and its explicit strategic objectives. In Practice 10.3 provides an example of this downstream, relationship.

However, what is lacking from this interpretation of strategic fit is the two-way, mutually supporting relationship that exists when HR activities also operate upstream of business strategy. This notion of two-way vertical strategic integration surfaces in the

In Practice   **10.3**

The use of SHRD to support a hotel's customer service strategy

René Angoujard, general manager of the Novotel London West hotel, challenges the commonly held view that training is a waste of time and money because it leads to staff leaving once trained. He presents a stark alternative: 'What if you don't train them and they stay?' (Morrison, 2004: 29). For him, training was at the heart of a culture change programme prompted by: client dissatisfaction; poor staff morale; a staff turnover rate of 78 per cent; and the need to profit from a major refurbishment programme and market repositioning of the hotel from a tourist to business customer base. The hotel had, in his opinion, lost sight of its service ethic and a 'comprehensive customer service strategy' was used to forge a service culture (Morrison, 2004: 29).

HRD interventions included formal training around a set of core service behaviours and the use of selected staff drawn from all levels of the hotel's hierarchy to act as on-the-job exemplars and coaches. Initial returns on HRD investment include: a 92 per cent drop in customer complaints; a 10 per cent increase in sales; achievement of a repeat booking level of 70 per cent; winning a number of training and customer service awards; and reducing staff turnover by over half to 34 per cent.

Source: Morrison (2004: 29).

more recent definitions. The capacity of SHRD to influence and shape corporate strategy in a mutually enhancing relationship is central to McCracken and Wallace's (2000) definition. Myers and Kirk (2005) refer to vertical linkage, which in many frameworks of SHRM assumes a two-way relationship. This fuller interpretation of strategic fit underscores much of the contemporary literature on SHRD and receives particular attention in Chapters 1 and 7. As will be seen a little later, this two-way vertical integration has been captured in a number of models of SHRD and can be seen reflected in Figures 10.3 and 10.7.

Another dominant theme arising from the above definitions is a focus on learning at the level of the individual and/or organisation. This finds particular expression when SHRD is promoted as the vehicle for establishing a learning culture (Stewart and McGoldrick, 1996; McCracken and Wallace, 2000) which resonates with the notion of the learning organisation. Learning is also interpreted as the vehicle for promoting the development of individuals towards their full potential so that there is mutuality between individual and organisational growth. This begins to surface a third theme, that to be effective SHRD has to respond to and reconcile the needs of a variety of different stakeholders. These emergent themes of: strategic integration; learning as an organisational orientation; and different stakeholder perspectives are central to the concept of SHRD and are adopted here as the main points of focus for the chapter.

Self-Check and Reflect Questions   **10.1**

Based on the story so far, what do you think are the essential characteristics of SHRD?

SHRD: a continuum of meanings and maturity

Characteristics of SHRD

In the analysis below, it is shown how McCracken and Wallace (2000) develop Garavan's (1991) nine characteristics of strategic HRD to arrive at a revised definition and model of SHRD. They present their construct of SHRD as being very strategically mature and compare and contrast this with HRD and training where, in their view, strategic maturity progressively decreases. In this sense their ideas on the development of SHRD can be presented as a continuum, working through training and HRD to the fullest expression of strategic maturity represented by SHRD (see Figure 10.2).

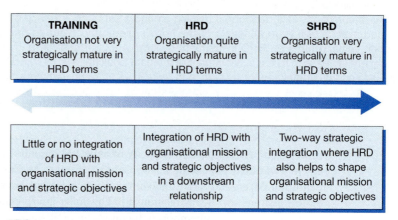

TRAINING	HRD	SHRD
Organisation not very strategically mature in HRD terms	Organisation quite strategically mature in HRD terms	Organisation very strategically mature in HRD terms
Little or no integration of HRD with organisational mission and strategic objectives	Integration of HRD with organisational mission and strategic objectives in a downstream relationship	Two-way strategic integration where HRD also helps to shape organisational mission and strategic objectives

Figure 10.2 A continuum of HRD strategic maturity
Source: adapted from McCracken and Wallace (2000).

This section uses the concept of a continuum of HRD strategic maturity as a useful way of getting to grips with what is meant by SHRD and further develops the three positions depicted along the continuum presented in Figure 10.2. It starts with a review of the work of Garavan (1991) and McCracken and Wallace (2000) before going on to explore how the concept of a continuum can be further developed within the context of SHRD. This will include going back to the very bedrock of HRD, as represented by the systematic approach to training. As identified in the chapter introduction, many readers will be familiar with this systematic approach and its depiction as a cycle of activities or stages and, in the following section, this is further developed to demonstrate its strategic possibilities.

Based on a comprehensive review of the literature, Garavan identified nine key characteristics that for him defined SHRD practice. These are summarised in Key Concepts 10.2.

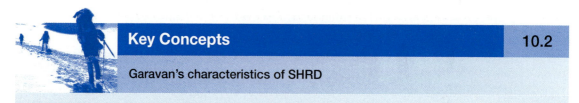

Key Concepts   10.2

Garavan's characteristics of SHRD

1. *Integration with organisational missions and goals* – where HRD is systematically integrated with wider business planning in a supporting role so that sight is not lost of organisational strategic objectives when developing HRD interventions.

2. *Top management support* – where the strategic integration of HRD requires the active support and participation of senior management in order to become a reality.

3. *Environmental scanning* – where the HRD function has the capacity to continuously analyse the external environment in order to identify both opportunities and threats to business and HRD strategies and thereby reinforce access to top table planning discussions.

4. *HRD plans and policies* – where systematic integration requires the formulation of HRD plans and policies to support wider business needs. For this planning to assume strategic status it must incorporate environmental scanning and scenario planning which, when used to regularly and systematically inform strategy formulation, can lead to HRD assuming a proactive, shaping function rather than simply a reactionary one.

5. *Line manager commitment and involvement* – consistent with the development of SHRM, the line manager takes centre stage in identifying and addressing the HRD needs of subordinates. This requires his or her active commitment and participation, where any relegation of their HRD roles and responsibilities in their list of managerial priorities will jeopardise its successful delivery.

6. *Existence of complementary HRM activities* – these cover such areas as improving HRP, recruiting higher-calibre employees, more exacting performance appraisal and identification of HRD needs, and individually and organisationally focused career development plans.

7. *Expanded trainer role* – where to support a strategic orientation HRD specialists need to develop their roles to become more proactive, interventionist, central and influential. This is likely to be embodied in the movement from training provider to a consultant, innovator role.

8. *Recognition of culture* – where the onus is on the HRD function to develop its activities in line not only with organisational strategy but also with organisation culture. This includes the key role of shaping HRD activities to maintain and change corporate culture.

9. *Emphasis on evaluation* – where, in order to develop its strategic relevance, the HRD function must evaluate its activities so that its strategic contribution and relevance can be assessed.

Source: Garavan (1991).

Self-Check and Reflect Questions   10.2

Before reading on, how would you critique Garavan's depiction of SHRD as summarised in Key Concepts 10.2?

Although Garavan's early work provides a very useful starting point to an exploration of SHRD, it can be critiqued on a number of grounds. These are summarised below:

- a specialist HRD function surfaces as a key SHRD stakeholder when in reality such a function may be absent from many organisations;

- the prominence given to the specialist HRD function downplays the significance of managers as SHRD stakeholders;

- this is at odds with the SHRM construct, which emphasises devolvement of responsibility to line managers;

- the potential for conflict between HRD specialists and managers as SHRD protagonists is not addressed;

- strategic integration is reduced to a vertical, downstream relationship that overlooks the importance of horizontal integration and the multi-dimensional, two-way interpretation of vertical strategic alignment;

- a very managerialistic standpoint is adopted which relegates the importance of the employee stakeholder perspective; and

- more prosaic areas such as needs analysis and approaches to HRD delivery are excluded from the analysis suggesting that they have little or no input into the training/SHRD debate.

McCracken and Wallace (2000) used Garavan's (1991) strategic portrayal of HRD as the starting point for their redefinition of SHRD. Following their review of his work, they concluded that, taken together, his identified characteristics of SHRD portrayed an approach that is not fully mature in terms of its strategic credentials. They went on to develop each one of his nine characteristics to reflect what a higher level of strategic maturity is for them. Their analysis is summarised in Key Concepts 10.3.

In some ways this reworking and redefinition of Garavan's characteristics of SHRD goes some way to addressing the earlier critique of his work. There is particularly more emphasis on the nature and importance of senior and line management involvement with a commensurate reduction in the emphasis on the role of the HRD function. McCracken and Wallace's rhetoric also points to the potential for the development of closer working relationships between managers and HRD specialists. Their characterisation of strategic integration also adopts and emphasises the importance of two-way vertical and horizontal integration. However, their analysis could still be said to reflect four potential limitations inherent in Garavan's work:

1. There remains a presumption that a professional HRD function is operating as an important stakeholder in support of HRD. This is unlikely to be the case in many, particularly small, organisations.

2. Strategic integration is represented as a single, two-way, vertical construct that does not reflect the multi-dimensional construct discussed in earlier chapters (particularly 1, 7 and 8).

3. Their ideas appear to be even more managerialist where SHRD is viewed as being less about addressing employee needs and more about focusing on the strategic imperatives of the organisation.

4. Issues around the employee stakeholder role, HRD needs analysis and approaches to HRD delivery do not feature in their analysis. However, this is not surprising as they were using Garavan's initial propositions as the platform for their redefinition of SHRD and Garavan was silent on these areas.

In one important respect it could be argued that Garavan's analysis reflects a greater level of strategic maturity than that offered by McCracken and Wallace. In their treatment of HRD evaluation, McCracken and Wallace emphasise the need for evaluation to have a harder, quantifiable edge, whereas Garavan places stress on the need for evaluation to focus on the strategic relevance of HRD. On the basis that a harder focus on cost effectiveness is likely to be a constituent element of evaluating the strategic contribution of HRD, Garavan's analysis arguably reflects the greater degree of strategic maturity.

Key Concepts **10.3**

Characteristics of strategically mature HRD

McCracken and Wallace argue that:

1. True *strategic integration* arises only when SHRD shapes and influences an organisation's missions and goals as well as supporting their effective implementation.

2. Top *management support* is too passive to fully enact SHRD and that what is required is top management leadership.

3. Consistent with this leadership role and as part of its *environmental scanning* responsibilities, senior management should assume responsibility for analysing the HRD implications of external and internal environment changes and take over this role from HRD specialists.

4. The formulation of *HRD plans and policies*, although strategically oriented, reflects an operational emphasis. To achieve a more strategic focus requires the development of HRD strategies from which the policies and plans would flow.

5. *Line manager commitment and involvement*, while necessary, is insufficient to achieve true integration of HRD into their broader managerial responsibilities. To achieve this integration requires closer collaboration with HRD specialists and the development of strategic partnerships between them.

6. Similarly, the *existence of complementary HRM activities* is insufficient in that it downplays the need for their close integration under the SHRM umbrella. This makes more explicit the necessity to ally vertical integration with horizontal integration and anticipates the development of strategic partnerships between HRD specialists and their other SHRM colleagues.

7. The *expanded role for HRD specialists* needs to be further extended to elevate their facilitation of organisational change function to a leadership of change role.

8. Similarly, the HRD function needs to extend its *recognition of organisational culture*, where training activities are shaped, in part, by an awareness of the current cultural context, to a position where it actively influences culture and, when necessary, plays a central role in culture change.

9. That the *emphasis on evaluation* needs to be interpreted more rigorously to include a harder, quantifiable edge, where HRD activities are evaluated in terms of their cost-effectiveness.

Source: McCracken and Wallace (2000).

One important feature of McCracken and Wallace's work is the emphasis they place on the relationship between SHRD and the development or existence of a learning culture within the context of a learning organisation. They argue that 'the existence of a learning culture would seem to be crucial to the existence of SHRD and likewise any organization where HRD has a role in influencing culture probably already has a learning culture in place' (McCracken and Wallace, 2000: 285). This they see as reflecting a two-way relationship between learning and organisational culture. On the one hand a learning culture is 'a means of transmitting culture' and on the other can be 'a product of [organisational] culture' (McCracken and Wallace, 2000: 285). As learning becomes institutionalised and an integral component of organisation development so, it is argued, the organisation adopts the characteristics of the learning organisation. This significant feature of SHRD is subjected to more detailed scrutiny later in the chapter.

Towards a continuum of HRD strategic maturity

The above analysis leads McCracken and Wallace to the view that SHRD embodies a proactive function where the emphasis is on shaping the strategic focus of the organisation supported by a strong learning culture. SHRD is characterised as being very mature in terms of strategic integration. In contrast, they interpret Garavan's analysis as representing HRD where the strategic connection is mainly conducted in a downstream supporting role within a relatively weak learning culture. HRD is characterised as being quite mature in terms of strategic integration. This they further contrast with training where 'The organization is strategically immature in HRD terms and has no discernible learning culture' (McCracken and Wallace, 2000: 286). Their representation of training as the provision of an ad hoc diet of standardised offerings is justified by its evident lack of connection with any of the nine characteristics as identified by Garavan (1991). This places training at the opposite end to SHRD on the continuum of HRD strategic maturity depicted in Figure 10. 2 and permits a clear comparison along this continuum between training, HRD and SHRD. The training end of the continuum reflects more a situation where its interventions are viewed as remedial and are designed to make good employee deficiencies, or fixing problems once they have arisen, in order to increase organisational efficiency (Garavan *et al.*, 1995; Daniels, 2003). These positions along the continuum of HRD strategic maturity are portrayed in Figure 10. 3.

Training and SHRD as a bi-polar construct

Notwithstanding the analysis above, the HRD territory is more commonly interpreted as a bi-polar construct with training at one end and SHRD at the other (see for example Muhlemeyer and Clarke, 1997; Horwitz, 1999; Holden, 2004). Figure 10.4 uses the introduction of new technology as an example to differentiate the two ends of this construct. At one end, training interventions are reactive and are directed at resolving specific problems resulting from the introduction of the new technology (what Muhlemeyer and Clarke refer to as problem-directed training and development). At the other end, SHRD interventions are proactive and help shape the decision-making process surrounding the introduction of the new technology (what Muhlemeyer and Clarke refer to as strategically oriented training and development). At the SHRD end, evaluation of HRD interventions operates as a continuous loop not only to support the introduction of new technology but also as an input into wider organisational learning that might impact, for example, on such areas as change and project management.

Muhlemeyer and Clarke's (1997) two approaches to HRD can be illustrated by reference to the introduction of computerised information systems into workplaces. This 'new technology' has been used, for example, by many organisations through the development and introduction of computerised personnel information systems or to underpin the operation of public sector bodies, such as the Child Support Agency and the Inland Revenue. The story line is that too frequently the technology fails to deliver expected efficiencies, leads to excessive backlogs and may even end up as a grossly expensive white elephant that has to be replaced by another computerised information system. Using Muhlemeyer and Clarke's analysis it would be interesting to know in such cases whether HRD was problem-directed or strategically oriented. Although only anecdotal, the authors' experience is that such computerised systems are introduced with little thought about the workforce's capability to operate them. This leads to operational

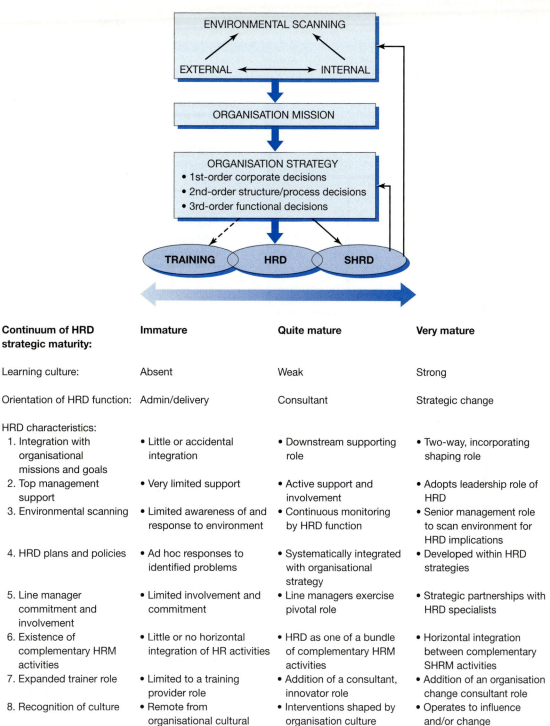

Continuum of HRD strategic maturity:	Immature	Quite mature	Very mature
Learning culture:	Absent	Weak	Strong
Orientation of HRD function:	Admin/delivery	Consultant	Strategic change
HRD characteristics:			
1. Integration with organisational missions and goals	• Little or accidental integration	• Downstream supporting role	• Two-way, incorporating shaping role
2. Top management support	• Very limited support	• Active support and involvement	• Adopts leadership role of HRD
3. Environmental scanning	• Limited awareness of and response to environment	• Continuous monitoring by HRD function	• Senior management role to scan environment for HRD implications
4. HRD plans and policies	• Ad hoc responses to identified problems	• Systematically integrated with organisational strategy	• Developed within HRD strategies
5. Line manager commitment and involvement	• Limited involvement and commitment	• Line managers exercise pivotal role	• Strategic partnerships with HRD specialists
6. Existence of complementary HRM activities	• Little or no horizontal integration of HR activities	• HRD as one of a bundle of complementary HRM activities	• Horizontal integration between complementary SHRM activities
7. Expanded trainer role	• Limited to a training provider role	• Addition of a consultant, innovator role	• Addition of an organisation change consultant role
8. Recognition of culture	• Remote from organisational cultural considerations	• Interventions shaped by organisation culture	• Operates to influence and/or change organisational culture
9. Emphasis on evaluation	• Little evident evaluation	• Cost effectiveness interventions evaluated	• Strategic contribution and relevance of interventions evaluated

Figure 10.3 Mapping the HRD strategic maturity continuum
Source: adapted from Garavan (1991); McCracken and Wallace (2000).

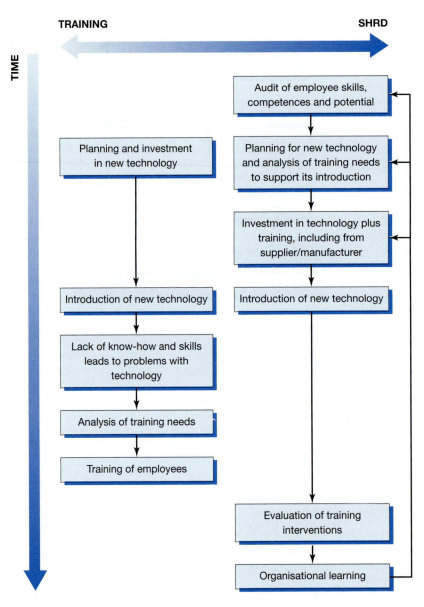

Figure 10. 4 Problem-directed versus strategically oriented HRD in the introduction of new technology
Source: adapted from Muhlemeyer and Clarke (1997).

failures that pinpoint the gaps in employee capability that are addressed retrospectively through problem-directed HRD. It is a moot point as to whether the adoption of a strategically oriented approach to HRD would lead to fewer operational failures and, perhaps, the saving of millions of pounds of taxpayers' money.

Perhaps somewhat depressingly for the adherents of SHRD, Muhlemeyer and Clarke found little evidence of strategically oriented practice. Citing a study by the University of Chemnitz (1995), they reported that only 18 per cent of organisations 'strategically plan their training and development requirements', with the vast majority of companies reporting that 'planning for training and development occurred only as a result of problems arising in the workplace' (Muhlemeyer and Clarke, 1997: 5). This pessimistic picture of SHRD take-up is echoed in analysis of empirical evidence reported elsewhere and particularly suggests that few organisations are actively developing a learning culture or an HRD infrastructure to support such a development (Horwitz, 1999; Ashton and Felstead, 2001; Harrison and Kessels, 2004). Taken at face value, this suggests that whatever the rhetoric underpinning the value of SHRD, strategically immature approaches to HRD dominate practice.

Systematic training approaches as a route to SHRD

The traditional, systematic approach to training

Having presented HRD strategic maturity as both a continuum and bi-polar construct, it is probably safe to say that readers will be more familiar with the training end of both these representations and will be well acquainted with what is commonly referred to as the systematic approach to training (or HRD, using the terminology adopted in this chapter). This approach to HRD is frequently depicted as a cycle of activities (as modelled in Figure 10.5) comprising:

- identification of HRD needs;
- planning and designing HRD interventions to meet identified needs;
- implementing the planned HRD interventions; and
- evaluating the outcomes of these interventions.

Such widely recognised and understood frameworks underpin the approach adopted by many organisations and can be illustrated by a couple of short examples. First, the extension of discrimination legislation to incorporate ageism will particularly impact on managerial behaviour. The identification of training needs may point to a need for managers to become conversant with the legislation and how it impacts on the way they manage their human resources, for example promotion decisions. HRD interventions to address these needs will be developed and implemented. The success of the HRD

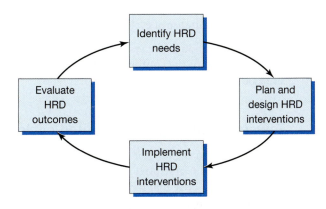

Figure 10.5 The systematic HRD model
Sources: Gibb and Megginson (2001); El-Sawed (2002).

interventions may then be evaluated in terms of the number of grievances and employment tribunal cases arising from age discrimination. Second, a move towards SHRM anticipates the devolvement of much of the responsibility for HR to line managers. Their performance appraisals may throw up a lack of competence to perform this role, with HRD needs in, say, employee involvement, giving and receiving feedback, interviewing, etc. emerging. HRD interventions to address these needs will be developed and implemented and their effectiveness perhaps assessed through the next cycle of performance appraisals.

However, as with so much else in the SHRM literature, the apparent simplicity of this HRD perspective can conceal a number of underlying complexities. A number of examples can be used to illustrate this point:

- Identification of HRD needs at its most basic level may be simply about identifying employee deficiencies related to their job performance. In contrast, at its broadest level of interpretation, the identification of HRD needs may adopt a strategic orientation. Here business strategies and goals are the starting point for an approach to HRD needs analysis that then cascades down the organisation to ensure integration between these needs and those of business units, workgroups and individuals. Indeed this approach is an important dimension of performance management as discussed in Chapter 9 and is captured in Holden's (2004: 318) depiction of the training cycle with his inclusion of the three sequential stages of 'organisation strategy', 'HRM strategy' and 'training development strategy'.

- The application of learning theory is needed both to inform the design of HRD interventions and to ensure that the method of HRD delivery matches (or develops) the learning styles of participants. Learning is thus critical to the HRD cycle.

- The evaluation stage of the cycle may be restricted to the lower levels of evaluation hierarchies or may alternatively vary across the whole range. Using Reid and Barrington's (1999) hierarchy, this might mean that the evaluation stage only measures the reactions of participants to their training or whether trainees have learned what was intended. Alternatively, the evaluation might range from these lower levels to the ultimate level where it seeks to assess the extent to which HRD interventions generate organisational benefits.

- When practised as a continuous cycle, the systematic HRD model mirrors the characteristics of the action research approach to evaluation as discussed in Chapter 4. This is also reflected in the HRD loops depicted in Figures 10.6 and 10.7 below, and echoes the strategic importance of evaluation captured in the models of SHRD discussed earlier.

Therefore, although the systematic HRD model may be thought of as residing at the less mature end of the continuum, it too can be developed to reflect different levels of strategic maturity.

Towards a strategically oriented cycle of HRD activities

This extension in the level of HRD strategic maturity is well illustrated by the work of Muhlemeyer and Clarke (1997). They are highly critical of the problem-directed application of the HRD cycle that for them epitomises the approach adopted by the majority of organisations. Their critique envisages a potential situation where failures to effectively transfer the know-how acquired through off-the-job training into the workplace means that 'every investment in training, whatever it costs, is a waste of money' (Muhlemeyer and Clarke, 1997: 5). They hold that their interpretation of the training cycle (illustrated in Figure 10.6) encapsulates a strategic orientation. This can be found particularly in their emphasis on the whole cycle being driven by organisational needs and securing knowledge transfer, and its exploitation, throughout the whole organisation. Their emphasis on knowledge transfer prevents HRD outputs being simply locked up in the heads of those directly involved in the training intervention and makes them available for others to utilise.

Figure 10.6 A strategically-oriented cycle of HRD activities

The importance they attach to knowledge transfer is summed up by their conclusion that it is 'this particular part of the training process, the transfer and subsequent use of know-how, that can be the key to success' (Muhlemeyer and Clarke, 1997: 7). This resonates with the principles underpinning a learning culture and, more recently, that of knowledge management. For them the development of organisational know-how occurs when the outputs from HRD interventions ('direct participant training') are disseminated and absorbed within the organisation ('know-how transfer and indirect participant training') which requires active organisational facilitation in order to overcome resistance to change (Muhlemeyer and Clarke, 1997: 9). However, the extent to which their ideas move the HRD cycle along the continuum of strategic maturity is restricted by two factors. First, the strategic connection represents one-way, downstream integration where HRD is cast in a supporting role. Second, the last of their four stages, controlling HRD and development, reflects an approach to evaluation that includes cost–benefit analysis but falls short of assessing effectiveness at the ultimate level of organisational contribution. Although less detailed in its depiction, this arguably places their positioning of training and development as a strategic task alongside McCracken and Wallace's (2000) portrayal of HRD, that is quite mature in strategic terms.

Harrison's (1993a) cycle of HRD activities moves further along the continuum of strategic maturity through its aim 'to transform people's learning and development into a corporate, business-led activity, relying on a collaboration between key parties to generate information, agree on strategies and plans and monitor, evaluate and act on outcomes'. Her portrayal of HRD, illustrated in Figure 10.7, carries many of the hallmarks of SHRD reflected in the later work of McCracken and Wallace (2000). It:

- has a long-term perspective;
- exhibits a heavy emphasis on learning;
- elevates evaluation to incorporate organisational learning;
- places the development of HRD plans and activities within a learning strategy;
- translates corporate vision, mission and goals into business strategies and key business processes from which employee development needs and learning strategies are sourced;
- is responsive to changing circumstances through its accommodation of emergent needs;
- addresses the potential for conflict between HRD stakeholders through forging agreement on responsibilities between them;
- anticipates two-way strategic integration where the output of corporate learning evaluation operates as an input to corporate vision, mission and goals; and
- is responsive to both the external and internal operating environment of the organisation.

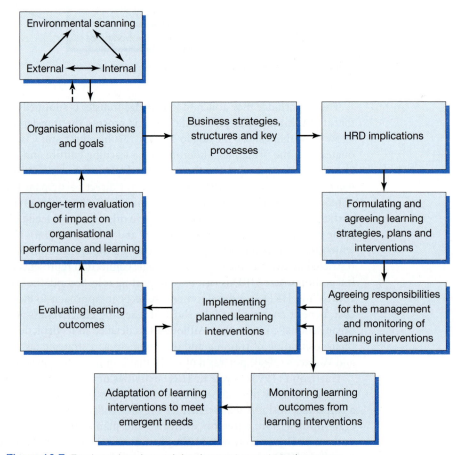

Figure 10.7 Employee learning and development as a strategic process
Source: adapted from Harrison (1993a: 326).

By way of example, an organisation may detect that it is entering a period of increased turbulence and instability in its field of operations (e.g. package holiday companies, branches of retailing such as Marks and Spencer, and the INA case featured at the end of the chapter). A response might be to develop a competitive strategy around innovation and recognition of the need to develop an employee capability and culture in the future that is adaptable and flexible. This then becomes the prime focus for HRD interventions to be supported by the parallel development of a learning organisation.

A revised continuum of HRD strategic maturity

These three depictions of systematic cycles of HRD activities broadly correspond to the levels of strategic maturity represented earlier by training, HRD and SHRD. However, while these positions on the continuum arguably cover the majority of HRD practice evidenced in organisations, they do not represent the full range of possibilities. Drawing further on the HRD literature, it is possible to delineate further positions along the continuum of strategic maturity as set out in Key Concepts 10.4, which also serve to extend the two extremes of the continuum.

Key Concepts 10.4

Levels of strategic maturity in HRD practice

1. No systematic training where employee development is likely to be ad hoc and at times accidental.
2. Isolated tactical training (as reflected by Muhlemeyer and Clarke's (1997) problem-directed approach).
3. Training integrated with operational management as part of planned structures for skill and career development.
4. Training as a vehicle for implementing corporate strategy and achieving change in a downstream, supporting role.
5. Training and learning as a vehicle for shaping strategy through two-way strategic integration.
6. Training and learning as a process through which strategy is formulated.
7. Learning and development processes are strategically directed to building and enhancing the organisation's core competences as the source of competitive advantage.

Sources: Burgoyne (1988); Lee (1996); Walton (1999).

The notion that SHRD can represent the process through which strategy can be formulated is developed by Luoma (2000). In an alternative approach to delineating different types of strategic integration, he identifies three HRD variants. The first – HRD driven by needs – adopts the familiar downstream stance where the strategic integration of HRD is defined by its ability to equip employees with the skills, knowledge and attitudes necessary to support the achievement of organisation objectives. The role of HRD here is to identify skill performance gaps that might frustrate the achievement of organisational strategy and then to close the gaps through appropriate HRD interventions. The second – HRD driven by opportunities – replaces this internal focus with one that concentrates on importing HRD strategies from the 'outer world of employee development' to act 'as catalysts for mental growth in organizations' (Luoma, 2000: 772–773). Cited examples include HRD associated with business process analysis, teamwork and total quality management (TQM) where their importation is designed not only to support the implementation of current organisational strategy but also to provide the capacity to orchestrate strategic and culture change. The third – HRD driven by capabilities – focuses on developing employee capabilities as the source of and route to competitive advantage. This is consistent with the resource-based theory of the firm and core competences discussed in earlier chapters. It is these organisational capabilities that become 'the primary object of strategy, and managerial attention should be focused on factors that support the capabilities' (Luoma, 2000: 775). These approaches, when operated in tandem, can, respectively, help support the efficient maintenance of the strategic status quo, provide the basis for new or revised strategic thinking or form the very basis of competitive strategy itself.

Taking all these perspectives into account, it is now possible to revise the continuum of HRD strategic maturity and identify the defining characteristics of points along it (Figure 10.8).

Increasing levels of strategic maturity in HRD

NO SYSTEMATIC TRAINING	ISOLATED TACTICAL TRAINING	SYSTEMATIC TRAINING	HRD	SHRD	SHRD+
• Ad hoc • Incidental	• Problem directed • Reactive	• Planned cycle of activities • Focus on employee needs	• Focus on needs arising from strategy • Downstream support role	• Two-way strategic integration • Contribution to strategy formulation	• The process through which strategy is formulated • Employee capabilities as the route to competitive advantage
Lee (1996)	Lee (1996) Muhlemeyer and Clarke (1997)	Gibb and Meggison (2001) El-Sawed (2002)	Garravan (1991) Muhlemeyer and Clarke (1997) Mabey et al. (1998)	Harrison (1993) McCracken and Wallace (2000)	Lee (1996) Luoma (2000)

Figure 10.8 Revised continuum of HRD strategic maturity

Defining characteristics of SHRD

Earlier in the chapter, three themes that emerged from an analysis of definitions of SHRD were identified: strategic integration; the centrality of a learning culture; and different stakeholder perspectives. The subsequent analysis of SHRD against different levels of strategic maturity and models of systematic HRD cycles not only reinforces these themes but builds on them to the point where it can be argued that they represent the defining characteristics of SHRD.

Strategic integration

Starting with strategic integration, it is not surprising that underpinning the concept of SHRD are the principles of vertical and horizontal strategic fit. Although not capturing the whole range of the multi-dimensional nature of strategic integration discussed in Chapter 1, the foregoing analysis embraces:

- the importance of two-way strategic integration where SHRD both supports the achievement of organisational strategies in a downstream relationship and can act to help shape strategic formulation in an upstream relationship;
- the role of SHRD in supporting (and being supported by) other SHRM activities and strategies in a mutually reinforcing coherent package; and
- the contribution of SHRD to strategic change through its emphasis on and exploitation of a learning culture.

Although not yet made explicit in this chapter, earlier coverage of vertical strategic integration (particularly in Chapters 1, 7 and 8) has established the position that the concept applies to the three levels (or orders) of strategy identified by Purcell (1991) and that vertical integration can operate in a two-way relationship. These four strands, together with horizontal integration and strategic change, delineate the six different strands of strategic integration discussed in Chapters 1 and 7. In Chapter 8, worked examples were used to show how these different strands of strategic integration could be applied to strategic recruitment and selection. This provides a template that can be applied to all HRM interventions to evaluate their strategic pedigree and you are encouraged to think through how these six different types of strategic integration can be applied to SHRD. However, the Self-Check and Reflect Question that follows should help you to get started.

Self-Check and Reflect Questions 10.3

How can SHRD help support second-order strategy changes designed to produce a flatter organisational structure through delayering?

What are new, however, are the attributes of SHRD embedded in the highest level of strategic maturity depicted in Figure 10.8. This portrays SHRD as the process through which strategy is formulated (Lee, 1997) and the driver of organisational capabilities that represent the route to sustainable competitive advantage (Luoma, 2000). These ideas increasingly find expression through such terms as intellectual capital and knowledge management, which require further exploration as a component part of the second theme: the centrality of a learning culture. For Walton (1999: 82), 'The measure of successful SHRD is that people development and the supporting learning processes should be considered to be one of the strategic capabilities and distinctive competences of those organisations that effectively undertake them'.

Centrality of a learning culture

The centrality and importance of organisation learning and SHRD are captured well in Harrison's (1993) schematic representation of learning and development as a strategic process (see Figure 10.7) and McCracken and Wallace's (2000) portrayal of SHRD (see Figure 10.3). Horwitz (1999: 188) argues that 'Learning occurs at individual, work group and organisational levels' and that 'A key focus of SHRD is the creation of a learning environment and structural design, which promotes learning and development for performance improvement and competitiveness'. This positions learning as an organisational capability such that those organisations that are able to learn more quickly than their rivals secure significant competitive advantage. It is this premise that has led to interest in the concept of the 'learning organisation'.

A multi-stakeholder perspective

The third theme, concerning different stakeholder perspectives, changes in emphasis as HRD moves along the continuum of strategic maturity. At the training end of the continuum the focus is very much on employee needs with the HRD function and specialists being held largely responsible for addressing them. Here the role of line managers is restricted mainly to identifying HRD needs. At the SHRD end of the continuum the focus is on organisational needs, senior management leadership, and strategic partnerships between line managers committed to HRD and HRD specialists. This positions senior and line managers as having a pivotal role to play in the effective delivery of SHRD. For Mabey et al. (1998) the support of senior managers and active involvement of line managers is an essential component of their model of SHRD because they constitute a dominant coalition of interests and represent and reflect the prevailing organisational culture.

The first of these defining characteristics of SHRD, strategic integration, is a constant throughout the book and, as indicated above, you will now be left to explore how the multi-dimensional nature of strategic integration, particularly developed in Chapters 1, 7 and 8, can be applied to SHRD. The remaining sections of the chapter go on to concentrate on important SHRD dimensions related to the two remaining themes identified above: the centrality of a learning culture; and different stakeholder perspectives. In the first of these, two distinct perspectives surfaced earlier are explored – the learning organisation and knowledge management. For the second the concentration on HRD stakeholders is directed at managers who are regarded by many as playing the pivotal role in SHRD (for example, Mabey *et al.*, 1998; McCracken and Wallace, 2000; Harrison and Kessels, 2004). Critical here is not only the development of managers themselves towards greater levels of competence to enhance their contribution to organisational success but also how they execute their personal HRD role responsibilities in support of the development of their staff.

These characteristics of SHRD, expressed through the three emergent themes, mirror what Harrison and Kessels (2004) conclude are the four key future challenges facing the HRD function:

- achieving strategic integration and thrust;
- facilitating culture change and building a learning culture;
- promoting workplace learning processes that build social as well as human capital;
- developing managerial and leadership capability to operate in changing organisational form.

The learning organisation: the chicken and egg paradox of SHRD?

A recurrent theme running through the management literature and reflected in this book is that organisations will need to learn how to adapt to endemic change if they are to survive and flourish. There is nothing essentially new in the notion that organisations learn to interact with their environment to varying degrees of success. Indeed, learning can be identified at the very foundation of many management change initiatives, such as TQM, culture change, and business re-engineering. Learning also lies at the heart of SHRD. Individual and/or organisational learning was a dominant theme arising from the definitions of SHRD considered at the beginning of the chapter such that the development of a learning culture is sometimes seen as being synonymous with SHRD (Stewart and McGoldrick, 1996; McCracken and Wallace, 2000). Such is the strategic significance of learning that in some quarters its status has been elevated to become the *modus operandi* of organisations finding popular expression in such terms as 'The Learning Organisation' or 'The Learning Company'.

Organisational learning or the learning organisation

The recent elevation in the status of learning can be attributed to at least two particular lines of argument. First is the notion that, to maintain competitive advantage, organisations through the collective interactions of their employees need to learn faster than the rate of change and faster than their competitors (Ashton and Felstead, 2001; Greer, 2001). Second, consistent with the principles of core competences and the resource-based view of the firm discussed in Chapter 1, is the notion that learning itself is one of the main sources, if not the main source, of competitive advantage (Ashton and Felstead, 2001; Sloman, 2002). Thus, learning can be viewed as both a means to an end and an end in itself. To an extent, these two perspectives have been reflected in the differentiation found in the literature between 'organisational learning' and the 'learning organisation'. In Key Concepts 10.5 an attempt is made to bring together the defining characteristics of these two concepts.

Organisational learning (the process of learning)	The learning organisation (the process of learning to learn)
• Focuses on learning that results in behavioural changes among employees, either individually or in workgroups	• Focuses on learning that results in changing the behaviour of the organisation itself as it anticipates or responds proactively to changes in its operational environment
• Concentrates on how individuals learn. Seeks to analyse the process involved in individual or collective learning in order to better understand how it can contribute to formalised HRD	• Concentrates on learning how to learn. Seeks to explore methods for improving the learning process in a continual quest to improve the ability of the organisation to learn
• Concerned with knowledge development in order to gain new insights that have the potential to influence the future behaviour of employees	• Concerned with enabling employee learning to generate positively valued outcomes such as innovation, managing change and the development of core competences
• Viewed as a means to an end where behavioural change is directed at supporting the achievement of organisational goals	• Viewed as an end in itself where the development of a learning organisation can become a strategic goal of the organisation

Sources: Garavan (1997); Mabey *et al*. (1998); Reynolds and Ablett (1998); Armstrong and Foley (2003); Betts and Holden (2003); Sun and Scott (2003).

The learning organisation has therefore a broader focus that builds on and thereby incorporates the principles underpinning organisational learning. The section now goes on to focus on the implications that this broader interpretation of the learning organisation has for organisational SHRD practice.

Characteristics of the learning organisation

A frequently quoted definition sees the learning organisation as one 'which facilitates the learning of all its members and continually transforms itself' (Pedler *et al.*, 1991: 1). Underpinning this definition is the creation of a learning climate where everybody is encouraged to learn and the organisation as a whole develops a capacity for learning. Drawing on the literature to unpack the concept further, it is possible to distinguish a number of features of the learning organisation, as seen in Key Concepts 10.6.

Learning: a problematic concept

Learning, however, is a difficult concept to get to grips with. Not least is that learning is difficult to evaluate and is arguably only evident when it results in some measurable behavioural outcome. This situation is further complicated by the premise that the

Key Concepts   10.6

Characteristic features of the learning organisation

- Learning can be derived from all experiences – accidental and deliberate/successes and failures – and used to shape future behaviour.
- Learning is valuable in its own right and learning how to learn is a critical part of the process.
- Learning from both the external and internal environment takes place at all levels of the organisation and therefore there is a premium on sharing knowledge across organisational boundaries.
- Learning is a continuous process and at its most powerful when it becomes habitual and internalised.
- Unlearning and the reconstruction and adaptation of an organisation's knowledge base is a key managerial task.
- Learning is used intentionally as an enabling mechanism for organisational transformation.
- Conscious organisational initiatives are necessary to translate learning, from whatever source, into a strategic force.
- An underpinning organisational philosophy, culture and supportive structure are necessary to create the right environment for experiential learning and its operational application.
- It embraces a multi-stakeholder approach with a reduced emphasis on formal HRD interventions and greater emphasis on employees accepting responsibility for their own learning and managers actively facilitating the processes of learning.

Sources: Pettigrew and Whipp (1991); Storey and Sisson (1993); Mabey and Salaman (1995); Lundy and Cowling (1996); Muhlemeyer and Clarke (1997); Walton (1999); Ashton and Felstead (2001); Sun and Scott (2003).

interaction between learning and outcomes can occur at a number of levels (Argyris and Schon, 1978, 1996; Walton, 1999; Harrison and Kessels, 2004). The first level, single-loop learning, focuses on improving current practice (i.e. doing what we currently do better). Essentially it involves a continual cycle of detecting errors in current practice, identifying potential areas for improvement and making incremental enhancements to work operations. For example, the manufacturing organisation cited in an earlier chapter (In Practice 8.6) was not able to meet its growth strategy because it could not fill its staff vacancies in a virtually full employment labour market. A single-loop response would anticipate incremental adjustments to recruitment and selection practice in an effort to match labour supply and demand. This could include, for example, changing recruitment media, redefining the person specification, or sourcing vacancies from abroad.

The second level, double-loop learning, focuses on questioning established practice (i.e. challenging what we currently do). Essentially it involves challenging existing aims, established beliefs and values with a view to reconstructing organisational systems and processes as organisations strive to adapt to changes in their internal and external environments. This response may be triggered when evaluation demonstrates that changes resulting from single-loop learning have not worked and could lead, for example, to changes to an organisation's core values, mission or strategy. Building on the above example, a continuing failure of single-loop adjustments to recruitment and selection practice to match labour supply and demand could lead to the organisation questioning its business practice in more fundamental ways. This might lead to outsourcing its production operations to eastern Europe, a wholesale relocation to another country or the capital intensification of work where labour is substituted by technology.

The third level, triple-loop learning, focuses on the processes of learning (i.e. learning what we can from single- and double-loop learning). Essentially it involves 'reviewing and reflecting on previous learning experiences and using such experiences as a basis for the formation of new learning activities and insights' (Walton, 1999: 389). It is synonymous with learning to learn and is directed at improving organisational learning processes. Double- and triple-loop learning are particularly identified with the concept of the learning organisation. Although not situated in an organisational context, you might like to think through the extent to which the no-diet approach to losing weight, summarised in 'In Practice' 10.4, relates to single-, double- or triple-loop learning.

In Practice   10.4

How to lose weight without dieting: the pot of gold at the end of the rainbow?

Clinical trials currently underway may point to an effective but novel way of losing weight. Early results include:

- an average weight loss after four months of more than 10lbs (4.54 kilos);
- an average weight loss of a further 2lbs (1 kilo) over the next six months;
- only a minority of subjects involved in the trials putting weight back on; and
- weight loss over a full year of up to 40lbs for some subjects.

These results have been achieved without any instructions with respect to diet or exercise regimes. The 'no-diet diet' starts from the assumption that most diets fail because people revert back to deeply ingrained habits. The approach being trialled requires subjects to behave in opposite ways to their habitual ways of behaving ('unlearning'), experimenting with behaviour in close relationships and changing activity patterns. So, for example, the subject might have to act as an introvert if they were an extrovert and vice versa, or might give up watching television and listen to the radio instead.

Although not an objective of this approach to behavioural modification, the weight loss seems to follow. The reasons for this are not yet fully understood but it is believed that being forced to change certain behaviours in this way results in subjects thinking more carefully about their other lifestyle habits.

Source: Persaud (2005).

The final paragraph of In Practice 10.4 probably gives the greatest insight into the type of learning being displayed. A diet based on changing the patterns of behaviour not ordinarily related to dieting at least elevates learning to double-loop. However, transferring this learning, even if subconsciously, to eating habits probably reflects triple-loop learning, where prior experiences are being used to develop new insights.

Translating the concept into practice: a critical analysis

The demanding nature of the concept and the complexities surrounding learning and its evaluation are likely to present significant obstacles to those organisations aspiring to become learning organisations. Indeed, the conceptual and practical difficulties surrounding its practical manifestation have led to something akin to the chicken and egg dilemma – it probably takes a learning organisation to produce a learning organisation! This has led to the conclusion that the learning organisation is better viewed as an aspirational vision that can at best be pursued as a never-ending journey and at worst will never be realised (Walton, 1999; Tjepkema *et al.*, 2002). This perspective is echoed well by Garavan's (1997: 26) view that 'It is perhaps more appropriate to suggest that organizations can develop in a progressive manner towards a learning organization but it is an idealized state which may never be attained'.

It is not surprising, therefore, that much of the literature on learning organisations tends to concentrate on those organisational practices and support mechanisms that help build towards a learning organisation (for example, Garavan, 1997; Walton, 1999; Griego *et al.*, 2000; Armstrong and Foley, 2003). These frequently coalesce around:

- the creation of a learning culture where learning and experimentation are actively promoted, as evidenced through such things as the resources allocated to learning and development activities and the recognition and reward of risk taking;

- structural mechanisms to support organisational learning, such as routines for collecting, analysing, disseminating and applying information, and identifying and addressing learning and development needs as well as the organisation structure itself (Chapter 5);

- the importance of evaluation as a continuous process that not only underpins the principles of the learning organisation and knowledge management but informs organisational investment in HRD/SHRD (Chapter 4); and

- the psychological maturity of an organisation's human resources such that, for example, employees at all levels are receptive to the greater levels of accountability, autonomy and responsibility that underpin the construct of the learning organisation.

Given the above analysis, it is not difficult to subscribe to the view that the learning organisation is perhaps best regarded as a 'convenient shorthand term for describing an overall philosophy for sustaining learning in organisations' (Walton, 1999: 409). This leads to the position where it could be argued that, while a learning organisation cannot exist in its idealised form, some organisations will exhibit some of the characteristics of learning organisations (Griego *et al.*, 2000). For those committed to the aspirational vision of the learning organisation this will represent a very pessimistic picture. However, it is a position largely supported by empirical evidence. Based on an analysis of case study and survey findings it can be concluded that there is little evidence of either the existence of learning organisations or, perhaps even more significantly, the support mechanisms necessary for their creation (Reynolds and Ablett, 1998; Ashton and Felstead, 2001; Tjepkema, 2002; Harrison and Kessels, 2004). In Practice 10.5 provides a sample of conclusions that can be drawn from the available evidence.

In the context of SHRD the whole philosophy of the learning organisation is disarmingly seductive. The underlying hypothesis is that where learning takes place all the time throughout the organisation, the organisation will be better able to cope with change and uncertainty and thereby sustain long-term competitive advantage (Lundy and Cowling, 1996). Where the continuous development of employees is inextricably linked to the process of strategic management they 'become a major source of competitive ability, positioned to take advantage of every opportunity, while taking a positive stance when confronted with adversity' (Harrison, 1993: 317). Others have gone further to argue that

In Practice   10.5

Evidence of the learning organisation or chasing rainbows?

- Interest in the concept of the learning organisation far exceeds its practical manifestation. In a survey of 60 organisations with a good record of investment in HRD, 84 per cent expressed an interest in the concept, 10 per cent claimed to have adopted the concept in practice but only 0.25 per cent were able to report on progress towards its implementation (Reynolds and Ablett, 1998).

- Little progress has been made towards the much heralded move towards a knowledge-based economy built on lifelong learning because: few employers provide the conditions necessary to support continuous employee development; apart from some professions, there is little interest among occupational groups for lifelong learning; and for most employees 'notions of employee development never mind continuous learning remain a fantasy' (Ashton and Felstead, 2001: 184–185).

- Even in organisations expected to exhibit high levels of HRD expertise and proactivity, little attention is being paid to developing learning cultures (Harrison and Kessels, 2004).

- The majority of managers lack preparation and training for their HRD role responsibilities (Cunningham and Hyman, 1999; Harrison and Kessels, 2004).

people are the only sustainable source of competitive advantage within a complex environment (West, 1994) and that organisational learning may be the only competitive advantage for firms in the future (Stata, 1989). For example, at the time of writing the cosmetic company Avon was about to diversify into the financial services sector using its door-to-door sales techniques to sell financial products. The company had awoken to the fact that its sales force was something of a sleeping giant with excellent customer access and sales competence that had hitherto been limited to the sale of cosmetics.

Viewed from these perspectives the learning organisation appears to offer the much sought after pot of gold at the end of the rainbow and application of its principles has been associated with the successful management of strategic and operational change (Pettigrew and Whipp, 1991). However, against this, as argued above, the concept may represent no more than an idealised construct rather than a practical working model (Storey and Sisson, 1993). One particular difficulty is that, as touched on earlier, the conditions thought to be conducive to learning organisations may not be readily found in practice. These conditions include: employees who are committed to and capable of managing their own continuous personal development; the presence of mechanisms that support mutual learning and which capture, disseminate and share learning; an appropriate culture that supports experimentation, risk taking, independent thinking, discord, authority based on expert knowledge rather than status; and, a pluralist ideology which accepts the fact that stakeholders within an organisation may have different interests to pursue. Organisations characterised more by bureaucracy, control and unitarism represent for many of us the reality of work. Messengers do get shot and even where senior management espouse openness and innovation, the reality may be that a blame culture (see Chapter 6) operates so that employees avoid risks and learn to keep their mouth shut.

Another difficulty is that the very concept of transformation underpinning Pedler *et al.*'s (1991) definition of the learning organisation, cited above, is open to criticism. In reality, organisational transformation is likely to be rare, and anyway, Mumford (1998) argues strongly that learning should be incremental rather than transformational. He questions whether employees can be equipped with the capacity for double-loop learning when arguably the HRD infrastructure has yet to deliver the widespread capacity for single-loop learning. The much-lamented parlous state of HRD in the UK would seem to lend weight to his view. In this context, single-loop learning may represent a rational approach to problem solving and should not be jettisoned until the superiority of new learning forms has been validated (Henderson, 1997).

Perhaps, then, a construct that appears from the literature to promise so much may in fact prove to be somewhat elusive in practice. However, the journey in pursuit of the rainbow's end, like so many journeys, may be rewarding in itself. Many of the ingredients of the learning organisation appear to have merit and arguably represent common sense even if common sense may in reality be a rare commodity!

Knowledge management

Knowledge management: the next big thing in HRD?

More recently the focus on approaches to HRD has moved on from learning organisations to knowledge management. Traced historically these represent the two latest approaches to HRD with knowledge management being the most recent to occupy centre stage in management discourse (In Practice 10.6).

This shift has been attributed to moves in developed economies away from low-tech, labour-intensive industries reliant on a relatively low skill base to high-tech industries reliant on knowledge workers. The argument runs that because such workers are in relatively short supply they have become identified as the key source of sustainable com-

In Practice   10.6

The recent HRD lineage

1. 1960s onwards – the systematic approach to HRD.

2. 1980s onwards – business orientation where the focus of the systematic approach concentrates on meeting organisational objectives consistent with a performance management framework.

3. Mid-1980s onwards – where frameworks for business approaches to HRD were built around competences.

4. Late 1980s onwards – emphasis on self-development where employees are given increasing autonomy over and responsibility for their learning as reflected in employee development and assistance programmes (EDAPs).

5. Early 1990s onwards – the learning organisation where the focus shifts from a concentration on individuals to adopt a holistic, systemic, whole-organisation perspective.

6. Mid-1990s onwards – knowledge management with a focus on developing human, intellectual and social capital.

Sources: Megginson *et al.* (1999); Walton (1999); Gibb and Megginson (2001).

petitive advantage consistent with the ideas of core competences and the resource-based view of the firm, discussed in Chapter 1. Given this rationale, it is not surprising that senior management may increasingly look towards HRD to build and help translate the knowledge and skills of its employees – the organisation's human capital – into intellectual capital to the benefit of the organisation (Blackler, 1995; Walton, 1999).

Interest in knowledge management would therefore appear to be predicated on at least two recent interrelated developments: the advent of the knowledge economy; and the focus on knowledge as the route to competitive advantage. Whereas in traditional economies added value is achieved through optimising the utilisation of the classic factors of production (capital, labour, material), in the knowledge economy added value is achieved through developing and utilising existing and new knowledge to enhance organisation efficiency, effectiveness and innovation. Where intangible, knowledge-based assets become the most important currency in the knowledge economy there is a premium on developing HRD processes strategically to capitalise on these assets (Harrison and Kessels, 2004). This position is captured by Skapinker (2002: 1):

> People at all levels have accumulated knowledge about what customers want, about how best to design products and processes, about what has worked in the past and what hasn't. A company that can collect all that knowledge and share it between employees will have a huge advantage over an organisation that never discovers what its people know.

Despite the attractiveness and plausibility of Skapinker's conclusion, there are two important difficulties that impact on its practical application. The first concerns the number of facets relating to knowledge that have to be managed. The second and related difficulty concerns the meaning and nature of knowledge itself.

Facets of knowledge management

With respect to the first concern it is possible to break down knowledge management into a number of interrelated strands. A fairly simplistic approach is to make a distinction between existing and new knowledge. Skapinker's conclusion relates principally to knowledge that already resides within the workforce, whereas earlier in the chapter the strategic importance of new knowledge and its effective utilisation were also stressed (Harrison and Kessels, 2004).

At a more detailed level of analysis Gibb and Megginson (2001) discern three interrelated strands in thinking. The first concerns the means for capturing, storing, retrieving and disseminating information. This information systems perspective particularly concentrates on the use of IT to facilitate these processes. Although seemingly straightforward, this dimension of knowledge management is not without its difficulties as exemplified by the exhortations of chief executives on the lines of 'if only we knew what we know' (Storey and Quintas, 2001: 340). Here auditing the existing workforce as part of HRP can make an important contribution to mapping existing knowledge (Matthewman, 1993; Heng, 2001; Herremans and Isaac, 2004).

Their second strand concerns the development of a learning culture as a facilitator of knowledge management. Viewed from this perspective it would appear that Gibb and Megginson are treating learning as a subset of knowledge management. However, it is also possible to adopt the opposite perspective where knowledge management is regarded as one step in the direction towards a learning organisation where the focus

In Practice   10.7

Global knowledge communities network to save millions and transform learning

Shell International Exploration and Production (SIEP) is a global knowledge-intensive business. This carries with it the potential that a problem faced in one country has already been encountered and solved in another. Without a mechanism to share and apply this knowledge a lot of money could be lost. To address this, SIEP established a series of web-based global knowledge communities focused on the core elements of its business. As a result, when the Brazil operation needed to retrieve broken tools from a borehole, local engineers were able to call down help from their international colleagues specialising in wells in order to help solve the problem. The ideas that poured in enabled the tools to be retrieved, the well being saved and an estimated monetary saving of US$7 million.

Source: Carrington (2002b).

moves from learning generally to concentrate on knowledge as the core competence (Storey and Quintas, 2001). Irrespective of the position taken, emerging from both is a clear emphasis on learning being critical to organisation success, particularly in the field of knowledge work. This leads to their third strand which focuses on the strategic perspective with its emphasis on the value of intellectual capital. However, before moving on it is worth noting that it is arguably the second strand that carries within it the potential to develop and effectively utilise new knowledge.

The strategic perspective (the third strand) has been a constant in the exploration of SHRD in this chapter and the elevation of knowledge management in the hierarchy of management thinking is well illustrated by reference to a small selection of commentaries. The Department for Education and Employment (DfEE) (1988) concluded that the foundation for economic success in the twenty-first century depended on investment in human capital. Stewart (1997) postulated that in recent years, within management and organisation theory knowledge, management had become a very important if not the most important development such that it was viewed in some quarters as the most important factor in economic life. For Prusack (1997: ix), 'a firm's competitive advantage depends more than anything on its knowledge, or, to be slightly

In Practice   10.8

Global knowledge communities as a strategic tool

Thames Water, serving over 50 million customers in more than 46 countries, is using knowledge-sharing communities that span global boundaries as part of its strategy for meeting one of its organisational objectives to 'profit from our knowledge, getting more value from our assets and capabilities'. Examples of these communities include water preservation experts who pool their ideas on preventing water loss, and contracting experts who share ways to improve bidding and negotiation processes.

Source: Lank and Windle (2003).

more specific, on what it knows, how it uses what it knows, and how fast it can know something new'.

Another way of delineating the various strands of knowledge management has been to distinguish between human capital, intellectual capital and social capital. Human capital refers to the knowledge, skills, experience and competence embodied in the workforce that, as an intangible asset, has value to the organisation. These individual and collective capabilities (know-how) are acquired through a process of lifelong learning and represent the focus of organisational HRD practice. However, it is increasingly recognised that, within the work context, everyday job experiences and professional and social networks contribute significantly to the accumulation of human capital. It is when the organisation is able to utilise this human capital to business advantage that it becomes intellectual capital. From a systems perspective, human capital represents the key input to knowledge management. When these inputs are converted into the tangible outputs on which an organisation trades, such as inventions, patents, market brands, reputation, problem solving, and research and development capability, etc., the outputs come to represent the intellectual capital of the organisation. Social capital represents the interpersonal glue that facilitates intra- and inter-group cooperation and comprises such things as social networks and shared values, norms and understandings. Interpreted through the systems construct, social capital is the process that facilitates the translation of human capital into intellectual capital through being a powerful conduit for learning and generator of unique and valuable knowledge (Figure 10.9).

Figure 10.9 A systems perspective of knowledge management

From this perspective it is social capital that builds and sustains knowledge-productive relationships within the workforce (Garavan *et al.*, 2001; Storey and Quintas, 2001; Harrison and Kessels, 2004; Herremans and Isaac, 2004). Therefore, as well as contributing to the development of human capital, SHRD also has an important role in helping to create, facilitate and sustain learning communities. However, consistent with the multi-stakeholder nature of SHRD, delivery of this role requires support from other quarters. This is particularly true of managers not only through their direct interventions but also through the work and organisational structures they build (Harrison and Kessels, 2004; Hedlund, 1994; MacNeil, 2004).

What is knowledge?

The second difficulty emerging from Skapinker's (2002) conclusion is that knowledge is a difficult concept to get hold of. There can be little disagreement that it is possible, in principle, to differentiate between occupations in terms of their knowledge intensity, i.e. the extent to which knowledge and other cognitive capacities impact on job performance. For example, jobs such as doctor, lawyer and lecturer can be classified as knowledge intensive relative to those of cleaner, checkout operator and footballer. Further, it is not a difficult step to accept that knowledge-intensive jobs can be differentiated according to the extent to which their underpinning knowledge is either relatively certain and complete or uncertain and incomplete. For example, the knowledge under-pinning the job of a pharmacist or lecturer in modern languages is relatively certain compared with that of an astronomer or ecologist. The extent to which such knowledge occupations operate in environments prone to endemic change will increase the significance of uncertain and incomplete knowledge to their effective performance. However, such simple distinctions based around knowledge intensity and the certainty of knowledge are relatively crude and do not adequately reflect the many theoretical perspectives available (see, for example, Blackler, 1995). However, for the purposes of this chapter they provide a useful template to which can be added the distinction between articulated and tacit knowledge (Hedlund, 1994).

Articulated knowledge mirrors that which is relatively certain and complete. It is known and can be expressed through verbal and written communication. Tacit knowledge as a concept, however, is far more amorphous. It represents that knowledge which it is difficult or impossible to articulate because it comprises intuition, values, etc. that are highly personal and relate to particular contexts (Hedlund, 1994; Garavan *et al.*, 2001). Imagine trying to articulate how to ride a bicycle or what it is to be in love and you will get somewhere close to tacit knowledge and why it is difficult to put it into words. Not surprisingly, therefore, knowledge management is likely to be largely directed at articulated knowledge and developing new knowledge. However, Baumard (1999) argues that, over time, what is currently tacit might become capable of articulation. He terms this implicit knowledge and differentiates it from that tacit knowledge which remains permanently closed to articulation. From an organisational perspective this carries with it the potential to bring some tacit knowledge under the umbrella of knowledge management. It has been argued that small teams have the potential to provide the forum for creating and sharing tacit knowledge through constant exposure to and communication between team members (MacNeil, 2004). This reinforces the role and value of social capital in knowledge management.

If the rhetoric of knowledge management is accepted, it is possible to advance a number of premises that place it securely within the SHRD arena. These are summarised in Key Concepts 10.7.

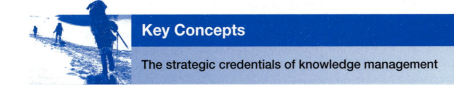

Key Concepts 10.7

The strategic credentials of knowledge management

- Within the SHRM construct superior human resources, i.e. the know-how embodied in the organisation's workforce, are a key source of competitive advantage.

- Knowledge, as a component of know-how, and social capital, if not the most important dimensions of HR competence are at least major contributors to human capital.

- The advent of the knowledge economy, particularly when allied to endemic change, places a premium on knowledge management where the utilisation of existing knowledge and the generation and application of new knowledge are used to generate intellectual capital from which organisations can profit.

- In advanced economies, the emphasis is increasingly directed towards 'developing knowledge workers capable of making rapid skills transitions and adjustments in response to unforeseen and unforeseeable contingencies' (Walton, 1999: 83).

▶

- This will necessitate that knowledge workers: possess a high level of job-specific capability; demonstrate commitment to and engagement in continuous personal development; and exhibit flexibility and cognitive agility to respond to conflicting demands and the challenge of the unknown.
- The HRD infrastructure can make important contributions to enable and support the development of human and social capital. However, this may well mean the need to transform learning and development to move it from an over-reliance on structured interventions to an infrastructure that can support lifelong learning as a route to human and social capital accumulation.
- Where such a transformation can take place, it will position HRD at the strategically mature end of the HRD continuum, depicted in Figures 10.3 and 10.8.

Sources: Lee (1996); Muhlemeyer and Clarke (1997); Walton (1999); Ashton and Felstead (2001); Garavan *et al*. (2001); Gibb and Megginson (2001); Harrison and Kessels (2004).

The problematic nature of knowledge management

Like the learning organisation, knowledge management appears to offer a route to the proverbial pot of gold but it carries with it similar question marks about its efficacy. To begin with, it is possible to question the extent of the knowledge economy itself and the preponderance of knowledge workers. Broad economic decisions are in the hands of government, and in the UK, at least, inconsistent signals have been sent out. In the early 1990s, for example, at one and the same time there was opposition to EU regulations that were seen to hamper organisations' ability to compete on the basis of cost while on the other there were drives to increase the participation rate of school leavers in higher education. For many workers, developments in IT can lead to a reduction in the knowledge component of their work, as evidenced in the financial services sector. Further, despite the clamour to increase the participation rate in higher education and thereby the number of graduates, it is among unskilled and skilled craft occupations that the severest shortages of labour have been experienced over the past decade, helping to explain the countervailing concern by government to develop the basic skills and competences of school leavers. The concept of knowledge management also smacks of unitarism. Employers may well be seeking to exploit the knowledge embedded in their workforce while at the same time undermining progressively their psychological contract. This throws up issues of ownership and power in relation to knowledge, and employees may not be willing to commit their intellectual capital beyond that which they are contracted to supply in the performance of their work contract.

The potential for SHRD to contribute towards the development of human and social capital is readily discernible, although the focus of knowledge management has arguably been largely directed internally at the intra-organisational level, although learning and the acquisition of knowledge clearly also derive from sources external to the organisation as part of lifelong learning and carries with it the same potential to be translated by employers into intellectual capital. This may mean that the HRD infrastructure, as part of social capital enhancement, will need to have an external focus. For organisations wishing to gain the maximum potential from this source of knowledge external networking promoted via employee membership of professional bodies is unlikely in itself to be sufficient. However, such moves to exploit externally generated knowledge outside of the work contract are likely to exacerbate issues around the ownership and exploitation of intellectual capital. In 'In Practice' 10.9 the example of a university HRM lecturer has been used to illustrate the relationship between externally generated knowledge and the principles of knowledge management.

In Practice **10.9**

Do knowledge workers routinely exploit external sources to enhance their job performance?

Travelling home from work, Jo, a university HRM lecturer, is listening to breaking news on her car radio. There has been an orchestrated series of terrorist attacks on transport systems in capital cities across the world. Those claiming responsibility say that the attacks are aimed at tourists from developed economies and will continue until those countries stop exporting capitalism. Not surprisingly the news story receives wall-to-wall coverage and engenders panic among those planning to travel abroad.

The following day, travelling into university, Jo decides to ditch her plan for the lectures that week on 'The virtues of human resource planning in a changing world'. Instead she decides to run each session as a discussion forum using this latest news as the catalyst for exploring the lecture title.

In relation to externally generated information and knowledge management, a number of points might be relevant:

- the predisposition of knowledge workers to keep their minds switched on when they leave work;
- whether the manipulation of non-work-specific knowledge and evaluating its relevance to work occurs naturally among knowledge workers;
- the extent to which this almost spontaneous importation and utilisation of knowledge is dependent on certain competences, a flexible disposition and the willingness to take risks;
- the extent to which Jo's actions add value, personally, for her students and for the organisation as a whole; and
- how Jo might have responded if this was an organisational expectation rather than a personal initiative over which she had full control.

A specific problem facing the development of knowledge management in the UK is the under-investment in HRD, evidenced at both the national (macro) and organisational (micro) level. The resources necessary to underpin knowledge acquisition, much of which is likely to be highly speculative, is unlikely to occur in all but a handful of organisations within this national context. Although HRD as a vital component of SHRM has its passionate advocates, it arguably remains a poor relation (Keep, 1992; Thornhill *et al.*, 2000). Ashton and Felstead's (2001) analysis points to evidence that, in terms of HRD investment, the UK is not catching up with its European competitors and is falling behind new competitors emerging from South East Asian economies. They conclude: 'If there is to be a significant move in the direction of lifelong learning or a knowledge economy, then it will require far more radical changes to the institutional framework than is currently envisaged in the policy debates' (Ashton and Felstead, 2001: 186).

Even if there is a commitment to knowledge management at the organisational level, it might be frustrated by the existing HRD infrastructure. The move towards SHRD, as discussed earlier, requires significant change in the strategies, roles and behaviours of the HRD function if it is to take place. This is likely to involve transforming HRD delivery systems from those characterised by standardised training packages and prescriptions to a focus on workplace learning with its greater emphasis on employee self-development facilitated by managers operating as mentors and coaches. Here there is likely to be a premium on HRD specialists working in partnership with senior and line managers, operating as facilitators rather than instructors, and actively developing and promoting support mechanisms to facilitate the development of learning and knowledge in the pursuit of continuous improvement and innovation (Walton, 1999; McCracken and Wallace, 2000; Harrison and Kessels, 2004). Key questions flowing from this analysis include:

- Will HRD specialists willingly make such transformations?
- Do they possess the necessary competences to successfully execute the change?

As with other HR interventions there is also the danger that knowledge management is likely to founder unless attention is paid to its full strategic integration. While the case for vertical alignment of knowledge management with organisational strategies has been well made, it is unlikely that it will be achieved if its horizontal integration with other dimensions of HR is not realised. A number of examples illustrate this point. Given the demanding set of competences required by knowledge workers, careful attention will need to be paid to their recruitment and selection (Chapter 8) and subsequent development. Reward structures (Chapter 11) will need to be able to recognise superior performance in the development of new knowledge and the successful application of this and existing knowledge to generating intellectual capital. The auditing and dissemination of knowledge will need to be incorporated into HRP as a key activity (Chapter 7). Learning cultures (Chapter 6) will be needed to support risk taking, innovation and entrepreneurial spirit, etc., which in turn will need to be supported by appropriate organisational structures (Chapter 5). Hierarchic structures based on command and control will need to be transformed into those that can accommodate and foster: temporary coalitions of employees and business units; an emphasis on lateral rather than vertical communication; delegation of responsibility for communication between functions, divisions and international operations from managers to line staff; job design incorporating the principles of self-organising teams; and sufficient formal regulation to capture the outputs of these more informal arrangements and translate them into intellectual capital (Hedlund, 1994; Harrison and Kessels, 2004).

Lastly, the capacity and competence of managers to meet the demands placed on them by SHRD, more generally, and knowledge management, specifically, is questioned. A core dimension of SHRM is the devolvement of responsibility for HR from specialist practitioners to, particularly line, managers and their internalisation of these responsibilities can be viewed as a component of strategic integration (Guest, 1987). In terms of social capital, line managers (or supervisors) have been identified as potentially the key players in fostering knowledge acquisition, transfer and exploitation in work teams. However, in addition to general concerns over the ability of managers to exercise their SHRD role responsibilities, MacNeil (2004) argues specifically that the potential supervisors provide for filling the missing communication link necessary to translate individual tacit knowledge into collective tacit knowledge receives insufficient attention.

Managers as SHRD stakeholders: linchpin or spanner in the works?

Arguably, the chapter to date provides plenty of rhetoric in support of the pivotal role played by managers in SHRD but it is left to you to work through these in response to the self-check question below. The focus of the section that follows is on two key inter-related perspectives: the critical relationship between organisational performance and

Self-Check and Reflect Questions   10.4

Why might it be argued that managers are the linchpin in the successful introduction and maintenance of SHRD?

the quality of its managers; and managers' role responsibilities for developing their staff. Central to these two perspectives is the management development component of SHRD.

Managerial HRD competence: a strategic linchpin?

The strategic importance of management development is readily discernible if it is accepted that an organisation's ability to secure current and future competitive advantage is dependent, in part, on the quality of its managers (Muhlemeyer and Clark, 1997; Sloman, 2002). Arguably, the importance attached to developing managers will increase the more dynamic an organisation's business environment becomes. It is not surprising, therefore, that in a survey of European companies commissioned by the Ashridge Management Research Group that 'managing on-going organisational change' was the most commonly cited priority when developing managers (Lundy and Cowling, 1996: 274). However, success in this arena is inextricably bound up with the ability of managers to secure effective performance from their staff. This obviously incorporates a number of human resource dimensions including HRD.

Development of their staff is seen here as one of the critical SHRM role responsibilities of managers. As they make operational the organisation's strategic plans, it is arguably line managers who are best placed to assess the current and future HRD needs of their staff (Garavan, 1991; Horwitz, 1999). In addition, they can play an important role in constructing and implementing HRD strategies designed to develop the requisite skills, knowledge and attitudes among the workforce. Particularly for job-related HRD, it will be necessary for managers to exhibit coaching and mentoring skills and to facilitate learning through shared experiences (Garavan, 1991).

In Practice   10.10

A case of two managers: Felicity

Felicity is a middle manager responsible for 15 technical and professional staff who can be classified as knowledge workers. She strongly believes that her performance as a manager is dependent upon the capability of staff who report to her and that their personal development also serves the interests of her organisation. She is therefore very committed to HRD even if it means that she may be participating in the development of tomorrow's managers who may be promoted ahead of her.

Although she is not against formalised off-the-job training, she particularly values using learning opportunities that present themselves from day-to-day work experiences. This means that she devotes a lot of her time to discussing work with her subordinates, identifying immediate HRD needs that arise from this and helping to develop their competence through coaching and mentoring.

Felicity is a strong advocate of learning derived from further education and is currently sponsoring two of her subordinates on an MBA programme. As part of her commitment to this she regularly meets with these staff to discuss: what they are learning on the programme; how it might be related to and used in their work; how their jobs might be reshaped to enable greater transfer of learning; how their learning challenges current organisational practice; and the feasibility of experimenting with practice to reflect their critique.

Felicity applies this same approach to staff undertaking an internal or external off-the-job HRD course. In addition, before she will approve course attendance, Felicity requires the member of staff concerned to propose how they will disseminate the outputs from the course, not only within her unit but more broadly across the organisation, and how they will evaluate its effectiveness. Delivery against this 'contract' is then incorporated into the six-monthly formal performance review she conducts with all her staff.

Although she recognises that this commitment to HRD is very time-consuming Felicity finds that she is increasingly able to delegate her operational tasks to her subordinates who, in return, seem increasingly keen for her to do this.

Managerial HRD competence: a spanner in the works?

Unfortunately, in comparison to countries such as Japan, this portrayal of managers' HRD role responsibilities sits rather uneasily in the context of the UK economy. As discussed earlier, the prevailing climate at both the national and individual organisation level is not particularly favourable to SHRD. A number of factors impact adversely on the quality of our managers and operate to marginalise their staff development responsibilities. An initial difficulty arises over role definition and the ownership of HRD. Managers may not necessarily regard HRD as part of their role either because they have not connected generally with their HR responsibilities or because they believe that its ownership resides elsewhere with HRD specialists. This position is likely to be reinforced where the customary response to identified HRD needs is to send the employee on a course rather than to undertake job-related HRD. For example, in developing managers' competence to manage poor performers, the organisation might either send them on a course to do this or exploit the learning opportunities presented by real cases of poor performers in their areas of responsibility. The first approach might be executed simply through HRD functional specialists, whereas the second approach requires the commitment of line and senior managers to their respective HRD role responsibilities.

However, even if dual responsibility for HRD is accepted, there is a danger that the two protagonists will conflict. Twigg and Albon (1992) reported that managers and HRD specialists are frequently critical of each other over, respectively, their lack of business focus and short-term profit mentality that precludes investment in the development of people. They have identified that these relationships can become so polarised that it is as if the two parties are operating in two different worlds – hardly a recipe for success. The reconfiguration of SHRD by McCracken and Wallace (2000) represents an interesting development and, with its emphasis on collaboration between HRD specialists and line managers, should not only avoid such polarisation but could generate very constructive working partnerships (Horwitz, 1999).

A further difficulty is that even managers who understand that HRD is an integral aspect of their staffing responsibility may fail to deliver against this role. At one level they may simply lack the motivation. This is not as irrational as it may sound because the longer-term payback strongly associated with HRD is not consistent with the predominantly short-term focus adopted by many organisations. For example, a sales manager assessed on the achievement of six-monthly sales targets by his or her sales team may be reluctant to release staff to undertake management development or to commit his or her own time and effort to developing their competence in this direction. Also, if the cynical view that you only get the behaviour that you either measure or pay for through performance management systems is accepted, then any failure to incorporate HRD performance objectives into a manager's performance criteria will result in the expenditure of minimum effort in this area. As Storey and Sisson (1993: 171) have lamented, 'Rarely is it the case in British companies that the extent to which a manager develops his or her own immediate staff is regarded as the critical measurement of how well that manager is doing the job'. Returning to the sales manager example, if the organisation was serious about managers executing their HRD role responsibilities then his or her performance-related pay could be made dependent on how well he or she performs in this arena.

At another level, managers may simply lack the necessary competences to execute their HRD roles effectively. Garavan (1991) cites the inability to appraise performance, identify HRD needs and empathise with subordinates, together with a lack of listening and counselling skills as the most commonly identified shortcomings. These competence deficiencies may reflect the relatively low education and training base of some managers and/or HRD approaches that rely more on throwing managers in at the deep end than on their methodical, continuous development (Storey and Sisson, 1993). This view is consistent with management development being seen as an avoidable cost such that it receives low priority in organisations (Greer, 2001).

In Practice   10.11

A case of two managers: Stanley

Stanley is a middle manager responsible for 15 technical and professional staff who can be classified as knowledge workers. He strongly believes that his performance as a manager is down to his own efforts and that he can get the best out of his subordinates through the force of his own personality. He has come up the hard way and believes that managers are born and not made. He is therefore very sceptical about expenditure of time, effort and money on HRD and will actively try to prevent any of his staff getting one jump ahead of him on the organisational promotion ladder.

Although he sees it largely as a waste of time, his standard response to any identified training need, if he cannot resolve it through threats and coercion, is to send subordinates on a course. However, he regards off-the-job courses as more like a holiday and resents the time staff spend away from their job. Stanley feels that the demands of his job do not allow him the luxury of spending time on the development of his staff. As far as he is concerned, throwing staff in at the deep end represents a sensible and efficient approach to HRD.

Stanley is proud of the fact that he has got where he is today without any management qualification and does not see the value in management education. He is aware that two of his staff are undertaking an MBA at their own expense. In the early days of their programme they had approached him wanting to discuss their course and its relevance to their work responsibilities. He had advised them to forget that theoretical nonsense and to get on with their jobs 'the way we do things around here'.

Stanley is generally critical of the competence of his staff and resents the fact that he cannot delegate work to them because they cannot be trusted to perform it effectively. His view is that if you want something doing well, then do it yourself.

Drawing on empirical evidence, it can be argued that it is a minority of organisations that effectively prepare their managers for their HRD role responsibilities. This applies to their leadership of HRD processes generally and the use of HRD as a strategic intervention particularly (Mabey *et al.*, 1998; Cunningham and Hyman, 1999; Harrison and Kessels, 2004). A particular difficulty is that what HRD activity there is tends to be concentrated towards the lower end of the management hierarchy (Garavan, 1991). Particular concern has been expressed that insufficient attention is paid to senior manager development given their critical contribution to organisation performance (Mumford, 1998). Where senior managers neglect their own personal development it can also establish poor role models, potentially reinforcing the negative attitudes line managers below them have towards HRD. Conversely, where senior managers demonstrate strong commitment to HRD, particularly through adopting an interventionist role in shaping its strategy and practice, learning transfer and higher levels of general commitment to HRD throughout the organisation are likely to be found (Horwitz, 1999; Ashton and Felstead, 2001).

Unfortunately a dilemma emerges in that managers may sustain an anti-HRD attitude out of rational self-interest, despite its potential for facilitating organisation change. Keep (1992) outlines a rather depressing scenario, where poorly educated and trained managers brought up within traditional authoritarian control and command structures conspire to deny subordinates training opportunities because their effective development may subsequently threaten their own managerial prerogative and/or managerial position.

Managerial HRD competence: another box for Pandora?

On a more optimistic note, it may be that the demands of strategic management will act as a catalyst on managers' attitudes towards HRD and galvanise them into action with respect to their own development needs and those of their subordinates. Research conducted in 91 large UK-based companies found that expenditure on management development was highest when it represented an integral element of corporate planning, was directly associated with the need to respond effectively to changing environments and the operating market was increasingly turbulent (Parkinson, 1990). More generally, management development appears to be receiving greater priority in the UK with an expectation that it will continue to increase (Stewart, 1997). Evidence of increased management development activity has also been linked explicitly with culture change programmes where it has been identified as an essential vehicle for engineering change (Storey and Sisson, 1993; IRS, 1997). Evidence drawn from across Europe, including the UK, also points to line managers increasingly accepting responsibility for their HRD role both in terms of identifying needs and the formulation of HRD policies (Mabey and Salaman, 1995).

Following on from the Pandora's box analogy in Chapter 7, it is possible that, despite the many obstacles to management engagement in HRD, strategic imperatives provide hope that they may re-evaluate their behaviour. It is to be hoped that, for example, through greater involvement in their own HRD, managers may adopt more positive attitudes to the development of their subordinates. A key element here may be to make HRD more accessible and relevant to their needs. In order to bridge the two worlds occupied by line managers and HRD specialists, Twigg and Albon (1992) suggest that HRD interventions need to switch from an emphasis on generic, off-the-job courses to work-based activities that have been designed collaboratively by the two parties to specifically address identified business needs. They particularly highlight the role organisational learning can play in drawing the two worlds together. Under this approach, business needs are increasingly linked to managing change and the requirement for managers to innovate and take risks. This they argue is more likely to happen in a learning climate where 'experiences, whether successful or not, are rapidly assimilated by others and form the basis of learning how to cope with change' (Twigg and Albon, 1992: 86).

Self-Check and Reflect Questions 10.5

What factors have contributed to the relatively low level of importance attaching to management development?

Summary

- It is possible to construct a continuum of HRD strategic maturity upon which different approaches to HRD can be positioned. At the strategically immature end HRD is conducted in isolation of organisational strategies. Here, any strategic linkage is accidental and HRD interventions represent isolated, tactical responses to operational problems encountered. At the strategically mature end HRD approaches and specific interventions reflect full strategic integration through their effective accommodation of two-way vertical and horizontal integration.

- In addition to strategic integration, SHRD is characterised by: senior management sponsorship; the commitment and active involvement of all levels of management; effective collaborative partnerships between HRD specialists and line managers; systematic environmental scanning to maximise the lead time for developing HRD responses to change; transformation in the role of HRD specialists from training providers to proactive change agents; a learning culture; and comprehensive evaluation of SHRD interventions.

- Although often positioned at the non-strategic end of the continuum of strategic maturity, it is possible for the more familiar systematic cycle of HRD to be modelled to incorporate the characteristics of SHRD.

- The learning organisation and knowledge management have emerged as two recent approaches to HRD that have a strong strategic connection. The learning organisation focuses on the process of learning to learn so as to enable learning within organisations and the rate of change to be faster than those achieved by competitors. Knowledge management adopts a narrower focus and seeks to capture, disseminate and utilise existing knowledge and generate new knowledge in order to sustain an organisation's competitive position and promote innovatory behaviour. Both concepts place a premium on human capital as the route to sustainable competitive advantage where learning and knowledge can assume the status of an organisation's core competence.

- Within a multi-stakeholder perspective, managers can be identified as the linchpin for the successful execution of SHRD. However, for a variety of reasons, their willingness and ability to assume this central role in SHRD are questionable.

Follow-up study suggestions

- Access and read the work of Luoma (2000), Mabey *et al.* (1998), McCracken and Wallace (2000) and Muhlemeyer and Clarke (1997) cited in the chapter and compare and contrast their views on what constitutes SHRD.
- Review the components of SHRD discussed in the chapter and produce your own conceptual model of SHRD. Critique your model in terms of its strengths and weaknesses.
- Select either the learning organisation or knowledge management, read more widely around the concept and its practise by organisations. Produce a critique of both its theory and practise.
- Revisit either Chapter 3 or 6 and explore how SHRD can contribute to the internationalisation of business or the strategic alignment of culture.
- Use the internet to source four or five examples of organisational SHRD practice (preferably relating to practise in a number of different countries). Using the continua of HRD strategic maturity depicted in Figures 10.3 and 10.8, analyse the cases and locate them on the continua providing justification for your decisions.

Suggestions for research topics

- Just how extensive is SHRD in practice? A comparative survey of SMEs and large organisations.
- Are you sitting comfortably? Evaluating HRD practice against a continuum of strategic maturity: a survey of organisational practice.
- Of what practical relevance is the concept of the learning organisation to organisations competing in today's global economy?
- What is meant by knowledge management and to what extent is it being practised by organisations?
- To what extent do managers hinder or help the development of SHRD practice?

Case Study

INA

INA Bearing Company is a medium-sized manufacturer of high-precision engine components for the automotive industry. Based in Llanelli, South Wales, it is one of a number of manufacturing companies across Europe owned by the multi-national Schaeffler Group.

In 2001 the company was facing a crisis. Its market position had been declining rapidly since the late 1990s as a result of orders being switched to low-cost producers in eastern Europe. This period resulted in successive reductions in the workforce from around 860 to 360 jobs. In 2001 prospects looked bleak. INA's German parent had plans to switch even more production capacity to units in eastern Europe which, if implemented, would have resulted in the loss of a contract accounting for around half the plant's output and further job losses of 120.

Faced with this bleak scenario, the personnel manager led a strategy workshop to reformulate the best way forward. It was accepted that competing with its European counterparts on the basis of cost was not a viable option. Instead INA decided to compete on the basis of quality with a vision to become the group's preferred location for high-tech production work. At the same time, it was recognised that this transformation in production orientation could not be achieved without radical realignment of the company's skill base. This led INA to a commitment to compete on the basis of workforce capability. Investment in machinery was to be switched to investment in human capital with the clear intent of building an employee skill base, developing a continuous improvement culture and building towards a learning organisation in order to realise the company's vision.

In effecting this transformation, INA had to confront a number of potential obstacles. The demands of continuous production severely limited the time available for staff development. The failure of previous turnaround initiatives had left the workforce cynical about management's intentions. Over time, the demands of production had resulted in the HR roles of managers, supervisors and team leaders becoming diluted. Team leaders spent too much time helping out with production, meaning that the management hierarchy was becoming distorted as supervisors operated as team leaders and managers as supervisors. The grapevine was rife and the works council operated more as a forum for discussing housekeeping issues. Previous attempts to build skills through NVQ (National Vocational Qualifications) programmes had foundered because of lack of time and commitment among supervisors to undertake the necessary assessments of employee competences. The workforce was characterised by long-serving employees who had received little task-based HRD. Lastly, employee relations had deteriorated to the point that some unresolved issues had prompted strike ballots.

In addressing these potential obstacles, INA took two early important steps towards facilitating the desired learning culture where survival was seen to depend on learning faster than the rate of change. First, one-to-one meetings were held with every employee to explain the company's vision and signal management's commitment to that vision. The emphasis was on communicating the company's position honestly, whereby if the company failed to achieve its vision its decision to base its strategy around HRD investment would have at least resulted in employees having been equipped with high-level, portable skills that would significantly enhance their employability. The second was to forge a partnership agreement with the trade union Amicus. This resulted in the union signing up to the change programme and securing funding for significant investment in the company's learning centre.

These two interventions have changed the employee relations climate and opened up a genuine two-way dialogue. The individual meetings allowed employees to share their perceptions on obstacles to the development of a learning culture. They particularly stressed the importance of a unified team. This resulted in the harmonisation of terms and conditions, the introduction of an inflation-linked pay system and the re-alignment of the works council. Shop stewards now report that collaboration has replaced confrontation, evidenced by the way that the works council now plays a key role in developing strategy. Also, the council's sub-committees have been charged with leading important initiatives. These include a review of internal communications and the development of systems to support company financed individual learning plans (similar to EDAPs).

The platform for skills development was the re-launch of the NVQ programme. This time around, the roles of managers, supervisors and team leaders have been redefined to enable them to commit to their HRD responsibilities. This surfaced a number of management skills gaps among these groups, such as communication, and led to the introduction of an NVQ level 3 in business improvement techniques for supervisors and an NVQ level 3 in management for team leaders. To reinforce their commitment to HRD, senior managers assist in customising training to meet INA's context and participate in its delivery to those with leadership roles. An NVQ level 2 pro-gramme in performing manufacturing operations is being delivered in collaboration with a local college. This is being taken by all the company's production operators, some of who are now progressing through levels 3 and 4 of the programme.

For some operators, gaining the NVQ award rep-resents their first ever external qualification. However, NVQs, while addressing identified skills gaps, repre-sent only one step in the direction of forging a learning culture. The development of the learning centre represents a significant milestone in this jour-ney. Computerised learning facilities provide a network of HRD possibilities for all staff and so far, for example, 100 employees have signed up for the government-initiated Learndirect courses. In-house continuous improvement courses further reinforce the focus on learning which is increasingly being supported by those already trained becoming involved as coaches, mentors and NVQ assessors in order to help cascade the outputs of the various training programmes throughout the organisation. As roles are redefined, HRD support is offered to help facilitate the changes. For example, programmes to develop meetings skills have supported the now active engagement of employees in the works coun-cil and its sub-committees. The trade union, Amicus, appoints and sponsors four learning representatives and uses TUC courses to support their role develop-ment. The company's investment in individual learning plans is yet another step along INA's journey towards internalising a learning culture throughout the company. Although some of the HRD outcomes of these plans involve employees attending non-work-related study in their own time, the message the company wishes to communicate is that learning is valuable for its own sake.

This process of transformation has already yielded substantial benefits. The works council has reported that the grapevine is now regarded as the least reliable information source by employees. Labour turnover has fallen from an already low 8.1 per cent in 2001 to 2.5 per cent and absence rates have been reduced by 50 per cent. Cost-reduction projects have produced savings in excess of £324,000, alongside improvements in productivity and the company's health and safety record. The company's efforts have also received external recognition, including a number of HR accolades. The company was named 'Welsh people develop-ment company of the year' in 2003 and shortlisted for CIPD's annual People Management Award in both 2003 and 2004.

Despite this progress, and representations made by employees to the German parent, by the end of 2003 INA did not know whether all of this would turn around its fortunes within the Schaeffler Group. However, the vision of becoming the Group's 'pro-duction location of choice' took a large step towards becoming reality when in 2004 it was announced that the Llanelli plant would not only retain production of the 'at risk' component but would also be commissioned to produce a new high-tech engine component for a prestigious car manufacturer.

Sources: Roberts (2003); Evans (2004).

Case study questions

1. How is INA trying to build a learning culture and how would you assess its success to date?

2. In a number of models of SHRD, employees, line managers and senior managers are identified as having important roles to play in its development (for example Mabey *et al*., 1998; McCracken and Wallace, 2000). To what extent do these stakeholders represent obstacles to the development of SHRD in INA and how are any such obstacles being addressed?

3. Where would you position INA along the HRD strategic maturity continuum (Figure 10.8) and how would you justify your placement decision?

4. *Either* – what recommendations would you make to help INA move further towards strategically mature HRD?

   Or – what further evidence would be needed to justify positioning INA at the SHRD end of the HRD strategic maturity continuum (see Figures 10.3 and 10.8)?

11 Strategic reward management:
Cinderella is on her way to the ball

Learning Outcomes

By the end of this chapter you should be able to:

- define reward management and strategic reward management;

- explain the factors in the external environment that have led to the increased interest in strategic reward management;

- analyse the links between intra-organisational factors that impact upon strategic reward management.

Introduction

Reward has always enjoyed something of a Cinderella status in the world of person-nel management. It has traditionally been about the rather dull but necessary concerns of wage and salary administration than the more exciting arena of strategy. Indeed, that tradition represents almost the opposite of strategic thinking as the fol-lowing quote from Smith (1983) illustrates:

> Repeated questions to managers and employees about why they pay and accept certain levels of remuneration usually result in replies which boil down to the same answer: that is the pay level is as it has always been or, in harsher terms, we don't really know. There are very few organisations where the answer is clear and positive.'
>
> *(Smith,1983: 12)*

This chapter covers evidence which suggests that the situation in many organisa-tions may not have changed that much in the last 20 years. However, for the more progressive organisations, times have changed; reward now plays a central part in HR strategy. According to one senior HR practitioner:

> Organisations are realising what a powerful lever reward is and how it needs to com-plement their other business strategies, whereas historically people have tended to view it in glorious isolation.
>
> *(Arkin, 2005)*

It is this change which is the theme of this chapter.

The term 'reward' rather than 'pay' is used in this chapter. This is an important point because employees expect more than pay for their efforts, so the definition of reward used in this chapter includes non-pay benefits, such as recognition and pensions, as well as wages and salaries. This broad definition of reward is examined in the first part of the chap-ter. It is followed by a definition of the term 'strategic reward management' which serves as the guiding framework for the rest of the chapter. The chapter continues with an analysis of the factors in the external environment that have led to the increased interest in strategic reward management. The main part of the chapter is about the environment internal to the organisation and the links between intra-organisational factors that impact upon strategic reward management. The chapter then concludes with a discussion of some of the ethical concerns which attend new types of reward.

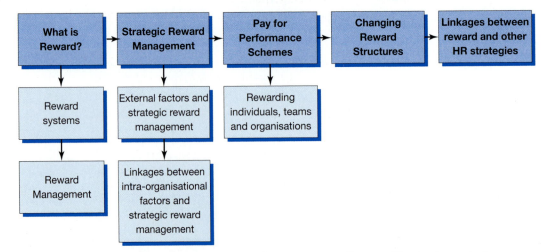

Figure 11.1 Mapping the strategic reward management territory: a summary diagram of the chapter content

What is reward?

Armstrong (2002: 3) defines reward as 'how people are rewarded in accordance with their value to the organisation. It is concerned with both financial and non-financial rewards and embraces the philosophies, strategies, policies, plans and processes used by organisations to develop and maintain reward systems.'

This definition is a useful point of departure for this chapter because it points the direction that much of the chapter will take. The first part of the definition notes that 'people are rewarded in accordance with their value to the organisation'. This is a significant point because it immediately raises the central concept in new reward thinking that it is *people* that are the focus of concern, not *jobs*. This is reflected, for example, in individual performance-related pay schemes. In addition, Armstrong's (2002) definition notes the importance of both financial and non-financial rewards. Including both financial and non-financial rewards in the reward system is recognition by the employer that non-financial rewards may play an important part in attracting, and, more particularly, retaining employees. It also represents what seems to us an important principle: that individuals require more for their efforts than simply monetary reward.

Financial and non-financial rewards

Armstrong (2002) notes that there are five areas where employees' needs may be met by non-financial rewards:

- achievement;
- recognition;
- responsibility;
- influence;
- personal growth.

Of these, it is likely that the first two – achievement and recognition – will apply to virtually all employees. The remaining three – responsibility, influence and personal growth – will apply to many more employees than may first be assumed. Most of us like to feel that we have accomplished something in our work and derive pride from our achievement. In addition, most managers realise that a simple 'thank you' and a pat on the back for a job well done has enormous motivational power.

It may seem strange to see responsibility in the list of non-financial rewards. We know that not all employees seek greater responsibility in their jobs, or greater influence over decisions that directly or indirectly influence those jobs. This may be related to the individual's personal characteristics, or it may be a consequence of a history of organisations not giving people the opportunity to exercise responsibility or influence. However, Semler's (1993) powerful account of the management style in his Brazilian company is an excellent example of how employees accept and welcome responsibility when they are treated in such a way that they are obviously valued. It may seem equally curious to see personal growth as a non-financial reward. Yet many individuals rate the opportunity for personal growth higher than financial reward.

Non-financial rewards are particularly important as motivational tools for some employees. Paying attention to these rewards increases the possibility of more positive employee attitudes and behaviours.

Employee involvement initiatives figure prominently as ways in which non-financial rewards may be delivered. For example, a communication strategy that broadcasts the successes of individuals and teams is often met with enthusiasm. Many organisations do this through their in-house magazines or their intranet. This, combined with special 'thank you' prizes (e.g. a weekend in Paris), often will have more motivational influence than direct financial rewards. Most of us like our colleagues to know when we are successful! Performance appraisal systems also have a significant role to play in meeting employees' needs for recognition and a feeling of achievement. As Chapter 9 emphasises, goal-setting and giving feedback to employees about their performance in pursuit of those goals are key performance appraisal activities. A developmental perspective to performance appraisal, rather than seeing it as a management control mechanism, is likely to result in employees defining their own training and career development needs. However, this approach to performance appraisal does depend on line managers having the appropriate attitudes and skills to manage in such a way that the individual is given sufficient autonomy for personal growth to be developed. This implies a clear training need for managers to shed the 'technician' label they often possess and embrace new ways of managing, which have leadership and facilitation as their guiding principles. These 'new ways of managing' are central to the concept of change given the key role line managers play in managing the change process.

Employees' needs for responsibility, influence and personal growth may also be met through imaginative job design. Armstrong (1993) advocates a number of elements of job design that may enhance the interest and challenge of work. These are:

- greater responsibility for employees in deciding how their work is done;
- reducing task specialisation;
- allowing employees greater freedom in defining their performance goals and standards of performance;
- introducing new and more challenging tasks.

In addition, more opportunities for employee involvement may also foster responsibility, influence and personal growth among employees. Achievement may be the result of involvement in such activities as quality circles and problem-solving groups.

Total reward

Non-financial rewards are the cornerstone of the concept of total reward. This concept emerged from the USA in the late 1990s. An internet-inspired booming economy generated a war for talent, and the consequent need to retain the most effective employees (IRS, 2003a) persuaded many organisations to look at their reward packages in new ways.

Total reward combines the traditional pay and benefits elements with the other factors that employees gain from employment. These may be skills, experience, opportunity and recognition. Therefore it is more than a flexible benefits package or a consideration of the combined value of basic pay, incentives and benefits. Total reward takes into account the less tangible benefits of employment (IRS, 2003c). The total reward package may differ between organisations, employee groups or individual employees. It may contain such considerations as a competitive base salary, development opportunities or flexible working hours. The aim is to construct the total reward package (see In Practice 11.1) in such a way that it is tailored to the desires of individual employees with the cost implications for the employer being minimal.

In Practice 11.1

Total reward at the Forestry Commission

The Forestry Commission awards its 21 senior staff 30 days holiday, while all other managers and staff (approximately 3,100) receive 25 days annual leave on entry and 30 days after ten years' service. However, it also offers a number of options for employees to take a longer break from work. These are in addition to the statutory rights to unpaid parental leave and fall into four broad categories:

Short breaks with pay. All employees are able to request short periods of time off work, regardless of their length of service. This allows staff to take time off to deal with life events, such as a family bereavement or domestic emergencies, or to participate in voluntary public service activities. However, employees are encouraged to take holiday to cover these and managers will take account of the person's untaken annual leave in deciding whether to grant special paid leave. Employees who have completed their probation – usually a year-long period – may apply for special leave without pay, of which there are several variations:

Short breaks. Employees are able to take an extended break of up to 40 days a year. 'This type of leave accommodates those employees who want to take a longer holiday, for example to visit relatives abroad. But such leave is limited in length and a return date must be agreed prior to the period of leave starting.

Open-ended. Employees can take an open-ended period of leave. While some organisations grant such sabbaticals for work-related or learning activities, the Forestry Commission does not place any restriction on what an employee can do during this time. Typically for no more than one year.

Career breaks. A scheme aimed at those with caring responsibilities provides the opportunity to take an unpaid employment break of up to five years. Again, employees must have completed their probationary period. Although not restricted to parents, that is the target group for this type of break and they are the most frequent takers.

Benefits all around

The head of HR at the Forestry Commission thinks that the breaks form part of the work–life balance approach that is continually being promoted within the organisation. He believes that having a range of options available to employees – subject to the business being able to cope with the absences, which he says it generally can – can only be advantageous because not only do the staff have the option of taking leave, but happy staff then make good workers for the organisation.

Source: IRS (2004a).

The examples in 'In Practice' 11.1 and Key Concepts 11.1 raise the total reward issue which is currently exercising the minds of many HR specialists: that of work–life balance.

Key Concepts 11.1

Foreword by Patricia Hewitt, Secretary of State for Trade and Industry, to CIPD *People Management Guide to Work–Life Balance*

'It's not political correctness, it is sound business sense'

Ten years ago, the phrase 'work–life balance' was virtually unheard of, and the idea of staggered hours and job sharing would have left most businesses baffled. Thankfully, times have changed. More and more organisations now operate on a 24/7 basis and traditional working practices are no longer an option.

▶

There is growing evidence that flexible working arrangements do help to lower absenteeism, reduce staff turnover, improve recruitment and widen the labour pool – all of which are tangible business benefits for companies looking for an edge in competitive and challenging markets. To give an example, stress-related sick leave costs British industry £370 million a year. It's a cost that we cannot afford.

I am therefore delighted that the term work–life balance is slowly but surely becoming a part of the everyday business vocabulary and that examples of good practice are becoming more widespread. It's my belief that it is not simply a matter of political correctness – it is sound business sense.

The argument for work–life balance is compelling. Since the launch of the DTI Work–Life Balance Campaign in 2000, the government has been committed to raising awareness of the business case for work–life balance and showing employers how they can implement effective policies.

We are committed to changing workplace culture, which is why we are bringing in new laws – developed in partnership with employers and employees – to create a new legal standard for flexible working. For example, from April 2003 parents of young or disabled children will gain the right to request to work flexibly and their employers will have to consider their requests seriously.

However, there is still work to be done to get more companies to seek and implement change. There are no off-the-shelf solutions to work–life balance issues. Our job is to enable a dialogue to take place between employers and employees that allows them to develop solutions that suit their individual workplace.

Work–life balance is about both empowering employees with control and choice over their working lives, and helping businesses to operate more efficiently, helping our economy become more productive. I believe that employers that instigate change will soon reap the bottom-line benefits that result from a happier workforce.

Source: Chartered Institute of Personnel and Development (2002).

Self-Check and Reflect Questions 11.1

What obstacles stand in the way of the more widespread adoption of work–life balance policies?

The philosophies, strategies, policies, plans and processes used to develop and maintain reward systems

In his definition of reward, Armstrong (2002) also notes that reward embraces the philosophies, strategies, policies, plans and processes used by organisations to develop and maintain reward systems. More particularly, writers such as Lawler (1995) have stressed the need for reward systems to play an important part in changing employee behaviours in order to complement business strategy. Such behaviours may be, for example, the acquisition of more 'commercially aware' attitudes and behaviours and greater preparedness and ability to undertake a wider range of tasks. This sits easily with the strategic HRM literature (see, for example, Mabey *et al.*, 1998), which also emphasises changed employee behaviours as the outcome of strategic HRM activities. It leads us to a more comprehensive definition of strategic reward management.

What is strategic reward management?

The strategic reward model in Figure 11.2 forms the basis of most of the content of this chapter. At the heart of the model is the theory that the HR strategy plays an important role in delivering the organisation's overall business strategy by creating in employees certain behaviours, the need for which are implied by the business strategy. These employee behaviours may be produced by an HR strategy, which includes a reward strategy as well as other HR strategies such as the cultural strategy; the structural strategy and other HR strategies (e.g. recruitment and selection, training, performance management, diversity).

The business strategy is based on the organisation's external and internal operating environments. Armstrong (1993) notes that the internal environment consists of the organisation's culture, structure, technology, working arrangements, processes and systems. In part, the model owes something to the thinking of Lawler (1995) who argues that the organisation's reward strategy can make a valuable contribution to the development of employee behaviours, although he, like us, concedes that reward is, of course, only part of the wider HR strategy.

Figure 11.2 Reward strategy and its relationship to business and other strategies

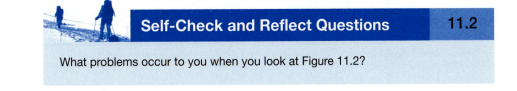

Self-Check and Reflect Questions   11.2

What problems occur to you when you look at Figure 11.2?

Factors in the external environment that have led to the increased interest in strategic reward management

Figure 11.2. suggests that reward strategy is increasingly being driven by the overall business strategy of the organisation, which is shaped by the external and internal environment in which the organisation operates. A recurrent them in this book is the changing nature of the external environment. In Table 11.1 some of the major environmental changes are considered and what they signal for an organisation's reward strategy.

Table 11.1 External environmental changes and their relationship to reward strategy

External environmental change	Relationship to reward strategy
More competitive product markets	The need to generate greater employee productivity through making this a key driver of reward strategy
More competitive product markets dictating need for greater cost control	Greater emphasis upon cash bonuses (e.g. in team pay or individual performance-related pay (IPRP) schemes) that are not consolidated into base pay
The drive for more customer-focused organisational cultures	Greater need for reward strategies that emphasise the demonstration of customer-focused behaviours as a key performance criterion
More competitive labour markets in key occupations	Reward strategies that are designed to attract and retain key employees (e.g. paying for competence acquisition, high performance). (See Schuster and Zingheim, 1999)
Low inflation economies	Greater need for self-financing reward mechanisms (e.g. output-related performance-related pay, gain sharing)
Adoption of new technologies	Need for reward strategies that are designed to pay employees for acquiring new competences
Increase in flexible organisation structures and work practices	Enhanced importance of flexible reward practices
Flatter organisational structures resulting in fewer promotion opportunities	Alternative ways of motivating effective employees in order to aid retention need to be adopted (e.g. IPRP)

Changing career expectations of employees	Declining likelihood of employees staying with organisations most of their career means loyalty is less important than effectiveness, so rewards schemes need to reflect individual effectiveness. Less attention paid to service-related pay
The decline of collective bargaining	Less emphasis upon across-the-board pay settlements to apply to all employees means greater opportunity for managers to differentiate between the pay of individuals and teams
The rise of HRM and high-commitment practices	Increase in initiatives, such as employee work involvement and teamwork, leads to search for reward initiatives that complement these

The fact that most of these external environmental changes have occurred is beyond dispute, although not all of them (e.g. the decline of collective bargaining) are significant in all organisations. To some degree, these environmental changes are reflected in the objectives for introducing new pay systems explained by organisations in the research conducted by Corby *et al.* (2005). Among these objectives were attraction and retention of staff; encouraging flexibility; and wanting to reward employees financially for remaining in their current posts rather than seeking higher pay through promotion. But the evidence suggests that the promotion of 'leading edge' reward strategies has not occurred to the extent that one may have expected. Lowe *et al.*'s (2002) international survey showed that the move to variable pay may not be as pronounced as it is tempting to think. Only three countries' managers (China, Japan and Taiwan) rated pay incentives as an important part of their current reward systems, much higher than the USA and Australia. However, all managers in all ten countries in their research were of the opinion that there should be greater dependence upon pay incentives in their reward systems. This suggests that actual reward practice is running behind management ambitions. When asked if incentives were a significant amount of pay, only Korea scored highly, whereas USA, Canada and Australia were low. This last finding is surprising given the national cultural value of individualism in these three countries. Again, managers in all ten countries thought incentives should be a more significant amount of pay. A similar result was evident when the focus turned to reward being contingent upon organisational or group performance. Again, only China and Taiwan reported relatively high dependence upon reward contingent upon organisational or group performance.

In another study, Brown (1999) notes that although 94 per cent of the respondent organisations in a Towers Perrin study of 460 organisations in 13 European countries reported that they had made 'significant' changes to their reward policies in the preceding three years and even more had changes planned,

> the reward package of the average European worker, in fact, looks very similar to that of three, five or even ten years ago, with base pay levels set using a job evaluation system in three-quarters of the companies; pay managed within ranges averaging between 20 and 40 per cent in width; an annual profit-sharing scheme; and an increasingly comprehensive bundle of benefits.
>
> *(Brown, 1999: 53)*

Brown argues that the impression gained from this study is one of incremental change with, for example, competences being used to improve traditional job evaluation schemes and team pay introduced alongside, rather than in place of, individual bonus schemes.

This lack of major change does raise questions as to what obstacles there may be to its introduction. Brown (1999) argues that there may be two such obstacles. The first is the lack of skill and commitment that many line managers have when it comes to the implementation of reward initiatives, particularly (as noted in Chapter 10) when they are linked to performance management. The second obstacle is the poor grasp that many employees have of such basic issues as how their base pay is set and the value of their reward packages. This is what the authors found (Lewis *et al.*, 2002) found in a study of the introduction a new reward scheme in a large UK company. Only eight of the 460 respondents to the Towers Perrin survey noted above were able to say that their employees had a strong understanding of the basic pay issues that relate to them.

The links between intra-organisational factors that impact upon strategic reward management and strategic reward management

The link with business strategy

Figure 11.2 makes clear that the purpose of the reward strategy (in its role as part of the overall HR strategy) is to assist in producing employee behaviours that are consistent with the organisation's business strategy. As such, the reward strategy plays its part in the quest for organisational change. As a preliminary stage prior to defining desired employee behaviours, the organisation may produce statements of intent similar to that of the company in the case study at the end of this chapter.

The strategic HRM literature (e.g. Beer *et al.*, 1984; Guest, 1987) reflects the desire for certain employee behaviours (or 'key HR outputs' as they call them) to be delivered by strategic HRM. These are: employee commitment to the organisation's aims; employee competence; flexibility; and the production of quality goods and services. Twenty years on from when this was written, these key HR outputs look so general and unspecific that they are of little value to most organisations. Many organisations have progressed from this level of generality by using these key HR outputs as general aims from which to develop statements of desired employee behaviours: behaviours that flow from the organisation's business strategy. These are often expressed as key competences for particular jobs. The movement towards competence acquisition is considered later in this chapter when we argue that the specification of competences is a key component of strategic reward management in that it links reward with other HR activities, such as recruitment, and selection and training.

At this point the assumption is raised which dominates reward management thinking in general and the model in Figure 11.2 in particular. This is that pay has the ability to motivate employees to behave in a way in which they may not otherwise behave. The theory here that tends to predominate is that of rational economic person. This has it roots in the work of F.W. Taylor (1911) who assumed that workers were lazy and needed money to motivate them to expend greater effort. The prevalence of payments-by-results schemes in the twentieth century, in particular for blue-collar workers, testifies to the influence of this way of thinking about the relationship between pay and employee effort. Later, this approach was questioned by the human relations school, which queried the over-reliance on money as a motivator and argued that social relationships were an important determinant of employee productivity.

Equally well-known are the theories of Maslow (1943) and Herzberg (1968). Maslow's 'hierarchy of needs' suggests that people's needs change as they ascend a hierarchy, which has basic needs for food, security, etc. at the lowest level, with self-actualisation at the highest. Herzberg argued that employees were more likely to be motivated by factors such as achievement and the work itself than simply by money. While money has only limited power to motivate, it does have the ability to demotivate employees if they are dissatisfied with the amount they receive or the way in which this amount is determined.

It is beyond the scope of this chapter to go into detail on these and the many other motivation theories. What is clear is that this is a highly complex issue. Perhaps the best we can say is that money may motivate some people to behave in particular ways some of the time, in some circumstances. What we cannot assume is a clear relationship between pay and motivation.

The links between reward strategy and cultural strategy; structural strategy; and other HR strategies

In Chapter 2, the point is made that in the matching models of strategic HRM, organisational culture, structure and HR activities (e.g. recruitment and selection, training) are important components of strategic HRM. This is true of both closed and open models. In the closed models of strategic HRM (e.g. Fombrun *et al.* (1984)) a particular type of business strategy (e.g. innovation or cost reduction) suggests the need for a specific organisational structure and differing HR practices. In addition, Schuler and Jackson (1987) suggest cultural change to match changed business strategies in terms of a series of required employee behaviours. In the open model (Mabey *et al.*, 1998) the organisational strategy's implied desired employee behaviours are pursued through the HR strategy, which consists of three 'key levers' (structural, cultural and personnel strategies) which are intended to subsume all aspects of organisation that impact upon employees' behaviour.

These three 'key levers' of the open model form the basis of the sections that follow and flow from Figure 11.2. First, organisation cultural strategy and the part that reward management may play in delivering a particular type of culture is dealt with. To achieve this what has been by far the most significant change in reward management in recent years is analysed: the linking of pay to performance. The section that follows deals with organisation structural strategy and the role of reward in achieving structural change. For this purpose we examine pay systems based on the principles of broad banding and job families. Both of these approaches to reward reflect the desire of organisations to move towards more flexible organisational structures to ensure greater responsiveness to change. The third section deals with HR strategies other than reward. Here we examine the issues of job competences. This has been a major feature of reward change in many organisations and has strong integrating links with the other major areas of HR.

The link with organisational culture: paying for performance

Rewarding performance, either individual job performance, team performance or organisational performance, has become, for many organisations, the most important component of reward strategy. What this means for many employees is a proportion of their salary is put at risk: something that is not guaranteed to be popular because most of us think about reward in terms of base pay (Schuster and Zingheim, 1992): the fixed amount which traditionally has increased yearly to reflect inflation and, often, length of service. Base pay will also change, of course, upon promotion to a more responsible job. Base pay embodies the values of predictability, security and permanency – none of which are characteristics consistent with the desire to change employee behaviours.

From a managerial perspective, base pay is not necessarily the best form of reward strategy because the element of permanency that it entails is expensive. Increasingly employers are asking themselves why they should build into their fixed salary costs a permanent salary bill that takes little account of changing external, organisational and individual circumstances. Reward strategies that rely exclusively on base pay built into salary scales, through which employees move annually until the top of the scale is reached, or promotion achieved, are typical in public-sector employment. Such strategies assume that length of service equates with experience and loyalty – neither of which tends to be as prized by organisations now as in the past. Indeed, such is the pace of change that yesterday's experience may be an impediment to change. Moreover, it is now generally accepted that loyalty to one employer, typified by a career spent with that employer, is an increasingly outdated concept in an age where employees may have a number of different careers as well as employers. Reward strategies that rely on promotions for employees to grow their salaries do not take into account the fact that organisations now have flatter structures, with the consequence that promotion is less available.

However, the decreasing interest in the dominance of base pay does raise an interesting question for HR specialists: 'how can the traditional reward objectives of attracting, retaining and motivating employees be achieved while making the pay budget more cost effective?' The answer for many organisations has been to make base pay reflect the market rate for the job and to supplement this with a variable pay element related to individual performance, team performance, organisational performance and individual competence acquisition – or a combination of these. One of the key decisions that needs to be taken into account is whether to pay the variable element as a lump sum bonus or to consolidate this into salary. The trend in both the USA and UK has been for a move towards one-off cash bonuses (IDS, 2003a). This is hardly surprising given the cost saving that the organisation enjoys. By not raising base pay, one-off cash bonuses do not affect future base pay increases or other associated payments such as overtime, and, of course, pensions.

Moving from all base pay to a combination of base and variable pay does, of course, signal the organisation's desire to move from paying for the job to paying for the person. Therefore, the reliance on traditional bureaucratic forms of job evaluation is less pronounced. However, job evaluation is still relevant. Base pay still needs to be set at a level consistent with jobs throughout the organisation and the external labour market. Therefore, some method of determining the relative importance of jobs is needed. It is that definition of importance that is likely to be different in the organisation which places more significance in a combination of base and variable pay. Such a definition is likely to reflect the changed employee behaviours the organisation wishes to encourage in order to meet its changed organisational circumstances. What is clear, according to Schuster and Zingheim (1992), is internal equity will no longer be the dominant consideration. The market value of jobs, and employees' skills and their impact on the organisation's strategy will take precedence over internal equity.

Self-Check and Reflect Questions 11.3

Moving from a situation where all pay is base pay to one where there is a combination of base and variable pay does carry with it threats. What may these be?

Rewarding individual performance

Appraisal-related pay (or, as we prefer to call it here, 'individual performance-related pay' (IPRP)) is defined by Acas as: 'a method of payment where an individual employee receives increases in pay based wholly or partly on the regular and systematic assessment of job performance' (Acas, 2005). It was adopted enthusiastically throughout the 1990s in the USA and UK in many areas of white-collar employment, for example education, local government and financial services. There is some evidence that the popularity of IPRP is spreading to many countries. In a survey of 460 organisations in 13 European countries by Towers Perrin, it was reported that only 25 per cent of non-management employees in the firms surveyed had general, across-the-board pay increases, while 93 per cent of the respondent firms had variable bonus schemes (Brown, 1999).

IPRP has been introduced in many organisations to change the culture towards a 'new performance culture' which many managers feel is necessary. There seems to be some support for the validity of this attempt. Lawler (1984: 128) notes that reward systems can lead to the culture of an organisation varying quite widely. Among the different types of culture that can be generated, Lawler suggests, are: human-resource oriented cultures, entrepreneurial cultures, innovative culture, competence-based cultures, and participative cultures. However, if you have studied Chapter 6 you will know that introducing IPRP and expecting a performance culture to be the inevitable consequence is somewhat naïve.

The proposition that IPRP will lead to culture change is based on two assumptions: first, that employees, in general, find the prospect of IPRP appealing and, second, that it is implemented effectively. The evidence suggests that the first may be valid. Most employees (Kessler, 1994) agree with the principle of IPRP: that the able and industrious employee should be rewarded more generously for that ability and industry than the idle and incompetent. However, there is ample evidence that the problems with IPRP concern implementation.

In a study of PRP for first-level managers in three UK financial services organisations (Lewis, 1998b) the author found evidence of implementation problems. Perceived unfairness was one which had a variety of causes. There was evidence of managers imposing objectives with the result that the objective-setting process was 'something that was done to them rather than something in which they played an active part' (Lewis, 1998b: 70). In another study, the employees interviewed by Procter et al. (1993) in an electronics plant expressed concerns about favouritism, in particular the arbitrary way in which managers applied measurement criteria and the ways in which grades were distributed. In two of the three organisations the authors researched (Lewis, 1998b) little attention was paid to the giving of performance feedback to employees. This may be because managers are put in a position where they must differentiate between the level of reward of their team members, a position many find uncomfortable. This decision process effectively creates increased dependency of the team member on the line manager, and less dependency on, for example, the trade union (Kessler, 1994).

Hand (2000) notes the growth of IPRP in Ireland. But he too notes implementation problems in Irish organisations. Among these are:

- poor design, implementation and communication;
- too much emphasis upon individual performance over a short timescale;
- an excessive focus on financial results;
- inadequate salary differentiation (particularly a problem in times of low inflation).

The outcome of these implementation weaknesses is that the value of paying for performance is not practised. What seems a good idea in principle becomes overtaken by perceived problems with the result that employees and managers lose faith in the concept. This then raises considerable doubts about the ability of IPRP to deliver the cultural change objectives planned by organisations (see Key Concepts 11.2 and In Practice 11.2).

Key Concepts   11.2

Acas on making appraisal-related pay effective

If appraisal-related pay is not suitably designed and introduced sensibly into an environment where trust is high and there is a readiness to adapt to the change, employee relations may suffer. It may not only fail to motivate but may in fact demotivate. Employees may soon become discouraged if they are not aware of the levels of performance they need to attain or where appraisal-related pay awards are not applied consistently across the eligible participants. There may be doubts about the credibility of the scheme where financial constraints, for example by the use of budgets or 'quotas', unnecessarily restrict the extent or amount of appraisal-related pay awards. A carefully developed scheme should minimise the scope for complaints about subjectivity in assessment and divisiveness in operation.

In particular, the appraisal-related pay scheme should be designed to avoid any tendency to mark higher each year to retain employees during periods of labour shortage. Any beneficial link between performance and reward may be lost with pay costs rising but without a corresponding rise in corporate or individual performance. Employers are also advised to consider how the scheme will fit with the management style and culture of the organisation.

Employers may also need to overcome a disinclination among some employees to move around an organisation where learning the skills required by a new job may jeopardise their appraisal-related pay awards. Employees may prefer to remain in a job where they have already been rewarded. Furthermore, employers who have operated a highly centralised method of pay determination may find a scheme that relies on openness and the judgement of line managers inappropriate.

Some trade unions and employee representatives remain hostile to appraisal-related pay as they see it as an individualised method of payment running counter to the principles of collective bargaining. These objections will best be overcome if, through negotiation and/or consultation, they have an opportunity to influence and agree management's proposals, develop confidence in the fairness of the scheme and the way it will operate, and if the potential benefits to their members are clearly demonstrated.

Appraisal-related pay should not be introduced retrospectively. Employees should be consulted at the earliest opportunity about any proposal to alter the established payment system in favour of appraisal-related pay. Employers will need to explain the need for such an initiative as well as how both the organisation and individual employees might hope to benefit from its introduction. Necessary research will need to be conducted to select the most suitable and flexible scheme that can accommodate the immediate and continuing needs of the organisation. Extensive communications and training will need to take place as far in advance of the scheme's implementation date as possible. Employees can only then know what is expected of them and in turn what to expect from the scheme.

The following points summarise some important ways in which appraisal-related pay may be made more effective.

- There must be commitment to appraisal-related pay from senior managers.
- The role of managers is critical.
- Adequate resources and suitable training should be provided.
- Employers should consult with managers, employees and their representatives before appraisal-related pay is introduced.

- All employees involved must receive full and clear information about how the scheme will operate.
- Appraisal-related pay should be fair and open and based on a formal system of performance assessment.
- The scheme should be carefully designed, simple to operate and should encourage consistency and objectivity.
- There should be an appeals procedure and the scheme should be regularly evaluated.

Source: Acas (2005).

In Practice   11.2

Mobile phone operator introduces individual performance-related pay

Mobile phone company O2 has reduced staff turnover by introducing performance-related pay for new workers in its UK call centres. The director of compensation and benefits at O2 said the new pay structure, which includes a performance-linked bonus and a revised career and pay progression framework, had 'dramatically reduced' staff attrition rates and the company's reliance on temporary staff.

O2 introduced the reward structure as part of a larger transformation programme to increase employee commitment and customer satisfaction following customer complaints about the complexity of its billing tariffs. Prior to the introduction of the new scheme, pay rises were linked to service and length of time in the role. There was no performance element and some of the salaries the company was paying were thought to be higher than the market rates.

Staff pay rises are now based on individual performance, monitored via phone-call observations and productivity levels. Employees can receive a target bonus of up to 10 per cent of their salary per annum, paid out twice yearly. They also sit down every month with their line managers to discuss their performance.

Currently only 30 per cent of O2's 3,300 UK call centre staff are on the new pay structure, with the remainder on a set salary up to £5,000 higher than those on the new pay scale. The difference is a result of O2's demerger from BT in 2001, because transferred staff were on the same terms and conditions that BT originally set in place.

O2's compensation director notes that the next task is to merge the existing employees onto the new terms and conditions. However, it was thought that the different pay scales had not caused problems between employees as the company had been very open about the two levels of pay.

Source: *People Management* (2004b).

Rewarding team performance

It is one of the contradictions of HRM in recent years that the expansion in IPRP has been accompanied by structural change that has emphasised team working. It would therefore be expected that team-based pay would have had similar growth to more individualised pay. But this has not been the case. Research by UK bodies, such as IRS, CIPD, the Institute for Employment Studies and the Industrial Society, suggest that, at most, 10 per cent of UK organisations operate team pay schemes, although the figure noted in the European-wide study by Towers Perrin was more than double that (see IRS, 2001).

Yet, as well as reinforcing the desire to move towards a team-oriented structure, team-based pay may play its part in fostering cultural values which support teamwork.

In team-based pay, payments, or other forms of non-financial reward, are made to team members on the basis of some predetermined criteria. These criteria may overcome one of the objections to team-based pay, that of differential contribution, by making differentiated rewards. Armstrong (2002: 336–337) notes that the purpose of team-based pay is to 'reinforce the sort of behaviour that leads to and sustains effective team performance by:

1. providing incentives and other means of recognising team achievements;
2. clarifying what teams are expected to achieve by relating rewards to the attainment of pre-determined and agreed targets and standards of performance or to the satisfactory completion of a project or the stage of a project;
3. conveying the message that one of the organisation's core values is effective teamwork.'

Thomson (1995) identified the types of teams that may be associated with team-based pay. He categorised these as temporary and permanent. The former may be a team set up to achieve a specific project-related goal. The team would consist of employees in different functions operating at different levels in the organisation. Permanent teams may be those based on a specific function (e.g. HR), a process (e.g. in manufacturing plants), a product market or a geographical area. What seems to be important for team-based pay to have a chance of success is that the team has a clear identity, a sense of autonomy, consists of members whose work is interdependent and are flexible, multi-skilled and good team players (Roberts, 1997: 570).

IRS (2001) argue that the slow take-up of team-based pay may be for five reasons:

1. the problem of identifying teams;
2. the difficulty is assessing individual contributions;
3. the effect that it may have in encouraging employees to stay in high-performing/rewarding teams thus prejudicing organisational flexibility;
4. group norms which encourage teams to perform at the level necessary to trigger the financial reward; and
5. the 'peaking out' effect, where teams reach a performance peak from which they decline after two or three years.

Rewarding organisational performance

The touchstone for the development of reward schemes that reward organisational performance is the statement by Chancellor Gordon Brown in his 1998 pre-budget report:

> I want to remove, once and for all, the old 'them and us' culture in British industry. I want to encourage the new enterprise culture of teamwork in which everyone contributes and everyone benefits from success … we will make it easier for all employees … to become stakeholders in their company. I want to double the number of firms in which all employees have the opportunity to own shares.
>
> *(cited in Hyman, 2000)*

Profit-related bonus schemes

The simplest, and traditionally most popular, of the schemes that reward organisation performance is the profit-related scheme (see an example in 'In Practice' 11.3). This popularity was due to the tax advantages that existed under UK tax regulations. Although

In Practice   11.3

Profit-related pay at The Big Food Group

The Big Food Group, a retail chain which includes Iceland stores, launched its scheme in 2001. It covers all employees and aims to link bonus to group and business unit profit.

For the majority of employees 75 per cent of the bonus potential is linked to the business unit profit target and the remaining 25 per cent to the group profit target. The annual payment is triggered when the group profit target is hit, since this covers the cost of the bonus payout. Additional payments are made for performance beyond target. Bonus potential depends upon role and seniority. In the initial year of operation all staff received a payment of £200. This amount could be doubled if the maximum profit target is achieved.

At the launch of the scheme, much effort was put into employee communication through briefings to managers and letters and leaflets to all employees. Progress towards targets is communicated to employees quarterly.

Source: IDS (2003a).

these tax advantages no longer remain, the link between profit and reward is a straightforward one which contributes to the Chancellor's ambitions.

In addition to linking bonus to profit, many organisations run employee share ownership schemes in which employees obtain shares in the company's stock.

Employee share ownership schemes

Hyman argues that there are three principal management rationales for the introduction of employee share schemes. These are that they:

1. offer property rights to employees;
2. help to unite employee and employer interests with resultant enhancements in employee satisfaction and, therefore, productivity;
3. buttress management attempts to seek control over the regulation of the employment relationship through, for example, moving pay away from predetermined formulae such as cost of living and connecting it more directly with company performance.

Hyman is dubious about the effect of the first two of these rationales. In general, the amount that is added to employees' salaries is modest, such that employees tend to see the share allocation as a bonus. In addition, there are usually no means for influencing organisational decision-making. Given these points, it is unlikely that significant gains in employee identification with the interests of the employer will result. That said, Hyman points out that there is some evidence to suggest the management ambition to retain key employees through the introduction of employee share ownership schemes is being realised. This view receives some support in a recent IRS study (IRS, 2003b). However, the same study notes that the administrative burden they impose is a potential disadvantage.

Key Concepts 11.3 and 11.4 outline the operational details of two employee share ownership schemes currently available in the UK.

Key Concepts   11.3

Share incentive plans (SIPs)

Prior to October 2001, SIPs were known as all-employee share ownership plans (AESOPs). SIPs provide for four types of share provision:

- free shares: given by the company to employees up to a limit of £3,000 in any tax year;
- partnership shares: purchased by employees out of their salary before it is subject to tax or national insurance to a limit of £125 per month (or 10 per cent of salary, whichever is the lower);
- matching shares: companies match partnership shares purchased by employees up to a limit of two matching shares for each partnership share purchased;
- dividend shares: dividends may be re-invested tax-free up to a limit of £1,500 per year depending on the rules in the company plan.

Employees who keep their shares in the scheme for five years pay no income tax or national insurance contributions on the shares. If the shares are withdrawn after three years, income tax and national insurance contributions must be paid on the initial market value of the shares. In addition, employees do not have to pay capital gains tax if their shares are kept in the scheme for five years.

Of the 27 large UK employers that participated in an IRS study in 2003 (IRS, 2003b), four were operating SIP schemes. One of these was the financial services organisation National Australia Group Europe. Ninety per cent of its employees participate in the scheme. The minimum monthly employee purchase of partnership shares is £10 and additional free shares are allocated, based on the company's performance (no matching shares are allocated as part of the scheme).

Key Concepts   11.4

Savings-related share option schemes

The savings-related share option scheme requires a contribution from the employee. In such schemes, the employee saves for a specified period of three, five or seven years. The scheme specifies that employees can buy shares at the end of the savings period with the savings fund accumulated. The price of the shares will be the market price at the start of the savings contract or at an agreed discount agreed at the start of the contract. The shares bought at the end of the savings contract attract tax relief.

With the three-year savings contract, the employee saves a fixed amount monthly (it cannot exceed £250) and at the end of the term a cash bonus of 2.75 months' payment is added. At the end of a five-year contract, a cash bonus of 7.5 months' payment is added. At the end of the three- or five-year term, the employee uses the amount saved and the bonus to buy shares in the company. For employees who have saved for five years there is the option of extending the term to seven years, in which case, 13.5 months' payments is added as a cash bonus. Employees who choose a seven-year contract do not have to make monthly contributions after five years but agree to leave their savings untouched for the final two years to qualify for the higher bonus.

The price at which employees have the opportunity to purchase shares must not be below 80 per cent of the market value at the start of the contract. This seemed to be the typical price determined by employers in an Incomes Data Services (IDS) study (IDS, 1998). At the end of the contract period, employees also have the option to have their contributions returned if the share price is not favourable, rendering the scheme risk-free.

As with profit-sharing schemes, all employees who have been employed by the company for five years must be eligible to participate in savings-related share option schemes if the scheme is to gain Inland Revenue approval.

The UK bank First Direct's savings-related share option scheme has a 61 per cent take-up among eligible employees (those with at least six months' service). Participating employees must make a minimum monthly payment of £5. The company offers a discount of up to 20 per cent on the market price of the shares purchased. Three- and five-year period options are available (IRS, 2003b).

Gainsharing

Gainsharing is more popular in the USA than in Britain. Gainsharing schemes differ from employee share ownership schemes in that the relationship between employees' efforts and their eventual reward is more direct. Gainsharing schemes are designed so that employees share the financial results of improvements in productivity, cost saving or quality. The resultant payment is paid from costs savings generated as a result of such improvements. The gainshare plan payment may be made in three ways: as a percentage of base pay; as a one-off cash bonus or as a payment per hour worked.

Schuster and Zingheim (1992) are careful to point out that the organisation must design safeguards to ensure that it derives financial value from the results generated from the project linked to gainsharing. This type of gainsharing differs from more traditional forms of gainsharing which have operated in manufacturing under the heading of Scanlon and Rucker plans. The principal difference is that the foundation of this new type of gainsharing is the future goals of the organisation, whereas that of more traditional gainsharing plans is the historical performance standards of the participating employees. The key point here, of course, is that historical performance standards may be achieved or exceeded while the organisation's overall goals are not met.

In Practice   11.4

Gainsharing at BP Grangemouth

BP's Grangemouth site has operated a gainsharing plan for several years. It covers all 2,300 employees at the site and is designed to focus the performance of employees on the site's performance objectives. The plan is divided into output measures and input measures. Output measures account for 80 per cent of the overall bonus and include a range of factors, such as:

● profits;
● costs;
● reliability; and
● safety.

Input measures cover:

● people and organisational objectives;
● the completion of projects on time; and
● the development of new strategy.

The financial, safety and reliability targets are annual or quarterly cash-based targets and a share of the savings generated by meeting or exceeding these targets is distributed among employees. The input targets are 'yes/no' targets, which yield payment only if they are fully achieved in the year.

The gainshare bonus is paid annually. In 2003 it was 15 per cent of salary.

Communication to employees is achieved by line managers explaining targets and regularly updating their teams on progress towards target achievement. Employees can also obtain information on targets and potential bonus payments from the site intranet.

Source: IDS (2003a).

The link with organisational structures

In the same way that reward has the potential to effect cultural change, it also has the capacity to contribute to structural change. Two of the most popular methods by which structural change strategies have been pursued are to construct reward structures on the principles of broad banding and job families. Organisations introducing these structures have a variety of reasons for doing so. But at the heart of the reforms is a desire to move towards more flexible organisational structures to ensure greater responsiveness to change.

A new reward structure reflects the particular circumstances of the organisation introducing it. Therefore, in the following section only give a general overview of broad banding and job families with a view to demonstrating how they play a significant part in strategic reward and SHRM can be given.

An understanding of new forms of reward structure is gained more easily by a brief introduction to traditional pay structures, typified by those that still exist for many employees in the public sector. Here, usually, a process of evaluating the 'worth' of each job leads to a pay structure that consists of a number of grades, each of which contains a pay spine with minimum and maximum pay levels for each spine. There is also a reference point which reflects the central position of the spine. In the example of the senior lecturer grade in the UK 'new' university sector, the pay spine contains ten pay points with a minimum pay point of £27,390 and a maximum pay point of £36,420 (there is no reference point as such). Employing universities determine the point at which a newly engaged lecturer enters the pay spine depending upon experience and market rate. However, the important point to bear in mind is that the lecturer progresses up the spine, usually by one point annually, until the top is reached. In such cases extra salary can only be obtained by promotion or cost of living adjustments to the scale.

Traditional pay structures do present the advantages of orderliness and the ability for employees to control costs.

Job-family-based reward structures

A job family is a group of jobs that may be similar in purpose and content although carried out at different levels in the organisation. They may be functional, in that they cover specific workgroups within a function such as marketing or HR; alternatively, they may be generic, encompassing jobs that entail similar types of work across functional boundaries, for example technicians or administrators. Armstrong and Murlis (1998: 208) note that there are a number of processes involved in job family modelling. These are:

● identifying groups of roles in which the type of work is similar but where it is carried out at different levels:

- analysing the essential nature of each of these groups or job families;
- establishing the levels of work carried out within each job family;
- defining the differentiating factors between each level in the family in terms of role size;
- producing functional or generic role specifications.

Job family-based structures offer specific advantages over more traditional pay structures, particularly the creation of career paths for employees who, in traditional pay structures, see promotion as a process of 'grade-jumping'. 'Grade-jumping' may have involved the employee in moving away from the type of job in which that employee had specialised, or from the particular function in which expertise and experience had been developed. In job-family-based reward structures the ambitious employee may grow his or her responsibilities and salary by remaining in similar work in the same function. This is particularly important in organisations that have been 'flattened' with fewer opportunities for promotion being evident.

By isolating particular jobs in separate groupings, job-family-based reward structures also present pay management advantages to the employer. Pressures on pay from the external labour market may be met more easily if jobs are put in 'market groups' (Armstrong and Murlis, 1998).

In Practice   11.5

Introducing a job-family-based reward structure at Norlife

Norlife is a supplier of retail financial services products in the UK. In recent years the financial services market has been characterised by intense competition following the deregulation of the market in the late 1980s. This competition led to the development of a strategy in which cost reduction was a cornerstone. In particular, it was felt to be of paramount importance that more value needed to be obtained from the organisation's employees. Obtaining more value from Norlife's employees was the driving force behind the new reward strategy that was introduced in 1998.

For some years Norlife operated a traditional pay system. The foundation of this was a conventional pay structure in which a sequence of job grades existed and jobs of broadly equivalent value were slotted into grades. A pay range was attached to each grade and pay progression was through that range which contained, typically, ten pay points. Grades were determined by job evaluation. While this provided an orderly basis for managing pay relativities, it led to a belief by employees that the only means of career and pay progression was by promotion through the grade structure.

The new structure is based on the principle of job families. All jobs at Norlife are grouped into eight families that are on six different levels. For example, staff who deal with customer queries in the company's call centre were placed in the job family 'sales support' at level 6 (the lowest level), whereas directors are in the 'strategy and policy' job family at level 1.

For each generic role (e.g. accounting technician) a set of competences was defined reflecting what role holders should be able to demonstrate as a 'starter', 'typical performer' or 'high performer'. Under the new system, pay is to be determined by market rate, acquisition of competences and the achievement of individual performance targets. In addition, Norlife management stressed that pay will be determined by job not grade. An important defining principle of the new system is that those employees who contribute more will progress faster through the pay scales than those who are average or below average performers. Stress was laid upon the fact that current pay and benefits were unaffected by the new system.

The company newsletter which announced the new job families system noted several advantages of the change.

▶

- employees would be better equipped to plan their own careers (within or outside the organisation) and their own training and development needs;
- broader job descriptions would give employees more opportunity to increase their skills and make their jobs more challenging;
- employees would not see grade promotions as the only way of furthering their salaries but be encouraged to think of skill acquisition as a means of career and salary progression;
- more effective employees would be able to earn more competitive salaries.

In the final analysis Norlife was seeking to develop a more competent and flexible workforce, better equipped to manage change and to meet the Norlife goal of increased efficiency and therefore, reduced cost.

Source: Lewis *et al.* (2004).

Broad-banded reward structures

Armstrong and Murlis (1998: 186) define broad banding as 'the compression of a hierarchy of pay grades or salary ranges into a small number of wide bands. Each of the bands therefore spans the pay opportunities previously covered by several separate pay ranges'.

Again the comparison with the traditional pay structure outlined at the beginning of this section will be taken as the focus of this brief discussion of broad banding.

The broad-banded pay structure may comprise as few as four or five bands to encompass all the employees covered by the pay structure. This contrasts with more than double that number of pay bands in the traditional pay structure. The broad bands are themselves much more comprehensive in their coverage of the pay span, which may extend to as much as 100 per cent or more above the minimum rate in the band. (In the senior lecturer example, noted above, the maximum pay point is only 30 per cent higher than the minimum point.) Compared with traditional pay structures the broad-banded structure will often depend less on the process of job evaluation to define small differences between job responsibilities. The pay differences that these produce may be catered for in a broad band that affords managers more opportunity to use their discretion in paying their employees what they think is the appropriate amount. Employees will be less concerned for higher status as a way of growing pay than in the traditional pay structure; this is replaced with a concern for career development through acquiring new competences. Therefore, the emphasis switches from the job in the traditional pay structure to the person in the broad-banded pay structure.

It is this last feature of broad-banded pay structures that relates most closely to strategic reward management and SHRM. One of the major advantages they offer is to encourage greater employee attention to career development through competence acquisition as well as fostering added organisational flexibility as employees are more likely to move around within their own bands than seek advancement through promotion to a higher band (see In Practice 11.6).

In Practice   11.6

Broad banding at English Welsh & Scottish Railway

English Welsh & Scottish Railway (EWS) is a rail freight operator running trains to and from British ports and into continental Europe. The company employs around 6,000 people. It emerged as a single entity from an international consortium that bought British Rail's freight operation in 1996. The company recognises four trade unions.

Original pay structure

The company inherited a reward structure based on allocation of a specific pay rate for a job that spanned 45 grade codes. Pay increases related to promotion and annual pay rises agreed by the associated trade unions, and had no direct link to performance, skills gained, or market rates. It was therefore a relatively inflexible system that did not easily accommodate sideways movement from one job to another within the organisation.

Because EWS had taken over what had been five separate companies, five different rates of pay for identical job types existed throughout the company. For instance, a chief clerk on grade five operating in one part of the company could be on £10,000, while a chief clerk at the same grade in another office was on £11,000.

Furthermore, salaries took no account of location. So, a senior administrator in Scotland could be earning the same as a senior administrator in a part of England where living costs are higher. The company also inherited a complex system of overtime pay and allowances based on rosters worked. These revolved around lengthy timesheets, which created the need for a complicated pay administration process.

Rationale for change

The reasons for change therefore hinged around the need to:

- provide more reward flexibility;
- provide a better base for rewarding growth in competence;
- reflect organisational changes and equalise the pay structure throughout the business;
- simplify the pay administration system to render it easier to run and less costly; and
- ensure that pay was in line with market rates.

The company felt that this pay system did not reflect the way the company wanted to do things. It felt that market rates should be paid; the right salary for the right person in the right place. So the decision was taken to discuss with the unions how a move away from the system of allocation of a specific pay rate for a job could be achieved.

A key factor in introducing the new system was that it focused staff on the need to acquire new competences in order to move up the salary band, rather than relying on promotion. A senior EWS manager explained that this enabled a pay structure to be created that allowed the company to say to staff 'the more responsibilities you take on, the more skills you gain, the more motivated you are, fine – you will move through the pay band. But if you are going to sit there and do the minimum job, we won't give you a pay rise.'

It also enabled the company to move away from formal job evaluation, which the company believed to be too rigid. It was felt that the new system was totally flexible and allowed the company to pay greater attention to what the market was paying.

New structure

The revised organisational structure consists of five bands or 'levels', ranging from the more junior roles in level one to the chief executive and director roles at level five. Broad-banded pay applies to the 1,200 white-collar workers only, leaving the remaining 4,800 employees in level one (largely train drivers, guards and ground staff) on a specific pay rate for a job.

Using external market data, EWS sets the range of pay attached to each level and this is further broken down into three sections: low (L), medium (M) and high (H). These salary ranges can be altered over time as and when changes occur in the market place. An outline of the general level, dimensions and accountabilities of the jobs that fall into each band was agreed with the unions and this is used by managers and HR as a guide to determine where each job sits within the framework.

Source: IRS (2004c).

The link with other HR strategies

Linking reward to other HR strategies is potentially the most problematic aspect of integrating reward with intra-organisational factors. Yet it is vital. It was noted at the beginning of the chapter that, historically, people have tended to view reward in glorious isolation. For example, it was evident in our discussion of team pay that progress towards its adoption has been slow despite the burgeoning of teamwork. In this final section competence-related pay is analysed. Competences highlight the employee attributes that may underpin a recruitment campaign and define those that selectors look for at selection stage. Competences structure the aims and objectives of training programmes and enable measurement criteria for performance management schemes to be defined accurately. They too may play an important part in promotion and redundancy decisions. Here we concentrate on competences in their direct link to pay.

Competence-related pay

Competence-related pay can be defined as 'a method of rewarding people wholly or partly by reference to the level of competence they demonstrate in carrying out their roles. It is a method of paying people for their ability to perform' (Armstrong, 2002: 289). It is not surprising that interest in competence-related pay should grow given the enormous amount of attention paid to the definition of competences for purposes of selection, training and appraisal in recent years. However, there is some evidence that take-up of competence-related pay is limited. Only 14 per cent of the 460 organisations in the Towers Perrin study noted above (Brown, 1999) reported that they related base pay increases to employees' competences.

As Chapter 9 details, perhaps the main reason for the low adoption of competence-related pay, in spite of the general interest in competences, is that managers often tend to concentrate on the 'hard' outputs (i.e. those performance indicators that can be calculated numerically) rather than the 'soft' processes (e.g. processes such as working with other team members) when measuring employee performance. Normally, managers are not too concerned with how the job is done provided that results are achieved. Yet competence-related pay overcomes this alleged weakness of IPRP by ensuring that, usually, both processes and outputs are taken into account when pay-related measurement is made.

Armstrong's definition of competence-related pay highlights the most important difference between competence-related pay and IPRP. This is that IPRP is essentially retrospective in that it measures performance over the past pay period (often one year). However, competence-related pay is forward-looking. It identifies those competences that are likely to be associated with effective current and future job performance.

Flannery *et al.* (1996: 92) define competences as 'sets of skills, knowledge, abilities, behavioural characteristics, and other attributes that, in the right combination and for the right set of circumstances, predict superior performance'. So the technical skill to do the job is insufficient. The successful job-holder must ally this skill (e.g. introducing clients to new products) with other attributes (e.g. the desire to enhance the perform-ance of the branch or team). In other words, competence-related pay is highly contextual. It also has, potentially, strong links to organisational strategy. Using the model of reward strategy in Figure 11.2, the question which may be asked at business strategy level is 'what employee behaviours/competences do we want our people to demonstrate in order that we may achieve our business goals?'

Competence-related pay need not necessarily ignore performance outputs at the expense of concentrating on competences. Many organisations introducing competence-related pay accompany competence-related ratings with performance output measurements, the market rate for the job, and the position of the individual on the pay scale in determining salary level. (A good example of such a reward programme is that of US giant Dow Chemical (Risher, 2000).)

One of the problems with IPRP is that managers can apply IPRP measurement crite-ria in an arbitrary way which creates in employees perceptions of a lack of fairness. This is no less true of competence-related pay. In fact, the more the approach moves from one where identifying discernible skills and outputs is possible, the more subjective the measurement process becomes. As yet, little empirical research has been done on the operation of competence-related pay but it would be surprising were it to uncover any-thing other than the same sort of employee dissatisfactions as found in relation to IPRP. However, the measurement criteria themselves may be more acceptable to employees than in the case of IPRP. This is often because there is some form of employee involve-ment in the development of the competence statements (Armstrong and Murlis, 1998), albeit that line managers are making the assessment of the extent to which the compe-tences have been demonstrated. This contrasts with IPRP where it is usually the manager who defines the performance objectives and assesses performance.

Self-Check and Reflect Questions   11.4

What may be some of the potential disadvantages of competence-based pay?

Summary

- Reward management is concerned with financial and non-financial rewards to employees and embraces the philosophies, strategies, policies, plans and processes used by organisations to develop and maintain reward systems. Strategic reward management plays an important role in delivering the organisation's overall business strategy by creating in employees certain behaviours, the need for which are implied by the business strategy. These employee behaviours may be produced by an HR strategy which includes a reward strategy as well as other HR strategies, such as the cultural strategy, the structural strategy and other HR strategies.

- A variety of factors in the external environment has led to the increased interest in strategic reward management. Principal among these are those factors which have impacted upon the commercial environment in which organisations operate creating the necessity to be more competitive and responsive to change.

- The intra-organisational factors that impact upon strategic reward management are the organisation cultural strategies, structural strategies and other HR strategies. In terms of reward, the principal contributors to the organisation's cultural strategies are pay for performance schemes. These may be at the level of the individual, the team, the business unit and the organisation.

- The reward contribution to the organisation's structural strategies involves changing reward structures. In this chapter the move from traditional pay structures to job family and broad-banded structures was examined. Competence-related pay was analysed as the means by which reward may complement other HR strategies.

Follow-up study suggestions

Use an organisation with which you are familiar, which may be one in which you are currently employed or have worked for, or one known to you, in order to study the following topics.

- Assess the degree to which the organisation has specific reward objectives.
- Using the model in Figure 11.2, evaluate the extent to which the organisation's reward management may be termed 'strategic'.
- Analyse the external factors that are impacting on the organisation's reward strategy.
- Evaluate the extent to which the organisation's pay structure fits the culture and structure of the organisation.
- Evaluate the extent to which the organisation's reward strategy complements the other HR strategies in place.

Suggestions for research topics

- What role do line managers play in the management of reward and how may this role be made more effective?
- How can employee involvement activities contribute to the effective management of reward?
- What constitutes an 'effective' reward scheme?

Case Study

Developing a global reward strategy at Tibbett and Britten Group

Business context

The Tibbett and Britten Group (TBG) is a UK-based international logistics service provider. Its main customers are retailers and manufacturers, to whom it provides warehouse, distribution and supply-chain management services under long-term contracts. The company directly employs 35,000 people in 35 countries, with the biggest markets in Europe and North America.

TBG employs people on a variety of contracts in different countries. Operating in a highly competitive sector, margins are low and the penalty to the business of passing on sudden rises in employment costs to customers is high. This is especially true where contracts are operated on an 'open book' basis, whereby a management fee is charged and other costs are agreed with the customer. The company's objective was, therefore, to reform group reward policy in a way that would be largely cost-neutral. Between 65 per cent and 70 per cent of the Group's overall operational costs relate directly to people, so staff reward management is key to business competitiveness.

The majority of TBG's employees were transferred from major customers such as Debenhams, Homebase or IBM. These employees retained their existing terms and conditions of employment. This meant that there was a wide variety of pay and grading arrangements in operation. These varied by country and contract. There were short- and long-term incentives and other benefits. There were also differing local relationships with trade unions. Local managers had traditionally agreed to vary certain arrangements locally and to pay upper quartile rates, for instance, or to use a particular form of competence-based pay. While the use of TBG incentives and benefits had become more consistent, many contracts were determined by the terms and conditions transferred from the customer. Most non-management employees were not on TBG terms and conditions. Managing this complexity was a key issue in the company's relationships with both employees and customers.

Developing a new strategy

The group started the process of reviewing its pay and benefits arrangements in 2002. The company had grown rapidly but there had been no attempt to introduce consistency in the way that managers in different countries were rewarded. The UK grading structure had been identified as an issue in need of attention, but it was felt that the best way to approach the problem was to take a step back and put a broader framework for reward in place across the company. The objectives were to:

- bring a measure of internal consistency to reward by establishing a group policy framework that would:
  - help managers communicate a coherent policy on reward;
  - guide country managers in the alignment of reward policies and projects within overall group principles;
  - initiate a cost-effectiveness review of current reward expenditure in light of what was identified as valued by employees; and
  - maintain the flexibility for local innovation and adaptability to customers' needs;
- address tactical issues impacting negatively on employee motivation and engagement, and create a culture where performance drove reward and recognition;
- create competitive advantage for TBG in the market place, particularly by improving its reputation as a contractor and employer of choice.

The key elements of the reward project were to:

- introduce a broad strategy focused on ten reward principles;
- review all elements of reward in line with these principles, project by project;
- move from the current grading structure to a new job level and job family structure, with five broad work levels, to be rolled out first in the UK; and
- continue to roll out a new voluntary benefits programme as part of the strategy, introduced in the UK in September 2003, to European countries.

TBG focused on a population of around 3,000 managers in developing the new reward strategy and introducing the new job levels. The approach was 'one step at a time'.

The overall reward strategy had been developed using focus groups, interviews with managers, and extensive organisational analysis conducted by the HR team.

Reward principles

In view of the complexity of the business it was felt that the reward strategy needed to be simple and easy to communicate in order to have any impact. Ten reward principles were proposed that formed the heart of the reward strategy, which were described as both a 'consistency benchmark' and a 'communications framework'.

The ten principles (see Appendix 1 at the end of the case study) were designed to be used to review current policies and practices, ensure that resources were being spent on company priorities and encourage greater internal consistency. For example, the company was nearing completion of a review of its short-term incentive programme for managers within Europe, from which eligible managers received an annual payment, based on local country, region and unit performance, linked also to performance against personal objectives. The review would reduce awards for poor and mediocre performance, while increasing awards for superior performance. A clearer framework for setting objectives and performance assessment was being introduced.

Grading project

An overhaul of the grading system used in the UK was the largest project being rolled out as part of the overall reward strategy. In the UK, TBG has historically operated a standard grading structure determined by job evaluation points. This was extended to evaluate jobs of managers in other countries.

The proposals for the new pay and grading structure meant moving from grades to five broad job levels and a job family structure. There were to be clear and structured capability statements for each level and descriptions of outputs that defined the scope of the role. Using the balanced scorecard approach, they were to cover four key areas:

- operational/functional scope;
- people/leadership challenge;
- financial impact; and
- customer/complexity challenge.

The levels were, however, underpinned by job evaluation, at least during early implementation of the new system. All management jobs were to be slotted into the new structure in the UK. Ultimately, managers throughout the business would be involved in agreeing the re-alignment of staff on their contract to the new system.

In order to set pay bands for job levels, extensive pay benchmarking research was carried out so that market data could be used to set a target rate for full competence in a particular role. It was thought that new pay rates, with a clear target rate and performance range, would be more transparent than the previous grading system. There would be greater emphasis on reward and access to incentives for high performers. The key principle was: 'This is the price for the job – the price you get depends on how good you are.'

The project involved the benchmarking of pay, benefits and incentives against appropriate comparator groups, both inside and outside the industry, with a longer-term aim of widening employment pools in certain areas and 'locking in' scarce talent in others.

The introduction

TBG planned to communicate the reward strategy and UK grading project within the company. The implementation required a thorough and painstaking process of one-to-one reviews, group meetings and written communications. A management panel was established to provide a permanent consultative forum to oversee the roll-out of the project to management grades. To encourage a move towards alignment with the reward principles, annual 'consensus meetings' were introduced, at which divisional heads met to compare and benchmark information on the reward systems currently operating in different customer contracts and countries.

Appendix 1   Ten reward principles

1. 'Think global, act local' by creating programmes that employ group principles and maintain optimum internal consistency and cohesion, while providing the flexibility to adapt to local market requirements and practices.
2. Develop and communicate total rewards policies and practices consistent with the stated group objective of attracting, motivating and retaining highly capable employees who regard Tibbett & Britten as their employer of choice.
3. Establish a competitive position for total compensation in the market place (fixed and variable pay and benefits) using appropriate comparator references, as well as internal benchmarks. Recognise that certain strategic roles and exceptional circumstances will drive variations from the norm without compromising the integrity of the established principles.
4. Pay for performance, strongly differentiating rewards, which reflect the underlying contribution of individuals through performance assessment against stretching objectives.
5. Establish and communicate accepted levels of operation that communicate clear career paths and development opportunities.
6. Ensure that all incentive programmes are exciting, 'SMART', credible and, where appropriate, tailored to the unique characteristics of different roles.
7. Implement rewards selectively and tactically, where justified, in recognition of the unique characteristics of certain roles.
8. Support and encourage all managers to 'recognise from the heart' the contribution of individuals and teams, as a critical component of the total rewards strategy.
9. Incorporate flexibility in the design of reward programmes, to provide the benefit of choice across our increasingly diverse workforce and to facilitate controlled tailoring to customer requests.
10. Exploit the Group's scale and available financial and fiscal opportunities in the delivery of benefit programmes for mutual advantage.

Appendix 2   Pay and grading: some big choices

Past approach	Future approach
A culture where relative status is reinforced through grades	A culture where individual performance drives recognition of contribution.
Externally validated, cumbersome job evaluation methodology: lengthier process, low risk, yet not transparent to managers	TBG bespoke job-levelling methodology: business responsive (and owned), greater discretion and transparency
Published pay bands drive pay decisions	Reliable market information drives pay
Grade changes and promotion naturally hand-in-hand	Greater emphasis on lateral job moves planned around building capability
Grades seen to drive pay	Individual performance seen to drive pay
Many grades and benefits thresholds, frequent requests for grading reviews	Fewer, significant job levels, with more benefits paid as cash
Grade increases reflect reporting lines	Some managers and their direct reports within the same level of operation
Grade thresholds are determined by job evaluation points ('tail wags dog')	So far as possible, grade levels reflect accepted differences in levels operationally ('dog wags tail')
Continue to roll out Hay grades to continental/rest of world operations	Reconsider, in light of where and how the interests of country operations and the Group are best served

Source: developed from IRS (2004b).

Case study questions

1. Why do you think that the creation of internal consistency was such an important objective of the new reward strategy?

2. Look again at the ten principles. Do you think there may be any potential contradictions inherent in these principles?

3. What potential benefits do you think may accompany the achievement of greater transparency in the new reward strategy?

12

Managing the employment relationship:
strategic rhetoric and operational reality

Learning Outcomes

By the end of this chapter you should be able to:

- explain the importance of the employment relationship to SHRM;

- define the employment relationship;

- evaluate the strategic approaches to managing the employment relationship;

- identify the various formats for organising the employment relationship at a range of levels;

- define employee involvement and voice;

- assess the linkages between SHRM and employee relations;

- evaluate the concepts of partnership and the psychological contract.

Introduction

The aim of this chapter is to consider how the management of the employment relationship can contribute to the achievement of SHRM. Essentially it has three key areas, the first area focuses on defining the changes that have taken place in the employment relationship. Central to this discussion has been the shift away from industrial relations to employee relations. The aim of this chapter is to explore and assess the linkages that exist between employee relations and SHRM. This exploration will emerge in the second and third areas of this chapter. In the second area an analysis of key theoretical discussions on the linkages between SHRM and employee relations will be presented. In the third area of the chapter evidence of the practices associated with a strategic approach to the management of the employment relationship will be presented. These practices are grouped around the central SHRM concept of employee involvement and participation.

The last 25 years in the HRM literature has seen significant focus and evaluation being placed on a 'strategic' approach to the development and implementation of HRM policies and practices (Legge, 1995b; Storey, 1995, Tyson, 1995; Schuler and Jackson, 1999a; Boxall and Purcell *et al.* 2003). Extensive discussions on this strategic approach have taken place in previous chapters of this book and the purpose of this chapter is to consider the management of the employment relationship and evaluate the strategic choices that are available to the various parties in this relationship. The term employment relationship can be defined most simply as the interaction between employers and employees. This simplistic definition highlights a potential problem in the employment relationship, if the relationship is merely based on interaction, at best it will be operational and as such have little strategic value for the parties involved. Traditionally, the management of the employment relationship has focused around the concept which is known as industrial relations. Industrial relations is generally understood to refer to the relationship between employers and employees collectively. The focus of industrial relations was firmly based on collective relationships that existed between individual or often groups of employees and the representatives of employees, namely trade unions. The CIPD (2005b) believe that the term industrial relations is no longer widely used by employers and refers to a set of employment relationships that no longer widely exist. So, do examples of traditional industrial relations exist?

- The first place to look would be within the public sector generally and in health, education, central and local government.
- Second would be in traditional industries, such as transport, heavy engineering and utility companies in the electricity, gas and water sectors.

These industries have had traditionally high levels of trade union membership. Industrial relations became the central element of personnel management from the mid-1940s until the late 1970s. This period can be characterised by widespread union membership, industry-level pay agreements, collective bargaining and widespread industrial disputes and strikes. Employers struggled to assert their authority and in many sectors collective bargaining was accepted as a form of 'joint regulation' that gave trade unions a say in many key management decisions. Over the last 25 years, a dramatic shift away from industrial relations towards employee relations has been witnessed. Employee relations is closely associated with SHRM and is often defined as an individual relationship between employer and employee. Employee relations can be considered as a way of describing a variety of employer policies and practices, which are aimed at improving workplace communications, for engaging employees directly or indirectly in decision-making and for securing employee compliance with management rules through disciplinary action. The key tool used by employers in managing employee relations is often employee involvement and participation (EI&P). This topic will be discussed in detail in a subsequent section but it is useful to introduce it at this point. Employee involvement and participation is seen as playing a central role in SHRM and is regarded as playing a central role in the development of high-performance work systems (Marchington, 2001). Bratton and Gold (2003) identify three aspects in relation to the contemporary debate on EI&P. These aspects are as follow:

- from a management perspective EI&P initiatives are seen as fundamentally transforming the climate of employment relations because they lead to long-term changes in workers' attitudes and commitment;

- communication plays a critical role in constructing and maintaining a 'strong' organisational culture, and, as a feature of the leadership process, 'communication style' is seen as being central to effective leadership;

- EI&P initiatives that promote the individual employee rather than employees' collective bodies deliberately undermine the role of trade unions; the exception to this is where the organisation uses partnerships agreements with trade unions to development and implement EI&P.

The concept of partnership will be discussed in more detail in a subsequent section of this chapter. In Key Concepts 12.1 the development of the employment relationship is explored.

Key Concepts   12.1

The development of the employment relationship

The concept of the employment relationship can be viewed as being a central element of a body of academic and practitioner writing in the field of employee relations. As Lewis *et al.* (2003a) highlight, a skim through the titles of books covering the relationship between employers and employees over the last 20 years will give an idea of the shift in emphasis that has taken place. In the 1970s and 1980s important authors such as Clegg (1979) and Bain (1983) used the term 'industrial relations' in their book and paper titles, while more recently the terms 'employee relations' (e.g. Rose 2001) and 'employment relations' (e.g. Gennard and Judge (2002)) have been used. Undoubtedly there is an element of fashion at work here. Lewis *et al.* (2003a) believe that 'industrial relations' is associated with the declining 'smokestack' industries and blue-collar workers and the accompanying emphasis upon collective bargaining between employers and trade unions. 'Employee relations' suggests that a wider employment canvas is being covered with equal importance being attached to non-union employment arrangements and white-collar jobs. Nonetheless, the emphasis still tends to be on the structure of 'perspectives, participants, processes and practices' adopted by Salamon (2000).

If the analysis presented in Key Concepts 12.1 is correct, the emerging employee relations concept with a strong strategic theoretical underpinning may be open to similar criticism to that expressed in relation to the general models of HRM.

These criticisms have been led by Legge (1995b). At this point it may be useful to consider the following issue: HRM and, in particular, the enhanced strategic focus of the concept in what is now called SHRM have had widespread coverage in both academic and practitioner publications but research collected in this field shows limited evidence regarding the reality of this process in observable organisational practice.

One of the key purposes of this chapter is to consider strategic approaches to managing the employment relationship both in theory and practice, and to present evidence of strategic practices in relation to the management of the employee relations. This issue will be explored throughout this chapter but it is useful to briefly consider it at this point. A central element of SHRM is the achievement of strategic integration. Strategic integration relates to linking HR policy choices with different types of business strategy. At the organisational level, one of the most effective ways of integrating HR and corporate strategy is through the management of the employment relationship. At a basic level, three strategic options that are aimed at gaining 'competitive advantage' can be identified:

- innovation;
- quality enhancement;
- cost reduction.

Each of these strategies will have an impact on HR strategy, and each will require the development and implementation of a series of HR policies and practices. The effective implementation of these policies and practices will require a series of SHRM behaviours. The choices available to the organisation will be dependent on a series of internal and external factors. At the internal level, the current and potential future employment relationship will have a major impact on how effectively the organisation develops its SHRM behaviours. So, for example, it may be more difficult to move to a more strategically focused approach in a unionised organisation as the union may resist attempts by management to make dramatic changes to the terms and conditions of workers.

Each of the basic strategic options has major SHRM implications, for example:

- A strategy that focuses on innovation will require multi-skilled employees, who are regularly appraised; the focus of the appraisal is on the achievement of long-term goals; pay rates tend to be low but employees may have the opportunity to individualise pay and rewards and link pay to performance.

- A quality enhancement strategy will require fixed explicit job descriptions and high levels of employee involvement and participation; pay is based on market evaluations to ensure equality; there is a high emphasis on team working.

- Finally, a cost reduction strategy will result in minimal levels of training and development, narrowly defined jobs and limited opportunities for career development; pay is based on market evaluations with the employer seeking to pay below the market average.

The strategy chosen and the associated SHRM policies will have a major impact on the employment relationship and will directly affect the psychological contract.

The psychological contract will be discussed in depth in the final area covered in this chapter, but it is useful at this point to offer a brief introductory definition. The psychological contract has been defined by Rousseau (1994, cited by Hiltrop, 1995: 287) as 'the understanding people have regarding the commitments made between themselves and their organisations'. It is therefore concerned with each party's perception of what the other party to the employment relationship owes them over and above that which may be specified in the contract of employment. As this contract is based upon perceptions, it is clear that the 'context' of this contract is not written and often not explicitly stated.

Having introduced the key themes to be addressed in this chapter it is now important to define the employment relationship.

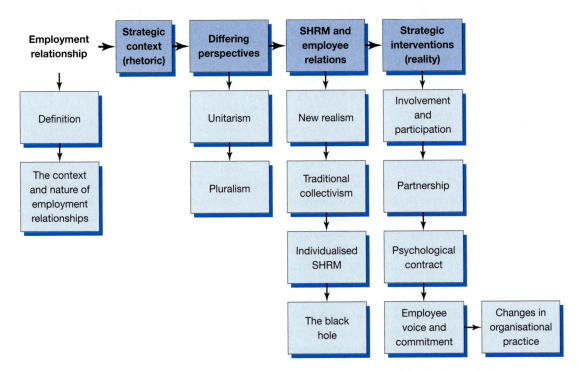

Figure 12.1 Mapping the employment relationship territory: a summary diagram of the chapter content

Defining the employment relationship

In Key Concepts 12.1, two terms that are central to developing an understanding of the employment relationship are highlighted. These terms are industrial relations and employee relations. Throughout this chapter, the term employment relationship is used. This is deliberate and aimed at supporting the successful achievement of learning outcomes. The term industrial relations is intrinsically linked to a collective orientation to the employment relationship and increasingly the term employee relations appears to focus on the individualised relationship that exists between employers and employees.

The use of the term employment relationship is used in this chapter to highlight the fact that a variety of collective and individual approaches are in operation in organisations across the UK and in many other economies. Moreover, organisations may decide, for a range of strategic and operational reasons, to implement individual and collective approaches across different divisions, departments and employee categories, thus creating an employment relationship that differs across the organisation. Rose (2004) highlights the fact that while employment relations is an academic subject area at undergraduate and postgraduate levels, it is also concerned with practical issue and processes that affect employers and employees, the government and other important institutions such as the Trades Union Congress (TUC) and the Confederation of British Industry (CBI). There is a clear research priority with regard to developing a greater understanding of the employment relationship within the UK. The nature of the interaction between employers and employees in the employment relationship deserves more attention than has traditionally been the case in the employee relations literature and research. Particular attention should be paid to:

- the expectations of parties to the employment relationship;
- the behaviours of managers and their employees;
- the ways in which the employment relationship is brought to an end.

Self-Check and Reflect Questions   12.1

Define the employment relationship and discuss the changes that have taken place to the relationship in recent years.

Gospel and Palmer (1993: 3) define the employment relationship as 'an economic, social and political relationship which provides manual and mental labour in exchange for rewards allocated by employers'. An important addition to this definition would be the psychological element of the employment relationship. Gospel and Palmer go on to note that there are certain characteristics of the employment relationship that mark it out as different from, say, the relationship between the customer and the supplier. The circumstances of the employment relationship may vary considerably. In the UK context, the evaluation and analysis of these factors is a significant area for study and discussion. These factors are presented in Key Concepts 12.2.

As Rose (2004) points out, 'the rewards from employment can be economic, social, and psychological, while the effort (the contribution the employee makes in his or her job) can range from skilled to unskilled and can be tightly controlled or left free to initiative and individual creativity'. A variety of employment relationships may exist to suit the needs of the employer and the employee; this has resulted in changes in the standard contract of employment to include short-term employment, part-time contracts, use of agency employees, subcontracting, casual labour and greater flexibility in terms of working hours, etc. Examples of the use of these methods can be found in the public and

Key Concepts   **12.2**

Factors influencing the employment relationship

Some of the variations are:

- the type of organisation in which the employment relationship is set;
- the wide range of purposes of the employment relationship and, consequently, the nature of the tasks performed by employees in the employment relationship;
- the location in which the tasks are performed;
- the amount of hours devoted to the employment relationship and the length of the relationship;
- the rewards that flow from the employment relationship;
- the way in which the main terms and conditions of the employment relationship are determined;
- the degree to which employees and employers possess and deploy power in the employment relationship;
- the effect that the degree of success of the employment relationship has on the employing organisation and the wider economy.

private sectors, manufacturing and services industries, international companies, SMEs and within unionised and non-unionised operating environments. The setting of the employment relationship is of particular importance, and the public and small business sectors are of vital importance and represent a major priority for study. The stability of the employment relationship in the rapidly growing service sector is also of interest as the practices operating in this sector may be reflective of future trends in the field. As graduates, many of you will actively seek employment within these sectors and the strategic underpinning of the employment relationship in these sectors will increase in importance beyond the area of academic study.

Having defined the employment relationship, it is important to now consider the changes that are taking place in the employment relationship.

The changing context and nature of the employment relationship

The traditional way of defining the employment relationship is through the contract of employment. Commentators would argue that in the UK the contract of employment is well defined and clearly established due to the rigorous fair employment legislation that exists. Torrington *et al.* (2005: 450) argue that all jobs in the labour market have the potential to become alienating. This alienation may manifest itself in a range of ways and can result in the job holder being indifferent or hostile to both the job and management, who are seen as being responsible for forcing the employee to do a job that they do not like.

Lewis *et al.* (2003a: 4) highlight the fact that the employment relationship can vary dramatically across organisations and this can be expressed in the range of jobs that exist. The wider the range of jobs, job descriptions and roles that exist across the organisation, the greater the differences in the employment relationship. Let us consider an organisational context with which you are all familiar. Within a university, there is a vast variety of jobs ranging from academics, functional administrative and managerial support for staff and students, technical staff in relation to information technology, learning resources (library), security, catering and cleaning operators. The job areas listed above are only indicative of the range of jobs and roles that exist within a university but the fact that each category will perform different tasks, require different training and qualifications and that the job will be performed in different locations means that the employment relationship varies enormously. The most visible element of difference can be in how the main terms and conditions of employment are determined. Two major variations can be identified. The first is an individualised approach focusing on direct negotiation between the employer and the employee, which in theory should have a strategic underpinning based on detailed negotiation between both parties. The practical reality of this individual approach is predominantly based on the employer laying out the terms and conditions they are prepared to offer to the potential employee with little or no opportunity offered to enter into any negotiations. The terms and conditions offered will focus on elements, such as starting salary, holiday entitlement, pension and sick pay entitlement, job description, performance and quality standards, etc. Although the terms and conditions offered should reflect the individual qualifications, expertise and knowledge of the employee, in many cases the organisations have standardised terms and conditions across a particular job type or category.

The second variation is based on a more distant collective arrangement between the employee's representative in the form of a trade union or professional body and the employer or the employer's representatives who jointly determine the main terms and conditions.

In recent years, there has been increasing interest in the non-legal aspects of the employment relationship. Lewis *et al.* (2003a: 12) believe this is particularly because the very foundations of the relationship, in many cases built upon years of mutual understanding, have been threatened. This has given rise to the psychological contract that exists between employer and employee, this concept will be considered in the final section of this chapter. Having considered changes occurring around the employment relationship, it is now useful to review and assess the differing perspectives on the employment relationship.

Differing perspectives on the employment relationship

In previous sections of this chapter, time has been spent defining the employment relationship. As Lewis *et al.* (2003a: 16) suggest, it is implicit in this definition that a number of different parties are involved in the operation of that relationship, employees, employers, trade unions and state agencies being the principal parties discussed above. Our understanding of the differing theoretical perspectives driving the employment relationship has been conceptualised by Fox (1966); the three concepts are *unitarism*, *pluralism* and *Marxism*. In the context of assessing a strategic approach to employee relations it is essential to examine the first two of these theoretical perspectives. It is important to note than the modern model of SHRM is largely based around the perspective of individualism and the traditional model personnel or industrial relations is based around the collective perspective. (For an evaluation of the concept of Marxism generally and individualism and collectivism specifically see Lewis *et al.* (2003a: 21–25).)

Unitarism

Fox (1966: 2) defined unitarism as a way of thinking about the organisation 'as a team unified by a common purpose', that common purpose being the success of the organisation. Among the principal characteristics of unitarism are the following:

- The employees of an organisation are seen as a team, unified by a common purpose with all employees pursuing the same goal.
- There is a single source of authority, that source being management.
- As all employees are pursuing the same goal, conflict is irrational, it must be the result of poor communication or 'troublemakers' at work who do not share the common purpose.
- The presence of third parties in the employment relationship is intrusive: therefore there is no place for trade unions (Lewis *et al.* (2003a).

Given this definition it is clear that unitarism is principally a management philosophy with regard to employee relations. As will be seen shortly, unitarism is very closely linked to the theory of SHRM that emerged in the USA in the early 1980s. It facilitates management to present an approach to managing the employment relationship that is well matched to their views and opinions. The outcome of this process in organisational terms is the creation of what has come to be known as *management prerogative* – which is described by Lewis *et al.* (2003a: 17) as the ability of management to make decisions without hindrance from those who may disagree with those decisions. If this is the case, the implementation of the unitary perspective can be considered as being consistent with the view that 'management knows best'. In this context Rose (2001) notes that the unitarist ideology may be useful for projecting to the outside world that management's decisions are right and any challenge to them comes from those who are either misguided or subversive.

A standard theme in many reviews of unitarism is that the concept bears little or no resemblance to organisational reality. Fox (1966: 4) argued that unitarism 'has long been abandoned by social scientists as incongruent with reality and useless for the purpose of analysis'. Lewis *et al.* (2003a: 17) argue that the view that unitarism is 'useless for the purpose of analysis' is questionable. They believe that it is a way of thinking about the employment relationship that has gained great currency in recent years, as it chimes with one of the central tenets of the so-called human resource management movement. Many of the well-established models of SHRM position the employment relationship firmly in the unitarist domain. An example of this is Storey's (1995) list of 25 dimensions that differentiate human resource management from personnel management. In this list, the nature of (employee) relations is 'unitarist'. Storey's checklist is presented in Key Concepts 12.3.

An analysis of Key Concepts 12.3 reflects Fox's (1966) definition of unitarism as a way of thinking about the organisation 'as a team unified by a common purpose' in several ways. A central theme running through many of the elements of SHRM is that of organisational culture. Lewis *et al.* (2003a: 18) believe that the development of a culture that is consistent with unitarist principles and in which the needs of individuals are of secondary importance to those of the organisation, dominates the thinking.

Key Concepts

12.3

Storey's 25 point checklist

Dimension	Beliefs and assumptions Personnel and IR	SHRM/ER
1. Contract	Careful delineation of written contract	Psychological contract
2. Rules	Importance of devising clear rules	'Can do' outlook:
3. Guide to management action	Procedures/consistency control	Business need/flexibility/commitment
4. Behavioural referent	Norms/customs and practice	Values/mission
5. Managerial task vis-à-vis labour	Monitoring	Nurturing
6. Nature of relations	Pluralist	Neo unitarist
7. Conflict (partnership)	Institutionalised	De-emphasised
8. Standardisation	High (parity an issue)	Low (parity not an issue) (Individualisation)
Strategic aspects		
9. Initiatives	Piecemeal	Strategic integration
10. Key relations	Labour management	Employer–employee
11. Corporate plan	Marginal to	HR strategy
12. Speed of decisions	Slow	Based on engagement
	Line management	
13. Management role	Transactional	Transformational leadership
14. Key managers	Personnel/IR specialists	Line managers
15. Prized management skills	Negotiation	Involvement and participation
	Key levers	
16. Attention on interventions	Personnel procedures	Cultural, structural and HR strategies
17. Selection	Separate, marginal task	Integrated, key skill
18. Pay	Job evaluation	Performance-related pay
19. Conditions	Separately negotiated	Harmonisation
20. Labour management	Collective	Individualised
21. Relations with stewards	Regularised, through negotiations	None or partnership
	Training and facilities	
22. Communication	Restricted flow/indirect	Direct
23. Job design	Division of labour	Team working
24. Conflict handling	Reach temporary truces	Partnership
25. Training and development	Controlled access to courses	Learning companies

Source: adapted from Storey (1992).

Unitarism presented in the guise that SHRM may be attractive and of significant value to some and it is unquestionable that it forms a core element in the majority of academic analysis in recent years. In the concept of SHRM, it is currently the most influential theme of analysis in relation to employment relationships. Among the rhetoric that has been developed in conjunction with the development of the SHRM models and theories is the concept that 'people are the organisation's most important asset'. With so much theoretical progression and sheer volume of analysis in this area, it would seem natural to assume that dramatic changes would have taken place in observable organisation policy and practice. For evidence of these dramatic changes the obvious starting point would be in the practices of UK companies, who would be actively developing and implementing policies and practices with the necessary strategic underpinning to transform employment relationships at a workplace level.

The key strategic tool that managers would utilise to achieve this transformation would, of course, be HRM and the strategic practices associated with it. So the rhetoric, in the form of key theories and models, tells us that the employment relationship will have a much greater strategic underpinning based on the pursuit by managers of a wide-ranging series of strategically underpinned HRM-based practices. So what is the reality? Following a review of survey evidence collected in the 1990s, Guest (2001) highlights very low adoption of high commitment human resource management work practice based upon the principles identified in the right-hand column of Key Concepts 12.3. This leads Guest (2001: 112) to conclude that 'the popular cliché that 'people are the organisation's most important asset' is patently untrue based on the current employment relations practices and actions of UK managers. Lewis *et al.* (2003a) argue that even if there had been wholesale adoption of the unitarist perspective by managers, it raises the question of whether it is consistent with the new psychological contract. A simple evaluation would suggest that the two ideas are contradictory. Unitarism stresses the absorption of the individual into the organisation, with the loss of their own identity and interests. The new psychological contract, on the other hand, suggests that the employee is 'on their own' to a significantly greater extent, and must respond to their own needs.

The psychological contract will be discussed in more detail in a subsequent section but in the context of this section of the chapter the new psychological contract recognises that there is a plurality of the different interests in the employment relationship rather than a common purpose. This is a view that has traditionally dominated employment relations thinking and practice and which will be analysed in the next section.

Pluralism

An understanding of the central tenets of pluralism is vital to the understanding of employee relations because many of the principal procedures, processes and practices that exist to manage the employment relationship are based on the principles of pluralism. Fox (1966: 2) defined pluralism as the organisation being a 'miniature' democratic state composed of sectional groups and divergent interests over which the government tries to maintain some kind of dynamic equilibrium. Lewis *et al.* (2003a: 19) believe that employing organisations are essentially a microcosm of society as a whole. They argue that the sectoral groups with divergent interests that exist in the organisational context are as easy to identify in this context as they are in society generally. Employers and managers represent obvious, potentially different, groups. The differences may be evident in how the two groups go about achieving certain common goals. In the plural-ists' ideology, the validity and legitimacy of these differing interests are recognised. Managers are responsible for ensuring the overall effectiveness of the organisation and the achievement of the organisation's goals. Employees, on the other hand, are more likely to be concerned with personal goals, in particular the wish to obtain better terms and conditions of employment. Within each organisation there will be a diverse range of sectional groups, at the employee level these will be determined by the nature of tasks performed by each group of employees and the terms and conditions each enjoy.

To give examples of this in a manufacturing environment, one group of employees will see their key tasks as being linked to performance in a production line environment, another may interact with clerical and admin staff whose key roles and tasks are quite different. A third group of employees in that organisation may be dealing directly with the company's customers or clients. At the management level, differences of interest will exist depending on each manager's function. The existence of the sectional groups with divergent interests in the organisation signals the potential for conflict, as their interests may clash over, say, the distribution of scarce resources. Each group makes a case for it to have what it sees as its 'fair' share of those resources. These discussions are often seen as healthy in an organisational context, and a small degree of internal conflict may well be necessary to achieve improvements and progression. The key strategic issue for organi-sations is to ensure that they have appropriate policies and procedures to ensure that these conflicts do not grow and escalate and create negative organisational cultures. Methods to ensure that these conflicts do not become unmanageable may be focused on a process of involvement and participation, and giving employees or sectional employee groupings a voice in the workplace strategic decision-making process. The concept of involvement and participation will be discussed in a subsequent section of this chapter.

The effectiveness of conflict handling mechanisms used by organisations is very much dependent on a key issue that Fox (1966) stressed: that the differences between the parties are not as 'fundamental or wide as to be unbridgeable' (Salamon, 2000: 8). These parties must have an interest in the survival of the organisation of which they are part. In strategic terms, simple survival may be a minimum goal but progression and devel-opment of the organisation should be in the interests of all parties involved. In periods of major economic problems in the UK, including the late 1970s and early 1980s, employees and, more frequently, the unions representing them were accused of being determined to destroy both individual organisations and complete industries. The late 1970s and early 1980s in the UK can be viewed as an era of mass industrial conflict, with a high number of strikes and widespread disputes in many industry sectors. In this con-text, virtually every conflict-handling procedure imaginable would be ineffective.

Self-Check and Reflect Questions   12.2

Fox (1966) clearly believed that the pluralistic perspective on employee relations was the most valid and realistic way to manage the employment relationship. Given the emergence of the HRM models of management in the 1980s do you believe that unitarism ia a more appropriate way of managing the employment relationship in the twenty-first century?

The starting point of the employment relationship in modern organisations is largely based on some overall shared view about the legitimacy of the organisation and its goals, and this forms the basis for common ground. This common ground may be further developed and made more sophisticated or strategic in organisations. The methods for doing this will depend on the employment relationship that exists. Unionised businesses may involve a partnership agreement between employers and a trade union, whereas in non-unionised businesses this may be based upon the principles of employee voice and involvement and participation. It may also be necessary to create a new psychological contract to provide the mechanisms for achieving common ground.

Before discussing these organisational elements it is important to develop an understanding of the theoretical discussion on the links between SHRM and employee relations.

SHRM and employee relations

Many analysts, including Guest (1995), and Beaumont (1995), have commented that the rising interest in SHRM throughout the 1980s coincided with a steady decline in the significance of industrial relations as a central element of economic performance and policy. It also coincided with a decline in the membership and influence of trade unions; during the 1980s, trade union membership density declined from 53 per cent to 33 per cent of the employed workforce. Industrial conflict displayed a similar decline, so that in the early 1990s strikes were at their lowest level for decades. As Guest (1995) suggests, it was tempting to seek an association between the apparent rise of SHRM and the decline of trade unions and industrial relations. Certainly many of the early models of SHRM were drawn mainly from successful American non-union firms. On closer examination, the changes that have occurred in industrial relations in the UK would, in all likelihood, have occurred with or without the emergence of SHRM, if perhaps at a more gradual pace. In the mid-1990s, for many organisations industrial relations were no longer a contingent variable helping to shape business policy and strategy in the way they might have done 10 or 15 years before. What emerges from the literature is that industrial relations (or employee relations) are of greater importance in the UK than in many of the other developed economies. A good example of this is the USA, where traditional industrial relations are now seen as a peripheral issue for many companies. Guest (1995) places the key themes that are discussed in the SHRM literature in regard to employee relations into three distinct categories. These categories are presented in Key Concepts 12.4.

Commitment, the theory of SHRM and employee relations

Guest (1995) describes the model of SHRM (particularly the Harvard model of Beer *et al.* (1985) and his own model (Guest, 1987)) as placing organisational commitment at SHRM's core. This is the central feature that distinguishes SHRM from traditional personnel management/industrial relations approaches. If the four key policy goals of SHRM, strategic integration, quality, flexibility and commitment are considered, then the focus on quality and flexibility can pose difficulties for trade unions but commitment to the organisation presents a direct challenge to trade unionism. Guest (1995)

Key Concepts   12.4

Key themes discussed in the SHRM literature

- The first is an examination of organisational commitment and dual commitment. Dual commitment refers to the fact that employees can be committed to both their employer and a trade union. The concepts of commitments and dual commitment can be used as a basis for considering the interaction between SHRM and trade unionism.
- The second examines the evidence on the choices being made by employers in the UK about the type of SHRM and employee relations they wish to pursue.
- The third considers strategy, taken from the trade union perspective, and explores the possible agendas available to trade unions in an environment where SHRM may be viewed as an opportunity as much as a major challenge.

(Table 12.1) suggests that this provides the basis for the contrasting values and assumptions underpinning the normative views of SHRM and industrial relations which have been presented by Walton (1985), Cradden (1992) and Storey (1992).

This dichotomy has been described as reflecting a soft view of SHRM (see Cradden, 1992; Guest, 1995), and is concerned with the full utilisation of human resources for the benefit of the organisation. It can be argued that the implementation of SHRM creates a shift away from industrial relations to employee relations. This is underpinned with the belief that the best way to ensure full utilisation of human resources is to take care of what Herzberg (1968) would term hygiene factors, such as job security and pay, through generous and fair provision, and to tap motivation by providing autonomy and challenge. Guest (1995) is of the opinion that to fill out the SHRM model, the organisation should invest in careful selection and extensive training to ensure the high quality of human resources. In many respects this has been the traditional means of managing and motivating managerial and professional staff. Guest believes that organisational commitment is central for a number of reasons:

Table 12.1 Key dimensions of industrial relations and SHRM

Dimension	Industrial relations	SHRM
Psychological contract	Compliance	Commitment
Behaviour referent	Norms, custom and practice	Values/mission
Relations	Low trust	High trust
	Pluralist	Unitarist
	Collective	Individual
Organisation and design	Formal roles	Flexible roles
	Hierarchy	Flat structures
	Division of labour	Teamwork/autonomy
	Managerial costs	Self-control

Source: adapted from Guest (1995).

- The belief is that committed workers will be highly motivated and will go beyond contract, delivering higher performance.
- Second, committed workers can be expected to exercise reasonable autonomy or self-monitoring and self-control, removing the need for supervisory and inspection staff and producing efficiency gains.
- Third, committed workers are more likely to stay with the organisation, thereby ensuring a return on the investment in careful selection, training and development.
- Finally, but correctly considered of greatest importance to the discussion of SHRM and employee relations, it is assumed that a worker who is committed to the organisation is unlikely to become involved in any type of collective activity which might reduce the quality and quantity of their contribution to the organisation.

Guest (1995) argues that placing organisational commitment at the core of the definition of SHRM acknowledges the deliberate attempt to win the hearts and minds of the workforce. In defining organisational commitment, he cites Mowday *et al.* (1982) as being the most relevant for any analysis involving HRM and industrial relations. They define organisational commitment as consisting of three components: identification with the goals and values of the organisation; a desire to belong to the organisation; and a willingness to display effort on behalf of the organisation. As Gordon *et al.* (1980) state, union commitment can be defined in precisely the same way. The key issue then becomes the compatibility of the goals and values of the company and the union. If they are compatible, then it is possible to display high commitment to both the union and the company. One good example is that of the union Amicus (formerly AEEU & MSF), which appears to have taken on board many SHRM ideas, with the honourable aim of maintaining at least a single union presence within the workplace. This of course raises questions about the role of the union and the nature of the values for which it stands. Guest (1995) believes an alternative scenario must be considered, based on workers being able to live with the inherent conflict and ambiguity of identification with two potentially opposing sets of values. Research by Reichers (1985, 1986) has suggested that workers can express loyalty and commitment to potentially conflicting targets such as a workgroup, career and company. This leads to the idea of a dual commitment, to both company and union, a subject often discussed in literature pertaining to HRM and industrial relations. The choices available to employees in relation to commitment to company and union are presented in a simple format in Figure 12.2.

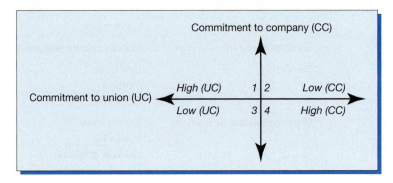

Figure 12.2 Employee choices in relation to commitment
Source: adapted from Guest (1995).

Guest (1995) believes that a matrix of this type is a useful starting point for analysis of commitment to company and union. It is important to bear in mind that it is an oversimplified specification in two respects. The first is that there may be intermediate levels of commitment to both company and union, reflecting, perhaps, a kind of conditional approval of both. The second, building on the work of Reichers and others, is that there are other potential foci of commitment. These include career, a profession and the family. Commitment to any of these may also conflict with commitment to either company and/or union.

Much of the research on this subject has been conducted in North America, where trade unionism has been in decline for a considerably longer time than in the UK. This might be expected to result in few, if any, employees feeling any commitment to a trade union and, as such, evidence of dual commitment minimal. The study of dual commitment in the work of Angle and Parry (1986) is probably the most important research evidence available. They identify the industrial relations climate as the key mediating variable. Where there was a cooperative and conflict-free climate, dual commitment was feasible. However, where the climate was hostile, workers were forced to confront the competing commitments to the company and union, and make a choice, or alternatively display a commitment to neither. This implies that, when conflict occurs, even though commitment to company and union may be caused by different factors, some choices among these factors have to be made.

During the 1980s, management in many UK organisations launched initiatives to win the hearts and minds of the workforce. Often, these fell under the broad umbrella of cultural change programmes. Guest believes that the evidence of limited dual commitment presents challenges for the unions. It would be unwise for unions to rely on one of the traditional bases of the commitment to the union, namely a presumed belief in trade unionism. The apparent failure of many companies to generate enthusiastic commitment among their workforce suggests that opportunities for unions still exist. If management is tempted to pursue a hard version of HRM, this might backfire, providing scope for unions to extend both membership and influence. Guest (1995) then considers recent developments at the interface of SHRM and industrial relations as a basis for understanding company policy and practice.

Developments in the employment relationship and SHRM: some potential approaches explored

The key areas that are discussed in the literature relating to this topic are presented in Key Concepts 12.5.

Guest (1995) identifies four possible approaches to managing the employment relationship. These are decribed below.

1. The new realism – a high emphasis on SHRM and employee relations

This is the subject most frequently discussed in the literature, the changes in practice that occurred in the 1980s resulting in what many have termed the new employee relations. The focus in this context was on developing and implementing SHRM in a context where unions had a role to play in the workplace and as such a collective approach is required. The approach mostly commonly adopted in this context is the

Key discussion areas

1. Union recognition and de-recognition.
2. Developments in the new employee relations, such as single-table bargaining and no-strike deals.
3. The role of unions in any changes affecting industrial relations.
4. The importance of employee relations as an issue.
5. The outcomes of employee relations, including levels of conduct activity, any union mark-up and productivity.

establishment of a partnership agreement between the employer and the union. Where the employment relationship is individualised and a trade union does not represent employees, the link between SHRM and employee relations will be developed through the psychological contract. Both these approaches will be discussed in a subsequent section of this chapter.

As with many of the other areas of employee relations, the terminology is changing. As already noted, industrial relations was traditionally the most significant area of human resource activity. Kochan *et al.* (1986), in proclaiming the transformation of American industrial relations, discuss a number of cases illustrative of the collaborative joint endeavour to shape a new relationship between management and union. These cases appear to fit well with the rhetoric of the Harvard approach to SHRM. Beer *et al.* (1984) discuss the coincidence of stakeholder interests and the importance of participation, power equalisation, trust and commitment. Walton's (1985) definition of mutuality emphasises this point. He argues that the new HRM model is composed of policies that promote mutuality: mutual goals; mutual influence; mutual respect; mutual rewards; and mutual responsibility. The theory is that policies of mutuality will elicit commitment, which in turn yields both better economic performance and greater human development.

Although this was the pattern that was described as emerging in employment relationships in the USA, it is also the pattern that may be expected to emerge in those organisations in the UK where attempts are being made by managers to pursue an approach that integrates HRM and employee relations. One of the most notable examples of recent decades is that of Nissan (Wickens, 1987). But Wickens account has been criticised by some commentators (Garrahan and Stewart, 1992) as being a story of implementation of a hard version of HRM, in the sense that tight control and performance systems operate. Many of the examples of serious attempts at a joint approach – the former MG Rover Corporation being a case in point – come from the car industry, where the unions were very well entrenched but market forces demanded improvements in productivity and quality. Guest (1995) proposes that these cases are similar to those cited by Kochan *et al.* (1986). In most older organisations, managers start from a position where the unions are entrenched. In the case of new plants or greenfield sites the choices are more open and these will be discussed in greater detail in a later section. However, Guest gives the example of Toyota and Bosch, both of which recognise a single union, and Honda who has decided to operate without any unions.

A phenomenon much associated with new plants, is the so-called beauty contest, where unions compete for recognition rights. From the union side, this constitutes a form of concession bargaining, based on who promises an agreement closest to the management's ideas.

Guest, following Storey (1995) in describing recent trends relating to HRM and industrial relations, concludes that there is little evidence of any frontal attacks on unions in the UK, but equally little attempt to involve the unions in the planning and implementation of change. In most cases, where unions have been well established in the past, the two systems – industrial relations and HRM – operate side by side but with little tendency for management to give increased weight to systems of employee involvement and, in particular, communication, which tends to bypass the union. Guest agrees with Storey's (1992) conclusion that the two systems can co-exist and remain relatively compartmentalised. Guest (1995) gave four possible explanations for employee relations remaining healthy in the context of SHRM, presented in Key Concepts 12.6.

Key Concepts   12.6

Employee relations in the era of SHRM

1. SHRM may be so ineffective that it is having a minimal impact on values and commitment; the hard version of SHRM is being used, and this leaves a level of anxiety such that workers continue to support the traditional industrial relations system and the trade union as a safeguard and safety net.

2. Management, while supporting SHRM, recognise the value of retaining collective arrangements because of their convenience, particularly in those establishments where large numbers are employed.

3. It is possible that the system of mutuality is viable and a mutually beneficial collaboration between management and unions can operate, resulting in the maintenance of both systems.

4. Employee relations systems may continue as a largely symbolic empty shell, insufficiently important for management to confront and eliminate, but retaining the outward appearance of health to the casual observer.

Management often set strategic agendas that are solely market-driven, while the employment relationship is relatively low on the list of concerns. It may thus be misleading to suggest that the two systems co-exist. Direct management channels of communication are receiving increased attention, while the union channels are in decline. There are, moreover, very few documented cases of a robust trade unionism in the context of enthusiastic SHRM policies. In the case of Rover, the unions were invited to participate but declined the invitation. The partnership described at Ford focused less on SHRM issues and more on the quality of working life. Guest (1995) describes the UK Ford example as fitting well with the analysis of the American model of Kochan *et al.* (1986), which included Ford in America as one of its cases. The underlying message, which the analysis of new realism reveals, is that managements and unions have made little attempt to forge new partnerships that give high priority to both SHRM and industrial relations through a process of integration. In recent years managers have implemented a significant number of the piecemeal SHRM initiatives, and in doing so ignored or bypassed the employee relations system. On the surface, it may appear that SHRM and employee relations are given high priority. Often, in the case of both, this will be an illusion, giving yet more credibility to the argument that much of the SHRM literature bears little resemblance to what is happening in reality. An example of an organisation that appears to place high emphasis on SHRM and employee relations is presented in 'In Practice' 12.1.

In Practice   12.1

Managing employee relations at ITV

ITV, the UK's major independent television company, bases its employee relations approach on engaging with its employees. It does this by a combination of methods: collective bargaining, consultation with elected employee representatives; and direct engagement with individuals. Engagement is regarded as being critical to the success of the company, which is using engagement to integrate its corporate and HR strategies. ITV uses a wide range of direct communication methods to engage with individual employees, these methods include:

- intranet;
- individual development reviews;
- briefings meetings;
- workshops;
- individual relationships between employees and their line managers;
- employee opinion survey.

This individualised approach can be considered as being reflective of an SHRM approach. The company also engages in collective consultations through elected representatives because, although 50 per cent of workers are covered by a collective bargaining arrangement, unions represent only 15 per cent of employees and the employer wants feedback from the whole workforce. ITV needs to consult employees frequently because of the scale of change within the organisation.

ITV uses collective bargaining as a means of securing employee agreement on new working practices. It believes that the collective relationships deliver significant change management benefits for the company and help to reassure employees that their interests are being respected. This can be considered a collective approach, associated with a high emphasis on employee relations.

Source: adapted from CIPD (2005b).

The ITV example gives a good insight into an organisational example of new realism. The company is using SHRM and employee relations to ensure that it engages with all its employees. ITV does this through consultation with individual employees and employee representatives and negotiation with the unions.

2. Traditional collectivism – priority to industrial relations without SHRM

Guest (1995) identifies the second main policy choice as being the retention of the traditional pluralist industrial relations arrangements within an essentially unchanged industrial relations system. Guest cites the evidence of Workplace Employee Relations Surveys (WERSs), which suggest that, in many places where trade unions are well established, the employee relations system appears to operate much as before. (For a detailed analysis of the WERSs see Millward *et al.* (2000).)

Management may continue to use the employee relations system, but afford it much less priority. This would appear to support the theory that managements view the marginalisation of the unions as a better strategy than formally to de-recognise them and risk provoking a confrontation; better to let them wither on the vine than receive a reviving fertiliser. A more optimistic view can also be offered, which appears more attuned to soft SHRM, in which the management decide that it is easier to continue to operate with a union. This may be based on the fact that it provides a useful well-established channel for communication and for the handling of grievance, discipline and safety issues. The strongest evidence that this type of industrial relations-centred system exists is mainly to be found in the public sector and in some industries which have been recently removed from public ownership. For examples of this approach look at the NHS trusts, all areas of the education sector and central government in the form of the UK civil service. There are also examples that have traditionally placed a high emphasis on collective industrial relations but are developing policies to move towards SHRM. An example of this is presented in 'In Practice' 12.2.

In Practice   12.2

Employee relations at South West Trains

The company has a well-established collective bargaining agreement with four trade unions. The unions involved are ASLEF, the RMT, TSSA and Amicus. The agreement gives the unions negotiating rights on a range of issues, including pay and terms and conditions of employment. They are also consulted on issues relating to performance and attendance, changes in working practices and redundancy. So traditional collectivism is well established in South West Trains.

The company also realises that if it is to implement SHRM it needs to ensure that it involves and engages all staff, not just its union members. South West Trains would prefer to adapt the current collective bargaining machinery to allow non-union representatives to be informed and consulted alongside a union representative. However, other options may be possible, including establishing employee forums which would be open to all staff.

Although the company has very good relationships with all the unions, it has moved away from relying solely on collective machinery. It uses a range of direct communication methods including email and intranet, undertakes regular staff surveys and is beginning to individualise the employment relationship by having face-to-face communication between line managers and employees.

While the unions are well established and professional the future employee relations strategy appears to focus on a partnership approach. The company sees this partnership as being between the employer and the individual employee and, as such, South West is a good example of a company which focuses on traditional collectivism but is moving towards an individualised SHRM approach.

Source: adapted from CIPD (2005b).

3. Individualised SHRM – high priority to SHRM with no employee relations

As detailed in a previous section, one of the key issues in considering the growth of SHRM is whether companies are taking SHRM seriously. This involves looking at the extent to which SHRM is being used in the organisational setting, and whether this involves operating without unions and an employee relations system. Guest (1993) notes that, in the UK, models of companies successfully practising SHRM are becoming somewhat dated. Analysis of new establishments in the WIRS (former name for the WERS, see above) sample by Guest and Hoque (1998) indicates that it is predominantly the North American-owned firms that appear to promote a high SHRM, non-union approach. A good example of this is presented in 'In Practice' 12.3.

In Practice   12.3

Employee relations at Dell

Dell is a US company that has grown rapidly since is formation 20 years ago, and is now the world's number one PC manufacturer. Dell is a non-unionised company and focuses its SHRM activities on an individualised and team-based partnership between employer, teams and the individual employee. The focus is on the team and on individual contributions to the team. People/line mangers are expected to interact with individuals, and their performance is closely monitored. Employee involvement and participation is the driving factor in the employment relationship. Key elements include:

- setting of performance plans;
- giving feedback to improve performance;
- work in each team on individual performance plans;
- ensuring employees understand the business challenges and priorities facing the company;
- ensuring employees are stakeholders in the business;
- ensuring employee and management skills development keeps pace with business changes;
- creating fair and open work environments where employees feel they have a voice and are treated fairly.

Implementation of each of these elements identifies Dell as an organisation with a strong individualised SHRM approach.

Source: adapted from CIPD (2005b) and *The Irish Times* (2006).

4. The black hole – no SHRM and no employee relations

What if the black hole scenario does occur? If SHRM loses its attractions as a policy priority, or at best becomes no more than a set of piecemeal techniques, and there is no compelling reason to operate within a traditional industrial system, the alternative is to emphasise neither. Guest (1995) offers pieces of evidence that suggest this option is becoming more prevalent. The first is the well-documented decline in trade union membership and trade union density. This decline is considered to be partly structural, and reinforced by the growth of de-recognition and the changing pattern of union recognition in new establishments. Unfortunately, if a union is not recognised, there is little evidence that management replaces it with an HRM strategy to obtain full utilisation of the workforce, by gaining its commitment to company goals and values. For examples of companies in which a black hole may exist, it may be useful to focus on many small and medium-sized enterprises (SMEs) that are too small to attract trade unions to organise in their workplace and where few or no strategic policies exist in relation to the management of people. Companies operating in sectors where staff can be poorly paid, such as retailing, hospitality and tourism, may also have this type of employment relationship.

In considering the four options presented, it becomes clear that the trend is away from the traditional collectivism of a representative industrial relations system, but the drift is towards the black hole of no industrial relations and no SHRM, rather than towards individualised SHRM or the new realism.

The major shift in employee relations occurred in the 1980s during a period of significant economic uncertainty and recession. Unemployment figures rose above 3 million, which provided a buyers' market where employers could find workers willing to accept management terms. Although many commentators have associated the emergence of SHRM with the demise of industrial relations, the political and economic contexts described previously have had a much more significant effect. In many organisational settings, traditional industrial relations no longer exist, but they have not been replaced by enlightened HRM: in other words the black hole effect described previously. This must have detrimental effects on employees' enthusiasm, as in this scenario more than any other they will be viewed as a liability, albeit one that can have positive inputs, but only when forced to do so. The acceptance and promotion of soft HRM may be the best strategy for trade unions in attempting to ensure managements do not renege on ensuring employees' rights are maintained. Although unions may not play as significant a role as they did in the 1960s and 1970s, they will still act as a safety valve in resisting management's adopting a hard approach to the management of human resources.

Self-Check and Reflect Questions 12.3

Choose an organisation with which you are familiar and, using Guest's evaluation of the four possible approaches to the management of the employment relationship, describe the current employment relationship.

Having considered SHRM and employee relations at a theoretical level it is now important to consider the policies and mechanism that can be used in organisations to create and implement strategic policies and practices at the organisational level. In the following section the focus will be on two key strategic concepts and mechanisms for achieving involvement and participation in employee relations, namely:

- partnership;
- the psychological contract including employee voice.

Involvement and participation: strategic concepts and practices

In this section a review the two key strategic concepts mentioned above will be presented. As has been the theme throughout this chapter, attempts will be made to differentiate between the rhetoric presented in literature and research and the reality that is observable in organisational practices.

Partnership

The TUC (Trades Union Congress) argues it has that longstanding commitment to partnerships between unions and employers. Partnerships at work can deliver higher productivity, improved performance and successful changes to workplace organisation. Partnership enables unions to play an active role in shaping an organisation's policy and strategy, and increases union involvement in organisational change. The TUC Partnership Institute, launched in January 2001, provides expertise, advice and support to unions and employers on developing successful workplace partnerships. Most partnerships that exist are at the workplace or organisational level and simply involve the employer and the trade union forming an agreement that is based on the concepts of partnerships.

Defining labour–management partnerships

Recent developments in the field of employee relations have focused a great deal of attention on the advent of partnership agreements between trade unions and employing organisations. Opinions differ as to the cause of such agreements, some arguing that they are born of the unions' latest strategy for survival and need for relevance, while others see them as a genuine social advance for working people and a vital contribution to the competitiveness of business organisations. Also, at the macro-level, it is possible to see partnership agreements as making a significant contribution to the economic performance of a country or region, or to view them as an alternative to legislative reform substituting voluntarism for statutory rights of consultation and company regulation.

At the enterprise level, a partnership agreement can be described as one in which management and trade union(s) agree to work together for mutual gain, and to create a climate of cooperative relations. They are characterised by management being expected to enhance job security and/or employability in return for employees accepting flexible work practices and increasing productivity. In some cases there has been a joint union/management approach, involving the re-writing or extension of existing written recognition and procedural agreements, and changing important aspects of collective bargaining and/or terms and conditions of employment. These would usually include the move to single-table bargaining and the introduction of single status for all employees, with harmonisation of rewards schemes, and equality policies. Frequently quoted examples in the UK include Rover, Blue Circle, Hyder Services, and in the US Saturn and NUMMI (see IDS (1998) and IRS (1998)).

At this point it is useful to briefly consider how one of these agreements developed. The agreement at Blue Circle emerged from a shared commitment to business success. The purpose of the agreement was to establish a framework within which constructive employee relations could be maintained and developed. The agreement was designed to support the business in its journey towards excellence.

There is no set pattern, and where such written agreements have emerged the importance of context is acknowledged, in that they are based specifically on a problem-solving approach within a plant or organisation. Neither is there agreement that trade union presence or recognition is necessary, and the Chartered Institute of Personnel & Development (CIPD) maintains that 'partnership has more to do with an approach to the relationship between employers and employees, individually and in groups, than it has to do with trade unions as such' (CIPD, 2006). The Institute of Directors (IOD) has taken a strongly unitarist stance towards partnerships, and the Confederation of British Industry (CBI) has warned of a 'possibly damaging build-up of trade union influence, hidden behind the new buzzword partnership' (CBI, 1999). Nonetheless, the TUC view is that 'partnerships between employers and trade unions can make a real contribution to company success' (Monks, 1998), and the Involvement and Participation Association (IPA) has produced evidence from case studies and surveys to show a direct link between partnership approaches and enhanced organisational performance (IPA, 1996, 1998).

The 'new realism' identified by Guest (1995) as one of four possible policy options for organisations on SHRM and employee relations matters, seeks to integrate them, with high priority being given by organisations to both, and cites the examples of Rover and Nissan in the UK (Guest, 1995). However, some scepticism also exists on the ideological left about the reasons for labour–management partnerships, it being argued that they have their origins in the extension of HRM practices, and are inherently unitarist. In this respect, some would say that union weakness is the reason behind unions seeking partnership agreements – as, as it were, a self-preservation measure. Kelly draws attention to this: 'Since it is difficult, if not impossible to achieve a partnership with a party that would prefer that you didn't exist, the growth of employer hostility is a major objection' (Kelly, 1996). He also refers to a significant number of writers in Europe and the USA who 'came to the conclusion that union survival and recovery turned on the willingness of unions and their members to behave "moderately" and to offer concessions to the employer as part of a new social partnership between labour and capital'. He goes on to point out that 'there is a striking parallel between the social partnership and human resource management literatures, evident most clearly in the way that employers' priorities have come to dominate the intellectual agenda of researchers' (Kelly, 1998).

Others have pointed to the two clear schools of thought that are emerging in academic circles, with some addressing the dynamics of labour–management partnerships only, and others taking a broad philosophical approach, examining employer, union and worker motives or responses. The former position is adopted by Kochan et al., (1996), the IPA (1998), Coupar and Stevens (1998), and by Kochan and Osterman, (1994). The latter position is adopted by writers such as Kelly (1996, 1998), Nissen (1997) and Parker and Slaughter (1997). This could be summarised as the 'incorporatist' approach, as in Allen and Haynes (1999), and Cressey and MacInnes (1980); this relies on the old socialist conventional wisdom that trade unions – and especially their paid officials or bureaucrats – can easily sell out and become incorporated in management's exploitative apparatus.

Before attempting to assess the extent to which these businesses are using a partnership approach, let us consider some views and experiences from the USA. In addressing the issue of labour–management partnerships and the implications for the UK and Ireland, McKersie (1996) has drawn attention to the possibility of transforming existing workplaces into modern, high-performance systems – as against the trend in the USA towards closing plants with traditionally strong adversarial cultures, and starting afresh with modern work practices and non-union labour on greenfield sites. He acknowledges that businesses and trade unions in the UK may be better able to manage change, and 'transform their industrial relationships for mutual gains' (McKersie, 1996) in order to be able to compete at a world-class level. Indeed, he is in no doubt that the UK experience of partnership will be different from that in the USA; Milsome (2001) has provided a valuable summary of the US experience, including a detailed description of one of the most celebrated successes of partnership: the General Motors (GM) Saturn Car project in Tennessee. The joint involvement of the United Auto Workers and GM from the initial planning stage, to full facilitation of the new plant on a joint basis on a greenfield site is in stark contrast to the evolutionary approach to partnership emerging in the UK.

At this point is useful to give an example of a partnership agreement. This example is presented in 'In Practice' 12.4.

In Practice   12.4

Bausch and Lomb partnership strategies

Bausch and Lomb is an American multi-national company that develops and manufactures health-care products for eyes. The company employs 12,000 people worldwide with annual revenues of $1.7 billion in sales. The company's plant at Waterford in the Republic of Ireland employs 1,750 people and is one of the few unionised plants in the company. The plant is the largest and most competitive manufacturing facility in the entire organisation. The plant operates a successful partnership forum that has been in place since 1998. The aim of the forum is to facilitate a two-way flow of information, giving all stakeholders an opportunity to shape the future of the company, for the common good. The forum is made up of management, elected and nominated members from the unions, and clerical and technical groups. They work on issues such as communications, pensions, training, finance and strategy.

The Waterford plant is clear about the practical benefits of the partnership and has improved communication. According to Bausch and Lomb the overall benefits of partnership are:

1. All stakeholders know the needs of the business and where it is heading.

2. Improved performance through discussion and debate.

3. Builds trust between employees, managers and unions.

4. Allows everyone to contribute to a constructive atmosphere.

5. Disclosure and communication of information leads to a better understanding of why decisions are made.

6. Widens the area of discussion and puts it on a strategic level and in a national and international context.

Source: adapted from *The Irish Times* (2006).

Key values for successful partnership

In a study of five cases of joint union–management cooperation in the USA in 1995, Roscow and Casner-Lotto (1998) identified the elements included in Key Concepts 12.7 as key elements of successful union–management partnerships.

Key Concepts   12.7

Key elements of a successful partnership

- Mutual trust and respect.
- A joint vision for the future and the means to achieve it.
- Continuous exchange of information.
- Recognition of job security and its link to productivity.
- Recognition of the central role of collective bargaining.
- Devolved decision-making.

Source: Roscow and Casner-Lotto (1998).

This work indicated that if all these matters were addressed successfully on a joint basis by management and unions, then companies could expect productivity gains, quality improvements, a better motivated and more flexible workforce, and a decline in absenteeism and labour turnover rates. Unions and their members could expect to gain improved job security, closer involvement in running the company and, ultimately, a better rewards package. While to some this may seem to be a wish list, and almost impossible to achieve all of the time, Roscow and Casner-Lotto (1998) believe that a win–win situation could be achieved, and that their research evidence shows that companies and unions really were managing to develop a successful partnership approach around these values.

It is interesting to compare the key values for labour–management partnerships identified in the USA with the behavioural aspects identified by Coupar and Stevens (1998) as distinguishing partnerships in the UK:

> … a commitment to working together to make the business more successful, understanding the employee security conundrum and trying to do something about it, building relationships at the workplace which maximise employee influence through total communication and a robust and effective employee voice.

They also identified some common elements in partnership agreements as:

> … a vision of the goal, a cultural change programme which began with managers, a systematic revision of reward, status and conditions, the development of new business-focused consultative arrangements from the workplace to the boardroom, a carefully thought out and agreed policy to manage employment security, and a major commitment to employee development and training.

Monks (1998) has also sought to identify the underlying values of a partnership agreement in practice as: 'employee security, employee voice, fair financial rewards, and investment in training'.

In economies close to the UK, such as the Republic of Ireland, partnership agreements are underpinned by and emphasise the notion of social partnership. This has resulted in national agreements dating back to 1986; the most recent of these agreements have been the Partnership 2000 agreement of 1996 and the Programme for Prosperity and Fairness of 2000. The aims of these agreements are based around building competitiveness through improved employee involvement at enterprise level. The National Centre for Partnership and a number of other support initiatives have been created to stimulate the roles of all stakeholders at enterprise level.

In the UK, most employer organisations, professional management associations and trade union interests have subscribed to the Department of Trade and Industry (DTI)/Department for Education and Employment (DfEE) initiative entitled 'Competitiveness through Partnerships with People' (DTI/DfEE, 1998). This was launched as part of the programme for implementing the Employment Relations Act 1999. It is built around the key values of:

- shared goals – understanding the business they are in;
- shared culture – agreed values binding them together;
- shared learning – continuously improving themselves;
- shared effort – one business driven by flexible teams;
- shared information – effective communication throughout the enterprise (DTI/DfEE, 1998).

Some modest financial incentives are provided by the DTI to assist implementation and improvement programmes (see http://www.gov.dti.uk/partnershipfund/).

Finally, there is wide agreement, first, that a direct trade-off exists between the important issues of security of employment and flexible working and, second, that all the employees in an enterprise are stakeholders, with a direct interest in enhancing its competitiveness.

Self-Check and Reflect Questions	12.4

Consider the arguments for and against the development and introduction of a partnership agreement in an organisation.

Having assessed the partnership concept, the psychological contract will now be considered.

The psychological contract

The *psychological contract* is a term first used by Argyris (1960). It refers to the expectations of employer and employee that operate in addition to the formal contract of employment. As highlighted earlier in this chapter, the psychological contract has been defined by Rousseau (1994, cited by Hiltrop, 1995: 287) as 'the understanding people have regarding the commitments made between themselves and their organisations'. It is therefore concerned with each party's perception of what the other party to the employment relationship owes them, over and above that which may be specified in the contract of employment. As this contract is based upon perceptions, it is clear that the 'context' of this contract is not written and often not explicitly stated. The aspect of the psychological contract that has been a major focus of attention in recent years is the traditional employee perception that the organisation promises a 'job for life' in return for employee loyalty and commitment. Such reciprocal expectations characterised (and to some extent still characterise) the employment relationship in many areas of employment. Typical examples of this can be found in local government and the civil service. Key Concepts 12.8 summarises the characteristics of the 'old and 'new' psychological contracts.

Key Concepts   12.8

The 'old' and 'new' psychological contracts

Characteristic	Old	New
Focus of employment relationship	Security and long-term career in the company	Employability driven by changes in this and future employment
Format	Structured and predictable	Flexible and unpredictable
Duration	Permanent	Variable
Underlying principle	Influence by tradition	Driven by market forces
Intended output	Loyalty and commitment	Value added
Employer's key responsibility	Fair day's work for a fair day's pay	High pay for high job performance
Employee's key responsibility	Good performance in present job	Making a difference to the organisation
Employer's key input	Stable income and career	Opportunities for self-development
Employee's key input	Time and effort	Knowledge and skills

Source: adapted from Hiltrop (1995: 290).

Much of the key research carried out on the psychological contract in the context of the UK has been undertaken by the CIPD. The structure of this section has been developed in the context of the key areas of discussion and analysis as presented by the CIPD (2006).

What is the psychological contract?

As highlighted above, the term 'psychological contract' was first used in the early 1960s, but became more popular following the economic downturn in the early 1990s. It has been defined by Guest and Conway (2002) as 'the perceptions of the two parties, employee and employer, of what their mutual obligations are towards each other'. These obligations will often be informal and imprecise: they may be inferred from actions or from what has happened in the past, as well as from statements made by the employer, for example during the recruitment process or in performance appraisals. Some obligations may be seen as 'promises' and others as 'expectations'. The important thing is that they are believed by the employee to be part of the relationship with the employer.

The CIPD (2006) believes that the psychological contract can be distinguished from the legal contract of employment. In many cases the latter will offer only a limited and uncertain representation of the reality of the employment relationship. The employee may have contributed little to its terms beyond accepting them. The nature and content of the legal contract may only emerge clearly if and when it comes to be tested in an employment tribunal.

The psychological contract, on the other hand, looks at the reality of the situation as perceived by the parties, and may be more influential than the formal contract in affecting how employees behave from day to day. It is the psychological contract that effectively tells employees what they are required to do in order to meet their side of the bargain, and what they can expect from their job. It may not – indeed in general it will not – be strictly enforceable, although courts may be influenced by a view of the underlying relationship between employer and employee, for example in interpreting the common law duty to show mutual trust and confidence.

A useful model of the psychological contract is offered by Guest (2002) (see Table 12.2). In outline, the CIPD (2006) believes that the model suggests that:

- the extent to which employers adopt people management practices will influence the state of the psychological contract;
- the contract is based on employees' sense of fairness and trust and their belief that the employer is honouring the 'deal' between them;
- where the psychological contract is positive, increased employee commitment and satisfaction will have a positive impact on business performance.

Table 12.2 A model of the psychological contract

Inputs	Content	Outputs
Employee characteristics	Fairness	Employee behaviour
Organisation characteristics	Trust	Performance
HR practices	Delivery	

Source: adapted from Guest and Conway (2002).

What happens if the contract is broken?

Research quoted by the CIPD (2006) shows that, where employees believe that management have broken promises or failed to deliver on commitments, this has a negative effect on job satisfaction, commitment to the company and on the psychological contract as a whole. This is particularly the case where managers themselves are responsible for breaches, e.g. where employees do not receive promised training, or performance reviews are badly handled. Managers cannot always ensure that commitments are fulfilled – for example where employment prospects deteriorate or organisations are affected by mergers or restructuring – but they may still take some blame in the eyes of employees.

The CIPD (2006) believes managers need to remember:

- Employment relationships may deteriorate despite management's best efforts: nevertheless, it is the managers' job to take responsibility for maintaining them.
- Preventing breach in the first place is better than trying to repair the damage afterwards.
- Where breach cannot be avoided it may be better to spend time negotiating or re-negotiating the deal, rather than focusing on delivery.

In Key Concepts 12.9 the changes currently affecting the workplace are highlighted.

Key Concepts   12.9

Changes currently affecting the workplace

- The nature of jobs: more employees are on part-time and temporary contracts; more jobs are being outsourced; tight job definitions are out, functional flexibility is in.
- Organisations have downsized and delayered: 'leanness' means doing more with less, so individual employees have to carry more weight.
- Markets, technology and products are constantly changing: customers are becoming ever more demanding, quality and service standards are constantly going up.
- Technology and finance are less important as sources of competitive advantage: 'human capital' is becoming more critical to business performance in the knowledge-based economy.
- Traditional organisational structures are becoming more fluid: teams are often the basic building block; new methods of managing are required.

Source: CIPD (2006).

What has persuaded people to take the psychological contract seriously?

This is a central element of the CIPD's (2006) discussion. It argues that the effect of these changes is that employees are increasingly recognised as the key business drivers. It believes that the ability of the business to add value rests on its front-line employees, or 'human capital'. Organisations that wish to succeed have to get the most out of this resource. In order to do this, employers have to know what employees expect from their work. As such, the psychological contract offers a framework for monitoring employee attitudes and priorities on those dimensions that can be shown to influence performance. The CIPD (2006) argues that in order to display commitment, employees have to feel that they are being treated with fairness and respect. It goes on to claim that many organisations have concluded they need to create a corporate personality, or identity, that employees as well as customers will recognise and relate to. This leads organisations to identify a set of corporate values or to set down the organisation's mission. The purpose of creating an 'employer brand' (sometimes referred to as the employment proposition) is to outline the positive benefits for employees of buying into the relationship with that employer. In practice, the employer brand can be seen as an attempt by the employer to define the psychological contract with employees so as to help in recruiting and retaining talent.

How do SHRM practices impact on performance?

The CIPD (2006) believes that the model of the psychological contact suggests that, by adopting 'bundles' of strategic HR practices, employers are likely to improve business performance. Research into high-performance working by Purcell *et al.* (2003) underlines how this process can occur. Many employees have substantial discretion as to how to do their jobs: it is more likely that they will use their discretion positively if they feel that they are being fairly treated. Simply adopting positive HR polices is not enough: policies need to be translated into practice if they are to influence employees' behaviour. The way in which they are implemented by line managers is critical to the way in which employees respond.

The changing employment relationship: is there a new contract?

The traditional psychological contract is generally described as an offer of commitment by the employee in return for the employer providing job security – or in some cases the legendary 'job for life'. The recession of the early 1990s and the continuing impact of globalisation are alleged to have destroyed the basis of this traditional deal, since job security is no longer on offer. The new deal is said to rest on an offer by the employer of fair pay and treatment, plus opportunities for training and development. On this analysis, the employer can no longer offer security and this has undermined the basis of employee commitment.

When considering this issue, the CIPD (2006) asks if this is the case, and is there a 'new contract'? Research suggests that in many ways the 'old' psychological contract is in fact still alive. Employees still want security: interestingly, labour-market data suggest that there has been little reduction in the length of time for which people stay in individual jobs. They are still prepared to offer loyalty, although they may feel less committed to the organisation as a whole than to their workgroup. In general, they remain satisfied with their job.

The kinds of commitments employers and employees might make to one another are given in the Key Concepts 12.10.

The CIPD (2006) argues that any study of collective agreements in the last few years would suggest that employers recognise employee concerns about security. Such agreements often state that compulsory redundancy will be used only as a last resort. However, employers know that they are unable to offer absolute security and employees do not necessarily expect it. Younger people – the so-called 'generation X' – want excitement, a sense of community and a life outside work. They are not interested, as some of their fathers and mothers were, in a 'job for life', nor do they believe any organisation can offer this to them. They expect to be treated as human beings.

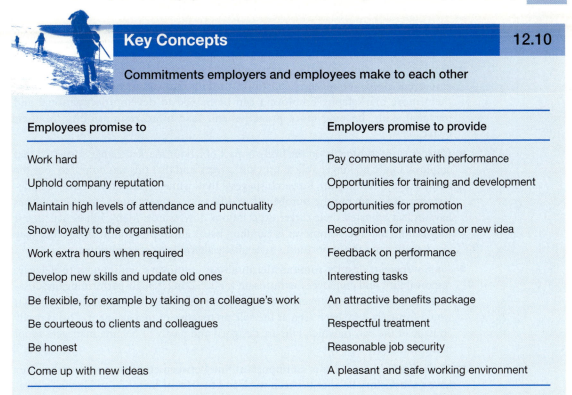

Key Concepts   12.10

Commitments employers and employees make to each other

Employees promise to	Employers promise to provide
Work hard	Pay commensurate with performance
Uphold company reputation	Opportunities for training and development
Maintain high levels of attendance and punctuality	Opportunities for promotion
Show loyalty to the organisation	Recognition for innovation or new idea
Work extra hours when required	Feedback on performance
Develop new skills and update old ones	Interesting tasks
Be flexible, for example by taking on a colleague's work	An attractive benefits package
Be courteous to clients and colleagues	Respectful treatment
Be honest	Reasonable job security
Come up with new ideas	A pleasant and safe working environment

Source: adapted from CIPD (2006).

The state of the psychological contract

Press reports suggest that UK employees are dissatisfied, insecure and lacking in commitment. Major national surveys, including those undertaken by the CIPD between 1996 and 2004, show that this picture is at best distorted. A simple overview of key survey findings is presented in Key Concepts 12.11.

Key Concepts   12.11

Employment relationship: what the surveys say

- There are continuing concerns about long hours and work intensity.
- A majority of employees consistently report that they are satisfied with their jobs.
- Four out of five employees are not worried about losing their job, and most expect that if they did lose their job they would be able to find another one at similar pay without having to move house.
- Levels of commitment have not shown any significant trend – whether up or down – in recent years.
- However, trust in the organisation has declined somewhat, in both private and public sectors.

However, CIPD (2006) research findings suggest that managers can usefully focus on other issues. In particular:

- *Employability:* although job security cannot be guaranteed, employers can recognise employees' need to build up a 'portfolio' of skills and competences that will make them more marketable. Employees can be helped to develop occupational and personal skills, become more proactive and take more responsibility for their own careers.

- *Careers:* early comments on the likely impact of labour market change suggested that employers were no longer able to provide 'careers' and that this was bound to sour the employment relationship. Research suggests that, while organisations have been de-layering and reducing the number of middle management posts, most employees have in fact adjusted their career expectations downwards. Many will be satisfied if they believe that their employer is handling issues about promotion fairly. They may also benefit from the opportunity to negotiate alternative career options.

- *Empowerment:* despite some cynicism about employers' willingness to delegate responsibility, and employees' enthusiasm for accepting it, high-performing organisations demand that employees make an important contribution to decisions that would formerly have been seen as the sole prerogative of management. This is partly an issue of the way in which jobs are designed and partly of helping managers adopt new behaviours.

- *Work–life balance:* there is an important link between employees feeling that they have a satisfactory balance between work and the rest of their life, and having a positive psychological contract. Employers need to think through how employees can be helped to achieve such a balance.

Source: CIPD (2006).

How do managers get commitment from employees?

Commitment has been the focus in a previous section of this chapter. The CIPD (2006) considers the strategic importance of achieving employee commitment as emerging clearly from the research into the impact of people management on performance. Traditional management theory focuses on reward and particularly pay as a prime source of motivation. However, Herzberg (1987) thought that employees were motivated to higher levels of performance by less material incentives, such as interesting work and the opportunity to develop their skills. Modern management thinking suggests that badly designed pay systems can demotivate employees but that getting pay right is no guarantee of commitment.

How important is employee voice?

As seen previously within the context of employee involvement and participation, the concept of 'employee voice or engagement' is of vital importance. Boxall and Purcell (2003: 162) believe that 'employee voice is the term increasingly used to cover a wide range and variety of processes and structures that enable, and in time empower, employees, directly and indirectly to contribute to decision-making in the firm, and occasionally in the wider society'.

Research into employee 'voice' by Marchington *et al.* (2001) shows the importance of communication and specifically of dialogue in which managers are prepared to listen to employees' opinions. Managers need to manage expectations, for example through systems of performance management which provide for regular employee appraisals. HR practices also communicate important messages about what the organisation seeks to offer its employers. However, employee commitment and 'buy-in' come primarily from listening not from telling.

The CIPD (2006) claims that employers are experimenting with a range of attitudinal and behavioural frameworks for securing employee inputs to management thinking as part of the decision-making process. This can be using a range of methods including:

- Face-to-face, for example through 'soap box' sessions, which encourage employees to speak their minds.

- Employee attitude surveys can also be an effective tool for exploring how employees think and feel on a range of issues affecting the workplace. In times of rapid change, managers and employees frequently hold contrasting opinions about what is going on.

- Two-way communication, both formal and informal, is essential as a form of reality check and a basis for building mutual trust.

What does employee commitment mean in practice?

Line managers have high expectations of employees. Examples of these expectations are presented in Key Concepts 12.12.

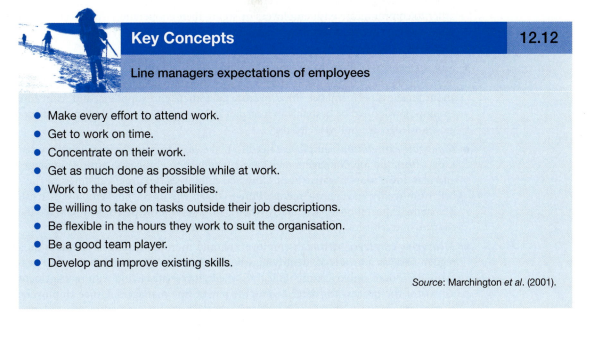

Key Concepts   12.12

Line managers expectations of employees

- Make every effort to attend work.
- Get to work on time.
- Concentrate on their work.
- Get as much done as possible while at work.
- Work to the best of their abilities.
- Be willing to take on tasks outside their job descriptions.
- Be flexible in the hours they work to suit the organisation.
- Be a good team player.
- Develop and improve existing skills.

Source: Marchington *et al.* (2001).

Strategic implications of the psychological contract

Basically, the psychological contract offers a metaphor, or representation, of what goes on in the workplace that highlights important but often neglected features. It offers a framework for addressing 'soft' issues about managing performance; it focuses on people, rather than technology; and it draws attention to some important shifts in the relationship between people and organisations.

Most organisations could benefit from thinking about the psychological contract. The first priority is to build the people dimension into thinking about organisational strategy. If people are bottom-line business drivers, their capabilities and needs should be fully integrated into business process and planning. The purpose of business strategy becomes how to get the best return from employees' energies, knowledge and creativity.

Employees' contribution can no longer be extracted by shame, guilt and fear: it has to be offered. Issues about motivation and commitment are critical. Yet many of the levers that managers have relied on to motivate employees are becoming increasingly unreliable.

The CIPD (2006) argues that the psychological contract may have implications for SHRM in a number of areas, for example:

- *Process fairness*: people want to know that their interests will be taken into account when important decisions are made; they would like to be treated with respect; they are more likely to be satisfied with their job if they are consulted about change. Managers cannot guarantee that employees will accept that outcomes on pay and promotion are fair, but they can put in place procedures that will make acceptance of the results more likely.

- *Communications*: although collective bargaining is still widely practised in the public sector, in large areas of the private sector trade unions now have no visible presence. It is no longer possible for managers in these areas to rely on 'joint regulation' in order to communicate with employees or secure their cooperation. An effective two-way dialogue between employer and employees is a necessary means of giving expression to employee 'voice'.

- *Management style*: in many organisations, managers can no longer control the business 'top-down' – they have to adopt a more 'bottom-up' style. Crucial feedback about business performance flows in from customers and suppliers, and front-line employees will often be best able to interpret it. Managers have to draw on the strategic knowledge in employees' heads.

- *Managing expectations*: employers need to make clear to new recruits what they can expect from the job. Managers may have a tendency to emphasise positive messages and play down more negative ones. However, employees can usually distinguish rhetoric from reality and management failure to do so will undermine employees' trust. Managing expectations, particularly when bad news is anticipated, will increase the chances of establishing a realistic psychological contract.

- *Measuring employee attitudes*: employers should monitor employee attitudes on a regular basis as a means of identifying where action may be needed to improve performance. Some employers use indicators of employee satisfaction with management as part of the process for determining the pay of line managers. Other employers, particularly in the service sector, recognise strong links between employee and customer satisfaction. However, employers should only undertake surveys of employee attitudes if they are ready to act on the results.

The psychological contract can help HR managers to make the business case for incorporating effective people management policies and practices into the change management process at an early stage, and to successfully manage their implementation. Research by CIPD (2006) shows that:

- A majority of workers in both public and private sectors report major organisational changes taking place.
- Employees are not necessarily hostile to change but major changes – particularly leading to redundancies – tend to cause negative attitudes.
- Most people say change in their organisation is badly managed.
- Employee trust in organisations has declined and this can make the process of managing change more difficult.

Breach of the psychological contract can seriously damage the employment relationship. It will not always be possible to avoid breach of the psychological contract but employees are more likely to be forgiving where managers explain what has gone wrong and how they intend to deal with it. The contract may need to be renegotiated.

Key lessons

Some of the key lessons that the CIPD (2006) believes emerge from research into the psychological contract are presented in Key Concepts 12.13.

Key Concepts   12.13

Key lessons from research on the psychological contract

1. Avoid redundancies whenever possible; redundancies lower morale.
2. Re-state the organisation's values; employees do not trust the organisation.
3. Train line managers in people management skills; employees are more likely to trust their line manager.
4. Ensure managers commit to key messages; mixed messages will have a negative influence on employee attitudes.
5. Inform and consult employees about proposed changes; they are more likely to see the outcome as fair.
6. Take care to fulfil commitments you make to employees; managers say employees show more commitment to their employer than vice versa.
7. Consider whether you need to renegotiate what employees are entitled to expect otherwise they may feel let down when circumstances change.
8. Put more effort into managing change; employees believe change is badly managed.
9. Give employees more responsibility: autonomy increases satisfaction.
10. Use employee attitude surveys to get a clear idea of what is happening in the organisation; employees often do not share senior managers' views of reality.

▶

11. Do not use tight management and close supervision; this will reduce employee satisfaction.

12. Use recruitment and appraisal processes to clarify the 'deal'; employee expectations are influenced by a number of factors.

13. If you cannot keep a promise, explain why; failure is often punished by loss of trust.

14. Trust employees to do a good job; most are highly motivated to do so and will respond to the trust you show in them.

15. Do not rely on performance management systems to motivate employees; you need to engage hearts and minds.

16. Be aware of changing expectations; for example more employees now want to work for organisations that behave responsibly.

17. Ensure consistency of treatment; perceived unfairness undermines trust.

18. Hold team meetings and focus groups; two-way dialogue will help flag issues at an early stage.

19. Review procedures for handing workplace conflict; mediation may offer a better outcome for both sides than an employment tribunal.

20. Encourage the growth of 'relational' contracts if you want employees to develop a long-term emotional attachment to the organisation.

Source: CIPD (2006).

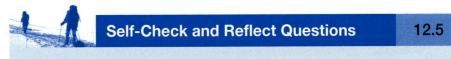

Self-Check and Reflect Questions   12.5

To what extent is the 'new' psychological' contract a myth dreamed up by HR commentators to add a new dimension to discussions about SHRM?

The psychological contract does not supply a detailed model of employee relations but it does offer important clues about how to maintain employee commitment. With the decline in collective bargaining, attention is more clearly focused on relations between the organisation and individual employees. The psychological contract reinforces the need for managers to become more effective at the communications process. Consultation about anticipated changes will help in adjusting expectations and, if necessary, renegotiating the deal.

Employees are becoming both more critical to business performance and more demanding of the organisations for which they work. In a 'winner takes all' economy, doing a good job is no longer enough: outstanding performance is essential to survival. This level of performance cannot be achieved by downsizing or cost control: it will only come from persuading employees to make a willing contribution.

The psychological contract provides a convincing rationale for 'soft HRM', or behaving as a good employer. It offers a perspective based on insights from psychology and organisational behaviour rather than economics. It emphasises that employment is a relationship in which the mutual obligations of employer and employees may be imprecise but have to be respected. The price of failing to fulfil expectations may be serious damage to the relationship and to the organisation.

In this chapter attempts have been made to consider both the theoretical rhetoric and the organisational reality in relation to the management of the employment relationship. At present there still appears to be a significant gap between the theories of SHRM and employee relations, and the observable practices evident in most UK and Irish workplaces. Students reading this book will hopefully become senior members of the HR professions in the future and may well take up executive positions within organisations. The reality is that it is only senior executives in companies and HR professional who can ensure that the employment relationship is managed in the most strategic manner. This is of vital importance not only in the context of the current internal and external operating environments that organisations are facing, but also with respect to the future challenges they are likely to face.

Summary

- The management of the employment relationship is a central area of discussion, research and organisational practice within the field of SHRM. Key concepts include the shift from traditional industrial relations to employee relations. Key parties to the employment relationship can be the grouped into bodies representing employers and employees.

- Two key differing perspectives in relation to a strategic approach to the management of the employment relationship – namely unitarism and pluralism – are identified and discussed.

- Key theoretical contributions in relation to strategic HRM and employee relations have been identified and grouped. Four possible organisational approaches to the management of the employment relationship are presented. These four approaches are: new realism, traditional collectivism, individualised SHRM and the black hole.

- Potential policies and practices in relation to managing employee relations in a strategic manner are discussed. This discussion is presented under the central theme of employee involvement and participation. Within this context, two key approaches are discussed in depth, namely partnership and the psychological contract. The practical realities of developing and managing partnership are discussed, as are the elements involved in the development of the psychological contract at the workplace and organisational level.

Follow-up study suggestions

- Use the internet to explore the employee relations' practices of two different 'case' organisations and develop explanations that account for similarities and differences between their practices.

- Use the internet to explore the employee relations' practices of two different national contexts and develop explanations that account for similarities and differences between their national practices.

- Interview a friend or colleague who is a member of a trade union and ask him or her why he or she joined the trade union and if that trade union plays a key role in the development of a strategic approach to the management of the employment relationship.
- Using the section titled 'Involvement and participation: strategic concepts and practices', in this chapter as your starting point, consider the practical implications for organisations generally and HR managers specifically of the emergence of concepts such as partnership and the psychological contract.

Suggestions for research topics

- Evaluate the management of the employment relationship within an industry of your choice. Consider how strategic or un-strategic the observable employment relationships are.
- Evaluate the development and implementation of a partnership agreement. The specific focus of your analysis should be on the employer.
- Discuss and analyse the psychological contract within an organisation or group of organisations. Specific attention in relation to discussion analysis should be paid to the views and opinions of both employers and employees.

Case Study

Strategic approaches to the employment relationship social partnership: the example of the Republic of Ireland

In other case studies presented in this book the focus of analysis has been at the organisational level and presented company-based cases. Managing the employment relationship in a strategic manner is important for both employers and employees, but can be a strategic issue that covers complete industries and sectors and, in exceptional cases, can have influence across complete national economies or even huge market places such as the European Union. Creating stability in the employment relationship at a national level can be of significant strategic importance. The benefits of such stability can be felt by all citizens who participate in the labour market, greater levels of job security may result, realistic increases in salaries and wages can be implemented on a regular basis, improvements in the employment relationship will occur at the workplace, company, sector, industry and national levels. Such an approach can create:

stability for both employers and employees; can allow indigenous businesses, particularly SMEs, to grow; and helps to attract and retain foreign direct investment (FDI) to the economy. In economies such as the UK, where unions still have a key role to play in many companies across a wide range of sectors, the most realistic strategic approach to developing a stable and flexible employment relationship may be through the partnership approach.

The case to be considered in this chapter focuses on social partnership in the Republic of Ireland. The reasons for choosing this case should become apparent after you have read it but there are a number of key factors which should be considered:

- There are many similarities between employee relations in the UK and Ireland, such as heavily unionised public sectors and traditional industry sectors.

- Modern private-sector industries and SMEs are largely non-unionised.

- Similarities exist in the UK and Irish governments' approaches to employee relations.

- Both economies are locations for major indigenous and foreign companies that face significant competition from emerging economies in China and India, for example.

- Similar education levels, age and gender breakdowns exist in most workplaces in both economies.

- Dramatic shifts have occurred that result in employment moving from traditional industries to new high-technology industries and the service sector.

Context

In the early 1980s the economy of the Republic of Ireland was in crisis, the traditional industries were in dramatic decline and unemployment was at record levels. In 1986 the National Economic and Social Council (NESC) (this Irish organisation is comparable with the UK's Economic and Social Research Council) produced a comprehensive prescription for economic recovery including most significantly, in the view of the government, the involvement of the unions. Implementation would, of course, only be possible with the agreement of the tripartite social partners – government, unions and employers. But why develop a national partnership agreement?

For the unions there were several considerations:

1. First, under a tripartite national agreement the weakest and lowest-paid members were protected by agreed minimum pay increases.

2. Second, wage dispersion in the1980s widened the gap between top and bottom, and threatened to undermine the solidarity of the TU movement.

3. Third, falling membership and increasing unemployment made leaders fear that what was happening to unions in Thatcher's Britain might also occur in Ireland.

The employers were represented by the Irish Business and Employers' Confederation (IBEC) and the government of the time was led by Fianna Fáil (FF) a major Irish political party. The three parties came together and despite their differences came to an agreement, which was to create a major strategic change in the direction of the employment relationship at the national level.

The Result was a three-year tripartite agreement grandly titled the Programme for National Recovery (PNR).

The PNR set sharp limits on pay, with only a 3 per cent pa increase on the first £120 per week of earnings, and 2 per cent thereafter – with an underpinning minimum of £4. The most significant features of PNR were competitive commitments to the control of public expenditure and a reduction in government borrowing. However, PNR included other broadly expressed 'classical' commitments: to promote increased employment through industrial development; to improve social welfare provision; and to reduce direct taxation on lower paid workers covered by the Pay As You Earn (PAYE) system.

From PNR to PESP

There was widespread recognition by employers and unions that the PNR had had beneficial effects; so it was followed by a similar agreement, the Programme for Economic and Social Progress (PESP), covering the period up to 1993. This allowed much the same percentage salary and increases, but also permitted an extra amount to be negotiated at enterprise or plant level. Although it seemed to be working well, there were some serious economic setbacks during the PESP period, including devaluation of the IR£ that government had tried hard to resist. As well as several pay-related crises, there were also major rows over income tax increases – and about cuts in social welfare benefits, which were argued by the unions to be in breach of the PESP. Yet the programme still held together, and also weathered change of government – when FF attempted to win a majority in a snap election in 1989, failed, and was obliged to make a coalition pact with the new Progressive Democrat party.

The Progressive Democrats, with only a very small number of TDs (equivalent of UK's MPs), had a 'new right', neo-liberal economic agenda. Yet this had no discernible effect on the government's approach to PESP.

From PESP to PCW

In 1992 that government was succeeded by a more left-leaning Fianna Fáil/Labour Coalition. Against the background of a recovering economy, a new agreement was fairly inevitable. So PESP was succeeded by the Programme for Competitiveness and Work (PCW).

Its tight pay provisions followed much the same pattern as in the two previous pacts, but more attention was given to non-pay issues.

As the title suggests, one of the main non-pay issues addressed by the PCW was unemployment. Another was employee involvement; for the Irish Congress of Trade Unions (ICTU) now wanted more than the lip service paid in the PNR and PESP. Significantly, an ICTU internal report on new management methods seemed to endorse 'bottom-up' employee involvement with a 'competitive edge' component.

What was wanted was for partnership at national level to be complemented by partnership in the enterprise, the plant and the office. But while there were more words about participation in the PCW, IBEC fought hard against anything too prescriptive. There was further disappointment for ICTU when post-agreement discussions produced little more. PCW ended on a sour note, with public service workers complaining loudly that they had done poorly in comparison with other groups.

P2000 – making partnership a priority

The tone was set by the name – Partnership 2000 (or P2000); it had a key part devoted to 'developing partnership in the workplace':

ICTU saw it 'as a watershed in the evolution of social partnership' and believed 'it would determine whether it develops or dies'. It was a last opportunity 'to widen and deepen the national partnership process into a genuine partnership at the level of the workplace'. The extent of new workplace partnership would be 'the union benchmark when it comes to assessing its success or failure'.

In order to meet the benchmark, a National Centre for Partnership was established to promote partnership in enterprises and workplaces. However, P2000 also included strong commitments to 'promoting enterprise' and the setting up of a National Competitiveness Council. Private-sector companies were also encouraged to reward employees by means of profit sharing.

With regard to the equality, employment and 'social inclusion' aspects, it was argued that economic growth had accelerated in a period marked by increasing income inequality, low pay and high levels of relative income poverty (Allen, 2000; Kirby, 2002).

In other words, there were too many marginalised people not enjoying any of the fruits of the 'Celtic Tiger'. Adding a more traditional or 'classical' neo-corporatist dimension, then, P2000 laid stronger emphasis on dealing with such issues. New agreement contained government commitments to spend £25 million on a range of important social projects before 2000. Targeted specifically were the long-term unemployed, the educationally disadvantaged, those on low incomes, and those living in the more deprived areas of the country. In addition, P2000 required the review of a number of economically important topics:

- modernising employee relations;
- modernising the public service;
- promoting enterprise – and it contained provision for a review mechanism on competitiveness.

Where to after P2000?

There were a number of other things to cheer supporters of social partnership. Although anecdotal evidence suggested wage drift beyond agreed norms, a survey of 1,000 pay settlements confirmed that the level of adherence was 'remarkably high'.

In addition, there were other achievements:

- agreement in broad terms to a procedure for union recognition;
- unemployment had dropped sharply;
- days lost due to disputes at all-time low;
- survey of IBEC members showed strong support for the continuation of social partnership;
- opinion poll in late 1999: 78 per cent of the public thought social partnership was 'very important' or 'quite important' to economic development and 80 per cent of employers believed that social partnership had been of vital importance to strategic developments in the way that people were managed at national, organisational and workplace levels;
- finally, spending in real terms on health, education and social welfare had increased by 117 per cent, 71 per cent and 45 per cent respectively since 1987 (IRS, 1998: 9, 18, 24 and 42).

Programme for Prosperity and Fairness

In January 2000, union leaders accepted a new agreement in the social partnership process. The new agreement was called the Programme for Prosperity and Fairness (PPF).

Under final PPF terms, workers on basic national minimum wage (NMW) were to receive pay increases worth 18.65 per cent over 33 months; workers on £200 would receive a 16.3 per cent pay rise and other workers would receive a 15.75 per cent pay rise.

The NMW started at IR£4.40 (€5.60) and rose to IR£4.70 (€5.80) in July 2001; it increased to IR£5 (€6.25) in October 2002.

There were several interesting 'non-pay' parts to the deal, including agreement to create new jobs for 1,500 primary school teachers. PPF also sought to deepen the workplace partnership measures begun under P2000.

At the time of writing this case the Irish government, IBEC and ICTU are currently in negotiation on a new partnership deal. It is useful to consider the arguments for and against a further partnership deal.

Stick with partnership? No!

First, the unions had 'pushed their luck' too far. Moreover ICTU was no longer the authentic, majority voice of Irish workers; it now represented predominantly public-sector employees and it had failed to convince most investors – especially US high-tech companies – to recognise trade unions.

Second, it was claimed that the strategic aims that prompted the birth of social partnership in the late 1980s had been almost fully realised. What was needed now was a dose of free market, employee relations – to sharpen up the act of the unions, management and employees.

Third, the pay agreement at the core of the PPF was becoming a fiction. Increases in the booming parts of the private sector appeared to be exceeding the PPF's pay norms and pay militancy was rising in the public sector. Could increases really be held to 2–3 per cent in a highly successful economy with real labour shortages?

Fourth, there was widespread 'partnership fatigue' arising from the 20+ working groups set up under the PPF on work, housing, gainsharing, etc. This demanded return to the 'leaner' and less complicated agreements of the late 1980s and 1990s.

Stick with partnership? Yes!

For all the factors against partnership there remain three main pressures for a continuation of social partnership.

First, a simple argument was that the cumulative strategic benefits and improvements in the employment relationship, that had occurred as a result of social partnership, were so obvious that it would foolish to throw them all away. It would be even more regrettable to abandon the uniquely Irish model for managing the employment relationship – one that incorporated both classical and competitive neo-corporatism, and represented, as it were, neo-liberalism with a social conscience.

Second, there was some apprehension that a return to unfettered free collective bargaining would be too much of a shock for the employee relations system. An associated worry was that many managers and union officials were ill-equipped to deal with face-to-face negotiating at firm and plant level.

Third, and perhaps most telling, it was argued that retaining neo-corporatism was essential in the face of an economic downturn. With so much US investment, Ireland was especially vulnerable to effects of the US recession of 2001 that was deepened by the 9/11 terrorist attacks.

To make economic matters worse, soon after the 2002 General Election – which returned the Fianna Fáil/PD coalition for a second term – suspicions about looming problems in public finances were proved justified, with expenditure running well beyond expectations but with tax receipts in serious decline. This was not the right moment, so it was argued, to make any radical change of approach. Social partnership might be essential to economic stability.

Sustaining Progress

In the event, the arguments for continuation of partnership finally won the day but there were several crisis points in the negotiations and it was only with the last-minute intervention of the Taoiseach (the Irish Prime Minister) that the most recent partnership agreement, entitled Sustaining Progress (SP), was concluded in February 2003. Like its predecessors, the SP was intended to cover a three-year period, however a degree of uncertainty was evident in the pay provisions from the start, which covered only an 'interim' period of 18 months. In late 2002 there was a 'benchmarking' (income comparison) process for public-sector employees. The aim was to redress a relative falling behind in the pay of the government's own employees during the course of the previous agreement. So SP dealt separately with public-sector pay, providing an implementation schedule for benchmarking, then a six-month pay pause. This was followed by a general increase of 7 per cent payable in three phases (3 per cent, 2 per cent and 2 per cent) ending in December 2004. For the private sector, SP provided an earlier but similarly phased implementation of the same 7 per cent. And the national minimum wage was increased to €7 with effect from February 2004. But, despite a focus on possible effects of SP on competitiveness, there remained a clear traditional commitment to social improvement – including a strong re-commitment to the development of workplace partnership.

Where to now?

All the old arguments – and a few new ones – were rehearsed in the run-up to the current negotiations. The start was delayed by a dispute in December 2005 between a major employer, Irish Ferries, and the largest Irish trade union, SIPTU, which represented over 85 per cent of Irish Ferries' 1,000+ employees. This dispute arose out of concern about a more general displacement of Irish workers by foreign nationals who were being paid significantly less.

At the time of writing it appears that employers hold the key to the successful creation of a new agreement. Employers appear to have regarding the fact that IBEC will only commit if a new agreement can restore the economy's competitive edge by controlling salaries and wages costs by:

● getting pay back into line with main trading partners, e.g. UK, USA and EU;
● maintaining a flexible labour market;
● improving productivity.

On employment standards employers say 'no more labour market regulation' – must maintain flexibility.

Will there be new agreement?

Eight out of 25 EU member states came to partnership pacts of a *competitive* kind in recent years (Belgium, Finland, Germany, Greece, Italy, The Netherlands, Portugal and Spain) but of course the new Irish pacts actually contained elements of both old *and* new approaches to managing the employment relationship:

● *Classical* – fairness and social justice.
● *Competitive (strategic)* – recognition of the importance of success of the national economy. Competitiveness obviously became a stronger component with the passage of time, but issues of justice and fairness have not been lost sight of.

The present Irish model of social partnership thus represents what might be call a *balanced* version of strategic management of the employment relationship.

Conclusions

Many analysts have concluded that the Irish social partnership model has played a vital role in the dramatic growth of the Irish economy in the last 20 years. This process of economic growth and development has driven economic and political analysts to use the term the 'Celtic Tiger' economy. Two clear benefits of social partnership can clearly be linked to economic growth:

1. low inflation – a key factor early on;
2. psychological effect – arguably the most important in the long term, for both Republic of Ireland employers and potential foreign direct investors who bring new employment with their investment.

It seems impossible, then, to conclude other than that social partnership was *a* key, if not *the* key, to recent economic strategic success of companies who are based in the Republic of Ireland. But, as well as those factors relating to employee relations and economic results, there is another wider lesson to be learned from social partnership – because the Irish experience shows that collective partnership is a real and demonstrably effective strategic policy alternative to an individualised approach to the strategic management of the employment relationship. That the collective social partnership-based employment relationship in Ireland and the free-market individualised employment relationship of the USA were among the best performing economies 1990s and early 2000s is adequate testimony to this.

Case study questions

1. Outline the main driving factors for the development of social partnership in Ireland.
2. Why do you think it was so important to have a tripartite agreement between the national government, employers and trade unions?
3. Why do you think it has been possible to develop and sustain social partnership in Ireland for such a long period?
4. Do you think it would be possible and/or beneficial for the UK to develop its own model of social partnership?

13 Diversity management: concern for legislation or concern for strategy?*
With Savita Kumra

Learning Outcomes

By the end of this chapter you should be able to:

- explain the differences between managing diversity and equal opportunities approaches to diversity management and the debates relating to these approaches;

- explore the interdependence of managing diversity and equal opportunities approaches in managing human resources strategically;

- evaluate the business case for diversity management;

- be able to integrate diversity management with other SHRM issues such as organisational culture;

- assess the implementation issues for organisations adopting diversity management as part of their strategy to manage human resources.

* This chapter was co-authored with Savita Kumra

Introduction

In today's highly competitive labour market, the ability to attract and retain talented people is now rated higher than market share in the top ten non-financial measures investors use to analyse company performance (Ernst and Young, 2000). Traditional markets for attracting talented people, however, are changing and becoming increasingly challenging for many organisations, owing to major shifts in the demographic composition of the workforce including age, gender and ethnicity. When Figure 13.1, is examined it can be seen that, although the total population of the EU's 15 member states (prior to the 2004 accessions) is predicted to remain stable over the next 25 years at approximately 380 million people, its composition will alter markedly. In particular, the number of people of traditional working age (16–59) will fall from 228 million in 2005 to 203 million by 2030, while the number aged 60 or over will rise from 86 million to 123 million, an increase of over 40 per cent (Eurostat, 2005a). As we read regularly in the newspapers, this has major implications for pension provision, in particular the ability of organisations and countries to fund them. However, these changes also have considerable strategic implications for organisations seeking to plan their future human resource requirements.

The EU predicts that such demographic changes will have considerable impact upon the composition of the Union's labour force (Eurostat, 2005b). Although these states' total labour force is predicted to rise slightly from 181 million in 2005 to 183 million by 2010, it will decline gradually to 170 million by 2030, the changes to full- and part-time worker numbers differing. Over the 2005–2030 period, the number of full-time (32 or more hours per week) workers in the labour force is predicted to decline by 8 per cent and, while the number of long part-time workers (20 to 31 hours per week) is predicted to remain reasonably constant, the number of short part-time (up to 19 hours per week) will grow by 5 per cent. These variations are even more dramatic when specific age groups are considered, in particular those aged 60 and over (Figure 13.2) where the numbers in the labour force are predicted grow by over 65 per cent.

Self-Check and Reflect Questions   13.1

Note down the changes in the EU's population highlighted by Figures 13.1 and 13.2.

1. How are these predicted changes likely to impact upon the composition of the labour force in relation to full- and part-time work, age and gender?
2. What implications do you consider these change are likely to have for SHRP (strategic human resource planning)?
3. What other demographic changes do you predict based upon your own knowledge of labour markets.

Many of the demographic changes you have probably highlighted in your answer to Self-Check Question 13.1 are likely to have been raised by other writers. For example, by 2006, the number of 16–24-year-olds in the UK labour market is likely to have fallen by 1 million compared with 1987. By 2010, 80 per cent of the UK workforce growth will be among women and only 20 per cent of the workforce will be white, able-bodied, male and under 45 years of age (Pearn Kandola, 2000).

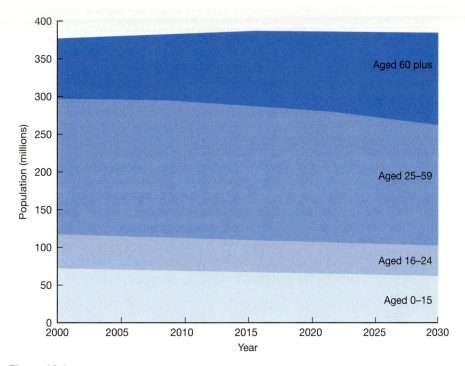

Figure 13.1 European Union* population, 2000–2030
Source: adapted from Eurostat (2005a), © 2005 European Communities, all rights reserved.
* All data relates to the 15 member states prior to the 2004 accession.

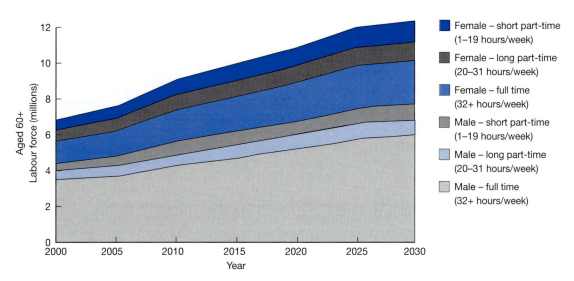

Figure 13.2 European Union* workforce aged 60 and over, 2000–2030
Source: adapted from Eurostat (2005b), © 2005 European Communities, all rights reserved.
* All data relate to the 15 member states prior to the 2004 accession.

Given these changes, it is not surprising that issues associated with the composition of organisations' workforces and their management have become a strategic imperative for HR managers and, as a consequence, their management a necessity. However, the way in which such issues associated with workforce diversity are tackled and the approach adopted is varied. Organisations have available to them a number of ways in which both to conceptualise the issue of diversity management and to operationalise their responses.

This chapter commences by considering the different ways in which diversity management has been conceptualised (Figure 13.3). Building upon this, equal opportunities and managing diversity approaches to diversity management are compared and contrasted, and the debates relating to these approaches discussed. As part of this, the question as to whether or not managing diversity represents a strategic shift from equal opportunities is addressed. After evaluating the business case for adopting diversity management, the issues for organisations wishing to implement a managing diversity approach to managing their human resources are assessed. The chapter concludes with a case study of a UK public-sector organisation, which explores the approaches used to promote the advantages of valuing diversity to their employees.

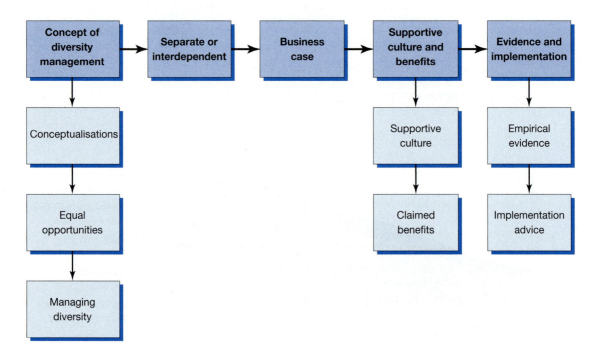

Figure 13.3 Mapping the diversity management territory: a summary diagram of the chapter content

The concept of diversity management

Conceptualisations

As has already been seen in our earlier discussions of SHRM (Chapter 2) and of SHRP (Chapter 7), a variety of definitions of the same concept are often put forward, the definition being dependent upon both organisational and individual interpretation. Diversity management has also been defined in different ways which are open to a range of interpretations. For some it is concerned with issues of managing differing national cultures within a multi-national organisation (Hofstede, 2001) (Chapters 3 and 6); for others it relates to further development and application of equal opportunities within the workplace (Liff, 1999); while for yet others it refers to a particular approach through which different parts of an organisation are integrated and/or the way in which people are managed strategically (Cox, 1991, 1993).

Much of the literature regarding diversity management emanates from the experiences of organisations in the USA, where the concept is particularly popular; a reflection perhaps of the more diverse workforce composition (Cassell, 1996). For example, a report by the US Department of Education (1999) described managing and valuing diversity as key components of effective people management, arguing that the focus on improving organisational performance and promoting practices that enhance the productivity of all staff were imperative to future organisational success. In this articulation of diversity management, dimensions of diversity included gender, race, culture, age, family/carer status, religion and disability. The definition provided also embraced a range of individual skills, such as educational qualifications, work experience and background, languages, as well as other relevant attributes and experiences that differentiate individuals.

Within the UK and Europe, the concept of diversity management is a more recent phenomenon, gaining prominence particularly since the mid-1990s. In the UK context, unlike equal opportunities, the term has no legislative definition. Rather, the term diversity is applied when describing a range of dimensions on which an organisation's employees may differ. These can include role, function and personality. In general, however, within the SHRM literature, diversity management is conceptualised usually in terms of differences that are particularly relevant to the issues of an individual employee's identity, such as gender, age, ethnicity, disability and sexual orientation (Hicks-Clark and Iles, 2000). This can be broadly categorised into two groups (Figure 13.4).

The first group, the equal opportunities approach, can be seen as contributing little more than a reiteration of the traditional arena of equality of status, opportunities and

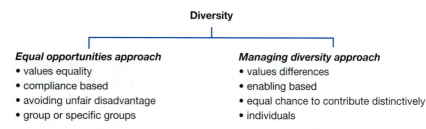

Figure 13.4 Conceptualisations of diversity in the literature

rights (Key Concepts 13.1) (for example, Cooper and White, 1995; Ellis and Sonnerfield, 1995; Copeland, 1988). Within this group, it is often argued that, although anti-discrimination legislation (sex, race and disability) has played some part in focusing attention on the practice of equal opportunities, these laws have had minimal impact despite, in the case of sex and race, being on the statute books for three decades (Ross and Schnieder, 1992). Thus, in this strand of the literature, diversity management is presented as providing the equal opportunities cause with some much needed revitalisation, broadening and reinvigorating a compliance-based perspective. Few would support the premise that this has met its stated objectives: to bring about equality in employment for groups facing particular disadvantage, such as women, those from ethnic minorities and people with disabilities (Johnson and Johnstone, 2000), differences in pay serving to emphasise this.

Key Concepts   13.1

Equality, discrimination and diversity

An examination of the definitions of these words in a dictionary highlights three distinct concepts:

Equality: being equal in status, rights and opportunities
Discrimination: unjust or prejudicial treatment of different groups of people
Diversity: being different or varied

The application of these concepts to SHRM has different foci, the first two emphasising similarity, and the third differences.

By contrast, the literature in the second group, the managing diversity approach, views diversity management as a paradigmatic shift from a conventional legislative focus upon equal opportunities to an explicit strategy of valuing differences, such as gender, age, social background, disability, personality, ethnicity and work style (Kandola and Fullerton, 1994a).

Whereas equality can be equated with equal status, rights and opportunities, diversity is equated with differences and variability among individuals and, to a lesser extent, groups of employees (Key Concepts 13.1). Within this, it is argued that, if these differences are managed properly, they are an asset to work being done more efficiently and effectively (Bartz *et al.*, 1990) and organisational goals being met (Kandola and Fullerton, 1994a). Consequently, a managing diversity approach focuses upon recognising both visible and non-visible differences and building upon the advantages that they

Self-Check and Reflect Questions   13.2

What do you consider to be the strengths and limitations of the equal opportunities and the managing diversity approaches to diversity management?

offer, rather than utilising legislation and targeted group initiatives to try to ensure that differences do not result in unjust or prejudicial treatment (Kandola and Fullerton, 1994a, 1998).

Mavin and Girling (2000) believe that, at its most simple, managing diversity can be viewed as a permissive concept, which is positive in emphasis and indicates a desire to do things. In contrast, they argue that equal opportunities is more restrictive, emphasising the negative with a focus on not doing things. Consequently, managing diversity is seen as an approach enabling all individuals to work in an environment that facilitates their development, releases their potential and encourages them to do all they can to support the organisation's progress by virtue of their differences. An equal opportunities approach is perceived as seeking to protect specific groups of employees in their work environment, usually supported by legislation, and tries to ensure, through compliance, that organisations do not behave in particular ways that are perceived as discriminatory to these individuals. The first piece of UK legislation to contain a more positive focus was the Race Relations (Amendment Act) 2000 (In Practice 13.1). This was introduced as part of the response to the Stephen Lawrence Inquiry's concern about institutional racism. It requires public-sector employers, including government departments, local authorities, the police, National Health Service, schools and the like to positively promote racial equality (Willey, 2003).

In Practice 13.1

The Stephen Lawrence Inquiry and institutional racism

Sir William MacPherson's (1999) report on the racist murder of Stephen Lawrence concluded that the UK's Metropolitan Police Service's investigation of the murder 'was marred by a combination of professional incompetence, institutional racism and a failure of leadership by senior officers' (MacPherson, 1999: para. 46.1). Institutional racism was defined as 'the collective failure of an organisation to provide an appropriate and professional service to people because of their colour, culture or ethnic origin' (MacPherson, 1999: para. 6.34). This, it was argued in the report, could be seen through the processes, attitudes and behaviours that amounted 'to discrimination through unwitting prejudice, ignorance, thoughtlessness, and racist stereotyping which disadvantage minority ethnic people' (MacPherson, 1999: para. 46.13). The report concluded that every organisation should examine their policies and the outcomes of these policies and practices to ensure that sections of communities were not disadvantaged.

Barmes and Ashtiany (2003) argue that the differentiation between equal opportunities and managing diversity on the basis of their respective emphases offers only a partial understanding of the nature of equality. In their view, equality entails more than the negative requirement of avoiding unfair disadvantage based on membership of a disadvantaged group. Rather it has a positive element, according to which each person should have an equal chance to make a distinctive contribution. Since individual circumstances differ, and perceptions of different groups within both society and the workplace are not the same, it follows that equality will sometimes require differential treatment among those drawn from different parts of society to ensure that their chances are equal. This argument is put succinctly by Fredman (2001), who observes that simply focusing on sameness of treatment does not require individuals to be treated well, they could all be treated the same but this could be badly.

SHRM thinking about diversity has other notable features (Industrial Society, 2000; Kandola and Fullerton, 1998). Within the managing diversity perspective, there is a strong emphasis on the individual represented by the aim of diversity management programmes for each individual's potential to be realised fully. This is particularly significant because it means that diversity strategies can be presented as applying to and including everyone. However, simply because individuals are the central focus, this does not mean that consideration at the group level becomes irrelevant. For example, membership of a group, such as older people, younger people or parents returning to work after a period of full-time care, needs to be taken into account when designing measures to promote diversity because of the major consequences such identities have for individuals' life chances and experiences (In Practice 13.2). Barmes and Ashtiany (2003) also emphasise that, although targeted measures to eliminate barriers faced by members of particular groups can and are contemplated, there is clear and emphatic rejection of benefits being awarded based solely on group membership (Thomas, 2002). In the UK context, both the managing diversity and the equal opportunities perspectives support positive action but reject completely positive discrimination (Key Concepts 13.2).

In Practice   13.2

Age discrimination in recruitment

In 2001 the CIPD undertook a study of age discrimination at work. In its survey one in eight respondents said that they had been discouraged from applying for a job due to an age limit or age range being specified in the advertisement or through the advertisement's wording, in particular the use of words such as 'young'. In the same survey, 7 per cent of those aged 16–24 said that they had been told they were 'too young' for the job, while a further 5 per cent suspected that this was the reason even though they had not been told.

Key Concepts   13.2

Positive action and positive discrimination

Positive action and positive discrimination are concerned with the position of individual job applicants or existing employees as well as wider patterns of discrimination within society.

Positive action refers to encouragement for under-represented groups to apply for vacancies and promotion and to participate in development opportunities. Within the UK it is commended in statutory codes of practice such as those published by the Equal Opportunities Commission.

Positive discrimination, sometimes known as *reverse discrimination*, refers to preferential treatment for under-represented groups. This reflects the American practice of affirmative action justified by a desire to eradicate historic patterns of disadvantage and to meet what are considered moral obligations and rights. It is unlawful in the UK.

The equal opportunities approach

Within the UK, the means to achieve equal opportunities has traditionally been a legislative compliance model. Various inequalities have been identified in the labour market, and successive governments have introduced a range of specific anti-discrimination rights aimed at promoting equality of opportunity, while at the same time assisting individuals in obtaining and retaining employment (Key Concepts 13.3). Existing legislation is being expanded considerably following the introduction of the EU's Equal Treatment Framework Directive 2000. This came into force in the UK in 2006 and extends existing law beyond protection for those with disabilities, those from racial minorities and women, to sexual orientation, religion or belief and age. The Directive requires organisations to think beyond observable differences (and the effect these have on the treatment of individuals within the organisation), to unobservable differences, which may nevertheless adversely affect individuals in the employment relationship. For example, under the new sexual orientation regulations, organisations that provide health insurance and pension schemes to unmarried heterosexual couples, will need to be sure that they provide the same benefits to same-sex couples (Hayfield, 2003).

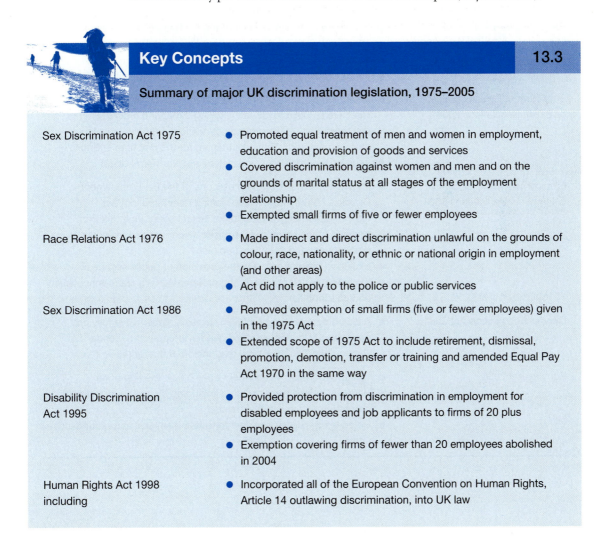

Key Concepts   13.3

Summary of major UK discrimination legislation, 1975–2005

Sex Discrimination Act 1975	● Promoted equal treatment of men and women in employment, education and provision of goods and services ● Covered discrimination against women and men and on the grounds of marital status at all stages of the employment relationship ● Exempted small firms of five or fewer employees
Race Relations Act 1976	● Made indirect and direct discrimination unlawful on the grounds of colour, race, nationality, or ethnic or national origin in employment (and other areas) ● Act did not apply to the police or public services
Sex Discrimination Act 1986	● Removed exemption of small firms (five or fewer employees) given in the 1975 Act ● Extended scope of 1975 Act to include retirement, dismissal, promotion, demotion, transfer or training and amended Equal Pay Act 1970 in the same way
Disability Discrimination Act 1995	● Provided protection from discrimination in employment for disabled employees and job applicants to firms of 20 plus employees ● Exemption covering firms of fewer than 20 employees abolished in 2004
Human Rights Act 1998 including	● Incorporated all of the European Convention on Human Rights, Article 14 outlawing discrimination, into UK law

Sex Discrimination (Gender Reassignment) Regulations 1999	• Made direct and indirect discrimination on the grounds of gender reassignment unlawful in employment and vocational training • Does extend to pay discrimination matters
Race Relations (Amendment) Act 2000	• Made the promotion of equality of opportunity, elimination of unlawful racial discrimination and the promotion of good race relations a statutory duty for all public-sector organisations and agencies
Sex Discrimination (Burden of Proof) Regulations 2001	• Introduced a new definition of indirect discrimination in the field of employment and vocational training • Definition of indirect discrimination was harmonised with that for the treatment of sex and racial harassment in October 2005. Subsequently there is only a need to show that a practice by an employer is inherently discriminatory and places women or men at a disadvantage
Race Relations Act 1976 (Amendment) Regulations 2003	• Implemented the provisions of the EU Race Directive into UK law, covering discrimination on the grounds of ethnic, racial or national group • Excluded discrimination on the grounds of nationality and colour
Employment Equality (Religion or Belief) Regulations 2003	• Implemented parts of the provisions of the EU Employment Directive (2000) into UK law, making direct and indirect discrimination on the grounds of religion and belief unlawful in employment and vocational training for the first time in Britain • Legislation was already in existence in Northern Ireland
Employment Equality (Sexual Orientation) Regulations 2003	• Implemented parts of the provisions of the EU Employment Directive (2000) into UK law, making direct and indirect discrimination on the grounds of sexual orientation towards persons of the same sex, opposite sex or both sexes unlawful in employment and vocational training • Excluded discrimination in the provision of public services • Excluded sexual practices and preferences (e.g. sado-masochism and paedophilia)
Gender Recognition Act 2004	• Allowed people who had taken decisive steps to live fully and permanently in their acquired gender to apply to a Gender Recognition Panel for legal recognition of that gender
Equality Act 2006	• Outlaws mandatory retirement ages below the age of 65 • Bans unjustified discrimination (including by age) in recruitment, promotion and vocational training • Removes the upper age limit for unfair dismissal and redundancy rights

The focus of equality legislation has been to remedy individual complaints rather than actively requiring employer action to promote equality (with the exception of the Race Relations (Amendment) Act 2000, discussed earlier). Within the UK context, there is a rather piecemeal approach to the issue of discrimination, legal regulation targeting specific groups such as women, ethnic minorities and people with a disability, and being used where a member or members of these groups feel unfairly treated in employment. What is lacking in the UK legislative framework (and present in the USA and Canada) is an overall right to fair and equal treatment for all individuals within employment. This is despite the fact that the UK's Human Rights Act 1998 incorporates all articles from the European Convention on Equal Rights, including Article 14 outlawing discrimination.

The combined focus of the UK's Sex Discrimination Acts of 1975 and 1986 and the Race Relations Act 1976 is to prioritise equal treatment, and the key legislative force is contained in the concepts of preventing both direct and indirect discrimination. The main legal obligation for organisations contained within the notion of direct discrimination is to treat people in the same situation the same, regardless of their membership of particular groups.

However, it is notable that no particular standard of conduct is imposed on organisations as the legislation only requires no differentiation to the detriment of a member of a protected group, in other words those from ethnic minorities, the disabled or women. Indirect discrimination is more complex as it recognises a need for differential treatment, where acting neutrally would put a person at a disadvantage because of their age, gender or race. As a consequence, treating people in the same situation in the same way will not always be lawful. However, rather than reducing the centrality of the concept in the traditional model of the equal treatment principle, the concept of indirect discrimination strengthens the principle because it tackles less obvious and unintentional discriminatory treatment that might arise as part of employment (Willey, 2003).

There are an estimated 8.9 million disabled people in the UK who frequently face discrimination and disadvantage in employment (Taylor, 2002) (In Practice 13.3). The Disability Discrimination Act 1995 seeks to ensure that such disadvantage is minimised, and has significant legal and training implications for employers. A period of

In Practice   13.3

Disability and employment statistics

Statistics on disability are notoriously difficult to compare between countries and, in some instances, to obtain. Different countries use different definitions of disability and have different degrees of political will to publicise such information. In many countries disability information is only collected every five or ten years as part of their national population census (International Labour Organisation (ILO), 2004). In addition, data sources often underestimate the number of people for whom a physical or mental impairment creates a substantial disadvantage when in or seeking employment (CSR Europe, 2005). The ILO estimates that there are 39 million disabled people living in Europe and 610 million disabled people worldwide. Within the UK, although nearly 20 per cent of the working age population have a disability, only 13 per cent of the workforce is disabled. A recent UK survey revealed that 15 per cent of young disabled people said that they had been turned down for a paid job, and told it was for a reason related to their disability or health problem (CSR Europe, 2005).

consultation led to a draft revised statutory code of practice, requiring those who provide goods and services to the public to make their premises accessible to disabled people. Section 3 of the Act, relating to goods, facilities, services and premises, has been in force since October 2004. This requires that services are physically accessible to all who wish to use them.

Employees are protected with reguard to age discrimination throughout the EU through member states' compliance with the EU's Equal Treatment Directive (2000). Within the UK, the Equality Act 2006 introduced age discrimination legislation from October 2006. Although it has been argued that these regulations will not affect the age at which people can claim their state pension, recent debate cast some doubt upon this. In summary the regulations will, in relation to age discrimination:

- outlaw mandatory retirement ages below the age of 65, other than where they can be objectively justified, while still allowing those under 65 to retire early if they wish;

- ban unjustified discrimination (including by age) in recruitment (In Practice 13.2), promotion and vocational training;

- remove the upper age limit for unfair dismissal and redundancy rights;

- introduce a duty for employers to consider requests to continue working beyond retirement.

Within the UK, these Acts are currently enforced through the Commission for Racial Equality, the Equal Opportunites Commission and the Disability Rights Commission. These aim to eliminate unfair treatment in the workplace, review existing legislation and lobby for change, and actively promote equality of opportunity in organisations. They also produce and publish codes of practice, which provide practical assistance and best practice benchmarks, and assist organisations to ensure they comply with their legislative obligations. However, the Equality Act 2006 has established the Commission for Equality and Human Rights (CEHR) that will come into being in October 2007. The CEHR will bring together this expertise to promote equality and tackle discrimination in relation to gender, disability, sexual orientation, religion or belief, age and human rights. It is planned to also include race by April 2009 (Commission for Equality and Human Rights, 2006).

In Practice   13.4

Linking racial targets to managers' bonuses

The UK's Environment Agency has an overall national target of recruiting 10 per cent of black and ethnic minority employees. This target is amended for each of its regions to reflect more closely the composition of the population it serves. In 2004 the Agency linked the bonuses it pays to its senior managers to these targets, setting them alongside other key performance indicators (Griffiths, 2005).

At the same time the Environment Agency introduced a toolkit to help raise awareness of diversity among recruiters and set up a national diversity, action group. Since this increased focus on diversity, the percentage of applicants for advertised vacancies has more than doubled from 3 to 7 per cent. The number of these applicants who have been offered jobs has also more than doubled (Griffiths, 2005).

However, the effectiveness of almost 30 years of anti-discrimination legislation based on legal compliance and consistency of treatment is a matter of some debate. Mackinnon, writing in 1987, observed that the focus of anti-discrimination laws had put the onus on individuals to seek redress through the courts if they feel they have suffered detriment to their working life based on some aspect of discriminatory treatment, and this observation still holds. The legislative requirement for a comparator to be referred to in order that discriminatory treatment can be judged, can be argued to neither challenge the prevailing norms nor promote the requirement to actively seek equality. As such, HR managers can be considered to have been placed in a reactive rather than proactive mode (Chapter 2), responding at an operational or tactical level, strategy often being little more than ensuring compliance with legislation. The result has been that males have been accessed as the 'norm' for comparator purposes and, for those from ethnic minorities, this has required individuals to subsume difference emanating from their membership of particular ethnic groupings in order to at least ensure 'equal' treatment (Parekh, 1998). As a consequence, it can be argued that the compliance-based equal opportunities approach does little more than reinforce previous or current discrimination as, in the attempt to promote sameness or similarity of treatment, established norms are left largely unchallenged and HR strategies unaltered.

Self-Check and Reflect Questions   13.3

Outline the strengths and limitations for diversity management of the equal opportunities approach.

The managing diversity approach: a paradigm shift?

Within the literature, there appears to be general agreement that organisations have become more interested in diversity management in response to the increased diversity apparent in both:

- their client or customer markets;
- the labour pool of potential and current employees (Frame and O'Connor, 2002).

Wilson and Iles (1999) assert that equal opportunities legislation has not managed to demonstrably produce race or gender employment opportunity, and they favour the diversity management approach. They argue that the drivers for equal opportunities have been external to organisations, compliance being driven by arguments of costs and moral and legal arguments rather than a strategic human resource imperative. Within this, differences among employees have been seen as problems. In contrast, managing diversity has been driven internally by a clear strategic business case in which diversity management is seen as an investment and differences regarded as an asset (In Practice 13.5). These views are summarised by the Industrial Society (2000: 3) which state in its report *Valuing Diversity: Managing Best Practice*:

> Where equality policies open doors, policies designed to value diversity offer a more strategic way of moving the business forward, backed up by a strong business and

ethical case. Valuing diversity goes further than equality. Equal opportunities policies are legislation led, remedial and based on the assumption that minority groups will assimilate into the dominant culture. By contrast, valuing diversity is visionary in aiming to create a positive work environment in which everyone benefits and can work to their full potential in pursuit of organisational goals, aims and objectives. This may involve changes in core values, mindsets and behaviours – supported by policies and strategies.

In Practice   13.5

A business case for age diversity

The CIPD (2005) reports that the cost of age discrimination to the UK economy is between £19 billion and £31 billion a year. It argues that, as life expectancy increases and the birth rate remains low, the proportion of the population aged 65 and over will increase (see also Figures 13.1 and 13.2) and society will increasingly depend upon the contribution these people can make. Based upon this, the CIPD highlights the following points:

- the difference in absenteeism between age groups is slight;
- older employees stay in the same job longer than younger people;
- findings from studies show that workers, both young and old, are equally effective in their work;
- given the right training, older people are as capable at learning new skills as younger employees;
- age discrimination leads to employees underachieving, a reduction in self-confidence and motivation and lower self-esteem.

Building upon this discussion, the underlying philosophy would seem to support the suggestion that managing diversity represents a shift in thinking about the cost of discrimination and disadvantage within the labour force. The focus shifts from the implications for individuals who are members of disadvantaged groups, to the cost to the organisation of the failure to fully recognise and utilise the talents and skills of all employees regardless of which segment of the labour force they are drawn from. The managing diversity approach implies that an organisation can gain competitive advantage and enhanced performance through a more strategic and inclusive deployment of all its human resources. This is based on the assumption that an organisation will be able to meet the needs of increasingly diverse customers, and tackle increasingly complex business and management problems by consciously fostering and effectively managing a diverse workforce (Cox, 1991; Stephenson and Lewis, 1996). Despite the pluralist ideal of valuing differences, from a managerial perspective managing diversity can therefore be seen as unitarist, promoting the importance of unifying people in organisations to the common purpose of organisational success.

Unification has parallels with the increase in the power of HR managers associated with the strategic aspects of HRM, the corresponding devolution of more operational aspects to line managers and their teams, and the expectation that employees will respond to diversity in their customers or clients, especially in the service sector (Agocs and Burr, 1996). At the same time, it should be noted that through devolvement of operational HR activities to line managers, the HR function is generally reduced in size and thus the HR manager's line management role is reduced. These and other differences when compared with the equal opportunities approach are summarised in Table 13.1.

Table 13.1 Managing diversity and equal opportunities approaches to diversity management

	Managing diversity	Equal opportunities
Concentrates upon	Maximising all employees' potential and overall contribution to the organisation	Issues of discrimination
Includes	Diversity factors relating to differences among all employees	Women, ethnic minorities and people with disabilities and other groups included in equal opportunities legislation
Emphasises	Positive perspective of employee differences	Negative perspective of disadvantage
Success is measured by	Organisational benefits such as cultural change and meeting business objectives	Compliance with legislation
Of concern to	All employees, especially managers within the organisation	Personnel or HR department
Targets	All employees	Particular sub-groups for positive action

Sources: Thomas (1990); Hall and Parker (1993); Mavin and Girling (1999); Maxwell *et al*. (2001).

Given our earlier discussion, it is therefore not surprising that, within the academic literature, managing diversity is considered a more holistic, strategic and more sophisticated organisational programme than equal opportunities or affirmative action (Cox, 1993). Such traditional concepts are viewed as being based on the recognition that employment discrimination exists, and a belief that, as highlighted in Table 13.1, the issue is best addressed by targeting groups with specific characteristics, which it is believed have led to their disadvantage. Consequently, for many, the managing diversity approach is seen as building upon the initiatives undertaken as part of equal opportunities (Gill, 1996).

In seeking to determine the organisational benefits to be gained from this interpretation of the managing diversity approach, Kandola and Fullerton (1994b) draw on literature and research from McEnrue (1993) and Cox and Blake (1991). They assert that this research provides proof of the benefits of diversity, in particular:

- the best candidates are employed;
- the organisational culture is one in which the potential of all employees is capable of realisation;

- flexible working arrangements are available;
- employees are valued, motivated and developed;
- employees are encouraged to actively progress in the organisation.

The benefits from an individual's perspective suggested by Kandola and Fullerton (1998) include:

- employees will freely give their best in such environments;
- employees are, by virtue of their diversity, automatically more in tune with the organisation's customer base;
- there is greater potential for innovation, creativity and problem solving;
- there is improved customer service of a higher quality.

The implied consequences of both the organisational and individual perspectives are therefore:

- a better public image for the organisation;
- a satisfying work environment for employees;
- improved employee relations;
- increased job satisfaction and higher employee morale;
- increased productivity;
- improved competitive edge.

These are undoubtedly far-reaching claims for a managing diversity approach. They emphasise individual and organisational benefits that most, if not all, HR strategies would wish to deliver. However, it must be noted that there is limited empirical support for their achievement either in the UK or in the USA. This issue will be explored in greater depth in the following section. However, until such time as robust research-based evidence is available, it is wise to treat such claims with caution.

Self-Check and Reflect Questions   13.4

Outline the strengths and limitations for diversity management of the managing diversity approach.

Managing diversity and equal opportunities: separate or interdependent approaches?

So far in this chapter a clear distinction between managing diversity and equal opportunities approaches to diversity management has been maintained. However, before moving on to a discussion of the business case for diversity management, it is important to offer a note of caution. From the preceding discussion it might appear that SHRM needs to adopt either an equal opportunities or a managing diversity approach. In reality they are often considered as interdependent, diversity management seeking to value individual differences, and equal opportunities seeking to ensure that specific groups and sub-groups are not discriminated against. McDougall (1996) suggests that, what in this chapter is termed managing diversity approach, should not be adopted instead of equal opportunities as, to focus on this alone, may mean the equal opportunities agenda is lost in the general search for valuing all aspects of difference. This is supported by research undertaken in the USA at IBM (In Practice 13.6). In addition, research undertaken with HR practitioners indicates that both approaches need to be considered together if they are to realise their strategic potential as organisational development tools and deliver an improvement in business results (Ford, 1996).

In Practice   13.6

Diversity management at IBM

Research undertaken by Child (1996) at IBM highlighted the interrelationships between three 'pillars' of diversity management:

- equal opportunities;
- affirmative action;
- work and personal life balance programmes.

Equal opportunities was found to enable employees to be employed and to work in a harassment-free environment. Affirmative actions taken helped enable individuals to compete on a level playing field without giving anyone an advantage but seeking to eliminate disadvantage. Work and personal life balance programmes aimed to eliminate attitudinal, policy and practice barriers that impacted upon employee productivity and prevented an individual's ability to balance work and personal life.

Liff (1993) argues that conventional equal opportunities approaches are deeply rooted in traditional approaches to personnel management, which have tended to see the employees as a collective. Equal opportunities approaches are considered bureaucratic, relying on setting rules for managers to follow and subsequently monitoring their compliance. To this extent, equal opportunities might be paralleled to personnel management, which is often viewed as largely legislatively driven, operating piecemeal initiatives assimilated into an existing culture. These aim to eradicate barriers and, with a focus on groups and numbers, normally remain the responsibility of the personnel function. In contrast, the diversity management approach, like SHRM in general, is driven by organisational needs, with a holistic strategy often requiring culture change and nurturing in order to improve the workplace environment (Chapters 1 and 2). Diversity therefore becomes a concern of the entire organisation. Liff (1993) further argues that, as SHRM focuses on the role of the individual and the importance of involvement and commitment, a diversity approach appears to fit more comfortably with this style. Like personnel management and SHRM, equal opportunities and managing diversity approaches can also be viewed as distinct concepts, yet remain organisationally interdependent.

Building upon these, Liff (1999) argues in later work that it is important for SHRM to offer both equal opportunities and managing diversity initiatives. Within this she suggests that equal opportunities, which she terms 'dissolving differences' (1999: 68) is probably a prerequisite for managing diversity, which she terms 'valuing differences' (1999: 68). The assertion is that diversity has become an increasingly important issue for organisations to manage. The significance of diversity appears to be in its relation to diverse markets and labour pools as opposed to the impact of legislation. This suggests that organisations will become more effective if they adopt a pluralist approach, paying attention to and utilising the different personal characteristics among their employees. However, this appears perhaps inconsistent with the unitarist business case for diversity management outlined earlier; unifying employees to the common purpose of organisational success. It is this business case for diversity management that is now considered.

The business case for diversity management

The business case supporting diversity management has been presented by numerous academics (for example, Liff, 1997, 1999; Foster and Newell, 2001; Schneider, 2001; Ward, 2001); and practitioners (for example, Johnson and Redmond, 2000; Bain, 2001; Elmes, 2001) as well as professional bodies such as the CIPD (2003). It is based on the argument that organisations will only survive and succeed in the current highly competitive and dynamic global environment if they respond positively to the increased heterogeneity of their markets, customers and employees. In essence, diversity management provides a competitive advantage, through differences being promoted as a positive source of innovation and improved organisational practice by, for example, utilising multiple perspectives. The business case therefore represents a strategic shift in focus to the management of difference which proposes that rather than engaging in equal opportunities activity to ensure social justice, or viewing equal opportunities as correcting an imbalance, an injustice or a mistake (Thomas, 1990), the activity is engaged in to gain business advantage. Robinson and Dechant (1997) caution, however, that this business case remains to be measured and documented (Frame and O'Connor, 2002).

From a managerialist perspective, diversity management means ensuring that every member of the workforce has the opportunity to perform to his or her full potential (Thomas, 1990). However, this definition lacks the consideration of the ways in which diversity management will benefit the individual employee and contains implications of organisational and managerial control. In contrast, Miller (1996) argues that the diversity management approach simply restates the 'neo-liberal' perspective where the maximisation of each individual's potential is the central principle. Within this model, diversity is to be used to add value to the organisation and a range of measures is deployed essentially to refocus corporate culture (In Practice 13.7). Articulating a business case for diversity therefore offers a way to operate equal opportunities as a strategic issue, a core value linked to the achievement of organisational competitiveness (Dickens, 1994). Consequently, a way to place diversity management on an organisation's strategic agenda is to position it as providing tangible benefit, rather than simply being socially and morally right.

Examination of the literature in relation to diversity management reveals that, over the past three decades, the overriding reason for a shift in emphasis from the promotion of equality of opportunity prevalent in the UK and other countries (such as the USA and Australia) has been business driven, and strategically and managerially focused. This is highlighted by training and development literature that increasingly frames diversity as a 'productive strategy' with 'bottom-line value' to create 'dividends', with the result that 'multiculturalism just makes good business sense' (Kirby and Harter, 2003: 29).

In Practice   13.7

Diversity and dignity at Ford

Although the Ford Motor Company has a long history of promoting equal opportunities, this image was tarnished in the 1990s by a number of incidents. In 1996 the Company was found to have super-imposed white employees' faces on four black employees in a photograph taken for an advertising campaign, while in the late 1990s allegations of abuse and harassment resulted in the prospect of formal investigation by the UK's Commission for Racial Equality (Burke, 2004).

Ford undertook wide-ranging measures to ensure that there would be a change in the organisation's culture. The negative events were used as a catalyst for positive change. A UK Diversity Manager was appointed and the organisation developed and implemented a Dignity at Work policy. Rather than focusing upon race or gender, this ensured that all employees are treated fairly and that all have a stake in Ford's reforms. A key feature in the success of this policy is getting universal buy-in from the entire organisation, which includes employees in eight salaried functions and ten manufacturing plants across the UK (Burke, 2004).

The business benefits of the Dignity at Work policy are that, if Ford's policies and practices and employee profiles relate to its customers, it will be able to avoid negative publicity and sell more motor vehicles (Burke, 2004).

In much of the diversity management literature, diversity is articulated as a resource to be managed and used to improve organisational performance, and organisations are encouraged to use their diversity to increase profits and achieve competitive advantage (Thomas, 1996). Cox and Beale (1997: 35) acknowledge, 'in most companies there is little chance of getting a genuine commitment by senior management to change their efforts concerning diversity unless they are convinced that investing in managing diversity is potentially a significant contributor to organisational performance'. Without the ability to frame diversity management in the language of improved business performance with measurable and tangible organisational outputs, senior management commitment and buy-in are unlikely to be forthcoming. Some diversity consultants even go so far as to recommend that previous rationales for affirmative action and valuing differences should be rejected.

It is this attempt to align diversity management with the realisation of performance and strategic outcomes that underpins the business case for diversity, and shifts the agenda from one in which equality and diversity promotion were the morally and ethically right things to do, to an agenda which purports that diversity management is the strategically sensible thing to do. Thus the focus shifts from equality being a cost to be borne, to diversity being a resource to be managed.

Proponents of this view highlight that, due in some degree to the diversity climate present within an organisation, the performance of organisations with diverse backgrounds is likely to differ from that of organisations with more traditional backgrounds.

Gender has often been found to have a negative effect on career progression, with women being less likely to be promoted than men (Kirchmeyer, 2002). Where women and those from ethnic minorities perceive this occurring in their organisations, they are likely to be less involved in their jobs (Grey and Healy, 2004).

Within the business case for diversity management, it is proposed that organisations willing to invest by harnessing the talent and ability of all their employees and in creating an environment that is positive and supportive of them, will reap a number of key organisational outcomes. These, in turn, will provide the organisation with competitive advantage. The main organisational benefits claimed to emanate from the creation of a positive and supportive environment for diversity management are summarised in Key Concepts 13.4.

Key Concepts   13.4

Organisational benefits claimed for diversity management

- Retained/gained market share by increasing marketing capabilities.
- Enhanced employee recruitment.
- Improved customer satisfaction.
- Reduced costs associated with high employee turnover and absenteeism.
- Increased employee productivity.
- Improved employee morale and commitment.
- Increased employee creativity and innovation.
- Improved decision-making.
- Decreased harassing behaviour and reduced discrimination suits.

Sources: Fernandez (1991); Henderson (1994); Esty *et al*. (1995); Hirsch (1995); Golembiewski (1995); Cox and Beale (1997); Graham (1997); Sonnenschein (1997); Cook Ross (2001); J. Howard and Associates (2001); The Diversity Group (2001).

Thus, the business case for diversity appears to be based upon a perceived necessity for organisations to move away from a piecemeal approach to equality and the management of difference. Simply implementing an equal opportunities awareness training programme without linking this with SHRM initiatives, such as cultural change (Chapter 6), is unlikely to bring about the permanence of attitudinal and organisational change. To gain the positive outcomes claimed, diversity management needs to address the issue in a coordinated and strategically integrated manner. As with other cultural changes and illustrated by the case at the end of this chapter, the benefits are likely to be long term rather than immediate. Thus, what is actually being proposed by diversity management is a cultural shift in the way organisations value employees' talents, whoever they are, and a questioning of many of the taken-for-granted assumptions about what talent is, how contributions are recognised and assessed, and how human resources are managed strategically. This issue of implementation is discussed in 'Evidence of the strategical adoption of diversity management and implementation advice' later in this chapter. However, before this we will consider the cultural context in which diversity management may be realised and the claimed benefits.

The need for a supportive culture and claimed benefits

The benefits claimed for diversity management are likely to be realised within the context of the re-alignment of an organisation's culture to one where diversity is valued (Doherty and Chelladurai, 1999). Although issues associated with organisational culture and its re-alignment have already been discussed in some detail in Chapter 6, there are some aspects that are worth reiterating. In particular it must be remembered that, within organisations, people are often reluctant to instigate culture change as this may lead to their own loss of power (Martin, 1992). However, if the culture is to be re-aligned to one in which diversity is truly valued, then it is likely that it will be necessary to persuade those in power that this will impact positively upon the organisation's effectiveness (Wright *et al.*, 1995; Robinson and Dechant, 1997).

Need for a supportive culture

For some, the change to valuing diversity is a moral obligation. This is based upon the argument that those in positions of power should structure the work environment so that all employees feel valued and are able to work with a sense of dignity (Cox, 1991; Morrison, 1992; DeSensi, 1995). These authors argue that organisations should adopt a culture in which diversity is valued because it is, put simply, the right thing to do. Indeed, for some of these authors the term 'managing diversity' is not one with which they feel comfortable. This is because the term has connotations of 'using' employee differences to bring additional organisational success (Prasad *et al.*, 1997). They contrast this with the belief that, through an understanding and appreciation of difference, both employees and their organisation will benefit. In contrast to this is the view that, whatever the moral arguments for developing a culture that values diversity, unless there is also a strong business case, it is unlikely that those in power will give their support. This is summarised by Robinson and Dechant (1997: 21) who argue 'business initiatives that present more compelling factual evidence of payback on investment win out over diversity initiatives'.

Given the earlier discussion it is not surprising that many authors have suggested that diversity management must be championed by top management to ensure successful implementation (Thomas 1991; Morrison, 1992; Dutton and Ashford, 1993; Golembiewski, 1995). Unfortunately, there are few empirical studies to support this. Rynes and Rosen (1995) found in a survey of 785 HR professionals that, where top management believed in the positive benefits of a diversity management approach, diversity management training was far more likely to have occurred. This supports Doherty and Chelladurai's (1999) contention that cultural diversity will be more beneficial in a culture that values diversity and that such a culture is heavily influenced by persons in positions of power. Consequently, although the evidence is limited, it appears likely that senior management's beliefs in the benefits of diversity will influence the extent to which diversity management is adopted.

To promote a positive climate for diversity in an organisation, Cox (1993) and Kossek and Zonia (1993) argue, then there must be an observable demographic mix of people at management and senior management level in the organisation. Indeed, Kossek and Zonia (1993) consider demographic mix to be an important determinant of a culture that values diversity, through the provision of role models to prospective recruits and existing employees, perhaps suggesting implicitly a need for affirmative action. Cox (1993) also asserts that, with the creation of a more supportive organisational environment, comes an increase in individual satisfaction and commitment. This can result in positive organisational outcomes, such as reduced industrial conflict, positive work attitude, increased cooperation and productivity gains (Harsis and Klenier, 1993).

Claimed benefits

In a UK study, Hicks-Clarke and Iles (2000), sought to assess whether the positive claims made for a culture supportive of diversity were evident in organisations. Based on a study of the retail and NHS sectors, they found a positive climate for diversity (indicated by perceptions of policy support, evidence of organisational justice, support for diversity and recognition of the need for diversity) was related strongly to the presence of positive employee job and career attitudes. In particular, there was a strong relationship between employees' perception of organisational justice and their organisational commitment. Positive perceptions of organisational justice were also predictive of increased job satisfaction, career planning, career commitment, satisfaction with manager and career satisfaction. Where employees felt that flexible working hours were available to them, this correlated strongly with organisational commitment, job satisfaction, satisfaction with manager, career satisfaction and career future satisfaction. Those in the study who had seen a copy of the organisation's equal opportunities policy were more likely to be satisfied with their manager, and the provision of career breaks strongly predicted satisfaction with future career opportunities. Finally, perceived organisational support for diversity was found to be linked to satisfaction with manager and future career opportunities. In Hicks-Clarke and Iles' view, these results confirm the importance of both a supportive climate for diversity in general and of specific associated policy dimensions such as flexible working hours, presence and sight of an equal opportunities policy, and career break policies in generating positive organisational and work-related attitudes and perceptions.

Despite such claims, others (for example, Barmes and Ashtiany, 2003) have argued the diversity agenda faces particular challenges if it is to be linked directly to a business case. Their concern is that, if financial business benefits are the key motivation for adopting the diversity perspective, then a diversity management strategy may be vulnerable to short-term economic conditions. By focusing instead upon non-economic justifications for the adoption of diversity management, continued investment in poorer economic conditions would allow business benefits to emerge and so provide an additional justification for promoting diversity (Practice 13.8). In addition, and more fundamentally, achieving the business advantage to be derived from diversity management is dependent upon a high-trust work environment. In such a context, each employee will have favourable expectations of the organisation's and other employees' motives and intentions, which will be manifest in their own resultant behaviours. The corollary of this is that trust is unlikely to exist unless organisational members and potential organisational members believe that commitment to their futures is genuine. Where the justification for valuing each person's distinctive contribution is based on economic considerations alone, such as within a business case, it is likely to be harder to

In Practice 13.8

Diversity management: a moral stance?

Over the past few years there has been increased awareness of the importance of a diverse workforce. A growing number of organisations have made their employees increasingly aware of the need and benefits of a more inclusive culture; employers have provided diversity workshops to advise employees of the benefits of a diverse culture, and foster a culture in which diversity is valued.

Kraft Foods is a good example of diversity management practice; it is also an example of an organisation that has embraced a diversity management approach because it is seen to be the 'right' thing to do, but, through its active approach has also reaped economic benefit through obtaining and retaining suppliers of high standards and quality (Forbes, 2002).

Kraft Foods is cited by the *Wall Street Journal* as being one of the key pioneers in the USA of supplier diversity. Kraft believes in doing business with suppliers and vendors who not only demonstrate a commitment to diversity in their own operations, but also show commitment to high standards of quality and ethical practice. Kraft actively manages its supplier diversity programme, which began in 1981 to ensure that goods and services are purchased from the widest possible pool of high-quality suppliers regardless of national origin, race or gender. The Kraft supplier diversity task force, seeks to encourage minority suppliers and provides assistance to such suppliers in understanding and taking advantage of the organisation's purchasing procedures. It has been argued that the high standards set for suppliers translate into these companies becoming excellent and attracting further business (Forbes, 2002).

believe that the focus on diversity management is genuine. Pursuing this argument to a logical end, the much sought after, and highly desirable, benefits articulated by the business case for diversity are therefore ultimately dependent upon an organisation focusing on diversity management because it fits with the culture's basic underlying assumptions (values), and not only because it promises future economic advantage.

Self-Check and Reflect Questions 13.5

To what extent is it appropriate to support a positive climate for diversity management for purely business-focused reasons rather than as part of its cultural values?

Based on this discussion, it is clear that diversity management is a strategic cultural choice for organisations in their approach to the management of difference. The move from piecemeal compliance-based initiatives to an integrated strategic programme is a challenge to any organisation. For those organisations for whom diversity management is part of their cultural values (Barmes and Ashtiany, 2003), implementation will be less of a challenge. For such organisations, existing policies and processes are more likely to consider automatically the diversity dimension and, given their overarching culture, strategic integration and alignment are more likely (Chapter 6). Despite this, evidence suggests that few organisations operate in quite this way. For these organisations, diversity management is seen as potentially providing business advantage requiring management of human resources in its delivery. The final section of this chapter considers evidence regarding the strategic adoption of diversity management and the advice available to organisations to manage diversity management programmes.

Evidence of the strategic adoption of diversity management and implementation advice

Despite discussion regarding the strategic adoption of diversity management, there is relatively little empirical evidence to support this process. Schneider (2001), for example, refers broadly to changing the organisation's culture thorough management development, change management and specific diversity awareness-raising, skills-building workshops. However, the tactics through which such major strategic re-alignments would be undertaken in practice, often require elaboration (Worman, 2001). This may be due to anticipated significant resource implications (Foster and Newell, 2001). When development opportunities are offered in company or by professional trainers, little evidence is present of a holistic, strategically aligned, culture-changing approach, as outlined in Chapters 6 and 10. Often what can be observed is an exclusive approach with an operational, or at best tactical, focus as opposed to the much discussed inclusive approach and strategic focus.

The exclusive approach is typified by diversity programmes that focus on gender and race-based scenarios, with trainees being invited to suggest appropriate actions as the scenarios unfold. The focus is therefore a particular theme, thereby excluding other aspects of diversity. Without careful management this may result in workshops being run to the exclusion of those who are not members of the group in question. In such circumstances, diversity initiatives differ little in substance from the equal opportunities approach outlined previously in this chapter.

Empirical evidence

Although rhetoric claims that there are differences between the managing diversity and equal opportunities approaches, the extent to which organisations have actually embraced these differences in their approach to managing diversity is less clear. Empirical evidence that assesses the extent to which the full diversity management agenda has really been adopted by organisations is limited. Kandola and Fullerton (1998) surveyed 445 organisations from 30 different industry groups from a perspective of promoting the adoption of managing diversity, and a belief that organisations should adopt this approach. They concluded that a managing diversity perspective was not being fully embraced. Rather, the majority of organisations were focusing only on those initiatives traditionally categorised as equal opportunities, for example placing emphasis on fair recruitment and selection processes. On the basis of this, Kandola and Fullerton (1998) argue that many organisations are using the banner of managing diversity when, in reality, they are undertaking equal opportunities initiatives.

Girling (1999) explored equal opportunities and managing diversity in 60 UK organisations across both the private and public sectors. Her survey asked about their organisations' approaches to diversity management, encompassing the strategy/policy, characteristics, aims and what was happening in practice with respect to equal opportunities and managing diversity. Respondents were also asked if they were aware of the two approaches and whether they appreciated the differences. She found that the majority of respondents were aware of equal opportunities and managing diversity approaches and some of the distinctions between them, this awareness coming from educational programmes. However, 25 per cent of the HR professionals were not sure if their organisation had a strategy/policy on managing diversity, whilst 78 per cent of the general line managers were also unaware of their organisations' responses (if any) to this issue.

In another study, respondents were asked to identify what they perceived as the main aims of equal opportunities and managing diversity (Mavin and Girling, 2000). Although 90 per cent of respondents believed adherence to legislation was the main aim of equal opportunities, there was still confusion between the terms. Eighty-one per cent of respondents considered that the responsibility for equal opportunities should fall predominantly to the personnel or HR function. Even for the low number of organisations following a managing diversity approach, it was interesting to note that diversity management was considered the primary responsibility of the personnel or HR function, rather than of senior management. This study also considered the methods being used by organisations to initially raise, and then progress, equal opportunities and managing diversity issues. The most frequently cited methods were:

- organisations were monitoring for equal opportunities (88 per cent);
- using personnel/HRM department to promote the issue (85 per cent);
- applying fair selection training (83 per cent);
- employing positive recruitment advertising (82 per cent).

Additionally, respondents were asked about the policies their organisations followed. These included:

- study leave provisions for those wishing to enhance their career through educational qualifications (95 per cent);
- special leave arrangements to assist individuals with personal issues as they arose (91 per cent);
- training and development initiatives (90 per cent);
- placing emphasis on recruitment and selection (88 per cent);
- implementing harassment and bullying policies (73 per cent).

However, in relation to extending and integrating the policies in a diversity management strategy, only 46 per cent had family friendly arrangements, while 5 per cent had work/life balance programmes. These results are therefore similar to those of Kandola and Fullerton (1998), where it was found that equal opportunities approaches were still the main method of raising awareness in UK organisations.

Such empirical research findings indicate that, for many organisations, the rhetoric of managing diversity remains as rhetoric rather than a distinct approach. This may be partially explained by Thomas's (1990) observation that it is impossible to manage diversity unless you actually have it. However, examination of the case study at the end of this chapter, shows that this need not be the case. For organisations where diversity among employees is visible, the characteristics of diversity management noted by respondents to the three research surveys described are based predominantly on established equal opportunities approaches. Collet and Cook (2000) believe that there are several reasons why organisations decide against such proactive management of diversity, the most frequent one being that the organisation believes it is already undertaking sufficient investment in ensuring equality of opportunity. Despite this, for those organisations considering implementation of a managing diversity approach within diversity management, advice is available.

Implementation advice

Ross and Schneider (1992) provide advice that enables organisations to grasp the holistic nature of implementing a diversity management approach. As part of this they stress the importance of adopting a strategic perspective. This, they argue, differentiates a diversity management approach to one that simply promotes equality of opportunity. In their view, the diversity management approach is:

- internally driven and not externally imposed;
- focused on individuals rather than groups;
- focused on a total culture change, rather than just change at systems or process level;
- the responsibility of all organisational members and not just those in the HR or personnel function.

To successfully implement diversity management, Ross and Schneider (1992) advocate six key stages (Figure 13.5). In the first of these, the current situation is assessed, using secondary data such as equal opportunities monitoring statistics, policy documents as well as organisational surveys. Based upon this, the key diversity issues and their likely causes are identified. The next stage uses the analysis to establish the aims of the diversity management programme. As part of this it has been argued that, as with

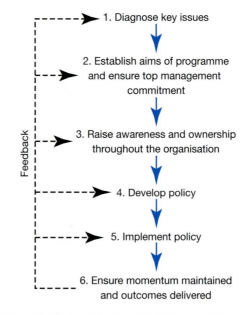

Figure 13.5 Stages in the implementation of diversity management
Source: adapted from Ross and Schneider (1992).

cultural realignment (Chapter 6), it is essential to ensure top management commitment is gained. In addition, Ross and Schneider highlight the importance of emphasising a business case for diversity management in which the key benefits the organisation could expect to gain through the adoption of the approach are highlighted.

The third stage involves ensuring that ownership for the programme is spread throughout the organisation, in other words a change of culture (Chapter 6). This stage also requires that awareness is raised through a programme encouraging the questioning of taken-for-granted attitudes and perceptions. As part of this it is important that awareness is raised at all levels in the organisation, and that diversity management is owned across the organisation (including by senior management) rather than just those in the HR function. Once awareness has been raised, it is possible to begin policy development (stage 4). It is important that this policy is developed through involvement and with an organisational understanding of where key priorities and issues lie, rather than the imposition from a central policy development unit.

The transition process, when the policy is implemented (Figure 13.5, stage 5), is likely to be difficult and involve a number of stages in itself. Positive action programmes may be instigated to provide specific development opportunities for key minority groups, policy implementation programmes may be more widely rolled out to enable all those in the organisation to appreciate the change in culture and the impact it will have on key policy areas such as recruitment and selection, performance appraisal and human resource development. Other programmes may also be required, such as further awareness training or initiatives directed at understanding the approach and reaction of those from differing cultures to the present and future organisational culture.

The final stage involves ensuring that the momentum is sustained, and that the programme delivers its intended outcomes. This requires 'champions', drawn from either the HR function or another part of the organisation. Their role is to ensure that the diversity management programme delivers the organisational positives articulated in the original business case. Involvement of key players, such as senior management and trade unions, continues to be critical at this stage. In addition, it is important that progress and success are communicated to all across the entire organisation. As with all culture re-alignment programmes, it is important to commit to the programme for the long term and to monitor, measure and ultimately communicate progress as the programme continues (Chapter 6). Without such monitoring, evaluation and communication, the aims of diversity management may be lost or overlooked in the highly dynamic reality that is organisational life.

Summary

- Conceptualisations of diversity management within the literature can be broadly categorised into two groups:
    - the equal opportunities approach, which has a legislative and compliance focus and is concerned with equality of status, opportunities and rights. This, it can be argued, is deeply rooted in traditional approaches to human resource management;
    - the managing diversity approach, which focuses upon an explicit holistic strategy of valuing differences, such as age, gender, social background, ethnicity and disability. This, it can be argued, is like SHRM, driven by organisational needs.

- The business case claimed for a managing diversity approach includes a better public image for the organisation, a satisfying working environment for employees, improved employee relations, increased job satisfaction and higher employee morale, increased productivity and, for the organisation, improved competitive edge. It is argued that organisations will only survive and prosper in an increasingly competitive and dynamic global environment if they respond to the heterogeneity of their markets. However, there is limited empirical evidence to support these claims in either the UK or USA.

- Despite a lack of evidence, it seems probable that the benefits of diversity management will only be realised within the context of the re-alignment of an organisation's culture to one where diversity is valued. For this to happen, it will be necessary to persuade those in power that this will impact positively on organisational effectiveness.

- Empirical evidence suggests that, for many organisations, diversity management remains a theoretical concept rather than a strategic reality, combining equal opportunities and managing diversity approaches. The most frequent reason advanced for this is that organisations believe they are already undertaking sufficient investment through ensuring equality of opportunity. However, for organisations considering the implementation of a managing diversity approach, advice is available.

Follow-up study suggestions

1. Choose an organisation with which you are familiar. If you are in full-time education, you may wish to choose your university or college. Obtain copies of the organisation's diversity management and/or equal opportunities policies. Based upon this evidence and what you have read, to what extent do you consider the organisation has adopted a strategy of diversity management?

2. Re-examine Table 13.1. Update this table in the light of the most recent UK legislation.

3. Visit the European Union's Eurostat statistical data web site (http://europa.eu.int/comm/eurostat/newcronos/). Using the demographic data available for member states choose two countries, one in western Europe and one country that joined the EU in 2004. To what extent do these data suggest different issues for diversity management with regard to workforce composition in relation to age and gender?

4. How persuasive do you think the business case for diversity management is? What information/evidence would you need to make the case more convincing?

5. To what extent do you think the recent emphasis on diversity management is entirely positive? Outline the key benefits of this recent emphasis, but also consider some of the less positive aspects of people working together that may be highlighted through such widespread emphasis.

Suggestions for research topics

1. To what extent do managing diversity and equal opportunities approaches exist in organisations?

2. To what extent is diversity management in XYZ aligned to the organisation's culture?

3. To what extent does an organisation's culture act as a barrier to diversity management? A case study of company XYZ.

4. What are the implications of European Union legislation for diversity management in company XYZ?

5. How does the impact of national legislation upon diversity management practices differ between countries?

Case Study

Making diversity an issue in leafy Elgarshire

Background

Worcestershire County Council is the local authority responsible for providing education; social services for children, older people and others in need; road maintenance and building; and libraries and strategic planning for the 542,000 people who live within Worcestershire. Worcestershire County Council employs approximately 17,500 people to provide these services. Of these, approximately 15,000 are based in schools and 2,500 in other establishments, the field (for example home care assistants), other offices or the County Council's headquarters on the outskirts of Worcester. Other local government services to the people of Worcestershire are provided by the six district councils of Bromsgrove, Malvern Hills, Redditch, Worcester, Wychavon and Wyre Forest. These include housing; development planning; leisure sports and museum services; and refuse collection and street cleaning.

Worcestershire is a predominantly rural county located south west of Birmingham within the UK's West Midlands region. The county's city, Worcester, has a population of 77,700; other large population centres being Redditch, a former new town (77,400), Kidderminster (55,200) and Bromsgrove (30,900) (Worcestershire County Council, 2004a). However, the majority of the population live in small towns and villages and the county's image is one of

The Malvern Hills, Worcestershire
© Mark Saunders 2006.

rural tranquillity, and the birthplace and home of the composer Edward Elgar. The county is home to over 21,000 companies, of which 85 per cent are small businesses employing less that ten people. Demographic data from the 2001 Census highlights that, in terms of gender and age, Worcestershire is very similar proportionally to the UK (Table 1). In contrast only 2.5 per cent of Worcestershire's residents are from an ethnic minority background compared with 7.9 per cent for the UK. Within Worcestershire this pattern differs markedly with over 30 per cent of the population in some wards in Redditch being from a Black or Black-British ethnic group and up to 10 per cent of the population in some wards in Redditch and Worcester being from an Asian or Asian-British ethnic background.

Table 1 Comparative demographic data

	Employees (2003) %	Worcestershire (2001 Census) %	UK (2001 Census) %
Gender			
Males	18.6	49.0	48
Females	81.4	51.0	51.3
Age			
0–15	–	19.5	20.2
16–64	99.9	64.1	63.8
65–74	0.1	8.6	8.4
75 and over	–	7.8	7.6
Health			
Limiting long-term illness	Comparable data	16.7	18.2
General health 'not good'	not available	8.0	9.2
Ethnicity			
White	97.5	97.5	92.1
All minority ethnic population	2.5	2.5	7.9
Total (= 100%)	17,458	542,107	58,789,194

Sources: developed from National Statistics (2003); Worcestershire County Council (2004a, 2004b).

The need to make diversity an issue

Simply considering the headline figures in Table 1, it might be argued that, within Worcestershire, diversity is 'not an issue' and is 'not something the County Council need to bother about'. Indeed this appears to be the perception of many, the much used 'leafy Elgarshire' description of Worcestershire, conjuring images of white rural prosperity associated with English shire counties. However, as the earlier discussion highlights, this is not the only reality for people within the county. For example, although the County Council's employees reflect the composition of the county in terms of ethnicity as a whole, for some parts of the county there is a marked mismatch between ethnicity of employees and that of residents in receipt of services. In addition, workforce monitoring has highlighted a lack of women in more senior positions within the organisation.

The County Council's Chief Officers' Management Board (COMB) was aware that the council was not serving some of the residents of Worcestershire as well as it should. It also recognised that, in order to get the best from all employees, there was a need to recognise diversity. COMB was determined to address these issues and raise the awareness of all staff to the diversity of needs of those living in Worcestershire and of their employees. In particular it was keen to be seen as not just 'ticking boxes' to meet legislative requirements, such as those set by the Disability Discrimination Act 1995 and the Race

Relations (Amendment) Act 2000. Rather, it wanted to be seen to be taking actions that actually made a difference to those living in the county and working for the County Council. COMB felt that an approach was needed that forced employees to recognise that diversity issues were important, needed to be addressed and, as part of this, challenged widely held perceptions. Through such an approach it aimed 'to produce observable changes in the behaviour and impacts upon underpinning beliefs and values' within the County Council (Britton, 2002: 1).

Worcestershire's approach
The County Council's approach was outlined in the internal document: Promoting Equality and Dignity at Work (Britton, 2002). Although this focused upon development and training activities required in response to Race Relations (Amendment) Act 2000, it also stressed that the County Council's commitment to equality and dignity was much broader, the underpinning principles of the proposed approach consisting of four interrelated and overlapping phases embracing all diversity issues:

● Phase 1 – capturing attention (awareness campaign);

● Phase 2 – addressing the issues (training);

● Phase 3 – operational briefings for managers;

● Phase 4 – embedding the learning.

The approach was led by the Director of Social Services, Jenny Bashforth, who took personal charge of the project and championed it actively.

Phase 1 was based on the belief that people learn best when they are motivated and interested. Consequently, all employees needed to know that the County Council was treating diversity and equality as special and important issues, and had been provided with thought-provoking information prior to commencing diversity awareness training (phase 2). This initiative was called 'Worcestershire. We all make it unique'. An ongoing poster campaign (begun in 2002) raised general awareness of the importance of diversity making use of both Commission for Racial Equality materials and Worcestershire specific materials. The latter, designed to capture the imagination of employees, used the headline 'Racism. Let's make it an issue'. An associated colour poster (Figure 1) consisted of 25 people's handprints and involved both the leader of the County Council and a wide range of employees directly in its creation. More detailed information to help provoke employee reaction was provided through displays in offices and in the employees' newsletter *Worcestershire Update*. At time of writing, this poster campaign is still continuing.

In the spring of 2002, 'mystery customer' surveys were undertaken across all County Council services to provide a clearer understanding of service users' experiences and identify any barriers that prevent their achieving equal access to good levels of service. The findings from these were used to inform the diversity awareness training which commenced in June 2002. The objectives of this one-day training event are to ensure that participants:

- develop general awareness and understanding of equal opportunities in general and race issues;
- define relevant issues and associated terms and language;
- review relevant legislation;
- identify the main oppressed groups in society;
- distinguish between personal and institutional discrimination and its impact on practice;
- develop a personal action plan to improve service delivery and promote good practice;
- establish their role in unit and directorate plans.

As emphasised by these objectives, this training has been designed to engage employees, challenge them to think about their own personal stance and perceptions in relation to ethnicity, as well as providing factual background and clarifying the County Council's position. Although the training is not compulsory, during the first year of operation over 2,000 employees attended.

Figure 1 'Racism. Let's make it an issue' poster

Source: © Worcestershire County Council 2002, reproduced with permission.

Since 2002, employee awareness of diversity as an issue has been maintained using a series of colour posters continuing the theme 'Worcestershire. We all make it unique'. These posters have used a similar design style to 'Racism. Lets make it an issue' (Figure 1) but have focused on other aspects of diversity, such as people's perceptions of disability. This poster posed the question, 'Is your inability to see my ability your disability?' alongside symbols representing 16 'disabilities', including being male and female, that an individual might possess (Figure 2).

At the same time, the County Council has incorporated diversity and equality issues into other training courses both directly and indirectly. For example, within recruitment and selection training the logic behind diversity-based legislation is explained explicitly. In addition, scenarios provided to participants to prompt discussion on issues such as team building use characters who reflect a diversity of employees. This process they believe is helping to embed the necessary learning more widely (phase 4).

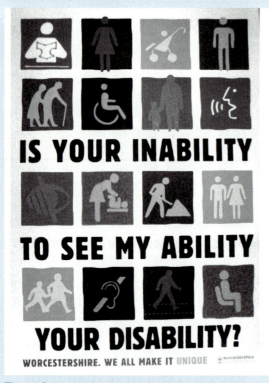

Figure 2 'Is your inability...' poster

Source: © Worcestershire County Council 2004, reproduced with permission.

Initial operational briefings (phase 3) for managers were linked directly to the phase 2 training activity. These briefings focus on their responsibilities under legislation and the framework of the Equality Standard for Local Government (Employers' Organisation for Local Government, 2001) who provide support and processes to carry forward actions relating to the mystery customer surveys and local audits. As with the diversity awareness training, the operational briefings concluded with action planning for each manager's area and were linked to practical team objectives as well as legislative targets. However, it was recognised in 2004 that the County Council's senior managers (some 200 people) needed to be re-energised and so a half-day conference was held. This has re-clarified the issues and challenges facing the County Council and both raised these managers' expectations and provided a clear focus on action.

Subsequently (in 2005) these senior managers and those employees reporting directly to them (some 700 people) attended a one-day training course. This focused on exploring personal perceptions as well as providing a factual background to issues associated with diversity. As part of this, the County Council's commitment to equality and dignity was re-emphasised along with the crucial role played by managers in promoting this.

Diversity appears to be becoming embedded within the County Council through a range of activities and events. Awareness-raising activities, such as those outlined above, are being continued as is employee training. In addition, the County Council has employed a Diversity Officer whose job is entirely concerned with diversity issues. Although the initiative is ongoing, the Development and Training Manager, Roger Britton, believes that the approach used to raise employees' awareness of diversity issues is working. As evidence for this, he highlights ongoing improvements to the ways in which services are delivered. He also emphasises how both race and disability have now become an issue of legitimate discussion among employees, being talked about widely.

Case study questions

1. Do you consider Worcestershire County Council to be adopting a managing diversity or equal opportunities approach to diversity management? Give reasons for your answer.

2. How has legislation impacted upon Worcestershire County Council's approach to diversity management?

3. Do you agree with Worcestershire County Council's phased approach to diversity management; what do you see as the key strengths and limitations of this approach?

4. If you were Worcestershire County Council's Diversity Officer, what specifically would you see as being the key focus of your role? What information/evidence do you think you would need to collect/disseminate to ensure the County Council makes progress towards its goal of better serving residents and of valuing diversity among its workforce to make a difference to people's lives, and not just to comply with legislation.

Acknowledgement

The considerable assistance of Roger Britton, Development and Training Manager (Human Resources), Worcestershire County Council in the development of this case is acknowledged gratefully.

14

Downsizing: proactive strategy or reactive workforce reduction?

Learning Outcomes

By the end of this chapter you should be able to:

- explain the purpose of downsizing and analyse the problems associated with its use;

- identify a range of organisational strategies to downsize and evaluate their implications;

- discuss the significance of employee involvement and influence in relation to the implementation of downsizing;

- describe the nature of survivors' reactions to downsizing and the existence of moderating variables affecting these, and evaluate their significance for organisations using this type of change strategy;

- discuss the role of organisational theories and HR interventions to provide strategies to manage the process of downsizing more effectively;

- explore the implications of outsourcing for SHRM;

- analyse the role downsizing plays in contributing to organisational HR strategies and the interrelationships with other HR interventions such as performance management, employee involvement and commitment, and training and development.

Introduction

Downsizing has become a major HR strategy used by organisations of all sizes. At a superficial level, downsizing appears a reassuringly simple and inviting strategy to consider. Reducing an organisation's headcount is a more concrete idea than, say, re-aligning an organisation's culture (Chapter 6) and appears to offer cost savings through fewer people being employed. However, although such a strategy may be easier to comprehend at this superficial level, in reality the process of downsizing is highly complex and can often generate a range of reactions that undermine the strategic objectives for downsizing. In this chapter we explore such reactions and their consequences for an organisation using this strategy (Figure 14.1). As a major organisational HR strategy, downsizing is also capable of promoting and contributing to other organisational strategies. Indeed, within this chapter it will be argued that the successful use of downsizing requires the implementation of and integration with other human resource strategies discussed in this book. Through doing this, possible negative reactions to downsizing may be avoided or reduced and the greatest bene-fits from its use gained. This chapter therefore focuses upon the human aspects of downsizing in order to maximise the positive and minimise the negative outcomes of using of this strategy.

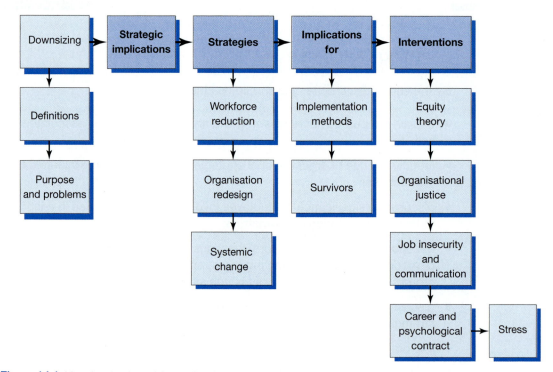

Figure 14.1 Mapping the downsizing territory: a summary diagram of the chapter content

Downsizing

What is downsizing?

Downsizing is an organisational strategy to reduce the size of an organisation's workforce. However, it is frequently used as a synonym for redundancy. You have almost certainly come across news reports where alternative terms such as rightsizing, restructuring and reorganisation have been used in relation to downsizing. The literature about downsizing recognises that it can use a range of methods. Consequently, downsizing can be seen as an HR strategy that includes some of the interventions or approaches to reducing headcount that have traditionally been seen as alternatives to redundancy. These include the use of natural wastage, early retirement, voluntary as opposed to compulsory redundancy, freezing recruitment, redeployment and retraining, as well as forms of work sharing, such as reduced working hours and job sharing. In recent years this appears to have been accompanied by changing employment practices through increased use of fixed-term and temporary employees (Guest, 2004) as organisations respond to sectoral shifts in the structure of employment and a need to cut costs. Freeman and Cameron (1993) offer two further distinguishing features of downsizing in relation to redundancy (or 'layoffs' as this is referred to in the North American literature). For them, downsizing is an organisational-level concept, whereas redundancy is approached at the level of the individual. Building upon this discussion, downsizing can be considered a strategic issue, whereas redundancy is one of a number of possible operational means to achieving it. Finally, downsizing differs from redundancy in the extent to which it is regulated. While redundancy is subject to tightly prescribed legislation associated with dismissal in many western countries; downsizing, because it may utilise a range of methods other than dismissal, not surprisingly falls outside dismissal legislation.

The purpose of and problem with downsizing

Downsizing is often justified as a means of improving organisational competitiveness (Kozlowski *et al.*, 1993). The strategic reasons behind this are varied, however the most common can be summarised under four headings (Labib and Appelbaum, 1994):

- the outcome of an acquisition or merger as duplicate and redundant functions are eliminated;
- a 'quick fix' to put off closure or bankruptcy;
- preparation for privatisation of state-owned organisations that wish to achieve high efficiencies prior to sale;
- the reduction of costs to maintain competitiveness in a global market.

These reasons obscure a more varied reality. For example, Worrell *et al.* (1991) observed that following an initial rise, stock market prices reacted negatively to redundancies. Similarly, Madison and Clancy (2000) found that while initial downsizing was associated with improved performance, subsequent downsizing was associated with poor performance. As can be seen from these, downsizing can be associated with either a short-term goal to cut costs, or a more fundamental and longer-term strategy to realise improvements related to greater effectiveness, efficiency, productivity and competitiveness. This distinction, and the fact that downsizing is frequently linked with both the former goal and the use of redundancy, leads to the fundamental problem associated with its intended purpose. In practice, pursuing short-term cost cutting through redundancy to reduce headcount is likely to lead to the loss of key skills and competences from the workforce and to the creation of lowered morale and insecurity. This outcome may adversely affect, rather than improve, aspects of the performance of an organisation. Even the use of a carefully managed and longer-term attempt to restructure and transform the organisation may still have adverse effects. Thus, downsizing is likely to be associated with the creation of negative psychological and behavioural consequences for survivors, no matter how well it is managed. The management of this HR strategy therefore needs to incorporate measures to alleviate the causes of such consequences as far as is possible and reduce their effects.

Organisations as well as human resource management theorists often recognise the importance of committed employees (Swailes, 2002). Alternatives to a strategy that encourages employee commitment to the goals of an organisation may be to muddle along or overtly increase the degree of managerial control over the workforce. However, the use of either of these approaches is likely to only work effectively in the short term, where no attempt is made to manage the issues that arise from downsizing. As can be seen in relation to BT (In Practice 14.1), survivors' commitment may also be affected. The need for organisational commitment and loyalty is likely to be more significant after downsizing, since those who remain become more important to the functioning of the organisation. However, this is likely to be threatened if the organisation does not foster continued commitment from those remaining, or unless its employees maintain some sort of third-party relationship with its customers, perhaps related to a sense of professional commitment.

Shaw and Barrett-Power (1997) recognise that the external measures typically used to assess the effectiveness of downsizing from a corporate perspective are clearly inadequate as a means to understand and manage the impact of this process on stakeholders, such as work groups and individual employees, who survive this event. Typically, corporate measures are related to profitability, productivity, investment returns, customer satisfaction ratings and the like. While these may indicate indirectly that downsizing has had a negative impact on those who survive as employees in the organisation, they can only imply the presence of psychological and behavioural consequences for survivors.

In Practice   14.1

Reactions to voluntary redundancies at BT

Between 1991 and 1995 BT's workforce fell from 215,000 to 137,000, a loss of 78,000 staff. During the early part of this period, the success of voluntary redundancy schemes led to many more BT staff applying than the targeted numbers. However, despite these release schemes being based on the principle of voluntary severance, a number of those who survived the event had negative reactions. The success of attracting so many volunteers for the redundancy terms being offered led to a situation where some of those retained felt 'angry and hurt' because they had not been allowed to leave (IRS, 1993: 14). This undoubtedly had an impact on the remaining employees' commitment to the company (Doherty *et al.*, 1996: 56), one employee stating, 'What drove us on to complete the project, even with its impossible targets, was our professionalism and our relationship with the customer to whom we were committed. It had little to do with loyalty to the company.' Subsequently, some of the survivors felt a sense of loss about colleagues with whom they had worked closely. For some this led to a sense of guilt about the fact they had kept their jobs while former colleagues had lost theirs (Thornhill *et al.*, 2000).

There is evidence of the existence of such consequences, and their adverse effect on expected corporate outcomes from downsizing, from the findings of a number of USA-based surveys. Mishra and Mishra (1994) cite Tomasko (1992) who found that just one-quarter of downsized organisations had realised their objective of improved productivity and higher returns on investment. Similarly, a survey by the Wyatt Company of 1,005 downsized organisations found that less than half were able to agree that they had achieved a particular organisational objective related to a desire to reduce costs, improve productivity, increase investment returns, or increase profits, etc. (e.g. Cameron, 1994a).

The continued commercial success of many organisations that have engaged in significant downsizing programmes means that there is a need to interpret the results of such surveys with a degree of caution. While a failure to achieve an objective following downsizing may indicate negative psychological and behavioural reactions from survivors, we believe that such consequences may be present even where corporate results do not point to this outcome. A range of contextual variables could affect, and disguise, the impact of survivors' negative reactions on the commercial performance of an organisation. These include the nature of the technology being used; the skills of the workforce; the nature of work processes; the need for innovative behaviour and level of redundancy payments made. Even within the EU, the minimum pay differs significantly between countries (In Practice 14.2) For this reason, the authors believe that the negative impact of survivors' reactions may often be hidden from an organisation's 'balance sheet', at least in the short-term.

In Practice   14.2

Minimum redundancy payments in the EU

Minimum redundancy payments in some EU countries are almost six times higher in some European countries than others (Mercer Human Resource Consulting, 2003). The graph below compares the minimum statutory paid notice period and number of weeks of severance pay for a typical non-manual employee aged 40 who was made redundant after ten years' service and with a salary of €30,000.

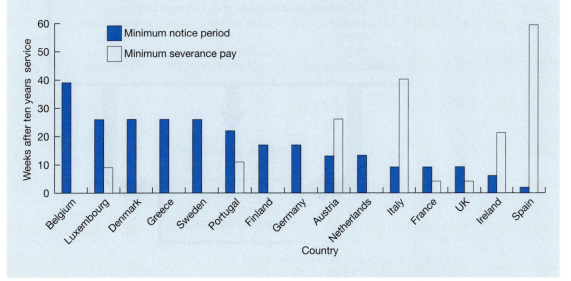

Thus, even where observable commercial costs are not considered, it may be the case that a significant adverse impact has occurred. This may be related to the creation of negative psychological consequences for survivors or to the altered profile of an organisation's workforce, which impairs its ability to demonstrate adaptability to altered circumstances in the future.

To summarise the discussion so far, it has been suggested that the intended purpose for organisations to downsize is to achieve an improvement in organisational performance. Despite this, the creation of psychological and behavioural reactions from those who survive this process may lead to the impairment, rather than the improvement, of the performance of the organisation. This suggests that downsizing needs to be examined as a 'bottom-up' process as well as a 'top-down' one. In other words, for the strategic outcomes of downsizing to be realised it will be necessary for the organisation to consider and manage the process from the perspective of affected individual employees and workgroups, and the stresses which this event creates. This type of approach has led Shaw and Barrett-Power (1997: 109) to propose a definition that focuses on this perspective: 'we define downsizing more broadly as a constellation of stressor events centering around pressures toward workforce reductions which place demands upon the organisation, work groups, and individual employees, and require a process of coping and adaptation.' The nature of these psychological and behavioural reactions is summarised in Figure 14.2 and discussed more fully, along with their implications, in 'Interventions to manage downsizing as a bottom-up process', later in this chapter.

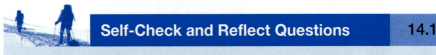

Self-Check and Reflect Questions   14.1

Using Shaw and Barrett-Power's (1997) definition of downsizing (outlined earlier), which of the following events would you classify as downsizing methods: compulsory redundancy, early retirement, induced redeployment, job share, natural attrition, recruitment freeze, voluntary redundancy, involuntary redeployment? Give reasons for your answer.

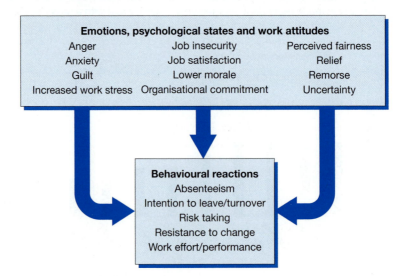

Figure 14.2 Survivor reactions to downsizing
Source: developed from Thornhill and Saunders (1998).

The strategic implications of downsizing

Downsizing is a powerful means to generate organisational change. As a strategy that adversely affects employees' jobs, its incidence will be highly transparent and its impact pervasive. Downsizing can also contribute to and impact upon other HR strategies. For example, it may be used as a means to help to bring about a re-alignment of an organisation's culture (Chapter 6), or to introduce a system of performance management (Chapter 9). Such HR strategies may be easier to apply when downsizing results in those remaining, re-evaluating their relationship with the organisation and, in particular, the way they perceive their psychological contract (Millward and Brewerton, 1999), discussed in Key Concepts 14.1. However, the use of downsizing may also impair an attempt to introduce another type of change strategy, where it produces negative reactions among those who survive. The process of downsizing also necessitates the development or amendment of other HR strategies. For example, as events such as restructuring, delayering, redundancy and redeployment occur, human resource development needs are likely to become apparent (Chapter 10).

Key Concepts	14.1

The psychological contract

Millward and Brewerton (1999) emphasise that psychological contracts can be described in terms of both the nature of the beliefs about the contract between employee and employer, and the process through which these beliefs arise.

Within the literature, the nature of employees' beliefs has been differentiated in terms of its transactional or relational orientation. A psychological contract with a transactional orientation has been argued to focus upon short-term, largely financial benefits to the employee (Rousseau, 1995). Perceived terms of employment are predicted to be calculative and instrumental with limited reciprocity, focusing upon beliefs about remuneration (Herriot and Pemberton, 1996). Within such contracts, affected employees will concentrate on distributive outcomes, there being limited identification and integration with the organisation (Millward and Brewerton, 1999). Thus, loyalty and commitment are unlikely to be an integral part of the transactional psychological contract.

A psychological contract with a relational orientation is likely to have evolved over time as a partnership develops between employee and employer (Rousseau, 1995), implying mutuality and reciprocity between them. Perceived terms of employment are therefore likely to be more than remunerative, incorporating beliefs about support from the employer, such as training, and personal and career development. Processes through which equity and fairness are affirmed are important in maintaining a relational contract, with the nature of beliefs becoming more pronounced as they are assessed over time (Herriot and Pemberton, 1996). Consequently, a relational psychological contract has been characterised for the employee as trusting his or her employer, high affective commitment, high integration and identification with the organisation, and long-term commitment (Rousseau, 1995). As argued earlier, organisational interventions such as downsizing may impact negatively upon these relational aspects, leading to a more transactional orientation.

Downsizing can therefore be seen as both a strategic intervention in its own right and a component of a wider business strategy. Implicit in this interpretation is the need for the process of and outcomes from downsizing to be managed proactively, and to try and ensure clear integration between different interventions. In practice, as we outline later, this may not happen, and the opportunity to achieve the strategic objectives intended from the use of downsizing is likely to be impaired. This will require reactive interventions to attempt to obtain the type of outcome that was originally intended. The need for a reactive intervention to overcome unintended and negative outcomes may also result from the use of inappropriate or ineffective interventions when downsizing was introduced. These types of events are illustrated in Figure 14.3.

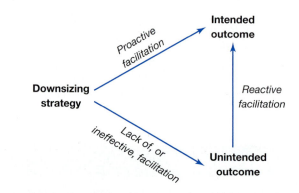

Figure 14.3 Outcomes of downsizing
Source: developed from Thornhill *et al.* (2000).

Strategies for organisational downsizing

Cameron and colleagues (e.g. Cameron *et al.*, 1991, 1993; Cameron, 1994b) have identified three organisational strategies to achieve downsizing (Figure 14.4). The first of these is the workforce reduction strategy, which focuses simply on reducing an organisation's headcount. This usually has an emphasis on cutting costs and is also known as convergent downsizing. The second is the organisation redesign strategy which, in addition to reducing headcount, involves elements of delayering, eliminating areas of work and job redesign, so that the amount of work is also reduced (In Practice 14.3). The third is the systemic change strategy which, in addition to workforce reductions and structural changes, is a longer-term approach. This is intended to promote a more fundamental change that affects the culture of the organisation (Chapter 6), for example by promoting employee involvement and adherence to a continuous improvement strategy. This and the second strategy are also known as reorientation strategies. Downsizing may thus be implemented solely through reducing an organisation's headcount (the most popular strategy) or in combination with one or more other strategies that seek to reduce the amount of work undertaken and bring about structural and cultural change to the organisation (In Practice 14.3).

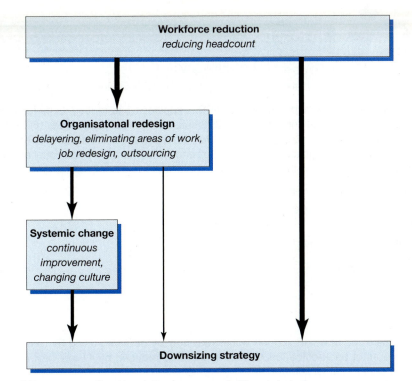

Arrow widths are proportional to relative frequency of different strategies.

Figure 14.4 Organisational strategies to achieve downsizing

Workforce reduction

Significantly, Cameron *et al.* (1993) found that the exclusive use of a workforce reduction strategy resulted in a reduction, rather than an improvement, in organisational performance. In a confirmatory study, Mishra and Mishra (1994) found that organisational performance was adversely affected in relation to both cost and quality, where this strategy was used exclusively. Such a strategy may lead to the loss of valued organisational competence, as discussed earlier, and negative consequences for those who remain. Its benefits are seen to be short term, whereas the attendant costs remain into the longer term as the organisation attempts to overcome the loss of required competence and negative survivor reactions.

Organisational redesign and systemic change

By comparison, the use of an organisation redesign and/or systemic change strategy has been positively related to organisational performance in terms of both cost reduction and quality improvement (Cameron *et al.*, 1993; Mishra and Mishra, 1994) and to survivors of downsizing having a positive learning orientation (Farrell and Mavando, 2004). Moreover, organisations relying exclusively on the use of a workforce reduction strategy have been found to be likely to repeat the use of this approach whenever cost reduction was deemed necessary (Cameron, 1994b). Repeated use of a workforce reduc-

In Practice   14.3

Downsizing HR at the BBC

BBC People, the HR department at the BBC, is planning to reduce its headcount from almost 1,000 to 450 posts in 2006 (Griffiths, 2005). Of these, 260 will be outsourced, 180 will be made redundant and other jobs will be transferred to other BBC divisions. Like many HR functions, BBC People already outsources services such as payroll and recruitment. The additional areas likely to be affected by this new outsourcing include:

- assessment and development;
- contracting of casuals;
- freelancers;
- HR advice and technical support;
- engineering training;
- occupational health;
- access services;
- relocation.

At the same time, HR support will increasingly be delivered using IT. Through the outsourcing, the headcount of back-office functions is likely to be reduced by 47 per cent and associated costs by 25 per cent (Griffiths, 2005).

tion strategy has been shown to further damage employee morale as subsequent downsizing programmes are revealed, resulting in anorexic organisations (Kinnie *et al.*, 1998).

The implications arising from an organisation's use of a downsizing strategy are also related to the extent to which the approach adopted is proactive or reactive (Kozlowski *et al.*, 1993) (see Figure 14.3). A proactive downsizing strategy is likely to be integrated with the organisation's business strategy, target organisational areas and competences for downsizing selectively, and recognise the potential consequences from both organisational and individual perspectives. The recognition of potential consequences is also likely to lead to the development of interventions to alleviate or manage their incidence. Proactivity, therefore, implies careful planning throughout the stages of downsizing.

In contrast, a reactive approach is unlikely to consider those aspects that a proactive approach is designed to address. It is therefore more likely to be used where the aim of downsizing is limited to reducing organisational costs, and lead to the creation of negative consequences in relation to remaining employees. The North American literature suggests that a reactive approach to downsizing may be more frequently used than a proactive one. For example, the small amount of time available to the HR managers in the study undertaken by McCune *et al.* (1988) meant that they had little opportunity to plan before downsizing. Managers faced with such a situation are unlikely to have sufficient time, if any, to plan and develop interventions to alleviate and manage the consequences of downsizing for those who survive. The HR implications are thus more likely to be negative and, in the event, more difficult to manage, where an organisation pursues only a workforce reduction strategy, especially where this is conducted on a reactive basis.

Self-Check and Reflect Questions 14.2

Why might the requirement to adopt a proactive downsizing strategy in order to minimise its negative consequences be difficult to achieve in practice?

Implications arising from downsizing

Implications of implementation methods

The earlier discussion highlighted the relationship between the strategy used to downsize and the consequences resulting from this process. This has suggested that a strategy that focuses only on workforce reductions, especially where this is reactive in nature, is less likely to achieve the organisational objectives established for downsizing and more likely to lead to unintended negative consequences related to survivors' reactions. A similar relationship also exists between the method or methods used to implement downsizing (Figure 14.5) and the nature of the reactions that occur.

The nature of survivors' reactions generated by use of a particular method is likely to be linked to the degree of managerial control that this method allows over the implementation of downsizing (Greenhalgh *et al.*, 1988). For example, a high level of managerial control over the implementation of downsizing is likely to promote a lack of perceived employee influence and greater feelings of job insecurity. The use of compulsory redundancy to achieve downsizing is therefore likely to lead to low employee influence and high levels of job insecurity (In Practice 14.4). In such situations, management exercises choice not only about method but also about selection of those to be made redundant.

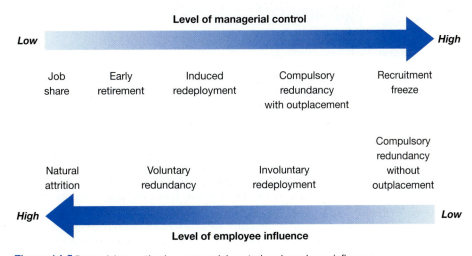

Figure 14.5 Downsizing methods, managerial control and employee influence
Source: developed from Thornhill *et al.* (2000).

The use of methods such as natural attrition or wastage or early retirement are likely to reduce the level of perceived managerial control. This should reduce levels of job insecurity for those below the early retirement age as well as concerns about low employee influence, since the use of such methods does not threaten these employees' continuity of employment. Greenhalgh *et al.* (1988) discuss five downsizing methods which they place on a continuum that emphasises employees' influence over their continuity of employment at one end and managerial control at the other. The authors have added job share, early retirement, voluntary redundancy and recruitment freeze to this continuum (Figure 14.5).

However, even where an organisation encourages early retirements or uses a voluntary approach to redundancy, a high level of managerial control may be exercised (Wass, 1996). All types of redundancy arise as the result of a managerial decision. Voluntary redundancy involves employees volunteering to be made redundant. This decision to volunteer may be in response to either a general request by the organisation or in response to specific targeting of individuals. Although voluntary redundancy involves a decision by an employee to accept an offer of a redundancy payment, and is differentiated from compulsory redundancy, which affects selected employees regardless of their wishes, managerial control over inducements to accept voluntarily have been shown to be highly persuasive (Wass, 1996). In most instances, those taking it feel that, although their choice was constrained, it was a voluntary process, financial incentives helping to make it an attractive proposition (Clarke, 2005). In addition, non-financial inducements to volunteer are likely to have an impact. For example, increasing the target number of staff to be made redundant may increase the pressure upon employees, reducing morale and resulting in more volunteers (Lewis, 1993). Work intensification and other changes may have a similar effect.

Perhaps the key point in this respect is the perception by employees of their level of influence over the downsizing process. While strategic targeting of the redundancy terms offered may allow organisations to exercise effective control over the implementa-

In Practice 14.4

Downsizing in Hong Kong's internet Industry

Soon after its return to Chinese sovereignty as a Special Administrative Region in 1997, Hong Kong, like neighbouring Asian economies, experienced an economic downturn. By 1999 a survey by the Hong Kong Institute of Human Resource Management found that 40 per cent of firms were reporting problems with surplus labour (Chu and Ip, 2002). In mid-1999, a sudden downturn in internet businesses prompted a series of layoffs in the workforce.

Downsizing in the internet businesses was more sudden than in other industries. Over two-thirds of those organisations making employees redundant communicated their decisions to employees in person, over half being dismissed immediately (Chu and Ip, 2002). According to Chu and Ip's research, employees' viewed the process as unfair. There had been no prior consultation or communication to explain the reasons for downsizing. Assistance with job search was not provided for those made redundant and, although some organisations used subcontracting to cover for lost employees, little was done to help those who remained in employment. These survivors felt uneasy and perceived little justice in the downsizing process or their own treatment.

tion of downsizing, even where the process is ostensibly voluntary, employees may perceive that they still exercise little choice in accepting redundancy. Alternatively, there may be an exchange relationship whereby employees are willing to trade their influence over the process for a sizeable compensatory payment. There may even be a sense that employees have exercised some degree of collective control in influencing management to offer relatively generous redundancy terms to avoid particular negative reactions. However, where the method to implement downsizing is presented as voluntary but is perceived not to be, the outcome is likely to be the creation of negative reactions. These may be created among survivors as well as leavers, with consequences for the future management of the organisation (Thornhill, *et al.*, 1997b). In this situation any sense of influence by employees would be perceived to be false, with the implication that survivors' reactions may be negatively affected through this type of organisational treatment. This may also mask underlying problems of morale and commitment (Clarke, 2005) as dissatisfied employees opt for voluntary redundancy.

Self-Check and Reflect Questions	**14.3**

Which factors related to the methods used to implement downsizing might affect managerial control and employee influence over the process?

Implications for those who survive the process

The process of downsizing, through the strategy adopted and the methods to implement it, has been linked to the psychological and behavioural reactions of those who survive this event remaining with the organisation. These may lead to the impairment of intended organisational objectives not being, or only partially being, met either in the short term or in the longer term. The need to approach downsizing as a 'bottom-up' process has been referred to in an earlier discussion. The implication is, that by doing this, an organisation will be more likely to recognise threats to the achievement of its objectives for downsizing, and therefore to understand how it might attempt to alleviate these or manage their effects.

In this section the psychological and behavioural reactions to this HR strategy are explored by adopting a 'bottom-up' approach to downsizing. The section commences by looking more closely at the nature of survivors' reactions to downsizing and the existence of moderating variables (Brockner, 1988), which affect the strength of survivors' reactions. These variables also highlight the scope for managers to intervene to manage this process. Subsequently, a range of organisational theories is used to suggest interventions to manage downsizing as a 'bottom-up' process.

The nature of survivors' reactions and the existence of moderating variables

Survivors' reactions to downsizing are affected not only by the actions of an organisation but also by psychological and social differences between individuals and broader environmental factors (Figure 14.6). Reactions to downsizing will vary between individuals because of psychological differences related to self-esteem, prior organisational

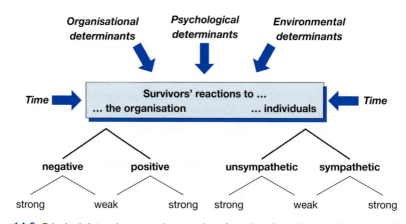

Figure 14.6 Principal determinants and categories of survivors' reactions to the advent of downsizing
Source: developed from Thornhill *et al.* (2000).

commitment, tolerance of insecurity and individual coping strategies. For example, Brockner *et al.* (1985) suggest that survivors' with low self-esteem may actually improve their work performance because they experience a high level of positive inequity (i.e. guilt) about the way in which a downsizing is conducted. Brockner *et al.* (1992) found that the survivors who are most likely to suffer from negative reactions are those who were highly committed to the organisation before downsizing, where they perceive the management of the process is unfair. Greenhalgh and Rosenblatt (1984) report that individuals who have a significant aversion to perceived threats, such as job insecurity, will experience strong reactions. Related to this last aspect, Armstrong-Stassen (1994) found that survivors who felt more in control of their situation adopted coping strategies that reflected this feeling. This suggests that those who do not feel this will be less likely to cope effectively.

Environmental conditions may also impact upon survivors' reactions (Brockner, 1988). Where their former colleagues are able to find comparable work in the labour market, survivors' reactions are likely to be less adverse. The occupational and geographical mobility of redundant employees and their economic need to work will also be likely to affect the strength of survivors' reactions (e.g. Greenhalgh and Rosenblatt, 1984).

These variables emphasise that survivors' reactions will vary between individuals in the same work setting. It also highlights that organisations need to be aware, in general terms, of the nature of differences between individual employees and prevailing environmental circumstances when they design interventions to alleviate negative survivor reactions to downsizing. However, this should not be interpreted as suggesting that these factors are outside of the influence of a downsizing organisation and therefore that any intervention is not possible. Rather, it highlights a need to lay particular emphasis on certain HR interventions, such as employee communication, and to provide an appropriate focus to other interventions, such as outplacement assistance for redundant staff, so that any threats posed by insecurity or lack of coping are alleviated. These types of intervention are discussed in the following section.

Individual differences and environmental factors are types of moderator variables. Such variables affect the incidence and strength of survivors' reactions to downsizing (e.g. Greenhalgh and Rosenblatt, 1984; Brockner, 1988). They help to explain why the incidence and strength of psychological and behavioural reactions vary in relation to different downsizing situations. The identification of moderator variables is therefore a very important step towards any attempt to manage a downsizing programme proactively and effectively. An understanding of possible moderator variables will permit possible effects to be identified and the use of appropriate procedures to avoid, or at least to seek to alleviate, the potentially negative consequences of downsizing.

Many moderator variables are related directly to events in an organisation. The nature and strength of survivors' reactions may thus be partly explained by prior work interdependence with those who are to leave or who have been made redundant (Brockner 1988). The strength of sympathetic survivors' responses is likely to be much greater where survivors and leavers have previously worked closely together. More broadly, these reactions may be partly explained by the existence or absence of shared attitudes, values and experiences (Brockner and Greenberg, 1990). Where survivors and leavers closely identify with one another there is likely to be a higher level of sympathetic survivor response.

Survivors' beliefs that they may be made redundant themselves may be another source of insecurity affecting the nature and level of their reactions. A further major determinant of survivors' reactions will be related to perceptions about the policies and procedures used by an organisation to implement downsizing. Related to this implementation variable are issues about employee expectations and avoidability. In particular, unexpected or avoidable redundancies may result in strong, sympathetic reactions, such as anger towards an organisation (Brockner, 1988).

The discussion so far about the nature of survivors' reactions and the existence of moderating variables points to a highly complex scenario within an organisation implementing a downsizing strategy. Moreover, these moderating variables will be likely to have a cumulative and compounding effect (Brockner, 1988). Nevertheless, managerial action focused at this level of downsizing should contribute towards the effective management of this type of HR strategy. Its intention would be to reduce the incidence or alleviate the consequences of negative survivors' reactions that can arise where downsizing is only conceived as a corporate-level (top-down) strategy. In this way, the strength of negative reactions may be weakened, while any sense of legitimacy in the downsizing process, combined with procedural fairness, may possibly lead to the creation of some positive reactions. Research by Allen *et al.* (2001) highlights that such attitudes are likely to alter over time. In particular, while survivors' attitudes are likely to be less positive immediately after a downsizing than prior to its occurrence, they can return to a more favourable level over a period of months.

Brockner and Greenberg (1990) present two opposing categories of reactions which survivors may exhibit, depending upon their perceptions of how leavers are selected and subsequently treated during their period of notice. These categories are labelled as 'sympathetic' and 'unsympathetic' and refer to survivors' reactions towards those who leave an organisation (Figure 14.6). In the context of downsizing, they suggest an unsympathetic reaction may include the belief that redundancies were justified, particularly in relation to those selected for redundancy, with survivors distancing themselves from the leavers and working harder. On the other hand, sympathetic reactions by survivors may include the belief that leavers have been unfairly selected and/or treated, resulting in negative emotions, attitudes and behaviours towards an organisation. These categories of survivors' reactions emphasise the need for managerial interventions (Thornhill and Saunders, 1998).

Self-Check and Reflect Questions   14.4

How would you react to the redundancy of colleagues in the organisation for which you work, or in an organisation for which you have worked? (Perhaps you have actually experienced this event. If you have, how did you react and why?)

Interventions to manage downsizing as a bottom-up process

Research using a number of applicable theories, such as those related to equity, organisational justice, job insecurity, job redesign and organisational stress, suggests a number of interventions for managers to consider. These would be designed to reduce the incidence and strength of negative survivor reactions and encourage more positive reactions to the downsizing organisation.

Equity theory, management decisions and work effort

Equity theory (Adams, 1965) has been used to evaluate the effects of employee perceptions about the fairness of management decisions related to the downsizing processes. For example, survivors' reactions are likely to be affected by their level of acceptance of:

- the need to downsize or make employees redundant;
- the lack of an alternative course of action;
- the level of prior notification provided by management;
- the selection criteria used and the decisions made by managers about who should be made redundant; and
- the way in which the leavers are treated during their period of notice and offered support to find alternative employment (Brockner, 1988, 1992).

Perceptions of fairness or equity about management decisions and procedures related to these aspects may help to reduce the incidence of negative reactions. On the other hand, perceptions of unfairness may lead either to positive inequity, where particular survivors feel that those made redundant had a greater claim to be retained than they did; or to negative inequity where, for example, survivors identified closely with those made redundant. Positive inequity may lead to survivors experiencing guilt, with the result that they work harder, whereas negative inequity may lead to affected survivors reducing their level of organisational commitment and working less hard (e.g. Brockner, 1988).

Organisational justice theory: management decisions, decision-making and managers' skills

Recognition of the importance of perceived fairness has been developed through the use of organisational justice theory (Brockner and Greenberg, 1990; Daly and Geyer, 1994), by categorising employees' views and feelings about their and others' treatment within an organisation (Morrison and Robinson, 1997). Distributive justice is related to employees' perceptions regarding the fairness of the decisions that are made – the 'outcomes' of the process. The elements of distributive justice promote an understanding of why survivors may not perceive the outcomes of redundancy decisions to be fair. Organisations are likely to make or promote redundancy selection decisions based on criteria related to business needs, efficiency and performance. However, in many, if not most, cases, such criteria will be unlikely to produce outcomes that match the economic need to maintain employment of those threatened by redundancy (Brockner and Greenberg, 1990). Explaining why criteria were chosen may help to reduce the consequences of redundancy decisions based on this mismatch between organisational and individual objectives. In addition, employees may perceive that the business-related criteria used for redundancy selection do not match their judgements about effective performance. The use of such criteria will lead to an outcome that is perceived to be unfair. The possibility of such an outcome has clear implications for the validity of selection criteria and the need to shape perceptions about this. Another aspect of distributive justice may relate to perceptions about whether downsizing and redundancy also affect management, or whether managers are seen to avoid redundancies (Brockner, 1992).

Perceptions about the processes used to arrive at, and to implement, these decisions form the basis of two further dimensions of justice that are sometimes treated as one in the literature: procedural justice and interactional justice (Cropanzano and Greenberg, 1997). Procedural justice focuses on employee perceptions about the fairness of the processes used to make decisions about downsizing and redundancies. This suggests that not only should the outcomes of downsizing decision-making be seen to be fair but so too should the procedures used to arrive at such decisions. Where negative reactions are created by outcomes that are perceived as unfair, these may be moderated by the use of procedures that are seen as fair (Brockner *et al.*, 1990). Studies related to procedural justice have focused mainly on two factors that affect perceptions about procedural fairness. These are 'voice', which is linked to employee involvement in the process (Chapter 8), and 'justification', which relates to education through explanation (Daly and Geyer, 1994). The promotion of involvement in this context may include the use of consultation and communication about the process; the use of a voluntary, as opposed to a compulsory, redundancy; affected employees being provided with options about redeployment and relocation; the provision of outplacement facilities and; interventions aimed at allowing survivors to adjust to downsizing-related changes. Guest and Peccei (1992: 55) evaluated the effects of involvement initiatives used during the closure of a British Aerospace site and found that 'employee involvement can work as a strategy for easing the process of plant closure'. However, they also found that certain groups were less involved, with the implication that these employees may have had less favourable perceptions about the fairness of the procedures used.

Involvement allows those affected to exercise some degree of influence in relation to the process, as we discussed earlier. This has been linked to a number of attitudinal and behavioural survivors' reactions. Davy *et al.* (1991) found that employee influence over the downsizing process positively affects perceptions about fairness and job satisfaction, which in turn affect level of commitment to the organisation and intention to stay. Organisations may therefore genuinely seek to engender employee involvement to promote perceptions that the process used is just (Davy *et al.*, 1991). Justification may also be promoted through an educative process to explain why downsizing is necessary. As with employee influence in relation to the process, justification has been found to be related positively to procedural fairness and, in turn, to intention to stay (Daly and Geyer, 1994). This may be explained through the finding that employees are more likely to accept a decision, even an unfavourable one related to redundancy, when they receive an adequate and genuine reason for it (Brockner *et al.*, 1990).

Procedural justice has been distinguished from interactional justice that focuses on employees' perceptions about fairness of interpersonal treatment received during the implementation of downsizing (Bies and Moag, 1986). However, there has been considerable debate concerning interactional justice. Initially, researchers (Bies and Moag, 1986; Greenberg, 1993) suggested that it consisted of two distinct types of treatment: treatment of people (interpersonal justice) and explanations provided to people (informational justice). Subsequently, it was argued that, as interactional justice produces the same type of perceptual outcomes as procedural justice, it should be considered a facet of procedural justice rather than as a separate dimension (Cropanzano and Greenberg, 1997). More recently, research has suggested that procedural, informational and interpersonal justice are three empirically distinct dimensions (Colquitt, 2001; Kernan and Hanges, 2002). Line managers have a potentially significant influence over the way their subordinates react to downsizing in terms of their treatment of those who leave and the survivors. Line managers therefore need to be able to demonstrate a range of skills that might be broadly described as change management skills. In addition, line managers need to be able to deal with issues that are specific to a redundancy situation. These will include communicating notification decisions and providing reasons for these (informational justice), as well as the sensitivity with which they treat leavers during their notice period (informational justice). It is therefore suggested that line managers will require preparation and training to be able to cope effectively and fairly (Thornhill *et al.*, 1997a).

Self-Check and Reflect Questions   14.5

Outline how perceptions of distributive, procedural, informational and interpersonal treatment may impact positively on downsizing survivors' reactions.

Job insecurity and the role of employee communication

The central role that effective communication may play in the management of downsizing and redundancy has already been highlighted through references to equity and organisational justice theories. Job insecurity theory develops our understanding of the role of communication in this context. Greenhalgh and Rosenblatt (1984) report that employees receive information through three channels: official organisational ones; organisational actions that provide them with clues, and informal channels such as rumours. Two points follow from this:

- information from the organisation may not focus on the specific concerns of those affected, whether they are leavers or stayers;
- in the absence of information, or appropriate information, employees will both infer what is likely to happen from organisational and managerial actions, and rely upon informal channels.

Where formal communications do not focus on the specific concerns of those affected, they will not alleviate their sense of powerlessness and perceived threat (Greenhalgh, 1983; Greenhalgh and Rosenblatt, 1984).

Earlier in this chapter it was highlighted that positive employee perceptions might follow from the exercise of employee involvement or voice during downsizing. In relation to job insecurity, perceptions about personal control related to the downsizing process may be positively affected through communicating how individuals will be affected, in particular:

- Most employees will benefit from knowing that they will not be affected, at least directly, such as when a downsizing strategy avoids the use of redundancy, at least in its compulsory form. An organisation may also use a carefully defined and targeted approach to reduce the pool of those potentially affected. Advance notification may be provided to those divisions or departments where redundancies will occur, thereby reducing insecurity about potential job losses for survivors, even though this introduces earlier issues for the management of those who are to leave.

- Both leavers and survivors will benefit from information about how they will be affected. Leavers will need information about how they will be treated during their period of notice, what will be expected from them and what further redeployment or outplacement support they may expect to receive. Survivors will need information about how they will be affected by the changes that result from downsizing. The provision of such information will be important for survivors who will now be less concerned about loss of their jobs, but may remain concerned about the removal of those job attributes that they found attractive before change was implemented.

Job insecurity, career progression and the psychological contract

Job insecurity, in this broader sense, refers to uncertainty about attributes such as career progression, contractual relationships, including the psychological contact (Key Concepts 14.1), and status. Downsizing and delayering may impair opportunities for career progression. Organisations will therefore need to consider the implications of this where it is likely to lead to the creation of negative survivor reactions and resulting intentions to leave. In attempting to avert this type of outcome, organisations will need to consider the competences that they require, the design and implementation of career management programmes to develop these and how they communicate these aspects to the survivors (Ebadan and Winstanley, 1997). More broadly, this threat to career progression and prior expectations about security may represent a breach of the psychological contract (Hendry and Jenkins, 1997: 39). This may signify a shift towards a 'transactional' contract, characterised by strict instrumentality where employee inputs are exchanged for financial reward, and there is a reduced willingness to participate in organisational citizenship behaviours (Key Concepts 14.2). It is likely to occur at the very time when the need for commitment to the organisation from survivors is at a premium (e.g. Murphy *et al.*, 2002). The implications of this may be particularly pronounced for middle managers as is now considered.

Studies conducted in North America (Belasen *et al.*, 1996) and the UK (Newell and Dopson, 1996; Campbell-Jamison *et al.*, 2001) found that work demands increase significantly for middle managers during and after downsizing. Such survivors have to work

Key Concepts   14.2

Organisational citizenship behaviour

Organisational citizenship behaviour (OCB) is the readiness of an employee to contribute to the organisation beyond that required by his or her contract. Such behaviour is not recognised formally by organisations' reward systems so, consequently, employees can decide whether or not to withhold OCB. OCB is multi-dimensional and includes employees' participation in activities that, while not formally required, help the image of the organisation as well as behaviours directed at individuals such as cooperative and constructive gestures (Coyle-Shapiro and Kessler, 2000; Murphy *et al.*, 2002).

harder and longer, and engage in a broader range of roles, and cope not only with their traditional management tasks but also with new aspects related to the implementation of change. This led Belasen *et al.* (1996) to report that the managers in their study needed to be 'hyper-effective' in order to cope. However, the sustainability of this requirement, its impact on these managers' psychological contracts, and their level of organisational commitment were questioned. Both studies found these managers felt they did not receive adequate information, leading to a sense of powerlessness, and that their psychological contracts had been unilaterally altered by the nature of the changes occurring within their organisations (Belasen *et al.*, 1996; Newell and Dopson, 1996). Newell and Dopson (1996) reported that the experiences of the managers in their study had led several of these to re-appraise the nature of their commitment, shifting the focus away from work irrespective of career progression.

All survivors may, of course, experience feelings of insecurity arising from uncertainty and unilateral changes to their psychological contracts. Kozlowski *et al.* (1993) used facets of job redesign, related to job enrichment or enlargement, to explore the relationship between an organisational strategy used to downsize and structural determinants of survivors' reactions following downsizing. In the earlier discussion of Figure 14.4, three organisational strategies to downsize were outlined. The first of these simply involved the use of a workforce reduction strategy, where the intention is to reduce organisational headcount and costs, as highlighted by In Practice 14.4. However, the amount of work that remains in the downsized organisation may not be reduced, at least on a commensurate basis. This will lead to a situation of job enlargement for survivors, where feelings of role stress and dissatisfaction may result in an altered commitment focus and intention to leave. This is likely to be associated with ineffective leadership, unclear job responsibilities, poor communication and feedback, and poorly defined performance standards, as well as role overload, following downsizing (Tombaugh and White, 1990). The use of an organisation redesign strategy (Chapter 5), in conjunction with a workforce reduction one, will instead be aimed at reducing the quantity of work in the downsized organisation. Where effective, this may lead to job enrichment enhancing personal control in relation to job roles (Kozlowski *et al.*, 1993; Cameron, 1994b).

Recognising and managing stress through the reactions of survivors

Research exploring the consequences of downsizing suggests that Lazarus and Folkman's (1984) theory of stress provides a useful framework to recognise and manage these issues (e.g. Brockner and Wiesenfeld, 1993). Shaw and Barrett-Power's (1997: 109) definition, cited earlier, emphasises that downsizing is a 'constellation of stressor events ... which ... require a process of coping and adaptation'. The changes that have been discussed in this chapter arising from downsizing have indicated a significant number of potential sources of stress for survivors. Lazarus and Folkman's (1984) theory centres on two key concepts: stress appraisal and coping. Individuals will cognitively appraise whether an event will lead to stress, how this may manifest itself and what they can do about it. Coping with an event that causes significant levels of stress, such as downsizing, may involve the use of one of two divergent strategies:

- problem-focused (or control oriented) coping;
- emotion-focused (or escape/avoidance) coping.

Strategies related to problem-focused coping involve an intention to confront the problem and to seek to solve it through attempts to exercise influence and control (Lazarus and Folkman, 1984; Latack, 1986). In contrast, emotion-focused coping involves focusing on emotional consequences and perhaps seeking to avoid stressful situations (Lazarus and Folkman, 1984; Latack, 1986), indicating withdrawal from the situation (Shaw and Barrett-Power, 1997).

There are therefore clear organisational and management implications from the application of stress theory to the downsizing context. In relation to stress appraisal, prior organisational treatment may be important to the way that individuals react to a potentially threatening or stressful situation (Naumann et al., 1995; Kernan and Hanges, 2002). Consequently, individuals who are employed in organisations that have proven to be supportive in the past, may appraise changes as less threatening and stressful. This may be particularly significant for survivors of downsizing. Organisational support throughout the downsizing is also likely to be important in relation to the type of coping strategy that affected individuals adopt. The aim of such support would be the encouragement of a problem-focused and control-oriented coping approach. Organisational support may be defined simply as the level of concern and care that an organisation shows in relation to the effects of its, and perhaps others', actions on its employees (Naumann et al., 1995). The most important source of this type of support is likely to be through employees' interactions with their line managers. In Armstrong-Stassen's (1994) study, survivors who performed better and were more committed and loyal to their organisation were those who also felt that they had highly supportive line managers. Survivors who demonstrated the same attributes towards commitment, performance and intention to stay were also found to be those who used control coping strategies. It therefore seems possible that some form of link exists between organisational support and survivors' coping strategies.

Summary

- Downsizing is an organisational strategy to reduce the size of an organisation's workforce. Its use is likely to generate a range of reactions from those who remain in an organisation, which may lead to adverse consequences.

- Three organisational strategies have been identified to achieve downsizing. These are: the workforce reduction strategy; organisation redesign strategy; and the systemic change strategy. An important distinction has also been drawn between the use of proactive and reactive approaches to downsizing. The use of a reactive, workforce reduction strategy has been found to impair, rather than improve, organisational performance. Even where this approach is not used there may still be a negative effect arising from the creation of negative survivors' reactions and the loss of organisational competence.

- Where organisations use methods to implement downsizing that emphasise managerial control at the expense of perceived influence by employees, this will generate further negative survivors' reactions leading to adverse consequences for the organisation.

- The incidence and strength of survivors' reactions are affected by the existence of moderating variables. These highlight the scope for downsizing organisations to intervene to seek to minimise their incidence or manage their effects.

- A range of organisational theories, related to equity, organisational justice, job insecurity, job redesign and organisational stress, can be used to suggest appropriate human resource interventions to manage the process of downsizing more effectively, depending on the characteristics of the organisational context.

Follow-up study suggestions

1. Using the search facilities of an electronic version of a quality daily newspaper obtain reports relating to recent downsizing at an organisation. Use these reports to discover the reasons for the downsizing and how it was implemented. How do you think the process might have been managed better?

2. Taking In Practice 14.2 as your starting point, explain the implications of variations in statutory redundancy requirements between member states in the EU.

3. Visit the government statistics web site for a country of your choice (for example http://www.statistics.gov.uk for the UK). Using that site's search facilities, obtain detailed data on redundancy rates. Find out what the overall trend in redundancy rates has been over the past few years. Explore how this trend differs between males and females and for different industry sectors.

4. Interview a friend or colleague whom you know has been made redundant from a previous job. Ask them to describe how they feel they were treated during the process. To what extent is organisational justice theory helpful in explaining their feelings?

Suggestions for research topics

1. Evaluate the management of the downsizing process at organisation XYZ paying special attention to the reactions of the survivors.

2. Evaluate the management of the downsizing process at organisation XYZ paying special attention to those who were made redundant.

3. Design a downsizing strategy for a large organisation to minimise the negative reactions from existing employees.

4. Explore the implications of variations in national legislation relating to redundancies for multi-national organisations facing the need to downsize their operations.

Case Study

The demise of MG Rover cars?

Financial Times cutting 1: MG Rover staff benefit from speedy payout

by Bob Sherwood
Financial Times, 3 May 2005

About 4,000 MG Rover workers who lost their jobs after the carmaker went into administration have received redundancy payments averaging £5,000 each.

The £20m-plus payout, which will ultimately be paid by the taxpayer, was speeded up by officials, Patricia Hewitt announced while campaigning for the general election in the West Midlands yesterday.

The trade and industry secretary said the total payments to former Rover workers would be closer to £50m than the £40m she had announced when the company collapsed last month.

Former workers at the Longbridge plant in Birmingham, where more than 5,000 jobs were lost, had complained they would receive payments up to £3,300. But the trade and industry secretary said the actual statutory redundancy payouts were larger. Speaking in the marginal constituency of Redditch, she said: 'I am delighted that my officials have put in a great deal of extra overtime and have made these payments in two weeks compared with the six weeks it can take to come through.'

The money is part of a £150m package pledged by the government to help the estimated 20,000 workers who have lost jobs at MG Rover and its suppliers.

The Transport and General Workers' Union said: 'It's excellent that the government has moved very fast. But it's awful that people with years of service have been left with the statutory minimum.'

The union also called for a quick settlement for the workers who were not paid their statutory 90-day notice period because of the speed of the redundancies.

Ms Hewitt said administrators had received a 'large number' of expressions of interest from companies contemplating acquiring assets or divisions of Rover, but it was uncertain whether they would save any jobs.

Financial Times cutting 2: New employment found by 1,250 ex-Rover workers

by Jonathan Guthriein
Financial Times, 22 June 2005

About 1,250 out of more than 5,000 workers who lost jobs when MG Rover collapsed in April have found new employment. A government-appointed taskforce said it was evidence that 'the West Midlands is fighting back from the biggest company closure in years'.

MG Rover, the last British-owned volume carmaker, went into administration after Shanghai Automotive Industry Corporation pulled out of collaboration talks. Yesterday's news on employment suggests the blow to the local economy will be lighter than many predicted. This reflects a tight labour market and diversification by suppliers after BMW sold Rover to local industrialists in 2000.

The MG Rover Taskforce, which updated the Prime Minister on its progress yesterday, said 2,200 MG Rover workers had signed up for training courses. About 1,000 have already started retraining. A few hundred MG Rover staff have been retained by the administrators to look after the Longbridge factory site, leaving about 1,000 other workers still looking for jobs or pondering their futures. The administrators have set today as the deadline for bidders to lodge their offers for MG Rover businesses

Tony Blair praised the taskforce, whose efforts could become a model for dealing with future mass redundancies, alongside such examples as the regeneration of Corby after steelworks closures. The body's task has been made easier by generous funding.

The Labour government, which was seeking re-election when MG Rover collapsed, has pledged £175m and the EU has put up £40m. That totals almost £36,000 per worker, though much of that money has not yet been spent.

JobCentre Plus, the government employment and benefits agency, set up an office on the Longbridge site and distributed information packs to redundant workers. A jobs fair was held on parkland beside the site and a register of manufacturing vacancies was set up. Small suppliers are receiving grants to retain workers dependent on MG Rover contracts while they diversify.

Margaret Hodge, minister for work and pensions, was embroiled in a row last week when she linked the MG Rover redundancies to vacancies at a local Tesco store. Some reports interpreted this as a call for former MG Rover workers to apply for jobs as shelf stackers. This hit a raw nerve with trade unionists worried by the replacement of well-paid manufacturing work with poorly-paid services jobs.

However Nick Paul, chairman of the MG Rover Taskforce, said many former MG Rover workers had found new jobs in manufacturing and that there were still 1,600 vacancies for skilled staff locally. Gerard Coyne, a member of the taskforce and regional secretary of the T&G union, said there would be a 'spike' in re-employment in three weeks, when compensation payments in lieu of notice ceased.

Many ex-MG Rover workers are learning construction industry skills, of which there is a national shortage.

Carl Lanchester, 56, previously a paint sprayer, will begin a plastering course this month. Mr Lanchester, who described Ms Hodge's comments as 'insulting', said he had felt 'frustrated' by delays to his retraining.

Mike Beasley, a taskforce member and chairman of the West Midlands Learning and Skills Council, agreed there had been a bottleneck in retraining, adding: 'You have to remember we are taking on over 3,000 new students, the equivalent of a whole new college being set up.'

Workers are mostly resigned to earning less in new jobs than they did at the Longbridge plant. Mr Lanchester, who received £21,000 a year, said: 'I will be lucky to get that anywhere else.' Average pay at MG Rover was about £22,000 with typical salaries for ex-workers beginning new careers estimated at £18,000.

Financial Times cutting 3: Waiting game ended in tears as SAIC deal for Rover failed to materialise

by James Mackintosh
Financial Times, 7 October 2005

When Tony Lomas, senior restructuring partner at PwC, arrived at the gates of MG Rover's Longbridge factory in Birmingham on a Saturday afternoon in April, he had already decided that a rescue of the company was close to impossible.

Colleagues at the professional services firm had worked through the night, after being appointed as administrators by the owners of the carmaker, to try to revitalise a deal with China's largest car manufacturer.

But Mr Lomas found attempts to contact executives at Shanghai Automotive Industry Corp had failed. He roped in colleagues from PwC's Shanghai office, spoke to NM Rothschild, SAIC's London-based investment banking adviser, and consulted Rover executives who had negotiated with the company.

Everything he discovered backed up the belief that a sale to SAIC – which had been under negotiation for a year – was 'highly unlikely' and even if possible could not be done quickly. He decided Rover could not risk its hoard of £17.2m cash and the workforce would have to be sacked on Monday. It was also unclear whether the money was pledged against loans or free to spend. 'We told both the union and the DTI that. That was our view on the Saturday morning and that was still our view on the Sunday.'

People close to SAIC had made clear in private ahead of the collapse of Rover that a deal was no longer on the table. Indeed, bankers at Rothschild had advised the Chinese company that if a deal was to be done, it was better to do it while Rover was still trading in order to avoid the brand damage. Anyone buying Rover would also have to contend with suppliers refusing to provide vital parts to the company until they were paid. Yet, late on the Sunday, with SAIC still out of contact, the Department of Trade and Industry decided to hand over £6.5m to stave off redundancies for a week while Chinese talks took place. This money, technically a loan, would only be repaid if the business was sold as a going concern.

Efforts to contact the Chinese company lasted four days before a letter arrived from Shanghai, addressed to Patricia Hewitt, the then trade and industry secretary, which made 'crystal clear' that no deal was possible. After that, job losses were inevitable. Mr Lomas brought in experts from PwC's human resources consultancy, who had handled the 3,000 job losses imposed during the restructuring of television rental company Boxclever.

'When you are trying to do the "hard" commercial things they made sure you deal with the human matters too,' he said.

As P45s landed on doormats, Mr Lomas heard from valuers that, apart from a few pieces of specialised equipment, most of Rover's machinery could only be sold as scrap metal. The 14,000 new and second-hand cars parked on disused airfields around Britain and Europe were the company's most valuable assets.

This meant finding a buyer that wanted to build MGs or Rovers and so needed the equipment. More than 700 bidders asked for information but by late June only a handful had proved serious, including Nanjing Automobile. Nanjing, which is struggling in its home market of China, demonstrated it was serious by sending a delegation, led by its second-in-command, to examine Longbridge.

At this point, two late bidders emerged: SAIC, which had wanted to buy only the Powertrain engine factory, realised that PwC preferred to sell Rover's assets as a package; and a consortium led by David James, who took over the troubled Millennium Dome in 2000, offered £40m for everything.

However, SAIC still did not believe Nanjing had the money and was finding it difficult to put in a serious bid. It finally lodged a bid just before a July 22 deadline but Mr Lomas said it was not as high as Nanjing's £53m offer and had conditions, unlike Nanjing.

Today, Chinese engineers are dismantling production lines to ship to Nanjing, where they plan to build MG cars. But Mr Lomas says Nanjing appears to be negotiating with GB Sports Car Co to build cars in Britain.

Case study questions

Before answering these questions read all three articles from the *Financial Times*.

1. Outline the organisational downsizing strategy that was adopted by Rover.

2. Outline the range of support offered to redundant Rover workers.
   Why do you believe this support was offered?

3. Why did the UK government become involved in the downsizing at Rover?

4. What were the intended and unintended outcomes of the downsizing strategy adopted?

Glossary

360-degree appraisal This type of appraisal is so called because it does not rely on assessment from the line manager only but from a number of sources. These may include, in addition to the line manager, other managers such as those responsible for projects; peers; employees for whom the individual may be responsible; internal and external customers; and self-assessment.

Achievement versus ascription A cultural dimension used by Trompenaars and Hampden-Turner that relates to relationships with people and, in particular, the way in which status is accorded.

Acquisitions *see* mergers and acquisitions.

Action research Evaluation strategy concerned with the management of a change and involving close collaboration between practitioners and researchers. The results flowing from action research should also inform other contexts.

Applied research Research of direct and immediate relevance to practitioners that addresses issues they see as important and is presented in ways they can understand and act upon.

Appraisal-related pay A method of payment when an individual employee receives increases in pay based wholly or partly on the regular and systematic assessment of job performance.

Artefact A manifestation of a culture that is relatively easy to discern but from which the true meaning is difficult to decipher because of its shallow or superficial nature. Material objects, physical arrangements, patterns of behaviour, stories and jokes are often described as artefacts. *See also* symbol.

Articulated knowledge The knowledge possessed by individuals that can be expressed verbally or in writing so that it can be passed on to others to assimilate.

Balanced scorecard This assumes that for an organisation to be successful it must satisfy the demands of its key stakeholders, investors, customers and employees. This suggests four key perspectives on business performance: finance; customers; internal business processes; and learning and growth.

Bandwagon effect This is where companies rush to emulate competitors by investing abroad for fear of losing competitive edge.

Base pay The basic, regular amount of wages or salary received by an employee without additional sums such as bonuses.

Basic research Research undertaken purely to understand processes and their outcomes, predominantly in universities as a result of an academic agenda, for which the key consumer is the academic community.

Basic underlying assumptions The deepest level of culture. These are the invisible 'theories in use' upon which more visible practices and artefacts of culture are built. They are so taken for granted that there will be little variation in them within a culture or subculture.

Best practice HRM Similar to the concept of universal models of SHRM, this suggests that there is 'one best way' of achieving HR effectiveness.

Best value An initiative in the UK public sector that requires local authorities (and other best value authorities) to seek to achieve continuous improvement by having regard to the efficiency, effectiveness and economy of their service delivery.

Big idea A key finding of one of the research projects on the extent to which HR impacts upon organisational performance showed the importance of a big idea (e.g. a dominant organisational imperative) that unified organisational thought and action.

Black box A term used in HR research to discover how the processes of people management influence employee and organisational performance.

Bottom-up Process typically initiated away from an organisation's headquarters, developed by employees and led by general managers. Tends to be approached incrementally.

Broad-banding The compression of a hierarchy of pay grades or salary ranges into a small number of wide bands.

Bundles (HR) Some of the studies treat HR practices as groups, or 'bundles', of activities, thus emphasising the importance of horizontal integration between practices.

Capability Refers to an individual employee's ability to perform the work expected of them to required standards.

Case study Evaluation strategy that involves the empirical investigation of a particular contemporary phenomenon within its real-life context, using multiple sources of evidence.

Closed question *see* question, closed

Collective agreement The outcome of the collective bargaining process; may be defined as an agreement between a trade union(s) and employer(s) that determines, among other things, the terms and conditions of employment of the employees and the employer who is party to the agreement.

Collective bargaining Voluntary, formalised procedure whereby employers and trade unions negotiate, for specific groups of employees, terms and conditions of employment, and the ways in which certain employment-related issues are to be regulated at national, organisational and workplace levels.

Collectivism (1) Refers to employees giving up their individual interests in favour of the interests of the workgroup, whether at workplace, company or national level. The employer may have little choice in this as it may be part of an arrangement where the employees' interests are progressed through a collective arrangement. (2) An approach to the management of the employment relationship that assumes that the employees' interests are pursued through the processes of collective representation to management, usually, but not exclusively, through trade unions

Commitment Widely used in current SHRM literature to describe the quality of being dedicated to the cause. Various methods are used to develop this quality among employees with the aim being a dedication to the cause of organisational success. Some employees may be committed to a career or to employment security that is associated with the success of the business, while other employees may be committed to their career, perhaps at the expense of the business. A final group of employees may have no commitment at all.

Competence-related pay A method of rewarding employees wholly or partly by reference to the level of competence they demonstrate in carrying out their roles.

Competitive advantage (1) A perceived association with a commodity or service of a tangible or intangible attribute of condition of supply, which makes that product or service more attractive to customers than the goods or services of a competitor. (2) The advantage enjoyed by an organisation over its competitors. This can arise accidentally as a result of the particular circumstance of an organisation but is often deliberately sought and pursued through strategic management. It may result from the positioning of an organisation in its market place, e.g. niche marketing or competing on the basis of quality, or from the exploitation of distinctive internal resources, e.g. an organisation's human capital.

Competitive environment The immediate competitive context in which an organisation operates.

Compulsory redundancy The selection of employees to be made redundant regardless of their wishes.

Confucian dynamism A cultural dimension used by Hofstede (and Bond) that relates to the long- or short-term orientation of cultures.

Contingency approach This approach suggests that there is no universal best way to design an organisation, that the design chosen is dependent on the current and future operating environment of the organisation.

Contract of employment Formed when an offer of employment is made and accepted. Traditionally, the terms and conditions included in the contract of employment create the central elements of the employment relationship.

Convergence, cultural *see* cultural convergence.

Core capabilities A set of organisation-specific capabilities that can lead to sustainable competitive advantage. These capabilities arise from the distinctiveness of internal resources and include an organisation's skill base, its processes and routines, and its assets and patents or intellectual capital. Frequently referred to as core competences. *See also* core competence.

Core competence A distinctive organisational capability that, if effectively exploited, can lead to an organisation achieving competitive advantage over its rivals if the competence cannot be easily copied. *See also* core capabilities.

Core values *see* basic underlying assumptions.

Corporate culture This is the pattern of values, beliefs and expectations shared by organisation members. It represents the taken-for-granted and shared assumptions that people make about how work is done and evaluated, and how employees relate to one another and to significant others, such as suppliers, customers and government agencies.

Corporate strategy The overall aims and objectives of an organisation and how the organisation plans and utilises its resources to achieve its strategy. *See also* strategic management; strategic planning; strategy.

Cross-sectional The study of a particular phenomenon (or phenomena) at a particular time, i.e. a 'snapshot'.

Cultural convergence The argument that, due to advances in technology, the growing number of multi-national organisations and the like cultures will converge.

Cultural divergence The argument that between-country differences, such as language, religious beliefs, laws, political systems and education, mean that cultures will diverge.

Cultural web The symbols, power structures, organisational structures, control systems, rituals and routines, and stories that, along with their interrelationships define the core values and beliefs of an organisation's culture.

Culture 'A pattern of shared basic assumptions that the group learned as it solved its problems of external adaptation and internal integration, that has worked well enough to be considered valid and, therefore, to be taught to new members as the correct way to perceive, think and feel in relation to those problems' (Schein, 1997: 12). *See also* national culture; organisational culture.

Differentiation perspective The perspective that different groups within, for example, an organisation are likely to have different beliefs and behaviours regarding some aspects of the organisation, resulting in manifestations of the culture being at times inconsistent.

Direct exporting This takes the form of a company producing and selling goods to foreign customers.

Discrimination Differential treatment of people in the same situation due to their membership of different groups.

Distributive justice The perception of the fairness of a decision that has been made in terms of that decision's outcomes.

Divergence, cultural *see* cultural divergence.

Diversity being different or varied. This is normally conceptualised using dimensions that are particularly relevant to an individual employee's identity such as gender, age, ethnicity, disability and sexual orientation.

Diversity, managing *see* managing diversity.

Diversity management Ensuring every member of the workforce has the opportunity to perform to his or her full potential. Diversity is therefore seen as a resource to be managed and used to improve organisational performance and competitive advantage.

Double-loop learning In contrast to single-loop learning, double-loop learning is the term used to explain the learning process where the main focus is not on improving current practice but on questioning the very basis of established practice. So, for example, if an HRD intervention fails to result in improved employee performance, rather than simply looking to see how that training intervention might be made more effective, the relevance of HRD itself in that situation might be challenged. *See also* single-loop learning.

Downsizing *see* organisational downsizing.

Downstream Denotes a later stage. When applied to rational strategic planning this would denote, say, that functional strategies developed to support corporate strategy would lie downstream from that corporate strategy. When applied to SHRM it denotes, for example, that strategic recruitment and selection lies downstream from the organisational competences it is designed to secure. Developing line management competence to manage their human resources would be a downstream activity necessitated by a prior decision to introduce SHRM.

Emergent strategy A strategy that evolves over time and as such has not been carefully planned. Such strategies can emerge from, for example, unexpected outcomes from the pursuit of a deliberate strategy or from initiatives developed at a local level that grow to take a hold over the organisation as a whole.

Employability A perspective on the employment relationship in which the onus is placed on the individual to ensure sufficient training and experience in order to remain attractive in the labour market. The employer may provide development opportunities but it is up to the individual to take advantage of them.

Employee behaviours This term refers to the repertoire of attitudes and actions held and performed by employees in pursuit of their duties.

Employee involvement A unitarist and business-centred concept, fostered by employer and managerial interests, designed to generate employee commitment and contribution. Employee involvement encompasses a range of practices that are focused directly on employees including forms of communicative involvement, task-level involvement and financial involvement, and is affected by managerial actions and styles of leadership.

Employee participation Power-centred concept, advanced by trade unions and through legislation in some cases. The focus is to allow employees to have a mechanism for offering their views about managerial proposals.

Employee relation/industrial relations These are not simply different terms for the same activities; they denote a significant change of emphasis. Concern with industrial relations developed when the emphasis was on collective relationships within industry, such as engineering, teaching, etc. Each business within that industry observed the terms and conditions agreed between employers' representatives and unions, which bound each employer. Employee relations have little regard for industry criteria and focus on collective or individual arrangements at the organisational, workplace or team/departmental levels.

Employee share ownership schemes A type of share incentive scheme whereby a special trust is established to purchase company shares.

Employee voice A term used to denote a series of practices (e.g. suggestion schemes) designed to ensure that employees have an input into the running of their organisation.

Employment relationship Economic, legal, social, psychological and political relationships in which employees devote their time and expertise to the interests of their employer in return for a range of financial and non-financial rewards and benefits.

Empowerment The granting to all staff of an organisation of as much scope for decision-making as feasible within the framework for a strategy.

End-loaded investment model Where the majority of financial investment in HR is directed at managing the performance of employees once recruited. This anticipates low levels of investment in the recruitment and selection process with more significant expenditure being sanctioned to rectify performance problems arising from unsatisfactory recruits.

Equal opportunities An approach to diversity management that is compliance based, values equality, and focuses on avoiding unfair disadvantage to specific groups utilising legislation and targeted group initiatives to try to ensure that differences do not result in unjust or prejudicial treatment.

Equality Being equal in status, rights and opportunities. Avoiding unfair disadvantage based on membership of a disadvantaged group and ensuring that each person has an equal chance to make a distinctive contribution.

Espoused value A value of a culture connected with moral and ethical codes that determines what people think ought to be done, rather than what they necessarily will do.

Ethnocentric orientation The main orientation of the MNC, here, is to direct foreign operations from parent-country HQ. Key jobs at both HQ and local operations are held by parent-country nationals.

European Foundation for Quality Management model (EFQM) European Excellence model This model posits that business results are a function of leadership driving people management, resources, and policy and strategy, which in turn drive business processes. The outcome is people satisfaction, customer satisfaction and, through these, business results.

Evaluation A process involving the systematic collection of data that are subsequently analysed, the findings being presented in a meaningful and useful form and contributing to organisational decision-making and improvement. This is sometimes referred to as planned evaluation or formal evaluation.

Evaluation, formative Evaluation where the focus is on improving and fine tuning. For formative evaluations, data collection is often part of regular ongoing monitoring of performance.

Evaluation, informal A process by which decisions are likely to be based on 'gut feeling' or unmethodical processes rather than the systematic collection, analysis and presentation of data.

Evaluation, summative Evaluation that occurs towards the later stages of a project, such as to assess impact, determine the extent to which goals have been met, or establish whether to continue with an intervention. For summative evaluations, data collection is unlikely to part of regular ongoing monitoring of performance.

Evaluation of human resource development *see* human resource development (HRD) evaluation.

Evaluation of recruitment and selection Where the return on investment in recruitment and selection processes and decisions is assessed to measure their effectiveness. Evaluation can take place at a number of levels, from assessing individual components of the process, e.g. the cost-effectiveness of advertising; the suitability of recruits; and the strategic contribution of the process.

Expatriates These employees are not citizens of the countries in which they are working.

Experiment Evaluation strategy that involves the definition of a theoretical hypothesis; the selection of samples of individuals from known populations; the allocation of samples to different experimental conditions; the introduction of planned change on one or more of the variables; and measurement on a small number of variables and control of other variables.

External labour supply The external labour market available to an organisation, comprising those available for work or those employed by other organisations.

External strategic integration *see* vertical strategic integration.

Fitting the job to the person Where the focus of recruitment and selection is on recruiting against sets of desired attributes or skills and then constructing, or allocating, jobs around those attributes or skills once recruited in order to maximise their utilisation.

Fitting the person to the job Where the attributes or skills necessary to effectively perform a job are identified first and then applicants and candidates are assessed against these attributes and selected where they fit this specification.

Fitting the person to the organisation Where the prime concern of recruitment and selection is to recruit employees against a set of organisational competences and values derived from the organisation's strategic objectives. Here, fit with the organisation takes precedence over the person–job fit where the fitting the job to the person approach is more likely to be adopted.

Foreign direct investment (FDI) This involves a company gaining a controlling interest in a foreign company, usually through acquiring 30 per cent or more of the foreign company's equity.

Formal (leader, organisation, system) A term used to designate a set of organisational relationships that are explicitly established in policy and procedures (e.g. the formal organisation). The term has been prefixed to many types of organisational phenomena.

Formal evaluation *see* evaluation.

Formative evaluation *see* evaluation, formative.

Fragmentation perspective Perspective that little consensus can be detected, regarding beliefs held and behaviours expected across all members of, for example, an organisation.

Franchising This is a type of licensing agreement whereby the franchiser allows the franchisee to use the franchiser's intellectual property to undertake a specific business activity.

Front-loaded investment model Where a significant financial investment in HR is made at the point of entry, i.e. recruitment and selection, in order to avoid letting unsatisfactory recruits into the organisation. This anticipates that lower levels of investment in managing the poor performance of unsatisfactory recruits will be necessary because of more effective selection in the first place.

Functional The terms used to describe those parts of an organisation that promote the attainment of goals. It comes from a mode of organisational analysis that seeks to explain organisations by understanding the effects that parts of the organisation have on one another and the mutual effect between the organisation and its environment.

Gainsharing Reward schemes designed so that employees share the financial results of improvements in productivity, cost saving or quality. The resultant payment is paid from cost savings generated as a result of such improvements.

Gap analysis In human resource planning terms, the difference in quantitative and qualitative terms between an organisation's demand for labour and its internal supply of labour. *See also* human resource planning (HRP).

Geocentric orientation The major concern of the MNC, here, is to employ the best people in key positions, irrespective of nationality.

Global mind-set A state of mind achieved by managers who are able effectively to work across organisational, functional and cross-cultural boundaries.

Hard human resource planning Where the human resource planning emphasis is on treating employees as resources to be exploited for the benefit of the organisation. There is a focus on the efficient, cost-effective, utilisation of employees through the exercise of management control and prerogative within a unitarist framework.

Hero A person associated with a well-known story about a culture's past whose actions are said to be a manifestation of that culture. Heroes are relatively easy to discern but the true cultural meaning may be difficult to decipher because of the story's shallow or superficial nature.

High-commitment management practices Involves such SHRM techniques as employee communication, employee involvement and profit sharing, designed to generate high employee performance and commitment to the job and the organisation.

High-performance work systems Management practices designed to provide employees with the skills, information, incentives and responsibility to make their own decisions, necessary for innovation, quality improvement and responses to change.

Horizontal integration A term that refers to integration between the various HR policies, procedures and practices (sometimes called 'internal' integration). *See also* horizontal strategic integration.

Horizontal strategic integration Where the activities of an organisation are not only directed at helping to achieve corporate strategy but where they interact with each other in a cohesive way. When applied to SHRM this refers to where the HR function integrates with other business functions and where the activities making up HR (such as HRP, R&S, performance management, HRD, reward management, employee relations, organisation structure, etc.) are developed as a coherent bundle so that they operate in a mutually reinforcing way to help deliver an organisation's strategic intent.

Host-country nationals (HCNs) These employees are citizens of the host country in which their employing organisation is operating (e.g. a Chinese working at VW in China).

Human capital The accumulated knowledge, skills experience and competence residing within the workforce that represents an intangible asset that adds value to the organisation. It can be argued that the overriding purpose of HRD is to increase an organisation's human capital.

Human relations school This school of thought argues that social relationships at work are an important determinant of employee productivity.

Human resource (HR) activities All those individual activities that come under the HR banner and are performed by managers and/or specialist staff, such as culture management, organisation restructuring, human resource planning, recruitment and selection, performance appraisals, etc.

Human resource (HR) consultants Support line managers with advice on the HR aspects of their roles.

Human resource development (HRD) Those organisational activities and interventions directly associated with developing its employees that, when employed generically, can be seen to cover education, learning and training.

Human resource development (HRD) evaluation Where the return on investment in human resource development processes and decisions is assessed to measure its effectiveness. Evaluation can take place at a number of different levels from, for example, a satisfaction rating of different HRD interventions, changes in the performance of trainees resulting from their HRD experiences to the strategic contribution of the HRD process.

Human resource development (HRD) function A dedicated unit, or part of an HR department, staffed by HRD specialists whose role is to support the organisation and its managers in the development of its employees.

Human resource development (HRD) stakeholders Stakeholders are all those people, groups and other organisations that have a vested interest in an organisation (i.e. those with a stake in that organisation) and can exert influence in it or be affected by it. When applied to HRD it refers to those who have a stake in the process and are affected by its outcomes.

Human resource forecasting Process of calculating the future *demand* for and *supply* of human resources in both quantitative and qualitative terms. Demand forecasting involves translating corporate strategic objectives into the human resource requirements needed to achieve that strategy using a variety of forecasting techniques. Supply forecasting involves calculating the internal supply of labour available to the organisation over the plan period, using such techniques as labour wastage analysis and demographic profiling, as well as the external labour supply available through the external labour market.

Human resource (HR) philosophy A term based on the well-known mission statement that portrays to stakeholders something of the nature of the organisation.

Human resource planning (HRP) As part of a staged process it means the development, implementation and evaluation of a coherent bundle of HR strategies designed to reconcile any mismatch between the organisation's projected demand for and supply of labour surfaced through gap analysis. More broadly, it can be interpreted as the process for securing the human capability to shape and achieve corporate strategic objectives.

Human resource preservation Steps taken by an organisation to retain the investment it has made in recruiting and developing its internal labour force. The emphasis is on reducing labour turnover and wastage and/or keeping it within acceptable parameters.

Human resource utilisation Steps taken by an organisation to reap the dividend from its investment in its labour force. From a hard human resource planning perspective this can be interpreted as getting more from less from the efficient utilisation of employees. A soft human resource planning perspective moves the emphasis from making labour more productive to 'winning hearts and minds' so that employees commit to the organisation and 'go the extra mile' willingly.

Incremental change Change that occurs gradually, dealing with one issue or part of the organisation at a time. Such change involves distinct modifications rather than radical changes.

Indirect discrimination Differential treatment of people in the same situation, where acting neutrally would put a person at a disadvantage due to their membership of a particular group or groups.

Indirect exporting This may be a domestic manufacturer importing goods from a foreign exporter, who then incorporates these goods as components in the manufacture of a product, which may in turn be exported.

Individualism An approach to the management of the employment relationship which assumes a one-to-one relationship with that employee's manager. It refers to the will of the individual to look after his or her own interests rather than relying on another person or body to do this for him or her and the desire of the employer to deal with his or her employees in the way he or she sees fit without outside interest.

Individualism versus communitarianism A cultural dimension used by Trompenaars and Hampden-Turner that relates to relationships with people and, in particular, emphasises that societies can be individualistic or collectivist.

Individualism–collectivism A cultural dimension used by Hofstede that relates to the views societies have about preferred ways of social organisation, as individual members or collective groups.

Industrial relations *see* employee relations.

Informal (leader, group, organisation, system) Term used to designate the set of organisational relationships that emerge over time from the day-to-day experiences that people have with one another. Informal relationships are expressive of the needs that people actually feel in situations, in contrast to the needs leaders think they should feel.

Informal evaluation *see* evaluation, informal.

Information asymmetry This occurs when managers control all the information relevant to performance management.

Informational justice The perception of the fairness of a decision that has been made in terms of the information received, in particular the explanations received during the implementation of the decision. Also considered a type of interactional justice.

Inner directed v. outer directed A cultural dimension used by Trompenaars and Hampden-Turner that relates to attitudes to the environment.

Institutional integration Where the human resource function is strategically integrated into the organisation and is more likely to occur where the head of function is a board-level appointment. This ensures that a meaningful dialogue about the relationship between people and strategy will take place.

Institutional racism 'The collective failure of an organisation to provide an appropriate and professional service to people because of their colour, culture or ethnic origin' (MacPherson, 1999: para. 6.34).

Integration The state of collaboration that exists among departments that are required to achieve unity of effort by demands of the environment. The term is primarily used in relation to contingency approaches to organisational design.

Integration perspective Perspective that all members of, for example, an organisation share a common culture with consensus regarding beliefs held and behaviours expected.

Intellectual capital The utilisation of human capital by an organisation to generate tangible benefits that can help it to obtain a business advantage and comprises such things as inventions, patents, market brands, reputation, problem solving, and research and development capability.

Intellectual property rights These may include technical expertise, patents, commercial knowledge and, most importantly, brand names.

Inter-unit linkages This refers to the way in which the MNC differentiates its operating units throughout the world and at the same time integrates, controls and coordinates its activities.

Interactional justice The perception of the fairness of a decision that has been made in terms of the treatment received during the implementation of that decision. Also considered a type of procedural justice. *See also* informational justice, interpersonal justice.

Internal labour supply That labour supply available to an organisation from its existing workforce in both quantitative and qualitative terms.

Internal strategic integration *see* horizontal strategic integration.

International investment This applies to the transfer by companies of resources in order that they may undertake business outside their country of origin.

International trade This term refers to the export and import of goods and services.

Internationalisation The increased interaction between national units, most often in international business transactions, taking the form of exports or foreign direct investment.

Interpersonal justice The perception of the fairness of a decision that has been made in terms of the interpersonal treatment received during the implementation of the decision. Also considered a type of interactional justice.

Interview Data collection technique in which an interviewer physically meets the respondent, asks him or her questions, and records the responses.

Interview, semi-structured Wide-ranging category of interview in which the interviewer commences with a set of interview themes but is prepared to vary the order in which questions are asked and to ask new questions in the context of the research situation.

Interview, structured Data collection technique in which an interviewer physically meets the respondent, reads them the same set of questions in a predetermined order, and records his or her response to each.

Interview, unstructured Loosely structured and informally conducted interview that may commence with one or more themes to explore with participants but without a predetermined list of questions to work through.

Job analysis The formalised study of how a job is conducted in order to determine the way of most effectively combining the job operations with the human capacities of the job holder, its operating environment and the use of tools and equipment necessary to perform the job. From a job analysis it is possible to construct a job description and person specification.

Job description A formal document, normally drafted following the job analysis, that summarises important dimensions of a job including: its overall purpose; performance objectives; key tasks; reporting relationships; responsibilities for staff; and financial or tangible resources. It may also include reference to the main terms and conditions of employment.

Job evaluation A systematic assessment of job content. It establishes the worth of a job in terms of salary or wage compared to other jobs.

Job family This is a group of jobs that may be similar in purpose and content although carried out at different levels in the organisation.

Knowledge-based economy An economy where the utilisation of existing and new knowledge is the basis for economic performance and success as opposed to adding value through the classic factors of: production capital; labour; and materials. Such economies are characterised by a high proportion of knowledge workers.

Knowledge economy *see* knowledge-based economy.

Knowledge management The development of human, intellectual and social capital as a route to securing sustainable competitive advantage based on knowledge utilisation, creation and transfer within an organisation.

Knowledge transfer The transfer of knowledge within an organisation so that it becomes available for others to utilise. Through transfer, it prevents knowledge from being simply locked up in employees' heads and lost to the organisation if those employees should depart. Within HRD, knowledge transfer assumes great importance as it is the transfer and subsequent use of know-how that can be the key to successful HRD interventions.

Knowledge workers Employees whose work requires the utilisation of their existing knowledge base, and the acquisition and utilisation of new knowledge in order to enhance organisational efficiency, effectiveness and innovation. Such workers would be expected to continuously learn from their experiences and to actively engage in knowledge transfer.

Labour preservation *see* human resource preservation.

Labour utilisation *see* human resource utilisation.

Layoff *see* redundancy.

Learning culture A culture residing within an organisation that promotes and facilitates individual, workgroup and organisational learning and development. The creation of a learning environment can constitute a key organisational capability.

Learning organisation An organisation that develops a capacity to learn more quickly than its rivals and that utilises that capacity to continually adapt itself to its business environment in order to secure sustainable competitive advantage.

Licensing This involves the licenser allowing the licensee to use the licenser's intellectual property rights in return for a fee.

Linear/sequential v. circular/synchronic A cultural dimension used by Trompenaars and Hampden-Turner that relates to attitudes to time.

Long-term–short-term orientation dimension (national culture) A cultural orientation that relates to the attitude that people have about long-term decisions, such as investment in training and development. Some countries traditionally have a focus on the future as opposed to those countries that have a shorter-term view.

Longitudinal The study of a particular phenomenon (or phenomena) over an extended period of time.

Managerialism A model of managing that assumes that management will conceive and implement strategies without considering the perspective of employees.

Managing diversity An approach to diversity management that focuses upon recognising both visible and non-visible differences between individuals and building upon the advantages they offer, rather than utilising legislation and targeted group initiatives to try to ensure that differences do not result in unjust or prejudicial treatment.

Manpower planning The precursor to human resource planning that essentially reflected a 'downstream', tactical response to strategy and emphasised a 'hard', quantitative approach with a focus on forecasting and controlling labour to ensure its efficient utilisation.

Market rate The 'standard' rate paid by employing organisations for a given occupation against which organisations may compare their pay rates.

Masculinity–femininity A cultural dimension used by Hofstede that relates to the importance societies put upon the values assertiveness or caring for others.

Matching models of SHRM closed There is a clear and mutually supportive relationship between organisational strategy and HR strategy and this relationship gives rise to the implementation of *specific* HR initiatives. That is to say the match between the organisational strategy and HR strategy is closed and prescribed in the sense that a particular type of organisational strategy suggests the need for a specific HR strategy and set of practices.

Matching models of SHRM open An approach that assumes the existence of a clear and mutually supportive relationship between organisational strategy and HR strategy. However, it differs from the closed approach in that the HR strategy initiatives should not be prescribed, following from the organisational strategy, but should be left open. The degree to which the HR strategy is truly 'strategic' is a test of its appropriateness to the organisational strategy.

Matrix organisation An approach for integrating the activities of different specialists while maintaining specialised organisational units.

Mergers and acquisitions Mergers involve the combination of two or more organisational entities of roughly equal standing into a new business entity, whereas acquisitions involve the takeover of one business entity by another.

Multi-national company (MNC) This type of organisation is characterised by the globalisation of its management systems, perspectives and approaches to strategic decisions.

Multi-stakeholder (approach to recruitment and selection) Stakeholders are all those people, groups and other organisations that have a vested interest in an organisation (i.e. those with a stake in that organisation) and can exert influence in it or be affected by it. When applied to recruitment and selection it refers to those who have a stake in the process and are affected by its outcomes, for example internal and external customers, managers, peers (particularly fellow group members), subordinates and HR professionals.

National culture The patterns of beliefs, values and learned ways of coping with experiences that have developed during the course of a nation's history, and which tend to be manifested in its material arrangements and in the behaviours of its members (after Brown, 1998).

Network organisation An organisational structure that involves managing an interrelated set of organisations, each specialising in a specific business function or task. The structure extends beyond the boundaries of any single organisation and involves linking different organisations to facilitate inter-organisational exchange and task coordination.

Neutral versus emotional A cultural dimension used by Trompenaars and Hampden-Turner that relates to relationships with people and, in particular, the extent to which it is acceptable to express emotions publicly, such as within interpersonal communications.

New-style managerialism This is characterised by less concern for the technical side of individuals' jobs than by talking to them about the help that is needed for them to do their jobs. The new-style manager is supportive, a team leader, a coach and facilitator. This is a style of management that is concerned with processes as well as outputs.

Non-financial rewards This term includes such factors as achievement, recognition, responsibility, influence and personal growth.

Observation The systematic observation, recording, description, analysis and interpretation of people's behaviour.

Observation, participant Observation in which the researcher attempts to participate fully in the lives and activities of the research subjects and thus becomes a member of the subjects' group(s), organisation(s) or community.

Observation, structured Observation in which the researcher observes and records the same predetermined set of activities or actions and records them, usually on a schedule.

One-way strategic integration (or linkage) Vertical (or external) strategic integration where, 'downstream', functions are shaped and managed to meet the strategic objectives passed down to them. Under this prescription the HR function would be charged with helping to achieve the, 'upstream', corporate strategy.

Open question *see* question, open.

Organic organisation This type of organisation is relatively flexible and relaxed. The organic style is most appropriate to unstable environmental conditions in which novel problems continually occur.

Organisation redesign strategy A downsizing strategy that, in addition to reducing headcount, involves elements of de-layering, eliminating areas of work and job redesign, so the amount of work is also reduced.

Organisational capabilities *see* core capabilities and core competence.

Organisational capability This focuses on the organisation's internal processes, systems and management practices to meet customer needs and directing the skills and efforts of the employees to achieving the goals of the organisation.

Organisational citizenship behaviour (OCB) The readiness of an employee to contribute to the organisation beyond that required by her or his contract.

Organisational culture 'The patterns of beliefs, values and learned ways of coping with experiences that have developed during the course of an organisation's history, and which tend to be manifested in its material arrangements and in the behaviours of its members' (Brown, 1998: 9).

Organisational design Involves bringing about a coherence or fit among organisational choices about strategy, organising mode, and the mechanisms for integrating people into the organisation. The greater the fit among these organisational dimensions, the greater will be the organisational effectiveness.

Organisational downsizing An organisational strategy to reduce the size of an organisation's workforce that may use a range of methods including early retirements, natural wastage, and voluntary and compulsory redundancy to achieve this outcome.

Organisational justice A set of related theories focusing on perceptions about fairness in organisations that seeks to categorise and explain the views and feelings of employees about their own treatment and that of others within an organisation. *See also* distributive justice; interactional justice; procedural justice.

Organisational re-orientation strategy An alternative name for organisation redesign strategies and systemic change strategies.

Output goals Relates to the product of the employee's performance.

Parent-country nationals (PCNs) A term used to denote the home country of an employee that is the same as the parent company (e.g. a German working for VW in China).

Participant observation *see* observation, participant.

Partnership An approach to trade union recognition and involvement in an employing organisation, where there is joint commitment by management and unions to work for its successive development, implying a model of mutual gain for the employer, employees and union.

Pay range Attached to each job grade, it specifies the minimum and maximum pay rates payable for any job in the grade and the points between the minimum and maximum rates.

Performance appraisal A process where an individual's performance and progress are assessed and performance feedback is given. Pay, promotions and training needs are often based on the information provided by the appraisal.

Performance culture Usually used to characterise an organisational culture in which employees have to perform; have to make a difference.

Performance feedback Information on the employee's performance usually given by the immediate manager.

Performance indicators Indicators of what may constitute effective performance, often expressed in numerical form.

Performance management A strategic and integrated approach to delivering sustained success to organisations by improving the performance of people who work in them and by developing the capabilities of teams and individual contributors.

Performance measurement The process of assessing performance against predetermined measures of performance. Based on key success factors which may include measures of deviation from the 'norm', measures to track past achievements and measures of output and input.

Person specification A formal document that specifies the personal attributes and skills required by prospective employees in order to effectively perform jobs as detailed in a job description.

Pilot test Small-scale study to test a data collection technique to minimise the likelihood of respondents having problems in answering the questions and of data recording problems, as well as to allow some assessment of the questions' validity and the reliability of the data that will be collected.

Planned evaluation *see* evaluation.

Pluralism A way of thinking about employee relations that conceptualises the organisation as being a 'miniature democratic state composed of sectional groups with divergent interests over which government tries to maintain some kind of dynamic equilibrium' (Fox, 1966). The most fundamental of these sectional groups is managers and employees. Many of the traditional institutions, principles, procedures, processes and practices that exist to manage the employment relationship are based on the principle of pluralism.

Polycentric orientation Here the MNC treats each separate foreign operation as a distinct national entity with some decision-making autonomy. Foreign subsidiaries manage local operations, albeit they are seldom promoted to parent-country HQ.

Positive action Encouragement for under-represented groups to apply for vacancies and promotions, and to participate in development opportunities.

Positive discrimination Preferential treatment for under-represented groups, also known as reverse discrimination. Positive discrimination is unlawful in the UK.

Power distance A cultural dimension used by Hofstede that relates to the views societies have about the exercise of power in organisations.

Practices A collective noun for the visible artefacts of culture symbols, heroes and rituals.

Procedural justice Theory concerned with perceptions about the fairness of the procedures and processes used to arrive at organisational decisions. *See also* distributive justice; interactional justice.

Process consultation The process where the consultant assists the client to perceive, understand and act upon the process events that occur within his or her environment in order to improve the situation as the client sees it.

Process goals Relates to the way in which employees perform their duties.

Profit-related bonus schemes Bonus schemes that reward employees according to the level of profit generated by their employing organisation.

Psychological contract The expectations of employee and employer, which operate in addition to the formal contract of employment. It therefore is concerned with each party's perceptions of what the other party to the employment relationship owes them. *See also* relational aspects; transactional aspects.

Psychometric model of recruitment and selection This model is based on the premise that it is possible to determine, through job analysis, the nature of jobs and the human qualities associated with their effective performance, and that these qualities can be measured in people so that their future job performance can be predicted.

Qualitative HR forecasting Forecasting the 'soft' human resource requirements (demand), and their availability (supply), necessitated by an organisation's strategic objectives. The emphasis is on the qualities required of an organisation's human resources, such as competences or skills, knowledge or intellectual capital, attitudes and values.

Quantitative HR forecasting Forecasting the 'hard' human resource requirements (demand), and their availability (supply), necessitated by an organisation's strategic objectives. The emphasis is on the numbers of employees required and their distribution across grades and jobs.

Question, closed Question that provides a number of alternative answers from which the respondent is instructed to choose.

Question, open Question allowing respondents to give answers in their own way.

Questionnaire General term, including all data collection techniques, in which each person is asked to respond to the same set of questions in a predetermined order.

Rational economic person A term used to describe a person who acts to obtain the highest possible well-being for him- or herself.

Realistic job preview The steps taken by an organisation to present potential applicants and shortlisted candidates with an honest and accurate portrayal of the job and its organisational context so that they may make informed decisions throughout the recruitment and selection process. It is a 'warts and all' approach. The rationale for this approach is that both parties need to be satisfied with their decision for recruitment to be deemed effective.

Recruitment Those activities performed to create a pool of applicants for a job vacancy from which subsequent selection can take place. At a more general level, and confusingly, the term can be used to mean the whole of the recruitment and selection process.

Redundancy This is defined in UK law as a dismissal due, wholly or mainly, to the complete closure of a business; the closure of the employee's workplace; or a diminishing need for employees to do work of a particular kind in the business as a whole, or at the employee's particular workplace.

Relational aspects Aspects of the psychological contract between an employee and an employer that focus upon mutual trust and commitment. *See also* psychological contract.

Reliability The extent to which the method produces the same result (e.g. measure of human attributes) irrespective of who is doing the measuring and when it is performed. For example, high reliability in interviews would mean that a candidate would be assessed similarly irrespective of who conducted the interview or when it was conducted.

Resource-based theory *see* resource-based view of the firm.

Resource-based view of the firm View presented as an alternative to the traditional view of strategy. Under the traditional view, strategy formulation is seen as a process of analysing the external environment of an organisation in order to devise a strategic direction that matches the opportunities that this offers. In contrast, the resource-based view shifts this perspective so that strategy making focuses on the internal capabilities of an organisation, including its people, so that these can be used as the basis of its strategic direction.

Reverse discrimination *see* positive discrimination.

Reward How people are rewarded in accordance with their value to the organisation. It is concerned with both financial and non-financial rewards and embraces the philosophies, strategies, policies, plans and processes used by organisations to develop and maintain reward systems.

Ritual A visible practice that is said to be a manifestation of a culture that is relatively easy to discern but from which the true meaning is difficult to decipher because of its shallow or superficial nature.

Scientific approach Approach that involves the systematic observation of and experiment with phenomena.

Secondary data Data used for evaluation that were originally collected for some other purpose.

Selection That part of the recruitment and selection process that assesses or measures the suitability of applicants for shortlisting or candidates for employment against the job description and person specification. There are many different selection methods that can be used to do this but arguably shortlisting from application forms and/or CVs, interviews and references are the most widely known and applied.

Semi-structured interview *see* interview, semi-structured.

Single-loop learning The learning process where the main focus is on improving current practice through operating a continual cycle of detecting errors in current practice, identifying potential areas for improvement and making incremental enhancements to work operations. *See also* double-loop learning.

Social capital The processes that facilitate intra- and inter-group cooperation that help translate human capital into intellectual capital, such as social networks and shared values, norms and understandings.

Soft human resource planning (HRP) Where the HRP emphasis is on treating employees as resourceful humans and on developing employee capability to the mutual benefit of both employees and employers. There is a focus on integrating employee values, beliefs and behaviours with organisational goals through culture management within a pluralistic framework.

Sophisticated selection The use of selection methods with demonstrable high reliability and predictive validity that may, at times, need to be tailor-made to obtain such measurements of particular attributes, for example honesty. As a consequence, they are relatively expensive and more likely to be used by organisations adopting a front-loaded investment model for recruitment and selection.

Specific versus diffuse A cultural dimension used by Trompenaars and Hampden-Turner that relates to relationships with people and, in particular, the relative importance ascribed by different cultures to focusing on the specific, for example analysing issues by reducing them to specific facts, tasks, numbers or bullet points.

Strategic business unit The units responsible for making strategy in a particular product area.

Strategic human resource development (SHRD) Where the thrust of an organisation's HRD processes and interventions are primarily directed at supporting the achievement of the organisation's strategic goals, as opposed to focusing on tactical responses to training needs identified at the level of individual employees.

Strategic human resource management (SHRM) Combines a stress on the integration of personnel policies both one with another and with business planning more generally.

Strategic human resource planning In essence, this means the same as human resource planning but where the addition of the word 'strategic' not only mirrors changes to HR terminology more generally but is also used to differentiate the process from short-term, tactical HRP approaches that are directed at resolving the human resource demands arising from operational concerns.

Strategic integration The state where the varied activities of a business are aligned to serve the overall strategic direction of the organisation, or the process of securing this alignment.

Strategic international human resource management (SIHRM) This relates to the HRM policies and practices that result from the strategic activities of MNCs and the impact that SIHRM has on the international concerns and goals of those organisations.

Strategic management Processes adopted and decisions and actions taken by an organisation that result in formulating, implementing and evaluating its chosen strategy.

Strategic planning Process of determining organisational strategy that involves making conscious choices between a number of different alternatives. The orthodox view reasons that strategy is formulated at the top of the organisation through a deliberate, rational process. An alternative perspective argues that strategy makers do not always act rationally, and that strategy may emerge over time so that it only becomes apparent through trying to make a pattern out of prior events.

Strategic recruitment and selection Whereas, under psycho-metric traditions, recruitment and selection is primarily directed at filling jobs with suitable employees, the strategic variant primarily seeks to recruit employees to help achieve the organisation's strategic goals. Such an approach places priority on the person–organisation fit rather than the person–job fit.

Strategic reward management Contributes to the achieve-ment of the organisation's overall strategy through the delivery of specific employee behaviours that are consistent with the organisation's overall strategy.

Strategy A deliberate course of action taken by an organisa-tion in order to utilise its resources to meet its long-term objectives developed to exploit opportunities presented by its external and internal environment.

Strategy formulation *see* strategic planning.

Strategy making *see* strategic planning.

Stretch goals Clear and challenging goals that lead to higher job performance.

Structure The formal arrangement of the different parts of an organisation and their interrelationships.

Structured interview *see* interview, structured.

Structured observation *see* observation, structured.

Summative evaluation *see* evaluation, summative.

Survey Evaluation strategy that involves the structured col-lection of data from a sizeable population. Although the term 'survey' is often used to describe the collection of data using questionnaires, it includes other techniques such as struc-tured observation and structured interviews.

Symbol A manifestation of a culture that is relatively easy to discern but from which the true meaning is difficult to deci-pher because of its shallow or superficial nature. Material objects, physical layouts and events are often described as symbols. See *also* artefact.

Systematic approach to training A term used to represent, or model, a particular approach to HRD (or training) that reflects a continuous cycle of identifying HRD needs, plan-ning and designing HRD interventions to address identified needs, implementing these HRD interventions and evaluat-ing their outcomes.

Systemic change strategy A downsizing strategy that, in addition to reducing headcount and involving elements of delayering, eliminating areas of work and job redesign, takes a long-term approach.

Tacit knowledge That implicit (as opposed to explicit) knowledge, which it is difficult or impossible to put it into words because it comprises intuition, values, etc. that are highly personal and relate to particular contexts.

Team-based pay Payments, or other forms of non-financial reward, are made to team members on the basis of some pre-determined criteria.

Temporal focus Time span of an organisation's focus and is frequently translated into three perspectives: short term; medium term; and long term. The locus of responsibility for personnel management no longer resides with specialist managers but is assumed by senior line management. The focus shifts from management–trade union relations to management–employee relations, from collectivism to indi-vidualism. There is stress on commitment and the exercise of initiative, with managers now donning the role of 'enabler', 'empowerer' and 'facilitator'.

Third-country nationals (TCNs) These employees are not citizens of the countries in which they are working and are not citizens of the country of the parent company (e.g. a UK employee working for a German organisation operating in China).

Top down Typically initiated and led by senior management.

Total reward This combines the traditional pay and benefits elements with the other factors that employees gain from employment. These may be skills, experience, opportunity and recognition. Total reward takes into account the less tan-gible benefits of employment.

Trade union Collective organisation of employees, a trade union's central function is to protect the interests of its mem-bers and to participate in job regulation of relations between these employees and their employer.

Training Planned actions (or interventions) designed to increase employees' job-related knowledge, skills and atti-tudes in order to enhance their performance in that job.

Training and development A term gradually being replaced by human resource development that embraces not only job-related training but also those actions that are oriented towards the future and designed to help employees towards personal growth and the realisation of their potential.

Transactional aspects Aspects of the psychological contract between an employee and an employer that focus upon the mutual instrumentality of the work–effort reward bargain. *See also* psychological contract; relational aspects.

Transformational change Change that is radical and overturns the status quo, often occurring throughout an organisation.

Triple-loop learning A learning process where the main focus is on the processes of learning itself (i.e. learning to learn more effectively). Essentially it involves 'reviewing and reflecting on previous learning experiences and using such experiences as a basis for the formation of new learning activ-ities and insights' (Walton, 1999: 389). *See also* double-loop learning; single-loop learning.

Two-way strategic integration (or linkage) Vertical (or external) strategic integration where 'downstream' functions are not only shaped and managed to help achieve corporate strategy but may also operate to influence strategy formation itself. This creates a more synergistic perspective to strategy making.

Uncertainty avoidance A cultural dimension used by Hof-stede that relates to actions members of societies take in respect of ambiguous and uncertain situations.

Unitarism A view of the employment relationship which assumes that the employees of the organisation are seen as a team, unified by a common purpose, with all employees pur-suing the same goal; there is a single source of authority, that source being management. Since all employees are pursuing the same goal, conflict is irrational and it must be the result of poor communication or 'troublemakers' at work who do not share the common purpose. The presence of third parties to the employment relationship is intrusive, therefore there is no place for trade unions.

Universal models of strategic human resource management This suggests that there is 'one best way' of achieving HR effectiveness.

Universalism versus particularism A cultural dimension used by Trompenaars and Hampden-Turner that relates to relationships with people and, in particular, the rigidity in which contractual agreements and rules are important in defining individuals' conduct within the workplace, as well as in the relationships between organisations.

Unplanned evaluation *see* evaluation, informal.

Unstructured interview *see* interview, unstructured.

Upstream Denoting an earlier stage. So, when applied to rational strategic planning, corporate strategy making lies upstream of functional strategy making. However, these 'classic' relationships can be reversed. So if, for example, an organisation's core competence was based around the unique capabilities of its employees and it was that core competence that was driving strategy formulation, then core competences would lie upstream of corporate strategy making (or corporate strategy making would lie downstream from the organisation's core competence).

Upward feedback A process in which performance feedback is provided to line managers in advance of their own development discussions and formal performance reviews. Usually, every member of the manager's team has the opportunity to give feedback to their manager.

Validity When applied to recruitment and selection there are many different types of validity but most commonly it refers to the extent to which a selection method produces an accurate prediction of a candidate's future job performance if recruited.

Values *see* basic underlying assumptions.

Variable pay That amount of the employee's salary or wages that varies according to a variety of factors, such as performance bonuses.

Vertical integration A term that refers to the link between wider business strategy and HR strategy (sometimes called 'external' integration).

Vertical strategic integration Where the different levels of an organisation are strategically aligned in a one-way or two-way relationship. Taking Purcell's (1991) three orders (or levels) of strategy, comprising first-order corporate strategy; second-order strategies relating to structures and organisational processes; and functional strategies, these would be developed in such a way that they integrated one with another.

Voice The opportunity for the subjects of organisational design to participate in the process of arriving at, including being able to influence, these decisions.

Voluntary redundancy The volunteering of employees to be made redundant in response to either a general request or the specific targeting of individuals.

Workforce reduction strategy A downsizing strategy that focuses simply on reducing an organisation's headcount.

Work–life balance This is about people having a measure of control over when, where and how they work. It is achieved when an individual's right to a full life inside and outside paid work is accepted and respected.

References

Abernathy, W., Clark, K. and Kantrow, A. (1981) The new industrial competition, *Harvard Business Review*, October: 68–81.

Acas (2004) *Discipline and Grievance at Work*. London: Acas.

Acas (2005) *Appraisal Related Pay*. London: Acas. Available online http://www.acas.org.uk/publications/B10.html#2f

Accounting Standards Board (2005) *Reporting Standard 1: Operating and Financial Review* (cited 18 January 2006). Available online http://www.asb.org.uk/images/uploaded/documents/ACF345.pdf

Adams, G. and Schvaneveldt, J. (1991) *Understanding Research Methods* (2nd edn). New York: Longman.

Adams, J.S. (1965) Inequity in social exchange, in Berkowitz L. (ed.) *Advances in Experimental Social Psychology*, Vol. 2, pp. 267–299. New York: Academic Press.

Agocs, C. and Burr, C. (1996) Employment equity, affirmative action and managing diversity: assessing the differences, *International Journal of Manpower*, 17(4/5), 30–45.

Ainsworth, C. (1995) Strategic human resource planning at Zeneca Pharmaceuticals, *Management Development Review*, 8 (2), 11–15.

Alkin, M. (1969) Evaluation theory development, *Evaluation Comment*, 2, 2–7.

Allen, A. (2004) High fidelity, *People Management*, 10(21), 48–51.

Allen, A. (2005) Metric conversion, *Human Capital Management – Enterprise Value Driven by People Performance*, pp. 6–7. London: Oracle and People Management.

Allen, M. and Haynes, P. (1999) *Partnership Unionism: A Viable Strategy?* Presented at BUIRA Conference, De Montford University, Leicester, July.

Allen, T.D., Freeman, D.A., Russell, J.E.A., Reizwnstein, R.C. and Rentz, J.O. (2001) Survivor reactions to organizational downsizing: does time ease the pain? *Journal of Occupational and Organizational Psychology*, 74, 145–164.

Amit, R.H. and Schoemaker, P.J.H. (1993) Strategic assets and organizational rent, *Strategic Management Journal*, 14 (1), 33–46.

Anderson, V. and Boocock, G. (2002) Small firms and internationalisation: learning to manage and managing to learn, *Human Resource Management Journal*, 12(3), 5–24.

Angle, H. and Parry, J. (1986) Dual commitment and labour management relationship climates, *Academy of Management Journal*, 29(1), 31–50.

Ansoff, H.I. (1965) *Corporate Strategy*. Harmondsworth: Penguin.

Appelbaum, S.H. and Gandell, J. (2003) A cross method analysis of the impact of culture and communications upon a health care merger, *The Journal of Management Development*, 22(5), 370–409.

Argyris, C. (1960) *Understanding Organisational Behaviour*. Homewood, IL: Dorsey Press.

Argyris, C. (1994). Good communication that blocks learning, *Harvard Business Review*, July–August, 77–85.

Argyris, C. (1995) Action science and organizational learning, *Journal of Managerial Psychology*, 10(6), 20–26.

Argyris, C. and Schön, D.A. (1978) *Organizational Learning*. Reading, MA: Addison-Wesley.

Argyris, C. and Schön, D.A. (1996) *Organizational Learning II*. Reading, MA: Addison-Wesley.

Arkin, A. (2005) Eyes on the prize, *People Management*, 10 February, 29–35.

Armstrong, A. and Foley, P. (2003) Foundations for a learning organization: organization learning mechanisms, *The Learning Organization*, 10(2), 74–82.

Armstrong, M. (1993). *Managing Reward Systems*. Buckingham: Open University Press.

Armstrong, M. (2002). *Employee Reward* (3rd edn). London: Chartered Institute of Personnel and Development.

Armstrong, M. (2003) *A Handbook of Human Resource Management Practice* (9th edn). London: Kogan Page.

Armstrong, M. and Baron, A. (1998) *Performance Management: The New Realities*. Wimbledon: Chartered Institute of Personnel and Development.

Armstrong, M. and Murlis, H. (1998) *Reward Management: A Handbook of Remuneration Strategy and Practice* (4th edn). London: Kogan Page.

Armstrong-Stassen, M. (1994) Coping with transition: a study of layoff survivors, *Journal of Organizational Behaviour*, 15, 597–621.

Asch, D. and Salaman, G. (2002) The challenge of change, *European Business Journal*, 14(3), 133–143.

Ashton, D. and Felstead, A. (2001) From training to lifelong learning: the birth of the knowledge society, in Storey, J. (ed.) *Human Resource Management: A Critical Text* (2nd edn), pp. 165–189. London: Thomson Learning.

Atkinson, J. (1984) Manpower strategies for the flexible organisations, *Personnel Management*, August.

Bach, S. (2000) From performance appraisal to performance management, in Bach, S. and Sisson, K. (eds) *Personnel Management: A Comprehensive Guide to Theory and Practice* (3rd edn). Oxford: Blackwell.

Bach, S. and Sisson, K. (eds) (2000) *Personnel Management: A Comprehensive Guide to Theory and Practice* (3rd edn). Oxford: Blackwell.

Bain, G. (1983) *Industrial Relations in Britain*. Oxford: Basil Blackwell.

Bain, T. (2001) *Doing Business in a Multicultural Britain: The Business Case*. Presentation by MD of JP Morgan Chase and Head of War for Talent at Diversity Seminar, London.

Baird, L. and Meshoulam, I. (1988) Managing two fits of strategic human resource management, *Academy of Management Review*, 13(1), 116–128.

Barmes, L. and Ashtiany, S. (2003) The diversity approach to achieving equality: potential and pitfalls, *Industrial Law Journal*, 32(4), 274–296.

Barney, J.B. (1986) Organizational culture: can it be a source of sustained competitive advantage?, *Academy of Management Review*, 11(3), 656–665.

Barney, J.B. (1991) Firm resources and sustained competitive advantage, *Journal of Management*, 17(1), 99–120.

Barney, J.B. (1995) Looking inside for competitive advantage, *Academy of Management Executive*, 9(4), 49–61.

Baron, A. and Armstrong, M. (2004) Get into line, *People Management*, 14 October.

Bartol, K.M. and Martin, D.C. (1994). *Management* (2nd edn). Maidenhead: McGraw-Hill International.

Bartz, D. Hillman, L., Lehrer, S. and Mayburgh, G. (1990) A model for managing workforce diversity, *Management Education and Development*, 21(5), 321–326

Bass, B.M. (1990) From transactional to transformational leadership: learning to share the vision, *Organizational Dynamics*, Winter, 19–31.

Bate, P. (1995) *Strategies for Cultural Change*. Oxford: Butterworth-Heinemann.

Baumard, P. (1999) *Tacit Knowledge in Organisations*, London: Sage.

Baverman, H. (1974) *Labor and Monopoly Capital The Degradation of Work in the Twentieth Century*. New York and London: Monthly Review Press.

BBC Online (1999) Teachers threaten appraisal boycott, 26 March. Available online http://news.bbc.co.uk/1/hi/education/specials/green_paper/273294.stm

BBC Online (2001) Pre-Christmas strikes hit Eurostar, 21 December. Available online http://news.bbc.co.uk/1/hi/business/1719389.stm

BBC News Online (2002) Dyson moves to Far East, 5 February. Available online http://news.bbc.co.uk/1/hi/business/1801909.stm

BBC News Online (2003) Strike threat over call centre closure, 11 December. Available online http://news.bbc.co.uk/1/hi/england/tyne/3308617.stm

BBC News Online (2004a) Police plans to boost ethnic ranks, 17 April. Available online http://news.bbc.co.uk/go/pr/fr/-/hi/uk/3634085.stm

BBC News Online (2004b) Boots aims to shed 1,000 jobs, 11 January. Available online http://news.bbc.co.uk/1/hi/business/3386947.stm

BBC News Online (2004c) Nemo breaks half-billion barrier, 27 January. Available online http://news.bbc.co.uk/1/hi/entertainment/film/3433069.stm

BBC News Online (2004d) HSBC routes calls to Philippines, 14 April. Available online http://news.bbc.co.uk/1/hi/business/3624851.stm

BBC News Online (2004e) RBS grows in US with $10.5 bn buy, 5 May. Available online http://news.bbc.co.uk/1/hi/business/3685105.stm

BBC News Online (2004f) New York HQ for Virgin US airline, 8 June. Available online http://news.bbc.co.uk/1/hi/business/3787987.stm

BBC News Online (2004g) Kia gives nod to Slovak car plant, 2 March. Available online http://news.bbc.co.uk/2/hi/business/3524497.stm

BBC News Online (2005a) Profits triple at animator Pixar, 6 May. Available online http://news.bbc.co.uk/1/hi/business/4520181.stm

BBC News Online (2005b) Tesco profits break through £2bn, 12 April. Available online http://news.bbc.co.uk/1/hi/business/4435339.stm#tescomap

BBC News Online (2006) HSBC strike to go ahead on 27 May, 23 May. Available online http://news.bbc.co.uk/1/hi/business/4573635.stm

Beardwell, J. (2004) Human resource planning, in Beardwell, I., Holden, L. and Claydon, T. (eds) *Human Resource Management: A Contemporary Approach* (4th edn), pp. 157–188. Harlow: Financial Times Prentice Hall.

Beardwell, I. and Holden, L. (eds) (1997) *Human Resource Management: A Contemporary Perspective* (2nd edn). London: Pitman.

Beardwell, I., Holden, L. and Claydon, T. (eds) (2004) *Human Resource Management: A Contemporary Approach* (4th edn). Harlow: Financial Times Prentice Hall.

Beardwell, J. and Wright, M. (2004) Recruitment and selection, in Beardwell, I., Holden, L. and Claydon, T. (eds) *Human Resource Management: A Contemporary Approach* (4th edn) pp. 189–229. Harlow: Financial Times Prentice Hall.

Beaumont, P.B. (1995) The European Union and developments in industrial relations, in Gunnigle, P. and Roche, W.K. (eds) *New Challenges in Irish Industrial Relations*. Dublin: Oak Tree Press.

Beaumont, P.B. and Hunter, L.C. (1992) Competitive strategy, flexibility and selection: the case of Caledonian Paper, *Industrial Relations Journal*, 23(2), 222–228.

Beckhard, R. (1992) A model for the executive management of transformational change, in Salaman, G., Cameron, S., Hamblin, H., Iles, P., Mabey, C. and Thompson, K. (eds) *Human Resource Strategies*, pp. 95–106. London: Sage.

Beer, M. and Eisenstat, R.A. (1996) American Medical Technologies Inc, in Storey, J. (ed.) *Blackwell Cases in Human Resource and Change Management*, pp. 124–143. Oxford: Blackwell,

Beer, M., Eisenstat, R.A. and Spector, B. (1990) Why change programs don't produce change, *Harvard Business Review*, November/December, 158–166.

Beer, M. Lawrence, P. Mills, Q. Walton, R. and Spector, B. (1984) *Managing Human Assets*. New York: Free Press:

Belasen, A.T., Benke, M., DiPadova, L.N. and Fortunato, M.V. (1996) Downsizing and the hyper-effective manager: the shifting importance of managerial roles during organizational transformation, *Human Resource Management*, 35(1), 87–117.

Bell, J. (2005) *Doing Your Research Project* (4th edn). Buckingham: Open University Press.

Bendell, T., Boulter, L. and Kelly, J. (1993) *Benchmarking for Competitive Advantage*. London: Pitman.

Bennet. R. (1999), *International Business* (2nd edn). London: Financial Times Management.

Betts, J. and Holden, R. (2003) Organisational learning in a public sector organisation: a case study in muddled thinking, *Journal of Workplace Learning*, 15(6), 280–287.

Bies, R.J. and Moag, J. (1986) Interactional justice: communication criteria of fairness, in Lewicki, R., Sheppard, B. and Bazerman, M. (eds) *Research on Negotiation in Organizations*, Vol. 1, pp. 43–55. Greenwich, CT: JAI Press.

bin Idris, A.R. and Eldridge, D. (1998) Reconceptualising human resource planning in response to institutional change, *International Journal of Manpower*, 19(5), 343–357.

Blackler, F. (1995) Knowledge, knowledge work and organizations: an overview and interpretation, *Organization Studies*, 16(6), 1021–1046.

Bloomfield, R, (2003) … deal with a blame culture, *People Management*, 9 (13) pp. 50–51.

Bond, M.H. (1988) Finding universal dimensions of individual variation in multicultural studies of values: the Rokeach and Chinese value surveys *Journal of Personality and Social Psychology*, 55(6), 1009–1015.

Borucki, C.C. and Lafley, A.F. (1984) Strategic staffing at Chase Manhattan Bank, in Fombrun, C.J., Tichy, N.M. and Devanna, M.A. (eds) *Strategic Human Resource Management*, pp. 69–86. New York: John Wiley.

Bowen, D.E., Ledford, G.E. and Nathan, B.R. (1991) Hiring for the organisation not the job, *Academy of Management Executive*, 5(4), 35–51.

Boxall, P. (1992) Strategic human resource management: beginnings of a new theoretical sophistication?, *Human Resource Management Journal*, 2(3), 60–78.

Boxall, P.F. (1996) The strategic HRM debate and the resource-based view of the firm, *Human Resource Management Journal*, 6(3), 59–75.

Boxall, P. and Purcell, J. (2003) *Strategy and Human Resource Management*. Basingstoke: Palgrave Macmillan.

BP (2004) Work Environment. Available online http://www.bp.com/sectiongenericarticle.do?categoryId=123&contentId=2002502.

Bramham, J. (1988) *Practical Manpower Planning*. London: IPM.

Bramham, J. (1997) *Human Resource Planning*. London: IPD.

Bratton, J. and Gold, J. (2003) *Human Resource Management: Theory and Practice* (3rd edn). Basingstoke: Macmillan.

Brews, P.J. and Hunt, M.R. (1999) Learning to plan and planning to learn: resolving the planning school/learning school debate, *Strategic Management Journal*, 20, 889–913.

Briscoe, D. and Schuler, R. (2004) *International Human Resource Management* (2nd edn). London: Routledge.

British Quality Foundation (2001) *Listen to your Employees … using the Excellence Model*. London: British Quality Foundation.

Britton, R. (2002) Promoting Equality and Dignity in Worcestershire, unpublished paper.

Brockner, J. (1988) The effects of work layoffs on survivors: research, theory and practice, in Staw, B.M. and Cummings, L.L. (eds) *Research in Organizational Behavior*, pp. 213–255. Greenwich, CT: JAI Press.

Brockner, J. (1992) Managing the effects of layoffs on survivors, *California Management Review*, Winter, 9–28.

Brockner, J., Davy, J. and Carter, C. (1985) Layoffs, self-esteem, and survivor guilt: motivational, affective, and attitudinal consequences, *Organizational Behavior and Human Decision Processes*, 36, 229–244.

Brockner, J., DeWitt, R.L., Grover, S. and Reed, T. (1990) When it is especially important to explain why: factors affecting the relationship between managers' explanations of a layoff and survivors' reactions to the layoff, *Journal of Experimental Social Psychology*, 26, 389–407.

Brockner, J. and Greenberg, J. (1990) The impact of layoffs on survivors: an organizational justice perspective, in Carroll, J.S. (ed.) *Applied Social Psychology and Organizational Settings*, pp. 45–75. Hillsdale, NJ: Erlbaum.

Brockner, J., Tyler, T.R. and Cooper-Schneider, R. (1992) The influence of prior commitment to an institution on reactions to perceived unfairness: the higher they are, the harder they fall, *Administrative Science Quarterly*, 37, 241–261.

Brockner, J. and Wiesenfeld, B. (1993) Living on the edge (of social and organizational psychology): the effects of job layoffs on those who remain, in Murnighan, J.K., *Social Psychology in Organizations*, pp. 119–140. Englewood Cliffs, NJ: Prentice Hall.

Brown, A. (1998) *Organisational Culture* (2nd edn). London: Financial Times Pitman.

Brown, D. (1999) States of pay, *People Management*, 25 November, 52–53.

Brunsson, N. and Olsen, J.P. (1998) Reform as routine, in Mabey, C., Salaman, G. and Storey, J. (eds) *Strategic Human Resource Management*, pp. 297–309. London: Sage.

Buono, A.F. and Bowditch, J.L. (1989) *The Human Side of Mergers and Acquisitions: Managing Collisions Between People, Cultures, and Organizations*. San Francisco, CA: Jossey-Bass.

Burgoyne, J. (1988) Management development for the individual and the organisation, *Personnel Management*, June, 40–44.

Burke, A. (2004) Mirror image, in Arkin, A. (ed.) *The Guide to Recruitment Marketing*, pp. 16–19. London: CIPD.

Burnes, B. (2004) *Managing Change* (4th edn). Harlow: Financial Times Prentice Hall.

Burns, T. and Stalker, G.M. (1961) *The Management of Innovation*. London: Tavistock.

Business Boffins (2005) Business help that works, 14 February. Available online http://www.businessboffins.com /achievements.html

Business Week (2003) Has Benetton stopped unravelling?, 23 June.

Calder, J. (1994) *Programme Evaluation and Quality*. London: Kogan Page.

Calder, S. (2004) Sick notes, stress, strife: crisis at British Airways, *The Independent*, 25 August, pp. 1 and 4.

Cameron, K.S. (1994a) Investigating organizational downsizing – fundamental issues, *Human Resource Management*, 33(2), 183–188.

Cameron, K.S. (1994b) Strategies for successful organizational downsizing, *Human Resource Management*, 33(2), 189–211.

Cameron, K.S., Freeman, S.J. and Mishra, A.K. (1991) Best practices in white-collar downsizing: managing contradictions, *Academy of Management Executive*, 5(3), 57–73.

Cameron, K.S., Freeman, S.J. and Mishra, A.K. (1993) Organizational downsizing, in Huber, G.P. and Glick, W.H. (eds) *Organizational Change and Redesign*. New York: Oxford University Press.

Campbell-Jamison, F., Worrall, L. and Cooper, C. (2001) Downsizing in Britain and its effects on survivors and their organisations, *Anxiety, Stress and Coping*, 14(1), 35–58.

Carnall, C. (1995) *Managing Change in Organisations*. London: Prentice Hall.

Carrington, L. (2002a) At the cutting edge, *People Management*, 8(10), 30–31.

Carrington, L. (2002b) Oiling the wheels, *People Management*, 27 June, 30–34.

Carrington, L. (2004) Laws of attraction, *People Management*, 10(12), 26–30.

Cassell, C. (1996) A fatal attraction? Strategic HRM and the business case for women's progression at work, *Personnel Review*, 25(5), 51–66.

Caulkin, S. (2001) The time is now, *People Management*, 7(17), 32–34.

Cave, A. (2004a) Abbey ready to back £8.5bn Spanish bid, *Daily Telegraph: Business*, 26 July, p. 32.

Cave, A. (2004b) Santander plans 'need 8,000 Abbey job losses', *Daily Telegraph: Business*, 13 August, p. 31.

CBI (1999) CBI President raises fears about trade union partnerships, Press Release June. Confederation of British Industry: London.

Chambers (1999) *Chambers 21st Century Dictionary*. Edinburgh: Chambers Harrap Publishers.

Chandler, A.D. Jr (1962) *Strategy and Structure: Chapters in the History of the Industrial Enterprise*. Cambridge, MA: MIT Press.

Chartered Institute of Personnel and Development (CIPD) (2001) *Performance Through People: The New People Management*. Wimbledon: Chartered Institute of Personnel and Development.

Chartered Institute of Personnel and Development (CIPD) (2002) *The People Management Guide to Work–Life Balance*, 26 September.

Chartered Institute of Personnel and Development (CIPD) (2003) *Diversity: Stacking up the Evidence: executive briefing*, London: CIPD.

Chartered Institute of Personnel and Development (CIPD) (2004a) Performance management, *Impact: Quarterly Update on CIPD Policy and Research*, 9, November.

Chartered Institute of Personnel and Development (CIPD) (2004b) *High Performance Working*. Available online http://www.cipd.co.uk/subjects/corpstrtgy/general /highperfwk.htm

Chartered Institute of Personnel and Development (CIPD) (2005a) *Age and Employment Factsheet*, 21 July. Available online http://www.cipd.co.uk/

Chartered Institute of Personnel and Development (CIPD) (2005b), *What is Employee Relations?* Change agenda. London: CIPD.

Chartered Institute of Personnel and Development (CIPD) (2006) *Managing Change: The Role of the Psychological Contract*. Change agenda. London: CIPD.

Chartered Management Institute (2004) *EFQM Business Excellence Model,* 24 February. Available online http://www.managers.org.uk

Child, J. (1972) Organizational structure, environment and performance: the role of strategic choice, *Sociology,* 6, 1–22.

Child, J. (1984) *Organization: A Guide to Problems and Practice.* London: Paul Chapman Publishing.

Child, J. (1991) A foreign perspective on the management of people in China, *International Journal of Human Resource Management,* 2(1), 93–107.

Child, J. (1994) *Management in China During the Age of Reform.* Cambridge: Cambridge University Press.

Child, J. (2005) *Organization: Contemporary Principles and Practice.* Oxford: Blackwell Publishing.

Child, J. (1997) Strategic choice in the analysis of action, structure, organizations and environment: retrospect and prospect, *Organization Studies,* 18(1), 43–76.

China Daily (2003) China stands out in Volkswagen's global sales, 12 November. Available online http://www.chinadaily.com.cn/en/doc/2003-11/12/content_280927.htm

Chinese Culture Connection (1987) Chinese values and search for culture-free dimensions of culture, *Journal of Cross Cultural Psychology,* 18, 143–174.

Chu, P. and Ip, O. (2002) Downsizing in the internet industry: the Hong Kong experience, *Leadership and Organization Development Journal,* 23(3), 158–166.

Clark, G. (1998) Performance management strategies, in Mabey, C., Salaman, G. and Storey, J. (eds) *Human Resource Management: A Strategic Introduction.* Oxford: Blackwell.

Clark, T. and Salaman, G. (1998) Telling tales: management gurus' narratives and the construction of managerial identity, *Journal of Management Studies,* 35(2), 137–161.

Clarke, A. (1999) *Evaluation Research.* London: Sage.

Clarke, M. (2005) The voluntary redundancy option: carrot or stick?, *British Journal of Management,* 16(3), 245–252.

Claydon, T. (2002) Human resource management in the USA, in Redman and Wilkinson, (eds) *The Informed Student Guide to Human Resource Management.* London: Thomson Learning.

Clegg, H. (1979) *The Changing System of Industrial Relations in Britain.* Oxford: Basil Blackwell.

Clegg, S.R. and Hardy, C. (1996) Organizations, organization and organizing, in Clegg, S.R., Hardy, C. and Nord, W.R. (eds) *Handbook of Organization Studies.* London: Sage Publications.

Cockerill, A. (1989) The kind of competence for rapid change, *Personnel Management,* September, 52–56.

Coghlan, D. and Brannick, T. (2005) *Doing Action Research in Your Own Organisation* (2nd edn). London: Sage.

Colquitt, J.A. (2001) On the dimensionality of organizational justice: a construct validation of a measure, *Journal of Applied Psychology,* 86, 386–400.

Commission for Equality and Human Rights (2006) *Commission for Equality and Human Rights,* 18 October. Available online http://www.cehr.org.uk/content/overview/rhtm

Commission for Racial Equality (2004) *A Formal Investigation of the Police Service in England and Wales: An Interim Report.* London: Commission for Racial Equality, 4 October, Available online http://www.cre.gov.uk/pdfs/PoliceFI_interim.pdf

Connor, K.R. (1991) A historical comparison of resource-based theory and five schools of thought within new organization economics: do we have a new theory of the firm?, *Journal of Management,* 17(1), 121–154.

Connor, K.R. and Prahalad, C.K. (1996) A resource-based theory of the firm: knowledge versus opportunism, *Organization Science,* 7(5), 477–501.

Conti, T. (1997) *Organizational Self-Assessment.* London: Chapman and Hall.

Cook, M. (2004) *Personnel Selection* (4th edn). Chichester: John Wiley.

Cook Ross (2001) *Cook Ross Homepage,* 9 May 2001. Available online http://www.CookRoss.com

Cooper, C.L., Cartwright, S. and Earley, P.C. (2001) *The International Handbook of Organizational Culture and Climate.* Chichester: John Wiley.

Cooper, C.L., Sloan, S.J. and Williams, S. (1994) *Occupational Stress Indicator.* Windsor: NFER-Nelson.

Cooper, M. and White, B. (1995) Organisational behaviour, in Tyson, S. (ed.) *Strategic Prospects for HRM.* London: Institute of Personnel and Development.

Copeland, L. (1988) Valuing diversity, part 2, Pioneers and champions of change, *Personnel,* July, 44–49.

Corby, S., White, G. and Stanworth, C. (2005) No news is good news? Evaluating new pay systems, *Human Resource Management Journal,* 15(1), 4–24.

Coupar, W. and Stevens, B. (1998) Towards a new model of industrial partnership: beyond the 'HRM versus industrial relations' argument, in Sparrow, P. and Marchington, M. (eds) *Human Resource Management: The New Agenda,* London: FT Pitman.

Cox, T. (1991) The multicultural organisation, *Academy of Management Executive,* 5(2), 34–47.

Cox, T. (1993) *Cultural Diversity in Organizations, Theory and Practice.* San Francisco, CA: Barrett-Koehler.

Cox, T. and Beale, R. (1997) *Developing Competency to Manage Diversity: Readings, Cases and Activities.* San Francisco, CA: Barrett-Koehler.

Cox, T. and Blake, S. (1991) Managing cultural diversity: implications for organizational competitiveness, *Academy of Management Executive,* 5(3), 45–56

Coyle-Shapiro, J. and Kessler, I. (2000) Consequences of the psychological contract for the employment relationship: a large scale survey, *Journal of Management Studies,* 37(7), 903–930.

Cradden, T. (1992) Trade unionism and HRM: The Incompatibles, *Irish Business and Administrative Research,* 13, 36–47.

Cressey, P. and MacInnies, J. (1980) Voting for Ford: industrial democracy and the control of labour, *Capital and Class*, 11, 5–13.

Croners, (1991) Capability v conduct, *Employment Digest*, 320, 7 October.

Croners (2004) Capability procedures for teachers. Available online http://www.croner.co.uk/cgi-bin/croner/jsp/Editorial.do?cache=true&channelId=-48501&contentId=53893

Cropanzano, R. and Greenberg, J. (1997) Progress in organizational justice: tunnelling through the maze, in Cooper C.L. and Robertson I.T. (eds) *International Review of Industrial and Organizational Psychology*, Vol. 12 pp. 243–298. Chichester: Wiley.

Crozier, M. (1964) *The Bureaucratic Phenomenon*, Chicago, IL: University of Chicago Press.

CSR Europe (2005) Disability: facts and figures, 26 May 2005 Available online http://www.csreurope.org/csrinfo/csrdisability/DisabilityFactsandfigures/

Cullen, P.C. (2001) *The Ladbroke Grove Rail Inquiry Report: Part 2*. Norwich: HMSO.

Cully, M., Woodland, S., O'Reilly, A. and Dix, G. (1999) *Britain At Work*. London: Routledge.

Cunningham, I. and Hyman, J. (1999) Devolving human resource responsibilities to the line: beginning of the end or a new beginning for personnel?, *Personnel Review*, 28(1/2), 9–27.

Cunningham, J.B. (1995) Strategic considerations in using action research for improving personnel practices, *Public Personnel Management*, 24(2), 515–529.

Cyert, R.M. and March, J.G. (1963) *A Behavioural Theory of the Firm*. Englewood Cliffs, NJ: Prentice Hall.

Dalton, M., Ernst, C., Deal, J. and Leslie, J. (2002) *Success for the New Global Manager. How to Work Across Distances, Countries and Cultures*, San Francisco, CA: Jossey Bass.

Daly, J.P. and Geyer, P.D. (1994) The role of fairness in implementing large-scale change: employee evaluations of process and outcome in seven facility relocations *Journal of Organizational Behaviour*, 15, 623–638.

Daniels, J., Radebaugh, L. and Sullivan, D. (2004) *International Business* (10th edn). NJ: Pearson Education.

Daniels, S. (2003) Employee training: a strategic approach to better return on investment, *Journal of Business Strategy*, 24(5), 39–42.

Davidow, W.H. and Malone, M.S. (1992) *The Virtual Corporation: Structuring and Revitalising the Corporation for the 21st Century*. New York: HarperCollins.

Davis, S.M. and Lawrence, P. R. (1977) *Matrix*. Reading, MA: Addison-Wesley.

Davy, J.A., Kinicki, A.J. and Scheck, C.L. (1991) Developing and testing a model of survivor responses to layoffs, *Journal of Vocational Behaviour*, 38, 302–317.

Deal, T.E. and Kennedy, A.A. (1982) *Corporate Culture: The Rites and Rituals of Corporate Life*. Reading, MA: Addison-Wesley.

Demetriou, D. (2004) Thousands left stranded on second day of airport chaos, *The Independent*, 25 August, p. 4.

DeMichillie, G. (2004) Shipping software: the end game. Available online http://www.directionsonmicrosoft.com/sample/DOMIS/update/2004/10oct/1004ssteg.htm

Department for Education and Employment (DfEE) (1998) *The Learning Age: A Renaissance for a New Britain*, Green Paper, Cm 3790. London: HMSO.

Department for Education and Employment (DfEE) (2000) *The Demand for Skills*. London: HMSO.

Department of Trade and Industry (2004) *News Release: Hewitt Announces New Plans to Strengthen Corporate Britain*, 21 February. Available online http://www.accountingforpeople.gov.uk

Department of Education (1999) *Initiative of the People Services, School Personnel Resources Divisions*. London: The Stationery Office.

Department of Employment and Productivity (1968) *Company Manpower Planning*. London: HMSO.

DeSensi, J. (1995) Understanding multiculturalism and valuing diversity: a theoretical perspective, *Quest*, 47, 34–43.

deVaus, D. (2001) *Research Design in Social Research*. London: Sage.

Dickens, L. (1994) The business case for women's equality: is the carrot better than the stick?, *Employee Relations*, 16(8), 5–18.

Dicom (2004) *Dicom Company Profile*, 3 December. Available online http://www.dicomgroup.com

Dierickx, I. and Cool, K. (1989) Asset stock accumulation and sustainability of competitive advantage, *Management Science*, 35, 1504–1511.

Ding, D., Fields, D. and Akhtar, S. (1997) An empirical study of human resource management policies and practices in foreign-invested enterprises in China: the case of Shenzen Special Economic Zone, *International Journal of Human Resource Management*, 8(5), 595–613.

Doherty, A. and Chelladurai, P. (1999) Managing cultural diversity in sport organizations: a theoretical perspective, *Journal of Sport Management*, 13, 280–297.

Doherty, N., Bank, J. and Vinnicombe, S. (1996) Managing survivors: the experience of survivors in British Telecom and the British financial services sector, *Journal of Managerial Psychology*, 11(7), 51–60.

Donaldson, L. (1996) The normal science of structural contingency theory, in Clegg, S.R., Hardy, C. and Nord, W.R. (eds) *Handbook of Organization Studies*. London: Sage Publications.

Dowling, P., Welch, D. and Schuler, R. (1999) *International Human Resource Management: Managing People in a Multinational Context*. Cincinatti, OH: South Western College Publishing.

Doyle, M., Claydon, T. and Buchanan, D. (2000) Mixed results, lousy process: the management experience of organizational change, *British Journal of Management*, 11, S59–S80.

Drucker, P. (1954) *The Practice of Management*, New York: Harper.

DTI/DfEE, (1998) *Competitiveness Through Partnerships with People*. Department of Trade and Industry and Department for Education and Employment London: HMSO.

du Gay, P. and Salaman, G. (1998) The cult(ure) of the customer, in Mabey, C., Salaman, G. and Storey, J. (eds) *Human Resource Management: A Reader*. London: Sage.

Dundon, T., Grugulis, I. and Wilkinson, A. (1999) Looking out of the black-hole: non-union relations in an SME, *Employee Relations*, 21(3), 251–266.

DuPont (2004) *DuPont's Heritage*, November. Available online http://heritage.dupont.com/

Dutton, J. and Ashford, S. (1993) Selling issues to top management, *Academy of Management Review*, 18, 397–428.

Dutton, J.E. (1993) Interpretations on automatic: a different view of strategic issue diagnosis, *Journal of Management Studies*, 30, 339–357.

Easterby-Smith, M. (1994) *Evaluating Management Development, Training and Education*. Aldershot: Gower.

Easterby-Smith, M., Thorpe, R., and Lowe, A. (2002) *Management Research: An Introduction* (2nd edn). London: Sage.

Ebadan, G. and Winstanley, D. (1997) Downsizing, delayering and careers – the survivor's perspective, *Human Resource Management Journal*, 7(1), 79–91.

Eden, C. and Huxham, C. (1996) Action research for management research, *British Journal of Management*, 7(1), 75–86.

Edwards, C. (2004) Portal combat, *People Management*, 10(22), 42–43.

Egan, J. (1998) *Rethinking Construction. The Report of the Construction Task Force to the Deputy Prime Minister on the Scope for Improving the Quality and Efficiency of UK Construction*, London: The Stationery Office.

Eisner, E. (1979) *The Educational Imagination*. New York: Macmillan.

Ellis, C. and Sonnerfield, J. (1995) Diverse approaches to managing diversity, *Human Resource Management*, 33(1), 79–109.

Elmes, P. (2001) *Diversity – Fad or Business Imperative?* Presentation by Barclays Capital Associate Director for Global Diversity at Diversity Day. London: STEPS.

El-Sawed, A. (2002) Human resource development, in Pilbeam, S. and Corbridge, M. (eds) *People Resourcing: HRM in Practice* (2nd edn), pp. 284–308. Harlow: Financial Times Prentice Hall.

Employers' Organisation for Local Government (2001) *Equality Standard for Local Government*, 2 November 2003. Available online URL:http://www.lg-employers.gov.uk /diversity/equality/

Ernst and Young (2000) *Parents at Work*. London: Ernst and Young.

Esty, K., Griffin, R. and Hirsch, M. (1995) *A Managers Guide to Solving Problems and Turning Diversity into a Competitive Advantage: Workplace Diversity*, pp. 7–12, Holbrook, MA: Adams Media.

European Foundation for Quality Management (2004) *European Foundation for Quality Management*, 12 November Available online http://www.efqm.org

Eurostat (2005a) *Eurostat Population Projection – Baseline Population Scenario* (1999 revision), 2 March. Available online http://europa.eu.int/comm/eurostat/newcronos/

Eurostat (2005b) *Eurostat Labour Force Projection – Baseline Population Scenario (1995)*, 8 March. Available online http://europa.eu.int/comm/eurostat/newcronos/

Evans, J. (2004) Bearing up brilliantly, *People Management*, 11 November, 32–33.

Evenden, R. (1993) The strategic management of recruitment and selection, in Harrison, R. (ed.) *Human Resource Management: Issues and Strategies* pp. 219–245. Wokingham: Addison-Wesley.

Exclusive Escapes (2005) *Hidden Turkey*.

Farmers' Weekly Interactive (2006) *Demand Makes Regional Cheese Big Opportunity*. Available online http://www.fwi .co.uk/Articles/2006/01/16/91806/Demand+makes+regional +cheese+big+opportunity.html

Farrell. M. and Mavondo, F.T. (2004) The effect of downsizing strategy and reorientation strategy on a learning orientation, *Personnel Review*, 33(4), 383–402.

Fernandez, J. (1991) *Managing a Diverse Workforce*. New York: Lexington Books.

Financial Times (2004) US United Nations Conference on Trade and Development and China find harmony on trade gap, 22 April.

Financial Times (2005a) FT Special Report by Ian Limbach, Digital Business News, 9 November, p. 6.

Financial Times (2005b) 10 November, p. 1.

Fineman, S. and Mangham, I. (1987) Change in organisations, in Warr, P. (ed.) *Psychology at Work* (3rd edn). London: Pelican.

Flannery, T., Hofrichter, D. and Platten, P. (1996) *People, Performance and Pay*. New York: The Free Press.

Flynn, R., McCombs, T. and Elloy, D. (1990) Staffing the self-managing work team, *Leadership and Organization Development Journal*, 11(1), 26–31.

Fombrun, C.J., Tichy, N.M. and Devanna, M.A. (eds) (1984) *Strategic Human Resource Management*, New York: John Wiley.

Forbes, L.H. (2002) Improving quality through diversity *Leadership and Management Engineering*, 2(4), 49–52.

Ford, V. (1996) Partnership is the secret of progress, *People Management*, February, Institute of Personnel and Development.

Foster, C. and Newell, S. (2001) *Managing Diversity and Equal Opportunities – Some Practical Implications*. Paper presented to the Fourth International Conference on Ethical Issues in Contemporary Human Resource Management, Middlesex University and Imperial College.

Fox, A. (1966) Industrial sociology and industrial relations, *Royal Commission Research Paper No. 3.* London: HMSO.

Frame, P. and O'Connor, J. (2002) From the 'high ground' of policy to 'the swamp' of professional practice: the challenge of diversity in teaching labour studies, *Society in Transition*, 33(2), 278–293.

Francis, A. (1994) The structure of organizations, in Sisson, K. (ed.) *Personnel Management: a Comprehensive Guide to Theory and Practice in Britain* (2nd edn). Oxford: Blackwell Publishers.

Franco, M.L.A. and Diaz, R.I. (1995) Strategic planning of human resources in the library system of the Pontifical Catholic University of Chile, *Library Management*, 16(3), 15–23.

Fredman, S. (2001) Equality a new generation?, *Industrial Law Journal*, 30(2), 145–168.

Freeman, S.J. and Cameron, K.S. (1993) Organizational downsizing: a convergence and reorientation framework, *Organization Science*, 4(1), 10–29.

Friedman, A. (1977) *Industry and Labour: Class Struggle at Work and Monopoly Capitalism.* London: Macmillan.

Fritz, R. (1994) *Corporate Tides: Redesigning the Organization.* Oxford: Butterworth-Heinemann.

Fulbrook, M. (2002) *A Concise History of Germany.* Cambridge: Cambridge University Press.

Galbraith, J. and Nathanson, D. (1978) *Strategy Formulation: Analytical Concepts.* St Paul, MN: West Publishing Co.

Galpin, T.J. (1999) When leaders really walk the talk: making strategy work through people, *Human Resource Planning*, 21(3), 38–45.

Gamble, J. (2003) Transferring human resource practices from the United Kingdom to China: the limits and potential for convergence, *International Journal of Human Resource Management*, 14(3), 369–387.

Garavan, T.N. (1991) Strategic human resource development, *Journal of European Industrial Training*, 15(1), 17–30.

Garavan, T.N. (1997) The learning organization: a review and evaluation, *The Learning Organization*, 4(1), 18–29.

Garavan, T.N., Costine, P. and Heraty, N. (1995) The emergence of strategic human resource development, *Journal of European Industrial Training*, 19(10), 4–10.

Garavan, T.N., Morley, M., Gunnigle, P. and Collins, E. (2001) Human capital accumulation: the role of human resource development, *Journal of European Industrial Training*, 25(2/3/4), 48–68.

Garrahan, P. and Stewart, P. (1992) *The Nissan Enigma: Flexibility at Work in a Local Economy.* London: Mansell.

Garvin, D. (1993) Building a learning organization, *Harvard Business Review*, July–August, 78–91.

Gennard, J. and Judge, G. (2002) *Employee Relations* (3rd edn). Wimbledon: Chartered Institute of Personnel and Development.

Gesteland, R. (1999) *Cross-cultural Business Behaviour Marketing, Negotiating and Managing Across Cultures.* Copenhahen: Handelshojskolens.

Ghauri, P. (2000) Internationalisation of the firm, in Tayeb, M. (ed.) *International Business: Theories, Policies and Practices.* Harlow: Financial Times Prentice Hall.

Gibb, S. and Megginson, D. (2001) Employee development, in Redman, T. and Wilkinson, A. (eds) *Contemporary Human Resource Management: Text and Cases*, pp. 128–167. Harlow: Financial Times Prentice Hall.

Gill, J. and Johnson, P. (2002) *Research Methods for Managers* (3rd edn). London: Sage.

Gill, P. (1996) Managing workforce diversity: a response to skill shortages?, *Health Manpower Management*, 22(6), 34–37.

Girling, J. (1999) To what extent is managing diversity a strategic approach to managing people? Unpublished HRM Master's Dissertation, Newcastle Business School, University of Northumbria at Newcastle.

Global Envision (2004) Available online http://www.globalenvision.org/index.php?fuseaction=home.google

Glover, L. and Siu, N. (2000) The human resource barriers to managing quality in China, *International Journal of Human Resource Management*, 11(5), 867–882.

Godard, J. and Delaney, J.T. (2000) Reflections on the 'high performance' paradigm's implications for industrial relations as a field, *Industrial and Labor Relations Review*, 53(3), 482–502.

Golden, K.A. and Ramanujam, V. (1985) Between a dream and a nightmare: on the integration of the human resource management and strategic business planning process, *Human Resource Management*, Winter, 26(4), 429–452.

Golembiewski, R. (1995) *Managing Diversity in Organizations*, Tuscaloosa, AL: University of Alabama Press.

Golembiewski, R.T., Billingsley, K. and Yeager, S. (1976) Measuring change and persistence in human affairs: types of change generated by OD designs, *Journal of Applied Behavioural Science*, 12, 133–157.

Goold, M. and Campbell, A. (1987) *Strategies and Styles: The Role of the Centre in Managing Diversified Corporations.* Oxford: Blackwell.

Gordon M., Philpot, J., Burt, R., Thompson, C. and Spiller, W. (1980) Commitment to the union: development of a measure and an examination of its correlates, *Journal of Applied Psychology*, 65, 749–799.

Gospel, H. and Palmer, G. (1993) *British Industrial Relations* (2nd edn). London: Routledge.

Grabham, A (2003) Composition of pay, *Labour Market Trends*, 297, August, 397–405.

Graham, L. (1997) *Proversity: Getting Past Face Value and Finding the Soul of People: A Manager's Journey.* New York: John Wiley.

Grant, R.M. (1991) The resource-based theory of competitive advantage: implications for strategy formulation, *California Management Review*, Spring.

Gratton, L. (1999) People processes as a source of competitive advantage, in Gratton, L., Hope Hailey, V., Stiles, P. and Truss, C. (eds), *Strategic Human Resource Management*, Oxford: Oxford University Press, 170–198.

Gratton, L. (2004) Means to an end, *People Management*, 2 September, 20–23.

Gratton, L., Hope Hailey, V., Stiles, P. and Truss, C. (1999) Linking individual performance to business strategy: the people process model, in Schuler, R.S. and Jackson, S.E. (eds) *Strategic Human Resource Management*, pp. 142–158. Oxford: Blackwell.

Gratton, L., Hope Hailey, V., Stiles, P. and Truss, C. (1999c) *Strategic Human Resource Management: Corporate Rhetoric and Human Reality*. Oxford: Oxford University Press.

Greenberg, J. (1987) A taxonomy of organisational justice theories, *Academy of Management Review*, 12(1), 9–22.

Greenberg, J. (1993). The social side of fairness: interpersonal and informational classes of organizational justice, in Cropanzano, R. (ed.) *Justice in the Workplace: Approaching Fairness in Human Resource Management*, pp. 79–103. Hillsdale, NJ: Erlbaum.

Greenhalgh, L. Lawrence, A.T. and Sutton, R.I. (1988) Determinants of work force reduction strategies in declining organizations, *Academy of Management Review*, 13(2), 241–254.

Greenhalgh, L. and Rosenblatt, Z. (1984) Job insecurity: toward conceptual clarity, *Academy of Management Review*, 9(3), 438–448.

Greer, C.R. (2001) *Strategic Human Resource Management: A General Managerial Approach* (2nd edn). Upper Saddle River, NJ: Prentice Hall.

Grey, S. and Healy, G. (2004) Women and IT contracting work – a testing process, *New Technology, Work and Employment*, 19(1), 30–42.

Grice, A. and Clement, B. (2004) Millions of workers to be given eight more days' holiday, *The Independent*, 26 July, p. 2.

Griego, O.V., Geroy, G.D. and Wright, P.C. (2000) Predictors of learning organizations: a human resource development practitioner's perspective, *The Learning Organization*, 7(1), 5–12.

Griffiths, J. (2005) The man from Auntie, *People Management*, 11(10), 16–17.

Griffiths, K. (2004) 2,500 jobs go at Co-operative Insurance, *The Independent*, 15 July, p. 28.

Guba, E. and Lincoln, Y. (1981) *Effective Evaluation: Improving the Usefulness of Evaluation Results Through Responsive and Naturalistic Approaches*. San Francisco, CA: Jossey Bass.

Guest, D. (1987). Human resource management and industrial relations, *Journal of Management Studies*, 24(5), 503–521.

Guest, D. (1991) Personnel management. The end of Orthodoxy?, *British Journal of Industrial Relations*, 29(2), 149–75.

Guest, D. (1992) Right enough to be dangerously wrong: an analysis of the in search of excellence phenomenon, in Salaman, G. (ed.) *Human Resource Strategies*. London: Sage.

Guest, D.(1995) Human resource management, trade unions and industrial relations, in Storey J. (ed) *Human Resource Management: A Critical Text*. London: Routledge.

Guest, D. (1997) Human resource management and performance: a review and research agenda, *International Journal of Human Resource Management*, 8(3), 265–276.

Guest, D. (2001) Human resource management: when research confronts theory, *International Journal of Human Resource Management*, 12(7).

Guest, D. (2004) Flexible employment contracts, the psychological contract and employee outcomes: an analysis and review of the evidence, *International Journal of Management Reviews*, 5/6(1), 1–20.

Guest, D. and Hoque, K. (1998) Are greenfield sites better at human resource management?, CEP Working Paper No. 435, London: London School of Economics.

Guest, D., Michie, J., Sheehan, M., Conway, N. and Metochi, M. (2000) *Effective People Management*. Wimbledon: Chartered Institute of Personnel and Development.

Guest, D. and Peccei, R. (1992) Employee involvement: redundancy as a critical case, *Human Resource Management Journal*, 2(3), 34–59.

Guest, D., Peccei, R. and Thomas, A. (1993) The impact of employee involvement on organisational commitment and 'them and us' attitudes, *Industrial Relations Journal*, 24(3), 191–200.

Guest, D.and Conway, N. (2002) *Pressure at Work and the Psychological Contract*. London: CIPD.

Gustafson, D.H., Sainfort, F., Eichler, M., Adams, L., Bisognano, M. and Steudel, H. (2003) Developing and testing a model to predict outcomes of organizational change, *HSR: Health Services Research*, 38(2), 751–776.

Halcrow (2003) *Corporate Report 2002*. London: Halcrow Group Ltd.

Halcrow (2004a) *About Halcrow*, 20 July. Available online http:www.halcrow.com/abouthalcrow.asp

Halcrow (2004b) *Act Now: Your Pocket Guide to Halcrow's Change Programme*. Swindon: Halcrow Group Ltd.

Hall, D. and Parker, V. (1993) The role of workplace flexibility in managing diversity, *Organizational Dynamics*, 22(1).

Hamblin, A.C. (1974) *Evaluation and Control of Training*. London: McGraw-Hill.

Hamel, G. and Prahalad, C. (1994) *Competing for the future*. Boston, MA: Harvard Business School Press.

Harris, H., Brewster, C. and Sparrow, P. (2003) *International Human Resource Management*. London: Chartered Institute of Personnel and Development.

Hand, D. (2000) Remuneration in the Republic of Ireland, *Benefits and Compensation International*, March, 21–24.

Handy, C.B. (1978) *The Gods of Management*, London: Penguin.

Handy, C.B. (1993) *Understanding Organisations*, London: Penguin.

Hannan, M.T. and Freeman, J. (1988) *Organizational Ecology*, Cambridge, MA: Harvard University Press.

Harris, H., Bewster, C. and Sparrow, P. (2003) *International Human Resource Mangagement*. London: Chartered Institute of Personnel and Development.

Harrison, A., Dalkiran, E. and Elsey, E. (2000) *International Business*. Oxford: Oxford University Press.

Harrison, R. (1972) Understanding your organization's character, *Harvard Business Review*, 50(May/June), 19–128.

Harrison, R. (1993) Developing people – for whose bottom line?, in Harrison, R. (ed.) *Human Resource Management: Issues and Strategies*, pp. 299–329. Wokingham: Addison-Wesley.

Harrison, R. and Kessels, J. (2004) *Human Resource Development in a Knowledge Economy: An Organisational View*, Basingstoke: Palgrave Macmillan.

Hassard, J. and Sharifi, S. (1989) Corporate culture and strategic change, *Journal of General Management*, 15(2), 4–19.

Hayfield, A. (2003) Meet the 'out' laws, *People Management*, 9(24), 21.

Hedlund, G. (1994) A model of knowledge management and the N-form corporation, *Strategic Management Journal*, 15, 73–90.

Heenan, D. and Perlmutter, H. (1979) *Multinational Organisation Development*. Reading, MA: Addison Wesley.

Heery, E. (1996) Risk, representation and the new pay, *Personnel Review*, 25(6), 54–65.

Henderson, G. (1994) *Cultural Diversity in the Workplace: Issues and Strategies*. Westport, CN: Quorum.

Henderson, S. (1997) Black swans don't fly double loop: the limits of the learning organization, *The Learning Organization*, 4(3), 99–105.

Hendry, C. (1995) *Human Resource Management: A Strategic Approach to Employment*. Oxford: Butterworth-Heinemann.

Hendry, C. (1996) Understanding and creating whole organisational change through learning theory, *Human Relations*, 49(5), 621–641.

Hendry, C. and Jenkins, R. (1997) Psychological contracts and new deals, *Human Resource Management Journal*, 7(1), 38–44.

Hendry, C. and Pettigrew, A. (1990) Human resource management: an agenda for the 1990s, *International Journal of Human Resource Management*, 1(1), 17–43.

Hendry, C., Pettigrew, A. and Sparrow, P. (1988) Changing patterns of human resource management, *Personnel Management*, November, 37–41.

Hendry, C., Woodward, S. , Bradley, P. and Perkins, S. (2000) Performance and rewards: cleaning out the stables, *Human Resource Management Journal*, 10(3), 46–62.

Heng, M.S.H. (2001) Mapping intellectual capital in a small manufacturing enterprise, *Journal of Intellectual Capital*, 2(1), 53–60.

Hercus, T. (1992) Human resource planning in eight British organizations: a Canadian perspective, in Towers, B. (ed.) *The Handbook of Human Resource Management*, pp. 404–425. Oxford: Blackwell.

Herremans, I.M. and Isaac, R.G. (2004) Leading the strategic development of intellectual capital, *Leadership and Organization Development Journal*, 25(2), 142–160.

Herriot, P. and Pemberton, C. (1996) Contracting careers, *Human Relations*, 49(6), 757–790.

Hertzberg, F. (1968) *Work and the Nature of Man*. London: Staples Press.

Hertzberg, F. (1987) One more time: how do you motivate employees?. *Harvard Business Review*, 65(5), September/October. 109–120.

Hewlett-Packard (2004) Company information – about us, 12 November. Available online http://www.hp.com/

Hicks-Clarke, D. and Iles, P. (2000) Climate for diversity and its effects of career and organisational attitudes and perceptions, *Personnel Review*, 29(3), 324–345.

Higginbottom, K. (2003) Image conscious, *People Management*, 9(3), 44–45.

Hiltrop, J,M. (1995) The changing psychological contract: the human resource challenge in the 1990s, *European Journal of Management*, 13(3), 286–294.

Hirsch, W. (1995) *Careers in Organizatons: Issues for the Future*, Brighton: Institute for Employment Studies.

Hofer, C.W. and Schendel, D. (1978) *Strategy Formulation: Analytical Concepts*, St Paul, MN: West Publishing.

Hofstede, G. (1980) *Culture's Consequences: International Differences in Work Related Values*. Beverly Hills, CA: Sage.

Hofstede, G. (1991) *Culture's and Organisations: Software of the Mind*. London: McGraw-Hill.

Hofstede, G. (2001) *Culture's Consequences: Comparing Values, Behaviours, Institutions and Organisations Across Nations* (2nd edn). Thousand Oaks, CA: Sage.

Hofstede, G. (2002) Dimensions do not exist, *Human Relations*, 55(11), 1355–1362.

Holden, L. (2004) Human resource development: the organisation and the national framework, in Beardwell, I., Holden, L. and Claydon, T. (eds) *Human Resource Management: A Contemporary Approach* (4th edn), pp. 313–360. Harlow: Financial Times Prentice Hall.

Hollinshead, G. and Leat, M. (1995) *Human Resource Management: an International and Comparative Perspective*. London: Pitman Publishing.

Horwitz, F.M. (1999) The emergence of strategic training and development: the current state of play, *Journal of European Industrial Training*, 23(4/5), 180–190.

Human Resource Management International Digest (2002) People: a key ingredient at Pret a Manger, 10(6), 6–8.

Huselid, M. (1995) The impact of human resource practices on turnover, productivity, and corporate financial performance, *Academy of Management Journal*, 38(3), 635–672.

Huselid, M., Becker, B. and Ulrich, D. (2001) *The HR Scorecard: Linking People, Strategy and Performance*. Boston, MA: Harvard Business School Press.

Hyman, J. (2000) Financial participation schemes, in White, G. and Druker, J. *Reward Management: a Critical Text*. London: Routledge.

IDS (1998) *Partnership Agreements*, Study 656, October.

IDS (2003a), *Bonus Schemes*, IDS Study 742, January.

IDS (2003b) *Building a High Performance Culture*, Study 748, April.

Iles, P. (2001) Employee resourcing, in Storey, J. (ed.) *Human Resource Management: A Critical Text* (2nd edn), pp. 133–164. London: Thomson.

Iles, P. and Hayers, P.K. (1997) Managing diversity in transnational project teams: a tentative model and case study, *Journal of Managerial Psychology*, 12(2), 95–117.

Industrial Society (2000) *Valuing Diversity, Managing Best Practice*, No. 78. London: Industrial Society.

Institute of Personnel Management (1992) *Performance Management in the UK*. London: Institute of Personnel Management.

International Labour Office. (2003) *Subcommittee on Multinational Enterprises*, 9 November. Available online http://www-ilo-mirror.cornell.edu/public/english/standards/relm/gb/docs/gb286/pdf/mne-3.pdf

International Labour Organisation (2004) Statistics on the employment situation of people with disabilities: a compendium of national methodologies, ILO Working Paper No. 40. Available online http://www.ilo.org/public/english/employment/skills/disability/download/wp40.pdf

IPA (1996) *Towards Industrial Partnership: A New Approach to Relationships*. London.

IPD (1998) *Employment Relations into the 21st Century*, An IPD position paper. London.

IRS (1991) The state of Selection 1, *Recruitment and Development Report 16*, April.

IRS (1993) Natural selection: BT's programme of voluntary redundancy, *IRS Employment Trends* 533, April, 11–15.

IRS (1997) Culture change, *IRS Management Review*, 1(4).

IRS (1998) *Employment Trends*, 652–660, March–September.

IRS (1999) Employment in the global village, *Employment Review* 689, 1 October.

IRS (2000) Added values, *Employment Review*, 711, 1 September.

IRS (2001) Whatever happened to team reward? *Employment Review*, 732.

IRS (2002) International assignments: the party's over, *Employment Review*, 752, 27 May.

IRS (2003a) Performance management: policy and practice, *Employment Review, Employment Trends*, 781, 1 August, 12–19.

IRS (2003b) Rules of engagement, *Employment Review*, 782, 5 September.

IRS (2003c) Totally rewarding, *Employment Review*, 782, 15 August, 34–36.

IRS (2003d), Sharing the spoils: profit-share and bonus schemes, *Employment Review*, 784, 18 September, 28–32.

IRS (2004a) Sabbaticals: the big break, *Employment Review*, 801, 4 June:

IRS (2004b) Developing a global reward strategy at Tibbett & Britten, *Employment Review*, 804, 23 July.

IRS (2004c) Broadbanded pay: on the right track at EWS, *Employment Review*, 796, 19 March.

IRS *Employment Trends* (1998) Gainsharing drives improvement process at Zircoa, 656, 1 May, 12–13.

Itami, H. (1987) *Mobilizing Invisible Assets*, Cambridge, MA, Harvard University Press.

J. Howard and Associates (2001) *J. Howard and Associates Homepage*. Available online http://jhoward.com

Jackson, N. and Carter, P. (2000) *Rethinking Organisational Behaviour*. Harlow: FT Prentice Hall.

Jacques, E. (1962) Objective measures for pay differentials, *Harvard Business Review*, January/February, 133–137.

Jenkins, J. (2002) Patterns of pay: results of the 2001 New Earnings Survey, *Labour Market Trends*, March 129–139.

Johnson, G. and Scholes, K. (2002) *Exploring Corporate Strategy: Text and Cases* (6th edn). Harlow: FT Prentice Hall.

Johnson, L. and Johnstone, S. (2000) The legislative framework, in Kitron, G. and Greene, A. (eds) *The Dynamics of Managing Diversity: A Critical Approach*. Oxford: Butterworth-Heinemann

Johnson, R. and Redmond, D. (2000) *Diversity Incorporated: Managing People for Success in a Diverse World*. Harlow: Pearson Education.

Kanari, N., Pineau, J.-L. and Shallari, S. (2003) End-of-life vehicle recycling in the European Union, *TQM*, August, 15–19. Available online http://doc.tms.org/ezMerchant/home.nsf/AutoFrameset?OpenAgent&url=http://doc.tms.org/servlet/ProductCatalog?category=JOM%202003%20August

Kandola, B. and Fullerton, J. (1994a) *Managing the Mosaic: Diversity in Action*. London: Institute of Personnel and Development.

Kandola, B. and Fullerton, J. (1994b) Diversity: more than just an empty slogan?, *Personnel Management*, November, 46–50.

Kandola, B. and Fullerton, J. (1998) *Diversity in Action: Managing the Mosaic* (2nd edn). London: CIPD.

Kanji, G. (2002) *Measuring Business Excellence*. London: Routledge.

Kaplan, R.S. and Norton, D.P. (1992) The balanced scorecard – measures that drive performance, *Harvard Business Review*, January/February, 71–79.

Keenoy, T. (1990) Human resource management: rhetoric, reality and contradiction, *International Journal of Human Resource Management*, 1(3), 363–384.

Keep, E. (1992) Corporate training strategies: the vital component?, in Salaman, G. (ed.) *Human Resource Strategies*, pp. 320–336. London: Sage.

Kelly, J. (1996) Union militancy and social partnership, in Ackers, P., Smith, C. and Smith, P. (eds) *The New Workplace and Trade Unionism*. London: Routledge.

Kelly, J. (ed.) (1998) *Rethinking Industrial Relations*, London: Routledge.

Kenton, B. and Moody, D. (2004) How to develop as an internal consultant, *People Management*, 26 February.

Kernan, M.C. and Hanges, P.J. (2002) Survivor reactions to reorganization: antecedents and consequences of procedural, interpersonal and informational justice, *Journal of Applied Psychology*, 87(5), 916–928.

Kessler, I. (1994) Performance pay, in Sisson, K. (ed.) *Personnel Management*. Oxford: Blackwell.

Kessler, I. and Purcell, J. (1995) Individualism and collectivism in theory and practice: management style and the design of pay systems, in Edwards, P. (ed.) *Industrial Relations: Theory and Practice in Britain*. Oxford: Blackwell.

Khoong, C.M. (1996) An integrated system framework and analysis methodology for manpower planning, *International Journal of Management*, 17(1), 26–46.

Kingsmill, D. (2003) *Accounting for People*. London: The Stationery Office.

Kinnie, N., Hutchinson, S. and Purcell, J. (1998) Downsizing: is it always lean and mean?, *Personnel Review*, 27(4), 296–311.

Kirby, E. and Harter, L. (2003) Speaking the language of the bottom-line: the metaphor of managing diversity, *The Journal of Business Communication*, 40(1), 28–49.

Kirby, P., (2002) *The Celtic Tiger in Distress*. London: Palgrave Macmillan.

Kirchmeyer, C. (2002) Gender differences in managerial careers: yesterday, today and tomorrow, *Journal of Business Ethics*, 37(1), 5–24.

Kirkpatrick, D.L. (1985) *How to Manage Change Effectively*. San Francisco, CA: Jossey Bass.

Knight, J. and Yueh, L. (2004) Job mobility of residents and migrants in urban China, *Journal of Comparative Economics*, 32, 637–660.

Knight, K. (ed.) (1977) *Matrix Management: A Cross-functional Approach to Organisation*. Farnborough: Gower Press.

Koch, M. and McGrath, R. (1996) Improving labor productivity: human resource management policies do matter, *Strategic Management Journal*, 17, 335–354.

Kochan, T.A. and Barocci, T.A. (eds) (1985) *Human Resource Management and Industrial Relations*. Boston, MA: Little Brown.

Kochan, T. Katz, T. and McKersie, R. (1986) *The Transformation of American Industrial Relations*. New York: Basic Books.

Kochan, T.A. and Osterman, P. (1994) *The Mutual Gains Enterprise: Forging a Winning Partnership among Labour, Management and Government*. Cambridge, MA: Harvard Business School Press.

Kochan, T., Katz, T. and McKersie, R.B (1996) *The Transformation of American Industrial Relations* (2nd edn). New York: Basic Books.

Koenig, P. and Kemeny, L. (2004) Burnt by soaring oil prices, *The Sunday Times: Business*, 8 August, p. 7.

Kossek, E. and Zonia, S. (1993) Assessing diversity climate: a field study of reactions to employer efforts to promote diversity, *Journal of Organizational Behavior*, 14(14), 61–81.

Kozlowski, S.W., Chao, G.T., Smith, E.M. and Hedlund, J. (1993) Organizational downsizing: strategies, interventions, and research implications, in Cooper, C.L. and Robertson, I.T. (eds) *International Review of Industrial and Organizational Psychology*, pp. 263–332. New York, John Wiley and Sons.

Kydd, C.T. and Oppenheim, L. (1990) Using human resource management to enhance competitiveness: lessons from four excellent companies, *Human Resource Management*, Summer, 29(2), 145–166.

Labib, N. and Appelbaum, S.H. (1994) The impact of downsizing practices on corporate success, *Journal of Management Development*, 13(7), 59–84.

Lam, S.S.K. and Schaubroeck, J. (1998) Integrating HR planning and organisational strategy, *Human Resource Management Journal*, 8(3), 5–19.

Lank, E. and Windle, I. (2003) Catch me if you can, *People Management*, 6 February, 40–42.

Lashley, C. (2000) Empowerment through involvement: a case study of TGI Fridays restaurants, *Personnel Review*, 29(6), 791–815.

Latack, J.C. (1986) Coping with job stress: measures and future directions for scale development, *Journal of Applied Psychology*, 71, 377–385.

Laurent, A. (1983) The cultural diversity of western conceptions of management, *International Studies of Management and Organization*, 13(1/2), 75–96.

Lawler, E. (1995) The new pay: a strategic approach, *Compensation and Benefits Review*, July–August, 14–22.

Lawler, E.E. (1984) The strategic design of reward systems, in Fombrun, C., Tichy, N.M. and Devanna, M.A. *Strategic Human Resource Management*. New York: John Wiley.

Lawler, E.E. (1994) From job-based to competency-based organisations, *Journal of Organizational Behaviour*, 15, 3–15.

Lawler, E.E. and Mohrman, S.A. (2003) HR as strategic partner: what does it take to make it happen?, *Human Resource Planning*, 26(3), 15–29.

Lawrence, P.R. and Lorsch, J.W. (1967) *Organization and Environment: Managing Differentiation and Integration*, Boston, MA: Harvard Business School Press.

Lazarus, R.S. and Folkman, S. (1984) *Stress, Appraisal, and Coping*, New York: Springer Publishing Company.

Lebas, M. (1995) Performance measurement and performance management, *International Journal of Production Economics*, 41(1), 23–35.

Lee, M. and Shao, G. (2000) Compensations and benefit trends – report from China, *Benefits and Compensation International*, January/February, 12–18.

Lee, R. (1996) The 'pay-forward' view of training, *People Management*, 8 February, 30–32.

Legge, K. (1978) *Power, Innovation and Problem-solving in Personnel Management*. Maidenhead, McGraw-Hill.

Legge, K. (1994) Managing culture: fact or fiction, in Sisson, K. (ed.) *Personnel Management: A Comprehensive Guide to Theory and Practice in Britain* (2nd edn), pp. 397–433 Oxford: Blackwell.

Legge, K. (1995a) HRM: rhetoric, reality and hidden agendas, in Storey, J. (ed.) *Human Resource Management: A Critical Text*. London: Routledge.

Legge, K. (1995b) *Human Resource Management: Rhetoric's and Realities*. London: Macmillan.

Legge, K. (2001) Silver bullet or spent round: assessing the meaning of the 'high commitment management/performance relationship', in Storey, J. (ed.) *Human Resource Management: A Critical Text*, London: Thomson Learning.

Legge, K. (2005) *Human Resource Management: Rhetorics and Realities* (2nd edn). Basingstoke: Palgrave Macmillan.

Lengnick-Hall, C.A. and Lengnick-Hall, M.L. (1988) Strategic human resources management: a review of the literature and a proposed typology, *Academy of Management Review*, 13(3), 454–470.

Leonard-Barton, D. (1992) Core capabilities and core rigidities: a paradox in managing new product development, *Strategic Management Journal*, 13(1), 111–125.

Leonard-Barton, D. (1998) *Wellsprings of Knowledge. Building and Sustaining the Sources of Innovation*. Boston, MA: Harvard Business School Press.

Lewin, K. (1952) *Field Theory in Social Science*. London: Tavistock.

Lewis, D. (1996) The organizational culture saga – from OD to TQM: a critical review of the literature. Part 2 – applications, *Leadership and Organization Development Journal*, 17(2), 9–16.

Lewis, P. (1993) *The Successful Management of Redundancy*. Blackwell: Oxford.

Lewis, P. (1999) Managing performance-related pay based on evidence from the financial services sector, *Human Resource Management Journal*, 8(2), 66–77.

Lewis. P. (1998b) Managing performance-related pay based on evidence from the financial services sector, *Human Resource Management Journal*, 8(2), 66–77.

Lewis, P. (2003a) Cultural barriers to the development of performance management in China, *International HRM Conference*, University of Limerick, June.

Lewis, P. (2003b) New China – old ways?: a case study of the prospects for implementing human resource management practices in a Chinese state-owned enterprise, *Employee Relations*, 25(1), 42–60.

Lewis, P., Thornhill, A. and Saunders, M. (2002) Family breakdown: developing an explanatory theory of reward system change. Paper presented to HRM in a Changing World conference, Oxford Brookes University, April.

Lewis, P., Thornhill, M. and Saunders, M. (2003a) *Employee Relations: Understanding the Employment Relationship*. Harlow: Pearson Education.

Lewis, P., Thornhill, A. and Saunders, M.N.K. (2003c) *Employee Relations: Understanding the Employment Relationship*. Harlow: Financial Times Prentice Hall.

Lewis, P., Saunders, M. and Thornhill, A. (2004) Family breakdown: developing an explanatory theory of reward system change, *Personnel Review*, 33(2), 174–186.

Liff, S. (1993) From equality to diversity: organisations, gender and power. Paper from an IRRU Workshop, *Warwick Papers in Industrial Relations*, No. 48, December.

Liff, S. (1997) Two routes to managing diversity: individual differences or social group characteristics, *Employee Relations*, 19(1), 11–26.

Liff, S. (1999) Diversity and equal opportunities: room for a constructive compromise?, *Human Resource Management Journal*, 9(1), 65–75.

Liff, S. (2000) Manpower or human resource planning – what's in a name?, in Bach, S. and Sisson, K. (eds) *Personnel Management: A Comprehensive Guide to Theory and Practice*, pp. 93–110. Oxford: Blackwell.

Littlefield, D. (2000) Four-stroke of genius, *People Management*, 3 February, 52–53.

Locke, E., Saari, L., Shaw, K. and Latham, G. (1981) Goal setting and task performance: 1969–1980, *Psychological Bulletin*, 90(1), 125–152.

Lockyer, C. and Scholarios, D. (2004) Selecting hotel staff: why best practice does not always work, *International Journal of Contemporary Hospitality Management*, 16(2), 125–135.

Love, A. (1991) *Internal Evaluation*. Newbury Park, CA: Sage.

Lowe, K., Milliman, J., De Cieri, H. and Dowling, P. (2002) International compensation practices: a ten country comparative analysis, *Human Resource Management*, 41(1), 45–66.

Lundy, O. and Cowling, A. (1996) *Strategic Human Resource Management*. London: Routledge.

Luoma, M. (2000) Investigating the link between strategy and HRD, *Personnel Review*, 29(6), 769–790.

Lupton, T. and Bowey, A. (1983) *Wages and Salaries* (2nd edn). Aldershot: Gower.

Mabey, C. and Iles, P. (1993) The strategic integration of assessment and development practices: succession planning and new manager development, *Human Resource Management Journal*, 3(4), 16–34.

Mabey, C. and Mallory, G. (1994/5) Structure and culture change in two UK organisations: a comparison of assumptions, approaches and outcomes, *Human Resource Management Journal*, 5(2), 28–45.

Mabey, C. and Salaman, G. (1995) *Strategic Human Resource Management*. Oxford: Blackwell.

Mabey, C., Salaman, G. and Storey, J. (1998) *Human Resource Management: A Strategic Introduction* (2nd edn). Oxford: Blackwell.

MacDuffie, J. (1995) Human resource bundles and manufacturing performance: organisational logic and flexible production systems in the world auto industry, *Industrial and Labor Relations Review*, 48(2), 197–221.

MacNeil, C.M. (2004) Exploring the supervisor role as a facilitator of knowledge sharing in teams, *Journal of European Industrial Training*, 28(1), 93–102.

MacPherson, W. (1999) *The Stephen Lawrence Inquiry*. London: The Stationery Office.

Madison, T.F. and Clancy, D.K. (2000) Downsizing and performance: an empirical study of the effects of competition and equity market pressure, in Epstein, M.J. and Lee, J.Y. (eds) *Advances in Management Accounting*, 9, 91–107.

Maitland, A. (2004) A mixed workforce can open up markets, FT Business and Diversity Special Report, *Financial Times*, 10 May, p. 1.

Manzini, A.O. (1988) Integrating human resource planning and development: the unification of strategic, operational, and human resource planning systems, *Human Resource Planning*, 11(2), 79–94.

Marchington, M. (2001) Employee involvement at work, in Storey, J. (ed.) *Human Resource Management: A Critical Text* (2nd edn). London: Thomson.

Marchington, M. and Grugulis, I. (2000) Best practice human resource management: perfect opportunity or dangerous illusion?, *International Journal of Human Resource Management*, 11(6), 1104–1124.

Marchington, M. and Wilkinson, A. (1996) *Core Personnel and Development*. London: IPD.

Marchington, M. and Wilkinson, A. (2002) *People Management and Development: Human Resource Management at Work* (2nd edn). London: CIPD.

Marchington, M., Wilkinson, A. and Ackers, P. (2001) *Management Choice and Employee Voice*. Research report. London: CIPD.

Marsden, D. and Richardson, R. (1992) *Motivation and Performance Related Pay in the Public Sector: a case study of the Inland Revenue*. Discussion Paper No. 75. Centre for Economic Performance, London School of Economics.

Martin, J. (1992) *Cultures in Organizations: Three Perspectives*. New York: Oxford University Press.

Maslow, A. (1943) A theory of human motivation, *Psychological Review*, 50, 370–396.

Matthewman, J. (1993) *HR Effectiveness*. London: IPM.

Mavin, S. and Girling, G. (1999) Of course I know what managing diversity is! Paper delivered to the British Academy of Management Conference, Manchester.

Mavin, S. and Girling, G. (2000) What is managing diversity and why does it matter?, *Human Resource Development International*, 3(4), 419–433.

Maxwell, G., Blair, S. and McDougall, M. (2001) Edging towards managing diversity in practice, *Employee Relations*, 23(5), 468–482.

Mayer, M. and Whittington, R. (2004) Economics, politics and nations: resistance to the multidivisional form in France, Germany and the United Kingdom, 1983–1993, *Journal of Management Studies*, 41(7), 1057–1082.

McCombs, T., Elloy, D.F. and Flynn, W.R. (1994) A procedure for staffing the autonomous work team, *Recruitment, Selection and Retention*, 3(1), 17–23.

McCracken, M. and Wallace, M. (2000) Towards a redefinition of strategic HRD, *Journal of European Industrial Training*, 24(5), 281–290.

McCune, J.T., Beatty, R.W. and Montagno, R.V. (1988) Downsizing: practices in manufacturing firms, *Human Resource Management*, 27(2), 145–161.

McDougall, M. (1996) Equal opportunities versus managing diversity, another challenge for public sector management, *International Journal of Public Sector Management*, 9(5/6), 62–72.

McEnrue, M. (1993) Managing diversity: Los Angeles before and after the riots, *Organizational Dynamics*, 21(3), 18–29.

McGregor, D. (1960) *The Human Side of Enterprise*. New York: McGraw-Hill.

McKersie, R.B. (1996) Labour–management partnerships: US evidence and the implications for Ireland, *IBAR – Irish Business and Administrative Research*, 17(1), 1–26.

McSweeney, B. (2002a) Hofstede's model of national cultural differences and their consequences: a triumph of faith – a failure of analysis, *Human Relations*, 55(1), 89–118.

McSweeney, B. (2002b) The essentials of scholarship, *Human Relations*, 55(11), 1362–1372.

Meek, V.L. (1988) Organizational culture: origins and weaknesses, *Organizational Studies*, 9(4), 453–473.

Megginson, D., Banfield, P. and Joy-Matthews, J. (1999) *Human Resource Development* (2nd edn). London: Kogan Page.

Mercer Human Resource Consulting (2003) *European Employment Conditions*, 10 Septmenber. Available online http://www.mercerhr.com

Miles, R.E. and Snow, C.C. (1984a) Fit, failure and the hall of fame, *California Management Review*, 26(3), Spring, 10–28.

Miles, R.E. and Snow, C.C. (1984b) Designing strategic human resources systems, *Organizational Dynamics*, 13(8), 36–52.

Miles, R.E., Snow, C.C., Mathews, J.A., Miles, G. and Coleman, H.J. Jr (1997) Organizing in the knowledge age: anticipating the cellular form, *Academy of Management Executive*, 11(4), 7–24.

Miller, D. (1996) Equality management: towards a materialist approach, *Gender, Work and Organization*, 3(4), 202–214.

Miller, E. (1984) Strategic staffing, in Fombrun, D.J., Tichy, N.M. and Devanna, M.E. (eds) *Strategic Human Resource Management*, pp. 57–86. New York: John Wiley.

Millmore, M. (2003) Just how extensive is the practice of strategic recruitment and selection?, *The Irish Journal of Management*, 24(1), 87–108.

Millmore, M. and Baker, B. (1996) Staff recruitment and selection: strategy for the future, *Managing HE*, Summer(3), 16–19.

Mills, D.Q. (1985) Planning with people in mind, *Harvard Business Review*, July–August, 97–105.

Millward, L.J. and Brewerton, P.M. (1999) Contractors and their psychological contracts, *British Journal of Management*, 10(3), 253–274.

Millward, N., Bryson, A. and Forth, J. (2000) *All Change at Work? British Employment Relations 1980–1998, as Portrayed by the Workplace Industrial Relations Survey series*. London: Routledge.

Milner, H. (2004) Expert views, in Morrison, D., What happens when employees can't get no job satisfaction, *The Daily Telegraph*, 28 September, p. 29.

Milsome, S. (2001) *New Forms of Work Organisation, the Benefit and Impact on Performance, Employment and Social Affairs*. European Commission, paper presented to the Director General Employment and Social Affairs by the European Work Organisation Network (EWON). Available online http://ukwon.net

Mintzberg, H. (1979) *The Structure of Organizations*. Englewood Cliffs, NJ: Prentice Hall.

Mintzberg, H. (1987) Crafting strategy, *Harvard Business Review*, July–August, 66–75.

Mintzberg, H. (1991) The effective organization: forces and forms, *Sloan Management Review*, Winter, 54–67.

Mintzberg, H. (1993) *Structure in Fives: Designing Effective Organizations*. London: Prentice Hall International.

Mintzberg, H. (1994) *The Rise and Fall of Strategic Planning*. Hemel Hempstead: Prentice Hall International.

Mintzberg, H., Ahlstrand, B. and Lampel, J. (1998) *Strategy Safari*. London: Prentice Hall Europe.

Mintzberg, H. and Waters, J.A. (1985) Of strategies, deliberate and emergent, *Strategic Management Journal*, 6, 257–275.

Mintzberg, H. and Waters, J. (1989) Of strategies deliberate and emergent, in Asch, D. and Bowman, C. (eds) *Readings in Strategic Management*. Basingstoke: Macmillan.

Mishra, A.K. and Mishra, K.E. (1994) The role of mutual trust in effective downsizing strategies, *Human Resource Management*, 33(2), 261–279.

Monks, J. (1998) Trade unions, enterprise and the future, in Sparrow, P. and Marchington, M. (eds) *Human Resource Management: The New Agenda*. London: FT Pitman.

Morgan, G. (1989) *Creative Organization Theory. A Resource Book*. London: Sage.

Morgan, G. (1997) *Images of Organization*. Thousand Oaks, CA: Sage.

Morris, J. (1974) Developing resourceful managers, in Taylor, B. and Lippiat, G. (eds) *Management development and Training Handbook*. New York: McGraw-Hill.

Morrison, A. (1992) *The New Leaders*. San Franciso, CA: Jossey Bass Inc.

Morrison, D. (2004) What happens when employees can't get no job satisfaction, *The Daily Telegraph*, 28 September, p. 29.

Morrison, E.W. and Robinson, S.L. (1997) When employees feel betrayed: a model of how psychological contract violation develops, *Academy of Management Review*, 23, 226–256.

Morrison, J. (2002) *The International Business Environment*. Basingstoke: Palgrave.

Mowday, R., Porter, L. and Steers, R. (1982) *Employee–Organisation Linkages: The Psychology of Commitment, Absenteeism and Turnover*. London: Academic Press.

Mueller, F. (1996) Human resources as strategic assets: an evolutionary resource-based theory, *Journal of Management Studies*, 33(6), 757–785.

Muhlemeyer, P. and Clarke, M. (1997) The competitive factor: training and development as a strategic management task, *Journal of Workplace Learning*, 9(1), 4–10.

Mumford, A. (1998) Managing learning and developing management, *Human Resource Development International: Enhancing Performance, Learning and Integrity*, 1(1), 113–118.

Murphy, G., Athanason, J. and King, N. (2002) Job satisfaction and organizational citizenship behaviour: a study of Australian human service professionals, *Journal of Managerial Psychology*, 17(2), 287–297.

Murray, S. (2004a) Age and experience, FT Business and Diversity Special Report, *Financial Times*, 10 May, p. 6.

Murray, S. (2004b) Banking on experience, FT Business and Diversity Special Report, *Financial Times*, 10 May, p. 6.

Myers, J. and Kirk, S. (2005) Managing processes of human resource development, in Leopold, J., Harris, L. and Watson, T. (eds) *The Strategic Managing of Human Resources*, pp. 351–379. Harlow: Financial Times Prentice Hall.

National Statistics (2003) *Census 2001: United Kingdom*, 11 November. Available online http://www.statistics.gov.uk /census2001/pyramids/pages/UK.asp

Naumann, S.E., Bies, R.J. and Martin, C.L. (1995) The roles of organizational support and justice during a layoff, *Academy of Management Best Papers Proceedings*, 55, 89–93.

Nelson, L. (2003) A case study in organisational change: implications for theory, *The Learning Organisation*, 10(1), 18–30.

Nevo, D. (1986) Conceptualisation of educational evaluation, in House, E. (ed.) *New Directions in Educational Evaluation* pp. 15–29. London: Falmer Press.

Newell, H. (2002) Accountco: small is beautiful? HR planning in a small firm, in Newell, H. and Scarbrough, H. (eds) (2002) *HRM in Context: A Case Study Approach*, pp. 79–105. Basingstoke: Palgrave.

Newell, H. and Dopson, S. (1996) Muddle in the middle: organizational restructuring and middle management careers, *Personnel Review*, 25(4), 4–20.

Newell, S. (2005) Assessment, selection and evaluation, in Leopold, J., Harris, L. and Watson, T. (eds) *The Strategic Managing of Human Resources*, pp. 140–177. Harlow: Financial Times Prentice Hall.

Newell, S. and Shackleton, V. (2001) Selection and assessment as an interactive decision–action process, in Redman, T. and Wilkinson, A. (eds) *Contemporary Human Resource Management: Text and Cases*, pp. 24–56. Harlow: Pearson Education.

Nicholson, M. (2004) The man who moved east to make rooms, *Financial Times*, 1 June, p. 11.

Nissen. B. (1997) Unions and workplace reorganisation, in Nissen B. (ed.) *Unions and Workplace Reorganisation*, Detroit, MI: Wayne State University Press.

Nkomo, S.M. (1986) The theory and practice of HR planning: the gap still remains, *Personnel Administrator Journal*, 31(8), 71–84.

Nkomo, S.M. (1987) Human resource planning and organizational performance: an exploratory analysis, *Strategic Management Journal*, 8(4), 387–392.

Nkomo, S.M. (1988) Strategic planning for human resources – let's get started, *Long Range Planning*, 21(1), 66–72.

O'Connell, D. (2004) BA courts passenger anger with £4m staff ticket giveaway, *The Sunday Times: Business*, 29 August, p. 1.

Office for National Statistics (2004) Mergers and acquisitions involving UK companies, 4 May. London: Office for National Statistics.

Office of the Deputy Prime Minister (2004) *Best Value FAQs*, Available online http://www.bvpi.gov.uk/pages/faq.asp

Ogbonna, E. (1993) Managing organizational culture: fantasy or reality?, *Human Resource Management Journal*, 3(2), 42–54.

Ohmae, K. (1994) *The Borderless World, Power and Strategy in the Interlinked Economy*. London: HarperCollins.

Oppenheim, A.N. (2000) *Questionnaire Design, Interviewing and Attitude Measurement*. London: Continuum International.

Organisation for Economic Cooperation and Development (OECD) (2005). *Foreign Direct Investment Outflows from US Hit Record $252 billion in 2004*. Available online http://www.oecd.org/document/54/0,2340,en_2649_33763_35033718_1_1_1_1,00.html

Paconowsky, M.E. and O'Donnell-Trujillo, N. (1982) Communication and organizational culture, *The Western Journal of Speech and Communication*, 46(1), 115–130.

Paddison, L. (1990) The targeted approach to recruitment, *Personnel Management*, November, 54–58.

Parekh, B. (1998) Integrating minorities, in Blackstone, T., Parekh, B. and Sanders, P. (eds) *Philosophy, Politics and Society* (2nd series). Oxford: Blackwell.

Parker, B. and Caine, D. (1996) Holonic modelling: human resource planning and the two faces of Janus, *International Journal of Manpower*, 17(8), 30–45.

Parker, M. and Slaughter, J. (1997) Advancing unionism on the new terrain, in Nissen, B. (ed.) *Unions and Workplace Reorganisation*. Detroit, MI: Wayne State University Press.

Parkinson, S. (1990) Management development's strategic role, *Journal of General Management*, 16(2), 63–75.

Paton, S. (1997) *Service Quality: Disney Style*. Available online http://www.qualitydigest.com/jan97/disney.html

Patrickson, M., Bamber, V. and Bamber, G. (1995) *Organisational Change Strategies*. Melbourne: Longman.

Patterson, M., West, M., Lawthom, R. and Nickell, S. (1997) *Impact of People Management Practices on Business Performance*. Wimbledon: Institute of Personnel and Development.

Patton, M.Q. (1997) *Utilization-focused Evaluation: The New Century Text*. Thousand Oaks, CA: Sage.

Patton, M.Q. (2002) *Qualitative Evaluation and Research Methods* (3rd edn). Thousand Oaks, CA: Sage.

Pavitt, K. (1991) Key characteristics of the large innovating firm, *British Journal of Management*, 2, 41–50.

Pearn Kandola (2000) *Cross-Government Statistics*. London.

Pedler, M., Burgoyne, J. and Boydell, T. (1991) *The Learning Company*. Maidenhead: McGraw–Hill.

Penrose, E.T. (1952) Biological analogies in the theory of the firm, *American Economic Review*, 42(5), 804–819.

Penrose, E.T. (1959) *The Theory of the Growth of the Firm*, New York, John Wiley.

People Management (1999) Fate of BAe merger hinges on exchange of knowledge, 22 April.

People Management (2004a) Home or away?, 3 June, 35–39.

People Management (2004b) O2 bonus helps to retain staff, 14 October.

People Management (2005a) Standard lacks staff value focus, *People Management*, 11(11), 11.

People Management (2005b) Pret eats into high levels of staff turnover, 14 July.

Perlmutter, H. (1969) The tortuous evolution of the multinational corporation, *Columbia Journal of World Business*, 1, 9–18.

Persaud, R. (2005) The no-diet diet: it's a question of habit, *The Daily Telegraph*, 4 January, p. 16.

Peteraf, M.A. (1993) The cornerstones of competitive advantage: a resource-based view, *Strategic Management Journal*, 14(3), 179–191.

Peters, T. and Waterman, R. (1982) *In Search of Excellence*. New York: HarperCollins.

Peters, T.J. and Waterman, R.H. (1995) *In Search of Excellence*, London: HarperCollins.

Petrovic, J. and Kakabadse, N. K. (2003) Strategic staffing of international joint ventures (IJVs): an integrative perspective for future research, *Management Decision*, 41(4), 394–406.

Pettigrew, A. and Whipp, R. (1991) *Managing Change for Competitive Success*. Oxford: Blackwell.

Pfeffer, J. (1981) *Power in Organizations*. Cambridge, MA: Pitman.

Pfeffer, J. (1992) *Managing with Power: Politics and Influence in Organizations*. Boston, MA: Harvard Business School Press.

Pfeffer, J. (1998) *The Human Equation: Building Profits by Putting People First*. Boston, MA: Harvard Business School Press.

Pfizer (2005) *Partners for Life*, Available online http://www .pfizer.co.uk/template4.asp?pageid=55

Pheysey, D.C. (1993) *Organizational Cultures: Types and Transformations*. London: Routledge.

Phillips, J. (1991) *Training Evaluation and Measurement Methods*. Houston, TX: Gulf Publishing.

Pierce, A., Evans, M. and Tendler, S. (2003) Senior judge heads inquiry to review security at Palace, *The Times*, 20 November, p. 6.

Poole, M. (1990) Editorial: human resource management in an international perspective, *International Journal of Human Resource Management*, 1(1), 1–15.

Porter, M.E. (1980) *Competitive Strategy: Techniques for Analyzing Industries and Competitors*. New York: Free Press.

Porter, M.E. (1985) *Competitive Advantage: Creating and Sustaining Superior Performance*. New York: Free Press.

Prahalad, C.K. and Hamel, G. (1990) The core competences of the corporation, *Harvard Business Review*, May–June, 79–91.

Prasad, P., Mills, A.J., Elmes, M. and Prasad, A. (1997) *Managing the Organizational Melting Pot: Dilemmas of Workforce Diversity*. Thousand Oaks, CA: Sage.

Preskill, H. and Torres, R. (1999) Building capacity for organisational learning through evaluative inquiry, *Evaluation*, 5(1), 42–60.

Price, R. (2001) *A Concise History of France*. Cambridge, Cambridge University Press.

Procter, S., McArdle, L., Rowlinson, M., Forrester, P. and Hassard, J. (1993) Performance related pay in operation: a case study from the electronics industry, *Human Resource Management Journal*, 3(4), 60–74.

Programme for Prosperity and Fairness (2000) Government of Ireland.

Prusack, L. (ed.) (1997) *Knowledge in Organizations*. Boston, MA: Butterworth-Heinemann.

Public Services Productivity Panel (2000) *Public Services Productivity: Meeting the Challenge*, HM Treasury. Available online http://www.hm-treasury.gov.uk/media/76E/19/241.pdf

Pugh, D.S., Hickson, D.J., Hinings, C.R. and Turner, C. (1968) Dimensions of organization structure, *Administrative Science Quarterly*, June, 65–104.

Purcell, J. (1989a) The impact of corporate strategy on human resource management, in Storey, J. (ed.) *New Perspectives on Human Resource Management*. London: Routledge.

Purcell, J. (1989b) The impact of corporate strategy on human resource management, in Storey J. (ed.) *New Perspectives on Human Resource Management*, pp. 67–91. London: Routledge.

Purcell, J. (1991) The impact of corporate strategy on human resource management, in Storey, J. (ed.) *New Perspectives on Human Resource Management*, pp. 67–91. London: Routledge.

Purcell, J. (1995) Corporate strategy and its link with human resource management strategy, in Storey, J. (ed.) *Human Resource Management: A Critical Text*, pp. 63–86. London: Routledge.

Purcell, J. (1999) Best practice and best fit: chimera or cul-de-sac?, *Human Resource Management Journal*, 9(3), 26–41.

Purcell, J. (2001) The meaning of strategy in human resource management, in Storey, J. (ed.) *Human Resource Management. A Critical Text* (2nd edn). London: Thomson Learning.

Purcell, J., Kinnie, N., Hutchinson, S., Rayton, B. and Swart, J. (2003) *Understanding the People and Performance Link: Unlocking the Black Box*. Wimbledon: Chartered Institute of Personnel and Development.

Purcell, J., Kinnie, N. and Hutchinson, S. (2003) *Understanding the People and Performance Link: Unlocking the Black Box*. Research report. London: CIPD.

Quinn, J.B. (1980) *Strategies for Change: Logical Incrementalism*. Homewood, IL: Irwin.

Quinn, J.B. (1993) Managing strategic change, in Mabey, C. and Mayon-White, B. (eds) *Managing Change*. London: Paul Chapman/Open University.

Quinn, R.E. and McGrath, M.R. (1985) The transformation of organizational cultures: a competing values perspective, in Frost, P.J., Moore, L.F., Louis, M.R., Lundberg, C.C. and Martin, J. (eds) *Organizational Culture*, pp. 315–334. Beverly Hills, CA: Sage.

Radnor, Z. and McGuire, M. (2004) Performance management in the public sector: fact or fiction, *International Journal of Productivity and Performance Management*, 53(3), 245–260.

Raimond, P. (1993) *Management Projects Design, Research and Presentation*. London: Chapman and Hall.

Randell, G. (1994) Employee appraisal, in Sisson, K. (ed.) *Personnel Management: A Comprehensive Guide to Theory and Practice in Britain*, pp. 221–252. Oxford: Blackwell.

Redman, T. (2001) Performance appraisal, in Redman, T. and Wilkinson, A. (eds) *Contemporary Human Resource Management*. Harlow: Financial Times Prentice Hall.

Redman, T. and Wilkinson, A. (eds) (2001) *Contemporary Human Resource Management: Text and Cases*, Harlow: Financial Times Prentice Hall.

Reichers, A. (1985) A review and reconceptualization of organizational commitment, *Academy of Management Review*, 10, 465-476.

Reichers, A. (1986) Conflict and organizational commitments, *Journal of Applied Psychology*, 71, 508–514.

Reichers, A.E., Wanous, J.P. and Austin, J.T. (1997) Understanding and managing cynicism about organisational change, *Academy of Management Executive*, 11(1), 48–59.

Reid, M.A. and Barrington, H. (1999) *Training Interventions*. London: CIPD.

Reigo, B. (2001) How to overcome the know-how shortage in a fast moving Telco, *Human Resources Solutions for Europe*, HR Summit Conference, Montreux, February.

Reuters (2005) Troubled Sony set for job cuts, new investments, 21 September. Available online http://today.reuters .com/business/newsArticle.aspx?type=technology&storyID =nT73539

Reynolds, R. and Ablett, A. (1998) Transforming the rhetoric of organisational learning to the reality of the learning organisation, *The Learning Organization*, 5(1), 24–35.

Richardson, R. and Thompson, M. (1999) *The Impact of People Management Practices on Business Performance: A Literature Review*. Wimbledon: Institute of Personnel and Development.

Risher, H. (2000) Dow Chemical's salary program: a model for the future?, *Compensation and Benefits Review*, May–June, 26–34.

Ritter, M. (2003) The use of balanced scorecards in the strategic management of corporate communication, *Corporate Communication*, 8(1), 44–59.

Ritzer, G. (1998) *The McDonaldisation Thesis*. London: Sage.

Ritzer, G. (2002), *McDonaldization: The Reader*. Thousand Oaks, CA: Pine Forge Press.

Robbins, S.P. (1987) *Organization Theory: Structure, Design and Applications*. Englewood Cliffs, NJ: Prentice Hall.

Roberts, I. (1997) Remuneration and reward, in Beardwell, I. and Holden, L. (eds) *Human Resource Management: A Contemporary Perspective*. London: Pitman Publishing.

Roberts, Z. (2003) Learning leads the way, *People Management*, 6 November, 34–35.

Robinson, G. and Dechant, K. (1997) Building a case for diversity, *The Academy of Management Executive*, 11(3), 21–31.

Robson, C. (2002) *Real World Research* (2nd edn). Oxford: Blackwell.

Ronen, S. and Shenkar, O. (1985) Clustering countries on attitudinal dimensions: a review and synthesis, *Academy of Management Review*, 10(3), 435–454.

Ronen, S. and Shenkar, O. (1988) Using employee attitudes to establish MNC regional divisions, *Personnel*, August, 32–39.

Roscow, J. and Casner-Lotto, J. (1998) *People Partnership and Profits: The New Labour–Management Agenda*, New York: Work in America Institute.

Rose, E. (2001) *Employment Relations*. Harlow: Pearson.

Rose, E. (2004) *Employment Relations*, (2nd edn), Harlow: Pearson Educational.

Ross, R. and Schneider, R. (1992) *From Equality to Diversity*. London: Pitman.

Rothwell, S. (1995), HRP, in Storey, J. (ed.) *Human Resource Management: A Critical Text*, pp. 167–202. London: Routledge.

Rousseau, D. (1994) cited by Hiltrop, J.M. (1995) The changing psychological contract: the human resource challenge in the 1990's, *European Journal of Management*, 13(3), 286–294.

Rousseau, D.M. (1995) *Psychological Contracts in Organizations*. London: Sage.

Rushmer, R.K. (1997) How do we measure the effectiveness of team building? Is it good enough? Team Management Systems – a case study, *Journal of Management Development*, 16(2), 93–110.

Russ-Eft, D. and Preskill, H. (2001) *Evaluations in Organizations*. Cambridge, MA: Perseus Publishing.

Rynes, S. and Rosen, B. (1995) A field survey of factors affecting the adoption and perceived success of diversity training, *Personnel Psychology*, 48(2), 248–270.

Sadler, P. and Milmer, K. (1993) *The Talent-Intensive Organisation: Optimising your Company's Human Resource Strategies*, Special Report No. P659. London: The Economist Intelligence Unit.

Salama, A., Holland, W. and Vinten, G. (2003) Challenges and opportunities in mergers and acquisitions: three international case studies – Deutsche Bank–Bankers Trust; British Petroleum–Amoco; Ford–Volvo, *Journal of European Industrial Training*, 27(6), 313–321.

Salamon, M. (2000) *Industrial Relations: Theory and Practice* (4th edn). Hemel Hempstead: Prentice Hall.

Saunders, M.N.K., Lewis, P. and Thornhill, A. (2007) *Research Methods for Business Students* (4th edn). Harlow: FT Prentice Hall.

Scarborough, H. (2003) *Human Capital: External Reporting Framework* London: Chartered Institute of Personnel and Development.

Schein, E.H. (1992a) *Organisational Culture and Leadership* (2nd edn), San Francisco, CA: Jossey-Bass.

Schein, E.H. (1992b) Coming to a new awareness of organisational culture, in Salaman, G., Cameron, S., Hamblin, H., Iles, P., Mabey, C. and Thompson, K. (eds) *Human Resource Strategies*, pp. 237–253. London: Sage.

Schein, E.H. (1997) (2nd edn) *Organizational Culture and Leadership*. San Francisco, CA: Jossey-Bass.

Schein, E.H. (1999) *Process Consultation Revisited*. Reading, MA: Addison-Wesley.

Schneider, B. and Konz, M.K. (1989) Strategic job analysis, *Human Resource Management*, Spring, 28(1), 51–63.

Schneider, R. (2001) Variety performance, *People Management*, 7(9), 26–31.

Schneider, S.C. and Barsoux, J.-L. (2003) *Managing Across Cultures* (2nd edn). Harlow: FT Prentice Hall.

Scholarios, D. and Lockyer, C. (1996) Human resource management and selection: better solutions or new dilemmas?, in Towers, B. (ed.) *The Handbook of Human Resource Management* (2nd edn), pp. 173–195. Oxford: Blackwell.

Schraeder, M. and Self, D.R. (2003) Enhancing the success of mergers and acquisitions: an organizational culture perspective, *Management Decision*, 41(5), 511–522.

Schuler, R., Dowling, P. and De Cieri (1993) An integrative framework of international strategic human resource management, *Journal of Management*, 19(2), 419–459.

Schuler, R. and Jackson, S. (1987) Linking competitive strategies with human resource management practices, *Academy of Management Executive*, 1(3), 207–219.

Schuler, R.S. and Jackson, S.E. (1989) Determinants of human resource management priorities and implications for industrial relations, *Journal of Management*, 15(1), 89–99.

Schuler, R. and Jackson, S. (1999) *Human Resource Management: Positioning for the 21st Century*, Cincinnati, MN: West Publishing.

Schuler, R.S., Jackson, S.E. and Storey, J. (2001) HRM and its link with strategic management, in Storey, J. (ed.) *Human Resource Management. A Critical Text*, (2nd edn). London: Thomson Learning.

Schuster, J. and Zingheim, P. (1992) *The New Pay: Linking Employee and Organisational Performance*. New York: Lexington.

Schuster, J. and Zingheim, P. (1999) Dealing with scarce talent: lessons from the leading edge, *Compensation and Benefits Review*, March/April, 31–44.

Scottish Enterprise (2004) *Scotland's Enterprise Minister Jim Wallace visits Amazon.co.uk's New Fully Operational Scottish Distribution Centre*, 12 October. Available online http://www.scottish-enterprise.com/sedotcom_home/news-se/news-fullarticle.htm?articleid=82513&

Scottish Executive (2004) *What is Best Value?* Available online http://www.scotland.gov.uk/about/FCSD/LG-PERF4/00014838/Home.aspx

Scriven, M. (1972) Pros and cons about goal free evaluation, *Evaluation Comment: The Journal Of Educational Evaluation*, 3(4), 1–7.

Seamark, M. (2003) Anyone recognise his name, shouted the barmaid. I do, said a regular. And that was enough to satisfy the Palace, *Daily Mail*, 20 November, pp. 6–7.

Seamark, M. and Greenhill, S. (2003) Palace is blamed for security farce, *Daily Mail*, 20 November, 6–7.

Semler, R. (1993) *Maverick! The Success Story Behind the World's Most Unusual Workplace*. London: Arrow Business Books.

Senior, B. (2002) *Organisational Change* (2nd edn). Harlow: FT Prentice Hall.

Shaw, J.B. and Barrett-Power, E. (1997) A conceptual framework for assessing organization, work groups and individual effectiveness during and after downsizing, *Human Relations*, 50(2), 109–127.

Shibata, H. (2002) Wage and performance appraisal systems in flux: a Japan–United States comparison, *Industrial Relations*, 41(4), 629–652.

Simon, H.A. (1976) *Administrative Behavior. A Study of Decision-Making Processes in Administrative Organizations* (3rd edn). London: Collier Macmillan Publishers.

Simpkins, E. (2004) BA at breaking point, *The Sunday Telegraph: Business*, 29 August, p. 3.

Sisson, K. (1990) Introducing the *Human Resource Management Journal*, *Human Resource Management Journal*, 1(1), 1–11.

Sisson, K. (1994) Personnel management: paradigms, practice and prospects, in Sisson, K. (ed.) *Personnel Management: A Comprehensive Guide to Theory and Practice in Britain* (2nd edn), pp. 3–50. Oxford: Blackwell.

Skapinker, M. (2002) *Knowledge Management: The Change Agenda*. London: CIPD.

Skills Foresight (2004) *Skills for Justice: Police Sector*. London: Skills for Justice, 4 October. Available online http://www.skillsforjustice.com/websitefiles/SF_2004_report(1).pdf

Skinner, D. (2004) Evaluation and change management: rhetoric and reality, *Human Resource Management Journal*, 14(3), 5–20.

Skinner, D. and Mabey, C. (1997) Managers perceptions of strategic HR change, *Personnel Review*, 26(6), 467–484.

Skinner. D., Saunders, M.N.K. and Duckett, H.R. (2004) Policies, promises and trust: improving working lives in the NHS, *International Journal of Public Sector Management*, 17(7), 558–70.

Skinner, D., Tagg, C. and Holloway, J. (2000) Managers and qualitative research: the pros and cons, *Management Learning*, 31(2), 163–180.

Sloan, A.P. (1963) *My Years with General Motors*. London: Sidgwick and Jackson.

Sloman, M. (2002) Ground force, *People Management*, 27 June, 42–46.

Smith, I. (1983) *The Management of Remuneration: Paying for Effectiveness*. London: Institute of Personnel Management.

Snow, C.C. and Hrebiniak, L.G. (1980) Strategy, distinctive competence, and organizational performance, *Administrative Science Quarterly*, 25, 317–335.

Snow, C. and Snell, S. (1993) Staffing as strategy, in Schmitt, N. and Barman, W. (eds) *Personnel Selection*, Vol. 4. San Francisco, CA: Jossey-Bass.

Snow, C.C., Miles, R.E. and Coleman, H.J. Jr (1992) Managing 21st century organizations, *Organizational Dynamics*, Winter, 5–19.

Sonnenschein, W. (1997) *The Practical Executive and Workforce Diversity*. Lincolnwood, IL: NTC Publishing Group.

Southco (2004) *Quality System Manual*. Philadelphia, PA: Southco.

Sparrow, P.R. (1994) Organizational competencies: creating a strategic behavioural framework for selection and assessment, in Anderson, N. and Herriot, P. (eds) *Assessment and Selection in Organizations: Methods and Practice for Recruitment and Appraisal, First Up-date and Supplement*, pp. 1–26. Chichester: John Wiley.

Sparrow, P., Brewster, C. and Harris, H. (2004), *Globalising Human Resource Management*. London: Routledge.

Sparrow, P.R. and Hiltrop, J.M. (1994) *European Human Resource Management in Transition*. Hemel Hempstead: Prentice Hall.

Sparrow, P. and Marchington, M. (1998) *Human Resource Management: The New Agenda*. London: FT Pitman.

Sparrow, P.R. and Pettigrew, A.M. (1988) Strategic human resource management in the UK computer supplier industry, *Journal of Occupational Psychology*, 61, 25–42.

Stacey, R.D. (1993) *Strategic Management and Organisational Dynamics*. London: Pitman Publishing.

Staniforth, D. (1996) Teamworking, or individual working in a team?, *Team Performance Management: An International Journal*, 2(3), 37–41.

Stata, R. (1989) Organizational learning – the key to management innovation, *Sloan Management Review*, Spring, 63–74.

Steffens-Duch, S. (2001) Employee commitment – evaluation, analysis, and enhancing as conditions for economic success, *Human Resources Solutions for Europe*, HR Summit Conference, Montreux, February.

Steinberg, R. (1998) No, it couldn't happen here, *Management Review*, 87(8), 68–73.

Stephenson, K. and Lewis, D. (1996) Managing workforce diversity, macro and micro level HR implications of network analysis, *International Journal of Manpower*, 17(4), 168–196.

Stern, E. (2004) Philosophies and types of evaluation research, in Descy, P. and Tessaring, M. (eds) *The Foundations of Evaluation and Impact Research*. Luxembourg: Office for Official Publications of the European Communities (Cedefop Reference Series 58).

Stewart, J. (1996) *Managing Change Through Training and Development* (2nd edn). London: Kogan Page.

Stewart, J. and McGoldrick, J. (eds) (1996) *Human Resource Development: Perspectives, Strategies and Practice*. London: Pitman Publishing.

Stewart, T.A. (1997) *Intellectual Capital: The New Wealth of Organizations*. London: Nicholas Brealey.

Stiles, P., Gratton, L., Truss, C., Hope-Hailey, V. and McGovern, P. (1997) Performance management and the psychological contract, *Human Resource Management Journal*, 7(1), 57–66.

Storey, J. (1989) *New Perspectives on Human Resource Management*. London: Routledge.

Storey, J. (ed.) (1991) *New Perspectives on Human Resource Management*. London: Routledge.

Storey, J. (1992) *Development in the Management of Human Resources: An Analytical Review*, Oxford: Blackwell Publishing.

Storey, J. (ed.) (1995) *Human Resource Management: A Critical Text*. London: Routledge.

Storey, J. and Quintas, P. (2001) Knowledge management and HRM, in Storey, J. (ed.) *Human Resource Management: A Critical Text* (2nd edn). London: Thomson Learning.

Storey, J. and Sisson, K. (1993) *Managing Human Resources and Industrial Relations*. Buckingham: Open University Press.

Sun, P.Y.T. and Scott, J.L. (2003) Exploring the divide – organizational learning and learning organization, *The Learning Organization*, 10(4), 202–215.

Swailes, S. (2002) Organizational commitment: a critique of the construct and measures, *International Journal of Management Reviews*, 4(2), 155–178.

Swanson, R.A. (1997) HRD research: don't go to work without it, in Swanson, R. and Holton, E. (eds) *Human Resource Development Research Handbook*. pp. 3–20. San Francisco, CA: Berrett-Koehler.

Tansley, C. (1999) Human resource planning: strategies, systems and processes in Leopold, J., Harris, L. and Watson, T. (eds) *Strategic Human Resourcing: Principles, Perspectives and Practices*, pp. 39–62. London: Financial Times Management, Pitman Publishing.

Tayeb, M.H. (1996) *The Management of a Multicultural Workforce*. Chichester: John Wiley.

Tayeb, M. (2000) National cultural characteristics, in Tayeb, M. (ed.) *International Business: Theories, Policies and Practices*, pp. 309–336. Harlow: FT Prentice Hall.

Taylor, F.W. (1911) *Principles of Scientific Management*. New York: Harper and Row.

Taylor, R. (2002) *Diversity in Britain's Labour Market*. London: Economic and Social Research Council.

Teece, D.J., Pisano, G. and Shuen, A. (1997) Dynamic capabilities and strategic management, *Strategic Management Journal*, 18(7), 509–553.

The Diversity Group (2001) *The Diversity Group Homepage*. Available online http://www.thediversitygroup.com

The Guardian (2001) Mine's a McLatte, 1 February.

The Guardian (2004) Halliburton faces Iran inquiry, 12 February.

The Irish Times (2006) *Business 2000* (6th edn). Dublin: The Irish Times.

Thomas, R. (1990) From affirmative action to affirming diversity, *Harvard Business Review*, March/April, 107–117.

Thomas, R. (1996) *Redefining Diversity*. New York: Amacom.

Thomas, R. (2002) *Profiles in Managing Diversity*. Atlanta: American Institute of Managing Diversity.

Thompson, K. (1992) Cultural strategies: introduction, in Salaman, G., Cameron, S., Hamblin, H., Iles, P., Mabey, C. and Thompson, K. (eds) *Human Resource Strategies*, pp. 189–191. London: Sage,

Thompson, M. (1992) *Pay and Performance: The Employer Experience*. Falmer, Brighton: Institute of Manpower Studies.

Thompson, M. (1995) *Team Working and Pay*. Institute of Employment Studies Report No. 281. Brighton: University of Sussex.

Thompson, P. and McHugh, D. (2002) *Work Organisations: A Critical Introduction* (3rd edn). London: Palgrave.

Thornhill, A., Lewis, P., Millmore, M. and Saunders, M.N.K. (2000) *Managing Change: A Human Resource Strategy Approach*. Harlow: FT Prentice Hall.

Thornhill, A. and Saunders, M.N.K. (1998) The meaning, consequences and implications of management of downsizing and redundancy: a review, *Personnel Review*, 27(4), 271–295.

Thornhill, A., Saunders, M.N.K. and Stead, J. (1997a) Downsizing delayering – but where's the commitment?, *Personnel Review*, 26, (1/2), pp. 81–98.

Thornhill, A., Stead, J. and Gibbons, A. (1997b) *Managing Downsizing and Redundancy*. London: FT Pitman Publishing.

Tjepkema, S. (2002) Conclusions from case studies and survey, in Tjepkema, S., Stewart, J., Sambrook, S., Mulder, M., ter Horst, H. and Schreens, J. (eds) *HRD and Learning Organisations in Europe*, pp. 156–177. London: Routledge.

Tjepkema, S., Stewart, J., Sambrook, S., Mulder, M., ter Horst, H. and Schreens, J. (eds) (2002) *HRD and Learning Organisations in Europe*. London: Routledge.

Tomasko, R.M. (1992) Restructuring: getting it right, *Management Review*, 81(4), 10–15.

Tombaugh, J.R. and White, L.P., (1990) Downsizing: an empirical assessment of survivors' perceptions in a post layoff environment, *Organisation Development Journal*, Summer, 8(2), 32–43.

Toracco, R.J. (1997) Theory-building and research methods, in Swanson, R.A. and Holton, E.F. (eds) *Human Resource Development Research Handbook*, pp. 114–137. San Francisco, CA: Berrett-Koehler.

Torres, R., Preskill, H. and Piontek, M. (1996) *Evaluation Strategies for Communicating and Reporting*. Thousand Oaks, CA: Sage.

Torrington, D., Hall, L. and Taylor, S. (2002) *Human Resource Management* (5th edn). Harlow: Financial Times Prentice Hall.

Torrington, D., Hall, L. and Taylor, S. (2005) *Human Resource Management* (6th edn). Harlow: FT Prentice Hall.

Trompenaars, F. (1993) *Riding the Waves of Culture: Understanding Cultural Diversity in Business*. London: Nicholas Brealey Publishing.

Trompenaars, F. and Hampden-Turner, C. (1997) *Riding the Waves of Culture: Understanding Cultural Diversity in Business* (2nd edn). London: Nicholas Brealey Publishing.

Trompenaars, F. and Hampden-Turner, C. (2004) *Managing People Across Cultures*. Chichester: Capstone.

Turner, P. (2002) *HR Forecasting and Planning*. London: CIPD.

Twigg, G. and Albon, P. (1992) Human resource development and business strategy, in Armstrong, M. (ed.) *Strategies for Human Resource Management: A Total Business Approach*, pp. 80–92. London: Kogan Page.

Tyson, S. (1995) *Human Resource Strategy*. London: Pitman Publishing.

Tyson, S. (1999) How HR knowledge contributes to organisational performance, *Human Resource Management Journal*, 9(3), 42–52.

Tyson, S. and Doherty, N. (1999) *Human Resource Excellence Report*. London: Financial Times Management.

uktradeinfo (2005) *UK Annual Imports and Exports*. Available online http://www.uktradeinfo.com/index.cfm?task =annualtrade

Ulrich, D. (1987) Strategic human resource planning: why and how?, *Human Resource Planning*, 10(1), 37–56.

Ulrich, D. (1998) A new mandate for HR, *Harvard Business Review*, January/February, 124–113.

Ulrich, D. (2000) From e-business to e-HR, *Human Resource Planning*, 23(2), 12–21.

United Nations Conference on Trade and Development (UNCTAD) (2003) *World Investment Report 2003*. Geneva, United Nations Conference on Trade and Development.

University of Chemnitz (1995) *Handelsblatt*, Vol. 12, K1.

US Department of State (2004) *1998 Country Report on Economic Policies and Trade Practices: India*. Available online http://www.state.gov/www/issues/economic/trade_reports /south_asia98/india98.html

van de Vliet, A. (1995) Asda's open plan, *Management Today*, December, 50–54.

Van Maanen, J. (1991) The smile factory: work at Disneyland, in Frost, P.J., Moore, L.F., Louise, M.R., Lundberg, C. and Martin, J. (eds) *Reframing Organizational Culture*, pp. 58–76. Newbury Park, CA: Sage.

Wagner, R., Hlavacka, S. and Bacharova, L. (2000) Hospital human resource planning in Slovakia, *Journal of Management in Medicine*, 14(5/6), 383–405.

Walsh, D. (1999) International human resourcing, in Leopold, J., Harris, L. and Watson, T. (eds) *Strategic Human Resourcing: Principles, Perspectives and Practices*, pp. 89–126. London: Financial Times Management, Pitman Publishing.

Walton, J. (1999) *Strategic Human Resource Development*. Harlow: Financial Times Prentice Hall.

Walton, R (1985) Towards a strategy of eliciting employee commitment based on policies of mutuality, in Walton, R. and Lawrence P. (eds) *Human Resource Management Trends and Challenges*, pp. 35–65. Boston, MA: Harvard Business School Press,

Ward, H. (2001) *Setting the Diversity Agenda Straight*. Paper presented to the Fourth International Conference on Ethical Issues in Contemporary Human Resource Management, Middlesex University and Imperial College.

Warner, M. and Witzel, M. (2003) *Managing in Virtual Organizations*. London: Thomson Publishing.

Wass, V. (1996) Who controls selection under 'voluntary' redundancy? The case of the redundant mineworkers payments scheme, *British Journal of Industrial Relations*, 34(2), 249–265.

Wernerfelt, B. (1984) A resource-based view of the firm, *Strategic Management Journal*, 5, 171–180.

Wernerfelt, B. (1989) From critical resources to corporation strategy, *Journal of General Management*, 14, 4–12.

Wernerfelt, B. (1995) The resource-based view of the firm: ten years after, *Strategic Management Journal*, 16, 171–174.

West, P. (1994) The concept of the learning organization, *Journal of European Industrial Training*, 18(1), 15–21.

Whipp, R., Rosenfeld, R. and Pettigrew, A. (1989) Culture and competitiveness: evidence from two mature UK industries, *Journal of Management Studies*, 26(6), 561–585.

Whittington, R. (1988) Environmental structure and theories of strategic choice, *Journal of Management Studies*, 25, 521–536.

Whittington, R. (2001) *What is Strategy – and Does it Matter?*, (2nd edn). London: Thomson Learning.

Wickens, P. (1987) *The Road to Nissan: Flexibility, Quality, Teamwork*. Basingstoke: Macmillan Press.

Willey, B. (2003) *Employment Law in Context* (2nd edn). Harlow: FT Prentice Hall.

Williams, A.P.O. and Dobson, P. (1997) Personnel selection and corporate strategy, in Anderson, N. and Herriot, P. (eds) *International Handbook of Selection and Assessment*, pp. 219–245. Chichester: John Wiley.

Williams, A., Dobson, P. and Walters, M. (1993) *Changing Culture, New Organizational Approaches* (2nd edn). London: Institute of Personnel Management.

Williams, S.L. (2002) Strategic planning and organizational values: links to alignment, *Human Resource Development International*, 5(2), 217–233.

Wilson, E and Iles, P. (1999) Managing diversity: an employment and service delivery challenge, *The International Journal of Public Sector Management*, 12(1), 27–48.

Wood, S. (1996) High commitment management and payment systems, *Journal of Management Studies*, 33(1), 53–77.

Wood, S. and de Menezes, L. (1998) High commitment management in the UK: evidence from the Workplace Industrial Relations Survey and the Employers, Manpower and Practices Skills Survey, *Human Relations*, 51(4), 485–515.

Woodward, J. (1965) *Industrial Organization: Theory and Practice*. London: Oxford University Press.

Worcestershire County Council (2004a) *2001 Census Key Statistics* 9 November. Available online http://www .worcestershire.gov.uk/home/cs-chief-exec/cs-research/cs -research-census/cs-research-census-key-statistics-wards.htm

Worcestershire County Council (2004b) Unpublished communication with Human Resources Department.

Worman, D. (2001) Taking diversity forward: Chartered Institute of Personnel and Development initiatives, Lecture presented at Middlesex University, London.

Worrell, L. Davidson, W.N. and Sharma, V. (1991) Layoff announcements and stockholder wealth, *Academy of Management Executive*, 34(3), 662–678.

Wright, A. (2004) *Reward Management in Context*. London: Chartered Institute of Personnel and Development.

Wright, M. and Storey, J. (1997) Recruitment and selection, in Beardwell, I. and Holden, L. (eds) *Human Resource Management: A Contemporary Perspective* (2nd edn), pp. 210–276. London: Pitman.

Wright, P., Ferris, S. and Hiller, J. (1995) Competitiveness through the management of diversity: effects on stock price valuation, *Academy of Management Journal*, 38, 272–287.

Wright, P.M. and McMahan, G.C. (1992) Theoretical perspectives for strategic human resource management, *Journal of Management*, 18(2), 295–320.

Wright, P.M., McMahan, G.C. and McWilliams, A. (1994) Human resources and sustained competitive advantage: a resource-based perspective, *International Journal of Human Resource Management*, 5(2), 301–326.

Wright, P. and Snell, S. (1998) Toward a unifying framework for exploring fit and flexibility in strategic human resource management, *Academy of Management Review*, 23(4), 756–772.

Wright, P.M. and Snell, S.A. (1999) Toward a unifying framework for exploring fit and flexibility in strategic human resource management', in Schuler, R.S. and Jackson, S.E. (eds) *Strategic Human Resource Management*, pp. 207–228. Oxford, Blackwell.

Youndt, M., Snell, S., Dean, J. and Lepak, D. (1996) Human resource management, manufacturing strategy, and firm performance, *Academy of Management Journal*, 39(4), 836–866.

ZDNetUK (2004), *Computer Sciences Want to Tripe Indian Staff*, 27 April. Available online http://news.zdnet.co.uk /business/employment/0,39020648,39148261,00.htm

Zeffane, R. and Mayo, G. (1994) Planning for human resources in the 1990s: development of an operational model, *International Journal of Manpower*, 15(6), 36–56.

Zukis, B. and Ushida, M. (1998) Japan's changing compensations and benefits structure, *Benefits and Compensation International*, September, 6–13.

Index